The University of Law

14 Store Street
London
WC1E 7

The Confli

9th Edition

The Conflict of Laws

9th Edition

David McClean, C.B.E., Q.C., D.C.L., Hon.Litt.D, F.B.A.
Bencher of Gray's Inn
Membre de l'institut de droit international
Emeritus Professor of Law, University of Sheffield

Verónica Ruiz Abou-Nigm, LL.M, Ph.D
Lecturer in International Private Law, University of Edinburgh

Originally by:

The late J.H.C. Morris, Q.C., D.C.L., LL.D, F.B.A.
Honorary Bencher of Gray's Inn
Honorary Fellow of Magdalen College, Oxford
Emeritus Reader in the Conflict of Laws in the University of Oxford

SWEET & MAXWELL

 THOMSON REUTERS

Published in 2016 by Thomson Reuters (Professional) UK Limited, trading as Sweet &
Maxwell, Friars House, 160 Blackfriars Road, London, SE1 8EZ (Registered in England &
Wales, Company No.1679046.
Registered Office and address for service: 2nd floor, 1 Mark Square, Leonard Street, London,
EC2A 4EG).

For further information on our products and services, visit *www.sweetandmaxwell.co.uk*.

Typeset by Letterpart Limited, Caterham on the Hill, Surrey, CR3 5XL.

Printed and bound in Great Britain by CPI Group (UK) Ltd, Croydon, CR0 4YY.

No natural forests were destroyed to make this product; only farmed timber was used and
re-planted.

A CIP catalogue record of this book is available for the British Library.

ISBN: 978 0 414 03816 5

Thomson Reuters and the Thomson Reuters logo are trademarks of Thomson Reuters.

Sweet & Maxwell ® is a registered trademark of Thomson Reuters (Professional) UK
Limited.

Crown copyright material is reproduced with the permission of the Controller of HMSO and
the Queen's Printer for Scotland.

Preface

It is forty-five years since this book first appeared; the preface to the first edition is dated April 1971. John Morris could not have foreseen the ensuing transformation of the English rules of the conflict of laws. In 1971, the rules were almost all judge-made. John Morris had few equals in his analysis of difficult case-law and, it has to be said, in his enjoyment of the extraordinary facts that cross-border and cross-cultural cases present. Statutory intervention had been very limited and the work of the Law Commission in the field of private international law lay ahead. So, a married woman had a domicile dependent on that of her husband; the rules on the recognition of foreign divorces and, especially, nullity decrees were in a chaotic state; those on choice of law in torts had just been addressed by the House of Lords in a decision that served only to produce debate and confusion. The United Kingdom was not yet a member of what was then the European Economic Community, and it was another 25 years before the European institutions acquired competence in private international law.

More recent editions of this book have reflected the growing Europeanisation of our subject. The most significant development since the last edition in 2102 has been the appearance of the Brussels I *bis* Regulation in 2015, a recasting of the European rules on jurisdiction and the recognition and enforcement of judgements in civil and commercial matters, less radical in some respects that some had hoped. The changes are of course fully reflected in this edition, as are the growing number of decisions on, for example, the interpretation of the Rome Regulations on choice of law in respect of contractual and non-contractual obligations.

European law has been influential in other ways. A series of decisions by the UK Supreme Court has adopted the European autonomous understanding of habitual residence, especially that of a child, as part of English law.

The book continues to seek to cover the principal areas of the conflict of laws. We repeat the observation in the preface to the 8th edition, that the tendency in some universities to reduce the scope of the subject to international commercial law (and so in practice for it to be almost wholly concerned with material from EU sources) deprives the student of the opportunity to see how this subject works across the whole field of law. We remain convinced that family law and property law remain important, not only in practice but to an understanding of the subject.

There has been some re-ordering of material for this edition. The theories and methods of the subject are no longer reserved to the very end of the book but form Chapter 2. We have expanded our treatment of jurisdiction, with a new introductory chapter 5, and have brought our introduction to the practice of international litigation into the run of chapters dealing with jurisdiction. Chapter 13, on finance and property during and after marriage, ends the separation in previous editions of the financial consequences of divorce from matrimonial property issues; in English legal practice they surely belong together (which indeed is one reason why the UK has not opted in to the EU work on choice of law regarding matrimonial property).

Throughout we have taken account of significant case-law and the implications for the conflict of laws of such developments as the introduction of same-sex marriage in England. And there has been a great deal of subtle re-writing to improve the clarity of our presentation.

There is a new cross-border aspect to the book in that Veronica Ruiz Abou-Nigm, whose domicile of origin is in the Oriental Republic of Uruguay, is now habitually resident in Scotland; David McClean can only lay claim to dual nationality. This remains a book on the conflict of laws rules of England, with only very occasional references to Scottish variants. We each accept responsibility for the whole book, each grateful for the kindly way the other corrected errors and infelicities. The text was completed in March 2016 and we aimed to state the law as reflected in the sources available to us at that date.

TABLE OF CONTENTS

3.   PERSONAL CONNECTING FACTORS

4.   THE EXCLUSION OF FOREIGN LAW

7. JURISDICTION: THE TRADITIONAL ENGLISH RULES

8. SOVEREIGN AND DIPLOMATIC IMMUNITY

9. THE CONDUCT OF INTERNATIONAL LITIGATION

10. RECOGNITION AND ENFORCEMENT OF FOREIGN JUDGMENTS

12. ENDING MARRIAGES

13. FINANCE AND PROPERTY DURING AND AFTER MARRIAGE

15. CONTRACTUAL OBLIGATIONS

16. TORTS AND OTHER NON-CONTRACTUAL OBLIGATIONS

20. SOME CONFLICTS TECHNICALITIES

TABLE OF CASES

TABLE OF CASES

TABLE OF STATUTES

TABLE OF STATUTORY INSTRUMENTS

TABLE OF INTERNATIONAL CONVENTIONS

TABLE OF EUROPEAN INSTRUMENTS

Directives

TABLE OF CIVIL PROCEDURE RULES

CHAPTER 1

INTRODUCTION TO THE CONFLICT OF LAWS

On many an office or seminar-room wall, there hangs a political map of the **1–001** world. Each state, except the very smallest, has its own colour. Sixty years ago, the colour scheme was rather simpler: pink for the British Empire, perhaps green for the French possessions, and some other colour for the many republics which made up the Soviet Union. The boundaries between the different colours once meant a great deal. Many individuals lived and died without ever visiting a foreign country. Patterns of trade and commerce tended to follow the Imperial colour schemes, so that British companies would have their branches in the colonies, where legal rules and commercial practice followed English models. All this is now dramatically different.

Mass tourism has made foreign travel commonplace. Students cross the world in search of higher education, or to offer voluntary service, or simply for adventure. Employees of British companies find themselves working in all corners of the world, and a trip to Brussels or Frankfurt has little novelty value. Many national boundaries, such as those in "Schengenland" can be crossed without formality. Love knows not national boundaries: tourist, student, or worker may find romance and marry someone whose home is on the other side of the world.

Independence may increase the number of colours on the map, but the old empires are replaced by regional common markets, such as those in Europe or the Caribbean. The regional organisations soon move beyond a concern with economic issues and acquire legislative powers. Each individual country nonetheless retains its own body of law, its own system of courts, its own legal personnel. Individual and corporate activity may be increasingly international, but there is no system of international courts to resolve legal issues and disputes that arise. They have to be addressed through the courts of a particular legal system and the legal rules which are applicable to cases with international elements in those courts. Those rules are the rules of the conflict of laws.

THE SUBJECT DEFINED

The conflict of laws is that part of a legal system which deals with cases having a **1–002** cross-border element. This cross-border element, sometimes referred to as 'the internationalising factor', is a contact with some system of law other than that of the "forum", that is the country whose courts are seised of the case. Such internationalising elements in the facts of a case are quite commonplace: a contract was made with a company based in another country or was to be performed in a country, or a tort was committed there, or property was situated there, or one of the parties is not English.

If a claim is made for damages for breach of a contract made in England between two English companies and to be performed in England, there is no cross-border element: the case is not a case in the conflict of laws. It will be dealt with by the English court applying the English internal or domestic law of contract. But if the contract had been made in France between two French companies and was to be performed in France, then the case would be (for an English court, but not for a French court) a case in the conflict of laws, and an English court (in the unlikely event of litigation taking place in England) would apply French law to most of the matters in dispute before it, just as a French court naturally applies French law to all such matters.

If we change the facts once more, and assume that the contract was made in France between an English company and a French company and was to be performed in Belgium, then the case is a case in the conflict of laws not only for an English court but also for a French court and a Belgian court, and indeed for any court in the world in which the contract is litigated. That court will have to use its "choice of law" rules to decide whether to apply English, French or Belgian law, deciding in effect whether the French or English or Belgian elements are the most significant.

As Lord Nicholls of Birkenhead explained[1]:

> "Conflict of laws jurisprudence is concerned essentially with the just disposal of proceedings having a foreign element. The jurisprudence is founded on the recognition that in proceedings having connections with more than one country an issue brought before a court in one country may be more appropriately decided by reference to the laws of another country even though those laws are different from the law of the forum court."

MEANING OF "COUNTRY"

1–003   In the conflict of laws, an internationalising element and a foreign country mean a non-English element and a country other than England. From the point of view of the conflict of laws, Scotland and Northern Ireland are for most (but not all) purposes as much foreign countries as are France or Germany. More generally, a state in the political sense, or as understood in public international law, may or may not coincide with a country (or "law district" as it is sometimes called) in the sense of the conflict of laws. Unitary states such as Sweden, Italy and New Zealand, where the law is the same throughout the state, are "countries" in this sense. England or Scotland, New York or California, although merely component parts of the UK and the US, are each a country in the sense of the conflict of laws, because each has a separate system of law.

England, Scotland, Northern Ireland, the Republic of Ireland, Guernsey, Jersey and the Isle of Man are each a separate country; so is each of the American and Australian states and each of the Canadian provinces, and each of the remaining dependencies of the UK. However, for some purposes larger units than these may constitute countries. Thus, the UK is one country for the purposes of the law of

---

[1] *Kuwait Airways Corp v Iraqi Airways Co (Nos 4 and 5)* [2002] UKHL 19; [2002] 2 A.C. 883 at para.[15].

negotiable instruments,[2] and Great Britain is one country for most purposes of the law of companies.[3] In federal states, the greater use made of federal legislative powers has resulted in Australia being one country for the purposes of the law of marriage and matrimonial causes, and Canada one country for the purposes of the law of divorce. However, the mere fact that the Parliaments of the various Australian states and Canadian provinces decide to enact uniform legislation on technical legal subjects (as an exercise of state or provincial rather than federal competence) does not mean that they cease to be separate countries for those purposes.

On the other hand, Wales is not yet a country, because its system of law is still the same as that of England. The enactment of the Government of Wales Act 1998 did not change the position, for the Welsh Assembly was not given the power to enact primary legislation, but the additional powers conferred by the Government of Wales Act 2006 will in time create a body of Welsh law on some subjects. A country in the sense of the conflict of laws may exist without having a separate legislature: this was the case with Scotland between the Union in 1707 and the restoration of the Scottish Parliament by the Scotland Act 1998; and Northern Ireland did not cease to be a country when its legislature was suspended, originally in 1972.

In this book, "England" includes Wales; "Great Britain" means England (as so defined) and Scotland. "The United Kingdom" means England, Scotland, and Northern Ireland.

"PRIVATE INTERNATIONAL LAW"

The conflict of laws is sometimes known as private international law to reflect that in spite of the fact the rules are English in their formal sources they are international in their roots and spirit. However, differently from public international law, the rules of the conflict of laws may differ from country to country. Nevertheless, some overlap exists between public international law and the conflict of laws: for instance, the topics of sovereign and diplomatic immunity from suit[4] and of governmental seizure of private property[5] are discussed in books on the conflict of laws as well as in books on public international law, and many rules of the conflict of laws are derived from international treaties or conventions.

The subject matter of this book is the English rules of the conflict of laws, which will not be identical with those of any other country. It is true that the common law countries of the Commonwealth adopt a similar approach, and the influence of English cases and textbooks persisted longer in the conflict of laws than in areas of law with more obvious political or economic importance. The work of law reform agencies and of appellate courts is causing the rules applied

1–004

---

[2] Bills of Exchange Act 1882.
[3] Companies Act 2006.
[4] See Ch.8.
[5] See Ch.17.

in different Commonwealth countries to diverge.[6] Even between England and Scotland[7] there are some significant differences, and development of the subject in the US has taken a rather different course.

The differences are much greater between the common law countries on the one hand and those in the civil law tradition. Civil law countries include most of the countries of mainland Europe, whose law is derived from Roman (and Napoleonic) sources; many of their former colonies in Latin America and elsewhere; and other countries which have chosen to use continental codes as models for their own. The common law uses "domicile" as a personal connecting factor[8]; the European civil law tradition had traditionally preferred nationality. The paradigmatic features of the civil law and the common law tradition have generated different approaches to some conflicts issues, particularly in the field of jurisdiction. The common law development thrives on judicial discretion; the civilian tradition has long-favoured hard-and-fast rules that leave little room for judicial manoeuvre. As we shall see, the development of EU law is leading to a reception of civil law ideas to an ever-increasing extent in the English conflict of laws.

As an Advocate General of the European Court explained[9]:

> "Private international law, whatever its name may suggest, is not a body of international law. It is a branch of the domestic law of each legal system. It provides a mechanism or, more accurately, a series of interlocking mechanisms for determining, where legal situations or relationships have links to more than one legal system, what courts or other authorities should have jurisdiction, what substantive law should apply and what effects or recognition should be given to decisions taken, or legal acts accomplished, in accordance with other legal systems.
>
> Because the situations or relationships concerned are by definition inter-jurisdictional, the machinery of each legal system necessarily interacts with the machinery of other systems. Sometimes the gears mesh, sometimes they clash. When they mesh (which is preferable), it may be because the legal systems concerned have compatible rules from the outset, it may be because they have worked together to achieve compatibility in the context of a body such as … the Hague Conference on Private International Law, or (within the EU) it may be because they have had compatibility thrust upon them by Community legislation. There remain, however, many areas in which compatibility or harmonisation is incomplete."

Generally speaking, the conflict of laws is concerned much more with private than with public law.[10] It is traditional that English books on the conflict of laws do not discuss such topics as the jurisdiction of criminal courts to try crimes committed abroad, or the extradition of persons accused of crime, or mutual assistance between states in the conduct of criminal prosecutions, or the immigration or deportation of aliens.

---

[6] See McClean, "A Common Inheritance? An Examination of the Private International Law Tradition of the Commonwealth", (1996) 260 *Recueil des Cours*, 1–98.

[7] Private international law is a devolved matter under the Scotland Act 1998 s.126(4)(a).

[8] See Ch.3.

[9] Sharpston Advocate General in Case C-353/06 *Grunkin and Paul* at paras [37–38].

[10] For the approach of the English courts to foreign public law, see below at para.4–008. On the relationship between public and private international law, see A. Mills, *The Confluence of Public and Private International Law: Justice, Pluralism and Subsidiarity in the International Constitutional Ordering of Private Law* (Cambridge: CUP, 2009); and Mills, (2006) 55 I.C.L.Q.1.

THE QUESTIONS TO BE ANSWERED

The questions which the rules of the conflict of laws seek to answer are of two main types: first, has the English court jurisdiction to determine this case, and secondly, if so, what law will it apply? Logically, they must be addressed in that order, for if the English court has no jurisdiction it follows that the second, choice of law, question cannot arise. In practice, this logical purity does not quite hold: it can often make sense to ask the question "what law governs this contract?" quite independently of any jurisdictional issue.[11]

    There may sometimes be a third question, namely, will the English court recognise or enforce a foreign judgment purporting to determine the issue between the parties? Of course, this third question[12] arises only if there is a foreign judgment, and thus not in every case. But the first two questions arise in every case with cross-border elements, though the answer to one of them may be so obvious that the court is in effect concerned only with the other. The law of every country has rules for dealing with these questions, the rules of the conflict of laws (or, less formally, "conflicts rules"), in contrast to its domestic or internal law.

1–005

JUSTIFICATION

What justification is there for the existence of the conflict of laws? Why should the English courts trouble themselves with cases which are, to a greater or lesser extent, "international" cases? Why should we depart from the rules of our own law and apply those of another system? The justification for the conflict of laws can best be seen by considering what would happen if it did not exist. Theoretically, it would be possible for English courts to close their doors to all except English litigants. ("Theoretically" because this ignores the obligations of the UK under EU law and international conventions, and any question of "denial of justice" under the concepts of public international law.) But if they did so, grave injustice would be done not only to foreigners but also to the English. An English company, a party to a contract with a Scottish or French company, would be unable to enforce it in England; if the courts of other countries adopted the same principle, the contract could not be enforced in any country in the world.

    Theoretically, it would be possible for English courts to apply English domestic law in all cases. But if they did so, grave injustice would again be done to both foreign and English parties. For instance, if two English people married in France in accordance with the formalities prescribed by French law, but not in accordance with the formalities prescribed by English law, the English court, if it

1–006

---

[11] Especially where all the countries concerned share the uniform choice of law rules of the Rome Convention or the Rome I Regulation; see Ch.15.

[12] These three questions relating to the three key issues that the conflict of law is all about—that is, jurisdiction, applicable law and the recognition and enforcement of foreign judgments—are sometimes referred as the three pillars of private international law. Note also that some authors refer to international judicial cooperation as the third pillar, and to the recognition and enforcement of foreign judgments as a part of that cooperation, see e.g. M.B. Noodt Taquela, *Applying the Most Favourable Treaty or Domestic Rules to Facilitate Private International Law Co-operation*, (2015) 377 *Recueil des Cours*, 121-318, at para [68], p.166.

applied English domestic law to the case, would may have to treat the parties as unmarried persons. This might have unexpected and unjust consequences, for example, in terms of matrimonial property rights.

Theoretically, it would be possible for English courts, while opening their doors to foreigners and while ready to apply foreign law in appropriate cases, to refuse to recognise or enforce a foreign judgment determining the issue between the parties. But if they did so, grave injustice would again be inflicted on both foreign and English parties. For instance, if a divorce was granted in a foreign country, and afterwards one party remarried in England, he or she might be convicted of bigamy. Or if an English claimant sued a foreigner in a foreign country for damages for breach of contract or for tort, and eventually obtained a judgment in his favour, the successful claimant might find that the defendant had surreptitiously removed all assets to England; the claimant would then have to start all over again.

It was at one time supposed that the doctrine of comity was a sufficient basis for the conflict of laws; and even today references to comity are sometimes found in English judgments.[13] In the EU context the general concept of comity has taken the shape of mutual trust and mutual recognition.[14] Regardless of the different justifications devised by different traditions to explain the sheer practical importance of the conflict of laws for the management of legal diversity, the justification of the English conflict of laws ultimately resides in doing justice between the parties, and systemic considerations have not necessarily assumed much importance beyond the context of the EU regime.

RANGE AND DIFFICULTY OF THE SUBJECT

1–007   Not the least interesting feature of the conflict of laws is that it is concerned with almost every branch of private law. "There is a sweep and range in it which is almost lyric in its completeness. It is the fugal music of law."[15] It is "one of the most baffling subjects of legal science", said the distinguished American judge Cardozo J,[16] who also remarked on another occasion that "the average judge, when confronted by a problem in the conflict of laws, feels almost completely lost, and, like a drowning man, will grasp at a straw."[17] "The realm of the conflict of laws", said an American writer, "is a dismal swamp filled with quaking quagmires, and inhabited by learned but eccentric professors who theorise about mysterious matters in a strange and incomprehensible jargon."[18] Although the conflict of laws is highly controversial, the number of permutations and

---

[13] *Spiliada Maritime Corp v Cansulex Ltd* [1987] A.C. 460 at 477; *Adams v Cape Industries Plc* [1990] Ch 433; *Airbus Industrie GIE v Patel* [1999] 1 A.C. 119. For a discussion of the doctrine of comity, see below, para.2–005.

[14] See Ch.6. See, inter alia, Mitsilegas, 'The Limits of Mutual Trust in Europe's Area of Freedom, Security and Justice: From Automatic Inter-State Cooperation to the Slow Emergence of the Individual' (2012) 31 *Ybk of Eur.L.*, 31 319–372; Weller, (2015) 11 J.Priv.Int.L. 64.

[15] Baty, *Polarized Law* (London: Stevens and Haynes, 1914), p.5.

[16] *Paradoxes of Legal Science* (New York: Columbia University Press, 1928), p.67.

[17] Cited in Cook, *Logical and Legal Bases of the Conflict of Laws* (Cambridge MA: Harvard University Press, 1942), p.152.

[18] Prosser, (1953) 51 Mich.L.Rev. 959 at 971.

combinations arising out of any given set of facts is limited, as is the number of possible solutions. In any given case, the choice of law depends ultimately on considerations of reason, convenience and utility: e.g. how will the proposed choice of law work in practice, not only in this case, but also in similar cases in which a similar choice may reasonably be made? In the conflict of laws, to a greater extent than in most other subjects, there is much to be learnt from the way in which similar problems have been solved in other countries with an historical and cultural background and legal tradition similar to our own. Conflict lawyers are naturally comparatists and there is much disciplinary cross-fertilisation between the conflicts of laws and comparative law, particularly in relation to the technique of the subject discussed below.

THE TECHNIQUE OF THE SUBJECT

If you are learning to ride a bicycle, you gain little benefit from abstract instruction in matters of technique given before you have actually handled the machine. The same may be true of the conflict of laws; and the analogy has its comforting aspect, in that, once familiar with its workings, you wonder why the technique once seemed so intimidating. But there are some matters which require at least a preliminary airing at this stage, using a commercial illustration: **1–008**

> A contract is made in Italy under which an English company will supply material to be used by the Italian party at its manufacturing plant in Belgium. The material supplied, it is claimed, is substandard, and the Italian company wishes to claim damages against the English supplier. Can the action be heard in the English courts? What law will be applied?

In tackling these questions, the conflict of laws uses legal categories and "localising" elements or "connecting factors".[19] On the facts of this problem, potential connecting factors include: to which country the parties belong; where the contract was entered into; where the legal duties it created, of making and delivering goods, were to be carried out.

Those factors may be of differing strength and may be allocated differing degrees of importance: for example, in these days of easy communication and electronic commerce it matters little where a contract is made. But the existence of the connecting factors makes it possible to devise rules which make sense of the infinite variety of possible fact-situations and allocate the issue to a particular legal system. The rules will identify the legal category into which the issues fall (performance or breach of contract) and the connecting factor, or sometimes factors, appropriate to that category.

Typical rules of the conflict of laws state that succession to immovables is governed by the law of the country in which the property is situated (often referred to by the Latin expression lex situs)[20]; that the formal validity of a

---

[19] This expression (first suggested by Falconbridge) is the English equivalent of the French and German technical terms, respectively, "*point de rattachement*" and "*Anknüpfungspunkt*".

[20] An attempt (not wholly successful) has been made in this book to avoid Latinisms, but they pervade much of the literature and are current tools in international debate. The principal expressions the reader may encounter are: *lex causae*, the law (usually but not necessarily foreign) which governs the question; *lex fori*, the domestic law of the forum, i.e. (if the forum is English) English law; *lex*

marriage is governed by the law of the place of celebration; and that capacity to marry is governed by the law of each party's ante-nuptial domicile. In these examples, the categories are succession to immovables, formal validity of marriage and capacity to marry, and the connecting factors are situation, place of celebration and domicile.

Connecting factors are important both for answering the jurisdictional and the applicable law issue; but different connecting factors may be relevant for the allocation of jurisdiction and the determination of the applicable law, respectively. In the example above, the connecting factors relevant to the jurisdictional issue may be that the defendant company has its "domicile" in England, and that the relevant obligation under the contract was to be performed principally in Belgium. In the choice of law context, the fact that the defendant's central administration is located in England may prove determinative. The reader will be able to give a fuller answer in due course; what is important here is the way in which connecting factors are used.

THE NEED TO PLEAD AND PROVE FOREIGN LAW

1–009   It is necessary at this point to introduce some features of English civil procedure which complicate, even to some extent undermine, that part of the conflict of laws process by which the applicable law is chosen, the choice of law process.

It is a general principle of English procedure that in the pleadings, the documents which state the claimant's and defendant's position and so identify the issues in dispute, the parties plead only facts and not law. It is for the court, once the facts have been found, to apply the law; and "the law" means the law which the court knows, English law. Prima facie, therefore, even if the facts indicate the presence of foreign elements, the court will apply English law. If either party wishes the court to apply foreign law, it must say so in the pleadings. In that sense the possible relevance of foreign law is asserted amongst the pleaded facts, rather than argued as a point of law.[21]

The implications of this are that the rules of choice of law, that a certain issue is to be governed by a specified foreign law (for example, where the parties were at the time the contract was made), apply only if one or other of the parties chooses to raise the point in the pleadings. Application of the choice of law rules is, to a striking extent, "voluntary"; by remaining silent, the parties can avoid their application.[22] Shocking in theory, this result is perhaps less significant in practice: the nature of the dispute is likely to be such that the application of foreign law will be to the advantage of one party, who will take pains to plead it.

---

domicilii (law of the domicile); *lex patriae* (law of the nationality); *lex loci contractus* (law of the place where a contract is made); *lex loci solutionis* (law of the place where a contract is to be performed or where a debt is to be paid); *lex loci delicti* (law of the place where a tort is committed); and *lex loci celebrationis* (law of the place where a marriage is celebrated).

[21] The origins of this rule are early: *Fremoult v Dedire* (1718) 1 P.Wms. 429; *Mostyn v Fabrigas* (1774) 1 Cowp. 161 at 174; *Nelson v Bridport* (1845) 8 Beav. 527. For a comparative study, see Hartley, "Pleading and proof of foreign law: the major European systems compared" (1996) 45 I.C.L.Q. 271.

[22] See Fentiman, *Foreign Law in English Courts* (Oxford: Oxford University Press, 1998); Geerooms, *Foreign Law in Civil Litigation* (Oxford: Oxford University Press, 2004). See also Ruiz Abou-Nigm,

If the application of foreign law has no advantage to either party, it will not feature and the case will, in practical effect, not be a case in the conflict of laws.

There is one statutory, and largely forgotten, exception to this principle. If a case is governed by the law of some "British territory", the court has power under the British Law Ascertainment Act 1859 to order that law to be ascertained in the manner prescribed in the Act, and has sometimes exercised this power on its own motion although the foreign law was not pleaded.[23]

However, that is not the end of the matter. If foreign law is pleaded, the English court is invited to apply law of which it is ignorant. English courts take judicial notice of the law of England and of "notorious" facts, but not of foreign law. An appellate court which has jurisdiction to determine appeals from the courts of several countries takes judicial notice of the laws of any of those countries when it hears an appeal from a court in one of them: so, the Supreme Court of the UK, when hearing an English appeal, takes judicial notice of Scots law,[24] and when hearing a Scottish appeal, takes judicial notice of the law of Northern Ireland[25] and of England. In other cases, foreign law must be proved (unless of course it is admitted).

A party seeking to rely on foreign law has, therefore, to produce evidence of the content of that foreign law. In this sense, too, foreign law is a matter of "fact" and has to be proved like any other fact. Here there is one more, rather startling, rule of practice: in the absence of proof to the contrary, the English court will assume that foreign law is the same as English law.[26] Foreign law must be both pleaded and proved before the court will do other than apply the familiar rules of internal English law. An English court will not conduct its own researches into foreign law. As the Court of Appeal put it in *Macmillan Inc v Bishopgate Investment Trust Plc (No.4)*[27]:

> "... the evidence of expert witnesses is necessary for the court to find that foreign law is different from English law. In the absence of such evidence, or if the judge[28] is unpersuaded by it, then he must resolve the issue by reference to English law, even if according to the rules of private international law the issue is governed by the foreign law."

No precise or comprehensive answer can be given to the question as to who, for this purpose, is a competent expert. A foreign judge or legal practitioner is of course always competent. But in civil proceedings there is no longer any rule of

---

'The Traditional Approach to Foreign Law in Civil Litigation in the Legal Systems of the United Kingdom' in Yuko Nishitani (ed.) *Treatment of Foreign Law: Dynamics towards Convergence?* (Springer, 2016, forthcoming).

[23] *Topham v Duke of Portland* (1863) 1 D.J. & S. 517.

[24] *Elliot v Joicey* [1935] A.C. 209 at 236; *MacShannon v Rockware Glass Ltd* [1978] A.C. 795.

[25] *Cooper v Cooper* (1888) 13 App.Cas. 88. The question whether a similar rule applied to the Privy Council was noted but not resolved in *Oakely v Osiris Trustees Ltd* [2008] UKPC 2.

[26] This is how the courts state the matter. Fentiman cogently argues (1998, p.147) that "to speak of [a presumption of similarity] at all, rather than admitting that English law applies as the *lex causae* where no other is proved, may rest on a conceptual mistake".

[27] Reported *sub nom MCC Proceeds Inc v Bishopsgate Investment Trust plc (No.4)* [1999] C.L.C. 417 at para.[10].

[28] Questions of foreign law, once decided by the jury are now reserved to the judge: Senior Courts Act 1981 s.69(5).

law (if indeed there ever was) that the expert witness must have practised, or at least be entitled to practise, in the foreign country.[29]

A witness may be competent, though his or her expertise is not that of a lawyer as such: any person who, by virtue of a profession or calling, has acquired a practical knowledge of foreign law may be a competent witness. Diplomatic and consular officers,[30] academic lawyers,[31] a bishop,[32] merchants and a bank manager[33] have all been held competent. Witnesses such as bishops, merchants and bank managers will, of course, be regarded as experts only in that part of the foreign law with which they are bound, by virtue of their profession or calling, to be familiar.

In *Macmillan Inc v Bishopgate Investment Trust Plc (No.4)* the Court of Appeal summarised the functions of the expert witness as being (1) to inform the English court of the relevant contents of the foreign law; identifying statutes or other legislation and explaining where necessary the foreign court's approach to their construction; (2) to identify judgments or other authorities, explaining what status they have as sources of the foreign law[34]; and (3) where there is no authority directly in point, to assist the English judge in making a finding as to what the foreign court's ruling would be were the issue to arise for decision there. The witness is there to predict the likely decision of a foreign court, not to press upon the English judge the witness's personal views as to what the foreign law might be.[35] Although matters of foreign law are issues of fact, they are factual issues "of a peculiar kind".[36]

The judge's role is not as passive as it may be in the case of issues of fact in the stricter sense. The foreign law, for example the law of an American state, may be in the English language, and it may make use of concepts and patterns of legal thought very similar to those of English law. In such a case, the English judge is entitled to make a legal input, using knowledge of the common law and of the rules of statutory construction. Unless the evidence shows that the foreign rules of construction are different, the English court interprets a foreign statute according to the English rules. If the expert witness advances an interpretation of

---

[29] See the Civil Evidence Act 1972 s.4(1).

[30] *Lacon v Higgins* (1822) Dowl. & Ry. N.P. 38; *In the Goods of Dost Aly Khan* (1880) 6 P.D. 6.

[31] *Brailey v Rhodesia Consolidated Ltd* [1910] 2 Ch. 95 (Reader in Roman-Dutch Law to the Council of Legal Education); *McCabe v McCabe* [1994] 1 F.L.R. 410 (Professor in the School of Oriental and African Studies, giving evidence on Ghanaian customary law).

[32] *Sussex Peerage Case* (1844) 11 Cl. & F. 85.

[33] *Vander Donkt v Thellusson* (1849) 8 C.B. 812; *De Beeche v South American Stores Ltd* [1935] A.C. 148. But the court may refuse to admit the evidence of such a witness where that of a qualified lawyer is readily available: *Direct Winters Transport Ltd v Duplate Canada* (1962) 32 D.L.R. (2d) 278.

[34] For the weight to be given to foreign case law, see e.g. *Beatty v Beatty* [1924] 1 K.B. 807; *Re Annesley* [1926] Ch. 692; *Bankers and Shippers Insurance Co of New York v Liverpool Marine & General Insurance Co Ltd* (1926) 24 Ll. L. Rep. 85; *Callwood v Callwood* [1960] A.C. 659; *In the Estate of Fuld (No.3)* [1968] P. 675 at 701–702. Where foreign decisions conflict, the court may be asked to decide between them, even although in the foreign country the question still remains to be authoritatively settled: *Re Duke of Wellington* [1947] Ch. 506; *Breen v Breen* [1964] P. 144.

[35] *G. & H. Montage GmbH v Irvani* [1990] 1 W.L.R. 667; *Macmillan Inc v Bishopgate Investment Trust Plc (No.4)* at para.23.

[36] *Parkasho v Singh* [1968] P. 233 per Cairns J at p.250. The implications of this for the role of the Court of Appeal, normally reluctant to differ from the trial judge on matters of fact, were discussed in *MacMillan Inc v Bishopgate Investment Trust Plc (No.4)*, citing Fentiman, above at pp.201–202.

a familiar concept which is "extravagant" or "impossible" the judge may decline to accept it.[37] More generally, if there is a conflict between the evidence of expert witnesses (as there may well be, the experts called by each side presenting differing opinions), the judge must look at the foreign material cited and form a judgment as best he or she may.[38]

There are three statutes and one international convention which provide alternative modes of establishing foreign law.[39] One statute, the British Law Ascertainment Act 1859, has already been mentioned; and a similar procedure exists as between parties to the European Convention on Information on Foreign Law, signed in 1968.[40] It is not well-known and is not used to obtain information for use in English cases. The certification of foreign law by a foreign authority, with no cross-examination of the author of the certificate, does not fit English procedures. The Convention is more attractive in civil law systems where the judge is typically responsible for ascertaining the content of foreign law and determining its application to the facts.[41]

By the Evidence (Colonial Statutes) Act 1907, copies of laws made by the legislature of any "British possession",[42] if purporting to be printed by its government printer, can be received in evidence in the UK without proof that the copies were so printed.

More significant is the Civil Evidence Act 1972. Section 4(2)–(5) of that Act provide that where any question of foreign law has been determined in civil or criminal proceedings at first instance in the High Court, the Crown Court, or in any appeal therefrom, or in the Privy Council on appeal from any court outside the UK, then any finding made or decision given on that question is admissible in evidence in any civil proceedings, and the foreign law shall be taken to be in accordance with that finding or decision unless the contrary is proved. The section does not apply if the subsequent proceedings are before a court which can take judicial notice of the foreign law. Thus a determination on a point of Scots law by the High Court or the Court of Appeal is not even prima facie evidence of that point in subsequent proceedings before the House of Lords. Nor is the determination prima facie binding if there are conflicting findings or decisions on the same question.

It may be that the harmonisation of law in the EU may one day affect the English common law approach to proof of foreign law.

---

[37] *Buerger v New York Life Assurance Co* (1927) 96 L.J.K.B. 930; *A/S Tallina Laevauhisus v Estonian State Steamship Line* (1947) 80 Ll.L.Rep. 99 at 108; *Macmillan Inc v Bishopgate Investment Trust Plc (No.4)*, above.

[38] *Bumper Development Corp v Commissioner of Police for the Metropolis* [1991] 1 W.L.R. 1362 (where the judge had wrongly rejected the agreed views of the expert witnesses).

[39] See also the possibilities presented by the European Judicial Network for informal consultation with foreign judges: *B.C. v A.C.* [2005] EWCA Civ 68, per Thorpe LJ at para.44.

[40] Any information obtained under the Convention is not binding on the requesting court.

[41] Some countries have a mixed system; e.g. the Chinese Act on Application of Law in Civil Relationships with Foreign Contacts 2010 provides for the judge to find the content of foreign law unless the foreign law has been chosen as applicable by the parties; in the latter case the parties must prove the content of the chosen law.

[42] i.e. "any part of Her Majesty's dominions exclusive of the United Kingdom": s.1(3).

SOME TECHNICAL PROBLEMS

1–010   In this book, some matters of fundamental importance and great difficulty have been reserved for discussion at the end, rather than at the beginning as they are in some other books. The reason for this treatment is that it would be daunting to the reader to embark on an examination of these matters before he or she knows enough about the subject to understand all their implications. Its disadvantage is that the reader is left in blissful ignorance of some fundamental matters until nearly the end of the book. Enough will be said here, by way of orientation, to enable the nature of the problems to be identified.

Characterisation

1–011   It has already been explained that the technique of the conflict of laws makes much use of legal categories: before the correct connecting factors can be identified we need to know into which legal category the facts of the case, or the particular issues, are properly placed. In the international context of our subject, this process of categorisation or characterisation, also known as classification, presents a special problem.

   The nature of this problem can best be shown by two examples. Suppose that a person buys a ticket in London for a train journey to Edinburgh, and is injured in a railway accident in Scotland. Is the passenger's cause of action against the railway company for breach of contract, in which case English law might apply, as the law governing the contract, or for tort, in which case Scots law will apply? By which law, English or Scots, is this question to be answered? Or suppose that a marriage is celebrated in England between two French people domiciled in France. The marriage is valid by English law but invalid by French law because neither party has the consent of his or her parents as required by French law. If this rule of French law relates to formalities of marriage, it will not apply to a marriage celebrated in England; but if it relates to capacity to marry, it will invalidate the marriage of a French couple. By which law, French or English, is the nature of the French rule to be determined? These and other similar problems are discussed in a later chapter.[43]

Renvoi

1–012   We have already seen that where the significant elements in a case are divided between two countries, e.g. France and England, the case is a case in the conflict of laws for any court in which it is litigated. If the English court applies French law, because it thinks that the French elements are more significant than the English ones, it may find that a French court would apply English law, because it thinks that the English elements are the more significant. The question then arises, does "French law" mean French domestic law, or does it mean the whole of French law, including its rules of the conflict of laws? This is the notorious problem of *renvoi*, possibly leading in this instance to a remission from French

---

[43] Below, Ch.20.

law to English law. If we change the facts and assume that the significant elements are divided, not between England and France, but between France and Germany, then an English court, if it applies French law, may find that a French court would apply German law. This also is a *renvoi* problem, but it leads not to a remission from French to English law, but to a transmission from French to German law, and possibly to a further reference from German to English or French law.

Suppose, for example, that a British citizen domiciled in France dies intestate leaving movables in England. In order to determine who are his next of kin, an English court will apply French law because he was domiciled in France; but it may find that a French court would apply English law because he was a British citizen. If the intestate had been a German national instead of a British citizen, a French court might have applied German law. The problem is whether French law means French domestic law, or the whole of French law including its rules of the conflict of laws. If it means the latter, there may be a remission to English law in the first of these cases, and a transmission to German law in the second.

It may be said at once that in the vast majority of cases the reference to the applicable law is a reference to the internal laws of a legal system, excluding its conflict of laws rules.[44] But there are a few exceptional cases, to be discussed in a later chapter, in which the reference is to mean the whole of the foreign law, including its rules of the conflict of laws.[45]

The incidental question

The nature of this problem also can best be shown by two examples. Suppose that a testator domiciled in France gives movables in England to his "wife". The main question here is one of succession to the movables; and it is governed by French law, because the testator was domiciled in France. But a subsidiary or incidental question may arise as to the validity of the testator's marriage: should this question be referred to the English or the French rules of the conflict of laws relating to the validity of marriages? Or suppose that the English court has to determine the capacity of a domiciled Italian to contract a second marriage after obtaining a divorce from his first wife in Switzerland. The Swiss divorce is recognised as valid in England, but not in Italy. The main question here is the question of capacity to remarry, and it is governed by Italian law, because the husband was domiciled in Italy. The incidental question is the validity of the divorce: should this question be referred to the English or the Italian rules of the conflict of laws relating to the recognition of divorces?

1–013

---

[44] See arts 20, Rome I Regulation and 24, Rome II Regulation.
[45] e.g. art.25 of the Brussels I *bis* Regulation, in relation to the applicable law to the material validity of choice of court agreements.

The time factor

1–014   The conflict of laws deals primarily with the application of laws in space; but problems of time cannot altogether be ignored. In the conflict of laws, the time factor is significant in various situations. The most important of these is when there is a retrospective change in the applicable law after the events have happened which gave rise to the cause of action. Should the English court apply the law as it was when the cause of action arose, or as it is at the date of the trial? This problem and others like it are also discussed in a later chapter.[46]

GLOBAL AND REGIONAL DEVELOPMENTS

1–015   There is no doubt that in an era of globalisation our subject has a future, and one of growing importance.[47] This is reflected in the expanding membership of the specialist international body, the Hague Conference on Private International Law. For more than a century, the Hague Conference has had a leading role in the development of our subject.[48] Its title conceals the fact that it is an intergovernmental organisation, styling itself as the World Organisation for Cross-border Co-operation in Civil and Commercial Matters, and not a "conference" in the more usual sense. It first met in 1893 under the leadership of T.C.M. Asser, a notable Dutch scholar, though it was the work of the Italian, Mancini, which first promoted the idea of such a meeting.

The Hague Conference was originally very much a European, and a civil law, club. After an interruption in its activities from 1928 to 1951, it was revived and its present Statute declares it to have a permanent character, with the object of "the progressive unification of the rules of private international law".[49] The membership of the Conference is now truly global, with 81 States in membership, plus the EU. This means it is now much more representative of the various legal traditions, with a number of Eastern European countries and China representing the socialist legal tradition, with Australia, Canada, Cyprus, Ireland, Malta, New Zealand, the UK and the US speaking from the common law perspective (though Cyprus, Ireland and the UK are bound to follow an agreed EU line in negotiations), and with much more active participation by the Latin American countries with their distinctive tradition of private international law. The significance of the work at The Hague lies primarily in the way it devises rules acceptable to all those different traditions.

Since the early 1990s the Conference has been pursuing a major Judgments Project. The original hope, of a global convention dealing with jurisdiction as well as the recognition and enforcement of foreign judgments, proved unachievable. The work was not wasted: a Convention on Choice of Court

---

[46] See para.20–028.

[47] See, inter alia, Harris and McClean in Hayton (ed.), *Law's Future(s)* (Oxford: Hart Publishing, 2000), Ch.9; McLachlan, (2004) 120 L.Q.R. 580.

[48] See Offerhaus, (1959) 16 *Annuaire Suisse de droit international* 27; van Hoogstraten, (1963) 12 I.C.L.Q. 148; North, (1981) 6 Dalhousie L.J. 417; McClean, (1992) 233 *Recueil des Cours* 271.

[49] Statute, art.1.

Agreements[50] was signed in 2005 and the Conference has resumed work on foreign judgments. Another major achievement was the successful conclusion in 2007 of work on family support and other forms of maintenance[51]; work done in close collaboration with the EU which was negotiating a Regulation on the same topic. The UK is party to 11 of the Conventions drafted at The Hague, in addition to two to which it became party via the EU; they have made a significant contribution to the development of the English rules of the conflict of laws.

However, the work of the EU is having an even greater impact on the English rules by the adoption of Regulations having direct effect as part of English law. The Treaty of Amsterdam of 1997 gave the EU competence in respect of "judicial cooperation in civil matters". Article 81(1) of the Treaty on the Functioning of the European Union (TFEU) provides:

> "The Union shall develop judicial cooperation in civil matters having cross-border implications, based on the principle of mutual recognition of judgments and of decisions in extrajudicial cases. Such cooperation may include the adoption of measures for the approximation of the laws and regulations of the Member States."

A series of important non-legislative documents has elaborated a programme for the development of European private international law instruments. These include the Conclusions of the European Council meeting at Tampere in 1999,[52] the Hague Programme of 2004,[53] and the Stockholm Programme of 2009,[54] with its associated Action Plan.[55]

There are now more than a dozen Regulations containing private international law rules applicable throughout the EU (subject to opt-out provisions for Denmark, Ireland and the UK). They deal with basic questions of jurisdiction and the recognition and enforcement of judgments in civil and commercial matters,[56] with many issues concerning divorce, separation and children[57]; contractual obligations[58]; torts and other non-contractual obligations[59]; civil procedure as to the service of process and the taking of evidence[60]; and the enforcement of claims.[61] They are referred to in almost every chapter of this book and now form

---

[50] See para.5–017.
[51] See para.13–013.
[52] Presidency Conclusions, especially nos 28–39. See a Communication, 'Area of freedom, security and justice: Assessment of the Tampere programme and future orientations', COM(2004) 401 final.
[53] The Hague Programme: strengthening freedom, security, and justice in the European Union, 13 December 2004, OJ 2005, C 53/1.
[54] The Stockholm Programme—An open and secure Europe serving and protecting the citizen, OJ 2010, C 115/1.
[55] Action Plan Implementing the Stockholm Programme, COM(2010) 171 final.
[56] Regulation 1215/2012 (Brussels I *bis*); see Ch.6 below.
[57] Regulation 2201/2003 (see Chs 11 and 14 below); Regulation 4/2009 (on maintenance; see Ch.13 below). Regulation 1259/2010 ('Rome III') on applicable law in divorce is not applicable in the UK.
[58] Regulation 593/2008 ('Rome I'); see Ch.15 below.
[59] Regulation 864/2007 ('Rome II'); see Ch.16 below.
[60] Regulation 1393/2007 (service); Regulation 1206/2001 (taking of evidence); see Ch.9 below.
[61] Regulation 805/2004 (European Enforcement Order); Regulation 1896/2006 (European Order for Payment Procedure); Regulation 861/2007 (European Small Claims Procedure); and Regulation 655/2014 (European Account Preservation Order).

the greater part of the conflict rules applying in England.[62] Work has been done to identify the gaps remaining if the EU is to have a comprehensive set of private international law rules, perhaps one day forming a single European Code of Private International Law.[63] The reader will note not only the extent to which topics are now covered by legislation derived from European sources but also the extent to which approaches and practices traditional in common law countries are being supplanted.[64] Those traditions continue, with local adaptations, in the many Commonwealth member states whose legal systems were derived from England

A ROAD MAP

1–016   Following this introductory chapter, Ch.2 examines the theories developed and the methodologies used in the operation of our subject. It is a chapter to which the reader may wish to return when he or she has greater familiarity with the English approach to, and rules of, the conflict of laws. Chapter 3 examines the complexities that lie behind seemingly simple statements that an individual or a company is, for example, English or French, and Ch.4 deals with a number of doctrines which may enable the English courts to refuse to apply a rule of foreign law.

Questions of jurisdiction, one of the main pillars of the subject, are treated in four chapters. Chapter 5 introduces the reader to the main ideas, Chs 6 and 7 with the two sets of jurisdiction rules used by the English courts, one derived from European law and the other the continued application in certain cases of the traditional approach of the English courts. Immunity from jurisdiction is dealt with in Ch.8.

A claimant may discover that the courts of a particular state have jurisdiction to rule on the claim. That is only the beginning of the matter: there are practical issues about the actual conduct of litigation across national boundaries (to which Ch.9 provides an introduction) and it may well be necessary to enforce any judgment obtained in a third state. Chapter 10 deals with the important question of the recognition and enforcement of foreign judgments.

Chapters 11 to 14 inclusive deal with international family law: the conflict of laws rules relating to marriage, matrimonial causes, the financial and property issues arising during and after the ending of a marriage, the care of children, and issues of legitimacy and adoption.

Choice of law rules relating to claims in contract and "non-contractual obligations", principally those in tort—both the subject of an EU Regulation—are the subject of Chs 15 and 16. Three chapters deal with property issues, a

---

[62] Exceptions are those dealing with insolvency, which is beyond the scope of this book; and succession (not applicable in the UK).

[63] See Study IP/C/JURI/IC/2012-009, 'A European framework for private international law: current gaps and future perspectives', European Parliament, September 2012; Kramer, *European Private International Law: The Way Forward* (2014).

[64] As to the reaction of common lawyers see inter alia, Hartley, "The European Union and the Systematic Dismantling of the Common Law of Conflict of Laws" (2005) 54 ICLQ 813; Harris, "Understanding the English Response to the Europeanisation of Private International Law" (2008) 4 J.Priv.Int.L. 347.

relatively static area of the subject: Ch.17 examines issues of title to property, Ch.18 the rules of succession and the administration of estates, and Ch.19 the choice of law rules as to trusts.

Finally, Ch.20 returns to examine more closely the technical problems outlined earlier in this introduction.

Chapter 2

THEORIES AND METHODS

In the opening chapter of this book, there was a brief discussion of the justification for the conflict of laws, and for the application in some cases by the courts of the forum state of rules derived from a foreign legal system. The justification traditionally advanced by English lawyers was a pragmatic one: a desire to do justice between the parties to the dispute, an exercise informed by perceptions of what the parties, or the wider public, would expect or feel to be an appropriate outcome. The point was also made, in discussing the term "private international law", that there is no single system of conflict of laws rules: they may differ from country to country. There is a fairly well-defined set of *questions* which constitute the remit of the subject, but the *answers* vary in different legal systems. In the European area of justice, there has been much harmonisation of these answers since the entry into force of the Treaty of Amsterdam in 1999, but there are still many answers that are, even within Europe, those of individual legal systems. Each legal system draws on its own tradition and experience in making a judgment as to what is just, or appropriate, or meets the legitimate expectations of the parties.

2–001

There are some matters of fact which every legal system has to take into account in developing its rules of the conflict of laws. An obvious example concerns land: from the earliest times, it has been recognised that land cannot in practice be dealt with except in accordance with the rules, or at least the mandatory rules, of the *lex situs*. We have seen, too, how developments in transport and communications have deprived the place in which the parties enter into a commercial contract of much of its former significance. In other areas, however, the content of legal rules is less clearly influenced by external factors and more by the internal logic of the law itself, for example in fixing the precise boundary between contract and tort. There is nothing inherent in the conflict of laws which dictates a "correct" answer, or which enables one to say that the approach taken by a particular legal system is or is not in accord with principle. It is true that academic commentators or even official law reform agencies may criticise a rule. They may believe it arose through some historical misunderstanding, or by some accident of litigation or legislation. It may be said to produce inconvenient or capricious results. But until the law is changed, it follows from state sovereignty that it remains in force and immune from effective challenge.

The conflict of laws is known for its ingenuity; many theoretical approaches have been advanced, and methods devised to provide answers to the complex legal issues that private cross-border scenarios generate. Some of these approaches are radically different from those used in England.

THEORIES

2–002   It is appropriate to begin with two of the founding fathers of our subject, Huber and Savigny. They each believed that there were principles of private international law of universal validity, from which the subject could be developed logically and scientifically.

Huber

2–003   Ulrich Huber (1636–1694) was successively a professor of law and a judge in Friesland. He was the author of the shortest treatise ever written on the conflict of laws[1] (only five quarto pages), but his influence on its development in England and the US has been greater than that of any other foreign jurist.

Huber laid down three maxims "for solving the difficulty of this particularly intricate subject". They are as follows[2]:

(1)   The laws of each state have force within the limits of that government, and bind all subject to it, but not beyond.

(2)   All persons within the limits of a government, whether they live there permanently or temporarily, are deemed to be subjects thereof.

(3)   Sovereigns will so act by way of comity that rights acquired within the limits of a government retain their force everywhere so far as they do not cause prejudice to the power or rights of such government or of its subjects.

In his first two maxims Huber states, more clearly than anyone before him, that all laws are territorial and can have no force and effect beyond the limits of the country where they were enacted, but that they bind all persons within that country, whether native-born subjects or foreigners. It was this insistence on the territorial nature of law that made Huber's doctrines so congenial to English and American judges. Then, in his third maxim, Huber offers, almost casually, two explanations of the apparent paradox that, despite the doctrine of territorial sovereignty, foreign law is applied beyond the territory of its enacting sovereign. His first explanation is that this is done simply by the tacit consent of the sovereign in whose territory the foreign law is applied. His second explanation is that what is enforced and applied is not foreign law as such but the rights to which the foreign law gives rise. Such thinking was to be expressed by later writers in terms of the doctrines of comity and of vested rights, discussed below. The third maxim also contains the seeds of the doctrine of public policy, discussed in Ch.4.

---

[1] *De Conflictu Legum* (1689). For translation and comment, see Lorenzen, *Selected Articles on the Conflict of Laws* (New Haven CT: Yale University Press, 1947), Ch.6; Davies, (1937) 18 B.Y.B.I.L. 49. Perhaps it is not fanciful to suggest that Huber's practical illustrations, which are such a feature of his work, were used as a model by Dicey and by the American Law Institute's *Restatements*.
[2] Section 2.

Savigny

The most influential writer on the conflict of laws in the civil law tradition (perhaps in any tradition) was Friedrich Carl von Savigny, who was born in Frankfurt in 1779 and died in 1861. He has been described as "a prince among the intellectuals of his age".[3] His treatment of the subject became very well known in England through the translation by William Guthrie,[4] with the title *A Treatise on the Conflict of Laws and the Limits of their Operation in Respect of Place and Time.*
   Savigny wrote[5]:

2–004

> "It is the function of the rules of law to govern legal relations. But what is the extent or sphere of their authority? What legal relations (cases) are brought under their control? The force and import of this question becomes apparent when we contemplate the nature of positive law, which does not happen to be one and the same all over the world, but varies with each nation and state; being derived in every community, partly from principles common to mankind, and partly from the operation of special agencies. It is this diversity of positive laws which makes it necessary to mark off for each, in sharp outline, the area of its authority, to fix the limits of different positive laws in respect to one another. Only by such demarcation does it become possible to decide all the conceivable questions arising from the conflict of different systems of positive law in reference to the decision of a given case.
>   The converse mode of procedure may also be followed, in order to find the solution of such questions. When a legal relation presents itself for adjudication, we seek for a rule of law to which it is subject, and in accordance with which it is to be decided; and since we have to choose between several rules belonging to different positive systems, we come back to the sphere of action marked off for each, and to conflicts resulting from such limitation. The two modes of procedure differ only in the points from which they start. The question itself is the same, and the solution cannot turn out differently in the two cases".

This exercise of "fixing the limits of different positive laws in respect to one another" is taken forward using a simple analysis of the subject matter of legal rules. They deal with *persons*, "their capacity for rights and capacity for acting, or the conditions under which they can have rights and acquire rights", and *legal relations*, including rights to specific things or to whole estates (i.e., succession), obligations and family relations.[6] Savigny concludes from this analysis that "the rule of law applicable to every given case is determined … first and chiefly, by the subjection of the person concerned to the law of a certain territory".[7]
   The assumption behind all this is surely that there is a single and correct answer to private international law questions. That is even plainer in Savigny's reformulation of the object of the exercise: "to ascertain for every legal relation (case) that law to which, in its proper nature, it belongs or is subject"[8]; or "to ascertain, for the legal relations of every class, to what territory it belongs, and therefore, as it were, to discover its seat", an inquiry to be based on "a comparative view of the legal relations themselves".[9]

---

[3] By Wieacker in his *Privatrechtsgeschichte der Neuzeit*, in the translation by Weir (as *A History of Private Law in Europe*, Clarendon Press, Oxford, 1995) p.304.
[4] 2nd edn, (Edinburgh: T. & T. Clark, 1880).
[5] ibid., 344; in Guthrie's translation, pp.47–48.
[6] ibid., para.345; p.56.
[7] ibid., para.345; p.57.
[8] ibid., para.348; p.70
[9] ibid., para.361; p.139.

Story and the doctrine of comity[10]

2–005   In 1835 Joseph Story, a professor at Harvard University and a justice of the United States Supreme Court, published his *Commentaries on the Conflict of Laws, Foreign and Domestic*.[11] It is a remarkable work, combining exposition of the case law developed in England and in the US with lengthy quotations from the leading writers in the civil law tradition. It has been described as "the most remarkable and outstanding work on the conflict of laws which had appeared since the thirteenth century in any country and in any language".[12]

There is an ambivalence in Story's treatment of the nature of the conflict of laws. Although he cites extensively from their writings, his opinion of the civilians of continental Europe is distinctly unflattering. "Their works ... abound with theoretical distinctions, which serve little other purpose than to provoke idle discussions, and with metaphysical subtleties which perplex, if they do not confound, the inquirer".[13] There speaks the authentic voice of the pragmatic common lawyer! Story took over Huber's doctrine of comity and made it the basis of his own system[14]:

> "The true foundation on which the subject rests is that the rules which are to govern are those which arise from mutual interest and utility; from the sense of the inconveniences which would arise from a contrary doctrine; and from a sort of moral necessity to do justice in order that justice may be done to us in return".

In England, Story's doctrine of comity was rejected by Dicey on the following grounds[15]:

> "If the assertion that the recognition or enforcement of foreign law depends upon comity means only that the law of no country can have effect as law beyond the territory of the sovereign by whom it was imposed, unless by permission of the state where it is allowed to operate, the statement expresses, though obscurely, a real and important fact. If, on the other hand, the assertion that the recognition or enforcement of foreign laws depends upon comity is meant to imply that ... when English judges apply French law, they do so out of courtesy to the French Republic, then the term 'comity' is used to cover a view which, if really held by any serious thinker, affords a singular specimen of confusion of thought produced by laxity of language. The application of foreign law is not a matter of caprice or option; it does not arise from the desire of the sovereign of England, or of any other sovereign, to show courtesy to other states".

Collins has traced the abandonment of the comity doctrine as a basis for private international law,[16] but he observes that while it may be discredited in the eyes of

---

[10] See Lorenzen, *Selected Articles on the Conflict of Laws* (1947) pp.138–139, 158–160, and 199–201; Cheatham, (1945) 58 Harv.L.Rev. 361 at 373–378; Anton, *Private International Law* (Edinburgh: W. Green and Son, 1970), pp.21–24; Yntema, (1966) 65 Mich.L.Rev. 1.

[11] 2nd edn (Boston: Little, Brown and Co, 1841).

[12] Lorenzen, *Selected Articles on the Conflict of Laws* (1947) pp.193–194. But for a ruthless attack on Story's postulates, which were an extension of those of Huber, see Cook, *Logical and Legal Bases of the Conflict of Laws* (Cambridge MA: Harvard University Press, 1942), Ch.2.

[13] para.11; p.10.

[14] Story, op. cit., s.35.

[15] Dicey, *The Conflict of Laws* (London: Stevens and Sons, 1896), p.10.

[16] Collins, in Fawcett (ed.), *Reform and Development of Private International Law* (Oxford: Oxford University Press, 2002), Ch.4.

text-writers it thrives in judicial decisions. The theory has performed, and may still perform, a useful function in freeing the conflict of laws from parochialism, and in making our judges more internationalist in outlook and more tolerant of foreign law than they might otherwise have been. In the European area of justice it has been supplemented and possibly supplanted by the principle of mutual trust[17].

Dicey and the theory of vested rights[18]

Dicey's treatise *The Conflict of Laws* was first published in 1896, though it had been in preparation since 1882. Dicey identified in Savigny, Bar, and other continental writers a theoretical approach, aiming to show what ought of necessity to be in any given case the rule of private international law. He admitted that the advantages of such an approach might be underrated by English lawyers "to whose whole conception of law it is at bottom opposed". But he then went on to identify its weakness[19]:

2–006

> "it rests on the assumption, common to most German jurists, but hardly to be admitted by an English lawyer, that there exist certain self-evident principles of right whence can be deduced a system of legal rules, the rightness of which will necessarily approve itself to all competent judges".

There is some irony in the fact that Dicey's survey concludes with the formulation of a set of General Principles of the subject.[20]

In Dicey's view, the growth of choice of law rules was "the necessary result of the peaceful existence of independent nations combined with the prevalence of commercial intercourse": these conditions compelled judges of every nation "by considerations of the most obvious convenience" to apply foreign laws.[21] Noting, and perhaps overstating, the similarity between the rules adopted in practice in different countries, Dicey explained this by the asserting that courts everywhere had in mind the same object. "All, or nearly all, the rules as to choice of law, which are adopted by different civilised countries, are provisions for applying the principle that rights duly acquired under the law of one country should be recognised in every country".[22]

This leads to Dicey's General Principle No.1:

---

[17] See paras 5–011. The principles of 'comity' and 'mutual trust' are undoubtedly related but wholly distinguishable, but are nevertheless often mentioned together. See e.g. Hennigan and Kenny, (2015) 64 I.C.L.Q. 197, p.199.

[18] See Dicey, 3rd edn, pp.11 at 23–33; Beale, *Treatise on the Conflict of Laws* (New York: Baker, Voorhis & Co, 1935), Vol. 3, pp.1967–1975; Cheatham, (1945) 58 Harv.L.Rev. 361 at 379–385; Carswell, (1959) 8 I.C.L.Q. 268.

[19] Dicey, op. cit., pp.18–19.

[20] cf. the observation by Cook, op. cit.; p.6, that both Story and Dicey do at times, without being fully conscious of it, revert to the theoretical method which professedly they had abandoned.

[21] Dicey, op. cit., p.8.

[22] Dicey, op. cit., p.12.

> "Any right which has been duly acquired under the law of any civilised country is recognised and, in general, enforced by English courts, and no right which has not been duly acquired is enforced or, in general, recognised by English courts".[23]

Savigny had many years before considered a not dissimilar proposition "that local law should always be applied by which vested rights shall be kept intact".[24] He dismissed it in a single sentence: "This principle leads into a complete circle; for we can only know what are vested rights, if we know beforehand by what local law we are to decide as to their complete acquisition".[25] Dicey acknowledged this criticism, but had no real answer to it.

It was left to Beale, the Reporter of the American Law Institute's first *Restatement of the Conflict of Laws*, to elevate the vested rights theory into a dogma and make it the theoretical basis of his system. Obsession with this theory led Beale to make some surprisingly trenchant statements, for example:

> "The question whether a contract is valid can on general principles be determined by no other law than that which applies to the acts [of the parties], that is, by the law of the place of contracting ... If ... the law of the place where the agreement is made annexes no legal obligation to it, *there is no other law which has power to do so.*"[26]

The vested rights theory has been effectively destroyed by Arminjon[27] in France and by Cook[28] and Lorenzen[29] in the US. Cook was trained as a physical scientist and he was something of a philosopher as well as a lawyer. Probably no more incisive mind than his has ever been applied to the problems of the conflict of laws. Certainly it is true that he "discredited the vested rights theory as thoroughly as the intellect of one man can ever discredit the intellectual product of another".[30] Objections to the vested rights theory include the following:

(1)   As Savigny noted long ago, the theory "leads into a complete circle; for we can only know what are vested rights if we know beforehand by what local law we are to decide as to their complete acquisition".[31]

(2)   The theory assumes that for every situation in the conflict of laws there is one[32] and only one "jurisdiction" which has power to determine what legal

---

[23] Dicey, op. cit., pp.23–24. There is a fascinating discussion (ibid., p.30) about which countries could be regarded for this purpose as "civilised". France, the US and Mexico qualified; but not Turkey and China. Dicey indicates no criteria.

[24] para.361; p.147.

[25] para.361; p.147.

[26] Beale, op. cit., vol. 2, p.1091 (italics added).

[27] (1933) II Hague *Recueil des cours*, 5–105.

[28] (1924) 33 Yale L.J. 457; reprinted in Cook, op. cit., Ch.1. See also Chs 13 and 14.

[29] (1924) 33 Yale L.J. 736; reprinted in Lorenzen, op. cit., Ch.1. See also pp.104–111.

[30] Currie, *Selected Essays on the Conflict of Laws* (Durham NC: Duke University Press, 1963), p.6, cf. Cavers, Book Review of Cook, (1943) 56 Harv.L.Rev. 1170, 1172: "the author's technique has enabled him to destroy the intellectual foundations of the system to the erection of which Professor Beale devoted a lifetime".

[31] Savigny, op. cit., p.147. Yntema, (1953) 2 Am.Jo.Comp. Law 297 at 313 states that Dicey "does not appear to have considered Savigny's objection that the principle [of vested rights] is circular". This is wrong, because Dicey quoted Savigny's statement (3rd edn, p.33), though his attempt to refute it is unconvincing.

[32] The theory affords no guidance when the cause of action arose, e.g., on the high seas.

consequences should follow in the given situation. It therefore led to the formulation of broad mechanical rules which had to be applied in order to select the relevant "jurisdiction", regardless of the content of its law and regardless of the social and economic considerations involved.

(3)   The theory derived whatever plausibility it had from simple cases where all the facts occurred in one country but the action was brought in another. If the facts are distributed between two foreign countries, or between one foreign country and the forum, the case presents a problem in the conflict of laws not only for the forum but also for the foreign country or countries concerned and indeed for any court in the world. Hence it is impossible to tell what rights have been acquired under the foreign law unless the forum inquires how the foreign court would decide this very case. This introduces the problem of *renvoi,* which according to the first Restatement[33] (but not according to Dicey[34]) is ordinarily to be rejected. Dicey, it would seem, "stuck to the logic of the vested rights theory to the bitter end".[35]

(4)   It is undeniable that the courts may decline, for a variety of reasons, to enforce the claimant's rights under the foreign law. Examples are cases in which the forum's public policy is invoked, or in which the forum classifies the foreign rule as procedural. The demolition of the vested rights theory was Cook's great contribution. In his original article,[36] published in 1924, which was never adequately answered and not at all by Beale, he discussed the famous case of *Milliken v Pratt,*[37] to which we shall return later in this chapter:

> A married woman, domiciled in Massachusetts, in that state signed and gave to her husband an offer addressed to the plaintiff in Maine, offering to guarantee payment by her husband for goods to be sold to him by the plaintiff. The husband posted the letter to the plaintiff in Maine, and the plaintiff accepted the offer there by sending the goods from that state. By the law of Massachusetts, a married woman had no capacity to make a contract of guarantee; by the law of Maine she had. The Massachusetts court held that the law of Maine governed because the contract was made there, and therefore the lady was liable.

Cook pointed out that, for the Maine court as well as for the Massachusetts court, this case presented a problem in the conflict of laws; and that the Massachusetts court could not have enforced a Maine-created right unless it undertook to discover how a Maine court would have decided this very case, which (since it contented itself with ascertaining the domestic law of Maine) it did not.

In the US, the *Restatement Second* has abandoned the vested rights theory and all its consequences. No longer is it said that the validity of a contract and the question of liability for torts are governed by the law of the place where the contract was made or the tort committed. Instead, the Restatement lays down that

---

[33] Sections 7, 8.
[34] 3rd edn, Appendix 1.
[35] Cook, op. cit., p.371.
[36] (1924) 33 Yale L.J. 457; reprinted in Cook, op. cit., Ch.1.
[37] 125 Mass.374 (1878).

both these questions are determined by "the local law of the state which has the most significant relationship to the occurrence and the parties".[38]

The local law theory[39]

2–007 Cook's positive contribution to doctrine in the conflict of laws is usually known as the local law theory. His method, congenial to an English lawyer, was not to start with preconceived ideas about the nature of law, but to proceed inductively by a method of scientific empiricism, stressing what the courts have done rather than what the judges have said. Noting the inescapable fact that in a case such as *Milliken v Pratt*[40] the court enforced a Massachusetts-created right and not a Maine-created right, and feeling the need to reconcile the application of foreign law with the doctrine of territorial sovereignty, Cook concluded that the forum always enforced rights created by its own law. In his own words[41]:

> "The forum, when confronted by a case involving foreign elements, always applies its own law to the case, but in doing so adopts and enforces as its own law a rule of decision identical, or at least highly similar though not identical, in scope with a rule of decision found in the system of law in force in another state or country with which some or all of the foreign elements are connected, the rule so selected being in many groups of cases, and subject to the exceptions to be noted later, the rule of decision which the given foreign state or country would apply, not to this very group of facts now before the court of the forum, but to a *similar but purely domestic group of facts involving for the foreign court no foreign element* ... The forum thus enforces not a foreign right but a right created by its own law".

Cook's theory was at first enthusiastically received in England, but enthusiasm has since waned. The theory seems sterile because there really is no need to reconcile the application of foreign law with the doctrine of territorial sovereignty, as Cook—no less than the protagonists of the vested rights theory—assumed.[42] For the law of England includes not only the domestic law of England but also its rules of the conflict of laws, which are just as much part of English law as the law of contract or the law of torts. Hence, it is no abdication of English sovereignty to apply foreign law in English courts if the English rules of the conflict of laws lay down that foreign law is applicable. To say that in such a case the English court is not applying foreign law but enforcing rights acquired under foreign law (vested rights theory), or modelling its rule of decision on that of the foreign law (local law theory), is really to play with words.

The reader may well conclude that the theoretical debates of the past centuries have made little real progress. There must remain practical questions as to how the courts actually go about the business of deciding cases which have international aspects. To these methodological questions we now turn.

---

[38] *Restatement Second*, s.145 (torts); s.188 (contracts). This is subject (in contracts) to a choice of law by the parties: ss.186 and 187.

[39] See Cook, op. cit., Ch.1; Cheatham, (1945) 58 Harv.L.Rev. 361 at 385–391.

[40] 125 Mass.374 (1878), the facts of which are given above.

[41] Cook, op. cit., pp.20–21 (his italics). Cook derived this local law theory from Judge Learned Hand's judgment in *Guinness v Miller* 291 F. 769 (1923), but cf. Cavers, (1950) 63 Harv.L.Rev. 822 on the differences between the two approaches.

[42] See Cook, op. cit., p.51 at n.9, where he accepted Story's version of Huber's first two axioms.

METHODS

Jurisdiction-selecting rules or rule-selecting rules?

The typical rules of the conflict of laws select a particular country whose law will govern the matter in question, irrespective of the content of that law. They do not select a particular rule of law. Theoretically at least, the court does not need to know what the content of the foreign law is until after it has been selected.[43] But that approach is not the only possible one.

2–008

Cavers

In 1933, Cavers published an important article[44] in which he deplored the "jurisdiction-selecting" technique (as he called it) of the traditional conflict of laws system. He pointed out that to apply the law of a particular jurisdiction without regard to the content of that law was bound to lead to injustice in the particular case and to generate false problems. "The court is not idly choosing a law; it is determining a controversy. How can it choose wisely without considering how that choice will affect that controversy?"[45] The court's duty is to reach a result which is a just one in the particular case and so it should not close its eyes to the content of the two conflicting rules of law.

2–009

As an illustration of what he had in mind, Cavers posed a hypothetical case based on *Milliken v Pratt*,[46] but with the laws of the two states reversed. Suppose that a married woman domiciled in Massachusetts makes a contract in Maine, and that by the law of Massachusetts she has capacity to make such a contract, but that by the law of Maine she has not. Does it make sense to say that the law of the place of contracting governs and therefore the contract is void? Surely not: for the Maine law was intended to protect married women domiciled or resident in Maine, not married women domiciled or resident in Massachusetts. The problem is therefore a false one.

At first sight Cavers's thesis seems an attractive one. Yet on closer inspection certain doubts arise. They are as follows:

(1) As he admitted in his original article,[47] the thesis may not be workable in international conflicts as opposed to interstate conflicts within the US, because in the former situation "the application of mechanical rules of law may be regarded as necessary to save the alien litigant from xenophobia. Discretion is a safe tool only in the hands of the disinterested. Such disinterestedness may more readily be credited to courts within the bounds of a federal union".

---

[43] There are cases in which neither the judge nor the reporter tells us what difference there was between the two systems of law between which a choice had to be made. Instances are: *Chatenay v Brazilian Submarine Telegraph Co* [1891] 1 Q.B. 79; *Re Duke of Wellington* [1947] Ch. 506; *The Assunzione* [1954] P. 150; *Tzortzis v Monark Line A/B* [1968] 1 W.L.R. 406.
[44] (1933) 47 Harv.L.Rev. 173.
[45] At p.189.
[46] 125 Mass.374 (1878); above, para.2–006.
[47] (1933) 47 Harv.L.Rev. 173 at 203.

(2)   If the courts are invited to choose between two competing rules of law without being given any guidance as to the principles which should influence their choice, there is a danger that they will choose what they consider to be "the better rule". There is an observable tendency for some American courts to do just that.

(3)   To expect the courts to discard the accumulated experience of centuries and to abandon the traditional system of the conflict of laws altogether is asking a great deal. Cavers envisaged that in course of time a new body of rules would emerge from the decisions of the courts if his thesis were adopted.[48] In his later writings he saw no objection to a jurisdiction-selecting rule if it is the product of two decisions choosing on policy grounds between competing rules in cases in which the law-fact patterns are reversed, provided the way in which it was put together is kept in mind.[49]

In 1965, Cavers took this last idea further in his book *The Choice of Law Process*. The central theme of the book is the presentation of seven "principles of preference" as guides for a court in cases where the conflict of laws is neither false nor readily avoidable.[50] Five of these principles relate to torts and two to contracts and conveyances. Cavers disclaimed any idea that his seven principles were intended to form a complete system even in these two fields of law. He also emphasised that if a particular case did not fall within any of his principles, this did not mean that a contrary choice of law must be made: it simply meant that the case posed a different problem from that covered by the principle and therefore required further consideration.

Cavers' five principles in the field of torts are as follows:

(1)   Where the law of the state of injury sets a higher standard of conduct or of financial protection than the law of the state where the defendant acted or had his home, the former law should be applied.[51]

(2)   Where the law of the state in which the defendant acted and caused an injury sets a lower standard of conduct or of financial protection than the law of the plaintiff's home state, the former law should be applied.[52] A sub-principle, not given a number, provides that if both plaintiff and defendant have their homes in a state or states other than the state of injury and the law of the state of injury sets a lower standard of financial protection than that afforded by the law or laws of the parties' home state or states, the law of that home state which affords the lower degree of protection should be applied.[53]

---

[48] (1933) 47 Harv.L.Rev. 173 at 193 et seq.

[49] (1963) 63 Col.L.Rev. 1219 at 1225–1226; Cavers, *The Choice of Law Process* (Ann Arbor: University of Michigan Press, 1965), p.9, fn.24.

[50] Cavers, Chs 5, 6, 7 and 8. For comments on his method, see Reese, (1966) 35 Fordham L.Rev. 153; Ehrenzweig, (1966) 80 Harv.L.Rev. 377; Baade, (1967) 46 Tex.L.Rev. 14 at 156–175; Scoles, (1967) 20 Jo.Leg.Ed. 111; von Mehren, (1975) 60 Cornell L.Rev. 927 at 952–963; Westmoreland, (1975) 40 Mo.L.Rev. 407 at 423–427 and 459–460; Leflar, *American Conflicts Law*, 3rd edn (Indianapolis: Bobbs-Merrill Co, 1977), s.95.

[51] Cavers, op. cit., pp.139–145.

[52] pp.146–157.

[53] pp.157–159.

(3)　　Where the state in which the defendant acted has established controls (including civil liability) over the kind of conduct in which the defendant was engaged when he caused a foreseeable injury to the plaintiff in another state having no such controls, the law of the former state should be applied.[54]

(4)　　Where the law of a state in which a relationship between two parties has its seat has imposed a standard of conduct or of financial protection on one party for the benefit of the other which is higher than that of the state of injury, the law of the former state should be applied.[55]

(5)　　Where the law of a state in which a relationship between two parties has its seat has imposed a standard of conduct or of financial protection on one party for the benefit of the other which is lower than that of the state of injury, the law of the former state should be applied.[56]

Cavers proposed no principles of preference for any fields of law other than torts and contracts and conveyances. But of course there are many other fields in which his method might be used; marriage for example. Despite Cavers's own statement to the contrary,[57] it is difficult to believe that his theory will work in international situations. He has articulated some of those choice-influencing factors to which judges consciously or unconsciously resort. But in an international case, how could a judge express a preference for the rules adopted by one country or another when those countries are not component parts of a federal system but are linked only by diplomatic relations or (perhaps) by a common cultural heritage?

The truth may well be that many of the traditional rules of the conflict of laws are the product of the type of process he describes. Take, for example, the rule that the formal validity of a marriage is governed by the law of the place of celebration. As it stands, this rule is a somewhat arid statement. In order to give it colour and texture, we need to split it up into its component parts, distinguishing between cases where the law of the place of celebration holds the marriage valid and cases where it holds the marriage void. We may also have to distinguish between cases where the marriage is celebrated in England and cases where it is celebrated abroad. We then find that our simple arid rule can be expanded into four propositions:

(a)　　A marriage celebrated in England in accordance with the formalities prescribed by English domestic law is valid.

(b)　　A marriage celebrated in England not in accordance with the formalities prescribed by English domestic law is void.

---

[54] pp.159–166.

[55] pp.166–177.

[56] pp.177–180. But Cavers disapproves of this as a principle, and says that it would probably not achieve general acceptance. The decisions of the New York Appellate Division in *Kell v Henderson*, 270 N.Y.S. 2d 552 (1966), of the Supreme Court of Wisconsin in *Conklin v Horner*, 38 Wis. 2d 468, 157 N.W. 2d 579 (1968) and of the Supreme Court of Minnesota in *Milkovich v Saari*, 295 Minn. 155, 203 N.W. 2d 408 (1973) are inconsistent with it.

[57] Cavers, op. cit., pp.viii, 117, 119n.

(c) A marriage celebrated abroad in accordance with the formalities prescribed by the law of the place of celebration is valid.

(d) A marriage celebrated abroad not in accordance with the formalities prescribed by the law of the place of celebration is void.

But, and this is the point of the present discussion, that final proposition was found to be too harsh, and so a number of exceptions to it have been created on policy grounds, some by statute and some by the courts.[58] So if we make the distinctions noted above, and bear in mind the exceptions to proposition (d), our simple, arid rule for the formal validity of marriage assumes a much less mechanical air.

It does not seem necessary to abandon the whole existing system of the conflict of laws, with its apparatus of concepts and rules, as long as it yields acceptable results. The particular history of the development of the rules of the conflict of laws in the US, where the influence of the vested rights theory led to the appearance of some indefensible rules, may have made a radically new approach inevitable. Elsewhere, there is no such urgent need, and it makes for economy of thought (and that means in practice judicial time, and so expense) to be able to apply a conflict rule instead of having to think out each problem afresh each time it arises. The great value of Cavers' contribution is that it does enable the "false conflict" to be identified and avoided. This is a matter which will be considered in more detail later in this chapter.

Currie: governmental interest analysis

2–010 An even more revolutionary opponent of the traditional system than Cavers was Brainerd Currie. In his opinion, "we would be better off without choice of law rules".[59] In a series of challenging articles, he inveighed again and again against "the system"; and he had some very hostile things to say about it. He deployed a rich array of adjectives: conceptualistic, irrational, mindless, ruthless, wretched, spurious, futile, arbitrary, hypnotic, mystical, intoxicating. The existing system was characterised as an apparatus, a machine, a field of sophism, mystery and frustration: "it has not worked and cannot be made to work".

Currie began his attack on "the system" by an analysis in depth of *Milliken v Pratt*.[60] Noting that the policies of the two states concerned were in conflict, he identified the policy of Massachusetts law as designed to protect Massachusetts married women, and the policy of Maine law as designed to protect the security of transactions by giving effect to the reasonable expectations of the parties. He then demonstrated with the aid of a number of ingenious tables that the application of the law of the place of contracting generated more false problems than there were real ones, and then solved the false problems, more often than not, in an obviously unacceptable way, by defeating the interests of both the states concerned, or by defeating the interests of one without advancing the interests of the other. He did not draw from this the conclusion which Cook had

---

[58] See below, para.11–007.
[59] Currie, *Selected Essays on the Conflict of Laws*, p.183.
[60] 125 Mass.374 (1878); see above, para.2–006. Currie's article now appears as Ch.2 of his book.

drawn,[61] namely, that the law of the domicile would be a better solution of the problem than the law of the place of contracting. He admitted that the application of this law would eliminate the false problems. But he rejected it on the grounds that "domicile is an intolerably elusive factor in commercial transactions"[62]; and that the application of the law of the domicile "would be commercially inconvenient and would consistently prefer the 'obsolete' to the 'progressive' policy".[63]

Instead, Currie proposed a radical new method for solving conflicts problems which would dispense with traditional conflict rules altogether. The latest statement of his thesis is as follows[64]:

(1) When a court is asked to apply the law of a foreign state different from the law of the forum, it should inquire into the policies expressed in the respective laws, and into the circumstances in which it is reasonable for the respective states to assert an interest in the application of those policies. In making these determinations the court should employ the ordinary processes of construction and interpretation.

(2) If the court finds that one state has an interest in the application of its policy in the circumstances of the case and the other has none, it should apply the law of the only interested state.[65]

(3) If the court finds an apparent conflict between the interests of the two states it should reconsider.[66] A more moderate and restrained interpretation of the policy or interest of one state or the other may avoid conflict.[67]

(4) If, upon reconsideration, the court finds that a conflict between the legitimate interests of the two states is unavoidable, it should apply the law of the forum.[68]

(5) If the forum is disinterested, but an unavoidable conflict exists between the laws of two other states, and the court cannot with justice decline to adjudicate the case, it should apply the law of the forum—until someone comes along with a better idea.

Currie claimed that acceptance of his "governmental interest" analysis would dispense not only with traditional conflict rules but also render obsolete such doctrines as *renvoi*, characterisation and public policy, which he regarded as devices required to make "the system" work.

Before we attempt to evaluate this revolutionary thesis, a few words of explanation are required. First, Currie was adamant that if the forum and the foreign state concerned each had an interest in the application of its law, the law

---

[61] Cook, op. cit., Ch.16.

[62] Currie, op. cit., p.103.

[63] Currie, op. cit., p.180.

[64] (1963) 63 Col.L.Rev. 1233 at 1242–1243. Other succinct statements of his thesis appear in Currie, op. cit., pp.183–184 and 188–189.

[65] This, says Currie, is what the court did in *Babcock v Jackson*, 12 N.Y. 2d 473, 191 N.E. 2d 279 (1963).

[66] This proposition formed no part of Currie's earlier statements of his position. It was added later.

[67] On the more moderate and restrained interpretation, see further below..

[68] This, says Currie, is what the court did in *Kilberg v Northeast Airlines*, 9 N.Y. 2d 34; 172 N.E. 2d 526 (1961).

of the forum must be applied, even though the foreign state had the greater interest. He refused to concede that the forum was entitled to weigh the interests of the two states. His reason was that assessment of the respective values of the competing legitimate interests of two sovereign states, in order to determine which is to prevail, is a political function of a very high order. This is a function that should not be committed to courts in a democracy. It is a function that the courts cannot perform effectively, for they lack the necessary resources.[69]

Second, as he himself admitted, Currie's method afforded no intellectually satisfying solution of "the intractable problem of the disinterested third state", that is cases where the forum has no interest in the outcome, but two foreign states have conflicting interests. He discussed this problem several times in his book,[70] and later devoted a special article to it.[71] In that article he minimised the practical importance of the problem by noting that actual cases involving it are extremely rare. He suggested that if possible the forum should avoid the problem by declining jurisdiction on forum non conveniens grounds; or, if that proved impossible, by construing it away by finding that the interest of one of the two foreign states did not really exist.[72] Lacking either of these solutions, the forum should either apply the law which it thinks Congress would apply if it legislated on the question, or should apply the law of the forum. He said, "If I were a judge I think I should prefer application of the law of the forum as the bolder technique. But then, I am a pretty old-fashioned fellow".[73] His contempt for traditional rules of the conflict of laws was such that he would not apply them even in this situation.

Old-fashioned or not, Currie's avowed object was to reduce the conflict of laws garden to ashes.[74] His ideas have been widely but not universally accepted in the US, not only by academics but also by courts; European writers, however, are more sceptical.[75] The following are among the difficulties which acceptance of his theory would present to an English court:

(1)   The conflict of laws deals mainly with private law and is concerned with the interests of private persons and not with the interests of governments. It may be doubted whether governments are really interested in having their law applied in a conflict of laws situation, unless indeed the government of

---

[69] Currie, op. cit., p.182.

[70] Currie, op. cit., pp.62–64, 120–121, 606–609 and 720–721.

[71] Currie, (1963) 28 Law and Contemporary Problems 754.

[72] This is what the court did in *Reich v Purcell* 63 Cal. 2d 31; 432 P. 2d 727 (1967).

[73] (1963) 28 Law and Contemporary Problems 754 at 780.

[74] Currie, op. cit., p.185.

[75] For a selection of comments on Currie's theory, see Hill, (1960) 27 U. of Chi.L.Rev. 463 (for Currie's reply, see Ch.12); Ehrenzweig, *Conflict of Laws* (St. Paul MN: West Publishing Co, 1962), pp.348–351; (for Currie's reply, see (1964) Duke L.J. 424 at 435–436); Leflar, op. cit., s.92; Kegel, (1964) Recueil des Cours, II, 95, 180–207; Reese, (1964) I Hague *Recueil des cours* 315, 329–333; Reese, (1965) 16 U. of Tor.L.J. 228; Chief Justice Traynor, (1965) Duke L.J. 426; Cavers, op. cit., pp.72–75, 96–102; Baade, (1967) 46 Tex.L.Rev. 141–151; Kahn-Freund, (1968) II Hague *Recueil des cours*, 5, 56–61; (1974) III *Recueil des cours*, 147, 413–415; von Mehren, (1975) 60 Cornell L.Rev. 927 at 935–941; Westmoreland, (1975) 40 Mo.L.Rev. 407 at 421–423 and 455–459; Fawcett, (1982) 31 I.C.L.Q. 189.

a country is a party to the action: and even then it may suit its purpose to argue that the foreign law and not its own should be applied.

(2)   Over one-third of Currie's book is devoted to a discussion of how his method is affected by the American Constitution, and in particular by the clauses dealing with full faith and credit, due process of law, privileges and immunities and equal protection of the laws.[76] Transplanted to a different environment, it is difficult to see how his theory would work in the absence of constitutional checks and balances.

(3)   It may be doubted whether Currie's refusal to concede that the forum is entitled to weigh its interests in the balance against those of the foreign state concerned is really consistent with his later and more refined view that, if the forum is confronted by an apparent conflict, it may be able to avoid the conflict by a "moderate and restrained interpretation" of its policy or that of the foreign state. For what is this but weighing in disguise?[77]

(4)   If the forum has an interest in the application of its law that cannot be construed away by a "moderate and restrained interpretation of its policy", Currie's method requires that the law of the forum should be applied, even if some other state has a much greater interest, and even if the result is to disappoint the reasonable expectations of the parties. Thus the interest of the forum prevails over all other considerations. And, as he freely admitted, his method sacrifices the goal of uniformity of result irrespective of the forum in which the action is brought, which has always been regarded as one of the most important objectives of the conflict of laws. For if there is a true conflict, and each state applies its own law as Currie's method requires, then the result will depend on the plaintiff's choice of forum. For this reason his method has been criticised as unduly orientated in favour of the *lex fori* and in favour of plaintiffs.

(5)   Currie's method requires that the "interest" of the forum and of the foreign state should be easily identifiable by counsel and court. This requirement is only fulfilled in the simplest of cases. In one of his articles,[78] Currie took nearly 40 pages to identify the policy behind a North Carolina statute of 1933 which prohibited actions on the personal covenant by certain kinds of mortgagee after foreclosure proceedings.

It is unrealistic to suppose that the purposes behind substantive rules of law are so clear, so unambiguous, and so singular that we can hope to discover them in the course of a trial with some degree of certainty and without risk of error. This is true of the substantive rules of the forum, and even more true of the substantive rules of foreign law. A rule of law is often the outcome of conflicting social, economic, political and legal pressures. It is an amalgam of conflicting interests. It does not express unequivocally a single "governmental interest" to the exclusion of all others. If it is an ancient rule of law, its original purpose may be lost in the mists of antiquity; and its continuance may simply be due to inertia or to lack of

---

[76] Currie, op. cit., Chs 5, 6, 10, 11. It may be noted that aliens as well as American citizens are within the protection of the due process and equal protection clauses.

[77] Currie's answer to this criticism is to be found in Currie, op. cit., pp.604–606, and in (1963) 28 Law and Contemporary Problems, 754, 756–761.

[78] Reprinted as Ch.8.

Parliamentary time to abolish it. Hence, what Currie said about the weighing of interests applies equally to the determination of policies: "it is a function that the courts cannot perform effectively, for they lack the necessary resources".[79]

(6) To expect the courts to abandon choice of law rules, and proceed on a case-by-case basis through governmental interest analysis, seems futile. Because of the doctrine of precedent, cases decided on the basis of governmental interest are bound to yield choice of law rules. These rules may differ from the traditional ones, but they are still rules, and as such are binding on the courts in future cases. Hence, as has been well said, "trying to throw away choice of law rules is like trying to throw away a boomerang".[80]

However, in spite of these criticisms, it must freely be admitted that Currie, like Cavers, did perform a useful service in enabling us to identify and avoid false problems. These will be discussed in more detail later in this chapter.

Choice-influencing factors

2–011 In 1952, Cheatham and Reese published an article in which they listed and commented on a number of policies which they believed should guide the courts in deciding choice of law questions and in formulating rules for the choice of law.[81] The American Law Institute adopted these policies (with some modifications) in the *Restatement Second of the Conflict of Laws,* of which Reese was Reporter.

Section 6 of the *Restatement* says that in the absence of direct guidance from a relevant statute, the factors to be weighed by a court include the following:

(1) *The needs of the interstate and international systems.* Choice of law rules should seek to further harmonious relations between states and nations and to facilitate commercial intercourse between them.

(2) *The relevant policies of the forum.* Every rule of law, whether embodied in a statute or in judge-made law, was designed to achieve one or more purposes. Therefore a court should have regard for these purposes in determining whether to apply its own rule or the rule of another country in the decision of a particular issue.

(3) *The relevant policies of other interested states.* The forum, says the *Restatement Second*, should give consideration not only to its own relevant policies but also to those of all other interested states. It should seek to reach a result that will achieve the best possible accommodation of these policies. It is usually desirable that the state whose interests are most deeply affected should have its law applied.

---

[79] Currie, op. cit., p.182, quoted above at p.32.
[80] Rosenberg, (1967) 67 Col.L.Rev. 459 at 464. cf. Cavers, op. cit., p.74.
[81] 52 Col.L.Rev. 959 (1952). See also Reese, (1963) 28 Law and Contemporary Problems 679; (1964) I Hague *Receuil des cours* 315, 340–356.

(4)   *The protection of justified expectations.* As a general rule, a person is entitled to expect that conduct regulated in accordance with the law of one country (for example, the country in which the conduct takes place) will not be called in question in another country.

(5)   *The basic policies underlying the particular field of law.* Situations sometimes arise where the policies of the interested states are largely the same but there are minor differences between their relevant local rules. In such instances, there is good reason for the court to apply the local law of that state which will best achieve the basic policy, or policies, underlying the particular field of law involved.

(6)   *Certainty, predictability and uniformity of result.* These values, says the *Restatement*, are important in all areas of the law; and to the extent that they are attained in choice of law, forum-shopping will be discouraged.

(7)   *Ease in the determination and application of the law to be applied.* Ideally, choice of law rules should be simple and easy to apply. Pushed to its logical conclusion, this policy would result in there being but one single rule, namely, that all cases should be decided in accordance with the *lex fori*. Hence, this policy should not be over-emphasised, since it is obviously of greater importance that choice of law rules should lead to desirable results. However, this policy does furnish the justification for applying the *lex fori* to questions of procedure.

A number of courts in the US have made use of this approach, or the similar development of a list of choice-influencing considerations produced by Leflar.[82] The generality of the language used in defining these factors, even with the explanations offered by their authors, makes them difficult to use. It is hard to see an English court having much patience with an argument based upon them.

False conflicts and foreign law as datum

As we have seen, the great merit of the methods of Cavers and Currie is that they enable false problems to be identified and avoided. What are these false problems, or false conflicts as they are more usually called, and how can they be identified?[83] The trouble is that no two writers agree on what constitutes a false conflict. Still, there is a large measure of agreement that false conflicts include the following:

2–012

(1)   The first class consists of cases where two countries have different laws, but one of them was obviously not intended to apply to the case in hand. Examples are: *Milliken v Pratt*[84] with the laws of the two states reversed (because the protective policy of Maine was not intended to apply to

---

[82] (1966) 41 N.Y.U.L. Rev. 267; (1966) 54 Calif.L.Rev. 1584. They are summarised in Leflar, op. cit., ss.103–107.

[83] Perhaps the most comprehensive survey is that by Westen, (1967) 55 Calif.L.Rev. 74, where copious references to the literature are given. For shorter statements, see Cavers, op. cit., pp.89–90; Leflar, op. cit., s.93. The whole notion of false conflicts is criticised by Kahn-Freund, (1974) III Hague *Recueil des cours*, 259–268.

[84] 125 Mass.374 (1878); above, para.2–006.

Massachusetts married women); the Englishman aged 20 who buys goods in a Ruritanian shop, minority ending in Ruritanian law at 21; *Babcock v Jackson*[85] (which concerned an Ontario statute limiting the liability of a host-driver giving a free lift to a passenger, because the Ontario statute was not intended to apply to New York hosts, guests and insurance companies); *Haumschild v Continental Casualty Co*[86] (because the Californian rule of interspousal immunity was not intended to apply to Wisconsin spouses). By contrast, the converse of each of these cases poses a true conflict: a married woman domiciled and resident in Massachusetts makes a contract in Maine which she is incapable of making by Massachusetts law (*Milliken v Pratt*); a Ruritanian aged 20 buys goods in an English shop; an Ontario host negligently injures an Ontario guest in New York[87]; an Illinois husband negligently injures an Illinois wife in Wisconsin.[88] The difference between false and true conflicts of this class can easily be perceived even by those who are sceptical of governmental interest analysis. In this situation, to say that one country's law was not intended to apply is only another way of saying that it had no interest in applying its law to the case.

(2)   The second class consists of cases where the laws of two countries are the same or would produce the same result. We shall see that there are some cases in which a conflict of characterisation leads to the law of neither country being applied.[89] A rather different illustration is provided by an Australian case *Koop v Bebb*[90]:

> The infant plaintiffs brought an action in the Supreme Court of Victoria for damages for the death of their father, who was a passenger in a motor vehicle driven by the defendant and who was killed as a result of the defendant's negligence. The accident occurred in New South Wales (where all parties were resident) and the father died in hospital in Victoria. Both Victoria and New South Wales had enacted legislation based on Lord Campbell's Act which permitted specified dependants to recover damages for the loss of their breadwinner. The statutes of the two states did not differ in any relevant respect.

Yet Dean J held that the action failed because the Victorian statute did not apply to wrongful acts occurring outside Victoria. His decision was reversed by the High Court of Australia; but the judges were not unanimous in their reasoning, and they made heavy weather of what should have been a simple case.

(3)   In some types of case, perhaps especially in the area of tort, the issues should be segregated and not necessarily resolved by reference to the same law.[91] This application of different laws to the separable issues is called *depeçage*. There is a danger that an undiscriminating court may segregate

---

[85] 12 N.Y. 2d 473; 191 N.E. 2d 279 (1963).
[86] 7 Wis. 2d 130; 95 N.W. 2d 814 (1959).
[87] *Kell v Henderson*, 270 N.Y.S. 2d 552 (1966).
[88] *Zelinger v State Sand and Gravel Co*, 38 Wis. 2d 98; 156 N.W. 2d 466 (1968); cf. *Johnson v Johnson*, 107 N.H. 30, 216 A. 2d 781 (1966), where on similar facts an opposite result was reached.
[89] See below, para.20–004.
[90] (1951) 84 C.L.R. 629.
[91] See para.16–003.

the issues improperly and so produce an unjust result which distorts the laws of both the countries concerned. In *Maryland Casualty Co v Jacek*[92]:

> A husband, resident with his wife in New Jersey, negligently injured her while both were travelling in the husband's car in New York. The husband was insured under a policy issued in New Jersey which provided that the insurer would satisfy any claim which the husband might become 'legally obligated to pay'. By the law of New York, a wife could sue her husband in tort but could not recover on his insurance policy unless express provision to that effect was specifically included in the policy. By the law of New Jersey, the policy would be construed to cover the wife's injuries, but wives could not sue their husbands in tort. Thus, if all the facts had occurred in New Jersey, the wife would be unable to recover because she could not sue her husband in tort; if all the facts had occurred in New York, she would be unable to recover because the policy did not cover her injuries.

Yet a lower federal court in New Jersey held that the wife could recover, because in its view the law of New Jersey governed the construction of the policy, and the law of New York governed the question whether the wife could sue her husband in tort.[93] The result seems wrong because the laws of both States were concerned with the danger of collusive suits by husbands or wives against insurance companies. The New York law permitting suits between spouses was enacted at the same time as the New York law restrictively interpreting insurance policies. There was a clear connection between the two laws, as the New York courts had observed[94]:

> "The purpose and policy of the legislature in making these simultaneous amendments is unmistakably clear. The object was to authorise personal injury actions between spouses, and at the same time to guard against the mulcting of insurance companies by means of collusive suits between husband and wife."

The federal court in New Jersey thus exploited the interstate situation unfairly, to the detriment of the insurance company.[95] Although the laws of the two states were different, the conflict was false.

(4) Another type of false conflict is where foreign law is referred to not for a rule of decision but for a *datum*. Currie emphasised that his governmental interest analysis was confined to cases of the first class.[96] The notion of foreign law being referred to not to furnish the rule of decision but as a *datum* is perfectly familiar to English law. Perhaps the simplest illustration is afforded by foreign rules of the road. These are not rules of decision but rules of conduct, non-compliance with which may amount to negligence. The foreign rules of conduct are incorporated in the English cause of action for negligence, just as the terms of a foreign statute may be incorporated in an English contract.[97]

---

[92] 156 F.Supp. 43 (1957). cf. *Lillegraven v Tengs*, 375 P. 2d 139 (1962).
[93] The case was decided two years before *Haumschild v Continental Casualty Co* 7 Wis. 2d 130; 95 N.W. 2d 814 (1959), where the rule of the *lex loci delicti* in this situation was abandoned.
[94] *Fuchs v London and Lancashire Indemnity Co*, 14 N.Y.S. 2d 387, 389 (1940).
[95] Contra, Reese (1973) 73 Col.L.Rev. 58 at 67–68, who approves of the result in this case.
[96] Currie, p.178.
[97] cf. *The Halley* (1868) L.R. 2 P.C. 193 at 203.

Currie's idea of foreign law being referred to as a *datum* was very much wider than this. He said that if a widow claims workmen's compensation in New York for the death of her husband there, or claims to be entitled as his widow under a New York will or intestacy, and the validity of her marriage is governed by Italian law, then this is not a case in the conflict of laws at all, since New York law in both cases furnishes the rule of decision, and Italian law furnishes no more than a *datum*.[98] This extremely narrow conception of what constitutes a case in the conflict of laws is certainly not adopted in England. If it were, it would mean that our choice of law rules for the validity of marriage could only be treated as true choice of law rules in the context of petitions for a decree of nullity or for a declaration as to status, and not in any other context. Apparently Currie would regard *Simonin v Mallac*[99] as a case in the conflict of laws, because the validity of the marriage was in issue in nullity proceedings brought by the wife against the husband. But he would not regard *Ogden v Ogden*[100] as a case in the conflict of laws, because the invalidity of the marriage was asserted as a defence to the second husband's petition for nullity on the ground of bigamy. This distinction seems very artificial.

There are three points on which all the modern American conflicts experts are agreed: first, the vested rights theory is dead; secondly, the mechanical place of contracting and place of tort rules of the first *Restatement* have rightly been abandoned; and thirdly, conflicts problems must be resolved in a flexible manner, case by case and issue by issue. But there agreement stops. In fact none of the new American methods is suitable for adoption by English courts in international cases. We would do better to build on what is good in the traditional system, as the *Restatement Second* seeks to do, rather than to abolish that system altogether and start again. The growth of a corpus of private international law derived from the EU can be seen as underlining that conclusion: the detailed rules may differ markedly from those of English common law, but the evolutionary[101] methodology is much the same. There is however one idea found in that European material which comes close to some of the American notions: that of the mandatory rule. The concept of mandatory rules[102] has found its way in the European area of justice, particularly in relation to the applicable law to contractual and non-contractual obligations. The developments in this regard are discussed in Chs 15 and 16.

---

[98] Currie, pp.69–72 and 177–178.
[99] (1860) 2 Sw. & Tr. 67.
[100] [1908] P. 46.
[101] See Symeonides, "The American Revolution and the European Evolution in Choice of Law: Reciprocal Lessons" and Michaels, "The New European Choice-of-Law Revolution" in (2008) 82 Tulane Law Rev. For an international comparative analysis see Symeonides, *Codifying Choice of Law Around the World* (Oxford: Oxford University Press, 2014).
[102] See further Ch.4.

Interdisciplinary and transdisciplinary[103] insights

Conflicts theory has also been the object of analysis of other legal disciplines, such as legal theory or public international law, and from disciplines beyond the law, such as anthropology, sociology or economics. There are various methodologies, that is, lenses, with which to study our very ingenious and fascinating discipline. It has been described as "a site of cosmopolitan progress on multicultural issues".[104] Responding to contemporary critique that perceives the conflict of laws as "a maze of legal technicalities", culturalist analysis with insights from anthropology provides tools for understanding the cultural background of the conflict of laws. Riles explains that the doctrines and methods of our discipline which implicitly recognise the importance of cultural conflict are sometimes the most difficult to implement and in some cases the most malleable and subject to criticism for that reason. As we have seen throughout this chapter some of these doctrines are particularly technical, not for the sake of technicality, but as a result of trying to address seriously the underlying problem of cultural conflict.

2–013

The consideration of cultural conflict is not new to the discipline; cultural conflicts have always been recognised as central to the matter. From Savigny and his search for the localisation of the legal relationship, these questions have been part of the theoretical framework of our discipline[105]. The contribution of Riles brings to the fore the global circulation of cultural elements in contemporary society: from the anthropological point of view 'culture' is more of a "constant act of translating and recreating or representing". This "translation" is an inherent methodological feature of the conflict of laws, perhaps more than of any other legal discipline.[106]

CONCLUSIONS

The approaches to the methodology of the conflict of laws can be bewildering in their variety. However, they do have some relatively simple lessons. The first is that conflict of law rules should be flexible and should be flexibly applied. The second is that they should never be applied without some regard to the content of the foreign law. Those simple axioms, and the notion of false conflicts, may serve to preserve all that is best in the traditional rule-selecting approach and to prevent it ossifying and becoming too inflexible to cope with the massive changes in society and commerce noted in the previous chapter.

2–014

---

[103] See the special issue edited by Michaels, Knop and Riles on "Transdisciplinary Conflicts" in (2008) 71 *Law & Contemporary Problems* 1.
[104] See A Riles, 'Cultural Conflicts' in *Law and Anthropology*, Current Legal Issues 12 (2009) 90.
[105] See A Riles, 'Cultural Conflicts' in *Law and Anthropology*, Current Legal Issues 12 (2009) 90.
[106] See A Riles, 'Cultural Conflicts' in *Law and Anthropology*, Current Legal Issues 12 (2009) 90.

CHAPTER 3

PERSONAL CONNECTING FACTORS

In the opening chapter, a number of examples referred to "English" or "French" parties, and the reader will have understood those terms as referring to people who, in some sense "belong to" or are connected to England or France. International travel means that some individuals move between countries very frequently, and while they may at all times regard themselves as English or French they have connections, stronger or weaker in character, with a range of countries. An illustration will make this clear:

> Carlos is a Venezuelan businessman working in the oil industry. He has dealings with Shell, which has offices in London and in the Netherlands. He flies to Europe for lengthy negotiations with Shell executives. Suppose that his aircraft is diverted from its intended direct route to Amsterdam by an incident of 'air-rage'[1] to Heathrow for the malefactors to be deplaned; it stays there for 45 minutes before resuming its journey. Or, he had all along booked via Heathrow, and he has one and a half hours in the transit lounge before his onward flight to Amsterdam. Or, he has two days in London, having preliminary discussions with Shell executives based in London.
>
> He arrives in Amsterdam and spends a fortnight in a hotel. Or two months in an apartment hotel. Or six months in a company flat. Or, as his brother works in the Brazilian embassy in The Hague, he stays for those periods with his brother and sister-in-law.
>
> Suppose further that he arranges to stay on in the Netherlands because of an economic downturn in Venezuela; or because he fears arrest there for some political offence; or because he wishes to marry a Dutch girl. Ten years later, he is still in the Netherlands.

Each variation of the basic facts indicates a link of a certain strength between Carlos ("a Venezuelan") and England or the Netherlands. At some point, the strength of these links may be such that he may no longer be thought of, by others or even by himself, as Venezuelan at all. The permutations are of course endless, but if we are to have a manageable system of rules we have to make use of a limited number of categories, which are explored in this chapter.

RESIDENCE

The most basic link between an individual and a country is mere physical presence, even if it be for 45 minutes spent wholly in an aircraft parked on an airport apron. Though factually clear-cut, it creates so limited a link as to have little or no significance in the conflict of laws. We will, however, hear rather more of "residence". Residence is basically a question of fact; in some contexts it means very little more than physical presence. But it does mean something more,

3–001

3–002

---

[1] Perhaps as in *Li v Quraishi*, 780 F Supp 117 (EDNY, 1992) where a drunken passenger exposed himself and urinated over some of his fellow-passengers.

for a person passing through a country as a traveller is clearly not resident there.[2] If someone becomes resident in a country, the link of residence may remain during brief periods of absence.[3]

It is difficult to be more specific, for a great deal depends on the context in which the term "residence" is used. In a case which held that university students were "resident" in their university town for electoral registration purposes,[4] Widgery LJ pointed out that, "In any seaside town in the summer the population divides itself into the residents who live there all the year round and the visitors who merely come for a period"; but the visitors' hotel-keeper would expect those visitors to use a room called the "residents' lounge". In the same way, "residence" means different things for different legal purposes.[5] To distinguish it from "ordinary residence" or "habitual residence" the concept is sometimes referred to as "residence *simpliciter*". It may be that a person will relatively easily be held resident in a country if the issue is one of the jurisdiction of that country's courts, but less easily if the context is one of residence during a fiscal year.[6] Even in a single context, "the pattern of, and reasons for, time being spent in the UK and elsewhere may be infinitely various. Decided cases illustrate a great variety of examples, and the result of one case cannot normally be used as a guide to how another should be decided, even if the two have some factors in common".[7]

ORDINARY RESIDENCE

3–003   Ordinary residence, a term often used in tax statutes, "connotes residence in a place with some degree of continuity and apart from accidental or temporary absences."[8] "If it has any definite meaning I should say it means according to the way in which a man's life is usually ordered."[9] It refers to a person's abode in a particular place or country which he has adopted voluntarily and for settled purposes, as part of the regular order of his or her life for the time being, whether of short or long duration.[10]

Ordinary residence can be changed in a day,[11] but there is no reason, on appropriate facts, for a person not to be held to be ordinarily resident in more than one country at the same time. Thus in *IRC v Lysaght*,[12] a man whose home was in the Republic of Ireland, and who came to England for one week in every month for business reasons, during which time he stayed in an hotel, was held to be

---

[2] *Matalon v Matalon* [1952] P. 233.
[3] *Sinclair v Sinclair* [1968] P. 189.
[4] *Fox v Stirk* [1970] 2 Q.B. 462.
[5] McClean, (1962) 111 I.C.L.Q. 1153.
[6] *Levene v IRC* [1928] A.C. 217; even there, relatively brief visits were held to amount to residence.
[7] *Grace v HMRC* [2009] EWCA Civ 1082 at [3] per Lloyd LJ.
[8] *Levene v IRC* [1928] A.C. 217 at p.225, per Lord Cave.
[9] ibid., at p.232, per Lord Warrington of Clyffe.
[10] *R.v Barnet LBC, Ex p. Nilish Shah* [1983] 2 A.C. 309.
[11] *Macrae v Macrae* [1949] P. 397, 403, per Somervell LJ.
[12] [1928] A.C. 234. It would be unfair to blame the House of Lords for this extraordinary decision, for they felt constrained to hold that a finding by the Special Commissioners was one of fact and so could not be disturbed on appeal.

resident and ordinarily resident in England for income tax purposes. But clearly he was also resident and ordinarily resident in the Republic.

It has been said that a child of tender years "who cannot decide for himself where to live" is ordinarily resident in his or her parents' matrimonial home, and that this ordinary residence cannot be changed by one parent without the consent of the other. If the parents are living apart and the child is, by agreement between them, living with one of them, the child is resident in the home of that parent and that ordinary residence is not changed merely because the other parent takes the child away from that home.[13]

It would, however, be wrong to assume that the term "ordinary residence" always bears the same meaning. As Lord Carnwath observed in *R. (on the application of Cornwall Council) v Secretary of State for Health*,[14] its meaning may be strongly influenced by the particular statutory context. Decisions in one context cannot be assumed to apply in others.

HABITUAL RESIDENCE

Habitual residence has long been a favourite expression of the Hague Conference on Private International Law. It appears in many Hague Conventions and therefore in English statutes giving effect to them; but it is increasingly used in other statutes as well. No definition of habitual residence has ever been included in a Hague Convention; this has been a matter of deliberate policy, the aim being to leave the notion free from technical rules which can produce rigidity and inconsistencies as between different legal systems. The expression is not to be treated as a term of art but according to the ordinary and natural meaning of the two words it contains.[15] However, there is a regrettable tendency of the courts, despite their insistence that they are not dealing with a term of art, to develop rules as to when habitual residence may and may not be established: "the English courts have been tempted to overlay the factual concept of habitual residence with legal constructs".[16] The Law Commission has spoken of the "allegedly undeveloped state" of habitual residence as a legal concept, citing, in particular, uncertainties as to the place of intention and as to the length of time required for residence to become habitual.[17]

The relationship between the two concepts of habitual residence and ordinary residence is an issue which the courts have frequently addressed, but the opinions expressed are bewildering in their variety. In *Mark v Mark*[18] Baroness Hale noted

3–004

---

[13] *Re P. (G.E.) (An Infant)* [1965] Ch. 568, 585–586.

[14] [2015] UKSC 46, [2015] 3 W.L.R. 213, at [43], a case on the National Assistance Act 1948. See, for another example, *R. v West Middlesex University Hospital* [2008] EWHC 855 (Admin.), (2008) 11 C.C.L. Rep. 358 for the meaning of ordinary residence for the purposes of the National Health Service Acts of 1997 and 2006.

[15] *ReJ (A Minor) (Abduction)* [1990] 2 A.C. 562; *Re M (Minors) (Residence Order: Jurisdiction)* [1993] 1 F.L.R. 495; Clive, 1997 Jur. Rev. 137. See also Resolution (72)1 of the Committee of Ministers of the Council of Europe on the Standardisation of the Legal Concepts of "Domicile" and "Residence" Annex, r.9.

[16] *A v A (Children: Habitual Residence)* [2013] UKSC 60; [2014] A.C. 1 at [39].

[17] *The Law of Domicile* (Law Com. No. 168), paras 3.5–3.8.

[18] [2005] UKHL 42; [2006] 1 A.C. 98, at [33].

that it was common ground that habitual residence and ordinary residence were interchangeable concepts; but also that habitual residence "may have a different meaning in different statutes according to their context and purpose."[19] In *Nessa v Chief Adjudication Officer*[20] Lord Slynn reserved the question whether the terms were always synonymous: each might take a shade of meaning from the context in which it was used, though they did share "a common core of meaning". Although the Court of Appeal expressly held in *Ikimi v Ikimi (Divorce: Habitual Residence)*[21] that the two concepts are synonymous where family law statutes are concerned, Baroness Hale's most recent observation[22] is that the Law Commissions deliberately adopted "habitual" rather than "ordinary" residence in reviewing family law issues,[23] because the latter frequently occurred in tax and immigration statutes and they thought that its use in the wholly different context of family law was a potential source of confusion.

It would seem that so far as the habitual residence of adults is concerned, especially in contexts other than those of EU law, the test to be applied will again be that of a person's abode in a particular country which he or she has adopted voluntarily and for settled purposes as part of the regular order of life for the time being[24]; the burden of proof being on the party alleging the change.[25]

As in the case of ordinary residence, the issue is essentially one of fact. From time to time, judgments place glosses on the concept of habitual residence; cited in subsequent cases, the judicial pronouncements seem to provide rules. Then comes along a case where the supposed "rule" is unhelpful, and it is discarded or qualified. So it was held in the House of Lords case of *Re J. (A Minor) (Abduction)*[26] that habitual residence cannot be acquired in a single day, as an appreciable period of time[27] and a settled purpose are required. The Supreme Court expressed doubts about these propositions in *A v A (Children: Habitual Residence)*[28]. They were, said Lord Hughes, much better regarded as helpful generalisations of fact than as propositions of law. Baroness Hale agreed; the propositions would usually but not invariably be true. She deplored the tendency to construe them as they were in a statute, and so debate the meaning of "appreciable time"; she would not accept that it is impossible to become habitually resident in a single day.[29] For many years it was thought that to acquire

---

[19] [2005] UKHL 42; [2006] 1 A.C. 98, at [15].
[20] [1999] 1 W.L.R. 1937 (HL).
[21] [2001] EWCA Civ. 873; [2002] Fam 72.
[22] *A v A (Children: Habitual Residence)* [2013] UKSC 60; [2014] A.C. 1 at [38].
[23] Law Com No 138, para.15.
[24] i.e.,the test adopted in *R. v Barnet LBC, Ex p. Nilish Shah* [1983] 2 A.C. 309, 344; *Kapur v Kapur* [1984] F.L.R. 920.
[25] *Re R (Wardship: Child Abduction)* [1992] 2 F.L.R. 481 at 487.
[26] [1990] 2 A.C. 562, strictly obiter as the issue in the case was the loss rather than the acquisition of habitual residence.
[27] In *Ikimi v Ikimi (Divorce: Habitual Residence)* [2001] EWCA Civ. 873; [2002] Fam 72, residence for 161 days in the year was sufficient in the circumstances for the acquisition of habitual residence; whereas 71 days in *Armstrong v Armstrong* [2003] EWHC 777 (Fam); [2003] 2 F.L.R. 375 was not. cf. *Re A (Abduction; Habitual Residence)* [2009] EWCA Civ 1021, [2010] 1 F.L.R. 1146 (seven–eight weeks sufficed; emphasis that movement between different EU countries).
[28] [2013] UKSC 60; [2014] A.C. 1.
[29] [2013] UKSC 60; [2014] A.C. 1 at [73] and [44] respectively.

habitual residence, a person's residence must be lawful,[30] but the House of Lords in *Mark v Mark*[31] has confirmed that it is indeed possible to acquire habitual residence, at least for tax purposes, even though the residence is not lawful. The person must live in the relevant country for a period which shows that the residence has become habitual[32]; the length of that period is not fixed; it must depend on the circumstances.[33] Habitual residence can, however, in appropriate circumstances, be lost in a day.[34] Habitual residence may continue during temporary absences,[35] but in most contexts a person can be without any habitual residence[36]; or have more than one habitual residence at any one time.[37] That habitual residence should be "adopted voluntarily" is not usually an issue; but in *Breuning v Breuning*[38] it was held that the continued presence in England of someone who had no choice but to remain in England for medical treatment did not constitute habitual residence. The Court of Session has doubted whether the element of voluntariness is always needed, using as examples the fictional case of Robinson Crusoe and the real example of Nelson Mandela as a prisoner.[39]

Although the "settled intent" has been identified as one to take up long-term residence in the country concerned,[40] the better view seems to be that evidence of intention or purpose may be important in particular cases (e.g., in establishing habituation when the actual period or periods of residence have been short) but is not essential. If long-term residence is established in a new country, the habitual residence will be there even if the individual concerned lives in an exclusively expatriate group (as in a forces' base) which simulates ordinary life in the individual's home country.[41]

---

[30] *R. v Barnet LBC, Ex p. Shah* [1983] 2 A.C. 309 at 343, Lord Scarman refusing unlawful ordinary residence on the grounds of public policy.

[31] *Mark v Mark* [2005] UKHL 42; [2006] 1 A.C. 98 at [36]. Baroness Hale did, however, leave open the caveat that a person's residence may need to be lawful for other purposes, for example, entitlement to State benefit. See *R. v Secretary of State for Health* [2009] EWCA Civ 225; [2010] 1 W.L.R. 279 (entitlement to health services; failed asylum seeker held not ordinarily resident).

[32] *Nessa v Chief Adjudication Officer* [1999] 1 W.L.R. 1937.

[33] ibid., citing the dictum of Butler-Sloss LJ in *Re AF (a Minor) (Child Abduction)* [1992] 1 F.C.R. 269, 277 that "a month can be . . . an appreciable period of time".

[34] *Re M. (Minors) (Residence Order: Jurisdiction)* [1993] 1 F.L.R. 495, 500; *Al Habtoor v Fotheringham* [2001] EWCA Civ. 186; [2001] 1 F.C.R 185.

[35] *Oundjian v Oundjian* (1979) 1 F.L.R. 198 (habitual residence throughout period of one year despite absences totalling 149 out of 365 days); *Re H (A Child) (Abduction: Habitual Residence: Consent)* [2000] 2 F.L.R. 294; *C v FC (Brussels II: free-standing application for parental responsibility)* [2004] 1 F.L.R. 317, where an absence of two years was not fatal to the continuance of habitual residence.

[36] *Hack v Hack* (1976) 6 Fam. Law 177: "unless one led a nomadic life" one had to have a habitual residence somewhere; *Re J (A Minor) (Abduction)* [1990] 2 A.C. 562. In some contexts, a piece of legislation may only be workable if there is no possibility of a gap in habitual residence: *Nessa v Chief Adjudication Officer* [1999] 1 W.L.R. 1937; *W and B v H (Child Abduction: Surrogacy)* [2002] 1 F.L.R. 1008.

[37] *Ikimi v Ikimi (Divorce: Habitual Residence)* [2001] EWCA Civ 873; [2002] Fam 72; *Armstrong v Armstrong* [2003] EWHC 777 (Fam), [2003] 2 F.L.R. 375; *C v FC (Brussels II: free-standing application for parental responsibility)* [2004] 1 F.L.R. 317; *Mark v Mark* [2005] UKHL 42; [2006] 1 A.C. 98.

[38] [2002] EWHC 236 (Fam); [2002] 1 F.L.R. 888.

[39] *Cameron v Cameron*, 1996 S.C. 17.

[40] *A v A (Child Abduction: Habitual Residence)* [1993] 2 F.L.R. 225, 235.

[41] *ReA (Minors) (Abduction: Habitual Residence)* [1996] 1 W.L.R. 25 (US serviceman in Iceland).

European autonomous meaning

3–005 The connecting factor of habitual residence has also been widely adopted by the legislators of EU law, and the leading ECJ case of *Swaddling v Adjudication Officer*[42] has held that, in the context of social security law, the term has a Community-wide meaning, being where the person's "habitual centre of their interests is to be found."[43] In *Tan v Choy*[44] this interpretation was considered as very influential. The common core of interpretation of the term 'centre of interests' is to be applied following the test set in *Marinos v Marinos*.[45]

In a particular social security context, the European legislation lists a number of factors to be considered in determining the centre of interests of the person concerned. They may include, as appropriate: the duration and continuity of presence on the territory of the Member States concerned; the person's situation (including the nature and the specific characteristics of any activity pursued, in particular the place where such activity is habitually pursued, the stability of the activity, and the duration of any work contract); his family status and family ties; the exercise of any non-remunerated activity; in the case of students, the source of their income; his housing situation, in particular how permanent it is; the Member State in which the person is deemed to reside for taxation purposes. If it is still impossible to reach agreement on the person's centre of interests, the person's intention, as it appears from such facts and circumstances, especially the reasons that led the person to move, is to be considered to be decisive for establishing that person's actual place of residence.[46]

Habitual residence of a child

3–006 The law on the habitual residence of a child was greatly changed by a series of decisions of the Supreme Court which aligned the English law with that adopted by the Court of Justice of the European Union (hereinafter CJEU). In *Proceedings brought by A*[47] that court held

> "The concept of 'habitual residence' under article 8(1) of Council Regulation (EC) No 2201/2003 must be interpreted as meaning that it corresponds to the place which reflects some degree of integration by the child in a social and family environment. To that end, in particular the duration, regularity, conditions and reasons for the stay on the territory of a member state and the family's move to that state, the child's nationality, the place and conditions of attendance at school, linguistic knowledge and the family and social relationships of the child

---

[42] Case C-90/97 [1999] E.C.R. I-1075. The case concerned social security entitlement under Regulation 1408/71. See Lamont [2007] 3 J.Priv.I.L. 261 where it is questioned whether the *Swaddling* definition can be suitably adapted for use in the family law context.

[43] At para.29.

[44] [2014] EWCA Civ 251; [2015] 1 F.L.R. 492 (habitual residence for the purposes of Regulation 2201/2003 art.3(1)(a) indent five; see further para.12–003.

[45] [2007] EWHC 2047 (Fam); [2007] 2 F.L.R. 1018 (at para.11).

[46] European Parliament and Council Regulation 987/2009 of 16 September 2009 laying down the procedure for implementing Regulation (EC) No.883/2004 on the coordination of social security systems, [2009] O.J. L 284, p. 1, Article 11.

[47] Case C-523/07 [2009] 2 E.C.R. I-2805; [2010] Fam. 42, developing the approach in Case C-497/10 *Mercredi v Chaffe* [2012] Fam 22.

in that state must be taken into consideration. It is for the national court to establish the habitual residence of the child, taking account of all the circumstances specific to each individual case."

The court also noted:

"An infant necessarily shares the social and family environment of the circle of people on whom he or she is dependent. Consequently, where … the infant is in fact looked after by her mother, it is necessary to assess the mother's integration in her social and family environment. In that regard, the tests stated in the court's case law, such as the reasons for the move by the child's mother to another member state, the languages known to the mother or again her geographic and family origins may become relevant."

That approach was endorsed by the Supreme Court in *A v A (Children: Habitual Residence)*[48]:

F and M married in Pakistan but then settled in England. Three children were born in England, but then the marriage broke down. F returned to Pakistan, M and the children remained in England. On a visit to Pakistan with her children, she was (on her account) forced by her family to return to live with F, by whom she then had a fourth child. She was eventually able to return to England, but on her own. The English court ordered the return of the children to her, holding that all the children were habitually resident in England for the purposes of section 3(1) of the Family Law Act 1986: applying a well-established rule of English law, the habitual residence in England of the three older children could not be changed by the unilateral action of one parent without the consent or acquiescence of the other. The youngest child, who had never been physically in England, was habitually resident there by reason of the habitual residence of his mother and siblings.

The Supreme Court rejected this reasoning.[49] It held that habitual residence was a question of fact and not a legal concept such as domicile. There was no legal rule akin to that whereby a child automatically took the domicile of his parents; nor a rule that a child's *habitual* residence could not be changed by the unilateral action of one parent without the consent or acquiescence of the other.[50] The essentially factual and individual nature of the inquiry should not be glossed with legal concepts that would produce a different result from that which the factual inquiry would produce. The approach of the European Court was preferable to that earlier adopted by the English courts, being focused on the situation of the child, with the purposes and intentions of the parents being merely one of the relevant factors. The test derived from *R. v Barnet LBC, Ex p. Shah*[51] should be abandoned when deciding the habitual residence of a child. Instead in cases under the Family Law Act 1986, the Hague Abduction Convention and the Brussels IIa Regulation, the approach of the European Court should be followed.

---

[48] [2013] UKSC 60; [2014] A.C. 1.
[49] See especially the summary by Baroness Hale at [54]. Note also Lady Hale's explanation at [51], approving the analysis in *DL v EL (Hague Abduction Convention: Effect of Reversal of Return Order on Appeal)* [2013] 2 F.L.R. 163, that any reference to "permanence" in the CJEU's judgment did in fact mean "stability".
[50] On this point, see also *Re H (Children) (Jurisdiction: Habitual Residence)* [2014] EWCA Civ 1101; [2015] 1 W.L.R. 863. This was reiterated in *Re R (Children)* [2015] UKSC 35; [2016] A.C. 76.
[51] [1983] 2 A.C. 309.

The Supreme Court addressed the issues again in *Re B (A Child)*.[52] The issue in that case concerned the possibility, recognised by the CJEU in *Proceedings brought by A*,[53] that it might be impossible to establish the Member State in which the child has his habitual residence. The Supreme Court interpreted this to refer to cases in which the child had no habitual residence, and not merely that it was difficult to establish where that was. It was not in the best interests of the child that it should be in a sort of limbo. Lord Wilson noted[54] that the test did not require the child's full integration in the environment of the new state but only a degree of it. He concluded[55] that the modern concept of a child's habitual residence, based on the European approach, operated in such a way as to make it highly unlikely, albeit conceivable, that a child would be in the limbo:

> "The concept operates in the expectation that, when a child gains a new habitual residence, he loses his old one. As, probably quite quickly, he puts down those first roots which represent the requisite degree of integration in the environment of the new state, up will probably come the child's roots in that of the old state to the point at which he achieves the requisite de-integration (or, better, disengagement) from it".

The views of the child

3–007   The state of mind of the child is relevant to the issue of integration. Lord Wilson addressed the issue in *Re LC (Children)*[56] and offered a very clear analysis:

> "Where a child of any age goes lawfully to reside with a parent in a State in which that parent is habitually resident, it will no doubt be highly unusual for that child not to acquire habitual residence there too. The same may be said of a situation in which, perhaps after living with a member of the wider family, a child goes to reside there with both parents. But in highly unusual cases there must be room for a different conclusion; and the requirement of some integration creates room for it perfectly. No different conclusion will be reached in the case of a young child. But, where the child is older, in particular one who is an adolescent or who should be treated as an adolescent because she (or he) has the maturity of an adolescent, and perhaps also where (to take the facts of this case) the older child's residence with the parent proves to be of short duration, the inquiry into her integration in the new environment must encompass more than the surface features of her life there. I see no justification for a refusal even to consider evidence of her own state of mind during the period of her residence there. Her mind may—possibly—have been in a state of rebellious turmoil about the home chosen for her which would be inconsistent with any significant degree of integration on her part. In the debate in this court about the occasional relevance of this dimension, references have been made to the 'wishes', 'views', 'intentions' and 'decisions' of the child. But, in my opinion, none of those words is apt. What can occasionally be relevant to whether an older child shares her parent's habitual residence is her state of mind during the period of her residence with that parent."

Baroness Hale and Lord Sumption felt that this applied not just to adolescent children but to all children.

---

[52] [2016] UKSC 4.
[53] Case C-523/07 [2009] 2 E.C.R. I-2805; [2010] Fam. 42, at [43].
[54] [2016] UKSC 4 at [39].
[55] [2016] UKSC 4 at [45].
[56] [2014] UKSC 1; [2014] A.C. 1038, especially at [37].

The case of the never-present child

An issue much discussed in *A v A (Children: Habitual Residence)* was whether a **3–008**
child could be said to be habitually resident in a country in which it had never
been physically present. This was the position of the fourth child in the instant
case; as another basis of jurisdiction was available, the court did not have to
resolve the issue.

The earlier cases were influenced by ideas, repudiated in *A v A (Children:
Habitual Residence)*, that a child's habitual residence followed that of whoever
had parental responsibility and could not be changed by the unilateral action of
one parent without the consent or acquiescence of the other. Reasoning of that
sort led Charles J to hold in *B v H (Habitual Residence: Wardship)*[57] (on facts
very similar to those in *A v A (Children: Habitual Residence)*) that a child who
was, at the date of the judgment, nearly two years old, having been born in
Bangladesh and having lived there all her short life, was habitually resident in
England. In *A v A (Children: Habitual Residence)* itself in the Court of Appeal,
Thorpe LJ gave the example of an English mother habitually resident in England
who gave birth to a child in France. As a result of complications mother and child
were hospitalised for an extended period before they are fit to come home; he
would hold the child habitually resident in England.[58]

On the other hand, in *W and B v H (Child Abduction: Surrogacy)*[59]:

> the relationship between an English surrogate mother and the Californian prospective parents
> broke down when they discovered that the mother was carrying twins, and the surrogate
> mother returned to England where she gave birth. The Californian couple applied under the
> Hague Convention on International Child Abduction for the summary return of the babies to
> the jurisdiction of the Californian court. The Convention could only apply if the twins had
> been habitually resident in California immediately before being brought to England.

Hedley J reiterated that habitual residence was a question of fact and that each
case must stand alone,[60] but that it was not possible for someone to acquire a
habitual residence in one country when they remain physically present in another
at all times. Therefore, on the particular facts of the case, the twins were not
habitually resident anywhere.[61]

In the state of the law as clarified in *A v A (Children: Habitual Residence)*,
there is much force in the view expressed by Baroness Hale, that presence is a
necessary pre-cursor to residence and thus to habitual residence.[62]

---

[57] [2002] 1 F.L.R. 388.
[58] [2012] EWCA Civ 1396; [2013] Fam. 232 at [29]. See also *Re T (A Child) (Care Proceedings:
Request to Assume Jurisdiction* [2013] EWHC 521 (Fam); [2013] 2 W.L.R. 1263.
[59] [2002] 1 F.L.R. 1008. See also *Re G (abduction: withdrawal of proceedings, acquiescence,
habitual residence)* [2007] EWHC 2807 (Fam.) and *Re F (Abduction: Unborn Child)* [2006] EWHC
2199 (Fam.); [2007] 1 F.L.R. 627.
[60] [2002] 1 F.L.R. 1008 at [23].
[61] This meant that the application under the Hague Convention failed. W then brought an action for
the summary return of the twins, and in *W and W v H (Child Abduction: Surrogacy) (No.2)* [2002] 2
F.L.R 252 the children were returned to California as the forum conveniens for their future to be
decided.
[62] [2013] UKSC 60; [2014] A.C. 1 at [55].

"It is one thing to say that a child's integration in the place where he is at present depends upon the degree of integration of his primary carer. It is another thing to say that he can be integrated in a place to which his primary carer has never taken him. It is one thing to say that a person can remain habitually resident in a country from which he is temporarily absent. It is another thing to say that a person can acquire a habitual residence without ever setting foot in a country. It is one thing to say that a child is integrated in the family environment of his primary carer and siblings. It is another thing to say that he is also integrated into the social environment of a country where he has never been."

DOMICILE

3-009   In most systems of the conflict of laws the notion of "belonging to" a country in some strong sense is of great importance: it identifies an individual's personal law, which governs questions concerning the personal and proprietary relationships between members of a family. Place of birth is an inadequate criterion by which to identify the personal law. In many (but not all) continental European countries, the personal law has traditionally been instead the law of an individual's nationality. In England and almost all common-law countries it is the law of the domicile.

Domicile is easier to illustrate than it is to define. The root idea underlying the concept is the permanent home. "By domicile we mean home, the permanent home", said Lord Cranworth,[63] "and if you do not understand your permanent home, I'm afraid that no illustration drawn from foreign writers or foreign languages will very much help you to it." The notion of home, or of permanent home, takes colour from particular facts. An Englishwoman aged 70 years, left a widow after living all her life in Somerset, goes to New Zealand to live with her married daughter; although that move may be, in practical terms, irreversible, is she not likely to regard England as her home country?

In fact, domicile cannot be equated with home, because as we shall see a person may be domiciled in a country which is not and never has been his home; a person may have two homes, but only have one domicile; a person may be homeless, but he or she must have a domicile. Indeed there is often a wide gulf between the popular conception of home and the legal concept of domicile. Domicile is "an idea of law".[64] Originally it was a good idea; but the once simple concept has been so overloaded by a multitude of cases that it has been transmuted into something further and further removed from the practical realities of life.[65] Important proposals for the reform of the law of domicile made by the Law Commission in 1987,[66] reflecting in part reforms adopted in a number of Commonwealth countries overseas[67] and examined at various points in this chapter, would narrow this gap; but unfortunately they were rejected by the Government in 1996. Partial reform has, however, been effected in Scotland with regard to the domicile of persons under the age of 16.[68]

---

[63] *Whicker v Hume* (1858) 7 H.L.C. 124, 160.

[64] *Bell v Kennedy* (1868) L.R. 1 Sc. & Div. 307, 320, per Lord Westbury.

[65] Anton, *Private International Law* (2nd edn) (Edinburgh: W Green & Son Ltd, 1990), p.125.

[66] *Law of Domicile* (Law Com. No. 168); this is a joint report with the Scottish Law Commission.

[67] See McClean, (1996) 260 *Recueil des cours* 36–54.

[68] Family Law (Scotland) Act 2006, s.22. cf McEleavy [2007] I.C.L.Q. 453.

Since the Civil Jurisdiction and Judgments Act 1982, there has been a further complication. This Act introduced a new concept which describes a certain type of link between an individual, or a company, and a country. It is called "domicile", but it is quite unlike the traditional, personal law, concept of domicile developed in English law and still important in many matters of family law and succession. It is very unfortunate that the same term had to be used to describe these two different concepts; in this chapter, it is the traditional concept which is to be examined.[69]

There are three kinds of domicile:

- *domicile of origin*, which is the domicile assigned by law to a child at birth is born;
- *domicile of choice*, which is the domicile which any independent person can acquire by a combination of residence and intention; and
- *domicile of dependency*, which means that the domicile of dependent persons (children under 16 and mentally disordered persons) is dependent on, and usually changes with, the domicile of someone else, e.g., the parent of a child.

The object of determining a person's domicile is to connect that person with some legal system for certain legal purposes. To establish this connection it is sufficient to fix the domicile in some "country" in the sense of the conflict of laws, e.g., England or Scotland, California or New York. It is not necessary to show in what part of such a country an individual is domiciled[70]; but it is usually insufficient to show that he or she is domiciled in some composite state such as the UK, the US, Australia or Canada, each of which comprises several "countries" in the conflict of laws sense. A person who emigrates, e.g., to the UK with the intention of settling either in England or Scotland, or to Canada with the intention of settling either in Nova Scotia or British Columbia, only acquires a new domicile by deciding in which country to settle and by actually settling there.[71]

This rule is unsatisfactory and the Law Commission recommended the adoption in England of rules based on those in the modern Australian legislation, so that a person who is present in a federal or composite state with the intention to settle in that state for an indefinite period should, if he is not held under the general rules to be domiciled in any country within that state, be domiciled in the country therein with which he is for the time being most closely connected.[72]

General principles

There are four general principles fundamental to the law of domicile.   **3–010**

---

[69] For domicile in the sense of the 1982 Act, see below, para.6–007.
[70] *Re Craignish* [1892] 3 Ch. 180, 192.
[71] *Bell v Kennedy* (1868) L.R. 1 Sc. & Div. 307; *Attorney General for Alberta v Cook* [1926] A.C. 444; *Gatty v Attorney General* [1951] P. 444.
[72] *The Law of Domicile*, paras 7.1–7.8.

(1) No person can be without a domicile.[73] This rule springs from the practical necessity of connecting every person with some system of law by which a number of legal relationships may be regulated.

(2) No person can at the same time have more than one domicile, at any rate for the same purpose.[74] This rule springs from that same necessity.

(3) An existing domicile is presumed to continue until it is proved that a new domicile has been acquired. Hence the burden of proving a change of domicile lies on those who assert it.[75] Varying views have been expressed as to the standard of proof required to rebut the presumption. According to Scarman J, the standard is that adopted in civil proceedings, proof on a balance of probabilities—not that adopted in criminal proceedings—proof beyond reasonable doubt.[76] There is little doubt that the test of balance of probabilities is applied in practice,[77] despite some dicta suggesting a higher standard.[78] However, as we shall see, the burden of proving that a domicile of origin has been lost is a very heavy one. Moreover, as Scarman J himself added,[79]

> "two things are clear: first, that unless the judicial conscience is satisfied by evidence of change, the domicile of origin persists; and secondly, that the acquisition of a domicile of choice is a serious matter not to be lightly inferred from slight indications or casual words."

The presumption of continuance of domicile varies in strength according to the kind of domicile which is alleged to continue. It is weakest when that domicile is one of dependency[80] and strongest when the domicile is one of origin, for "its character is more enduring, its hold stronger, and less easily shaken off".[81] More recently, Cazalet J reviewed this dictum and concluded that as far as the abandonment and acquisition of a domicile of choice is concerned "... the standard is the civil standard of proof; but ... the judicial conscience will need particularly convincing evidence to be satisfied that the balance of probabilities has been tipped."[82] Similarly, Arden LJ, dealing

---

[73] *Bell v Kennedy* (1868) L.R. 1 Sc. & Div. 307, 320; *Udny v Udny* (1869) L.R. 1 Sc. & Div. 441, 448, 453, 457.

[74] *Udny v Udny* (1869) L.R. 1 Sc. & Div. 441, 448; *Garthwaite v Garthwaite* [1964] P. 356, 378–379, 393–394.

[75] *Bell v Kennedy* (1868) L.R. 1 Sc. & Div. 307, 310, 319; *Winans v Attorney General* [1904] A.C. 287; *Ramsay v Liverpool Royal Infirmary* [1930] A.C. 588; *In the Estate of Fuld (No.3)* [1968] P. 675, 685; *Irvin v Irvin* [2001] 1 F.L.R. 178, 185B; *Cyganik v Agulian* [2006] EWCA Civ. 129, [2006] 1 F.C.R. 406.

[76] *In the Estate of Fuld (No.3)* [1968] P. 675, at pp.685–686; cf. *Re Flynn (No.1)* [1968] 1 W.L.R. 103, 115; *Re Edwards* (1969) 113 S.J. 108; *Buswell v IRC* [1974] 1 W.L.R. 1631, 1637.

[77] See, e.g., *Holliday v Musa* [2010] EWCA Civ 335; [2010] 3 FCR 280; *Haji-Ioannou vFrangos* [2009] EWHC 2310 (QB); [2010] 1 All E.R. (Comm) 303.

[78] *Henderson v Henderson* [1967] P. 77, 80 per Sir Jocelyn Simon P: "the standard of proof goes beyond a mere balance of probabilities"; *Steadman v Steadman* [1976] A.C. 536, 563.

[79] *In the Estate of Fuld (No.3)* [1968] P. 675, at p.686.

[80] *Harrison v Harrison* [1953] 1 W.L.R. 865; *Re Scullard* [1957] Ch. 107; *Henderson v Henderson* [1967] P. 77, at pp.82–83.

[81] *Winans v Attorney General* [1904] A.C. 287, 290, per Lord Macnaghten; cf. *Henderson v Henderson* [1967] P. 77, 80 per Simon P.

[82] *Irvin v Irvin* [2001] 1 F.L.R. 178, 189, per Cazalet J.

with the standard of proof, concluded: "... there is no need for any higher standard of proof ... because the civil standard has the inbuilt flexibility to take the seriousness of an allegation into account. Accordingly the more serious an allegation the more substantial will need to be the evidence to prove it on a balance of probabilities."[83]

The Law Commission's proposals for the reform of the law of domicile would leave unchanged the rule that the burden of proving the acquisition of a new domicile falls on the person alleging it. However, the normal civil standard of proof on a balance of probabilities would apply in all disputes about domicile and no higher or different quality of intention would be required when the alleged change of domicile was from one acquired at birth than when it was from any other domicile.[84]

(4) For the purposes of a rule of the conflict of laws, "domicile" means domicile in the English sense. The question as to where a person is domiciled is determined solely in accordance with English law. Thus, persons domiciled in England may acquire a French domicile of choice regardless of whether French law would regard them as domiciled there,[85] and English law alone determines when a Frenchman acquires a domicile in England.[86]

It is too wide a formulation to say that in an English court, domicile means domicile in the English sense. Under the *renvoi* doctrine,[87] English courts sometimes refer to the whole law of a foreign country, including its rules of the conflict of laws, and then accept a reference back to English law either because (i) the foreign conflict rule refers to the law of the nationality, and the person concerned is a British citizen; or (ii) because the foreign conflict rule refers to the law of the domicile, and the foreign court regards the person as domiciled in England. In the latter case, it is not true that domicile in an English court always means domicile in the English sense; but it is still true that it means domicile in the English sense for the purpose of an English rule of the conflict of laws.

---

[83] *Henwood v Barlow Clowes* [2008] EWCA Civ 577; [2008] N.P.C. 61 at para.88.
[84] *The Law of Domicile*, paras 5.4, 5.6, 5.9.
[85] *Collier v Rivaz* (1841) 2 Curt, 855; *Bremer v Freeman* (1857) 10 Moo.P.C. 306; *Hamilton v Dallas* (1875) 1 Ch.D. 257; *Re Annesley* [1926] Ch. 692. Article 13 of the Code Napoléon, which required a foreigner to obtain the authorisation of the French Government before he could establish a domicile in France, was repealed in 1927. See, by way of exception, Family Law Act 1986 s.46(5), which refers, in the alternative, either to domicile in a country in the English sense, or domicile in a country in the sense of that country's law.
[86] *Re Martin* [1900] P. 211.
[87] Below, para.20–011.

Acquisition of a domicile of choice

3–011   The content of the notion of domicile is probably best understood from the rules governing the domicile of choice.[88] Every independent person (i.e., one who is not a child under 16 or a mentally disordered person) can acquire a domicile of choice by the combination of (a) residence and (b) the intention of permanent or indefinite residence, but not otherwise.

These two factors must coincide before the law will recognise a change of domicile. Residence, however long, in a country will not result in the acquisition of a domicile of choice there if the necessary intention is lacking.[89] Conversely, intention, however strong, to change a domicile will not have that result if the necessary residence in the new country is lacking.[90] "A new domicile is not acquired until there is not only a fixed intention of establishing a permanent residence in some other country, but until also this intention has been carried out by actual residence there."[91] Hence a domicile cannot be acquired *in itinere*[92]; it is necessary not only to travel, hopefully or otherwise, but to arrive.

It is very difficult to keep the two requirements of residence and intention in watertight compartments, but in the interest of clarity of exposition they must be considered separately.

Residence

3–012   The meaning of residence as an independent concept has already been examined.[93] A person can acquire a domicile in a country, if he or she has the necessary intention, after residence for even part of a day.[94] The length of the residence is not important in itself; it is only important as evidence of intention. Thus an immigrant can acquire a domicile in a country immediately after arrival there. "It may be conceded that if the intention of permanently residing in a place exists, residence in pursuance of that intention, however short, will establish a domicile."[95] In order to be resident in a country a person need not own or rent a house there. It is sufficient to live in an hotel,[96] or in the house of a friend,[97] or even in a military camp.[98] For many years it was held that a person could not

---

[88]   For a critical assessment, see Trakman, (2015) 11 J.Priv.Int.L. 317.

[89]   *Jopp v Wood* (1865) 4 D.J. & S. 616; *Winans v Attorney General* [1904] A.C. 287; *Ramsay v Liverpool Royal Infirmary* [1930] A.C. 588; *IRC v Bullock* [1976] 1 W.L.R. 1178.

[90]   *In the Goods of Raffenel* (1863) 3 Sw. & Tr. 49; *Harrison v Harrison* [1953] 1 W.L.R. 865; *Willar v Willar,* 1954 S.C. 144, 147 ("one cannot acquire a domicile of choice by wishful thinking").

[91]   *Bell v Kennedy* (1868) L.R. 1 Sc. & Div. 307, 319, per Lord Chelmsford.

[92]   *Udny v Udny* (1869) L.R. 1 Sc. & Div. 441, 449–450, 453–454.

[93]   Above, para.3–002.

[94]   For striking illustrations, see *White v Tennant,* 31 W.Va. 790, 8 S.E. 596 (1888); *Miller v Teale* (1954) 92 C.L.R. 406. See the Law Commission's confirmation of the policy behind this rule: *Law of Domicile,* para.5.7.

[95]   *Bell v Kennedy* (1868) L.R. 1 Sc. & Div. 307, 319, per Lord Chelmsford.

[96]   *Levene v IRC* [1928] A.C. 217; *IRC v Lysaght* [1928] A.C. 234; *Matalon v Matalon* [1952] P. 233.

[97]   *Stone v Stone* [1958] 1 W.L.R. 1287.

[98]   *Willar v Willar,* 1954 S.C. 144.

acquire a domicile of choice if their residence was unlawful.[99] However, the House of Lords in *Mark v Mark* has held that, although it may be a relevant factor in establishing the intention to permanently remain in a country, there is no reason why unlawful residence in itself would prevent the acquisition of a domicile of choice.[100]

In the Law Commission's proposed statutory reformulation of the rules as to domicile, the term "presence" was used in place of "residence".[101]

Intention

The intention which is required for the acquisition of a domicile of choice (often **3–013** referred to as the *animus manendi)* is the intention to reside permanently or for an unlimited time in a particular country. "It must be a residence fixed not for a limited period or particular purpose, but general and indefinite in its future contemplation."[102] If a person intends to reside in a country for a fixed period (e.g., an engineer accepts a three-year contract to work on a civil engineering project in Saudi Arabia), the intention necessary to acquire a domicile there is lacking, however long the fixed period may be.[103] The same is true where a person intends to reside in a country for an indefinite time (e.g., until passing an examination) but clearly intends to leave the country at some time.[104]

The result of these principles is that the burden of proving a change of domicile is a very heavy one. Indeed, if we confine our attention to cases decided by the House of Lords, there appears to be an almost irrebuttable presumption against a change, because in the 13 disputed cases of domicile that have reached the House since 1860, there are only two in which it was held that a domicile of origin had been lost.[105] Two leading decisions of the House of Lords in particular have attracted much criticism. These are *Winans v Attorney General*[106] and *Ramsay v Liverpool Royal Infirmary.*[107]

In *Winans v Attorney General*:

---

[99] *Puttick v Attorney General* [1980] Fam. 1 (German terrorist in England on false passport). But query whether this is a rule of English public policy so that it would not apply to illegal residence in a foreign country. See Pilkington, (1984) 33 I.C.L.Q. 885.

[100] *Mark v Mark* [2005] UKHL 42; [2006] 1 A.C. 98. See *Henwood v Barlow Clowes* [2008] EWCA Civ. 577; [2008] N.P.C. 61 at para.119 where Arden LJ stated that the inability to live in Mauritius on a permanent basis without the permission of the Mauritian government made his residence there precarious and subsequently the acquisition of a domicile of choice less likely.

[101] The Law of Domicile, para.5.7.

[102] *Udny v Udny* (1869) L.R. 1 Sc. & Div. 441, 458, per Lord Westbury. See *Cramer v Cramer* [1987] 1 F.L.R. 116.

[103] *Attorney General v Rowe* (1862) 1 H. & C. 31.

[104] *Jopp v Wood* (1865) 4 D.J. & S. 616; *Qureshi v Qureshi* [1972] Fam. 173.

[105] *Casdagli v Casdagli* [1919] A.C. 145. The other cases are: *Aikman v Aikman* (1861) 3 Macq. 854; *Moorhouse v Lord* (1863) 10 H.L.C. 272; *Pitt v Pitt* (1864) 4 Macq. 627; *Bell v Kennedy* (1868) L.R. 1 Sc. & Div. 307; *Udny v Udny* (1869) L.R. 1 Sc. & Div. 441; *Winans v Attorney General* [1904] A.C. 287; *Huntly v Gaskell* [1906] A.C. 56; *Lord Advocate v Jaffrey* [1921] 1 A.C. 146 (where it was conceded that the husband had lost his domicile of origin, and the dispute was as to the domicile of dependency of the wife); *Ross v Ross* [1930] A.C. 1; *Ramsay v Liverpool Royal Infirmary* [1930] A.C. 588; *Wahl v Attorney General* (1932) 147 L.T. 382; *Mark v Mark* [2005] UKHL 42; [2006] 1 A.C. 98.

[106] [1904] A.C. 287: the case of the anglophobe American millionaire.

[107] [1930] A.C. 588: the case of the human jellyfish (or sponge).

Mr Winans was a man of eccentric ideas, self-centred and strangely uncommunicative. He was born in the United States in 1823 with a domicile of origin in Maryland or New Jersey. The two ruling passions of his life were hatred of England and the care of his health. As Lord Macnaghten described him 'He nursed and tended it' (i.e., his health, not England) 'with wonderful devotion. He took his temperature several times a day. He had regular times for taking his temperature, and regular times for taking his various waters and medicines'.

His opportunity for gratifying his hatred of England came in 1850, when he went to Russia and was employed by the Russian Government in equipping railways and in the construction of gunboats to be used against England in the Crimean War. But nemesis overtook him in 1859, when his health broke down. He was advised by his doctors that another winter in Russia would be fatal, and that he must spend the winter in Brighton. Very reluctantly he accepted this advice, spent the winter in a Brighton hotel, and in 1860 took a lease of a house there. However, he held aloof from English people, whom he continued cordially to dislike. From then on until his death in 1897 he spent more and more time in England, living in furnished houses and hotels, and less and less time elsewhere. From 1893 until 1897 he lived entirely in England.

He entertained a grandiose dream of constructing in Baltimore, Maryland, a large fleet of cigar-shaped vessels which, being proof against pitching and rolling (or so he thought), would gain for the United States the carrying trade of the world and give her naval superiority over Great Britain. He also dreamed of acquiring control of 200 acres of wharves and docks in Maryland to accommodate the cigar-shaped vessels, and a large house in which he would live and superintend the whole scheme. He was working night and day on the scheme when he died, a millionaire several times over.

Mr Winans had thus lived mainly in England for the last 37 years of his life, and never revisited the United States after his departure in 1850.

On these facts, six judges held that he died domiciled in England; but a bare majority of two to one in the House of Lords held that he never lost his domicile of origin. "When he came to this country", said Lord Macnaghten,[108] "he was a sojourner and a stranger, and he was I think a sojourner and a stranger in it when he died." Lord Lindley, equally robust, said[109]: "He had one and only one home, and that was in this country; and long before he died I am satisfied that he had given up all serious idea of returning to his native country." Lord Halsbury was unable to make up his mind, and fell back on the presumption of continuance.

In *Ramsay v Liverpool Royal Infirmary*[110]:

George Bowie was born in Glasgow in 1845 with a Scottish domicile of origin. In 1882, at the age of 37, he gave up his employment as a commercial traveller and did no work for the remaining 45 years of his life. At first he lived with his mother and sisters in Glasgow. In 1892 he moved to Liverpool and sponged on his brother and another sister. He died unmarried in 1927. Thus he lived in England for the last 36 years of his life. During all that time he left England only twice, once on a short visit to the United States, and once on a short holiday in the Isle of Man. Though he often said he was proud to be a Glasgow man, he resolutely refused to return to Scotland, even to attend his mother's funeral. On the contrary, he expressed his determination never to set foot in Glasgow again, and arranged to be buried in Liverpool. His will, which gave the residue equally between three Glasgow charities and one Liverpool one, was formally valid if he died domiciled in Scotland, but formally invalid if he died domiciled in England.

On these facts the House of Lords, affirming both the Scottish courts below, unanimously reached the astonishing conclusion that he died domiciled in Scotland. The ratio decidendi evidently was that he was such a low form of life as

---

[108] At p.298.
[109] At p.300.
[110] [1930] A.C. 588.

to be incapable of forming the necessary intent to change his domicile. "The long residence of George Bowie", said Lord Thankerton,[111] "is remarkably colourless, and suggests little more than inanition".

Unfortunately, we cannot dismiss these two cases as mere aberrations of the House of Lords, because in 1976 the Court of Appeal reached a similar decision. In *IRC v Bullock*[112] it was held that a Canadian with a domicile of origin in Nova Scotia who had lived mainly in England for more than 40 years had not acquired an English domicile of choice, because he intended to return to Canada after the death of his English wife. Ironically, this decision meant that (as the law then stood) the wife also was domiciled in Nova Scotia at the time in question (1971–1973), although she disliked the place. On the other hand, in *Re Furse*[113] the home of an American for the last 39 years of his life was on a farm in England. He declared an intention to return to the US if he became unable to lead an active physical life on the farm, where he remained until his death aged 80. The contingency was held to be so vague and indefinite that it did not prevent the acquisition of an English domicile of choice.

Fentiman has argued that *Re Furse* taken with some other cases can be read as indicating a shift towards an understanding of domicile as the place with which an individual has his most real and substantial connection.[114] Existing factual links, he argues, are becoming more important than reliance on intention as to future plans. This would effectively bring domicile closer to habitual residence, or at least to domicile as understood in many US jurisdictions, but there is little sign that the courts intend to depart from the traditional English principles, which require a close examination of the evidence as to the propositus' intentions.

Evidence of intention

Most disputes about domicile turn on the question as to whether the necessary intention accompanied the residence; and this question often involves very complex and intricate issues of fact. This is because:

    3–014

> "there is no act, no circumstance in a man's life, however trivial it may be in itself, which ought to be left out of consideration in trying the question whether there was an intention to change the domicile. A trivial act might possibly be of more weight with regard to determining this question than an act which was of more importance to a man in his lifetime".[115]

---

[111] At p.595.

[112] [1976] 1 W.L.R. 1178; criticised by Carter, (1976–77) 48 B.Y.I.L. 362.

[113] [1980] 3 All E.R. 838.

[114] (1991) 50 C.L.J. 445. The other cases he cites are *Brown v Brown* (1981) 3 F.L.R. 212 (U.S. businessman resident in England for 14 years and belonging to London clubs held domiciled there; the links with English society were in sharp contrast with those in *Winans v Attorney General)* and *Plummer v IRC* [1988] 1 W.L.R. 292.

[115] *Drevon v Drevon* (1864) 34 L.J.Ch. 129, 133, per Kindersley VC. See *Henwood v Barlow Clowes* [2008] EWCA Civ 577; [2008] N.P.C. 61 where the Court of Appeal criticised the trial judge for failing to consider certain elements of the propositus' life.

There is, furthermore, no circumstance or group of circumstances which furnishes any definite criterion of the existence of the intention[116]; for example, naturalisation is not conclusive as "it is not the law either that a change of domicile is a condition of naturalisation, or that naturalisation involves necessarily a change of domicile".[117] A circumstance which is treated as decisive in one case may be disregarded in another, or even relied upon to support a different conclusion.

The questions which the court has considered include the following: where did the propositus live and for how long? Was it in a fixed place or several different places? Did he build or buy a house, or live in furnished lodgings or hotels? What was his lifestyle? Was he accompanied by his wife, or unmarried partner, and children? Did he vote in elections there? Was he naturalised there? Did he arrange to be buried there? What churches did he attend? What clubs did he belong to? Of course, this list is far from being exhaustive: a person's "tastes, habits, conduct, actions, ambitions, health, hopes and projects" are all regarded as "keys to his intention."[118] Thus the law, instead of allowing long-continued residence to speak for itself, insists on proof of a person's intention, that most elusive of all factors. The resulting uncertainty has given rise to much criticism and to proposals for reform of the law.

Declarations of intention

3–015   The person whose domicile is in question may give evidence of his or her intention, but the court will view the evidence of an interested party with suspicion[119]; though in one case[120] such evidence was decisive. As Lord Buckmaster put it[121]:

> "Declarations as to intention are rightly regarded in determining the question of a change of domicile, but they must be examined by considering the persons to whom, the purposes for which, and the circumstances in which they are made, and they must further be fortified and carried into effect by conduct and action consistent with the declared expression".

---

[116] As Mummery LJ observed in *Cyganik v Agulian* [2006] EWCA Civ. 129; [2006] 1 F.C.R. 406 at para 46: "... the court must look back at the whole of the deceased's life, at what he had done with his life, at what life had done to him and at what were his inferred intentions in order to decide whether he had acquired a domicile of choice in England".

[117] *Wahl v Attorney General* (1932) 147 L.T. 382 (H.L.) per Lord Atkin at p.385. A decision to take British nationality when faced with a choice was held to be a "clear pointer" of the acquisition of a domicile of choice in England: *Bheekhun v Williams* [1999] 2 F.L.R. 229, per Chadwick LJ at p.239B; but the acquisition of British citizenship together with a British passport was not enough was not enough in *F v IRC* [2000] W.T.L.R. 505, 528.

[118] *Casdagli v Casdagli* [1919] A.C. 145, 178, per Lord Atkinson, commenting on *Winans v Attorney General* [1904] A.C. 287.

[119] *Bell v Kennedy* (1868) L.R. 1 Sc. & Div. 307, 313, 322–323; *Re Craignish* [1892] 3 Ch. 180, 190; *Qureshi v Qureshi* [1972] Fam. 173, 192; *Gaines-Cooper v Revenue and Customs Commissioners* [2007] S.T.C. (S.C.D.) 23 (decision upheld by the High Court [2007] EWHC 2617 (Ch); [2008] S.T.C., 1665); *Henwood v Barlow Clowes* [2008] EWCA Civ 577; [2008] N.P.C. 61 at para.81.

[120] *Wilson v Wilson* (1872) L.R. 2 P. & M. 435. The Scottish court arrived at an opposite conclusion on the same facts: *Wilson v Wilson* (1872) 10 M. 573; but the husband's evidence was not then admissible in Scotland.

[121] *Ross v Ross* [1930] A.C. 1, 6–7. "Expression" the last word in the quotation, seems to be a misprint for "intention".

A statement made for tax purposes may not be as cogent as entries in personal diaries showing a different intent.[122] The courts are particularly reluctant to give effect to declarations as to domicile made by testators in their wills, since the testator is unlikely to understand the meaning of the word, while to allow the solicitor drafting the will to determine the question of domicile would be to oust the jurisdiction of the court.[123]

Motive and intention

It is important to distinguish between motive and intention. As a general rule it does not matter whether a person's motive in leaving one country and living in another is good or bad: the question is whether or not there is the requisite intention for a change of domicile. The motive may be, for instance, to enjoy the benefit of a lower rate of taxation,[124] or of a better climate, either for the person concerned or for a troupe of performing chimpanzees,[125] to get a divorce,[126] to prevent his wife from getting maintenance,[127] or to facilitate international travel.[128] In none of these cases has the particular motive prevented the acquisition of a new domicile. But if the motive is suspect, the court may be reluctant to concede a change of domicile. It may conclude that there really was no change at all, but merely the appearance of a change made to secure some personal advantage.[129]

3–016

Intention freely formed

In order that a person may acquire a domicile of choice, it has been said that "there must be a residence freely chosen, and not pre-scribed or dictated by any external necessity, such as the duties of office, the demands of creditors, or the relief from illness."[130] That is a somewhat misleading statement. It certainly does not mean that only a person able to exercise the most perfect freedom of choice can acquire a domicile of choice: if it did, the acquisition of a domicile of choice would be a rare event. It is submitted that the rules as to the acquisition of a domicile of choice apply to everyone, but that the position of certain groups of people who go to another country (persons liable to deportation; fugitives from justice; refugees; invalids; and employees, diplomats and members of the armed forces) is such that they are markedly less likely, as an observation of fact, to form the necessary intention to remain in that country.

3–017

---

[122] *Holliday v Musa* [2010] EWCA Civ 335; [2010] 3 FCR 280.
[123] *Re Steer* (1858) 3 H. & N. 594; *Re Annesley* [1926] Ch. 692; *Attorney General v Yule* (1931) 145 L.T. 9; *Re Liddell-Grainger* (1936) 53 T.L.R. 12; *Dellar v Zivy* [2007] EWHC 2266 (Ch); [2007] I.L.Pr. 868.
[124] *Wood v Wood* [1957] P. 254.
[125] ibid.
[126] *Drexel v Drexel* [1916] 1 Ch. 251; *Wood v Wood*, above; *Chaudhary v Chaudhary* [1985] Fam. 19.
[127] ibid.
[128] *F v IRC* [2000] W.T.L.R. 505.
[129] See *White v White* [1950] 4 D.L.R. 474, affirmed [1952] 1 D.L.R. 133.
[130] *Udny v Udny* (1869) L.R. 1 Sc. & Div. 441, 458, per Lord Westbury.

(i)   Persons liable to deportation

3–018   A person who resides in a country from which he or she is liable to be deported may lack the necessary intention because the residence is precarious. But if in fact the necessary intention is formed, a domicile of choice will be acquired.[131] Once such a person has acquired a domicile of choice, it is not lost merely because a deportation order has been made.[132] It is lost only when there is actual deportation *and* the deported person can no longer be said to have an intention to return as a lawful resident.

(ii)   Fugitives from justice

3–019   A person who leaves a country as a fugitive from criminal justice, or in order to evade creditors, has a special motive for leaving it, but no special motive for living in any other country. In the case of a fugitive from justice, the intention to abandon the previous domicile will readily be inferred, unless perhaps the punishment sought to be avoided is trivial, or by the law of that country a relatively short period of prescription bars liability to punishment. In *Re Martin*,[133] a French professor committed a crime in France in connection with his professorship[134] and fled to England where he remained for the next 20 years. Two years after the French period of prescription had expired, he returned to France. The Court of Appeal by a majority held that he had acquired an English domicile six years after his arrival in England. A similar conclusion was reached in *Moynihan v Moynihan (No.2)*,[135] where a peer of the realm fled England to avoid arrest on serious fraud charges, and was held to have acquired a domicile of choice in the Philippines where he "was in the nature of a king", owning a hotel and at least one massage parlour. Similarly, a person who leaves a country in order to evade his creditors may lose a domicile there[136]; but if the debtor plans to return as soon as the debts are paid or have been cancelled, there is no change of domicile.[137]

(iii)   Refugees

3–020   If a political refugee intends to return as soon as the political situation changes, he or she remains domiciled there. There may, of course, come a point at which the prospect of return becomes so remote that the court will treat a declared intention to return as an exercise in self-deception, inconsistent with reality. A refugee who has decided *not* to return even when the political situation does change, may acquire a domicile of choice in the country of refuge.

---

[131] *Boldrini v Boldrini* [1932] P. 9; *Zanelli v Zanelli* (1948) 64 T.L.R. 556; *Szechter v Szechter* [1971] P. 286, 294; *Mark v Mark* [2005] UKHL 42; [2006] 1 A.C. 98.
[132] *Cruh v Cruh* [1945] 2 All E.R. 545.
[133] [1900] P. 211.
[134] The report is tantalisingly silent as to what this might have been.
[135] [1997] 1 F.L.R. 59, 63.
[136] *Udny v Udny* (1869) L.R. 1 Sc. & Div. 441.
[137] *Re Wright's Trusts* (1856) 2 K. & J. 595; *Pitt v Pitt* (1864) 4 Macq. 627.

Thus in *Re Lloyd Evans*[138]

> an Englishman with a Belgian domicile of choice returned to England very reluctantly in June 1940 because of the German invasion, and lived in furnished flats in England until he died in 1944. He always intended to return to Belgium after the war. It was held that he retained his Belgian domicile.

On the other hand, in *May v May*[139]

> a Jew fled from Germany to England in 1938 to escape persecution by the Nazis. He originally intended to immigrate to the United States, but his hope of doing so was frustrated by the outbreak of war in 1939. In 1941, the idea of going to the United States gradually faded from his mind. He declared that he would never return to Germany, even if the Nazis were overthrown. It was held that he had acquired an English domicile of choice by the beginning of 1942.

(iv) Invalids

If a person moves to live in a new country for health reasons, is there a change of domicile? Different judges have given different answers to this question. Since illnesses vary greatly in intensity, no general rule can be laid down. Each case turns on its own facts. A person who goes to a country for the temporary purpose of undergoing medical treatment there clearly lacks the necessary intention for a change of domicile. So does a person who is terminally ill and decides to move to a country to alleviate his last sufferings or to be cared for by relatives.[140] On the other hand, a person who moves to a new country in the belief that the move will ensure better health may well intend to live there permanently or indefinitely, but of course not necessarily.   3–021

In *Hoskins v Matthews*[141]

> a man whose domicile of origin was English went to Florence at the age of 60, and lived there, except for three or four months in each year in a villa that he had bought, until he died 12 years later. He was suffering from an injury to the spine and left England solely because he thought that the warmer climate of Italy would benefit his health. His housekeeper gave evidence that he would have returned to England if he had been restored to health. Nevertheless it was held that he had acquired a domicile in Tuscany (as it then was), because he was "exercising a preference and not acting upon a necessity.[142]

(v) Employees

The question whether an employee who is sent to a country by his or her employer intends to reside there permanently or indefinitely remains in the last resort a question of fact. If someone goes to a country for the temporary purpose   3–022

---

[138] [1947] Ch. 695.

[139] [1943] 2 All E.R. 146.

[140] *Allen v Revenue and Customs Commissioners* [2005] S.T.C. (S.C.D.) 614.

[141] (1855) 8 D.M. & G. 13. See *Haji-Ioannou v Frangos* [2009] EWHC 2310 (QB); [2010] 1 All E.R. (Comm) 303 (medical treatment in Athens; domicile in Monaco retained).

[142] cf. *Re James* (1908) 98 L.T. 438 where the continued ownership of a farm in Wales seems to have been decisive.

of performing the duties of office or employment,[143] he does not acquire a domicile of choice there; but if he goes not merely to work but also to settle,[144] he may acquire a domicile of choice.

The same principles apply to diplomats and members of the armed forces. It is a question of fact whether diplomats intend to reside permanently or indefinitely in the country to which they are accredited. Generally, of course, they form no such intention,[145] but occasionally they may do so and thus acquire a domicile of choice there.[146] Members of the armed forces are likely to have even less freedom of choice as to where they are stationed. Nonetheless, a member of the armed forces can, during service, acquire a domicile of choice in the country in which he is stationed[147] or elsewhere,[148] provided he has established the necessary residence and formed the necessary intention. But in the great majority of cases he does not intend to make his permanent home where he is stationed, and retains the domicile which he had on entering service.[149]

Loss of a domicile of choice

3–023   A person abandons a domicile of choice in a country by ceasing to reside there and by ceasing to intend to reside there permanently or indefinitely, and not otherwise.[150] It is not necessary to prove a positive intention not to return: it is sufficient to prove merely the absence of an intention to continue to reside.[151] A domicile of choice is lost when both the residence and the intention necessary for its acquisition are given up. It is not lost merely by giving up the residence,[152] nor merely by giving up the intention.[153]

Domicile of origin

3–024   "It is a settled principle", said Lord Westbury in a leading case,[154] "that no man shall be without a domicile, and to secure this result the law attributes to every individual as soon as he is born the domicile of his father, if the child be legitimate, and the domicile of the mother if illegitimate".[155] This has been called

[143] e.g., *Attorney General v Rowe* (1862) 1 H. & C. 31 (English barrister appointed Chief Justice of Ceylon).
[144] e.g., *Gunn v Gunn* (1956) 2 D.L.R. (2d) 351.
[145] *Niboyet v Niboyet* (1878) 4 P.D. 1.
[146] As in *Naville v Naville,* 1957 (1) S.A. 280.
[147] *Donaldson v Donaldson* [1949] P. 363; *Willar v Willar,* 1954 S.C. 144.
[148] *Stone v Stone* [1958] 1 W.L.R. 1287.
[149] *Cruickshanks v Cruickshanks* [1957] 1 W.L.R. 564; *Sellars v Sellars,* 1942 S.C. 206.
[150] *Udny v Udny* (1869) L.R. 1 Sc. & Div. 441, 450; *IRC v Duchess of Portland* [1982] Ch. 314.
[151] *Re Flynn (No.1)* [1968] 1 W.L.R. 103, 113–115; *Qureshi v Qureshi* [1972] Fam. 173, 191; *Morgan v Cilento* [2004] EWHC 188 (Ch); [2004] W.T.L.R. 457.
[152] *Bradford v Young* (1885) 29 Ch.D. 617; *Re Lloyd Evans* [1947] Ch. 695; *Breuning v Breuning* [2002] EWHC 236 (Fam); [2002] 1 F.L.R. 888.
[153] *In the Goods of Raffenel* (1863) 3 Sw. & Tr. 49; *Zanelli v Zanelli* (1948) 64 T.L.R. 556.
[154] *Udny v Udny* (1869) L.R. 1 Sc. & Div. 441, at p.457.
[155] There is no English authority on the domicile of origin of a posthumous child or of a foundling; but it is generally assumed that the former takes the domicile of the mother and that the latter has domicile of origin in the country where he or she is found.

the domicile of origin, and is involuntary. In many cases, the domicile of origin will be in the country in which the child is born but this is coincidental as the place of birth is in no way determinative.[156]

Since the domicile of the child's father may be the father's domicile of origin which itself may be derived from the father's father, it follows that a domicile of origin may be transmitted through several generations no member of which has ever lived in the country of his or her domicile of origin,[157] and during which time national borders may have changed.[158] The Law Commission proposed new rules for determining the domicile of a child, under which the concept of the domicile of origin would disappear.[159]

No person can legally be without a domicile, but a person may in fact be without a home, being for instance a wanderer or a sailor, with no home except a cabin. To meet such situations, the law has to resort to fictions; and it draws a sharp distinction between the domicile of origin and a domicile of choice.

A domicile of origin possesses a very adhesive quality[160] and cannot be lost by mere abandonment. It can only be lost by the acquisition of a domicile of choice. Thus in *Bell v Kennedy*[161]:

> Mr Bell was born in Jamaica of Scottish parents domiciled in Jamaica. In 1828 he married in Jamaica. In 1837, at the age of 35, he left Jamaica for good and went to Scotland, where he lived with his mother-in-law and looked around for an estate on which to settle down. He found one in 1839, and from then on was admittedly domiciled in Scotland. But until then he was undecided whether to settle in Scotland or in England or elsewhere. He was dissatisfied with Scotland, mainly due to the bad weather—so different from what he was used to in Jamaica. The question was where was he domiciled in September 1838 when his wife died? The House of Lords held that he had not lost his Jamaican domicile of origin.

On the other hand, a domicile of choice can be lost by abandonment; and if it is, and a new domicile of choice is not simultaneously acquired, the domicile of origin revives to fill the gap.[162] The reasons given for this rule (often referred to as "the rule in *Udny v Udny*") are not very convincing,[163] and its artificiality has often been criticised. If, for instance, an Englishman emigrates to New York at the age of 25, remains there for the next 40 years and then decides to retire to California, but is killed in an air crash en route, it does not make much sense to

---

[156] See, e.g., cases of children born to expatriates working away from the country of their domicile such as *M v M (Divorce; Domicile)* [2010] EWHC 982 (Fam.); [2011] 1 F.L.R. 919 (child born in Kenya had English domicile of origin).

[157] See *Peal v Peal* (1930) 46 T.L.R. 645; *Grant v Grant*, 1931 S.C. 238.

[158] See *Al-Bassam v Al-Bassam* [2004] EWCA 857; [2004] W.T.L.R. 757.

[159] This reform has been implemented in Scotland, Family Law (Scotland) Act 2006 s.22.

[160] *Winans v Attorney General* [1904] A.C. 287; *Ramsay v Liverpool Royal Infirmary* [1930] A.C. 588. See above para.3–013; *R v R (Divorce: Jurisdiction: Domicile)* [2006] 1 F.L.R. 389; *Cyganik v Agulian* [2006] EWCA Civ 129, [2006] 1 F.C.R. 406.

[161] (1868) L.R. 1 Sc. & Div. 307.

[162] *Udny v Udny* (1869) L.R. 1 Sc. & Div. 441; *Harrison v Harrison* [1953] 1 W.L.R. 865; *Re Flynn (No.1)* [1968] 1 W.L.R. 103, 117; *Tee v Tee* [1974] 1 W.L.R. 213; *Henwood v Barlow Clowes* [2008] EWCA Civ 577, [2008] N.P.C. 61.

[163] In *Udny v Udny* (1869) L.R. 1 Sc. & Div. 441, Lord Westbury said (at p.458): "as the domicile of origin is the creature of law, and independent of the will of the party, it would be inconsistent with the principles on which it is by law created and ascribed, to suppose that it is capable of being by the act of the party entirely obliterated and extinguished."

say that he died domiciled in England, especially as an American court would undoubtedly hold that he died domiciled in New York. Yet the opposite American rule, that a domicile of choice continues until a new one is acquired, sometimes produces equally bizarre results. For instance, in the leading American case, *Re Jones' Estate*[164]:

> Evan Jones was born in Wales in 1850 with an English domicile of origin. In 1883, he put a Welsh girl in the family way and she threatened him with affiliation proceedings. To escape this prospect he emigrated to the United States, where he acquired a domicile of choice in Iowa, became a naturalised American citizen, and married an American wife. He was 'a coal miner, an industrious, hardworking, thrifty Welshman who accumulated a considerable amount of property.' In 1915, after the death of his wife, he decided to return to Wales for good and live there with his sister. He sailed from New York on May 1 in the *Lusitania,* and was drowned when she was torpedoed by a German sub-marine off the south coast of Ireland. He died intestate. By English law, his brothers and sisters were entitled to his property; by the law of Iowa, it went to his illegitimate daughter, from whom he had fled over 30 years ago, and with whom he had never had anything to do. The Supreme Court of Iowa held that he died domiciled in Iowa and that the daughter was entitled.

Short of holding that he died domiciled in the *Lusitania,* and therefore (since she was registered at Southampton) in England, there would appear to be no satisfactory solution to this problem. The truth is that the American rule is as much a fiction as the English one.

The detailed nature of the investigation of the family circumstances needed in domicile cases is illustrated by *Sekhri v Ray*[165]:

> A couple met via an internet dating site while in England. H was about to take up a post in a law firm in Singapore and W agreed to go with him. They married in India and spent some three years in Singapore before the marriage broke down. For the English court to have jurisdiction in divorce it was necessary that both parties were domiciled in England.
>
> H was born in England in 1971, but his domicile of origin depended on that of his father, whose own domicile of origin was in India. The court held that by 1971 the father had demonstrated an intention to reside in England which was fixed and was for the indefinite future. He had chosen to 'settle' there and to bring up his family in England. His continued contemplation of living once again in India at some distant future time was no more than a 'pipe dream'. It followed that H had a domicile of origin in England. His move to Singapore was of an insufficient quality to establish a fresh domicile of choice in Singapore, given the 'adhesive' and 'tenacious' character of a domicile of origin.
>
> W was born and brought up in India, which was her domicile of origin. She travelled to England in 2002, obtained work and further qualifications in England and bought a house there. She had for many years dreamt of living and working in England. She had had an unsuccessful arranged marriage in India which ended in divorce, the result of which was to place social pressure upon her as a single separated woman in Indian society. This circumstance hardened her resolve to leave India and put all her energy into developing her career. The court held that she had acquired a domicile of choice in England by 2008 at the latest: her residence was settled and not fixed for a limited period or particular purpose, but was general and indefinite in its future contemplation. The question was therefore whether W had abandoned her domicile of choice by moving to Singapore. The court found that she had not, as the move to Singapore was for a time limited period and that she expected and intended to return to England and resume her career and residence there.

---

[164] 192 Iowa 78, 182 N.W. 227 (1921).
[165] [2014] EWCA Civ 119; [2014] 2 F.L.R. 1168.

Domicile of dependency

Dependent persons cannot acquire a domicile of choice by their own act. As a general rule, the domicile of such persons is the same as, and changes with, the domicile of the person (if any) on whom they are legally dependent. For this purpose, the category of dependent persons now comprises children and the mentally disordered; it formerly included all married women, and it is still necessary to know something of a rule which now seems a prime example of political incorrectness.

The rules applying to each group will be examined in turn.

3–025

Children

At common law, the domicile of a child below the age of majority was the same as, and changed with, the domicile of the appropriate parent, the father in the case of a legitimate child, and the mother in the case of an illegitimate child or a legitimate child whose father was dead.[166] One decision suggests that the rule was not quite so strict in the case of an illegitimate or fatherless child as it was in the case of a legitimate child whose father was alive. In *Re Beaumont*,[167] a widow, domiciled in Scotland with her minor children, remarried and went to live with her second husband in England, taking all but one of the children with her, leaving the one behind in Scotland in the care of an aunt; it was held that the domicile of this child continued to be Scottish. Although there is no authority on the point, it seems likely that the domicile of a legitimated child would be dependent on that of its father, at any rate if the legitimation was effected by the subsequent marriage of the parents.

3–026

The modern law is contained in the Domicile and Matrimonial Proceedings Act 1973, s.3(1) of which provides that a child becomes capable of having an independent domicile when he or she attains the age of 16 or marries under that age.[168]

At common law, the child was treated as dependent upon the father even if the parents had separated and the child was living with the mother. Section 4 of the 1973 Act sought to introduce greater flexibility into the rules as to dependency, enabling the child to be dependent upon its mother in appropriate circumstances. It provides that the domicile of a dependent child whose parents are alive but living apart shall be that of his mother if (a) he has his home with her and no home with his father, or (b) he has at any time had her domicile by virtue of (a) above and has not subsequently had a home with his father. "Living apart" does not imply any breakdown in the relationship between the parents, who may be living apart because of the demands of one parent's job. "Home" is also

---

[166] A female minor who married took her husband's domicile in place of her father's or mother's.

[167] [1893] 3 Ch. 490. Given that at that date a married woman had no power over her own domicile, the suggestion that she might have a discretion as to that of her children is surprising.

[168] In English domestic law, a marriage between persons either of whom is under 16 is void (Marriage Act 1949 s.2); but a child may be regarded as validly married under foreign law even if under that age.

undefined: the home of a pre-school child[169] may be more easily identifiable than that of a young teenager being educated at a boarding school. Section 4(3) provides that the domicile of a dependent child whose mother is dead shall be that which she last had before she died if at her death he had her domicile by virtue of s.4(2) and he has not since had a home with his father. The main object of this enactment is to increase the number of cases in which the domicile of dependency of a child will be that of the mother; previously existing rules of law to that effect (e.g., those relating to illegitimate children and legitimate children whose fathers are dead) are preserved by s.4(4).

Adopted children are now treated in law as if they had been born as the legitimate child of the adopter or adopters.[170] Accordingly the domicile of an adopted child under 16 will be determined as if he or she were the legitimate child of the adopted parent or parents.

The domicile of a legitimate child whose parents are both dead, or of an illegitimate child whose mother is dead, probably cannot be changed at all. But there is no authority on the point.

When the domicile of a dependent child is changed as a result of a change in the parents' domicile or as a result of its legitimation, the new domicile acquired by the child in this way is a domicile of dependency and not a domicile of origin.[171] Hence, it is not this domicile but the one acquired at birth that will revive if in later life he or she abandons one domicile of choice without at the same time acquiring another. On the other hand, it would seem to follow from what has been said above about adopted children, that the domicile of origin of an adopted child is deemed to be the domicile of the relative adoptive parent at the time of the child's birth[172] since s.67(1) of the Adoption and Children Act 2006 provides that an adopted person is to be treated in law as if born as the child of the adopters or adopter. It is submitted that this extends the fiction of the domicile of origin too far. If domicile is based on the concept of 'permanent home' and the domicile of origin denotes being born to a family, a community, then if the domicile of origin is to change at all upon adoption, it should be to the domicile of the relevant parent at the time of adoption, not changed retrospectively to whatever domicile the adoptive parent may have had at the time the child was born to his biological parents.

In its 1987 report,[173] the Law Commission recommended new and simpler rules to replace those in the 1973 Act. A child should be domiciled in the country with which he or she is, for the time being, most closely connected. Where the child's parents were domiciled in the same country and the child had its home with either or both of them, it would be presumed, unless the contrary were shown, that the child was most closely connected with that country. Where the child's parents were not domiciled in the same country and the child had its home

---

[169] 'Where the child keeps its toys' may once have been a relevant question to ask in the days when toys were few and treasured, but for today's children this is less likely to be a determinative factor; some families may have children's toys in different countries.

[170] Adoption and Children Act 2002 s.67.

[171] *Henderson v Henderson* [1967] P. 77.

[172] If this is correct, it is the only instance in English law in which a domicile of origin can be changed.

[173] Law of Domicile Pt VI.

with one of them, but not with the other, it would similarly be presumed that the child was most closely connected with the country in which the parent with whom it had its home was domiciled. No presumption would apply in cases in which the parents were domiciled in separate countries and the child had a home with both of them; nor in cases where the child had a home with neither parent. For the purposes of these rules, "parent" would include parents who are not married to one another; there would no longer be separate rules applying to legitimate, illegitimate and legitimated children.

Mentally disordered persons

A mentally disordered person cannot acquire a domicile of choice and, as a general rule, retains the domicile which he or she had when becoming mentally incapable.[174] Since such a person cannot exercise any will, he or she lacks the capacity to acquire or lose a domicile; nor can the domicile be changed by a person taking charge of or caring for the mentally disordered person,[175] nor by the court.[176] The rules governing who lacks the mental capacity to form the necessary intention to change their domicile are now contained in the Mental Capacity Act 2005. Had the Law Commission's proposals[177] been accepted, special rules would have applied to mentally incapable adults. Such persons would be domiciled in the country with which they were for the time being most closely connected. When that capacity was restored, they would retain the domicile held immediately before it was restored, but could of course then acquire a new domicile under the rules applying to adults generally.

3–027

Married women

Before 1974 there was an absolute rule, to which there were no exceptions, that the domicile of a married woman was the same as, and changed with, the domicile of her husband.[178] This rule reflected social conditions and attitudes of a past age, and it was abolished by s.1(1) of the Domicile and Matrimonial Proceedings Act 1973.

3–028

Section 1(1) of the Act is retrospective in the sense that it applies to women married before as well as after 1 January 1974. Hence, a transitional provision was needed. Section 1(2) provides that where immediately before that date a woman was married and then had her husband's domicile by dependence, she is to be treated as retaining that domicile (as a domicile of choice, if it is not also her domicile of origin) unless and until it is changed by acquisition of another domicile either on or after that date.

---

[174] *Bempde v Johnstone* (1796) 3 Ves. 198; *Urquhart v Butterfield* (1887) 37 Ch.D. 357; *Crumpton's Judicial Factor v Fitch-Noyes*, 1918 S.C. 378.

[175] However, if a dependent child becomes insane and remains so after attaining the age of 16, the appropriate parent has power to change his or her domicile even after he or she attains that age: *Sharpe v Crispin* (1869) L.R. 1 P. & M. 611; *Re G* [1966] N.Z.L.R. 1028.

[176] See *Westminster City Council v C* [2008] EWCA Civ 198; [2009] Fam. 11 at [14]–[15].

[177] The Law of Domicile Pt VI.

[178] *Lord Advocate v Jaffrey* [1921] 1 A.C. 146; *Attorney General for Alberta v Cook* [1926] A.C. 444.

In *IRC v Duchess of Portland*[179]

> a woman with a domicile of origin in Quebec married a domiciled Englishman in 1948. She lived with her husband in England but retained links with Quebec, visiting it for ten to 12 weeks every summer, keeping a house which she owned there ready for immediate occupation, and retaining Canadian citizenship. She intended to return permanently to Quebec with her husband when he retired from business, but continued to live in England. It was held that the effect of s.1(2) was that she retained her English domicile of dependency as a domicile of choice. In effect, the pattern of her own life before 1974 was given no weight.

The Law Commission subsequently recommended a much more satisfactory form of transitional provision, that the domicile of any person at any date after the enactment of the new rules should be determined as if those rules had always been in force.[180]

Section 1(1) is not retrospective in any other sense. Hence, in considering the domicile of a married woman as at any time before 1 January 1974, the old law will still apply.

DOMICILE OF CORPORATIONS

3–029 The English law of domicile was evolved almost entirely with individuals in mind. It can only be applied to corporations with a certain sense of strain. A corporation is not born (though it is incorporated); it cannot marry (though it can be amalgamated with or taken over by another corporation); it cannot have children (though it can have subsidiaries); it does not die (though it can be dissolved or wound up). Hence in the case of corporations, most of the occasions for determining the domicile of an individual do not arise. But it may be important to know whether a so-called corporation possesses corporate personality, whether it has been amalgamated with another corporation, or whether it has been dissolved. These questions are determined by the law of its domicile.

A corporation is domiciled (for purposes other than those of the Civil Jurisdiction and Judgments Acts 1982 and 1991)[181] in its place of incorporation. Unlike an individual, it cannot change that domicile, even if it carries on all its business elsewhere.[182]

It may be asked, if questions concerning the existence, amalgamation, or dissolution of a corporation are governed by the law of its place of incorporation, why not say so and dispense altogether with the fiction that it has a domicile? That question is unanswerable; but the difficulty is that tax statutes sometimes speak of the domicile of a corporation, and the reference has to be given some meaning.

---

[179] [1982] Ch. 314; criticised by Wade, (1983) 32 I.C.L.Q. 1 and by Thompson, ibid., 237.
[180] Law of Domicile para.8.7.
[181] See below, para.6–010.
[182] *Gasque v IRC* [1940] 2 K.B. 80.

DOMICILE AND NATIONALITY[183]

Until the beginning of the nineteenth century, domicile was universally regarded   **3–030**
as the personal law for purposes of the conflict of laws. The change from
domicile to nationality on the continent of Europe started in France with the
promulgation of the Code Napoléon in 1804. One of the principal objects of the
codifiers was to substitute a uniform law throughout the whole of France for the
different *coutumes* of the French provinces. In matters of personal status these
coutumes applied to persons domiciled within the province, wherever they
happened to be. It was natural that the new uniform law should apply to French
people everywhere, and art.3(1) of the Civil Code provided that "the laws
governing the status and capacity of persons govern Frenchmen even though they
are residing in foreign countries." No provision was expressly made for the
converse case of foreigners residing in France, but the French courts held that in
matters of status and capacity foreigners too were governed by their own national
law. The provisions of the French code were adopted in Belgium and
Luxembourg; similar provisions were contained in the Austrian code of 1811 and
the Netherlands code of 1829.

The change from domicile to nationality on the continent of Europe was
accelerated by Mancini's famous lecture delivered at the University of Turin in
1851. In his lecture, he advocated the principle of nationality on the ground that
laws are made more for an ascertained people than for an ascertained territory. A
sovereign (he said) in framing laws for his people should consider their habits
and temperament, their physical and moral qualities, and even the climate,
temperature and fertility of the soil. This was heady wine for a people preparing
to throw off a foreign yoke and unify all the small states of Italy into a new
nation. Under Mancini's influence, art.6 of the Italian Civil Code of 1865
provided that "the status and capacity of persons and family relations are
governed by the laws of the nation to which they belong." Mancini's ideas also
proved extremely influential outside Italy, and in the second half of the nineteenth
century the principle of nationality replaced that of domicile in code after code in
continental Europe, until today only Norway and Denmark retain the principle of
domicile. The result is that the nations of the world have become divided in their
definition of the personal law, and it is this fact more than any other which
impedes international agreement on uniform rules of the conflict of laws. What
then are the arguments in favour of nationality or domicile as the personal law?

The advocates of nationality claim that it is more stable than domicile because
nationality cannot be changed without the formal consent of the State of new
nationality. However, as has been well said,[184] "the principle of nationality
achieves stability, but by the sacrifice of a man's personal freedom to adopt the
legal system of his own choice. The fundamental objection to the concept of
nationality is that it may require the application to a man, against his own wishes
and desires, of the laws of a country to escape from which he has perhaps risked
his life."

---

[183] See Nadelmann, (1969) 17 Am.Jo.Comp. Law 418.
[184] Anton, *Private International Law* (Edinburgh: W Green & Son Ltd, 1970), p.123.

It is also claimed that nationality is easier to ascertain than domicile because it involves a formal act of naturalisation and does not depend on the subjective intentions of the person concerned. This is undoubtedly true, though there may be difficult cases of double nationality or of statelessness. But it does not follow that the most easily ascertained law is the most appropriate law. Many immigrants who have no intention of returning to their country of origin do not take the trouble to apply for naturalisation.

The decisive consideration for countries such as the UK, the US, Australia and Canada is that, save in a very few respects, there is no such thing as UK, American, Australian, or Canadian law. Since the object of referring matters of status and capacity to the personal law is to connect a person with one legal system for legal purposes, nationality breaks down altogether in the case of a federal or composite state containing more than one country.[185]

---

[185] See *Re O'Keefe* [1940] Ch. 124.

CHAPTER 4

THE EXCLUSION OF FOREIGN LAW

In any system of the conflict of laws, and the English system is no exception, the courts retain an overriding power to refuse to enforce, and sometimes even to refuse to recognise, rights acquired under foreign law on grounds of public policy. This notion is related to that of mandatory rules.[1] However, mandatory rules operate in priority to the normal conflicts process, whereas public policy operates when that process has led to an unacceptable result. The exclusion of foreign law represents an exception to the normal functioning of any conflict of laws system therefore it must operate only when tolerance towards the effects of foreign law would produce a result that the adjudicating court considers to be against fundamental values that the system is there to protect.[2] In the English conflict of laws we need to consider first the general doctrine of public policy, which is necessarily somewhat vague; and secondly, some more specific applications of this exception.

4–001

PUBLIC POLICY

The nature and scope of the public policy doctrine was fully examined by Lord Nicholls of Birkenhead in *Kuwait Airways Corp v Iraqi Airways Co (Nos 4 and 5)*.[3] The case concerned the seizure by the Iraqi Government, in the immediate aftermath of the Iraqi invasion of Kuwait in 1990, of aircraft belonging to the claimant company, and the effect of an Iraqi Government Resolution transferring the ownership of the aircraft to the defendants.

4–002

Lord Nicholls described the normal workings of the conflict of laws, which often lead to the application of the laws of another country even though those laws are different from the law of the forum.[4] That was "overwhelmingly" the normal position, but "blind adherence to foreign law can never be required of an English court".[5] He continued:

> "Exceptionally and rarely, a provision of foreign law will be disregarded when it would lead to a result wholly alien to fundamental requirements of justice as administered by an English court. A result of this character would not be acceptable to an English court. In the

---

[1] These are examined below, para.15-022.
[2] See Fresnedo de Aguirre, (2016) 379 *Recueil des Cours* 181.
[3] [2002] UKHL 19; [2002] 2 A.C. 883. See Rogerson, (2003) 56 *Current Legal Problems* 265; Briggs, (2002) 73 B.Y.B.I.L. 490.
[4] See *Harding v Wealands* [2004] EWHC 1957 (New South Wales rules as to calculation of damages differed from those in England; but not contrary to English public policy).
[5] *In the Estate of Fuld, decd (No.3)* [1968] P. 675, 698, per Scarman J.

conventional phraseology, such a result would be contrary to public policy. Then the court will decline to enforce or recognise the foreign decree to whatever extent is required in the circumstances".[6]

In English domestic law it is now well settled that the doctrine of public policy "should only be invoked in clear cases in which the harm to the public is substantially incontestable, and does not depend upon the idiosyncratic inferences of a few judicial minds".[7] In the conflict of laws it is even more necessary that the doctrine should be kept within proper limits, otherwise the whole basis of the system is liable to be frustrated. As Justice Cardozo, a distinguished American judge once said,

"the courts are not free to refuse to enforce a foreign right at the pleasure of the judges, to suit the individual notion of expediency or fairness. They do not close their doors unless help would violate some fundamental principle of justice, some prevalent conception of good morals, some deep-rooted tradition of the common weal".[8]

Lord Nicholls held that the English courts had a residual power, to be exercised exceptionally and with the greatest circumspection, to disregard a provision in the foreign law when to do otherwise would affront basic principles of justice and fairness which the English courts seek to apply. Gross infringements of human rights were an important example, but the principle could not be confined to one particular category of unacceptable laws. In the *Kuwait Airways* case, the seizure of Kuwaiti assets was held to involve flagrant violations of rules of international law of fundamental importance; the breach of established principles of international law was plain and ultimately acknowledged by the Iraqi Government. In those circumstances, recognition of the Iraqi Government Resolution was contrary to public policy.

The doctrine of public policy has assumed far less prominence in the English conflict of laws than have seemingly corresponding doctrines, often referred to as *ordre public,* in the laws of some continental European countries.[9] One reason for this may be that English courts invariably apply English domestic law in many types of family proceedings, such as those involving divorce, maintenance, or the care or adoption of children. Thus, foreign law is inapplicable in many important departments of family law in which, in continental European countries, it is frequently excluded on grounds of public policy.

It is only on the rarest occasions that a foreign law itself can be regarded as contrary to English public policy.[10] What is usually in question is not the foreign law in the abstract, but the results of its enforcement or recognition in England in the concrete case. Everything turns on the nature of the question which arises. Thus, until 1972, no polygamously married spouse could obtain a divorce from the English courts but the spouses were treated as married persons and thus

---

[6] *Kuwait Airways Corp v Iraqi Airways Co (Nos 4 and 5)* [2002] UKHL 19; [2002] 2 A.C. 883, at para.[16].

[7] *Fender v St. John Mildmay* [1938] A.C. 1, 12 per Lord Atkin.

[8] *Loucks v Standard Oil Co* (1918) 224 N.Y. 99, 111; 120 N.E. 198, 202, cited with approval in *Kuwait Airways Corp v Iraqi Airways Co (Nos 4 and 5)* [2002] UKHL 19; [2002] 2 A.C. 883, at para.[17].

[9] See Mills, (2008) 4 J.Priv.I.L. 201.

[10] Traditional illustrations are laws licensing slavery and (perhaps now more arguable) prostitution.

incapable of contracting a valid marriage in England and the children were regarded as legitimate; and the wife was entitled to assert rights of succession and other rights on the footing that she was a wife.[11] Again, to take an improbable but striking example, if a foreign law allowed a bachelor aged 50 to adopt a spinster aged 17, an English court might hesitate to give the custody of the girl to her adoptive father; but that is no reason for not allowing her to succeed to his property as his "child" on his death intestate.[12] In other words, public policy is not absolute but relative; the recognition of a foreign status is one thing, and the recognition of all its incidents another.

The doctrine of public policy may not only lead a court to refuse to enforce or recognise, for example, a contract or a marriage when it would be valid under the appropriate foreign law. It may also produce the opposite effect, leading to the enforcement or recognition of a contract or a marriage that under the applicable foreign law would be invalid. Thus, a foreign law that invalidates a marriage will be disregarded if it is discriminatory and so adjudged penal.[13] On the other hand, the effect of the doctrine of public policy is always to exclude the application of foreign law that would otherwise be applicable. In one case,[14] the doctrine was anomalously applied so as to invoke the application of a foreign law which would otherwise have been inapplicable; but this case has since been held to have been wrongly decided.[15]

The reservation of public policy in conflict of laws cases is a necessary one, but "no attempt to define the limits of that reservation has ever succeeded".[16] All that can be done, therefore, is to enumerate the cases in which the recognition or enforcement of rights arising under foreign laws has been refused on this ground. It will be found that the doctrine has been usually invoked in two classes of case, namely those involving foreign contracts; and those involving a foreign status.

Contracts

Under Art.21 of the Rome I Regulation,[17] the application of a rule of law otherwise applicable by virtue of the Convention may be refused if its application is manifestly incompatible with the public policy (*ordre public*) of the forum.[18] So in *Duarte v Black and Decker Corp*,[19] the English court would have refused to apply a covenant in restraint of trade had it been enforceable under the law governing the contract. In earlier cases, English courts refused to enforce

4–003

---

[11] See below, para.11–029 ff.
[12] See below, para.18–010 ff.
[13] Below, para.11–022.
[14] *Lorentzen v Lydden & Co Ltd* [1942] 2 K.B. 202.
[15] *Bank voor Handel en Scheepvart N.V. v Slatford* [1953] 1 Q.B. 248, 263–264; *Peer International Corp v Termidor Music Publishers Ltd* [2003] EWCA Civ 1156; [2004] 2 W.L.R. 849 (noted Briggs, (2003) 74 B.Y.B.I.L. 522).
[16] Westlake *Private International Law* (London: Sweet and Maxwell, 1925), p.51.
[17] See below, para.15–054. The same provision was in the predecessor provision, Rome Convention art.16.
[18] The English text of the Regulation includes the French term.
[19] [2007] EWHC 2720; [2008] 1 All E.R. (Comm.) 401.

champertous contracts,[20] contracts entered into under duress or coercion,[21] contracts involving collusive and corrupt arrangements for a divorce,[22] or trading with the enemy,[23] or breaking the laws of a friendly country.[24] On the other hand, they enforced contracts for the loan of money to be spent on gambling abroad,[25] and for foreign loans which contravened the English Moneylenders Acts.[26]

Status

4–004   English courts will not give effect to the results of any status existing under a foreign law which is penal, i.e. discriminatory. Examples are the status of slavery or civil death,[27] and the disabilities or incapacities which may be imposed on priests, nuns, Protestants, Jews, persons of alien nationality, persons of certain ethnic groups,[28] and divorced persons. Some of the disabilities referred to above are obviously imposed as a punishment,[29] e.g. the inability under some systems of law of persons divorced for adultery to remarry while the innocent spouse remains single,[30] or the disabilities imposed on Jews by the Nazi regime in Germany.[31] Others equally obviously are not, e.g. the inability under the laws of some Catholic countries of priests and nuns to marry at all.[32] None of these disabilities will be recognised in England, the true reason being that recognition would be contrary to English public policy.

The treatment of "prodigals" in civil law systems has sometimes been treated by the English courts as contrary to public policy, but it is arguable that the limitation of a person's normal powers of dealing with property to prevent it being dissipated is protective in nature not penal.[33]

---

[20] *Grell v Levy* (1864) 10 C.B. (N.S.) 73.

[21] *Kaufman v Gerson* [1904] 1 K.B. 591, a much-criticised decision.

[22] *Hope v Hope* (1857) 8 D. M. & G. 731.

[23] *Dynamit A/G v Rio Tinto Co* [1918] A.C. 260.

[24] *Foster v Driscoll* [1929] 1 K.B. 470; *Regazzoni v K.C. Sethia Ltd* [1958] A.C. 301 (in both of which the contract was governed by English law).

[25] *Saxby v Fulton* [1909] 2 K.B. 208.

[26] *Schrichand v Lacon* (1906) 22 T.L.R. 245.

[27] *Re Metcalfe's Trusts* (1864) 2 D. J. & S. 122.

[28] See *Wolff v Oxholm* (1817) 6 M. & S. 92; *Re Friedrich Krupp A.G.* [1917] 2 Ch. 188; *Re Helbert Wagg & Co Ltd's Claim* [1956] Ch. 323, 345–346.

[29] See *Sottomayor v De Barros (No.2)* (1879) 5 P.D. 94, 104.

[30] *Scott v Attorney General* (1886) 11 P.D. 128, as explained in *Warter v Warter* (1890) 15 P.D. 152, 155; below, para.11–022.

[31] See *Frankfurther v W.L. Exner Ltd* [1947] Ch. 629; *Novello & Co Ltd v Hinrichsen Edition Ltd* [1951] Ch. 595; *Oppenheimer v Cattermole* [1976] A.C. 249, 277–278; *Kuwait Airways Corp v Iraqi Airways Co (Nos 4 and 5)* [2002] UKHL 19; [2002] 2 A.C. 883, at para.[19]. cf. *Oppenheimer v Rosenthal & Co* [1937] 1 All E.R. 23; *Ellinger v Guinness Mahon & Co* [1939] 4 All E.R. 16.

[32] *Sottomayor v De Barros (No.2)* (1879) 5 P.D. 94, 104.

[33] Compare *Worms v De Valdor* (1880) 49 L.J.Ch. 261 (Frenchman declared a prodigal and unable in French law to sue without approval of his *conseil judiciaire* held free to sue in England) and *Re Selot's Trusts* [1902] 1 Ch. 488 (French status of prodigal apparently not recognised). See also *Re Langley's Settlement* [1962] Ch. 541 (status of "incompetent" under Californian law did not prevent dealings in England; criticised by Grodecki, (1962) 11 I.C.L.Q. 578; Collier, [1962] C.L.J. 36. In all these cases, English law seems to have been the *lex causae,* and the results might have been different if the foreign law had been the *lex causae.*

Public policy may sometimes require that a capacity existing under foreign law should be disregarded in England[34] but the circumstances have to be extreme before such a course is taken. An example of such extreme circumstances is provided by *City of Westminster Social and Community Services Dept v C*[35]:

> C had very limited mental capacity. In many respects his intellectual functioning was below that of an average three-year-old. At the behest of his family, he was married in an Islamic ceremony conducted by telephone, the bride being in Bangladesh. The marriage was valid under the law of Bangladesh.

The English court received evidence that the marriage was potentially highly injurious to C, and noted that any sexual activity he was encouraged to engage in would be a criminal offence under English law. In its duty to prevent abuse to C, the marriage was refused recognition on the ground of public policy. Although marriages by proxy had been held not contrary to public policy,[36] some qualification was required were such a procedure to be used for abusive purposes.

English courts do recognise the validity of polygamous marriages,[37] and of marriages within the prohibited degrees of English law,[38] provided of course they are valid under the applicable foreign law. But they might refuse to recognise a marriage between persons so closely related that sexual intercourse between them was incestuous by English criminal law,[39] or with a child below the age of puberty.[40]

The mere fact that a foreign status or relationship is unknown to English domestic law is not a ground for refusing to recognise it.[41] Thus, legitimation by subsequent marriage was recognised and given effect to in England long before it became part of English domestic law.[42] The recognition of polygamous marriages and of same sex marriages are other examples.

Other cases

Apart from cases of contract and status, examples of the exclusion of foreign law on the grounds of public policy are rare. It is not contrary to public policy to recognise foreign decrees confiscating private property,[43] but it may be otherwise if the decree is "penal" in the sense of being directed against the property of a particular individual or a particular company or a particular family or persons of

4–005

---

[34] *Cheni v Cheni* [1965] P. 85, 98.
[35] [2008] EWCA Civ 198; [2009] Fam. 11.
[36] *Apt v Apt* [1948] P. 83.
[37] See below, para.11–034.
[38] *Re Bozzelli's Settlement* [1902] 1 Ch. 751 (marriage in 1880 with deceased brother's widow); *Re Pozot's Settlement* [1952] 1 All E.R. 1107, 1109 (marriage with step-daughter); *Cheni v Cheni* [1965] P. 85 (marriage between uncle and niece).
[39] *Brook v Brook* (1861) 9 H.L.C. 193, 227–228; *Cheni v Cheni* [1965] P. 85, 97.
[40] cf. *Mohamed v Knott* [1969] 1 Q.B. 1, where such a marriage was recognised. See Karsten (1969) 32 M.L.R. 212.
[41] *Phrantzes v Argenti* [1960] 2 Q.B. 19; *Shahnaz v Rizwan* [1965] 1 Q.B. 390, 401.
[42] Below, para.14–046.
[43] *Luther v Sagor* [1921] 3 K.B. 532, 559; *Princess Paley Olga v Weisz* [1929] 1 K.B. 718.

a particular race or a particular alien nationality.[44] It is not contrary to public policy to recognise foreign exchange control legislation,[45] but it may be otherwise if the legislation, even though originally passed with the genuine object of protecting the state's economy, has become an instrument of oppression and discrimination.[46] The recognition of a foreign decree of divorce or nullity of marriage[47] and the enforcement of a foreign judgment in personam[48] may be refused on grounds of public policy, but instances are extremely rare. There is no general principle that the application of a foreign law is contrary to public policy merely because it operates retrospectively.[49] However, the *Kuwait Airways* case[50] established that breaches of public international law could attract the public policy doctrine.

PENAL LAWS

4–006   It is well settled that English courts will not directly or indirectly enforce a foreign penal law. "The courts of no country execute the penal laws of another",[51] said Chief Justice Marshall of the US. The reason has been thus explained by the Privy Council[52]:

> "The rule has its foundation in the well-recognised principle that crimes, including in that term all breaches of public law punishable by pecuniary mulct or otherwise, at the instance of the State Government, or of someone representing the public, are local in this sense, that they are only cognisable and punishable in the country where they were committed. Accordingly no proceeding, even in the shape of a civil suit, which has for its object the enforcement by the State, whether directly or indirectly, of punishment imposed for such breaches by the *lex fori*, ought to be admitted in the courts of any other country."

Although this principle is almost universally accepted, modern state practice requires some qualification of its more expansive formulations. There are a growing number of international treaties under which states, including the UK, provide mutual assistance in the conduct of criminal prosecutions. For example, compulsory measures available under the law of one state may be exercised at the request of a foreign state to search and seize evidence, or to freeze and confiscate the profits of drug-trafficking. International practice is reflected in English law in legislation such as the Crime (International Co-operation) Act 2003.

A "penal" law, in the present context, is a criminal law imposing a penalty recoverable at the instance of the State or of an official duly authorised to prosecute on its behalf.[53] The fact that a particular piece of legislation contains provisions creating criminal offences does not mean that the whole Act is

---

[44] Below, para.17–033.
[45] *Kahler v Midland Bank* [1950] A.C. 24; *Zivnostenska Banka v Frankman* [1950] A.C. 57.
[46] *Re Helbert Wagg & Co. Ltd's Claim* [1956] Ch. 323, 352.
[47] Below, para.12–037.
[48] Below, paras 10–004, 10–023.
[49] Below, para.20–031.
[50] *Kuwait Airways Corp v Iraqi Airways Co (Nos 4 and 5)* [2002] UKHL 19; [2002] 2 A.C. 883.
[51] *The Antelope* (1825) 10 Wheat. 66, 123.
[52] *Huntingdon v Attrill* [1893] A.C. 150, 156.
[53] *Huntingdon v Attrill* [1893] A.C. 150, 157–158.

necessarily penal.[54] The word "penal" here has quite a different meaning from that which it bears in the contexts examined earlier in this chapter, where "penal" means merely discriminatory. It is for the English court to determine for itself whether the foreign law in question is a penal law, and it is not bound by the interpretation placed upon the law by the courts of the foreign country.[55]

Since "the essential nature and real foundation of a cause of action are not changed by recovering judgment upon it",[56] the court will not enforce a foreign judgment based upon a foreign penal law.[57] A striking illustration of the rule is afforded by *Banco de Vizcaya v Don Alfonso de Borbon y Austria*[58]:

> The King of Spain deposited securities with the Westminster Bank in London. A decree of the Constituent Cortes of Spain declared the ex-King to be guilty of high treason, and ordered all his properties, rights and grounds of action to be seized for its own benefit by the Spanish State. An action by a nominee of the State to recover the securities was dismissed.

An important distinction was drawn by the Irish courts in *Larkins v National Union of Mineworkers*[59]:

> A part of the funds of the National Union of Mineworkers was transferred to Ireland during the miners' strike of 1984. After the Union had refused to obey English court orders, its assets were made the subject of sequestration, and the sequestrators began proceedings in Ireland to recover sums in Irish bank accounts. A receiver was later appointed by the English court with general powers to take control of the Union's assets; the receiver began similar proceedings in the Irish courts. It was held that the sequestrators' action was a means of enforcing a penal process of English law, and could not be allowed; the receivership rested on other grounds, and the receiver's action could continue.

REVENUE LAWS

"No country ever takes notice of the revenue laws of another", said Lord Mansfield in *Holman v Johnson*,[60] and though (as will be seen below) this proposition is too widely stated, it has ever since been assumed by English lawyers that foreign revenue laws will not be enforced in England. Authority for this more limited proposition was sparse until the decision of the House of Lords in *Government of India v Taylor*[61] placed the matter beyond doubt. The reason for

4–007

---

[54] *Islamic Republic of Iran v Barakat Galleries Ltd* [2007] EWCA Civ 1374; [2008] 3 W.L.R. 486.

[55] *Huntingdon v Attrill* [1893] A.C. 150

[56] *Wisconsin v Pelican Insurance Co*, 127 U.S. 265, 292 (1888).

[57] *Huntingdon v Attrill* [1893] A.C. 150. See *Blue Holding (I) Pte Ltd v United States* [2014] EWCA Civ 1291; [2015] 1 W.L.R. 1917 (foreign proceedings to recover assets the subject of money-laundering; any eventual judgment would be penal).

[58] [1935] 1 K.B. 140. Compare *Huntington v Attrill* [1893] A.C. 150 (New York statute making company directors signing certificates false in any material respect personally liable for company debts held not to be penal). See the decision of the US Supreme Court in *Huntingdon v Attrill*, 146 US 657 (1892).

[59] [1985] I.R. 671. cf. the distinction drawn in a rather different context in *Williams & Humbert Ltd v W.&H. Trade Marks (Jersey) Ltd* [1986] A.C. 386.

[60] (1775) 1 Cowp. 341, 343.

[61] [1955] A.C. 491, 514. The coming of the Brussels and Lugano Conventions (and the Brussels I and Brussels I *bis* Regulations) has made no difference: it remains a fundamental principle: *QRS 1 Aps v Frandsen* [1999] 1 W.L.R. 2169 (see Briggs, (1999) 70 B.Y.I.L. 341).

non-enforcement is that "tax-gathering is not a matter of contract but of authority and administration as between the state and those within its jurisdiction".

A foreign revenue law is a law requiring a non-contractual payment of money to the state or some department or sub-division thereof. It includes income tax,[62] capital gains tax,[63] customs duty,[64] death duties,[65] local rates or council taxes,[66] compulsory contributions to a State insurance scheme[67] and a profits levy.[68]

The traditional rule of English law was that English courts will not enforce foreign revenue laws either directly or indirectly. Direct enforcement occurs when a foreign state or its nominee seeks to recover the tax by action in England. Indirect enforcement occurs, for example, where a company in liquidation seeks to recover from one of its directors assets under the director's control which the liquidator would use to pay foreign taxes due from the company,[69] or where a debtor pleads that the debt has been attached by a foreign garnishee order obtained by a foreign state claiming a tax.[70] The status of this rule as to indirect enforcement is now uncertain in that the CJEU has held, on particular facts, that an action by the revenue authorities to recover damages in respect of losses caused by a VAT fraud is within the concept of "civil and commercial matters" for the purposes of the Brussels I *bis* Regulation.[71]

Where neither direct nor indirect enforcement arises, foreign revenue laws are freely recognised.[72] Thus Lord Mansfield's proposition that "no country ever takes notice of the revenue laws of another" is now seen to be too widely stated. The difference between enforcement and recognition was explained by Lord Simonds in *Regazzoni v K.C. Sethia Ltd*[73]:

> "It does not follow from the fact that today the court will not enforce a revenue law at the suit of a foreign State that today it will enforce a contract which requires the doing of an act in a foreign country which violates the revenue law of that country. The two things are not complementary or co-extensive. This may be seen if for revenue law penal law is substituted. For an English court will not enforce a penal law at the suit of a foreign State, yet it would be surprising if it would enforce a contract which required the commission of a crime in that State".

---

[62] *USA v Harden* (1963) 41 D.L.R. (2d) 721.

[63] *Government of India v Taylor* [1955] A.C. 491.

[64] *Attorney General for Canada v Schulze* (1901) 9 S.L.T. 4.

[65] *Re Visser* [1928] Ch. 877.

[66] *Municipal Council of Sydney v Bull* [1909] 1 K.B. 7.

[67] *Metal Industries (Salvage) Ltd v Owners of S.T. Harle,* 1962 S.L.T. 114. cf. *The Acrux* [1965] P. 391, where this point was overlooked.

[68] *Peter Buchanan Ltd v McVey* [1954] I.R. 89.

[69] ibid.

[70] *Rossano v Manufacturers Life Assurance Co Ltd* [1963] 2 Q.B. 352.

[71] Case C-49/12 Revenue and Customs Commissioners v Sunico ApS [2014] Q.B. 391. See Collins, (2014) 130 L.Q.R. 353. For "civil and commercial matters", see para.6–006.

[72] *The State of Norway's Application (Nos 1 and 2)* [1990] 1 A.C. 723.

[73] [1958] A.C. 301, 322.

OTHER PUBLIC LAWS

English courts will not enforce other public laws of a foreign state but the scope   **4–008**
of this principle is unclear.[74] In *Attorney General of New Zealand v Ortiz*,[75]
which concerned the unauthorised export of an ancient Maori carving from New
Zealand, Lord Denning MR recognised the existence of this "other public law"
category, but when the decision was affirmed in the House of Lords the
discussion of this point was regarded as obiter.[76]

It is perhaps best to limit the scope of "other public law" to the enforcement of
claims by the foreign state relating to the exercise of its governmental power.
That it is so limited is suggested by a number of decisions in several jurisdictions.
The High Court of Australia recognised the existence of such a principle in
Attorney General for the UK v Heinemann Publishers Australia Pty Ltd[77]:

> Mr Wright, a former member of the British Civil Service, wrote his memoirs under the title
> *Spycatcher*. The British Government sought to restrain their publication, relying on the duty of
> confidentiality arising from his employment.

The Australian court refused to grant the British Government an injunction, a
decision which has been trenchantly (and, it is submitted, rightly) criticised[78] as
going beyond the proper limits of the principle. The court regarded the principle
as including an action to protect and enforce the "interests" of the British
Government, a marked and undesirable extension of a principle which, as one
limiting access to the courts, should be cautiously applied.

The *Spycatcher* principle was examined in the Court of Appeal in *Mbasogo v
Logo Ltd*[79]:

> After what was alleged to have been a conspiracy to overthrow the Government of Equatorial
> Guinea, the President of that state and the Republic itself sought remedies in the English
> courts against the conspirators. The defendants argued that this would be to enforce the public
> laws of a foreign state.

The Court of Appeal sought to go behind the language of "public law". In its
judgment, the critical question was whether in bringing a claim, a claimant was
doing an act which was of a sovereign character or which was done by virtue of
sovereign authority; and whether the claim involved the exercise or assertion of a
sovereign right. If so, then the court would not determine or enforce the claim.
On the other hand, if in bringing the claim the claimant was not doing an act
which was of a sovereign character or by virtue of sovereign authority and the
claim did not involve the exercise or assertion of a sovereign right and the claim
did not seek to vindicate a sovereign act or acts, then the court would both
determine and enforce it.

---

[74] See Collins, (2007) 326 *Receuil des Cours* 11.
[75] [1984] A.C. 1. See now the Dealing in Cultural Objects (Offences) Act 2003.
[76] [1984] A.C. 1, 41.
[77] (1988) 165 C.L.R. 30.
[78] Mann, (1988) 104 L.Q.R. 497.
[79] [2006] EWCA Civ 1370; [2007] QB 246. For earlier related proceedings, see *President of the
Republic of Equatorial Guinea v Bank of Scotland International* [2006] UKPC 7.

That distinction was central to *Islamic Republic of Iran v Barakat Galleries Ltd*.[80] Like *Attorney General of New Zealand v Ortiz*[81] it involved the unlawful export of antiquities, and the Republic claimed remedies in conversion. The Court of Appeal found that the goods were the property of the Republic under Iranian law, and held that where the foreign state had acquired title under its law to property within its jurisdiction in cases not involving compulsory acquisition of title from private parties, so that it owned property in the same way as a private citizen, there was no reason in principle for the English court not to recognise its title in accordance with the general principle that the *lex situs* governed.[82]

It is increasingly the case that states, including the UK, use what are ostensibly civil proceedings to recover the proceeds of crime. The courts have had to examine how this practice relates to the rule about foreign penal laws. In *United States Securities and Exchange Commission v Manterfield*[83] the applicant for a freezing order was a US regulator which was seeking in US civil proceedings both the "disgorgement" of huge profits made in what was alleged to be a fraudulent scheme, the sums obtained to be returned to the victims of the fraud, and also a monetary penalty. The Court of Appeal upheld the freezing order in respect of the disgorgement, the applicant having given an undertaking not to enforce any penalty. However, that case was distinguished in *Pocket Kings Ltd v Safenames Ltd*.[84] The judge held that a foreign order requiring the forfeiture of assets used in the commission of crime under local foreign law, even if categorised by the foreign state as a civil remedy under its law, was "distinctly penal in nature, requiring the confiscation without compensation of an asset on the ground that the owner, or user of it, was guilty of a criminal offence"; the fact that the purpose of the forfeiture was ostensibly to protect the public rather than to punish the wrongdoer did not alter the position.

It is still difficult to be sure how this part of the law will develop. It would be wise for the courts to maintain a flexible approach which recognises the great variety and the continuing capacity for development within the field of "governmental power".

---

[80] [2007] EWCA Civ 1374; [2008] 3 W.L.R. 486.

[81] [1984] A.C. 1. See Council Directive (EEC) 93/7 on the return of cultural objects unlawfully removed from the territory of a member state, the Return of Cultural Objects Regulations 1994, SI 1994/501, and the Dealing in Cultural Objects (Offences) Act 2003. For the cross-border recovery of cultural objects from an EU member state. see Gillies (2015) 11 J.Priv.Int.L. 295.

[82] On that principle, see para.17-015.

[83] [2009] EWCA Civ 27; [2010] 1 W.L.R. 172.

[84] [2009] EWHC 2529 (Ch.); [2010] Ch. 438.

CHAPTER 5

JURISDICTION IN THE CONFLICT OF LAWS

Jurisdiction is a multifaceted concept[1] that has generated a wealth of literature in various disciplines.[2] In the conflict of laws, the rules as to jurisdiction determine whether or not a court can hear a case. More precisely, they identify the country or countries whose courts can appropriately deal with a case.

The jurisdictional question is the first to impact the process of international litigation; and it is of the utmost importance. In a pragmatic approach, questions such as the following arise: Where should the claimant initiate the proceedings? Is it possible for the defendant to object to the jurisdiction chosen by the claimant? What happens in cases where proceedings on the same issue(s) and between the same parties are initiated in more than one country? Will the eventual judgment obtained in a country be enforceable against the assets of the defendant elsewhere? These are very important issues for international legal practice.[3] From a theoretical perspective, understanding the foundations of jurisdictional principles is required if one is to envisage ways forward towards further harmonisation in this field. Such harmonisation is happening regionally and internationally. In Europe, this is the result of the Europeanisation of private international law, and particularly the direct application of the Regulations containing jurisdictional rules in all the Member States of the EU. Internationally, the Hague Conference on Private International Law has long taken the lead in this as in many other fields of our subject. This chapter looks at some of these issues, and seeks to explain the centrality of jurisdiction in serving the overall objectives of the conflict of laws. It seeks to clarify the terminology and concepts used in the provisions examined in the next two chapters. Two caveats are necessary at the start of this discussion. First, in this sphere, strictly conflict of laws considerations, such as the quest for the appropriate forum, become intertwined with considerations of procedural efficiency, such as case management powers, particularly in cases of conflicts of jurisdiction.[4] Secondly, this is an area that bridges private and public international law.

---

[1] It has been considered an 'omnibus' term, as it comprises several theoretical and doctrinal principles about the authority of the law, not all of which can easily be read together. See A. Kaushal, (2015) 78 M.L.R. 759-792, 761, referring to I. Brownlie, *Principles of Public International Law,* 6th edn (Oxford: Oxford University Press, 2003).

[2] See e.g. C. Ryngaert, *Jurisdiction in International Law,* 2nd edn (Oxford: Oxford University Press, 2015) a monograph on jurisdiction from the (public) international law perspective.

[3] Another set of issues, also very important in this context, relate to the conduct of international litigation. See further Ch.9.

[4] For a more holistic analysis of this topic, including insights from (public) international law, see French and Ruiz Abou-Nigm, 'Jurisdiction: Betwixt Unilateralism and Global Interest' in *Private and Public International Law: Strengthening Connections* (forthcoming).

THE APPROPRIATE FORUM

5–002   The notion of an "appropriate forum" for the resolution of a dispute is a complex one, and is understood in different ways in different legal traditions. Clearly there must be limits to the jurisdiction of the courts of any country. It would be entirely appropriate for the English court to have jurisdiction over an action arising out of a fight between two English students in the middle of an English city. It would be entirely inappropriate for that court to deal with an action arising out of a fight between two Chinese students in the middle of Beijing. In practice, cases seldom have the simplicity of such textbook examples: they may concern corporations operating in several countries, or events causing loss or damage in several countries. There is also the time factor: if a claim is brought against a defendant now based wholly within a single country, and having assets solely in that country, it may well be appropriate to have the claim heard there. That will be true even if the underlying dispute has no connection with that country and neither party had any such connection when the dispute first arose.

Before the rules as to jurisdiction are examined more closely, it should be noted that in federal countries, and countries which have courts operating on a regional basis, similar issues may arise in deciding how cases are to be allocated between the various component parts. As we shall see, many rules give jurisdiction to the courts of the UK, but it is then necessary to decide whether the case is to be heard in England, Scotland or Northern Ireland. Students of legal history may recall the old rules as to "venue" which identified the English county within which a trial was to be held. There are still some rules assigning cases to particular local courts but they are regarded as domestic rules and not part of the conflict of laws.

DIRECT AND INDIRECT JURISDICTION

5–003   In the conflict of laws the notion of jurisdiction involves not only jurisdiction to adjudicate, but also a court's decision to recognise and enforce the judgments of a foreign court. The former is sometimes referred to as "direct" jurisdiction; the latter as "indirect jurisdiction". The exercise of direct jurisdiction is about hearing and deciding the case, whereas the exercise of indirect jurisdiction involves the court asked to recognise or enforce a judgment (the requested court) deciding whether or not to recognise the direct jurisdiction of the court that adjudicated the case and issued the judgment (the court of origin). International instruments dealing with jurisdiction, such as currently the Brussels I *bis* Regulation in the European regime, usually deal also with the recognition and enforcement of foreign judgments, and they are referred to as "double" instruments as they deal with both direct and indirect jurisdiction.[5]

---

[5] Michaels, 'Some Fundamental Jurisdictional Conceptions as Applied in Judgment Conventions' in E. Gottschalk, R. Michaels et al (eds), *Conflict of Laws in a Globalizing World* (Cambridge: Cambridge University Press, 2007).

"Direct" jurisdictional bases have been divided into three categories: "consensual" jurisdiction; "connected" jurisdiction; and "universal" jurisdiction.[6] In turn, four different strands of the "connected" bases have been distinguished, i.e. exclusive, general, special and protective jurisdiction.[7] Some of these concepts and many of the provisions providing for these different kinds of jurisdictional bases are examined either in this chapter or in one of the following two chapters dedicated to the European regime of jurisdiction and the English traditional rules of jurisdiction, respectively.

Direct jurisdiction: choice by the claimant

In the conflict of laws the existence of concurrent jurisdictional bases is the rule rather than the exception. That is to say, in many cases, there will be two or more countries with jurisdiction, each of which could properly provide the forum in which the matter could be tried. It is the claimant who decides whether and where to begin legal proceedings, and the claimant's choice of forum may have a crucial effect on the outcome of the case. The choice is influenced by a whole series of factors of greater or lesser sophistication.

5–004

One is simply a wish to "play on one's home ground". Particularly to the individual or small firm claimant, it seems only natural to sue in the local courts down the road. Litigation is never comfortable, but it seems less alarming in one's home-town, or at least one's home country, before local judges, speaking one's own language. There is perhaps the subconscious feeling that the court is more likely to be on your side if you are the local party, a feeling that may even be justified.

The home ground factor shades into considerations of convenience. It is easier to sue locally in most cases—but not always. It may depend on the location of the evidence and of potential witnesses. A corporate claimant may have in-house lawyers: if not, much may depend on the location of the legal firm that understands the special features of the particular company or the particular business.

A more sophisticated analysis will take into account differences in the substantive law applied in the possible fora including, of course, their choice of law rules. The law that would be applied might, for example, make liability strict or require a claimant to prove negligence; it might provide for compensatory damages only or exemplary ("punitive") damages as well. There might be a difference in the limitation periods applicable in the different countries, and different categories of persons eligible to sue, as a result, for example, of varying definitions of "relatives" able to claim in fatal accident cases, or the existence of strict privity of contract rules, or the availability of claims by "third-party beneficiaries".

Other relevant factors include differences in procedural law, including the law of evidence and pre-trial procedures such as the extensive rights of "discovery"

---

[6] Hill, 'The Exercise of Jurisdiction in Private International Law' in P. Capps, M. Evans & S. Konstadinidis (eds) *Asserting Jurisdiction: International and European Legal Perspectives* (Oxford: Hart Oxford, 2003) 39 at 49.

[7] Hill (2003) 49.

available to claimants and potential claimants in US jurisdictions, and differences in professional practices, such as rights of audience and the rules as to costs or contingent fees.

All these factors put the claimant in a strong position. It is natural to assume that the claimant is the person asserting that someone else is liable for a particular act or omission, but that is not necessarily the case. Someone who appears to be the potential defendant may attempt a pre-emptive strike by seeking a negative declaration, a ruling that there is no liability to the claimant, and the proceedings for such a declaration would be in a forum chosen by the applicant, the potential defendant.

Can the claimant's choice be challenged?

5–005   The claimant is able to take many matters into account so as to select the most favourable forum. The forum which is most favourable to the claimant may not be the forum which is, on more objective criteria, the most appropriate for the trial of the case. A defendant may well feel that the claimant, by selecting a forum which is relatively inappropriate, is "playing the system", manipulating it to the claimant's own advantage. In the common law tradition, various devices were developed which enabled defendants to influence the choice of forum, and which enabled the judges themselves to steer a case to what they considered the most appropriate court.[8]

Under the doctrine of forum non conveniens, originating in Scots law,[9] a defendant might ask the court chosen by the claimant not to exercise its jurisdiction on the ground that the case could more appropriately be tried elsewhere.[10] In some cases the defendant could prevent the claimant suing in a foreign court by obtaining an anti-suit injunction.[11] Developments within the EU have greatly limited the use that can be made of these procedures by the English courts.[12]

---

[8] See *Stonebridge Underwriting Ltd v Ontario Municipal Insurance Exchange* [2010] EWHC 2279 (Comm); [2011] Lloyd's Rep. I.R. 171.

[9] The doctrine took various tags when it first appeared: forum non conveniens, forum conveniens and *forum non competens*. The earliest cases identified as the origins of the doctrine date from the 1830s. In *Sim v Robinow* (1892) 19 R. 665 Lord Kinnear, at 668, made the doctrine "fit for export", providing the world with a valuable device to secure the ends of justice; and particularly, to restrain the use of far-reaching general jurisdictional bases. The doctrine was successfully developed in the US; see among the leading cases *Canada Malting Co Ltd v Paterson Steamships Ltd* 285 U.S. 413 (1932); and later in England.

[10] See below, para.7–032.

[11] See below, para.7–036.

[12] See further paras 7–033 and 7–037.

BASES OF JURISDICTION

In the conflict of laws, a jurisdictional basis is a link between a forum and a dispute that is in some sense international. In principle, that connection contributes to establishing the level of appropriateness of the courts[13] of that particular country to hear the merits of that particular international dispute. The bases for exercising adjudicatory jurisdiction rest on different kinds of relationship between: (i) the forum and the dispute, or (ii) the forum and the parties to the dispute. The strength of these links vary from minimal, for example a defendant's transitory presence in the forum State, to strong, when the claim has a close connection with the forum State, based on that State's relationship with the parties and/or the dispute. In most cases, the stronger the connection the more appropriate is the forum to adjudicate the merits of that particular dispute.[14]

5–006

This notion of "appropriateness" is expressed in different ways by writers and by the courts of particular legal systems. Some have developed notions such as "the natural forum", or "the forum in which the case might be suitably tried in the interests of the parties and for the ends of justice", or "the forum with which the action had its most real and substantial connection". Others prefer to speak of "reasonableness"[15] or "proximity".[16] Different considerations have been identified as justifying the allocation of jurisdiction internationally in particular types of case.[17] They include, for example, the location of the property the subject of the dispute, party autonomy (a respect for the choice of jurisdiction made by the parties), and the right of access to justice. Those considerations, it will be seen, operate in different ways; it is very difficult to construct an overall statement of priority as between different considerations. It has been argued that the one consideration on which there is consensus is that the exercise of jurisdiction should serve the proper administration of justice[18]. However, in the international sphere that is not without difficulties, for "the proper administration of justice" may not be understood in the same way in different legal traditions.

---

[13] Conflict of laws rules of jurisdiction designate as appropriate the courts of a particular country, but they do not provide specifically for a particular court within the territory of that country; that is in most cases for the national legal system to determine.

[14] If the English traditional rules apply to the case the assessment of the appropriateness of a certain forum in international civil and commercial litigation is not limited to the consideration of the strength of the link as such but includes several other factors such as the availability of witnesses, the governing law, the residence or place of business of the parties (*Spiliada Maritime Corp v Cansulex Ltd (The Spiliada)* [1987] 1 Lloyd's Rep 1, HL). The suitability of the *Spiliada* test for determining the appropriateness of the forum was confirmed by the UK Supreme Court in *VTB Capital Plc v Nutritek International* [2013] UKSC 5; [2013] 2 A.C. 337.

[15] Ryngaert, *Jurisdiction in International Law* (2015).

[16] P Lagarde, *Le principe de proximité dans le droit international privé contemporain* (1986) 196 *Recueil des Cours* 9, 131-132; Ruiz Abou-Nigm (2011).

[17] See Diego P Fernández Arroyo, *Compétence exclusive et compétence exorbitante dans les relations privées internationales,* (2008) 323 *Recueil des cours* 13.

[18] See e.g. R Fentiman, *International Commercial Litigation* 2nd edn (Oxford: Oxford University Press, 2015) at 32. See further para.6–068.

General and special jurisdiction

5–007   This classification was first coined more than 50 years ago.[19] It distinguishes, on the one hand, jurisdictional grounds based on the relationship between the forum and the person or persons whose legal rights are to be affected (general jurisdiction, or jurisdiction *ratione personae*) and, on the other hand, jurisdictional grounds based on the relationship between the forum and the dispute (special jurisdiction, subject-matter jurisdiction or jurisdiction *ratione materiae*).[20]

In terms of general jurisdiction, there is wide recognition of the principal enshrined, not very clearly, in the Latin statement *actor sequitur forum rei*. Literally it requires the claimant to sue where the property is to be found; more generally it means that there is jurisdiction where the defendant can properly be sued. Because of the advantages generally possessed by the claimant, this basic rule of "general jurisdiction" requires a link between the *defendant* and the chosen court, for example the habitual residence of the defendant and not of the claimant. In the US this has been elevated to a constitutional rule, as an application of the Due Process clause.

This principle of resort to what is sometimes called "the defendant's forum" is qualified in a number of ways. What is an appropriate jurisdiction may depend on the subject matter as much as on the identity and characteristics of the parties, so there are additional rules of "special jurisdiction", for example taking into account where an obligation was to be performed. In international civil and commercial litigation in Europe, this other category—special jurisdiction—includes the jurisdictional grounds based on an objective link between the forum and the dispute, such as the place where the harmful event occurred or may occur for tort/delict claims,[21] or the place where the property is situated for jurisdiction regarding proceedings concerning rights in rem in relation to immovable/heritable property.[22] A court exercising special jurisdiction "may adjudicate only disputes which are related to the particular connecting factor on which jurisdiction is based".[23] Choice of court agreements can also be considered as a source of special jurisdiction: the agreement of the parties determines the scope of competence of the chosen court, so that it may adjudicate only disputes that are within the competence attributed to the court by the choice of court agreement.

Protective jurisdiction

5–008   The notion of jurisdictional protection has sometimes been considered as relatively new in the conflict of laws. Private international law, as the discipline is also referred to as, has traditionally been conceived as 'neutral' in relation to its

---

[19] von Mehren and Trautman, (1966) 79 Harvard L. Rev. 1121.
[20] de Winter, (1968) 17 I.C.L.Q. 706 at 718. Note that in the US "special jurisdiction" is known as "specific jurisdiction". The term used in the Brussels regime, i.e. special jurisdiction (art.7 of the Brussels I *bis* Regulation), is the one used throughout this book.
[21] Brussels I Regulation art.7(2).
[22] Brussels I Regulation art.24(1).
[23] Hill, (2003) 52.

three main spheres, that of jurisdiction, choice of law, and the recognition and enforcement of foreign judgments. However, the rationale of 'protecting' the defendant is at the root of the most well established principle of jurisdiction: that of general jurisdiction based on the domicile of the defendant. Moreover, the underpinning of the principles recognised in the European regime of jurisdiction as a whole is indeed to 'protect' the defendant from having to defend a claim in a place remote from where he or she is based, if that place is not somehow connected with the parties or the dispute. Nevertheless, relatively new in the history of the conflict of laws are the protective rules of jurisdiction addressing the imbalance that may affect certain category of parties that are deemed to be in need of protection ('weaker parties'), both in the sphere of jurisdiction, as well as in the context of choice of law. Changes in the vision of the role that private international law should deploy in Europe—and in the world at large—have had an impact on the provisions of the European regime of jurisdiction, as they have also had in the sphere of choice of law.

Weaker parties in need of jurisdictional protection are consumers seeking to sue commercial firms with which they have had unhappy dealings; employees in dispute with their employers (though some employees may be rich and powerful: labels can mislead); or policy-holders with a claim against an insurance company. In many of these cases, there may be "protective" jurisdiction.[24] Contrary to the usual rule, claimants in these categories may be allowed in certain circumstances to sue in his or her home jurisdiction (*forum actoris*) even if the defendant is based elsewhere.

Exclusive jurisdiction

The term has a special meaning in the context of the conflict of laws, reflecting that in an instrument on jurisdiction, such as an international convention or a European regulation, it is possible for contracting States or Member States to agree that where a case concerns a particular subject matter the courts of one country, and one country only, it is only appropriate for the courts of that jurisdiction to adjudicate the case. This is usually related to the nature of the dispute on the merits. Typically, for example, in disputes about title to land, the location of the subject matter is of more importance than any other factor, therefore it justifies the limitation of jurisdiction to the courts of the country in which the property is to be found.[25] Party autonomy is also recognised as a source of exclusive jurisdiction where the parties have entered into a choice-of-court agreement, designating a court as having exclusive jurisdiction over the dispute.

5–009

---

[24] See para.6–038 and following.
[25] Advocate General Jacobs, writing in Case C-37/00 *Weber v Universal Ogden Services* [2002] Q.B. 1189 of the application of the basic principles of jurisdiction in the European legislation, could not resist tracing their ancestry to a national source: "The principles ... are not new. Already in the sixteenth century, Sir James Balfour of Pittendreich wrote in his *Practicks*: 'Na man may be Judge in ony cause, bot gif defendar be within his jurisdiction, be resson of his dwelling place within the same, or in respect of contract of obligation made thair; or be resson of tresspas committit within the boundis thairof, or in respect of the thing that is askit and clamit, quhilk is and lyis within his jurisdictioun; because the persewar sould follow the defendar's jurisdictioun, and persew him befoir his awin competent Judge' (*Of jugeis*, Ch.15, p.284 in the printed editions)".

The role of party autonomy in the field of jurisdiction is ever increasing and the changes introduced in the Brussels I *bis* Regulation[26] and the entering into force of the Hague Convention on Choice of Court Agreements[27] are clear signs of that phenomenon.

Excessive or exorbitant jurisdiction

5–010   In general terms it can be said that when the balance between the interests of the claimant(s) and the defendant(s) is not even, to the extent that one or the other faces something close to a practical denial of justice, the situation is unacceptable. Certain excessive or exorbitant jurisdictional rules can create such a situation. Even though it is difficult to give a clear definition of what constitutes an excessive or exorbitant jurisdictional basis, exorbitance in this field has been equated to a lack of reasonableness.[28] It is argued, therefore, that a judgment rendered in such conditions in one State should not be recognised or enforced elsewhere. This reflects the understanding that principles of international jurisdiction should aim to ensure "juridical continuity" in international legal relations.

Traditionally, there have been clear cases of exorbitant jurisdictional bases in many legal systems. The best known examples include the nationality of the claimant,[29] the presence of a non-resident defendant's assets within the jurisdiction,[30] the domicile of the claimant,[31] and arrestment of movables belonging to non-residents as in the Scottish rules of jurisdiction. All of these jurisdictional grounds as bases of general jurisdiction met with disapproval as considered excessive or exorbitant.[32]

Different States have their own understanding of when their courts can properly take jurisdiction. It is, however, important for jurisdictional bases to meet with international approval. The reason lies in the inherent relationship between direct and indirect jurisdiction. The more the bases for the exercise of direct jurisdiction are recognised and accepted internationally, the easier it becomes for courts to exercise indirect jurisdiction, that is, to accept the direct jurisdiction of the court of origin and therefore recognise and/or enforce the judgment issued by that court. The continuing international effort to agree defined bases for the exercise of direct jurisdiction is not an end in itself; its aim is rather to achieve a freer circulation of judgments, in a certain region such as the EU and potentially globally.

---

[26] See further para.6–054 and following.

[27] See below, para.5–017 and following.

[28] Fernández Arroyo, 'Exorbitant and Exclusive Grounds of Jurisdiction in European Private International Law' (2004) 170; (2008) 323 *Recueil des cours* Ch 3.

[29] e.g., art.14 of the French Civil Code.

[30] e.g., art.23 of the German Code of Civil Procedure and art.99 of Austrian Court Jurisdiction Act.

[31] e.g., art.126(3) of the Dutch Code of Civil Procedure.

[32] In the EU, these 'exorbitant' jurisdiction rules are to be listed in the Official Journal following notification to the European Commission (reg.1215/2012; art.76). Some excessive jurisdictional bases were listed in Annex I to Brussels I Regulation (reg.44/2001), but that list was not exhaustive.

DIFFERENT MODELS OF JURISDICTIONAL REGIMES

In the field of jurisdiction, there is what has been called a "clash of mentalities" between the common law tradition and the civilian approach enshrined in the European Regulations.[33]

5–011

Traditional English thinking about jurisdiction is dramatically different from the European paradigm. Long-established rules include a wide range of jurisdictional bases. These rules are shaped by judicial discretion[34]; but the emphasis on judicial discretion, and a liking for tailor-made solutions crafted to meet individual circumstances are alien to the European legal mind-set. English courts exercise their discretion both positively and negatively with the respective doctrines of forum conveniens and forum non conveniens. These doctrines, together with the powers of case management (seeking to prevent waste and to promote the expediency of the litigation process), are at the heart of English courts' inherent discretion in the jurisdictional sphere. These doctrines and powers are used as a "flexible weapon" showing "the inclination of the English courts to adopt flexible structures that are at odds with the more certain but also more rigid rules of the [then] Brussels I Regulation".[35]

In contrast, the civilian, and so the European, approach seeks to resolve jurisdictional problems through an integrated framework of rules. The role of judicial discretion is rather limited.[36] The system is based on narrowly-defined bases of jurisdiction, which a claimant is entitled to invoke as of right. Central to the European regime is the aim to avoid parallel proceedings that could result in inconsistent decisions ('irreconcilable judgments').[37] This is a result of the ultimate purpose of the European regime, that of the free circulation of judgments in the European area of justice.

Another essential component of the European model is the mutual trust principle, developed first in relation to substantive European law on the functioning of the common market, but which permeates the functioning of the system as a whole. As was early recognised in the Jenard Report on the Brussels Convention, the regime is based on "complete confidence in the Court of the State in which the judgment was given and the assumption that that court correctly applied the rules of jurisdiction".[38] The case law of the CJEU leaves

---

[33] See, e.g., Harris, 'Understanding the English Response to the Europeanisation of Private International Law' (2008) 4 J.Priv.Iint.L. 347, at 352.

[34] *Spiliada Maritime Corp v Cansulex Ltd* [1987] 1 Lloyd's Rep 1 (HL).

[35] Harris, (2008) 347, at 393.

[36] Note, however, arts 33 and 34 of the Brussels I *bis* Regulation, introducing what it may be considered as an opening to the doctrine of forum non conveniens in certain (limited) circumstances where proceedings in a non-EU country have already commenced. See further paras 6–068 and 7–033.

[37] Fentiman argues that the emphasis put on this point by the European legislator is misguided. His argument is based on the fact that at least in international commercial litigation the litigants are not looking for judgments, they are in search of settlements. See R Fentiman, *International Commercial Litigation* (2015).

[38] Jenard Report, (Report on the Convention of 27 September 1968 on jurisdiction and the enforcement of judgments in civil and commercial matters, OJ C 59, 5.3.1979), 46.

room for little doubt in this regard.[39] Following that it has been said that European jurisdictional thinking is "international"; what matters is the relation between nations.[40] This normative role of mutual trust has featured particularly in the interpretation and application by the CJEU of the rules on *lis pendens*.[41]

"Legal certainty" is also at the heart of the European regime. The interest of the parties is sought to be protected by the predictability achieved by the system.[42]

Finally, the ultimate goal of promoting the good functioning of the internal market constitutes the justification for EU action in jurisdictional issues.[43]

THE APPLICABLE SETS OF JURISDICTIONAL RULES

5–012   Four different sets of rules govern the jurisdiction of the English courts. The first is the Brussels regime, comprising the Brussels I Regulation (Regulation 44/2001)[44] regulating proceedings instituted in the courts of Member States of the EU, including Denmark[45], before 10 January 2015, and the Brussels I *bis* Regulation (also known as the Brussels I Recast) (Regulation 1215/2012)[46] regulating proceedings instituted in the courts of Member States of the EU on or after 10 January 2015.[47] The Brussels I *bis* Regulation contains the latest version of rules first established in the Brussels Convention of 1968.[48] The 1968 text reflected, as one would expect, the civil law traditions of the original signatory Member States, and it was adjusted in 1978 to facilitate the accession of the UK, Ireland, and Denmark, states whose legal traditions are not in the classical civil law form.

The second is the Lugano Convention. The third is the Intra-UK regime. The fourth set is made up of the English traditional rules of jurisdiction. A brief

---

[39] See e.g. Case C-159/02 *Gregory Paul Turner v Felix Fareed Ismail Grovit* [2004] ECR I-03565 ('*Turner*'); Case C-116/02 *Erich Gasser GmbH v MISAT Srl* [2003] ECR I-14693 ('*Gasser*'), Case C-185/07, *Allianz SpA (formerly Riunione Adriatica di Sicurtà SpA) and Generali Assicurazioni Generali SpA v West Tankers Inc* [2009] ECR I-663 ('*West Tankers*').

[40] Michaels, 'Two Paradigms of Jurisdiction' (2006) 27 Mich.Jo.Int.L. 1003.

[41] See para.6–060.

[42] The main aim of the Regulations is to facilitate the sound administration of justice by making rules on jurisdiction highly predictable. See Brussels I *bis*, Recitals (15) and (16). Legal certainty and predictability in the European regime are connected with the ability of the defendant to foresee the possibility of being sued before a particular court.

[43] Article 81 of the Treaty on the Functioning of the EU (OJ C 115, 9.5.2008).

[44] Provisions making the necessary adjustments to the law of the UK were made in the Civil Jurisdiction Order 2001, SI 2001/3929.

[45] For Denmark, see the Agreement of 19 October 2005 between the European Community and the Kingdom of Denmark on jurisdiction and the recognition and enforcement of judgments in civil and commercial matters, OJ L 299/62, 16.11.2005, which entered into force 1 July 2007.

[46] European Parliament and Council Regulation 1215/2012 on jurisdiction and the recognition and enforcement of judgments in civil and commercial matters, OJ L 351/1, 20.12.2012; also known as the Brussels I Recast.

[47] Regulation 1215/2012, art.66(2). For Denmark see the Agreement between the European Community and the Kingdom of Denmark on jurisdiction and the recognition and enforcement of judgments in civil and commercial matters, OJ L 79/4, 21.3.2013.

[48] Formally the Convention on Jurisdiction and the Enforcement of Judgments in Civil and Commercial Matters of 27 September 1968; it came into force on 1 February 1973.

account of their respective scopes of application is given in this chapter. The following two chapters give a detailed analysis of the European regime and of the English traditional rules of jurisdiction.

The Lugano Convention

On 16 September 1988, an international convention, closely based upon but not identical to the then current text of the Brussels Convention, was signed at Lugano. The signatories were Member States of the EU and of the European Free Trade Association ("EFTA"), and the object of what was sometimes called "the Parallel Convention" was to apply the principles of the earlier Convention throughout the wider area covered by the two groups of States. As most of the EFTA signatories have since become Member States of the EU, the Lugano Convention now applies only as between the Member States and Iceland, Norway and Switzerland. It was given effect in the UK by the Civil Jurisdiction and Judgments Act 1991. A revised version of the Convention was agreed on 30 October 2007. The Lugano Convention 2007 entered into force for the EU (including Denmark) and Norway on 1 January 2010; for Switzerland on 1 January 2011 and for Iceland on 1 May 2011.[49] The 2007 Lugano Convention's text is for the most part identical to that of the Brussels I Regulation.[50]

5–013

Intra-United Kingdom jurisdictional rules

There is one more variant of the European rules, based on Ch. II of the Brussels regime, allocating jurisdiction as between different parts of the UK.[51] It is considered in Ch.6,[52] but as a general rule the position before the English courts of a person domiciled in another part of the UK is similar to that of one domiciled in another Contracting State.

5–014

English traditional rules of jurisdiction

So far, all the sets of rules are derived from European initiatives. When the UK joined the EU, it had to decide whether to apply the principles underlying the European instruments universally, in all cases coming before the English courts. A contrary position prevailed: there should be no change in the existing practice of the English courts in what could broadly be described as "non-European"

5–015

---

[49] The Civil Jurisdiction and Judgments Regulations 2009 (SI 2009/3131) amended the Civil Jurisdiction and Judgments Act 1982 to reflect the entry into force of the 2007 Lugano Convention.
[50] See the Explanatory Report by Pocar ("the Pocar Report"), [2009] OJ C319/1; for the relationship between the Brussels I Regulation and the 2007 Lugano Convention, see art.64 of the latter and the Pocar Report at para.18–22.
[51] Civil Jurisdiction and Judgments Act 1982 Sch.4 as substituted by the Civil Jurisdiction Order 2001 (SI 2001/3929), amended by the Civil Jurisdiction and Judgments Regulations 2009 (SI 2009/3131) and further amended in light of the Brussels I Recast by the Civil Jurisdiction and Judgments (Amendment) Regulations 2014 (SI 2014/2947) and the Civil Jurisdiction and Judgments (Amendment) (Scotland) Regulations 2015 (SSI 2015/1).
[52] See para.6–071.

cases.[53] So, the fourth set of rules governing the jurisdiction of the English courts contains the "traditional rules" developed by the judges and now to be found in the Civil Procedure Rules. The Rules of Court of many Commonwealth countries are based on the principles underlying these traditional rules. In civil and commercial matters, that is, within the scope of application of the European regime in this context, the technical basis on which the English courts apply the traditional rules is art.6 of the Brussels I *bis* Regulation, which allows national law to apply in cases not caught by the other provisions of the Regulation. The traditional rules are examined in Ch.7.

THE HAGUE JUDGMENTS PROJECT

5–016   It has for long been an ambitious project of the Hague Conference on Private International Law to produce a potentially world-wide convention on jurisdiction and the recognition and enforcement of judgments. An instrument of this kind could provide on a much larger scale the benefits of a systematic recognition and enforcement of foreign judgments now found in Europe. By harmonising globally the way jurisdiction is exercised it could enhance the juridical continuity of legal relations across frontiers. The mere idea of a global system of jurisdiction poses some fundamental questions. Is there, or will there be, a move towards universal ideals and common goals, or will the reciprocity and narrow bilateralism implicit in the notions of mutual trust and mutual recognition continue to prevail as the underpinning narrative of comparative private international law jurisprudence.

The preliminary discussions on the Judgments Project go back to a proposal made in 1992.[54] From then until 2001 great efforts were devoted to devising a double convention, combining direct rules of jurisdiction, addressing the issue of exorbitant bases of jurisdiction, and rules on indirect jurisdiction, i.e. on the recognition and enforcement of foreign judgments. However, consensus could not be achieved across the whole field, and the Conference turned to the issues where consensus could be reached. This led to the adoption of the Hague Convention on Choice of Court Agreements.[55]

In 2011 the Judgments Project gained renewed impetus, and the Hague Conference has since been working towards a new global instrument, limited essentially to the recognition and enforcement of judgments. In October 2015 a Working Group competed its work on a draft proposal.[56] The objectives of the proposed draft text are to "enhance access to justice through the recognition and enforcement of judgments given by courts which the parties could reasonably have expected to determine their rights and obligations in the circumstances of the particular case" and to "facilitate trade and investment, thus contributing to

---

[53] cf. the situation in Scotland: Maher and Rodger, *Civil Jurisdiction in the Scottish Courts* (Edinburgh: W. Green & Son Ltd, 2010).

[54] The history of, and information on recent progress can be found on the Hague Conference website, *https://www.hcch.net*.

[55] See below para.5–017

[56] See Report of the Fifth Meeting of the Working Group on the Judgments Project (26—31 October 2015), Prel Doc No 7A, HCCH, November 2015.

economic growth by enhancing legal certainty and reducing costs and uncertainties associated with cross-border dealings, and with the resolution of cross-border disputes". The proposed draft takes account of existing international instruments, including regional instruments, and in particular is intended to be complementary to the Hague Convention on Choice of Court Agreements.

HAGUE CONVENTION ON CHOICE OF COURT AGREEMENTS[57]

The Hague Convention on Choice of Court Agreements was concluded under the auspices of the Hague Conference on Private International Law on 30 June 2005, and is in force in all Member States of the EU from 1 October 2015. The Convention applies in international cases to exclusive choice of court agreements concluded in civil and commercial matters, with the exclusion of consumer and employment contracts. The scope is further defined by the express exclusion of a whole range of other matters. An exclusive choice of court agreement is defined as the one concluded by two or more parties to designate the courts (or one or more specific courts) of one contracting state as having jurisdiction in disputes relating to a particular legal relationship. Such an agreement is considered to be exclusive, unless otherwise specified by the parties to the agreement.

5–017

Direct jurisdiction to adjudicate

The court or courts of a Contracting State designated in an exclusive choice of court agreement has jurisdiction to decide a dispute to which the agreement applies, unless the agreement is null and void under the law of that State. Any other court of a Contracting State must stay or dismiss the proceedings, except in cases where (a) the agreement is null and void under the law of the State of the chosen court; (b) a party lacked the capacity to conclude the agreement under the national law of the court seised; (c) giving effect to the agreement would contravene the public policy of the State of the court seised; (d) the agreement cannot be performed; or (e) the chosen court declines to hear the case based on the provisions of the law of the forum.

5–018

Indirect jurisdiction—recognition and enforcement of judgments

Contracting states must recognise and enforce a judgment given by the court designated in the exclusive choice of court agreement.[58] However, the judgment to be recognised must be effective in the state of origin; a judgment to be enforced must be enforceable there.[59]

5–019

---

[57] See Civil Jurisdiction and Judgments (Hague Convention on Choice of Court Agreements 2005) Regulations 2015, SI 2015/1644. See, inter alia, P. Briza, 'Choice-of-court agreements: could the Hague Choice of Court Agreements Convention and the reform of the Brussels I Regulation be the way out of the Gasser-Owusu disillusion?' (2009) 5(3) J.Priv.Int. L. 537.
[58] Convention on the Choice of Court Agreements 2005 art.8.
[59] Convention on the Choice of Court Agreements 2005 art.8(3).

Recognition or enforcement of a judgment may be refused when: (a) the agreement is null and void in the State of the chosen court; (b) a party lacked the capacity to conclude the agreement under the law of the requested State; (c) the document instituting the proceedings was not presented in sufficient time to the defendant; (d) the manner in which the document instituting the proceedings was presented to the defendant is in conflict with the fundamental principles of the requested State on serving documents; (e) the judgment was obtained by fraud in a matter of procedure; (f) recognition or enforcement is manifestly incompatible with the public policy of the requested state; (g) the judgment is not consistent with an earlier one given by the requested State in a dispute between the same parties; (h) the judgment is not consistent with an earlier one given by another State (and entitled to recognition in the requested State) in a dispute between the same parties and on the same cause of action. The law governing the procedure for recognition, declaration for enforceability or registration for enforcement and the enforcement of the judgment is that of the requested State.[60]

---

[60] Convention on the Choice of Court Agreements 2005 art.9.

CHAPTER 6

JURISDICTION: THE EUROPEAN REGIME

The European regime of jurisdiction consists of the Brussels I Regulation   **6–001**
(Regulation 44/2001)[1] regulating proceedings instituted in the courts of Member
States of the EU, including Denmark,[2] before 10 January 2015, and the Brussels
I *bis* Regulation (also known as the Brussels I Recast) (Regulation 1215/2012)[3]
regulating proceedings instituted in the courts of Member States of the EU on or
after 10 January 2015.[4] The Lugano Convention of 2007, replacing an earlier
Convention of 1988, applies to proceedings instituted in EFTA states (Iceland,
Norway and Switzerland)[5]. The provisions of the Lugano Convention are for the
most part identical to those of the original Brussels I Regulation.

The Brussels I *bis* Regulation contains the latest version of rules first
established in the Brussels Convention of 1968.[6] The 1968 text reflected the civil
law traditions of the original signatory Member States, and it was adjusted in
1978 to facilitate the accession of the UK, Ireland, and Denmark, states whose
legal traditions are not in the classical civil law form. Nevertheless it is still
possible to assert that the European regime is for the most part modeled on a
civilian conception of jurisdiction.

The civilian approach seeks to resolve jurisdictional problems through an
integrated framework of rules. The role of judicial discretion is rather limited.[7]
The system is based on narrowly defined bases of jurisdiction, which a claimant
is entitled to invoke as of right. Central to the European regime is the aim to

---

[1] Council Regulation (EC) 44/2001 of 22 December 2000 on Jurisdiction and the Recognition and
Enforcement of Judgments in Civil and Commercial Matters, [2001] OJ L 12/1, 16.1.2001 ("Brussels
I Reg"). Provisions making the necessary adjustments to the law of the UK were made in the Civil
Jurisdiction Order 2001, SI 2001/3929.

[2] For Denmark, see the Agreement of 19 October 2005 between the European Community and the
Kingdom of Denmark on jurisdiction and the recognition and enforcement of judgments in civil and
commercial matters, OJ L 299/62, 16.11.2005, which entered into force 1 July 2007.

[3] European Parliament and Council Regulation 1215/2012 on jurisdiction and the recognition and
enforcement of judgments in civil and commercial matters, [2012] OJ L 351/1, 20.12.2012; also
known as the Brussels I Recast. For Denmark see the Agreement between the European Community
and the Kingdom of Denmark on jurisdiction and the recognition and enforcement of judgments in
civil and commercial matters, OJ L 79/4, 21.3.2013. See generally Dickinson and Lein, *The Brussels
I Regulation Recast* (2015).

[4] Regulation 1215/2012 art.66(2).

[5] Convention on jurisdiction and the enforcement of judgments in civil and commercial matters of 30
October 2007. For the text see [2007] OJ L 339/1, 21.12.2007. See also reg.1215/2012, art.73(1).

[6] Convention on Jurisdiction and the Enforcement of Judgments in Civil and Commercial Matters of
27 September 1968; it came into force on 1 February 1973.

[7] Note, however, arts 33 and 34 of the Brussels I *bis* Regulation, introducing what it may be
considered as an opening to the doctrine of forum non conveniens in certain (limited) circumstances
where proceedings in a non-EU country have already commenced.

avoid parallel proceedings that could result in inconsistent decisions ('irreconcilable judgments').[8] This contributes to the ultimate purpose of the European regime, that of the free circulation of judgments in the European area of justice.

Another essential component of the European model is the mutual trust principle discussed in the previous chapter,[9] which permeates the functioning of the system as a whole. The principle is based on the assumption that the courts of all the Member States are equally competent to adjudicate jurisdiction according to the regime. The landmark case of *Turner v Grovit*[10] leaves room for little doubt in this regard. Following that it has been held that European jurisdictional thinking is 'international'; what matters is the relation between nations.[11]

Legal certainty is also at the heart of the regime. The interest of the parties is sought to be protected by the predictability achieved by the system.[12] Furthermore, the ultimate goal of promoting the good functioning of the internal market constitutes the justification for the EU action in jurisdictional issues.[13]

This chapter analyses the provisions of the Brussels I *bis* Regulation. It is concerned with jurisdiction in actions in personam. An action in personam is an action brought against a person to compel him or her to do a particular thing, e.g. the payment of a debt or of damages for breach of contract or for tort, or the specific performance of a contract; or to compel a person not to do something, e.g. when an injunction is sought. It does not include Admiralty actions in rem, probate actions, administration actions, petitions in matrimonial causes, or cases concerning guardianship or custody of children, or proceedings in bankruptcy or for the winding up of companies.

JURISDICTION IN CIVIL AND COMMERCIAL MATTERS

6–002   The law of civil and commercial jurisdiction is a matter where competence rests exclusively with the EU. However, art.71 of the Brussels I *bis* Regulation provides that the Regulation shall not affect any convention to which the Member States are parties and which, in relation to particular matters, govern jurisdiction or the recognition or enforcement of judgments.[14]

---

[8] Fentiman argues that the emphasis put on this point by the European legislator is misguided. His argument is based on the fact that at least in international commercial litigation the litigants are not looking for judgments, they are in search of settlements. See R Fentiman, *International Commercial Litigation*, 2nd edn (Oxford: Oxford University Press, 2015).

[9] See para.5–011.

[10] Case C-159/12 *Turner v Grovit* [2005] 1 A.C. 101 (CJEU).

[11] Michaels, 'Two Paradigms of Jurisdiction' (2006) 27 Mich.Jo.Int.L. 1003.

[12] The main aim of the Regulations is to facilitate the sound administration of justice by making rules on jurisdiction highly predictable See Brussels I *bis*, Recitals (15) and (16). Legal certainty and predictability in the European regime are connected with the ability of the defendant to foresee the possibility of being sued before a particular court.

[13] Article 81 of the Treaty on the Functioning of the EU (OJ C 115, 9.5.2008).

[14] *Owners of Cargo Lately Laden on Board the Deichland v Owners and/or Demise Charterers of the Deichland (The Deichland)* [1990] 1 Q.B. 361 (CA) 370; see also *The Tatry* [1995] 1 Lloyd's Rep 302 (CJEU); cf. *The Anna H* [1995] 1 Lloyd's Rep 11 (CA). However, on the possible 'interference' of the European regime, see Case C-533/08 *TNT Express Nederland BV v AXA Versicherung AG*, judgment of the Court (Grand Chamber) of 4 May 2010. For a detailed analysis of the jurisdictional aspects

In relation to the interpretation of the provisions of the European regime, under the Treaty on the Functioning of the European Union ("TFEU"), where a court of final appeal in any Member State finds that a decision on the interpretation of any of these Regulations is necessary for it to give judgment, it must refer the matter to the CJEU.[15] Other courts, trial or appellate, may make such a reference[16] and must apply the principles laid down by the CJEU.[17] The courts must also consider the explanatory reports published in the *Official Journal*.[18]

In interpreting the provisions the CJEU must take into account general principles governing the effects of EU law and its relationship with national laws, having in mind the overall aim behind the adoption of these Regulations, that is, promoting the development of the internal market.[19]

The Brussels I *bis* Regulation

The Brussels I *bis* Regulation (also known as the Brussels I Recast) is the result of a process of thorough revision of the functioning of the European regime of jurisdiction throughout the lifetime of the Brussels I Regulation and the Brussels Convention 1968. It is not revolutionary but evolutionary and its main improvements include the enhancement of choice of court agreements and the introduction of some leeway in the exercise of discretionary powers when there is parallel litigation already instituted in the courts of a non-EU Member State.

6–003

Territorial scope of application

Article 6 of Brussels I *bis* Regulation establishes that the regime applies in principle to defendants domiciled in a Member State of the EU. This has two important qualifications. According to art.25 of the Regulation the exercise of jurisdiction deriving from a jurisdiction agreement choosing the courts of a Member State extends to those where one or both of the parties to the agreement are domiciled outside the EU.[20] Furthermore, it also extends beyond the domicile connection with the EU in cases of exclusive jurisdiction as provided for in art.24

6–004

---

related to the arrest of ships see Ruiz Abou-Nigm, *The Arrest of Ships in Private International Law* (Oxford: Oxford University Press, 2011). There are many International Conventions to which the UK is party that contain provisions on jurisdiction.

[15] Treaty on the Functioning of the European Union (TFEU) art.267. The number of referrals to the CJEU has grown considerably in the past few years.

[16] This is a possibility introduced by the Treaty of Lisbon, in force since 1 December 2009.

[17] The Lugano Convention is not subject to interpretation by the CJEU, but Protocol 2 to the Convention requires a court interpreting the Convention to "take account of" any principles laid down in a relevant decision in another Contracting State.

[18] Civil Jurisdiction and Judgments Act 1982 ss.3(3) (as amended by SI 1989/1346 and SI 1990/2591). The reports are the Jenard report on the 1968 text (O.J. 1979, C59); the Schlosser report on the 1978 Accession Convention (ibid.); and the reports on the 1982 and 1989 Accession Conventions (O.J. 1986 C298 and 1990 C189).

[19] For the identification of general (first-order) and jurisdiction-specific (second-order) principles, see R. Fentiman, *International Commercial Litigation* (2015) paras 8-09 to 8-25.

[20] Regulation 1215/2012 art.25.

of the Regulation.[21] Hence, the Regulation applies if (1) the defendant is domiciled in a Member State of the EU; or when (2) there is a valid choice of court agreement conferring jurisdiction to the courts of a Member State; or (3) if the courts of a Member State have exclusive jurisdiction pursuant to the Regulation, regardless of domicile.

Material scope of application

6–005   Article 1 provides that the Brussels I *bis* Regulation is to apply in civil and commercial matters whatever the nature of the court or tribunal but that it is not to extend, in particular, to revenue, customs or administrative matters.[22] It does not apply to (a) the status or legal capacity of natural persons, rights in property arising out of a matrimonial relationship or out of a relationship deemed by the law applicable to such relationship to have comparable effects to marriage; (b) bankruptcy, the winding-up of insolvent companies and analogous proceedings[23]; (c) social security; (d) arbitration[24]; (e) maintenance obligations arising from a family relationship, parentage, marriage or affinity; or (f) wills and succession.

Arbitration remains one of the express exclusions of the scope of application of the Brussels I *bis* Regulation.[25] After extensive discussion on the relationship between arbitration and the Brussels I Regulation, the Brussels I *bis* Regulation did not change for the most part the scope of application of the Regulation in relation to arbitration. The scope of the arbitration exclusion was uncertain under the original Brussels I Regulation with results that attracted severe criticisms. In *West Tankers Inc v Allianz SpA*[26] the scope of the exclusion was considered.

> The claimant applied in the English courts for an anti-suit injunction to restrain the defendant from pursuing legal proceedings in the Italian courts, proceedings allegedly brought in breach of an arbitration agreement between the parties. As the purpose of the anti-suit injunction was to enforce the arbitration agreement, the claimant argued that the English proceedings fell outside the scope of the Regulation. However, the CJEU ruled that despite the arbitration agreement, the Italian proceedings, involving a claim based on non-contractual obligations, concerned civil and commercial matters within the scope of the Brussels I Regulation.[27]

---

[21] Regulation 1215/2012 art.25; reg.44/2001 art.22.

[22] Regulation 1215/2012 art.1(1); reg.44/2001 art.1(1).

[23] See Case 133/78 *Gourdain v Nadler* [1979] E.C.R. 733; *Polymer Vision R&D Ltd v Van Dooren* [2011] EWHC 2951 (Comm).

[24] Case C-190/89 *Marc Rich & Co AG v Societa Italiana Impianti pA, The Atlantic Emperor* [1991] E.C.R. I-3855; Case C-185/07 *Allianz SpA (formerly Riunione Adriatica di Sicurtà SpA) and Generali Assicurazioni Generali SpA v West Tankers Inc* [2009] E.C.R. I-663; [2009] 1 A.C. 1138; Case C-536/13 *Gazprom OAO* [2015] 1 W.L.R. 4937. There is a vast amount of specialised commentary on the relationship between arbitration and the Brussels I Reg, inter alia, Van Houtte [2005] Arb. Int. 509; Pullen, (2009) 12 I.A.L.R. 56; Hess, [2010] P.J.I.A. 17; Schlosser, (2009) 12 I.A.L.R. 45; Pinsolle, (2009) 12 I. A. L.R. 62; Fentiman, (2007) 66 C. L. J. 493; Magnus and Mankowski, [2010] 1 Zeitschrift für Vergleichende Rechtswissenschaft 21; Radicati di Brozolo, [2010] IPRax 121 and (2011) 7 J.Priv.Int.L. 423.

[25] Regulation 1215/2012 art.1(2)(d); reg.44/2001 art.1(2)(d). There is a similar exclusion in the 2007 Lugano Convention and in Sch.4 to the 1982 Act (intra-UK cases).

[26] Case C-185/07, [2009] E.C.R. I-663; [2009] 1 A.C. 1138.

[27] See also *Youell v La Réunion Aérienne* [2009] 1 Lloyd's Rep. 586.

Hence, the claim was within the scope of the Regulation (and the requested anti-suit injunction was held to be incompatible with the Regulation).[28]

The position of the CJEU is well established and it was confirmed in the *Gazprom*[29] case. There the CJEU held that the exclusion "must be interpreted as not precluding a court of a Member State from recognising and enforcing, or from refusing to recognise and enforce, an arbitral award prohibiting a party from bringing certain claims before a court of that Member State, since that regulation does not govern the recognition and enforcement, in a Member State, of an arbitral award issued by an arbitral tribunal in another Member State".

In the Brussels I *bis* Regulation the exclusion of arbitration extends to civil proceedings ancillary to arbitration.[30] This clarification, introduced in Recital 12 of the Brussels I *bis* Regulation, aims to strengthen the arbitration exclusion.[31]

Civil and commercial matters: European autonomous interpretation

The text of the Brussels I *bis* Regulation does not define the key term, "civil and commercial matters". In common law countries, this term is not in general use. To a common lawyer, it appears to cover everything that is not a criminal matter, and its use in international conventions such as those negotiated at the Hague Conference on Private International Law has given rise to difficulties as a result.[32] In civil law countries, the more usual contrast is with public law, though the precise boundary is an unclear and shifting one. For this reason, the CJEU held that the concept was among what has become quite a long list of terms which must be given a European "autonomous" meaning, not tied to the understanding of any national legal system but to the European system. The rationale behind a "European autonomous interpretation" is the aim to attain uniformity in the allocation of jurisdiction throughout the European area of justice. So in the *Eurocontrol* case[33]:

6–006

> Eurocontrol, an international agency supplying air traffic control services to civil aviation in Western Europe, claimed route charges allegedly owed by Lufthansa. Eurocontrol was clearly a public body, but that did not necessarily take the claim outside the 'civil and commercial' category. The Court held that the question had to be asked whether the public body was acting in the exercise of its powers. If it were *not*, the matter would be a 'civil and commercial' one.

The reference to the public body acting in the exercise of its powers is not to the English law notion of acting intra or ultra vires. The contrast is between a claim arising out of the primary purposes of a public authority, in the *Eurocontrol* case the provision of air traffic control services, and a claim arising out of

---

[28] Not surprisingly, this decision has been severely criticised in England, see e.g. Briggs, [2009] L.M.C.L.Q. 161; Peel, (2009) 125 L.Q.R. 356; Fentiman, [2009] C.L.J. 278.

[29] Case C-536/13 *Gazprom OAO* [2015] 1 W.L.R. 4937. See Hartley (2015) 64 I.C.L.Q. 965; Kajkowska (2015) 74 C.L.J. 412; Briggs [2015] L.M.C.L.Q. 284; Ojiegbe (2015) 11 J. Priv. Int. L. 267.

[30] Regulation 1215/2012, recital 12.

[31] See *Toyota Tsusho Sugar Trading Ltd v Prolat Srl* [2014] EWHC 3649 (Comm); [2015] 1 Lloyd's Rep. 344.

[32] See *Re the State of Norway's Application (Nos 1 and 2)* [1990] 1 A.C. 723; below, para.9–013.

[33] Case 29/76 *LTU GmbH v Eurocontrol* [1976] E.C.R. 1541.

activities not specific to those purposes, for example the purchase of food for consumption in the organisation's staff canteen. It is not surprising that issues concerning the acts of German armed forces in Greece during the Second World War should be regarded as outside the scope of "civil and commercial matters" as military operations are a direct exercise of state sovereignty.[34] Other cases are more difficult.[35] So it has been held that claims relating to clearance of a wreck in a public waterway by the public authority charged with that responsibility[36] and a claim against a central bank charged with supervisory duties over the registration of companies[37] were not civil or commercial matters; but a claim concerning the actions of a teacher in a state school taking pupils on climbing trip was, as it did not involve an exercise of public authority powers.[38] In *Realchemie Nederland BV v Bayer Cropscience AG*[39] the CJEU held that a party's right to exclusively exploit the invention protected by its patent was clearly within the autonomous concept.

In *Land Berlin v Sapir*[40] the CJEU considered a case in which a public body was required, by an authority established by legislation designed to provide compensation for acts of persecution carried out by the Nazi regime, to compensate victims by making over part of the proceeds of the sale of land. By mistake, the body paid to those persons the total sale price and not the share to which they were entitled and sought to recover the over-payment. It was held that the claim was included in the concept of 'civil and commercial matters'. In *Revenue and Customs Commissioners v Sunico ApS*[41] the CJEU further developed the autonomous concept considering that it covered an action whereby a public authority of one Member State claimed, as against natural and legal persons resident in another Member State, damages for loss caused by a tortious conspiracy to commit value added tax fraud in the UK.

---

[34] Case C-292/05 *Lechouritou v Dimisio tis Omospondiakis Dimokratias tis Germanias* [2007] 2 All E.R. (Comm) 57.

[35] See Betlem and Bernasconi, (2006) 122 L.Q.R. 124. See also in Cases C-226/13, C-245/13, C-247/13 and C-578/13 (joined) *Fahnenbrock v Greece*, CJEU judgment of 11 June 2015, about reg.1(1) of reg.1393/2007 of the European Parliament and of the Council of 13 November 2007 on the service in the Member States of judicial and extrajudicial documents in civil or commercial matters (service of documents). The CJEU held, against the opinion of the Advocate General Bot, that "civil and commercial matters" in this context had to be interpreted as meaning that legal actions for compensation for disturbance of ownership and property rights, contractual performance and damages brought by private persons who are holders of government bonds against the issuing State, fall within the scope of that regulation in so far as it does not appear that they are manifestly outside the concept of "civil and commercial matters". Even though this decision is not about the Regulations on jurisdiction, the divergence of reasoning between the opinion of the General Advocate Bot and the decision of the CJEU shows the difficulty that the scope of 'civil and commercial' matters may present in certain circumstances.

[36] Case 814/79 *Netherlands State v Ruffer* [1980] E.C.R. 3807.

[37] *Grovit v Nederlandesche Bank* [2007] EWCA Civ 953; [2008] 1 W.L.R. 51.

[38] Case C-172/91 *Sonntag v Waidmann* [1993] E.C.R. I-1963. See also Case C-435/06 *C* [2008] 3 W.L.R. 419 (taking child into care a "civil matter" for purposes of Brussels II Revised (reg.2201/2003 concerning jurisdiction and the recognition and enforcement of judgments in matrimonial matters and matters of parental responsibility).

[39] Case C-406/09, 18 October 2011, [2012] I.L.Pr.1.

[40] *Land Berlin v Sapir* (C-645/11) [2013] C.E.C. 947; [2013] I.L.Pr.29.

[41] *Revenue and Customs Commissioners v Sunico ApS* (C-49/12) [2014] Q.B. 391; [2014] 2 W.L.R. 335.

Domicile: the primary connecting factor in the European regime

Domicile is the key connecting factor in the scheme of the European regime. The Brussels I *bis* Regulation provides a uniform definition to be used to determine the domicile of companies and other "legal persons",[42] and leaves the determination of the domicile of individuals to national law.

6–007

Domicile of individuals

(i)   In the Member State whose courts are seised of a matter

Article 62 of the Brussels I *bis*[43] Regulation provides that in order to determine whether a party is domiciled in the Member State whose courts are seised of a matter, the court is to apply its internal law. So, if the English court has to determine whether an individual party is or is not domiciled in England, it is English law that supplies the applicable definition of domicile. It was recognised that it would be unsatisfactory, indeed absurd, to use in this context the traditional understanding of domicile. Domicile in that sense can be very artificial, notably as a result of its emphasis on permanent home and on the domicile of origin, and it is often difficult to ascertain. It describes a long-term association between an individual and a country: there is no reason to insist on such an association before an individual can, for example, be sued for breach of contract. Instead a definition of domicile was needed that could be applied more readily and would be closer to the understandings of domicile in the states of mainland Europe as something not dissimilar from habitual residence. So, s.41 of the Civil Jurisdiction and Judgments Act 1982 supplied a new definition in the context of the Brussels Convention, and the same rules are applied to the Regulation in the Civil Jurisdiction and Judgments Order 2001.[44]

6–008

The rules provide that an individual is domiciled in the UK if and only if he or she is resident in the UK and the nature and circumstances of the residence indicate that the individual has a substantial connection with the UK.[45] There is no definition of "residence" or of "substantial connection" but the English courts speak of a "settled or usual place of abode".[46] This can involve a time-consuming assessment of all the circumstances. To minimise the need for this, the rules provide that in the case of an individual who is resident in the UK and has been so resident for the last three months or more, the requirement of substantial connection is presumed to be fulfilled unless the contrary is proved.[47] This, very convenient, rule resolves most domicile issues, but the "substantial connection"

---

[42]   Regulation 1215/2012 art.63; reg.44/2001 art.60.
[43]   Regulation 1215/2012 art.62; reg.44/2001 art.59. In the process leading to the negotiation of Brussels I *bis* it had been suggested that it should include an autonomous rule for determining the domicile of individuals as it does for companies (see European Commission, Brussels I Green Paper, COM (2009) 175 final, p.10); however, this proposal did not materialise in the Brussels I *bis* Regulation.
[44]   SI 2001/3929 Sch.1, para.9.
[45]   Civil Jurisdiction and Judgments Order 2001 Sch.1, para.9(2).
[46]   *Bank of Dubai Limited v Fouad Haji Abbas* [1997] I.L.Pr. 308 (CA).
[47]   Civil Jurisdiction and Judgments Order 2001 Sch.1, para.9(6).

test is relevant if it is sought either to defeat the presumption or to establish the acquisition of a domicile within the three month period. *Petrotrade Inc v Smith*[48] provides an illustration of that last type of case:

> Mr Smith, born in England and of British nationality, had lived for some eight years in Switzerland; his work was there and he had a Swiss wife. He came to England on what was intended to be a four-day visit. He was arrested and was bailed on condition that he remained in England. He remained on bail for two years, and once the criminal proceedings were dropped decided to stay on in England. The issue was his domicile 21 days after his initial arrival in England, and it was held that his enforced presence in England did not indicate a substantial connection.

It is almost always necessary to show that someone is domiciled not merely in the UK as a whole but in a particular part of it, for example in England. An individual is domiciled in a particular part of the UK if, and only if, he or she is resident in that part and the nature and circumstances of the residence indicate that the individual has a substantial connection with that part.[49] Furthermore, an individual is domiciled in a particular place in the UK if, and only if, he or she is (a) domiciled in the part of the UK in which that place is situated; and (b) is resident in that place.[50]

The presumption based on residence for three months applies in this context.[51]

In *Daniel v Foster*[52] the defendant spent regularly short periods of time attending his business in Scotland and the remainder of his time at his principal residence in Sussex. In this case the Scottish court held that the three months residence presumption operated even when the three months residence were not continuous.

There may well be cases in which the three-month presumption is unhelpful. Suppose D is appointed by his German company to come to the UK to set up a marketing and distribution network for the company's products. He has been in the UK for six months, dividing his time as to two-fifths in England, two-fifths in Scotland, and one-fifth in Northern Ireland. He has never spent a continuous period of three months in any of them, and may well be found not to have a substantial connection with any one part. To deal with this type of case, the rules provide that if an individual is domiciled in the UK but has no substantial connection with any particular part, he is to be treated as domiciled in the part of the UK in which he is resident.[53]

(ii) In a Member State other than the Member State of the court hearing the case

6–009 The Brussels I *bis* Regulation provides that if a party is not domiciled in the state whose courts are seised of the matter, then, in order to determine whether the

---

[48] [1998] 2 All E.R. 346.

[49] Civil Jurisdiction and Judgments Order 2001 Sch.1, para.9(4).

[50] Civil Jurisdiction and Judgments Order 2001 Sch.1, para.9(3).

[51] Civil Jurisdiction and Judgments Order 2001 Sch.1, para.9(6).

[52] *Daniel v Foster* 1989 SLT (Sh.Ct.) 90; see also *Relfo Ltd (In Liquidation) v Varsani* [2010] EWCA Civ 560; *Work Legal E-Ltd v Allen Court of Session* [2015] CSOH 12.

[53] Civil Jurisdiction and Judgments Order 2001 Sch.1, para.9(5).

party is domiciled in another Member State, the court is to apply the law of that state.[54] This contrasts with the approach under the traditional domicile rules, where English law is always applied. There is another contrast: under the European regime an individual may have more than one domicile. It may be, for example, that French law would regard an individual as domiciled in France, and Belgian law would accept him or her as a Belgian domiciliary. In such a case, an action may be begun in either country. For the purposes of the Regulation, the CJEU has held that defendants with unknown domicile are domiciled at their last known domicile.[55] The European regime does not address the determination of the domicile of a person in a state other than a Member State. The rules in the Civil Jurisdiction and Judgments Order 2001 provide that an individual is domiciled in such a state if and only if he is resident in that state and the nature and circumstances of his residence indicate that he has a substantial connection with that state.[56] In this case, there is no presumption based on three months' residence.

Domicile of corporations and associations

A different approach is taken in the case of a company or other legal person or association of natural or legal persons; this will include partnerships[57] and clubs with a defined membership. In the Brussels I *bis* Regulation art.63(1)[58] provides that, for the purposes of the Regulation, such an entity is domiciled at the place where it has its statutory seat, or central administration, or principal place of business. Although it is unlikely in practice, this can mean that the entity is domiciled in three different countries.[59]   **6–010**

The notion of "statutory seat" is unknown in common law countries, so the Regulation has a special rule that for the purposes of the UK, Cyprus and Ireland: "statutory seat" means the registered office or, where there is no such office anywhere, the place of incorporation or, where there is no such place anywhere, the place under the law of which the formation took place.[60]

There is one further complication. Article 24(2) of the Regulation, considered below,[61] gives exclusive jurisdiction over certain disputes about the constitution, dissolution or acts of a company or association to the courts for the "seat" of that entity. In order to determine the seat, a court is to apply its rules of private international law.[62] The relevant English rules are set out in the Civil Jurisdiction and Judgments Order 2001.[63] For the purposes of the European regime on jurisdiction, a company, legal person or association has its seat in the UK if and

---

[54] Regulation 1215/2012 art.62(2); reg.44/2001 art.59(2).
[55] Case C-327/10 *Hypotecni banka as v Lindner* [2011] E.C.R. I-11543; [2012] C.E.C. 975.
[56] Civil Jurisdiction and Judgments Order 2001 Sch.1, para.9(7).
[57] *Phillips v Symes* [2001] 1 W.L.R. 853.
[58] Regulation 1215/2012 art.63(1); reg.44/2001 art.60(1).
[59] For example, *The Deichland* [1990] 1 Q.B. 361 (Brussels Convention case: company incorporated in the Republic of Panama, but its central management and control exercised in Germany).
[60] Regulation 1215/2012 art.63(2); reg.44/20011 art.60(2). For cases under the Brussels and Lugano Conventions, see the Civil Jurisdiction and Judgments Act 1982 s.42.
[61] See para.6-050.
[62] Regulation 1215/2012 art.24(2); reg.44/2001, art.22(2).
[63] Civil Jurisdiction and Judgments Order 2001 Sch.1, para.10.

only if (a) it was incorporated or formed under the law of a part of the UK; or (b) its central management and control is exercised in the UK. A company, legal person or association has its seat in another state to which the Regulation applies if and only if (a) it was incorporated or formed under the law of that state; or (b) its central management and control is exercised in that state. But it will not be regarded as having a seat in such a state if it was incorporated or formed under the law of a part of the UK or if the courts of that other state would not regard it as having its seat there for the purposes of the relevant provision of the Brussels regime.

Domicile of trusts

6–011   Article 63(3) of the Brussels I *bis* Regulation[64] provides that in order to determine whether a trust is domiciled in the Member State whose courts are seised of the matter, the court must apply its rules of private international law. The 2001 Order provides that a trust is domiciled in a part of the UK if the system of law of that part is the system of law with which the trust has its closest and most real connection.[65] The Court of Appeal has indicated that where there is a choice of English law to govern a trust, it is very difficult to see what other circumstance would be sufficient to outweigh it in assessing which was the system of law which the trust had its closest and most real connection.[66] Of course it is artificial and novel to speak of the domicile of a trust at all. But it is a convenient form of shorthand.

GENERAL JURISDICTION

6–012   The principal basis for jurisdiction is that set out in art.4(1) of the Brussels I *bis* Regulation[67], that persons domiciled in a Member State must, whatever their nationality, be sued in the courts of that state. This accords with what has been identified in the previous chapter as a basic rule of "general jurisdiction", requiring a strong connection between the defendant and the chosen court. The European regime requires that jurisdiction to be always available on this ground save in a few well-defined situations in which the subject-matter of the dispute[68] or the autonomy of the parties[69] warrants a different connecting factor. The domicile of the defendant in England is thus the primary basis for the jurisdiction of the English courts under the European regime of jurisdiction. The relevant time for establishing the defendant's domicile in the Member State is at the time of the issue of proceedings, which in England means the time of the issue of the claim form rather than its service on the defendant.[70]

---

[64] Regulation 1215/2012 art.63(3); reg.44/2001, art.60(3).
[65] Civil Jurisdiction and Judgments Order 2001 Sch.1, para.12(3).
[66] *Gomez v Encarnacion Gomez-Monche Vives* [2008] EWCA Civ 1065; [2009] Ch. 245.
[67] Regulation 1215/2012 art.4(1); reg.44/2001 art.2(1).
[68] See para.6–013 below.
[69] See para.6–059, below.
[70] *Canada Trust Co. v Stolzenberg (No.2)* [2002] 1 A.C. 1.

If the proposed defendant is domiciled in another Member State, he or she may be sued in England only in accordance with the rules set out in ss.2 to 7 of Ch.II of the Brussels I *bis* Regulation, i.e. arts 7 to 26 inclusive. These rules, shortly to be examined, include cases where the defendant submits to the jurisdiction, various cases of "special" jurisdiction, and cases in which there is a valid choice of court agreement in favour of the courts of a Member State. Reliance on the traditional English rules as to service of process on a defendant during the defendant's temporary presence in England is expressly excluded by art.5(2) of the Brussels I *bis* Regulation,[71] along with bases for jurisdiction under other legal systems judged equally 'exorbitant'.[72]

Where the defendant is *not* domiciled in another Member State, the jurisdictional rules applicable are those of the national law of the forum,[73] in England, the traditional rules,[74] subject always to the rules of the European regime[75] which confers exclusive jurisdiction on the courts of particular Member States regardless of the domicile of the parties.

SPECIAL JURISDICTION

Article 7 of the Brussels I *bis* Regulation[76] deals with a number of cases of "special" jurisdiction: the European regime identifies a limited number of special jurisdictional grounds providing the claimant with alternative fora to institute the proceedings, in addition to the courts of the defendant's domicile. The identification of these special grounds is based on a strong connection between the dispute and the designated forum that justifies the exercise of direct jurisdiction by the latter to hear and determine the case.

6–013

Special jurisdiction rules in 'matters relating to a contract'[77]

Article 7 of the Brussels I *bis* Regulation provides:

6–014

"A person domiciled in a Member State may be sued in another Member State:

---

[71] Regulation 1215/2012 art.5(2); reg.44/2001 art.3(2).
[72] Even though there is no definition of what constitutes an exorbitant jurisdictional basis, it can be said that when the balance between the interests of the claimant and the defendant is not even, and one or the other is put into a position which is close to a practical denial of justice, the situation is unacceptable from an international point of view. See Fernández Arroyo, *Compétence exclusive et compétence exorbitante dans les relations privées internationales*, (2006) 323 Recueil des cours (Martinus Nijhoff, Leiden, 2008). Cf. the position of the UK Supreme Court in *Abela v Baadarani* [2013] UKSC 44 in relation to service out of the jurisdiction ("It should no longer be necessary to resort to the kind of muscular presumptions against service out which are implicit in adjectives like 'exorbitant'. The decision is generally a pragmatic one in the interests of the efficient conduct of litigation in an appropriate forum." Lord Sumption, at [53]).
[73] Regulation 1215/2012 art.6; reg.44/2001 art.4.
[74] See Ch.7.
[75] Regulation 1215/2012 art.24; reg.44/2001 art.22.
[76] Regulation 1215/2016 art.7; reg.44/2001 art.5.
[77] For insurance, consumer and employment contracts, see paras 6–038 and following.

(1)(a) in matters relating to a contract, in the courts for the place of performance of the obligation in question[78];"

The first phrase to be considered is "matters relating to a contract".[79] This will include cases where there is a disagreement as to the very existence of the contract,[80] but not cases in which the subject matter is a duty to conduct pre-contractual negotiations in good faith.[81]

'Contract': European autonomous interpretation

6–015 The notion of "contract" is not identical in every legal system, with different understandings of the boundary between contract and tort or property law. For this reason, "contract" in the text of the Regulation is given a European autonomous meaning, independent of the categories in national legal systems; it covers any matters having their basis in an agreement.[82] So, in *Peters v Zuid Nederlandse Aannemers Vereniging*,[83] the dispute was between a Dutch trade association and one of its members. Under the association's rules, a percentage of any earnings within the association's area was to be paid to the association. The issue would clearly be contractual in English law, but Dutch law treated the relationship between members of an association as sui generis. The CJEU held that, as membership of an association creates between the members close links of the same kind as those which are created between the parties to a contract, their obligations should be regarded as contractual for the purpose of the application of the special rules on jurisdiction in the European regime.

The CJEU case law emphasises the central requirements of the existence of a direct relationship between the parties, and the undertaking of a voluntary obligation by one party towards the other.[84] That suggests that benefits conferred on others, as third party beneficiaries or as sub-purchasers, under some national legal systems will not be treated as arising under a contract. However, the Court of Appeal held in *WPP Holdings Italy Srl v Benatti*,[85] without any full examination of the European case law, that where two contracting parties confer a benefit on a stranger to the contract, intending that the stranger may enforce the

---

[78] Regulation 1215/2012 art.7(1)(a); reg.44/2001 art.5(1)(a).

[79] See e.g. Case 375/13 *Kolassa v Barclays Bank Plc* [2015] CEC 753; [2015] I.L.Pr. 14.

[80] Case 38/81 *Effer SpA v Kantner* [1982] E.C.R. 825; *Boss Group Ltd v Boss France SA* [1997] 1 WLR 351 (CA).

[81] Case 334/00 *Fonderie Officine Meccaniche Tacconi SpA v Heinrich Wagner Sinto Maschinenfabrik GmbH* [2002] E.C.R. I-7357. cf. the position where an insurance contract is challenged for non-disclosure: *Agnew v Länsförsäkringsbolagens AB* [2001] 1 A.C. 223.

[82] Case 9/87 *Arcado Sprl v Haviland SA* [1988] E.C.R. 1539 (agency dispute involving allegations of bad faith held contractual); Case 334/00 *Fonderie Officine Meccaniche Tacconi SpA v Heinrich Wagner Sinto Maschinenfabrik GmbH* [2002] E.C.R. I-7357.

[83] Case 34/82, [1983] E.C.R. 987.

[84] Case 26/91 *Ste Handte et Cie GmbH v Traitements Mecano-Chimiques des Surfaces* [1992] E.C.R. I-3967 (sub-purchaser unable to sue the original manufacturer-supplier of goods); Case 419/11 *Ceska Sporitelna AS v Gerald Feichter* [2013] I.L.Pr. 22. (promisory note, aval, guarantee provided for a credit contract). See also Case 375/13 *Kolassa v Barclays Bank Plc* [2015] C.E.C. 753; [2015] I.L.Pr. 14 and Case 147/12 *OFAB, Ostergotlands Fastigheter AB v Koot* [2015] Q.B. 20.

[85] [2007] EWCA Civ 263; [2007] 1 W.L.R. 2316.

benefit in his own right, the claim by the stranger under the Contracts (Rights of Third Parties) Act 1999 was a contractual matter for the purposes of the Brussels I Regulation.

A difficult issue was addressed by the House of Lords in *Kleinwort Benson Ltd v Glasgow City Council*[86]:

> Financial dealings called 'interest swap agreements' had been undertaken by a number of local authorities until the House of Lords in a separate decision held that they were all void as ultra vires the local authorities. The plaintiff bank claimed the return of the money it had paid to the Council under the invalid contract, a claim classified in English law as one for restitution, or for unjust enrichment. The issue was whether the claim for restitution fell within art.5(1).[87]

A bare majority (Lords Goff, Clyde and Hutton) held that the claim did not fall within art.5(1) of the Brussels I Regulation: it had already been decided there was no contractual obligation on which the claim could be founded, and that was not now in dispute between the parties. Because of that unusual feature of the case, it is not authority for a general proposition that restitution claims can never be within this special jurisdiction basis of the Brussels regime. Lords Mustill and Nicholls dissented, principally to avoid having to draw awkward distinctions depending on how claims were worded: the view taken by the majority means that a claim for damages for non-performance is within the concept of 'matters related to a contract' but an additional claim in the same case for the return of sums paid in advance will not be.

The obligation in question

It would seem obvious that "the obligation in question" means that which is relied upon as the basis for the claim. This was the interpretation placed upon the text by the CJEU in *De Bloos Sprl v Bouyer SA*,[88] where the claim concerned an alleged breach of the condition of exclusivity in an agreement appointing the claimant sole distributor of the defendant's products in Belgium. It was immaterial that other obligations under the contract fell to be performed in France.

6–016

It is of course possible for a claim to relate to several distinct obligations, with different places of performance. When in trouble, lawyers revert to Latin: *accessorium sequitur principale*, which means that the court has to identify the principal obligation and let those other obligations accessory to the principal obligation be swept up with it.[89]

Identifying the principal obligation may not be at all easy. An example is *Union Transport Group Plc v Continental Lines SA*[90]:

> The plaintiffs claimed that the defendant ship owners had agreed to nominate a vessel suitable for the carriage of telegraph poles from Florida to Bangladesh and then to execute the carriage.

---

[86] [1999] 1 A.C. 153.

[87] The issue arose under Sch.4 of the 1982 Act, the Convention as applied to intra-UK cases rather than the Convention text itself; the CJEU had for that reason refused to rule on the matter.

[88] Case 14/76 [1976] E.C.R. 1497.

[89] Case 266/85 *Shenavai v Kreischer* [1987] E.C.R. 239.

[90] [1992] 1 W.L.R. 15.

The defendants had failed to do so. When sued in England, the defendants argued that the English courts had no jurisdiction: they were domiciled in Belgium, and the place of performance must be the port of loading, in Florida.

The House of Lords held that under a "tonnage to be nominated" charter, the principal obligation is to nominate the vessel, and on the facts that had to be done in London. Jurisdiction therefore existed under art.5(1).[91]

The CJEU has had to recognise that there can be cases in which the claim concerns obligations of equal importance, where it is impossible to identify one as "principal" and the others as "accessory". In such a case, a court can take jurisdiction under art.7(1) only in respect of the obligation the place of performance of which is within its territory.[92] Although this can produce inconvenience, the claim being divided between two or more courts, the claimant always has the option of relying on art.4 and bringing action in the country of the defendant's domicile.

Place of performance

6–017 Under the 1968 Brussels Convention the identification of the place of performance had to be done according to the interpretation of that phrase in national law.[93] That opening to the diversity of national legal systems did not enhance the functioning of the system but made its application rather difficult for national courts. Take the apparently simple facts of *Barry v Bradshaw*[94] which was decided under the Brussels Convention:

> Mr and Mrs Barry retired from business in 1989 and went to live in the Republic of Ireland. Mr and Mrs Barry employed tax advisers, including Mr Young. They sued Mr Young for negligence and breach of contract in failing to secure capital gains tax retirement relief in respect of certain years. Mr Young argued that the English courts had no jurisdiction: he was domiciled in Ireland and the place of performance under art.5(1) was also in Ireland.

However, the Court of Appeal held that, as the tax claim had to be delivered to the Inland Revenue in England, the place of performance was there.

Another, and more difficult, case involving an exclusive distributorship agreement is *Boss Group Ltd v Boss France SA*[95]:

> An English company, manufacturers of fork-lift trucks, set up a French subsidiary to act as sole distributor of its products in France. Both companies were later sold, the English manufacturing company to a German corporation which had its own distribution network in

---

[91] For other examples, see *Source Ltd v Rheinland Holding AG* [1998] Q.B. 54 (English company prepared to grant credit on imported goods, subject to inspection in country of origin; principal obligation in that country); *AIG Group (UK) Ltd v The Ethniki* [2000] 2 All E.R. 566 (reinsurance of earthquake risks in Greece; notification of damage to be in England, and that held principal obligation).

[92] Case 420/97 *Leathertex Divisione Sintetici SpA v Bodetex BVBA* [1999] E.C.R. I-6747 (agency contact; commission payable in Italy, notice of termination to be given in Belgium).

[93] Case 12/76 *Industrie Tessili Italiana Como v Dunlop A.G.* [1976] E.C.R. 1473; Case 288/92 *Custom Made Commercial Ltd v Stawa Metallbau GmbH* [1994] E.C.R. I-2913; Case 440/97 *GIE Groupe Concorde v The Suhadiwarno Panjan* [1999] E.C.R. I-6307.

[94] [2000] I.L.Pr. 706.

[95] [1996] 4 All E.R. 970.

France, and the French company to a French businessman. He claimed that the distribution of the fork-lift trucks was now routed through the distribution network of the German parent company, in breach of the exclusive distributorship agreement.

The English company applied to the English court for a negative declaration, that there was no distributorship contract or, if there were, it had been terminated. At first sight, a contract for exclusive distributorship rights in France is to be performed there. The court, however, finding that the trucks were delivered to the distributors at the factory gates, held that the obligation was to be performed either in England (the place of delivery) or possibly everywhere (because it was a duty not to deliver to anyone else), and "everywhere" included England. The last idea now seems untenable: the CJEU has held that a negative obligation applying everywhere cannot be located in a Member State at all.[96]

Dissatisfaction with art.5(1) as it stood in the text of the Brussels Convention grew: in too many cases, it seemed to identify an inappropriate forum. Additional connecting factors were added at the time of the conversion of the Brussels Convention into the Brussels I Regulation to provide greater certainty in this field.

Contracts of sale

Article 7(1)(b) of the Brussels I *bis* Regulation provides: **6–018**

> "(b)   for the purpose of this provision and unless otherwise agreed, the place of performance of the obligation in question shall be:
> —   in the case of the sale of goods, the place in a Member State where, under the contract, the goods were delivered or should have been delivered,"[97]

This additional provision has been the object of further interpretation by the CJEU. In *Car Trim GmbH v KeySafety Systems Srl*[98] the European court held that art.5(1)(b) of the Brussels I Regulation had to be interpreted:

> "as meaning that contracts for the delivery of goods to be produced or manufactured are to be classified as a sale of goods, notwithstanding specific requirements by the customer with regard to the provision, fabrication and delivery of the components to be produced, including a guarantee of the quality of production."[99]

Furthermore, where a sale involved the carriage of goods, the place where the goods were, or should have been, delivered under the contract was to be determined on the basis of the provisions of that contract; or, if it was not possible to do so, then that place was the place of physical transfer of the goods to the

---

[96] Case 265/00 *Besix AG v Wasserreinigungsbau Alfred Kretzschmar GmbH & Co KG* [2003] 1 W.L.R. 1113. It followed that there was no jurisdiction under art.5(1) of the Brussels I Regulation (reg.44/2001).

[97] In cases to which this new provision does not apply, the matter is governed by the general words of art.5(1)(a): see art.5(1)(c).

[98] Case 381/08, *Car Trim GmbH v KeySafety Systems Srl* [2010] E.C.R. I-1255.

[99] See paras 16–26 of judgment.

buyer. *Car Trim* was followed in *Electrosteel Europe SA v Edil Centro SpA*[100] where the application of the provision for cases of distance selling was further clarified.

Electrosteel involved proceedings arising out of a contract for the sale of goods by an Italian company (C) to a French company (E). The contract was concluded in Italy, and the goods were delivered to E's headquarters in France. C claimed that E had failed to pay for the goods and began proceedings in the Italian court. The issue was whether the Italian court had jurisdiction as the "place of delivery". C claimed that the court had to take account of a clause in the contract which contained the words "delivered free ex our business premises". It asserted that those words corresponded to the "ex works" clause in the Incoterms. On that basis it argued that Italy was the place of delivery.

The CJEU held that in the case of distance selling, in order to verify whether the place of delivery was determined "under the contract", the national court had to take account of all the relevant terms and clauses of the contract that were capable of clearly identifying that place, including terms that were generally recognised and applied through the usages of international trade or commerce, such as the Incoterms. If it was impossible to determine the place of delivery on that basis, without referring to the substantive law applicable to the contract, the place of delivery was the place where the physical transfer of the goods took place, as a result of which the purchaser obtained, or should have obtained, actual power of disposal over those goods.[101]

More generally, by locating the various obligations arising under contracts to which it applies in a single country, the new provision minimises some of the difficulties discussed above: it may no longer be necessary to struggle with the identity of the "principal" and "accessory" obligations, as all will have a common location attributed to them. But some problems remain. They can be illustrated by the facts of a Brussels Convention case, *Viskase Ltd v Paul Kiefel GmbH*[102]:

> Eight machines were to be supplied for a particular purpose. In the case of seven of the eight machines, delivery had taken place in Germany, but in the case of one machine delivery was at the National Exhibition Centre in Birmingham, England. The Court of Appeal held that the place of the obligation to deliver goods fit for the purpose was the place of delivery. The English court had jurisdiction only in respect of that machine.

In *Color Drack GmbH v Lexx International Verbriebs GmbH*[103] the CJEU held that where there are several places of delivery all within the same Member State, the "principal place of delivery" is the relevant one, failing which the claimant could sue at any delivery place.[104] The rationale behind this approach, sometimes referred as the "*Color Drack* test" is to attribute jurisdiction to the courts with the "closest linking factor" with the contract in question; in the case of contracts for

---

[100] Case 87/10, *Electrosteel Europe sa v Edil Centro SpA* [2011] I.L.Pr. 28.
[101] ibid.
[102] [1999] 1 W.L.R. 1305, noted Briggs, (2000) 70 B.Y.B.I.L. 336. See also *M.B.M. Fabri-Clad Ltd v Eisen Und Huttenwerke Thale AG* [2000] I.L.Pr. 505.
[103] Case 386/05, [2007] E.C.R. I-3699; see Harris, (2007) 123 L.Q.R. 522.
[104] See also *Scottish & Newcastle International Ltd v Othon Ghalanos Ltd* [2008] UKHL 11; [2008] 2 All E.R. 768 (place of shipment is place of delivery in F.O.B. contracts); see Merrett [2008] C.L.J. 244 and Hare and Hinks [2008] L.M.C.L.Q. 353.

the provision of services, the place where, pursuant to that contract, the main provision of services was to be carried out.[105]

Provision of services

The second indent of art.7(1)(b) of the Brussels I *bis* Regulation provides:　　　**6–019**

> "(b)　　for the purpose of this provision and unless otherwise agreed, the place of performance of the obligation in question shall be:
> —　　in the case of the provision of services, the place in a Member State where, under the contract, the services were provided or should have been provided."

The extent of the phrase "provision of services" has exercised the CJEU. Many commercial contracts will fall under this provision, for example, commercial agency agreements, franchise contracts, distribution agreements[106]; however, a contract under which the owner of an intellectual property right granted its contractual partner the right to use that right in return for remuneration was not a contract for services within the meaning of that provision.[107]

In proceedings concerning the breach of an exclusive distributorship agreement, it was established that the services are provided where the distributorship obligation is to be performed.[108]

The *Color Drack* approach developed originally for contracts of sale was followed in *Wood Floor Solutions Andreas Domberger GmbH v Silva Trade SA*,[109] a case involving a contract for services in which the defendant had to perform services in more than one country. The proceedings related to a contract of commercial agency under the terms of which the agent undertook to provide services in more than one Member State. The CJEU held that the court which has jurisdiction is the court of the place where the "main provisions of services" is performed. However, in many types of case, including a commercial agency contract, that criterion may link the case with more than one jurisdiction; hence the CJEU added, with no basis for such addition in the text of the Brussels I Regulation, that where that place cannot be established, the courts that have jurisdiction are the courts of the place where the agent is domiciled[110]:

> "if the place of the main provision of services cannot be determined on the basis of the provisions of the contract itself or its actual performance, the place must be identified by another means which respects the objectives of predictability and proximity pursued by the legislature. For that purpose, it will be necessary for the purposes of the application of the second indent of article 5(1)(b) to consider, as the place of the main provision of the services provided by a commercial agent, the place where that agent is domiciled. That place can always be identified with certainty and is therefore predictable. Moreover, it has a link of proximity with the dispute since the agent will in all likelihood provide a substantial part of his services there."

---

[105] Case 204/08, *Rehder v Air Baltic Corp* [2009] E.C.R. I-6073.
[106] Case C-9/12 *Corman-Collins SA v La Maison du Whisky SA* [2013] ELR (D) 513; [2014] Q.B. 431; [2014] 2 W.L.R. 494.
[107] Case C-533/07 *Falco Privatstiftung v Weller Lindhorst,* [2009] E.C.R. I-3327.
[108] Case C-9/12 *Corman-Collins SA v La Maison du Whisky SA* [2013] ELR (D) 513 (preliminary ruling referral from a Belgium court); [2014] Q.B. 431; [2014] 2 W.L.R. 494.
[109] Case C-19/09, [2010] 1 W.L.R. 1900. See *Costas Stamatiou* [2010] ICCLR 43.
[110] At paras 41–42.

In relation to the same question in the context of air travel, the CJEU held in *Rehder v Air Baltic Corp*[111] that the only places which had a direct link to those services were those of the departure and arrival of the aircraft. Accordingly, the claimant had an option to sue the defendant in the court in whose jurisdiction one of those places was situated. Hence, it seems that in the case of provision of services related to an air transport contract, there would be always concurrent jurisdiction at the courts of the place of departure and arrival and the claimant has the option of suing at the courts of either place.

Other contracts

6–020   Article 7(1)(c) of the Brussels I *bis* Regulation provides:

> "(c)   if point (b) does not apply then point (a) applies;"

In relation to contracts other than contracts of sale and provision of services, for example, financial contracts including sale of securities and debts, sale of intellectual property rights, licensing agreements, joint-venture agreements, etc., the determination of the place of performance is to be done according to the unqualified connecting factor of 'the place of performance of the obligation in question'. That is to be determined in accordance with the law applicable to the contract under the conflicts rules of the forum. If, for example, English law is the applicable law, the place of payment is deemed to be the place of the debtor's residence. This approach adopted under the Brussels Convention 1968 remains under the Brussels I *bis* Regulation.[112] The law applicable to the contract also determines the effects of contractual stipulations as to the place of performance.[113]

Special jurisdiction rules for claims in tort, delict or quasi-delict

6–021   Article 7(2) of the Brussels I *bis* Regulation provides:

> "7.   A person domiciled in a Member State[114] may be sued in another Member State:
> (2)   in matters relating to tort, delict or quasi-delict in the courts for the place where the harmful event occurred or may occur.[115]"

The phrase "tort, delict or quasi-delict" uses the varying terms found in national legal systems. Despite this, the phrase has a European autonomous meaning unrelated to those in national systems. It covers actions calling into

---

[111] Case C-204/08, [2009] E.C.R. I-6073. See George and Harris [2010] L.Q.R. 30, arguing that there is a fundamental difference between contracts of sale and contracts for the provisions of services and that extension of the *Color Drack* test to services performed in cross-border cases militates against predictability.

[112] R. Fentiman, *International Commercial Litigation* (2015) para.9.48 at 335.

[113] Case 12/76 *Industrie Tessili Italiana Como v Dunlop AG* [1976] E.C.R. 1473; Case C-288/92 *Custom Made Commercial Ltd v Stawa Metallbau GmbH* [1994] E.C.R. I-2913; Case C-440/97 *GIE Groupe Concorde v The Suhadiwarno Panjan* [1999] E.C.R. I-6307.

[114] Case 292/10 *G v de Visser* [2013] Q.B. 168.

[115] Regulation 1215/2012 art.7(2); reg.44/2001 art.5(3).

question the liability of the defendant outside the field of matters relating to contract.[116] The effect of so defining the scope of actions in tort is to exclude the possibility, which exists in English domestic law and in other national legal systems, of the action being available in either contract or tort at the claimant's option; if the claim arises out of a legal relationship of a contractual nature, it must be pursued as a claim in contract.[117]

One aspect of *Kleinwort Benson Ltd v Glasgow City Council*,[118] the restitution claim after the invalid "interest swap" agreements considered above in the context of the contract head, was whether the claim could be brought alternatively as a claim in tort. The House of Lords answered in the negative because a claim based on unjust enrichment "does not, apart from special circumstances, presuppose either a harmful event or a threatened wrong". The result is to leave at least some restitution claims wholly outside art.7, and the claimant must sue under art.4 in the country of the defendant's domicile.[119]

The place of the tort

"The place where the harmful event occurred"

The "place where the harmful event occurred", as a connecting factor for special jurisdiction, is intended to provide a high degree of predictability for all parties.[120] However, the vexed question of the place of the tort has been the object of abundant jurisprudence from the very early times of the Brussels Convention. In *Bier v Mines de Potasse d'Alsace*[121]:

6–022

> A market gardener in the Netherlands complained that his plants were damaged by pollutants in the Rhine water he used for irrigation purposes. He brought an action in the Dutch courts against the defendants, a company domiciled in France, alleging that the damage was caused by their pumping chlorides into the river from its French bank. The CJEU held that under art.5(3) the claimant had an option to sue either at the place where the damage occurred or the place of the event giving rise to it.

Hence, art.7(2) gives a claimant the option of instituting proceedings against the tort-feasor[122] in the courts of either place, i.e. the courts of the country where the

---

[116] Case 189/87 *Kalfelis v Shroder, Munchmeyer, Hengst & Co* [1988] E.C.R. 565; *Swithenbank Food Ltd v Bowers* [2002] 2 All E.R. (Comm) 974; Case 167/00 *Verein für Konsumenteninformation v Henkel* [2003] All E.R. (EC) 311; Case 18/02 *Danmarks Rederiforening v Landsorganisationen i Sverige* [2004] All E.R. (EC) 845; Case 548/12 *Brogsitter v Fabrication de Montres Normandes EURL* [2014] Q.B. 753; Case 375/13 *Kolassa v Barclays Bank Plc* [2015] CEC 753; [2015] I.L.Pr. 14.
[117] Case C-47/14 *Holterman Ferho Exploitatie v F.L.F. Spies von Büllesheim* [2015] I.L.Pr. 789 at [70].
[118] [1999] 1 A.C. 153.
[119] See *Casio Computer Co Ltd v Sayo (No.3)* [2001] EWCA Civ 661; [2001] I.L.Pr. 694, noted Yeo, (2001) 117 L.Q.R. 560 (constructive trust based on knowing assistance; claim held within art.5(3)).
[120] *OFAB, Ostergotlands Fastigheter AB v Koot* (C-147/12) [2015] Q.B. 20.
[121] Case 21/76, [1976] E.C.R. 1735; [1978] Q.B. 708.
[122] This special jurisdictional basis cannot be interpreted extensively as to ground jurisdiction in a country where an 'accomplice or joint participant' who is not a defendant has committed a harmful act, see Case C-228/11 *Melzer v MF Global UK Ltd* [2013] Q.B. 1112.

event giving rise to the damage happened, or the courts of the country where the damage was suffered. The ruling in the *Bier* case has been applied repeatedly by the CJEU in several different contexts.

In *Cartel Damage Claims (CDC) Hydrogen Peroxide SA v Akzo Nobel NV*,[123] an action for damages brought against defendants domiciled in various Member States as a result of a single and continuous infringement of EU competition law, in which the defendants participated in several Member States, at different times and in different places, the CJEU interpreted the *Bier* principle and held that the harmful event occurred in relation to each alleged victim on an individual basis and each of the victims could choose to bring an action before the courts of the place in which the cartel was definitively concluded or, as the case may be, the place in which one agreement in particular was concluded which was identifiable as the sole causal event giving rise to the loss allegedly suffered.[124] It was also held in that decision that the location of the harmful event must be assessed in relation to each claim for damages independently of any subsequent assignment or consolidation of those claims.[125]

"The place where the damage occurs"

6–023   In the context of product liability, it was held in *Zuid-Chemie BV v Philippo's Mineralenfabriek NV/SA*[126] that "the place where the damage occurs" was the place where the initial damage occurred as a result of the normal use of a product for the purpose for which that product was intended. It seems to follow that consequential or secondary economic loss suffered in a Member State should not be enough to confer jurisdiction under art.7(2); however there is room for further refinement of the interpretation of this provision in relation to economic loss.[127]

The place of damage for this purpose is where the relevant physical damage or economic loss is *directly* sustained. For example, had the claimant in the *Bier* case been a company with English shareholders, it could not have invoked this special jurisdiction provision[128] as giving the English court jurisdiction even though it might have suffered consequential financial loss. Had the rule been otherwise, almost every business claim could be brought in the claimant's forum.[129] So in *Dumez France v Hessische Landesbank*[130]:

---

[123] Case C-352/13 *Cartel Damage Claims (CDC) Hydrogen Peroxide SA v Akzo Nobel NV* [2015] 3 W.L.R. 909.

[124] ibid. at [56].

[125] Case C-352/13 *Cartel Damage Claims (CDC) Hydrogen Peroxide SA v Akzo Nobel NV* [2015] 3 W.L.R. 909, at [36].

[126] Case C-189/08, [2009] E.C.R. I-6917.

[127] See Case 12/15 (pending before the CJEU) *Universal Music International Holding BV v Michael Tetreault Schilling* [2015] O.J. C89 (request for a preliminary ruling from the Hoge Raad in The Netherlands lodged on 14 January 2015, where the question put forward to the CJEU is "Must Article 5(3) be interpreted as meaning that the 'place where the harmful event occurred' can be construed as being the place in a Member State where the damage occurred, if that damage consists exclusively of financial damage which is the direct result of unlawful conduct which occurred in another Member State?".

[128] Regulation 1215/2012, art.7(2); reg.44/2001, art.5(3).

[129] See Case C-364/93 *Marinari v Lloyd's Bank Plc* [1995] E.C.R. I-2719.

[130] Case 220/88, [1990] E.C.R. I-49.

D, a French company, had German subsidiary companies engaged in a building project, financed by loans from the defendant bank. After a dispute, the bank suspended the loans and the project came to a halt. D sued in France, arguing that it sustained loss at its registered office in Paris.

The CJEU held that jurisdiction must be limited to where the harmful event "directly produced its harmful effect on the person who is the immediate victim of that event" and would not normally cover the domicile of an indirect victim.

The same principle applies to further losses suffered by the original victim. In *Henderson v Jaouen*[131]:

> The claimant, an Englishman, was injured in a road traffic accident in France and was awarded damages by a French court in an action against the other driver and his insurers. He began fresh proceedings in England some 17 years later, claiming that his state of health had deteriorated in the ensuing years as a direct result of the accident: this, he argued, was a 'harmful event' occurring in England.

The Court of Appeal applied the *Dumez France* principle. The only "harmful event" was that which occurred in France.

The CJEU has justified this narrow definition of 'damage' by the need to avoid a multiplicity of courts with jurisdiction that would heighten the risk of irreconcilable judgments. An alignment with art.4(1) of the Rome II Regulation on the law applicable to non-contractual obligations is sometimes pointed at by commentators in relation to this justification.[132] However, it is important to note that whilst concurrent jurisdiction is the rule rather than the exception in relation to the allocation of jurisdiction to adjudicate in a multilateral instrument such as the Brussels I or Brussels I *bis* Regulations, the same cannot be said about conflict-of-laws instruments in relation to choice of law, the underlying objective of the latter is to point to 'the' applicable law to the merits. The narrow interpretation seems to be more crucial in relation to the latter than the former.

In *Deutsche Bahn AG v Morgan Advanced Materials Plc (formerly Morgan Crucible Co Plc)*,[133] a claim instituted, in the lifetime of the Brussels I Regulation, by multiple claimants for damages under the Competition Act 1998 against several defendants, following a decision by the European Commission establishing that the defendants had been engaged in a cartel, the Court of Appeal found that:

> "There was no justification for imposing a gloss upon art.5(3) to the effect that in order to be a relevant connecting factor between defendant and putative jurisdiction, a harmful event had to be one of which the putative claimant was an immediate victim. That would involve a search for a connecting factor between the claimant and the putative jurisdiction, rather than a connecting factor between the defendant and the putative jurisdiction, which was what the Regulation was concerned with. The authorities were essentially concerned with situations where the adverse consequences of an event which had already caused damage in one legal district were additionally felt in another legal district. The decision in Dumez France SA v Hessische Landesbank (220/88) [1990] E.C.R. I-49 had not said that it was only the immediate victim of a harmful event who might rely upon that harmful event as founding jurisdiction

---

[131] [2002] 1 W.L.R. 2971, noted Briggs, (2002) 73 B.Y.B.I.L. 458. See also *Brownlie v Four Seasons Holdings Inc* [2015] EWCA Civ 665; [2015] C.P. Rep. 40.

[132] See Bergson, (2016) L.Q.R. 132, 42–46.

[133] *Deutsche Bahn AG v Morgan Advanced Materials Plc (formerly Morgan Crucible Co Plc)* [2013] EWCA Civ 1484.

under art.5(3). The court in that case had concluded that the place identified by art.5(3) was the place where the event giving rise to the damage, and entailing liability, directly produced its harmful effects upon the immediate victim of that event".

"The place of the event giving rise to the damage"

6–024   In *Kainz v Pantherwerke AG*,[134] where a manufacturer was sued for liability for a defective product, the "place of the event giving rise to the damage" was the place where the product in question was manufactured.

The CJEU has confirmed that the option conferred on the claimant according to the *Bier* interpretation of the effects of this special jurisdictional basis need not be read as limited to physical damage, and can be applied to (for example) damage to reputation in a defamation context, as in *Shevill v Presse Alliance*[135]:

> A Yorkshire woman, the plaintiff, worked in a bureau de change in Paris. *France Soir* carried a story that that bureau was used for money laundering in the drugs trade. The plaintiff's name was mentioned. The paper sold 200,000 copies in France, and some 230 in England (perhaps 10 of them in Yorkshire). S sued in England relying on art.5(3), and it was held that jurisdiction existed under art.5(3) both where the article was originally published (the place of the event giving rise to the damage)[136] and where damage to reputation was sustained.

In *Shevill* the CJEU explained that the *Bier* principle was essential if the special jurisdiction provision in relation to tort, delict and quasi-delict in the Brussels regime was to have any real effect. If jurisdiction under that provision were limited to the place the defendant acted, it would so often overlap with the general jurisdiction rule based on the domicile of the defendant, rendering it worthless in many occasions. But the court placed a new limitation on the effect of the special jurisdiction rule. If the action was brought in the Member State where the publisher of the libel was established, the court could award damages for all the damage sustained by the plaintiff, wherever it occurred; if the action were in one of the states where her reputation was damaged (on the periphery, as it were), the court could award damages only in respect of the damage sustained in that state.

That kind of limitation on the award of damages has also been regarded as applicable to claims for damages based on the infringement of copyright resulting from the placing of protected photographs online. In *Hejduk v EnergieAgentur.NRW GmbH*[137] the CJEU held that in such a cases a court has jurisdiction only to rule on the damage caused in the Member State within which the court is situated.

---

[134] Case 45/13 *Kainz v Pantherwerke AG* [2015] Q.B. 34; [2015] Q.B. 54.

[135] Case C-68/93, [1995] E.C.R. I-415; [1995] 2 A.C. 18.

[136] For similar results in a misrepresentation context, see *Domicrest Ltd v Swiss Bank Corp* [1999] Q.B. 548 and *Sunderland Marine Mutual Insurance Co Ltd v Wiseman (The "Seaward Quest")* [2007] EWHC 1460 (Comm); [2007] 2 Lloyd's Rep. 308.

[137] Case C-441/13 *Hejduk v EnergieAgentur NRW GmbH* [2015] Bus. L.R. 560.

"Harmful event": broad interpretation

The notion of the "harmful event" itself is, however, to be given a broad interpretation.[138] It has been held to include the "undermining of legal stability" by the use of unfair contract terms, a ruling coloured by the need to give practical effect to the Directive on unfair terms in consumer contracts. In cases where the "harmful event" is the lack of payment to which the claimant was entitled, the harm occurs at the place where the payment should have been made.[139]

6–025

"Or may occur"

The final words of this special jurisdiction provision,[140] "or may occur", have no counterpart in the earlier Brussels Convention text but probably reflect their intent. It is now clear that an action to prevent a tort occurring is within the remit of this special jurisdiction basis.

6–026

The CJEU has clarified the concept in cases involving an alleged infringement of personality rights by means of content placed online on an internet website.[141] The Court recognised that the placing online of content on a website is to be distinguished from the regional distribution of media e.g. in a physical newspaper, in that it is intended, in principle, to ensure the ubiquity of that content.

> "Consequently, ... in the event of an alleged infringement of personality rights by means of content placed online on an internet website, the person who considers that his rights have been infringed has the option of bringing an action for liability, in respect of all the damage caused, either before the courts of the Member State in which the publisher of that content is established or before the courts of the Member State in which the centre of his interests is based. That person may also, instead of an action for liability in respect of all the damage caused, bring his action before the courts of each Member State in the territory of which content placed online is or has been accessible. Those courts have jurisdiction only in respect of the damage caused in the territory of the Member State of the court seised".

Special jurisdiction rules for civil claims in criminal proceedings

Article 7(3) of the Brussels I *bis* Regulation provides:

6–027

> "A person domiciled in a Member State may be sued in another Member State:
> (3)   as regards a civil claim for damages or restitution which is based on an act giving rise to criminal proceedings, in the court seised of those proceedings, to the extent that that court has jurisdiction under its own law to entertain civil proceedings."[142]

---

[138] Case C-167/00 *Verien fur Konsumenteninformation v Henkel* [2002] E.C.R. I-8111. See *Future Investments SA v FIFA* [2010] EWHC 1019 (Ch); [2010] I.L.Pr. 34.
[139] *Dolphin Maritime & Aviation Services Ltd v Sveriges Angfartygs Assurans Forening* [2009] EWHC 716 (Comm); [2009] 2 Lloyd's Rep. 123.
[140] Regulation 1215/2012 art.7(2); reg.44/2001 art.5(3).
[141] Joined Cases C-509/09 *eDate Advertising GmbH v X* and Case C-161/10 *Martinez v MGN Ltd* [2012] Q.B. 654.
[142] Regulation 1215/2012 art.7(3); reg.44/200 art.5(4).

This relates to such claims as those of a *partie civile* intervening in French criminal cases; there is no direct English equivalent.

Special jurisdiction rules for claims for the recovery of cultural property

6–028   Article 7(4) of the Brussels I *bis* Regulation provides:

> "A person domiciled in a Member State may be sued in another Member State:
> (4)   as regards a civil claim for the recovery, based on ownership, of a cultural object as defined in point 1 of Article 1 of Directive 93/7/EEC initiated by the person claiming the right to recover such an object, in the courts for the place where the cultural object is situated at the time when the court is seised[143];"

Special jurisdiction rules for claims arising out of operations of a branch, agency or other establishment

6–029   Of greater importance is the provision in the Brussels I *bis* Regulation about branches and agencies:

Article 7(5) of the Brussels I *bis* Regulation provides:

> "A person domiciled in a Member State may be sued in another Member State:
> (5)   as regards a dispute arising out of the operations of a branch, agency or other establishment, in the courts for the place where the branch, agency or other establishment is situated."[144]

It is an entirely familiar feature of economic life that businesses established in one country will also operate in other countries. This is true by definition of the big multinationals, but a relatively small company may decide to set up a manufacturing, assembly or distribution plant abroad, or at least to have a representative office in a foreign capital to help in marketing its products. It may operate in the foreign country directly, or through the agency of another company, or it may establish its own subsidiary company for the purpose. A fundamental aim of European integration is the facilitation of just this type of activity. The question is how many of these arrangements are within the scope of this part of the Regulation. It is important to note that it applies only where the defendant is domiciled in a Member State, and not, for example, to a branch of a United States corporation.[145]

The terms "branch, agency or other establishment" have European autonomous meanings. The court must ask whether a particular entity acts as an extension of the parent body, is subject to its direction and control of the parent body, and has "the appearance of permanence".[146] A mere sales agency, especially where the agent may represent several firms and merely transmits

---

[143] See Gilles, (2015) 11 J Priv Int L 295.
[144] Regulation 1215/2012 art.7(5); reg.44/2001 art.5(5).
[145] Contrast the position under the special rules for insurance, consumer and employment contracts (arts 11(2), 17(2) and 20(2) of the Brussels I *bis* Regulation), all considered below.
[146] Case 14/76 *De Bloos Sprl v Bouyer SA* [1976] E.C.R. 1497; Case 33/78 *Somafer SA v Saar-Ferngas AG* [1978] E.C.R. 2183.

orders to the relevant principal, will not qualify.[147] In this context, the corporate structure of a group of companies may not be decisive; an entity may be an extension of the "parent" body in this sense even though the "parent" body is actually one of its subsidiaries; commercial realities are to be examined.[148] This special jurisdiction basis refers to claims arising out of the "operations" of the branch, agency or other establishment. This notion includes matters concerning the management of the agency or branch itself, such as those concerning the situation of its premises or the local engagement of staff to work there; to undertakings entered into there in the name of the parent body; and to non-contractual obligations arising from the activities in which the branch or agency has engaged.[149]

Special jurisdiction rules for claims against a settlor, trustee or beneficiary of a trust

There were no provisions as to trusts in the original Brussels Convention as the trust device was unknown in the law of the signatory States. The text has made provision for trusts since the Accession Convention of 1978.

6–030

Article 7(6) of the Brussels I *bis* Regulation provides:

> "7.   A person domiciled in a Member State may be sued in another Member State:
>   (6)   as regards a dispute brought against a settlor, trustee or beneficiary of a trust created by the operation of a statute, or by a written instrument, or created orally and evidenced in writing, in the courts of the Member State in which the trust is domiciled.[150]"

The trust must have been created by statute or by a written instrument: resulting or constructive trusts are not included. Nor are trusts arising under wills or intestacies, because wills and intestacies are outside the scope of the Regulation.[151] This special jurisdiction basis applies to disputes relating to the internal relationships of the trust, such as disputes between beneficiaries or between trustees and beneficiaries, and not to disputes relating to its external relations, such as the enforcement by third parties of contracts made by trustees.[152] It must be restrictively interpreted, and while the word "trustee" has an autonomous meaning under the Regulation that meaning is strongly influenced by the understanding of the concept in the common law countries which gave birth to the trust.[153]

The domicile of a trust has already been considered[154]; it is tested as at the time when proceedings are commenced.[155]

---

[147] *De Bloos Sprl v Bouyer SA* [1976] E.C.R. 1497; Case 139/80 *Blanckaert and Willems PVBA v Trost* [1981] E.C.R. 819.
[148] Case 218/86 *SAR Schotte GmbH v Parfums Rothschild* [1987] E.C.R. 4905.
[149] Case 33/78 *Somafer SA v Saar-Ferngas AG* [1978] E.C.R. 2183.
[150] Regulation 1215/2012 art.7(6); reg.44/2001 art.5(6).
[151] Article 1; Schlosser, para.52.
[152] Schlosser, para.120.
[153] *Gomez v Encarnacion Gomez-Monche Vives* [2008] EWCA Civ 1065; [2009] Ch. 245.
[154] See above, para.6–011.
[155] *Chellaram v Chellaram (No.2)* [2002] EWHC 632 (Ch); [2002] 3 All E.R. 17.

Special jurisdiction rules in relation to disputes involving the arrest of cargo or freight[156]

6–031   Article 7(7) of the Brussels I *bis* Regulation provides:

> "A person domiciled in a Member State may be sued in another Member State:
> (7)   as regards a dispute concerning the payment of remuneration claimed in respect of the salvage of a cargo or freight, in the court under the authority of which the cargo or freight in question:
> (a)   has been arrested to secure such payment; or
> (b)   could have been so arrested, but bail or other security has been given;
> provided that this provision shall apply only if it is claimed that the defendant has an interest in the cargo or freight or had such an interest at the time of salvage."

Where the action is concerned not with the ship itself but with the salvage of cargo or freight, this specific provision of special jurisdiction applies.

CONNECTED JURISDICTION: MULTI-PARTY CASES AND COUNTERCLAIMS

6–032   The jurisdiction grounds identified on the basis of what was discussed in the previous chapter as 'connected jurisdiction' are placed in the Brussels I *bis* Regulation in art.8, within the section providing for 'special jurisdiction', therefore, it has been understood that these 'connected' grounds are to be narrowly construed.[157]

The underpinnings of connected jurisdiction are rather different to that of special jurisdiction, since the rationale behind these provisions on multi-party cases and counterclaims is more related to procedural efficiency than it is with the notion of the appropriate forum, i.e. the underlying justification of jurisdictional bases. There is no doubt that these two types of consideration are closely related, but it is important to bear in mind that the main rationale behind the provisions of arts 8 and 9 of the Brussels I *bis* Regulation is the systemic efficiency and expediency of the European free area of justice considered as a whole.

Centralisation of jurisdiction[158]: several defendants

6–033   Article 8 (1) of the Brussels I *bis* Regulation provides:

> "8.   A person domiciled in a Member State may also be sued:
> (1)   where he is one of a number of defendants, in the courts for the place[159] where any one of them is domiciled[160], provided the claims are so closely connected

---

[156] See Jackson, *Enforcement of Maritime Claims* (LLP 2005).
[157] Case 145/10 *Painer v Standard Verlags GmbH* [2011] E.C.D.R. 13; Case 645/11 *Land Berlin v Sapir* [2013] I.L.Pr.29.
[158] Case C-352/13 *Cartel Damage Claims (CDC) Hydrogen Peroxide SA v Akzo Nobel NV* [2015] 3 W.L.R. 909.
[159] One of the few points in the Regulation at which domicile at particular place must be established.
[160] At the time of the issue of the claim form rather than its service: *Canada Trust Co v Stolzenberg (No.2)* [2002] 1 A.C. 1. See also *Latmar Holdings Corp v Media Focus Ltd* [2013] EWCA Civ 4; [2013] I.L.Pr.19.

that it is expedient to hear and determine them together to avoid the risk of irreconcilable judgments resulting from separate proceedings[161];"

Article 8 does not extend to co-defendants who are not domiciled in the EU, in the cases where they are sued in proceedings brought against several defendants, some of whom are domiciled in the EU.[162]

In *Freeport Plc v Olle Arnoldsson*,[163] the CJEU held, on facts which involved claims based on contract and tort, that the fact that claims brought against a number of defendants had different legal bases did not preclude the application of this 'connected' jurisdiction ground.[164]

The CJEU has held that it cannot be interpreted in such a way as to allow a claimant to make a claim against a number of defendants for the sole purpose of removing one of them from the jurisdiction of the courts of the Member State in which that defendant is domiciled.[165] This basis cannot be abused by the claimant, and if there is clear evidence of collusion a court can refuse to exercise its jurisdiction against the 'connected' co-defendant despite that the application in principle meets the requirements of art.8(1)[166].

In *Cartel Damage Claims (CDC) Hydrogen Peroxide SA v Akzo Nobel NV*, the CJEU held that the rule applies even where the applicant has withdrawn its action against the sole co-defendant domiciled in the country of the court seised, unless it is found that, at the time the proceedings were instituted, the applicant and that defendant had colluded to artificially fulfil the applicability of the rule on centralisation of jurisdiction.[167]

The core consideration is the risk of irreconcilable judgments (inconsistent judgments); whether that risk is latent or not if the related actions are heard in separate proceedings is for the court of the anchor claim to assess objectively.[168] The same considerations apply in relation to interpretation of the same concept, 'related actions', i.e. 'closely connected actions', for the purposes of the *lis pendens* rule in art.29 of the Brussels I *bis* Regulation.[169]

Centralisation of jurisdiction: third parties

Article 8 (2) of the Brussels I *bis* Regulation provides: 6–034

---

[161] Regulation 1215/2012 art.8(1); reg.44/2001 art.6(1); the proviso was new in the Brussels I Regulation, but it reflects earlier case-law: Case 189/87 *Kalfelis v Schroder, Munchmeyer, Hengst & Co* [1988] E.C.R. 5565. See also, e.g. *Shetty v Al Rushaid Petroleum Investment* [2011] EWHC 1460 (Ch).
[162] Case 645/11 *Land Berlin v Sapir* [2013] I.L.Pr.29.
[163] Case C-98/06, [2007] E.C.R. I-8319.
[164] As to the degree of connection see also *Gascoine v Pyrah* [1994] I.L.Pr. 82; Case 645/11 *Land Berlin v Sapir* [2013] I.L.Pr.29.
[165] Case C-103/05 *Reisch Montage AG v Kiesel Baumaschinen Handels GmbH* [2006] E.C.R. I-6827.
[166] *Sibir Energy Ltd v Chalva Pavlovich Tchigirinski* [2012] EWHC 1844 (QB); [2012] I.L.Pr. 52 (on the application of the 2007 Lugano Convention, art.6).
[167] Case C-352/13 (CJEU) 2015 3 W.L.R. 909, at [33].
[168] *Gard Marine and Energy Ltd v Tunnicliffe* [2010] EWCA Civ 1052; [2011] 2 All E.R. (Comm) 208 (on the application of this proviso in the Lugano Convention); *FKI Engineering Ltd v Stribog Ltd* [2011] EWCA Civ 622; [2011] 1 W.L.R. 3264.
[169] See further below, para.6–060.

"8.   A person domiciled in a Member State may also be sued:
         (2)   as a third party in an action on a warranty or guarantee or in any other
                 third-party proceedings[170], in the court seised of the original proceedings,
                 unless these were instituted solely with the object of removing him from the
                 jurisdiction of the court which would be competent in his case[171];"

Given the purpose of these provisions in the Regulation, to avoid the risk of irreconcilable judgments, it is necessary for there to be a close connection between the original claim and the third party proceedings (in English practice, a "Part 20 claim", referring to the relevant provisions in the Civil Procedure Rules). That a mere factual link is not enough is shown by the facts of *Barton v Golden Sun Holidays Ltd*[172]:

The claimants, a group of holidaymakers on a holiday arranged by the defendant company, stayed at a hotel in Cyprus. Its low standards of hygiene led to the claimants suffering gastrointestinal infections. The defendants admitted liability and agreement was reached on the damages payable and the basis on which costs were to be quantified. At that point the defendants sought leave to bring a Part 20 claim against the hotel operators.

It was held that the case fell outside the 'connected' basis in relation to third parties in the European regime of jurisdiction. The main claim had been entirely a matter of English law, but the claim against the hotel company also involved the law of Cyprus. The main claim was now effectively dealt with, so that there was no realistic possibility of the two claims being heard together and there was no risk of irreconcilable judgments.

Centralisation of jurisdiction: counterclaims

6–035   Article 8 (3) of the Brussels I bis Regulation provides:

"8.   A person domiciled in a Member State may also be sued:
         (3)   on a counter-claim arising from the same contract or facts on which the original
                 claim was based, in the court in which the original claim is pending[173];"

Centralisation of jurisdiction: the interface of contract and property

6–036   Article 8 (4) of the Brussels I *bis* Regulation provides:

"8.   A person domiciled in a Member State may also be sued:
         (4)   in matters relating to a contract, if the action may be combined with an action
                 against the same defendant in matters relating to rights *in rem* in immovable
                 property, in the court of the Member State in which the property is situated."

---

[170] Whether the basis for jurisdiction in the original proceedings was the defendant's domicile or some other basis: Case C-365/88 *Kongress Agentur Hagen GmbH v Zeehage BV* [1990] E.C.R. I-1845.
[171] Regulation 1215/2012 art.8(2); reg.44/2001 art.6(2). These provisions cannot be relied upon to deprive the third party of the benefit of a jurisdiction agreement under art.25: *Hough v P&O Containers Ltd* [1999] Q.B. 834.
[172] [2007] EWHC 3455 (QB); [2007] I.L.Pr. 57.
[173] Regulation 1215/2012 art.8(3); reg.44/2001 art.6(3).

Centralisation of jurisdiction: liability from the use or operation of a ship

Article 9 of the Brussels I *bis* Regulation establishes that where a court of a   **6–037**
Member State has jurisdiction under the Regulation in actions relating to liability
from the use or operation of a ship, that court, or any other court substituted for
this purpose by the internal law of that Member State, must also have jurisdiction
over claims for limitation of such liability.[174]

PROTECTIVE JURISDICTION[175]

The protective jurisdiction rules in relation to the categories identified by the   **6–038**
European regime share several common features. One of the key notions is the
so-called *forum actoris*, that is, the possibility for the 'weaker' party to bring
proceedings in his or her own country of residence.

Protective rules in relation to jurisdiction in certain insurance claims

The original text of the Brussels Convention 1968 made special provision for
jurisdiction in matters of insurance[176] in order to protect the policy-holder, the
supposedly weaker party. As Schlosser says,[177] the accession of the UK
introduced a totally new dimension to the insurance business as it had hitherto
been practised within the EU. This was because the London insurance market has
such a large share of worldwide insurance business, particularly in the
international insurance of large risks. In such a business the policy-holder is
likely to be a powerful multinational corporation which does not need the
protection given by the original Convention to an individual policy-holder
insuring his or her house, car, or life. Changes to take account of the new
situation were made at the time the UK acceded and again when the Brussels I
Regulation was formulated. The result is the very complicated law currently
contained in arts 10 to 16 of the Brussels I *bis* Regulation.[178]

These provisions provide an almost exclusive code governing jurisdiction "in
matters relating to insurance"[179] and with two exceptions other bases of
jurisdiction cannot be relied upon: the exceptions are arts 6 (application of
national jurisdictional rules in certain cases) and 7(5) (disputes concerning the
operations of a branch, agency or other establishment). In addition, the general

---

[174] Regulation 1215/2012 art.9; reg.44/2001 art.7.

[175] See para.5–008.

[176] For the scope of this phrase, see Case C-412/98 *Universal General Insurance Co v Group Josi Reinsurance Co SA* [2001] 1 Q.B. 68; *Agnew v Länsforsäkringsbølagens* [2001] 1 A.C. 223.

[177] Schlosser Report (Report on the Convention of 9 October 1978 on the accession of Denmark, Ireland and the UK, OJ C 59, 5.3.1979), para.136.

[178] Regulation 1215/2012 arts 10–16; reg.44/2001 arts 8–14.

[179] As between insurer and insured: actions between insurers are not covered and the general rules apply: *Youell v La Réunion Aérienne* [2008] EWHC 2493 (Comm); the issue was not taken on appeal.

rule giving jurisdiction to the court of a Member States before which a defendant enters an appearance[180] applies to insurance as to other cases.

The basic rule is that an insurer domiciled in a Member State may be sued (a) in the courts of the Member State where the insurer is domiciled[181] (a basis corresponding to that in art.4 of the Brussels I *bis* Regulation), or (b) in the case of a co-insurer, in the courts of a Member State in which proceedings are brought against the leading insurer[182] (a provision similar to the "co-defendants" provision in art.8(1), but distinguishing between "leading" and other insurers), or (c) in another Member State, in the case of actions brought by the policyholder, the insured or a beneficiary, in the courts for the place where the claimant is domiciled.[183] The effect of these rules is enlarged by the provision that an insurer who is not domiciled in a Member State but has a branch, agency or other establishment in one of the Member States is, in disputes arising out of the operations of the branch, agency or establishment, deemed to be domiciled in that Member State.[184]

In respect of liability insurance or insurance of immovable property, the insurer may in addition be sued in the courts for the place where the harmful event occurred.[185] The same applies if movable and immovable property are covered by the same insurance policy and both are adversely affected by the same contingency[186]; and in respect of liability insurance the insurer may also, if the law of the court permits it, be joined in proceedings which the injured party has brought against the insured.[187]

On the other hand, an insurer[188] may bring proceedings against a policyholder, the insured or a beneficiary only in the courts of the Member State in which the defendant is domiciled.[189] This rule is subject to a number of exceptions: where the applicable rules governing direct actions between injured party and insurer so provide[190]; when a counterclaim is brought against the original plaintiff[191]; and in certain cases in which the parties have given jurisdiction to a court by

---

[180] Regulation 1215/2012 art.26; reg.44/2001 art.24. See Case C-111/09 *Ceska Podnikatelska Pojistovna as, Vienna Insurance Group v Bilas* [2010] Lloyd's Rep IR 734.

[181] Regulation 1215/2012 art.11(1)(a).

[182] Regulation 1215/2012 art.11(1)(c).

[183] Regulation 1215/2012 art.11(1)(b); reg.44/2001 art.9(1). See *Jones v Assurances Générales de France (AGF) SA* [2010] I.L.Pr. 4 (English victim of road accident in France entitled to sue French insurer of Irish negligent driver in England).

[184] Regulation 1215/2012 art.11(2); reg.44/2001 art.9(2).

[185] Regulation 1215/2012 art.12; reg.44/2001 art.10.

[186] Regulation 1215/2012 art.12; reg.44/2001 art.10.

[187] Regulation 1215/2012 art.13(1); reg.44/2001 art.11(1). For direct actions between injured party and insurer, see art.11(2)(3) and Case C-463/06 *FBTO Schadeverzekeringen NV v Odenbreit* [2007] E.C.R. I-11321. See also Case C-347/08 *Vorarlberger Gebietskrankenkasse v WGV-Schwabische Allgemeine Versicherungs AG* [2009] E.C.R. I-8661.

[188] Whether or not domiciled in a Member State: *Jordan Grand Prix Ltd v Baltic Insurance Group* [1999] 2 A.C. 127.

[189] Regulation 1215/2012 art.14(1); reg.44/2001 art.12(1); *New Hampshire Insurance Co v Strabag Bau AG* [1992] 1 Lloyd's Rep. 361.

[190] Regulation 1215/2012 art.13(3), 14(1); reg.44/2001 arts 11(3), 12(1).

[191] Regulation 1215/2012 art.14(2); reg.44/2001 art.12(2); *Jordan Grand Prix Ltd v Baltic Insurance Group* [1999] 2 A.C. 127.

agreement.[192] This last possibility is hedged about by complex rules designed to protect individuals: cases of marine, aviation and "large risks" insurance are treated differently.[193]

In insurance cases, an agreement as to jurisdiction departing from the rules in s.3 of the Brussels I *bis* Regulation is effective only if it is entered into after the dispute has arisen; or allows the policyholder, the insured or a beneficiary to bring proceedings in courts other than those indicated in s.3; or which is entered into by the policyholder and the insurer, both of whom are at the time of conclusion of the contract domiciled or habitually resident in the same Member State, and which confers jurisdiction on the courts of that Member State even if the harmful event were to occur abroad, provided that such an agreement is not contrary to the law of that Member State; or which is concluded with a policyholder not domiciled in a Member State, except in so far as the insurance is compulsory or relates to immovable property in a Member State; or which relates to a contract of insurance in so far as it covers certain types of risk listed in art.16.[194]

Protective rules in relation to jurisdiction in certain consumer contracts

Section 4 (arts 17–19) of the Brussels I *bis* Regulation contains special provisions for jurisdiction over consumer contracts in order to protect consumers, the economically weaker party. These provisions provide an almost exclusive code, and other bases of jurisdiction cannot be relied upon, with two exceptions: the exceptions are arts 6 (application of national jurisdictional rules in certain cases) and 7(5) (disputes concerning the operations of a branch, agency or other establishment). In addition, the general rule giving jurisdiction to the court of a Member State before which a defendant enters an appearance[195] applies in the consumer context as elsewhere.

6–039

There are important definitions of "consumer" and "consumer contract" in art.17.

"Consumer"

A person is a "consumer" only if he or she concluded the contract for a purpose which can be regarded as being outside his or her trade or profession.[196] The CJEU has held that this brings within the consumer contract category only contracts concluded[197] for the purpose of satisfying an individual's own needs in

6–040

---

[192] Regulation 1215/2012 art.16; reg.44/2001 art.13.

[193] See reg.1215/2012 art.16(5); reg.44/2001 arts 13(5).

[194] Regulation 1215/2012 art.16; reg.44/2001 art.13.

[195] Regulation 1215/2012 art.26; reg.44/2001 art.24.

[196] Regulation 1215/2012 art.17(1); reg.44/2001 art.15(1). Assignees of the original consumer are not included: Case C-89/91 *Shearson Lehman Hutton Inc v TVB Treuhandgesellschaft fur Vermogensverwaltung* [1993] E.C.R. I-139; nor are consumer associations: Case C-167/00 *Verien fur Konsumenteninformation v Henkel* [2002] E.C.R. I-8111.

[197] Case C-96/00 *Gabriel v Schlank & Schick GmbH* [2000] E.C.R. I-6367; Case C-27/02 *Engler v Janus Versand GmbH* [2005] E.C.R. I-481; Case C-180/06 *Ilsinger v Dreschers* [2009] E.C.R. I-3961.

terms of private consumption.[198] In many cases an item is bought for mixed purposes: a professor may buy a computer partly to use in editing a student textbook but also for playing computer games. The professor could claim the benefit of the special rules as to consumer contracts only by showing that the trade or professional purpose was so limited as to be negligible in the overall context of the supply, and even in that case not if he or she had acted in such a way as to lead the supplier reasonably to believe that the supply was for business purposes.[199]

"Consumer contract"

6–041   A "consumer contract" includes a contract for the sale of goods on instalment credit terms[200]; a contract for a loan repayable by instalments, or any other form of credit, made to finance the sale of goods; or any other contract (wherever concluded) with:

> "a person who pursues commercial or professional activities in the Member State of the consumer's domicile or, by any means, directs such activities to that Member State or to several states including that Member State, and the contract falls within the scope of such activities."[201]

"Directing activities"

6–042   The CJEU has produced abundant interpretative rulings trying to provide further guidance as to the meaning of "directing activities".[202] The idea behind this provision is that a business which seeks to enter the consumer market in a particular country cannot complain if it finds itself exposed to litigation there. This applies even if the transactions which the business seeks to promote have effects in another country: for example, a French company advertising in the English press time-share arrangements for the use of apartments in Spain could be sued by an English consumer. Although US law does not have this type of protective jurisdiction for consumers, the Regulation has echoes of the American notion of jurisdiction based on "doing business" in a State.

The ever-increasing reality of ecommerce continues to put forward challenges in this context. The European Commission observed, in making the proposal on which the Brussels I Regulation was based,[203] that:

---

[198] Case C-269/95 *Benincasa v Dentalkit Srl* [1997] E.C.R. I-3767.
[199] Case C-464/01 *Gruber v BayWa AG* [2006] Q.B. 204 (E.C.J.) (tiles for a farmhouse which was used both as a private house and for farm purposes).
[200] See Case 150/77 *Société Bertrand v Paul Ott KG* [1978] E.C.R. 1431 (decided under an earlier text of the Convention).
[201] Regulation 1215/2012 art.17(1)(c); reg.44/2001 art.15(1)(c). Contracts of transport are excluded (art.15(3)) (but not packages covering both transport and accommodation) because there are specific rules in the various international transport conventions.
[202] See e.g. Case C-297/14 *Rüdiger Hobohm v Benedikt Kampik Ltd & Co*, judgment of 23 December 2015.
[203] See O.J. C 376E/1, 28.12.1999; Kennett, (2001) 50 I.C.L.Q. 725 and, more generally, Øren, (2003) 52 I.C.L.Q. 665.

"The concept of activities pursued in or directed towards a Member State is designed to make clear that [art.15(1)(c)][204] applies to consumer contracts concluded via an interactive website accessible in the State of the consumer's domicile. The fact that a consumer simply had knowledge of a service or possibility of buying goods via a passive website accessible in his country of domicile will not trigger the protective jurisdiction. The contract is thereby treated in the same way as a contract concluded by telephone, fax and the like ...".

In *Pammer v Reederei Karl Schlüter GmbH* and *Hotel Alpenhof GmbH v Heller*[205] the CJEU was asked for a preliminary ruling on, inter alia, the interpretation of "directing activities" in the context of what was then art.15 of the Brussels I Regulation. Both cases involved consumers purchasing services via the internet from companies based in different Member States, having obtained information about them from the internet. One of the questions referred was whether the fact that the website of an intermediary, or of a party with whom a consumer had concluded a contract, could be consulted on the internet was sufficient to justify a finding that activities were being "directed" to the Member State of the consumer's domicile within the meaning of this provision. The Court held that the protection afforded in this section was not absolute because the directing of activities to a Member State had been laid down as a condition for the application of the rules relating to consumer contracts, not the mere existence of a website.[206] In order to determine whether the rule applied to a particular trader, it had to be ascertained whether, before the conclusion of any contract with the consumer, it was apparent from the trader's websites and the trader's overall activity that the trader envisaged doing business with consumers domiciled in one or more Member States, including the Member State of that consumer's domicile, "in the sense that it was minded to conclude a contract with them".

The CJEU went on to enumerate a non-exhaustive list of matters capable of constituting evidence from which it might be concluded that the trader's activity was directed to the Member State of the consumer's domicile: the international nature of the activity; mention of itineraries from other Member States for going to the place where the trader was established; use of a language or currency other than the language or currency generally used in the Member State where the trader was established; mention of telephone numbers with an international code; outlay of expenditure on an internet referencing service in order to facilitate access to the trader's site by customers domiciled in other Member States; use of a top-level domain name other than that of the Member State in which the trader was established; and mention of an international clientele composed of customers domiciled in various Member States. However, the mere accessibility of the trader's or intermediary's website in the Member State where the consumer was domiciled was insufficient, as was mention of an email address or other contact details and use of the language or currency generally used in the Member State where the trader was established.[207]

In *Muhlleitner v Yusulfi*[208] the Austrian domiciled consumer searched online for a car of a German make. She contacted the retail business in Germany that

---

[204] Regulation 1215/2012 art.17(1)(c); reg.44/2001 art.15(1)(c).
[205] Joined Cases C-585/08 and C-144/09, [2012] All E.R. (EC) 34.
[206] See paras 60–61, 63–64, 66–68, 70–71 of the CJEU's decision.
[207] ibid., paras 69, 76–77, 80–84, 89–94.
[208] Case 190/11 *Muhlleitner v Yusulfi* [2013] C.E.C. 595; [2012] I.L.Pr.46.

was selling the car. She used the telephone number, including the international dialling code that she found in the retailer's website. After that, she went to Hamburg and bought another vehicle from this same retailer. On her return to Austria she found that the vehicle was defective and asked the retailer to repair it. When the retailer refused to repair it, she initiated proceedings in Austria against the retailer for rescission of the contract of sale, which she alleged was a consumer contract protected under the Regulation. The defendants argued that they did not direct their activities to Austria, and that the contract was not protected because the claimant had concluded the contract at their premises in Germany. On a reference from the Austrian court for an interpretative ruling the CJEU held that the provisions of the Regulation were not limited to distance contracts.

Furthermore, in *Emrek v Sabranovic*[209] the CJEU made clear that there was no need for a causal link between the directing of the activities and the conclusion of the contract; that is, it is sufficient for the application of the protective rule in this context that the professional has directed his activities to the Member State of the consumer's domicile, even if such activities did not impact on the conclusion of the contract that was the basis of the claim.

How is the consumer protected in these scenarios?

6–043   Article 18 of the Brussels I *bis* Regulation provides:

> "1.   A consumer may bring proceedings against the other party to a contract either in the courts of the Member State in which that party is domiciled or, regardless of the domicile of the other party, in the courts for the place where the consumer is domiciled.
>
> 2.   Proceedings may be brought against a consumer by the other party to the contract only in the courts of the Member State in which the consumer is domiciled.
>
> 3.   This Article shall not affect the right to bring a counter-claim in the court in which, in accordance with this Section, the original claim is pending."

The effect of art.18 is that a consumer may bring proceedings against the other party to a contract either in the courts of the Member State in which that party is domiciled or in the courts of the Member State in which the consumer is domiciled[210] (*forum actoris*).[211] This latter possibility is the core 'protection'. Under the Brussels I Regulation the protective rule applied only on the basis that both parties to the contract were EU-domiciled or that the professional had a branch or agency in the EU. Article 18(1) of the Brussels I *bis* Regulation has extended the *forum actoris* reach to non-EU domiciled defendants ("regardless of the domicile of the other party").

On the other hand, proceedings may be brought against a consumer by the other party to the contract[212] only in the courts of the Member State in which the

---

[209] Case 218/12 *Emrek v Sabranovic* [2014] I.L.Pr.39.
[210] See Case C-327/10 *Hypotecni banka as v Lindner* [2011] E.C.R. I-11543; [2012] C.E.C. 975 (last known domicile within the EU, in the absence of evidence of domicile outside the EU, as affording *forum actoris* jurisdiction for a consumer for the purposes of art.16(2) of the original Brussels I Regulation).
[211] Regulation 1215/2012 art.18(1); reg.44/2001 art.16(1).
[212] Case 478/12 *Maletic v lastminute.com GmbH* [2014] Q.B. 424.

consumer is domiciled.[213] A consumer who enters into a contract with a party who is not domiciled in a Member State but who has a branch, agency or other establishment in one of the Member States, has the benefit of a special rule: that party is, in disputes arising out of the operations of the branch, agency or establishment, deemed to be domiciled in that state.[214]

Finally, there is further protection of the consumer, against the effect of jurisdiction clauses. The rules as to jurisdiction over consumer contracts may be departed from only by an agreement (a) which is entered into after the dispute has arisen; or (b) which allows the consumer to bring proceedings in courts other than those indicated in those rules; or (c) which is entered into by the consumer and the other party to the contract, both of whom are at the time of conclusion of the contract domiciled or habitually resident in the same Member State, and which confers jurisdiction on the courts of that state, provided that such an agreement is not contrary to the law of that state.[215]

Protective rules in relation to jurisdiction in cases concerning individual contracts of employment[216]

Article 20 of the Brussels I *bis* Regulation provides: **6–044**

"1.   In matters relating to individual contracts of employment, jurisdiction shall be determined by this Section, without prejudice to Article 6, point 5 of Article 7 and, in the case of proceedings brought against an employer, point 1 of Article 8.

2.   Where an employee enters into an individual contract of employment with an employer who is not domiciled in a Member State but has a branch, agency or other establishment in one of the Member States, the employer shall, in disputes arising out of the operations of the branch, agency or establishment, be deemed to be domiciled in that Member State."

The 1968 Brussels Convention did not contain special provisions governing jurisdiction in employment contracts, so that jurisdiction was given to the court of the defendant's domicile or the place of performance of the obligation in question. In a series of cases,[217] the CJEU ignored the plain language of the text and held that in the case of individual contracts of employment there had to be a single place of performance: that in which the employee's duties were performed. The justification offered for this exercise of judicial creativity was that contracts of employment have special features: they create a lasting bond which brings the worker to some extent within the organisational framework of the business of the undertaking or employer, and they are linked to the place where the activities are pursued, which determines the application of mandatory rules and collective agreements.[218]

---

[213] Regulation 1215/2012 art.18(2); reg.44/2001 art.16(2). Article 18 does not affect the right to bring a counterclaim in the court in which, in accordance with s.4, the original claim is pending: art.18(3).
[214] Regulation 1215/2012 art.17(2); reg.44/2001 art.15(2).
[215] Regulation 1215/2012 art.19; reg.44/2001 art.17.
[216] See Grušić, *The European Private International Law of Employment* (Cambridge: Cambridge University Press, 2015).
[217] Beginning with Case 133/81 *Ivenel v Schwab* [1982] E.C.R. 1891.
[218] Case 266/85, *Shenavai v Kreischer* [1987] E.C.R. 239 at [16].

The existence of mandatory rules designed to protect employees and of collective agreements, made the fragmentation of employment cases between jurisdictions especially undesirable. In the Brussels I and Brussels I *bis* Regulations, provisions reflecting this earlier case-law form section 5 of each Regulation.[219]

As is the case with the comparable provisions as to insurance and consumer contracts, the Section provides an almost exclusive code, and with two exceptions other bases of jurisdiction cannot be relied upon: the exceptions are arts 6 (application of national jurisdictional rules in certain cases); 7(5) (disputes concerning the operations of a branch, agency or other establishment) and 8(1) (co-defendants)[220] In addition, the general rule giving jurisdiction to the court of a Member States before which a defendant enters an appearance[221] applies in the employment context as elsewhere.

The scope of this protective code has been understood to be quite extensive.[222] "Matters *relating to* individual contracts of employment" has been given a broad interpretation: a dispute could *'relate to'* a contract of employment even though the claim itself sounded in tort.[223]

An employer domiciled in a Member State may be sued in the courts of the Member State where the employer is domiciled (a rule corresponding to that in art.4 of the Brussels I *bis* Regulation). If an employee works at different times for two companies, in the same group but with different domiciles, it is possible for an employee instituting proceedings to make use of the co-defendants rule of art.8 of the Brussels I *bis* Regulation.[224] This is a welcome improvement on the Brussels I Regulation, where this possibility was not expressly indicated by the text of the Regulation and the ECJ held, for frankly unconvincing reasons, that it was not possible.[225]

The Regulation does not define "employer", "employee" or "individual contract of employment" and the CJEU has held that these legal concepts that must be given an independent interpretation common to all the Member States.[226] A "contract of employment" may pre-suppose a relationship of subordination of the employee to the employer.[227] The essential feature of an employment

---

[219] Regulation 1215/2012 arts. 20-23; reg.44/2001 arts. 18-21. See Grušić, (2012) 61 I.C.L.Q. 91.
[220] Regulation 1215/2012 art.20(1); reg.44/2001 art.18(1).
[221] Regulation 1215/2012 art.26; reg.44/2001 art.24.
[222] *Alfa-Laval Tumba AB v Separator Spares International Ltd* [2012] EWCA Civ 1569; [2013] I.C.R. 455; *Petter v EMC Europe Ltd [2015] EWCA Civ 828; [2015] C.P. Rep. 47.*
[223] *Alfa-Laval Tumba AB v Separator Spares International Ltd* [2012] EWCA Civ 1569; [2013] I.C.R. 455.
[224] See para.6–033.
[225] Case C-462/06 *GlaxoSmithKline v Rouard* [2008] E.C.R. I-3965; see Harris, (2008) 124 L.Q.R. 523.
[226] See, inter alia *Mahamdia v Algeria* (C-154/11) [2014] All E.R. (EC) 96, at [42]; *Holterman Ferho Exploitatie v F.L.F. Spies von Büllesheim* (C-47/14) *[2015] I.L.Pr. 789; Petter v EMC Europe Ltd* [2015] EWCA Civ 828; [2015] C.P. Rep. 47.
[227] Jenard Report, OJ 1990 C 189, p. 57.

relationship is that for a certain period of time one person performs services for and under the direction of another in return for which he receives remuneration.[228]

How is the employee protected in these scenarios?

Article 22 of the Brussels I *bis* Regulation provides: 6–045

> "1.   An employer may bring proceedings only in the courts of the Member State in which the employee is domiciled.
> 2.   The provisions of this Section shall not affect the right to bring a counter-claim in the court in which, in accordance with this Section, the original claim is pending."

Article 23 of the Brussels I *bis* Regulation provides:
The provisions of this Section may be departed from only by an agreement:

> "1.   which is entered into after the dispute has arisen; or
> 2   which allows the employee to bring proceedings in courts other than those indicated in this Section."

The scope of the jurisdiction over actions against employers is extended by the rule that where an employee enters into an individual contract of employment with an employer who is *not* domiciled in a Member State but has a branch, agency or other establishment in one of the Member States, the employer is, in disputes arising out of the operations of the branch, agency or establishment, deemed to be domiciled in that Member State.[229]

Forum actoris

Article 21 of the Brussels I *bis* Regulation provides: 6–046

> "1.   An employer domiciled in a Member State may be sued:
> (a)   in the courts of the Member State in which he is domiciled; or
> (b)   in another Member State:
> (i)   in the courts for the place where or from where the employee habitually carries out his work or in the courts for the last place where he did so; or
> (ii)   if the employee does not or did not habitually carry out his work in any one country, in the courts for the place where the business which engaged the employee is or was situated.
> 2.   An employer not domiciled in a Member State may be sued in a court of a Member State in accordance with point (b) of paragraph 1."

Thus the employer may also be sued in a Member State other than that of the employer's domicile:

(a)   in the courts for the place where the employee habitually carries out his work or in the courts for the last place where he did so, or

---

[228] Case C-47/14 *Holterman Ferho Exploitatie v F.L.F. Spies von Büllesheim* [2015] I.L.Pr. 789, at [41] referring to concepts used in EU law more generally.
[229] Regulation 1215/2012 art.20(2); reg.44/2001 art.18(2).

(b)   if the employee does not or did not habitually carry out his work in any one country, in the courts for the place where the business which engaged the employee is or was situated.[230]

The approach taken to the rule in sub-paragraph (a) reflects a concern that where work is performed in more than one Member State, it is important to avoid any multiplication of courts having jurisdiction, so that the rule should not be read as conferring concurrent jurisdiction on the courts of each of the states involved.[231]

The *forum actoris* protection has been extended expressly to non-EU domiciled employers by virtue of art.21(2) allowing the employee to institute proceedings against an employer not domiciled in a Member State in a court of a Member State in accordance with points (a) and (b).

In *Rutten v Cross Medical Ltd*[232] the plaintiff had an office in the Netherlands to which he returned after each business trip, but spent only two-thirds of his time in that country, the rest in other States. The Court equated the place where the employee habitually carries out his work with the place in which the employee had "established the effective centre of his working time and where, or from which, he in fact performs the essential part of his duties *vis-à-vis* his employer" (in that case, the Netherlands). The Court noted that that is the place where it is least expensive for the employee to commence proceedings against the employer or to defend himself in such proceedings. The courts for that place are also best placed and, therefore, the most appropriate to resolve the dispute relating to the contract of employment.

This development was taken further in *Weber v Universal Ogden Services*[233] where the Court held that the place where the employee actually performed the essential part of his duties was normally the place where, the whole of the term of employment being taken into account, the employee spent most of his working time engaged on the employer's business, but that it could be otherwise if there were circumstances showing that the subject matter of the dispute was more closely connected with a different place. That might involve looking at the nature and importance of the work done in each place.

The employee is further protected by the rule that an employer may bring proceedings only in the courts of the Member State in which the employee is domiciled.[234] The employee is also protected against the effect of jurisdiction clauses. The rules as to jurisdiction over employment contracts may be departed from only by an agreement (a) which is entered into after the dispute has arisen; or (b) which allows the employee to bring proceedings in courts other than those indicated in those rules.[235]

---

[230] Regulation 1215/2012 art.21(2); reg.44/2001 art.19(2).

[231] Case C-125/92 *Mulox IBC Ltd v Geels* [1993] E.C.R. I-4075.

[232] Case C-383/95, [1997] E.C.R. I-57 (dealing with the equivalent phrase which then formed part of art.5(1) of the Brussels Convention.

[233] Case C-37/00, [2002] Q.B. 1189.

[234] Regulation 1215/2012 art.22(1); reg.44/2001 art.20(1). But the provisions of s.5 do not affect the employer's right to bring a counter-claim in the court in which, in accordance with the section, the original claim is pending: art.22(2).

[235] Regulation 1215/2012 art.23; reg.44/200 art.21.

EXCLUSIVE JURISDICTION

The Regulation sometimes gives "exclusive jurisdiction"[236] to the courts of a   **6–047**
particular country. The term has a special meaning in the Regulation, reflecting
the fact that the Member States have agreed that where a case concerns a
particular subject matter the courts of one country within the EU, and one country
only, can hear the case. The allocation of exclusive jurisdiction operates
regardless of the defendant's domicile.[237] If a court of one Member State finds
itself seised of a claim which is principally concerned[238] with a matter over which
the courts of another Member State have exclusive jurisdiction, it must declare of
its own motion that it has no jurisdiction.[239] The types of case in which there is
exclusive jurisdiction are set out in art.24 of the Brussels I *bis* Regulation.[240]

Before that provision is examined, it is necessary to identify and distinguish
two other situations arising under the Regulation. The first is where the parties
have reached a choice-of-court agreement, under which a court is identified as
having exclusive jurisdiction over the dispute. Rather different rules apply in this
type of case, and they are considered below.[241] The second situation is one in
which the Regulation provides that a certain claim (by an insurer, or against a
consumer or employee) may only be brought in the country in which the
defendant is domiciled. This is not strictly a case of exclusive jurisdiction, not
least because, as we have seen, the defendant may be domiciled in more than one
country.

Exhaustive list of exclusive jurisdiction bases

In considering whether any particular claim falls within the jurisdictional rules of   **6–048**
the European regime, it is wise to begin with art.24 of the Brussels I *bis*
Regulation on exclusive jurisdiction. This Article applies regardless of the
domicile of the defendant; that means that it is relevant even if the defendant is
domiciled in, say, New Zealand, a non-Member State. The cases in which a court
has exclusive jurisdiction under art.24 are defined by reference to the "object" of
the relevant proceedings, which refers to the nature of the subject matter,[242] not to
the purpose of the claimant in bringing the action.[243] A court that has exclusive
jurisdiction under art.24 of the Brussels I *bis* Regulation ousts the jurisdiction of
other potentially competent courts.

---

[236] See para.5–009.

[237] For example, Case C-73/04 *Klein v Rhodos Management Ltd* [2005] E.C.R. I-8667.

[238] What is the principal issue in a case may be difficult to determine, especially at the outset; see *Newtherapeutics Ltd v Katz* [1991] Ch. 226 (issue of whether a resolution of a Board of Directors authorised acts appeared the principal issue, not the issue of breach of duty involved in the acts themselves).

[239] Regulation 1215/2012 art.27; reg.44/2001 art.25.

[240] Regulation 1215/2012 art.24; reg.44/2001 art.22.

[241] At paras 6–054 and following.

[242] See Case C-103/05 *Reisch Montage AG v Kiesel Baumaschinen Handels GmbH* [2006] E.C.R. I-6827; Case 73/77 *Sanders v Van del Putte* [1977] E.C.R. 2383; Case C-8/98 *Dansommer A/S v Gotz* [2000] E.C.R. I-393; [2001] 1 W.L.R. 1069; Case C-343/04 *Land Oberosterreich v CEZ* [2006] E.C.R. I-4457.

[243] *Newtherapeutics Ltd v Katz* [1991] Ch. 226.

Article 24 grants exclusive jurisdiction to the following courts:

Exclusive jurisdiction in certain cases involving immovable property

6–049
"in proceedings which have as their object rights in rem in, or tenancies of, immovable property; the courts of the Member State in which the property is situated;"

This is subject to qualifications in respect of certain short-term lettings, and the matter is more fully examined in the context of immovables.[244]

Exclusive jurisdiction in proceedings involving validity of the constitution, nullity or dissolution of corporations

6–050
"in proceedings which have as their object the validity of the constitution, the nullity or the dissolution of companies or other legal persons or associations of natural or legal persons, or the validity of a decision of their organs; the courts of the Member State in which the company, legal person or association has its seat."[245]

This head of jurisdiction includes proceedings for the winding-up of solvent companies, but the winding-up of insolvent companies is outside the scope of the Regulation.[246] Where the proceedings have as their object a decision of an organ, the jurisdiction of the English courts is not exclusive as against the courts of other parts of the UK.[247] In *Hassett v South Eastern Health Board*,[248] the CJEU held that proceedings where the issue was whether a decision adopted by the organ of a company had infringed the rights of one of the parties under that company's articles of association did not concern the "validity of a decision" for the purposes of this exclusive jurisdiction provision. In *Berliner Verkehrsbetriebe (BVG) v JP Morgan Chase Bank NA*,[249] the CJEU explained that what was then art.22(2) did not apply to proceedings in which a company pleaded that a contract could not be relied upon against it because the contract's conclusion by its organs was invalid on account of infringement of its statutes. It is apparent from the case law of the CJEU that, as in the case of other "special" jurisdictional grounds that represent an exception to the "general" rule of jurisdiction based on the defendant's domicile, the interpretation given to exclusive jurisdiction grounds is narrow and should not be extended.[250]

---

[244] See para.17–005.

[245] An example is a dispute about the appointment of directors: *Speed Investments Ltd v Formula One Holdings Ltd (No.2)* [2004] EWCA Civ 1512; [2005] 1 W.L.R. 1936. For the seat, see above, para.6–010.

[246] Regulation 1215/2012 art.2(b); reg.44/2001 art.1(2)(g). See the Schlosser report, paras 57–58.

[247] See Civil Jurisdiction and Judgments Act 1982 Sch.4, r.11(b) as substituted by SI 2001/3929.

[248] Case C-372/07 [2008] E.C.R. I-7403.

[249] Case C-144/10 *Berliner Verkehrsbetriebe (BVG) v JP Morgan Chase Bank NA* [2011] 1 W.L.R. 2087. See also *UBS AG v Kommunale Wasserwerke Leipzig GmbH* [2010] EWHC 2566 (Comm); [2010] 2 CLC 499.

[250] Contrast this with the broad interpretation given by the English courts to the European regime in connection with heads of protective jurisdiction in matters in relation to contracts of employment, see above, para.6–044.

Exclusive jurisdiction in proceedings concerning the validity of entries in public registers

"in proceedings which have as their object the validity of entries in public registers, the courts of the Member State in which the register is kept."

6–051

The scope of this head is limited in the English situation, given that cases involving the registration of land will usually be covered by the first head; an example might be a case involving the Register of Aircraft Mortgages kept by the Civil Aviation Authority.

Exclusive jurisdiction in proceedings concerning Intellectual property rights

"in proceedings which concern the registration or validity of patents, trademarks, design or other similar rights required to be deposited or registered, the courts of the Member State in which the deposit or registration has been applied for or has taken place (or is deemed by virtue of a European instrument or an international convention to have taken place), or in which a European patent has been granted."

6–052

Infringement proceedings may be included, where the substance of the dispute is the validity of the patent or other right allegedly infringed, regardless of which party raises the validity issue.[251] In *Lucasfilm Ltd v Ainsworth*[252] the UK Supreme Court decided that this provision did not apply to infringement actions where there was not a validity issue.[253] Copyright actions are likely to be outside the scope of this provision.[254]

Exclusive jurisdiction for the enforcement of judgments

"in proceedings which concern the enforcement of judgments, the courts of the Member State in which the judgment has been or is to be enforced."[255]

6–053

This provision on exclusive jurisdiction ranks most highly in the pyramid of jurisdictional grounds of the European regime. It cannot be derogated from by the voluntary submission by the defendant to the courts of another Member State, and it cannot be contracted out by a choice of court agreement by the parties. It is a mandatory rule.

---

[251] *Coin Controls Ltd v Suzo International (U.K.) Ltd* [1999] Ch. 33; Case C-4/03 *Gesellschaft für Antriebstechnik mbH & Co KG v Lamellen und Kupplungsbau Beteilings KG* [2006] E.C.R. I-6509.
[252] [2011] UKSC 39; [2012] 1 A.C. 208.
[253] ibid., paras 105–110.
[254] ibid.
[255] See *Kuwait Oil Tanker Co SAK v Qabazard* [2003] UKHL 31; [2004] 1 A.C. 300; *Masri v Consolidated Contractors International (UK) Ltd (No.2)* [2009] QB 450.

CONSENSUAL JURISDICTION: CHOICE OF COURT AGREEMENTS AND
SUBMISSION TO THE JURISDICTION

Choice of court agreements[256]

6–054 Any well-drafted contract which has factual links with more than one country will contain a choice of court agreement or jurisdiction clause. This is often in an "exclusive" form, providing that all disputes between the parties arising out of the contract *must* be referred to a named court or the courts of a named country. Less frequently it takes a "non-exclusive" form, the parties agreeing that disputes *may* be referred to such a court, without seeking to preclude any other possible forum. Whether a jurisdiction clause is exclusive or "non-exclusive" is a matter of construction of the contractual terms and in principle this construction should be done according to the law governing the agreement.[257] The court selected may be the English court or a foreign court. Different considerations apply to these different categories of case. As the case law discussed below reveals, the essential component of any choice of court agreement is the existence of consent.[258]

This is a sphere where the changes introduced in the Brussels I *bis* Regulation are most significant.[259] With a view to enhance the effectiveness of choice of court agreements,[260] and in line with the international developments in this field,[261] the relevant provision has been revised and changed to address the needs of international commerce, and the interaction between this provision and other provisions in the Regulation has been altered to tackle problems observed in the functioning of the system during the lifetime of the previous instruments, i.e. the 1968 Brussels Convention and the original Brussels I Regulation, such as abusive litigation tactics that often undermined the effect of jurisdiction agreements.[262]

Article 25 of the Brussels I *bis* Regulation provides:

> "1.　If the parties, *regardless of their domicile*, have agreed that a court or the courts of a Member State are to have jurisdiction to settle any disputes which have arisen or which may arise in connection with a particular legal relationship, that court or those courts shall have jurisdiction, *unless the agreement is null and void as to its substantive validity under the law of that Member State*. Such jurisdiction shall be exclusive unless the parties have agreed otherwise. The agreement conferring jurisdiction shall be either:
>
> (a)　in writing or evidenced in writing;
> (b)　in a form which accords with practices which the parties have established between themselves; or

---

[256] See Hartley, *Choice-of-court Agreements under the European and International Instruments* (Oxford: Oxford University Press, 2013).

[257] See *Bank of New York Mellon v GV Films* [2009] EWHC 2338 (Comm.); [2010] 1 Lloyd's Rep 365.

[258] See, inter alia, C-543/10 *Refcomp SpA v Axa Corporate Solutions Assurance SA* (third party sub-buyer, claim against the manufacturer).

[259] See Hartley (2012) 128 L.Q.R. 197; Ratkoviæ and Zgrabljiærotar (2013) 9 J Priv. Int. L. 245; Ballesteros (2014) 10 J. Priv. Int. L. 291; Bowen (2014) 24 S.L.T. 99; Queirolo (2013/2014) 15 Yb. P.I.L. 113.

[260] Regulation 1215/2012, recital 22.

[261] The Hague Convention on Choice of Court Agreements has been discussed in the previous chapter, paras 5–017 and following.

[262] Case C-111/01 *Erich Gasser GmbH v MISAT Srl* [2003] E.C.R. I-14693; [2005] Q.B. 1.

(c)   in international trade or commerce, in a form which accords with a usage of which the parties are or ought to have been aware and which in such trade or commerce is widely known to, and regularly observed by, parties to contracts of the type involved in the particular trade or commerce concerned.

2.   Any communication by electronic means which provides a durable record of the agreement shall be equivalent to 'writing'.

3.   The court or courts of a Member State on which a trust instrument has conferred jurisdiction shall have exclusive jurisdiction in any proceedings brought against a settlor, trustee or beneficiary, if relations between those persons or their rights or obligations under the trust are involved.

4.   Agreements or provisions of a trust instrument conferring jurisdiction shall have no legal force if they are contrary to Arts 15, 19 or 23, or if the courts whose jurisdiction they purport to exclude have exclusive jurisdiction by virtue of Art.24.

5.   An agreement conferring jurisdiction which forms part of a contract shall be treated as an agreement independent of the other terms of the contract.
        The validity of the agreement conferring jurisdiction cannot be contested solely on the ground that the contract is not valid."

The main changes can be summarised as follows:

(1)   Under art.23 of the Brussels I Regulation, a choice of court agreement did not have priority in the event of prior parallel proceedings in another Member State. Accordingly, a court having jurisdiction pursuant to a choice of court agreement could not hear the case if a court in another Member State was first seised and assumed jurisdiction. In the Brussels I *bis* Regulation jurisdiction based on art.25 may not be declined in the event of parallel proceedings, unless the courts of another state has overriding exclusive jurisdiction (as provided in art.24 of this instrument) or in the event of subsequent submission to the jurisdiction (as indicated in art.26 of the Brussels I *bis* Regulation).

(2)   Article 23 of the Brussels I Regulation applied only if at least one of the parties was domiciled in the EU, therefore, agreements where both parties were non-EU domiciles were governed by national law. Article 25 of the Brussels I *bis* Regulation applies regardless of the domicile of the parties.

(3)   Under art.23 of the Brussels I Regulation, where the parties neither of whom was domiciled in a Member State had agreed to the jurisdiction of the courts of a Member State, the courts of another Member State had to stay its proceedings unless the designated court had declined jurisdiction. This type of agreement is now covered by the extended approach of art.25 of the Brussels I *bis* Regulation.

(4)   In the Brussels I Regulation there was uncertainty as to the law governing the substantive validity of the choice of court agreement. Article 25(1) of the Brussels I *bis* Regulation clarifies the point by establishing that the applicable law to the substantive validity of the choice of court agreement shall be the law of the chosen forum.

Furthermore, art.31 of the Brussels I *bis* Regulation provides:

"1.   Where actions come within the exclusive jurisdiction of several courts, any court other than the court first seised shall decline jurisdiction in favour of that court.

2.   Without prejudice to Art.26, where a court of a Member State on which an agreement as referred to in Art.25 confers exclusive jurisdiction is seised, any court of another

Member State shall stay the proceedings until such time as the court seised on the basis of the agreement declares that it has no jurisdiction under the agreement.

3. Where the court designated in the agreement has established jurisdiction in accordance with the agreement, any court of another Member State shall decline jurisdiction in favour of that court.

4. Paragraphs 2 and 3 shall not apply to matters referred to in Sections 3, 4 or 5 where the policyholder, the insured, a beneficiary of the insurance contract, the injured party, the consumer or the employee is the claimant and the agreement is not valid under a provision contained within those Sections."

The effect of the provisions in art.31 is to reverse the effect of *Erich Gasser GmbH v MISAT Srl*.[263] Article 31 gives priority (except in the case of insurance, consumer and employment contracts, where the jurisdiction agreement is not effective under the relevant provisions) to the court of the designated Member State to decide whether the jurisdiction agreement is effective.

Clauses selecting the courts of an EU Member State

6–055 A clause giving jurisdiction to the English courts or those of another Member State will often fall within art.25 of the Brussels I *bis* Regulation.[264] Subject to the operation of the Hague Convention on Choice of Court Agreements,[265] art.25(1) applies to agreements as to jurisdiction between parties, regardless of their domicile, and which meet certain formal requirements. These are that the clause must be (a) in writing or evidenced in writing, any communication by electronic means which can provide a durable record of the agreement being treated as in writing[266]; or (b) in a form which accords with practices which the parties have established between themselves[267]; or (c) in international trade or commerce, in a form which accords with a usage of which the parties are, or ought to be, aware and which in such trade or commerce is widely known to, and regularly observed by, parties to contracts of the type involved in the particular trade or commerce concerned.[268] National law may not invalidate agreements by requiring additional formalities to those prescribed by art.25.[269]

The meaning of "evidenced in writing" has exercised the courts. The courts have repeatedly emphasised that the real issue is that of consensus between the

---

[263] Case C–116/02, [2005] Q.B. 1; [2003] E.C.R. I-14693.

[264] See Camilleri, (2011) 7 J.Priv.Int.L. 297; Steinle and Vasiliades, (2010) 6 J.Priv.Int.L. 565; on the difficulties in relation to asymmetrical and unilateral optional choice of court agreements see Keyes and Marshall, (2015) 11 J.Priv.Int.L 345.

[265] Article 26(6). See para.5–017.

[266] Regulation 1215/2012 art.25(1)(a); reg.44/2001 art.23(2).

[267] This possibility eases some practical problems, e.g. that of the tacit renewal of written clauses which have in their own terms expired; see Case 313/85 *Iveco Fiat SpA v Van Hool NV* [1986] E.C.R. 3337.

[268] See Case C-106/95 *Mainschiffahrts-Genossenschaft eG v Les Gravieres Rhenanes SARL* [1997] E.C.R. I-911.

[269] Case 150/80 *Elefanten Schuh v Jacqmain* [1981] E.C.R. 1671.

parties; the written material is evidence of that consensus.[270] General references to standard conditions of contract will not suffice; more specific evidence of agreement is required.[271]

So, in *Estasis Salotti de Colzani Amo e Giammario Colzani v RUWA Polstereimaschinen GmbH*[272]:

> A German company, R, wrote to C, an Italian company, offering for sale a number of machines used in making furniture. The letters referred to R's general conditions of sale which were printed on the back. Those conditions permitted R to bring any claim in the courts of Cologne. The offer was accepted and a written contract drawn up, again with the conditions on the reverse. C refused to take delivery of the machines. R began proceedings in Cologne, where the court held it had no jurisdiction.

The CJEU held that where a clause conferring jurisdiction is included among the general conditions of sale of one of the parties, printed on the back of a contract, the "in writing" requirement of what is now art.(1) is fulfilled only if the contract signed by both parties contains an express reference to those general conditions.

In *Crédit Suisse Financial Products v Société Générale d'Entreprises*[273] and *7E Communications Ltd v Vertex Antennentechnik GmbH*[274] the Court of Appeal applied that decision, holding that a guarantee that the relevant party has "really consented to the clause" exists where there is an express reference to the terms and conditions which include the jurisdiction clause. It is not necessary for there to be a specific reference to the jurisdiction clause itself. The fact that the relevant party does not have a copy of the terms and conditions or the jurisdiction clause in his possession is not relevant.[275]

In *El Majdoub v CarsOnTheWeb.Deutschland GmbH*[276] the CJEU held that the method of accepting the general terms and conditions of a contract for sale by 'click-wrapping' (i.e. a licence agreement which appears as an icon during the setup of a software program or online service and must be clicked on to agree to its terms (ticking a box online)), which contains an agreement conferring jurisdiction, constitutes a communication by electronic means which provides a durable record of the agreement, within the meaning of the provision, where that method makes it possible to print and save the text of those terms and conditions before the conclusion of the contract.[277]

---

[270] *Deutsche Bank AG v Asia Pacific Broadband Wireless Communications Inc* [2008] EWCA Civ 1091; [2008] 2 Lloyd's Rep 619.

[271] Case 24/76 *Estasis Salotti de Colzani Amo e Giammario Colzani v RUWA Polstereimaschinen GmbH* [1976] E.C.R. 1831; Case 25/76 *Galeries Segoura sprl v Rahim Bonakdarian* [1976] E.C.R. 1851.

[272] Case 24/76, [1976] E.C.R. 1831.

[273] [1997] CLC 168.

[274] [2007] EWCA Civ 140; [2007] 1 W.L.R. 2175.

[275] See *Coys of Kensington Automobiles Ltd v Pugliese* [2011] EWHC 655 (QB); [2011] 2 All E.R. (Comm) 664; *Sherdley v Nordea Life and Pension SA* [2012] EWCA Civ 88.

[276] Case C-322/14 *El Majdoub v CarsOnTheWeb.Deutschland GmbH*, Judgment of the CJEU (Third Chamber) of 21 May 2015.

[277] At [40].

A case in which agreement could not be shown is *Lafarge Plasterboard Ltd v Fritz Peters & Co KG*[278]:

> L was an English company making gypsum plasterboard. F was a German company, supplying liner paper for gypsum plaster-board. F approached L offering to supply liner paper. An order was placed. On the back were L's terms of trade including a clause giving exclusive jurisdiction to the English courts. There was nothing on the face of the order form drawing attention to the fact that there were conditions printed on the back. L had different conditions in other documents; F's conditions conflicted with L's. L sued in England and F contested the jurisdiction; L relied on (what is now) art.25.

The Court noted that if the requirements of the article were satisfied, the choice was mandatory.[279] Before it could apply, the Court had to be satisfied that there had been a consensus between the parties[280]; the detailed requirements as to formalities were designed to help the court in making that assessment. On the facts, there was no consistent practice on which the parties could rely. There was no document in which the defendant had expressed in writing consent to the conditions containing the jurisdiction clause: the mere printing of a jurisdiction clause on the reverse of a bill of lading did not satisfy the requirements of the Regulation, as such a procedure gave no guarantee that the other party had actually consented to the clause derogating from the ordinary jurisdiction rules of the Regulation.

A written document confirming the oral agreement need not be produced by the party bound by the clause so long as there is evidence of acceptance by that party[281]; in one case the articles or statutes of a company were relied upon.[282] A more common practice where the agreement is essentially oral is for one party to confirm the agreement by fax or email; if the other party receives the confirmation and does not object, agreement may be established.[283] The choice of forum may be upheld even if the contract within which it is contained, or by which it is evidenced, is void or vitiated by misrepresentation or want of authority.[284] An agreement meeting these requirements and specifying a court or courts of a Member State[285] gives that court or those courts jurisdiction for the purposes of the Regulation. Unless the parties have agreed otherwise, such jurisdiction is exclusive.

---

[278] [2000] 2 Lloyd's Rep. 689.

[279] See also *Equitas Ltd v Allstate Insurance Co* [2008] EWHC 1671 (Comm.); [2009] 1 All E.R. (Comm) 1137; *UBS AG v HSH Nordbank AG* [2009] EWCA Civ 585; [2009] 2 Lloyd's Rep 272.

[280] See also Case C-543/10 *Refcomp SpA v Axa Corporate Solutions Assurance SA* [2013] 1 All E.R. (Comm) 1201.

[281] Case 71/83 *Partenreederei MS Tilly Russ v Haven & Vervoebedrijf Nova NV* [1985] Q.B. 931; Case 221/84 *Berghoefer GmbH v ASA SA* [1985] E.C.R. 2699. See also *Calyon v Wytwornia Sprzetu Kommunikacynego PZL Swidnik SA* [2009] EWHC 1914 (Comm); [2009] 2 All E.R. (Comm) 603. cf. *Lafarge Plasterboard Ltd v Fritz Peters & Co KG* [2000] 2 Lloyd's Rep 689.

[282] Case 214/89 *Powell Duffryn v Petereit* [1992] E.C.R. I-1745.

[283] Case 221/84 *Berghoefer GmbH v ASA SA* [1985] E.C.R. 2699.

[284] *Deutsche Bank AG v Asia Pacific Broadband Wireless Communications Inc* [2008] EWCA Civ 1091; [2008] 2 Lloyd's Rep 619.

[285] See Case C-387/98 *Coreck Maritime GmbH v Handelsveem BV* [2000] E.C.R. I-9337 (clause named no country but referred to country where party had its principal place of business; that held sufficient to meet requirements of art.23).

It remains unclear how a claim that apparent consent to the clause was vitiated by fraud or duress should be treated. The CJEU has asserted that the formal requirements required by the European regime are a sufficient safeguard,[286] but that seems to fly in the face of logic: formal compliance can be secured by fraud. The case of *Deutsche Bank AG v Asia Pacific Broadband Wireless Communications Inc*[287] is illustrative in this context.

> The case involved a credit agreement including an exclusive jurisdiction clause in favour of the English courts. The claimant bank brought proceedings in England. The defendants argued that the credit agreement was void, alleging that it was part of a large-scale fraud. The Court of Appeal relied on the doctrine of severability or separability: a jurisdiction clause is a separable agreement from the agreement as a whole. It was only if the jurisdiction clause was itself under some specific attack (e.g. were fraud or duress to be alleged in relation specifically to the jurisdiction clause) that the jurisdiction clause could be challenged.

Separability of choice of court agreements

The principle of separability or severability of choice of court agreements has been expressly recognised in the Brussels I *bis* Regulation. Following the lead of the Hague Convention on Choice of Court Agreements[288] and adopting a principle that is well-established in the practice of arbitration, art.25(5) provides that a jurisdiction clause in a contract is to be treated as an agreement independent of the other terms of the contract. Hence, a challenge to the validity of the main contract will not prevent the chosen court from hearing the merits in relation to that challenge or any other claim arising out of that contract.

6–056

Scope of jurisdiction clauses

So far as the scope of jurisdiction clauses is concerned, the courts seek to give effect to the will of the parties as effectively[289] as possible. Therefore jurisdiction clauses are usually interpreted as to cover all disputes between the contracting parties[290] in the belief that the parties are likely to intend than any dispute arising out of their relationship should be decided by the same court.[291] On these lines, choice of court agreements should be interpreted "widely and generously".[292]

6–057

---

[286] Case C-159/97 Soc. *Trasporti Castelletti Spedizioni Internazionali SpA v Hugo Trumpy SpA* [1999] E.C.R. I-1597; and see Case C-269/95 *Benincasa v Dentalkit Srl* [1997] E.C.R. I-3767.

[287] [2008] EWCA Civ 1091; [2008] 2 Lloyd's Rep. 619.

[288] See paras 5–017 and following.

[289] See *Deutsche Bank AG v Asia Pacific Broadband Wireless Communications Inc* [2008] EWCA Civ 1091; [2008] 2 Lloyd's Rep. 619.

[290] ibid.; *UBS AG v HSH Nordbank AG* [2009] EWCA Civ 585; [2009] 2 Lloyd's Rep. 272; *Cinnamon European Structured Credit Master Fund v Banco Commercial Portugues SA* [2009] EWHC 3381 (Ch); [2010] I.L.Pr. 11.

[291] *Premium Nafta Products Ltd v Fili Shipping Co Ltd* [2007] UKHL 40; [2007] 4 All E.R. 951, at para.13.

[292] *UBS AG v HSH Nordbank AG* [2009] EWCA Civ 585; [2009] 2 Lloyd's Rep. 272, at para.82. For a thorough discussion on the scope of jurisdiction agreements see R Fentiman, International Commercial Litigation (2015) paras 2.53 and following.

It is possible for a defendant to waive the clause, e.g. by submitting to the jurisdiction of another court selected by the claimant.[293]

Exclusive jurisdiction clauses choosing the English courts

6–058 An exclusive jurisdiction clause satisfying the requirements of art.25[294] and naming the English courts will plainly give those courts exclusive jurisdiction. There can be no question of the English court refusing to exercise jurisdiction. Should proceedings be begun in another Member State, the court in that state will be required to stay its proceedings, but there is no possibility of the English court restraining those proceedings by an anti-suit injunction.[295]

Submission to the jurisdiction

6–059 Article 26 of the Brussels I *bis* Regulation[296] provides that apart from jurisdiction derived from other provisions of the Regulation, a court of a Member State before which a defendant enters an appearance has jurisdiction. This rule does not apply where appearance was entered to contest the jurisdiction,[297] or where another court has exclusive jurisdiction. But it does apply where the parties have chosen another court under Art.25;[298] thus, if there is a conflict, the provisions of art.26 prevail over those of art.25.

In *Deutsche Bahn AG v Morgan Advanced Materials Plc (formerly Morgan Crucible Co Plc)*[299] the claimants argued that the defendant had submitted to the jurisdiction by taking steps in the proceedings to contest jurisdiction whilst contesting the merits. The English Court of Appeal, in line with the case law of the CJEU,[300] made clear that, provided that the intention to contest jurisdiction was evinced at the outset, a submission that also contested the merits was not to be considered as submission for the purposes of attribution of jurisdiction.

CONCURRENT JURISDICTION: THE POSSIBILITY OF PARALLEL PROCEEDINGS

6–060 Within the framework of the European regime of jurisdiction, it is plainly possible for the courts of two or more Member States to have jurisdiction (concurrent jurisdiction). In a contractual claim for example, one State may be

---

[293] Case 150/80 *Elefanten Schuh v Jacqmain* [1981] E.C.R. 1671.

[294] Regulation 1215/2012 art.25; reg.44/2001 art.23.

[295] Under the principle of Case C-111/01 *Erich Gasser GmbH v MISAT Srl* [2003] E.C.R. I-14693; [2005] Q.B. 1.

[296] Regulation 1215/2012 art.26; reg.44/2001 art.24.

[297] See Case 150/80 *Elefanten Schuh v Jacqmain* [1981] E.C.R. 1671 (but note that the Regulation, unlike the earlier texts does not speak of appearance entered *solely* to contest the jurisdiction).

[298] Case 150/80 *Elefanten Schuh v Jacqmain* [1981] E.C.R. 1671.

[299] *Deutsche Bahn AG v Morgan Advanced Materials Plc (formerly Morgan Crucible Co Plc)* [2013] EWCA Civ 1484. See also *Future New Developments Ltd v B&S Patente Und Marken GmbH* [2014] EWHC 1874 and *Deutsche Bank AG London Branch v Petromena ASA* [2015] EWCA Civ 226; [2015] 1 W.L.R. 4225.

[300] Case 150/80 *Elefanten Schuh v Jacqmain* [1981] E.C.R. 1671.

the country in which the defendant is domiciled, and its courts will have jurisdiction under art.4 of the Brussels I bis Regulation, and the courts of another State may have special jurisdiction under art.7(1) as the place of performance of the obligation in question. The two parties may each seek to begin proceedings, selecting the courts of different Member States. In terms of legal technique, determining the most convenient jurisdiction in cases of concurrent jurisdiction is a difficult task for conflict of law rules. In most cases, as the example just given illustrates, the courts involved will be internationally competent to hear the merits, there being a close connection between the forum and the parties, or the forum and the dispute. In the Brussels I bis Regulation, the resulting problems are addressed in s.9 of Ch.II (arts 29–31). Articles 29 and 30 provide the courts with mechanisms to deal with the issues that may arise in these circumstances; these provisions apply regardless of the domicile of the parties[301] and independently of the basis of jurisdiction on which the proceedings are founded.[302]

Parallel proceedings: *lis alibi pendens*

The term *lis alibi pendens*, which is found in many of the older cases, refers to the situation in which what is essentially the same dispute is the subject of litigation in two or more countries. This is plainly undesirable, from the point of view of the courts as well as the parties, because of the extra costs involved and the risk that the two courts may make different and conflicting decisions.   **6–061**
Article 29 provides[303]:

> "Where proceedings involving the same cause of action and between the same parties are brought in the courts of different Member States, any court other than the court first seised shall of its own motion stay its proceedings until such time as the jurisdiction of the court first seised is established. Where the jurisdiction of the court first seised is established, any court other than the court first seised shall decline jurisdiction in favour of that court."

The same parties

The two sets of proceedings must involve the same parties, and it is immaterial whether or not either party is domiciled in a Member State.[304] This rule is easy to apply where the parties are single companies or individuals, but much litigation involves multiple parties, and it is not uncommon for proceedings to be commenced in different countries by different groups of claimants with overlapping membership. The CJEU has held, logically but inconveniently, that what was then art.27 has to be applied only where there is complete identity of parties.[305] This identity, it seems, is not entirely a question of names: an insurer   **6–062**

---

[301] Case C-351/89 *Overseas Union Insurance Ltd v New Hampshire Insurance Co* [1991] E.C.R. I-3317.
[302] *Trademark Licensing Co Ltd v Leofelis SA* [2009] EWHC 3285 (Ch); [2010] I.L.Pr. 16.
[303] The same provision is to be found in art.21 of the Brussels and Lugano Conventions.
[304] Case C-351/89 *Overseas Union Insurance Ltd v New Hampshire Insurance Co* [1991] E.C.R. I-3317.
[305] Case C-406/92 *The Tatry* [1994] E.C.R. I-5439 (actions by different groups of cargo-owners arising out of a single incident of cargo contamination). The Court suggested that flexible application of what is now art.28 (see below) would minimise the practical inconvenience of its decision.

and its insured, having identical interests, may be treated as the same party in this context[306] as may a company and its wholly-owned subsidiary.[307]

The Court of Appeal examined the interpretation of this proviso in *Kolden Holdings Ltd v Rodette Commerce Ltd*[308]:

> In March 2004, a group of companies sold their shareholdings in a Russian company to the defendants. A dispute arose, the seller companies maintaining that under the terms of the contract the defendants were obliged to pass on their newly-acquired shares to another company, but had not done so. In July 2006 the seller companies began an action in England seeking a declaration reflecting their position. On 14 February 2007 the defendants began proceedings in Cyprus (where all the relevant companies were incorporated) seeking a negative declaration on the same issues; the defendants were the seller companies and K. In November 2006 the seller companies assigned all their rights under the contract to K, and on 16 February 2007 (and so two days after the commencement of the Cyprus action) permission was given by the English court for K to be substituted as claimant in the English action.

The Court of Appeal held that the essential issue was whether there were on 14 February 2007 two sets of proceedings between "the same parties". If so, the subsequent substitution of K for the seller companies would not matter. It summarised the jurisprudence of the CJEU as saying that the term "between the same parties" had an autonomous meaning. In considering whether two entities were the "same party", the court looked to the substance, and not the form. Although the parties had to be "identical", that identity was not destroyed by the mere fact of there being separate legal entities involved. Whether they were identical might depend on whether there was such a degree of identity between the interests of the entities that a judgment given against one of them would have the force of res judicata as against the other. It would also depend on whether the interests of the entities were identical and indissociable, and it was for the national court to ascertain whether that was in fact the case. The test to determine whether parties were "the same parties" for this purpose was the "good arguable case" test. On the facts, that test was satisfied. A decision against K or against the seller companies, one would be res judicata as against the other; the interests of the seller companies and K were identical. It followed that the English court was the court first seised and the defendant's attempt to have the English proceedings stayed failed.

The same cause of action

6–063   Another problem is that of deciding, given the variety of legal categories used in different states, when the proceedings do involve "the same cause of action". This must be interpreted independently of any one national system, and attention will be paid to the underlying issue rather than the forms in which it is presented. It is not necessary that the cause of action should be absolutely identical: proceedings for specific performance of a contract may be regarded as based on the same

---

[306] Case C-351/96 *Drouot Assurances SA v Consolidated Metallurgical Industries* [1998] E.C.R. I-3057.

[307] *Berkeley Administration Inc v McClelland* [1995] I.L.Pr. 210. See *Turner v Grovit* [2000] Q.B. 345, CA (companies in same group treated as "same parties").

[308] [2008] EWCA Civ 10; [2008] 1 Lloyd's Rep. 434.

cause of action as proceedings seeking the annulment of the relevant contract.[309] Actions in personam and in rem may be treated as resting on the same cause of action if the subject matter and object of the proceedings do in fact coincide.[310] On the other hand, an action for infringement of a trademark and an action for passing off have been held not to be the same cause of action.[311] In *Lehman Brothers Bankhaus AG I. Ins v CMA CGM*[312] it was held that an action to determine the quantum of a debt was not the same as proceedings to suspend the duty of repayment.[313] In *The Alexandros T*[314] the UK Supreme Court held that a claim for a declaration that Greek proceedings were brought in breach of an exclusive jurisdiction clause in favour of the English courts was not the same cause of action as the tortious claim brought in Greece.

When is a court seised of a case?

The approach of giving priority to the court first seised makes it crucial to discover when exactly a court is "seised". The Brussels and Lugano Conventions offered no definition of the term and the CJEU interpreted it as requiring the case to be "definitively pending", itself a matter to be determined by the national law of each court.[315] In England, although the issue of the claim form has considerable procedural significance, the claim was held not to be "definitively pending" until it had been served.[316] This is no longer the position: the Brussels I and the Brussels I *bis* Regulations contains detailed rules to that effect,[317] which cater for the variant procedures found in Member States. A court is deemed to be seised: (1) in countries following procedures of the English type, at the time when the document instituting the proceedings is lodged with the court, i.e., when the claim form is issued, provided that the claimant has not subsequently failed to take the steps required to have service effected on the defendant, or (2) in other countries, if the document has to be served before being lodged with the court, at

6–064

---

[309] Case 144/86 *Gubisch Maschinenfabrik AG v Palumbo* [1987] E.C.R. 4861.

[310] See Case C-406/92 *The Tatry* [1994] E.C.R. I-5439 (where there were claims in rem for compensation for damage to cargo and an action by the shipowner for limitation of liability); *Republic of India v India Steamship Co Ltd (No.2)* [1998] A.C. 878.

[311] *Mecklermedia Corp v DC Congress GmbH* [1998] Ch. 40.

[312] [2013] EWHC 171 (Comm.).

[313] See also *Irish Bank Resolution Corp Ltd v Higgins* [2013] IEHC 178 (action to determine liability on a debt not the same as proceedings as to recoverable interest in consumer contracts).

[314] [2013] UKSC 70; [2014] 1 All E.R. 590 (reversing [2012] EWCA Civ 1714; [2013] 1 Lloyd's Rep. 217 *sub nom. Starlight Shipping Co v Allianz Marine & Aviation Versicherungs AG (The "Alexandros T")*.

[315] Case 129/83 *Zelger v Salintrini (No.2)* [1984] E.C.R. 2397.

[316] *Dresser (UK) Ltd v Falcongate Freight Management Ltd* [1992] Q.B. 502; *Neste Chemicals SA v DK Line SA, The Sargasso* [1994] 3 All E.R. 180; but cf. *Phillips v Symes (No.3)* [2008] UKHL 1; [2008] 1 W.L.R. 180 (Lugano Convention; procedural defect in service later cured by court order).

[317] Regulation 1215/2012 art.32; reg.44/2001 art.30. In *Debt Collect London Ltd v SK Slavia Praha-Fotbal AS* [2010] EWCA Civ 1250; [2011] 1 W.L.R. 866 the English court was deemed to be the court first seised where Czech proceedings had been lodged first but there had been a failure to take a step required for effecting service within the Brussels I Regulation art.30(1): the Czech court fee had not been paid.

the time when it is received by the authority responsible for service, provided that the claimant has not subsequently failed to take the steps required to have the document lodged with the court.

Practical implications

6–065   Article 29 is the main *lis pendens* (parallel proceedings) rule establishing the priority of the court first seised. It is often referred to as the "court first seised" rule, and its critics see it as mechanical and as encouraging a race to the court-house: each party may see an advantage in "getting in first" in its chosen forum. It has encouraged the so-called "torpedo action" litigation tactic. In these respects it stands in sharp contrast to the highly discretionary practice in the common law tradition, no longer available in cases within the scope of the Regulation,[318] which enabled the courts to steer cases to the most appropriate forum regardless of the speed with which the various parties may have acted.

The "court first seised" rule is strictly applied. It may sometimes happen that the court first seised does not in fact have jurisdiction under the Regulation: it may be that another court has exclusive jurisdiction, either under art.24 or under a choice of court agreement. The choice of court case arose under the 1968 Brussels Convention in *Erich Gasser GmbH v MISAT Srl*[319]:

> A contractual dispute arose between Italian and Austrian companies. The Italian company began proceedings in Italy, in effect for a negative declaration, asserting that the contract had been terminated and that it had not failed to carry out its obligations under the contract. Some eight months later, the Austrian company began proceedings in Austria, claiming sums due under the contract. The Austrian courts had exclusive jurisdiction by virtue of a clause in the contract.

The CJEU held that art.21 of the Brussels Convention, had to be interpreted as meaning that a court second seised whose jurisdiction had been claimed under an agreement conferring jurisdiction must nevertheless stay proceedings until the court first seised had declared that it has no jurisdiction.[320] The Court discussed and in effect overruled an English Court of Appeal decision to the contrary.[321]

This has dramatically changed in the Brussels I *bis* Regulation. As outlined above, the Brussels I *bis* Regulation in a welcomed innovation to enhance the effect of choice of court agreement has given priority to the chosen court in case of parallel proceedings.

Article 32 (2) of the Brussels I *bis* Regulation provides:

> "Without prejudice to Article 26 (exclusive jurisdiction), where a court of a Member State on which an agreement as referred to in Article 25 confers exclusive jurisdiction is seised, any

---

[318] See para.6–068 below.

[319] Case C-111/01, [2003] E.C.R. I-14693; [2005] Q.B. 1, noted Mance, (2002) 120 L.Q.R. 357, Fentiman, [2004] C.L.J. 312; Hartley in *Mélanges en l'honneur de Paul Lagarde* (Dalloz, Paris, 2005) at p.383. See *JP Morgan Europe Ltd v Primacom* [2005] EWHC 508 (Comm); [2005] 2 Lloyd's Rep. 665.

[320] The CJEU also ruled that long delays in the court first seised could not be relied on as justifying a departure from the "court first seised" rule.

[321] *Continental Bank NA v Aeokos Cia Naviera SA* [1994] 1 W.L.R. 588.

court of another Member State shall stay the proceedings until such time as the court seised on the basis of the agreement declares that it has no jurisdiction under the agreement."

A similar issue arises in the context of exclusive jurisdiction as provided in the exhaustive list of art.24 of the Brussels I *bis* Regulation (formerly art.22 of the original Brussels I Regulation). In *Weber v Weber*[322] the CJEU considered the extent to which a court second seised is obliged to stay its proceedings in order to allow the court first seised to determine its jurisdiction, where the second court has exclusive jurisdiction under the Regulation. It was held that where the jurisdiction of the court second seised is based on the exclusive jurisdiction rules, the second court must examine whether the judgment of the court first seised would be recognised or not; it would not if the court first seised lacked jurisdiction by virtue of the relevant exclusive jurisdiction provision. If it finds that a decision of the court first seised would, for that reason, not be recognised, the second court is not entitled to decline jurisdiction or stay its proceedings pursuant to the lis pendens provision, but must rule on the substance.

Parallel proceedings: related actions

Article 30 of the Brussels I *bis* Regulation, unusual in the context of the Regulation in giving a discretion[323] to the court, provides as follows:

6–066

"1. Where related actions are brought in the courts of different Member States, any court other than the court first seised may stay its proceedings.
2. Where these actions are pending at first instance, any court other than the court first seised may also, on the application of one of the parties, decline jurisdiction if the court first seised has jurisdiction over the actions in question and its law permits the consolidation thereof.
3. For the purposes of this Article, actions are deemed to be related where they are so closely connected that it is expedient to hear and determine them together to avoid the risk of irreconcilable judgments resulting from separate proceedings."

The discretion is two-fold, first, there is discretion as to whether or not the parallel proceedings are related; and second, if they are considered to be related, the 'secondary' court has discretion as to the decision whether or not to stay the proceedings.[324] Article 30(3) gives guidance as to when actions are deemed to be related—that is when they are so closely connected that it is preferable to hear them together, as separate proceedings could result in irreconcilable judgments

---

[322] Case C–438/12 *Weber v Weber* [2015] Ch. 140 (first proceedings in Italy; German court second seised but claimed exclusive jurisdiction as dispute involved a right in rem over immovable property in Germany).

[323] See *FKI Engineering Ltd v Stribog Ltd* [2011] EWCA Civ 622; [2011] 1 W.L.R. 3264.

[324] See *Starlight Shipping Co v Allianz Marine & Aviation Versicherungs AG (The Alexandros T)* [2013] UKSC 70; [2014] 1 All E.R. 590 (reversing [2012] EWCA Civ 1714; [2013] 1 Lloyd's Rep. 217 *sub nom. Starlight Shipping Co v Allianz Marine & Aviation Versicherungs AG.*) See Baatz (2014) L.M.C.L.Q. 159; McComish [2014] C.L.J. 270; Ahmed (2015) 11 J. Priv. Int. L. 406. See also *S E T Select Energy GmbH v F & M Bunkering Ltd* [2014] EWHC 192 (Comm.); [2014] 1 Lloyd's Rep. 652.

(inconsistent decisions). This discretion is for the courts other than the court first seised; that is, the court first seised has no discretion to stay proceedings under art.30.

"Risk of irreconcilable judgments"

6–067   The courts have sought to clarify the notion of a "risk of irreconcilable judgments". The CJEU has held that the risk is of conflicting decisions, even if there are no mutually exclusive legal consequences.[325] If two courts might give conflicting interpretations of identical contractual wording used in related transactions between different sets of parties, this would present a risk of irreconcilable judgments, even though each court's judgments could be executed. It is not always possible to predict the precise issues which a court may address, but in *Sarrio SA v Kuwait Investment Authority*[326] the House of Lords said that "a broad common sense approach" should be taken, and that it was not essential for a party seeking to rely on these provisions to show that a court would inevitably deal with certain issues.

As the Court of Appeal explained in Research in *Motion UK Ltd v Visto Corporation*,[327] the effect of this proviso is not entirely mechanical:

> "It requires an assessment of the degree of connection, and then a value judgment as to the expediency of hearing the two actions together (assuming they could be so heard) in order to avoid the risk of inconsistent judgments. It does not say that any possibility of inconsistent judgments means that they are inevitably related. It seems to us that the article leaves it open to a court to acknowledge a connection, or a risk of inconsistent judgments, but to say that the connection is not sufficiently close, or the risk is not sufficiently great, to make the actions related for the purposes of the article. Mechanics do not, for once, provide a complete answer."[328]

Article 31 of the Brussels I *bis* Regulation deals with the case in which two courts each have exclusive jurisdiction over the same case; the case must be heard by the court first seised.

The European regime of jurisdiction and non-Member States

6–068   One of the most controversial issues under the European regime of jurisdiction is whether the English court may, in cases where its jurisdiction is based on the jurisdictional grounds provided for by Ch.II of the Brussels I *bis* Regulation, stay proceedings or decline jurisdiction in favour of the courts of a non-Member State.[329]

---

[325] Case C-406/92 *The Tatry* [1994] E.C.R. I-5439.

[326] [1999] 1 A.C. 32.

[327] [2008] EWCA Civ 153; [2008] 2 All E.R. (Comm) 560.

[328] See *FKI Engineering Ltd v Stribog Ltd* [2011] EWCA Civ 622; [2011] 1 W.L.R. 3264 where members of the Court of Appeal expressed rather different views as to way in which the courts should address the issue.

[329] In the process of recasting the Brussels I Regulation, the EU Commission had included originally in its Proposal the extension of the scope of the Regulation to defendants domiciled outside the EU. This would have eliminated the possibility of English courts applying the English traditional rules of

The Brussels I *bis* Regulation includes discretionary *lis pendens* rules for disputes on the same cause of action and between the same parties (art.33) or related actions (art.34) which are pending before the courts of a third country.

In relation to parallel proceedings before the courts of a non-EU country involving the same cause of action and the same parties, the court of the Member State may stay the proceedings if: (a) it is expected that the court of the third State will give a judgment capable of recognition and, where applicable, of enforcement in that Member State; and (b) the court of the Member State is satisfied that a stay is necessary for the proper administration of justice. The court of the Member State may continue the proceedings at any time if: (a) the proceedings in the court of the third State are themselves stayed or discontinued; (b) it appears to the court of the Member State that the proceedings in the court of the third State are unlikely to be concluded within a reasonable time; or (c) the continuation of the proceedings is required for the proper administration of justice.[330] Further, the court of the Member State must dismiss the proceedings if the proceedings in the court of the third State are concluded and have resulted in a judgment capable of recognition and, where applicable, of enforcement in that Member State.[331] It is noteworthy that this discretion can be exercised on the application of one of the parties and even on the initiative of the court if that is possible under the procedural rules of the forum.[332]

As regards related actions pending in the courts of non-EU country, the court of the Member State may stay the proceedings if: (a) it is expedient to hear and determine the related actions together to avoid the risk of irreconcilable judgments resulting from separate proceedings; (b) it is expected that the court of the third State will give a judgment capable of recognition and, where applicable, of enforcement in that Member State; and (c) the court of the Member State is satisfied that a stay is necessary for the proper administration of justice.[333] However, the court of the Member State may continue the proceedings at any time if: (a) it appears to the court of the Member State that there is no longer a risk of irreconcilable judgments; (b) the proceedings in the court of the third State are themselves stayed or discontinued; (c) it appears to the court of the Member State that the proceedings in the court of the third State are unlikely to be concluded within a reasonable time; or (d) the continuation of the proceedings is required for the proper administration of justice.[334] In the same fashion as in the case of parallel proceedings, the court of the Member State may dismiss the proceedings if the proceedings in the court of the third State are concluded and have resulted in a judgment capable of recognition and, where applicable, of enforcement in that Member State.[335] And also in relation to this kind of scenario,

---

jurisdiction altogether. It had also proposed to create two new jurisdictional grounds that would have only apply to non-EU defendants: one based on the non-EU defendant's movable or immovable property in the State; and the other a *forum necessitatis*, designed to prevent abuses of human rights through a denial of justice. These proposals did not materialise in the Brussels I *bis* Regulation.

[330] Regulation 1215/12 art.33(2).
[331] Regulation 1215/12 art.33(3).
[332] Regulation 1215/12 art.33(4).
[333] Regulation 1215/12 art.34(1).
[334] Regulation 1215/12, art.34(2).
[335] Regulation 1215/12, art.34(3).

this discretion can be exercised on the application of one of the parties or on the initiative of the court if that is possible under the procedural rules of the forum.[336]

Differences between European and non-European litispendence

6–069   The solution adopted in arts 33 and 34 differs from the rules on *lis pendens* and related actions that apply as between Member States under arts 29 and 30 of the Brussels I *bis* Regulation. On the one hand, in relation to non-Member States, the *lis pendens* provisions of arts 33 and 34 only apply to cases in which the jurisdiction of the court of the Member State is invoked on the general ground of the domicile of the defendant (art.4) or on the basis of a ground of special jurisdiction (arts 7–9). They do not apply where the court of the Member State exercises jurisdiction in cases involving insurance, consumer and employment contracts (arts 10–23). Nor do they apply where the court of the Member State exercises exclusive jurisdiction under art.24 or by virtue of a choice of court agreement under art.25. On the other hand, the rules for *lis pendens* and related actions applicable as between the courts of Member States in principle apply to all cases of parallel and related proceedings.

The new provisions embed a welcome component of discretion into a system that otherwise favours the mandatory application of hard and fast rules. Guidance as to the exercise of that discretion is provided for in Recital 24 of the Brussels I *bis* Regulation. The Recital indicates that the court of the Member State concerned should assess all the circumstances of the case before it, particularly (a) the connections between the facts of the case and the parties and the third State concerned, (b) the stage to which the proceedings in the third State have progressed by the time proceedings are initiated in the court of the Member State and (c) whether or not the court of the third State can be expected to give a judgment within a reasonable time. That assessment may also include consideration of the question whether the court of the third State has exclusive jurisdiction in the particular case in circumstances where a court of a Member State would have exclusive jurisdiction.[337]

It will be interesting to see whether developments in the application of these provisions in English courts will be aligned with the more general concept of case management or whether an international understanding of "the proper administration of justice" emerges as a result of these new provisions, enabling a truly international understanding of justice and procedural efficiency to underpin the general principles of *lis pendens*.

---

[336] Regulation 1215/12, art.34(4).
[337] Regulation 1215/12, recital (24).

ANCILLARY JURISDICTION: PROVISIONAL AND PROTECTIVE MEASURES

Article 35 of the Brussels I *bis* Regulation[338] provides that application may be made to the courts of a Member State for such provisional, including protective, measures as may be available under the law of that State, even if, under the Regulation, the courts of another Member State have jurisdiction as to the substance of the matter.

6–070

International judicial co-operation in this field is two-fold. On the one hand, a court that has no jurisdiction to hear the merits of a case can still exercise jurisdiction for the sole purpose of granting provisional and protective measures in support of foreign proceedings. There is a clear distinction between jurisdiction on the merits and jurisdiction for the purposes of interim relief in the European regime.

Article 35 of the Brussels I *bis* Regulation meets this situation by enabling protective measures to be applied for in, for example, the courts of the state where the property is situated. It may be important in the interests of the claimant to achieve a surprise effect; but it is equally important in the interests of the defendant (and of third parties) that such measures should be rapidly brought to the notice of all concerned and that they should have the opportunity to take immediate counter-measures.

In English practice the most important "protective measure" is the *Mareva* injunction or freezing order,[339] which may be granted to a claimant who can show a good arguable case on the merits to restrain the defendant from dealing with, disposing of, or removing assets out of the jurisdiction in which they are to be found. Its purpose is to prevent the dissipation of the assets so as to prevent them being available to satisfy the judgment.

In the European regime, the availability and the requirements concerning provisional, including protective measures are for the most part left to the law of the court granting the provisional measure (*lex fori*). The possibility of relying on national jurisdictional grounds, including exorbitant jurisdictional grounds, has generated real concern about the role of what is now art.35 of the Brussels I *bis* Regulation. It has been suggested that this provision has the potential to undermine the objectives pursued by the scheme, enabling circumvention of its core provisions.[340]

Article 35 imposes no conditions on jurisdiction in the case of provisional, including protective measures. However, certain limitations have been established by the case law of the CJEU.[341]

---

[338] Regulation 1215/12, art.35; reg.44/2001, art.31.

[339] Named after one of the first cases in which it was used, *Mareva Compania Naviera SA v International Bulkcarriers SA* [1975] 2 Lloyd's Rep. 509.

[340] Dickinson (2010) 6 J.Priv.Int.L. 530.

[341] See Case 143/78, *De Cavel v De Cavel I* [1979] E.C.R. 1055 and Case 120/79, *De Cavel v De Cavel II* [1980] E.C.R. 731; Case 125/79, *Denilauler v Couchet Frères* [1980] E.C.R. 1553; Case C-261/90, *Reichert v Dresdner Bank II* [1992] E.C.R. I-2149; Case C-391/95, *Van Uden Maritime BV v Firma Deco Line* [1998] E.C.R. I-7091; Case C-99/96, *Mietz v Intership Yachting Sneek BV* [1999] E.C.R. I-2277; Case C-80/00, *Italian Leather SpA v WECO Polstermöbel GmbH* [2002] E.C.R. I-4995 and Case C-104/03, *St Paul Dairy Industries NV v Unibel Exser BVBA* [2005] E.C.R. I-3481.

In *Van Uden Maritime BV v Firma Deco Line*[342] the CJEU developed the distinction between the powers of a court exercising merits jurisdiction according to the Brussels scheme and a court exercising its power to order provisional measures in support of proceeding on the merits in another court. Certain limitations were introduced by requiring the existence of a "real connecting link" between the subject matter of the measures sought and the territorial jurisdiction of the court granting the measure. There has been much discussion about the appropriateness of this requirement. One view is that it may provide "a manageable (i.e., sufficiently flexible to reflect the variety of measures available and of the circumstances in which courts may be asked to grant them) outer limit upon the exercise of national rules of jurisdiction and procedure under Article 31".[343] A more prevalent view is that the *Van Uden* requirement should merely be a factor for consideration in the court's discretion.[344]

A few changes were introduced in this regard in the Brussels I *bis* Regulation. Recital (33) together with the definition of 'judgment'[345] clarify that a provisional measure ordered by the court with jurisdiction over the merits of the dispute can be recognised and enforced under the Regulation (provided that the defendant has been given the opportunity to appear before the court or the judgment has been served on him prior to enforcement). However, provisional measures issued by the court of any other Member State (in the exercise of ancillary jurisdiction exclusively rather than direct jurisdiction on the merits) are confined to the territory of that State.[346]

INTRA-UK JURISDICTION[347]

6–071   Section 16 of the Civil Jurisdiction and Judgments Act 1982[348] applies a modified form of the jurisdictional provisions of the European regime as between the different parts of the UK. This is set out in Sch.4. It applies where (a) the subject matter of the proceedings is within the scope of the Brussels I *bis* Regulation and (b) the defendant is domiciled in the UK or the proceedings are of a kind mentioned in art.24 (exclusive jurisdiction).[349]

The principal differences between the rules set out in Sch.4 and those of the European regime are as follows:

---

[342] Case C-391/95, *Van Uden Maritime BV v Firma Deco Line* [1998] E.C.R. I-7091.

[343] Dickinson, (2010) 6 J.Priv.Int.L. 546. See also the suggestion of Hess, Pfeiffer and Schlosser, Report on the Application of Regulation Brussels I in the Member States (Study JLS/C4/2005/03) (the *Heidelberg Report*), para.783.

[344] See *Dicey, Morris & Collins*, 15th edn (London: Sweet & Maxwell, 2012) para.8.031; see also *Masri v Consolidated Contractors International (UK) Ltd (No.2)* [2009] Q.B. 450 per Collins LJ (obiter) at para.106.

[345] Regulation 1215/2012, art.2(a).

[346] Regulation 1215/2012, Recital (33).

[347] See Hood, *Conflict of Laws within the UK* (Oxford: Oxford University Press, 2007).

[348] As amended by the Civil Jurisdiction and Judgments Order 2001 (SI 2001/3929).

[349] Regulation 1215/2012, art.24; reg.44/2001, art.22; Civil Jurisdiction and Judgments Order 2001 (SI 2001/3929) s.16 (1) as amended from time to time.

(1) The rules of special jurisdiction in matters relating to a contract refer simply to "the courts for the place of performance of the obligation in question"[350] and omits the words clarifying this notion which from part of the corresponding Regulation provision[351];

(2) Rule 3(h), which does not have a counter-part in the European regime, gives the English courts jurisdiction in proceedings to enforce a debt secured on immovable property or to determine proprietary or possessory rights or rights of security in or over movable property, in each case where the property is situated in England.

(3) Rule 4 confers jurisdiction, in proceedings which have as their object a decision of an organ of a company or association, on the courts of that part of the UK in which the company or association has its seat.[352]

(4) There is no equivalent to s.3 of the Regulation on insurance contracts, and jurisdiction in such cases must be allocated under the other aspects of the Regulation system such as the domicile basis or the special jurisdiction rules as to contracts in general or the operations of a branch or agency.

(5) Rule 11 corresponding to art.24 on exclusive jurisdiction omits any reference to patents, trademarks, etc.

(6) In rule 12 corresponding to art.25 (jurisdiction agreements),[353] there is no requirement as to writing.

(7) The provisions relating to *lis pendens* and related actions are omitted (in the intra-UK system forum non conveniens has been preserved as the way to tackle parallel proceedings).[354]

Rule 7 deals with allocation of jurisdiction in proceedings brought in the UK by virtue of art.7 (6) of the Brussels I *bis* Regulation (trust domiciled in the UK) or of art.17(1) (consumer domiciled in the UK), allocating jurisdiction to the courts of the part of the UK in which the trust is domiciled and the courts of the part of the UK in which the consumer is domiciled.

The CJEU has no jurisdiction under art.267 of the Treaty on the Functioning of the EU in relation to the interpretation of Sch.4.[355] However, the principles adopted by the CJEU in the interpretation of the rules contained in the Brussels Convention and the Brussels I Regulation, which have been adopted as part of Sch.4, must be considered by the UK courts when applying these provisions.[356]

---

[350] See *MacRitchie Bros Ltd v Commercial Power Ltd* (unreported, Sh.Ct, 2010) (Scotland was not the place of performance of the obligation in question; the obligation in question was the providing of advice by the English defendants and the place of performance was not *solely* Scotland).

[351] Schedule 4, r.3(a).

[352] The seat will be determined in accordance with para.10 of Sch.1 to the Order; see above, para.6–010.

[353] See above, paras 6–004 and following.

[354] *Cook v Virgin Media Ltd* [2015] EWCA Civ 1287; [2016] I.L.Pr. 6.

[355] Case C-346/93 *Kleinwort Benson Ltd v City of Glasgow District Council* [1995] E.C.R. I-615.

[356] 1982 Act ss.16(3) and 20(5).

CHAPTER 7

JURISDICTION: THE TRADITIONAL ENGLISH RULES

The traditional English approach to civil jurisdiction is based on the principle that **7–001** the exercise of jurisdiction to adjudicate is essentially discretionary. This discretion is used cautiously and with a view to enhance efficiency and procedural justice.[1] The traditional approach is based on a set of well-established rules and it is subject to a number of important qualifications. First and foremost, where a claim relates to a civil and commercial matter[2] within the meaning of the European regime, the traditional rules apply to the extent that the Brussels I *bis* Regulation permits. As discussed in the previous chapter, art.6(1) of the Brussels I *bis* Regulation enables the national courts of Member States to apply their own jurisdictional rules in certain circumstances not falling within the Regulation. These cases are where the defendant is not domiciled in a Member State and art.24 (exclusive jurisdiction) does not apply and there is no valid choice of court agreement conferring jurisdiction to the courts of a Member State.[3] It is important to appreciate that the jurisdictional rules of the European regime and the "traditional rules" now to be considered apply to different categories of case. The first step in considering the issue of jurisdiction is always to decide which set of rules applies. If there turns out to be no jurisdiction under the applicable rules that is the end of the matter: there can be no switching to the other (by definition inapplicable) set of rules. Furthermore, it has been held that the exercise of jurisdiction under the English traditional rules is potentially qualified by the principles underpinning the Regulation, including the *lis pendens* rules provided in arts 29 and 30 of the Brussels I *bis* Regulation.[4]

The traditional rules, enshrined in the Civil Procedure Rules, base jurisdiction on (a) the presence of the defendant in England; (b) the submission of the defendant to the jurisdiction; and (c) several special jurisdiction grounds connecting the forum to defendants outside of the jurisdiction, justifying in certain circumstances, the service of process abroad.

It is well established that ultimately the foundation of jurisdiction in personam in England is service of process.[5] Viewed critically, and especially through the eyes of foreign lawyers, this appears to rest upon a confusion of ideas. Service of

---

[1] R. Fentiman, *International Commercial Litigation*, 2nd edn (Oxford: University Press, 2015) p.299.
[2] See para.6–006.
[3] European Parliament and Council Regulation 1215/2012 on jurisdiction and the recognition and enforcement of judgments in civil and commercial matters, OJ L 351/1, 20.12.2012, (hereafter "reg.1215/2012"), art.25.
[4] Fentiman, *International Commercial Litigation* (2015) p.293.
[5] See Dicey, Morris and Collins, *The Conflict of Laws,* 15th edn (London: Sweet & Maxwell, 2012) rule 29(1); [11-02] p 412.

a claim form, in the jurisdiction or abroad, serves a vital procedural purpose, that of putting the defendant upon notice of the claim being brought, and every legal system makes some provision to that end (in this chapter these rules are examined under the headings on 'effecting service', in England and abroad, respectively). But there is a distinct logical leap in moving from the proposition that a claim form is a necessary procedural step to that which makes it a sufficient basis for jurisdiction. As a basis for jurisdiction, it is sometimes regarded as exorbitant,[6] and its use is excluded under the European regime.[7] Technically, it would be possible to argue that the basis of jurisdiction in the case of defendants present in England and Wales is the actual presence in the jurisdiction, and service of the claim form is the mechanism to give legal notice to a defendant of a court's exercise of its jurisdiction over the defendant, enabling him to respond to the proceedings before the court. On the same lines, there is a range of jurisdictional bases identified in the Civil Procedural Rules as potentially enabling the court to exercise jurisdiction over defendants located outside the jurisdiction; these connecting factors constitute the bases of jurisdiction and service of process abroad materializes the exercise of that jurisdiction.

PRESENCE OF THE DEFENDANT IN THE JURISDICTION

7–002 Every civil action governed by the Civil Procedure Rules, whether in the High Court or a county court, is started when the court issues a claim form at the request of the claimant.[8] The claim form must then be served on the defendant in England within four months of the date of issue.[9] When a claim form cannot be served on a defendant, the court cannot exercise jurisdiction over the claim; conversely, when a defendant has been served with the claim form, the court can in principle exercise jurisdiction, although in certain scenarios the defendant may request the court to decline jurisdiction based on forum non conveniens.[10]

The rule that service of the claim form establishes jurisdiction is a central feature of the traditional rules. In general, therefore, in any case to which those traditional rules apply, any person who is in England and served there with the claim form is subject to the in personam jurisdiction of the court. The application of this principle depends on whether the defendant is an individual, a partnership firm, or a corporation.

---

[6] See Fernández Arroyo, *Compétence exclusive et compétence exorbitante dans les relations privées internationales*, (2006) 323 *Recueil des cours* 9 (Leiden: Martinus Nijhoff, 2008). But cf. Collins, (1991) 107 L.Q.R. 10, 13–14; Fentiman, *International Commercial Litigation* (2015) p.301; *Abela v Baadarani* [2013] UKSC 44.

[7] These 'exorbitant' jurisdiction rules are to be listed in the Official Journal following notification to the European Commission (reg.1215/2012; art.76). These rules were previously listed in Annex I to the Brussels I Regulation.

[8] CPR r.7.2.

[9] CPR r.7.5; the period may be extended: r.7.6. The period is of six months in cases of service out of the jurisdiction: r.7.5(2).

[10] See para.7-031.

Individuals

Any individual who is present in England is liable to be served with a claim form, however short may be the period for which he or she is present in the jurisdiction, and irrespective of nationality, or domicile, or usual place of residence, or of the nature of the cause of action. **7–003**

Thus in *Maharanee of Baroda v Wildenstein*[11]:

> An Indian princess, resident in France, brought an action against an American art dealer, also resident in France, for rescission of a contract to sell her a picture. The contract was made in France and governed by French law. The writ (the document now known as the claim form) was served on the defendant at Ascot races during a temporary visit to England. It was held that the court had jurisdiction.

Effecting Service in England: individuals

A claim form may be served on an individual by (a) personal service, by leaving it with that individual[12]; (b) first class post, document exchange or other service which provides for delivery on the next business day; (c) in certain cases, leaving it at the address of the defendant's solicitor or "European Lawyer", or at an address the defendant has given as an address at which service may be effected, or at the defendant's usual or last known residence[13]; (d) fax or other means of electronic communication including email.[14] In *Varsani v Relfo Ltd*[15] the determination of the defendant's "usual" residence for this purpose was not based on the consideration of duration of periods of occupation of that address as compared to the defendant's other residences. The defendant was a British citizen who had a business in Kenya. His family lived in a property owned by him and his wife in London and he visited as work permitted, staying for a month or two in each of the few years previous to the case. The court held that it was possible to have more than one "usual" residence; the fact that the premises were occupied permanently by the defendant's family was considered as material, hence the premises could be described as his "usual" residence.[16] **7–004**

Where it appears to the court that there is a good reason to authorise service by some other method or at some other place, the court may make an order for "service by an alternative method",[17] for example publication in newspapers. It is common practice for the claimant to serve the claim form to the defendant,

---

[11] [1972] 2 Q.B. 283. The actual decision would now be different because the case would fall under the Brussels I Regulation as a result of the defendant's domicile in France; cf. *Colt Industries Inc v Sarlie* [1966] 1 W.L.R. 440.

[12] CPR r.6.5(3)(a).

[13] CPR rr.6.7 and 6.8; "European Lawyer" has a technical meaning set out in the European Communities (Services of Lawyers) Order 1978 (SI 1978/1910) art.2.

[14] CPR r.6.3(1) which needs to be read with Practice Direction 6A.

[15] [2010] EWCA Civ 560; [2010] 3 All E.R. (Comm)1045.

[16] See *Levene v Inland Revenue Commissioners* [1928] A.C. 217.

[17] CPR r.6.15 (formerly known as "substituted service").

although the court is in principle responsible for service.[18] However, in the Commercial Court service is to be effected by the parties and not the court registry.[19]

Partnerships

7–005 Claims against partners of any nationality[20] who carried on business within England and Wales when the cause of action arose must in principle be brought against the partnership.

Effecting Service in England: partnerships

7–006 Where partners are being sued in the name of their firm, the claim form can be served on any partner or any other person who, at the time of service, has the control or management of the partnership business at its principal place of business.[21] Where personal service is not effected, because the defendant does not give an address at which it may be served, and the claimant does not wish to effect personal service, it is possible to serve the individual being sued in the business name of a partnership, in the usual or last known residence of the individual; or principal or last known place of business of the partnership.[22] In fact, this may result in an extension of the exercise of jurisdiction over defendants who are not present in the jurisdiction. A partnership without a place of business in England cannot be sued in the firm's name. A limited liability partnership may also be served by any of the methods of service permitted under the Companies Act 2006.[23]

Companies and other corporations

7–007 The notion of service on a defendant "present" in England is readily understood when the defendant is an individual, but the presence of a corporation is, like its nationality or domicile or residence, to some extent a fiction.[24] Companies registered in England are deemed to be "present" in the jurisdiction by virtue of its incorporation. In relation to foreign companies the situation may differ depending on the company's domicile. If the foreign company is domiciled in an EU Member State or a Lugano Convention State, jurisdiction will depend on the rules of the European regime. In cases outside the scope of the European regime, if a foreign company has a branch in England, it may be served in England even

---

[18] CPR r.6.4.

[19] Practice Direction 58 para.9; Admiralty and Commercial Courts Guide (2014), para.B.7.1.

[20] *Worcester, etc Banking Co v Firbank* [1984] 1 Q.B. 784 (CA).

[21] CPR r.6.5(3)(c).

[22] CPR r 6.9(2)–(3).

[23] CPR r.6.3(3). For these modes of service see below; their application is subject to modification by regulations made under the Limited Liability Partnerships Act 2000.

[24] See Fawcett, (1988) 37 I.C.L.Q. 644, and the exhaustive treatment in *Adams v Cape Industries Plc* [1990] Ch. 433.

if the claim has no connection with the branch or with England.[25] Neither the Civil Procedure Rules nor the Companies Act 2006 provide a definition for the connecting factor 'place of business'[26] but it is interpreted widely.[27]

Effecting Service in England: Companies and other corporations

The Companies Act 2006 contains special rules as to service on companies. The Civil Procedure Rules preserve those statutory options,[28] but it is almost always preferable to use the simpler methods in the CPR.

7–008

If the company is registered in England under the companies legislation, it is present in the jurisdiction, even if it only carries on business abroad, and service of a claim form can always be effected by leaving it at, or sending it by post to, the company's registered office in England.[29] Similarly, if a company registered in Scotland carries on business in England, a claim form may be served on it by leaving it at, or sending it by post to, the company's principal place of business in England, with a copy to the company's registered office in Scotland.[30] An overseas company whose particulars are registered may be served by leaving the claim form at, or sending it by post to, the registered address of any person resident in the UK who is authorised to accept service of documents on the company's behalf, or if there is no such person, or if any such person refuses service or service cannot for any other reason be effected, by leaving it at or sending by post to any place of business of the company in the UK.[31]

Service under these provisions does not depend upon the subject matter of the action being substantially concerned with the activity of the place of business in the UK.[32]

Under the Civil Procedure Rules, a document is served personally on a company or other corporation by leaving it with a person holding a senior position within the company or corporation,[33] or by leaving it at the company's principal office or any place of business within the jurisdiction which has a real connection with the claim.[34] Service may be effected on a company other than one registered in England at any place within the jurisdiction where it carries on its activities, or at any place of business of the company within the jurisdiction.[35]

---

[25] CPR r.6(9); however, the lack of connection of the claim with the branch or place of business in England may be a ground for a stay of proceedings under CPR r.38.

[26] *Saab v Saudi American Bank* [1999] 1 W.L.R. 1861 (CA); see also *Actavis Group HF v Eli Lilly & Co* [2013] EWCA Civ 517; [2013] R.P.C. 985.

[27] See further Dicey, Morris and Collins, para.[11-118].

[28] CPR r.6.3(2)(b).

[29] Companies Act 2006 s.1139(1).

[30] Companies Act 2006 s.1139(4). However, see the different applicable periods: The time limit for serving a claim form on a company whose registered office is in Scotland is six months, rather than the four months that would have applied for service within the jurisdiction (*Ashley v Tesco Stores Ltd* [2015] EWCA Civ 414; [2015] 1 W.L.R. 5153).

[31] Companies Act 2006 s.1139(2), (3).

[32] *Saab v Saudi Arabian Bank* [1999] 1 W.L.R. 1861.

[33] CPR r.6.5(3)(b); "person holding a senior position" is defined in Practice Direction 6A, para.6.2 as including, in the case of a company, a director, the treasurer, secretary, chief executive, manager or other officer of the company.

[34] CPR r.6.9(2). Similar rules apply to corporations which are not companies.

[35] CPR r.6.9(2); *Lakah Group v Al Jazeera Satellite Channel* [2003] EWHC 1231(QB).

Whether the defendant is an individual, a partnership firm, or a corporation, where a dispute arises out of a contract, and a claim form is issued containing only a claim relating to that contract, it may be served by any method specified in the contract.[36]

Service by contractually agreed method

7–009   Whether the defendant is an individual, a partnership firm, or a corporation, where a dispute arises out of a contract, and a claim form is issued containing only a claim relating to that contract, it may be served by any method specified in the contract.[37]

Service on agent of overseas principal

7–010   In respect of a particular contract entered into within the jurisdiction with or through an agent of a defendant who is overseas, the court may on application permit a claim form to be served on an agent of an overseas principal.[38] A copy of the claim form and of the order permitting service on the agent must be sent to the principal[39] but the effective service is that within the jurisdiction. Service in these circumstances is regarded as exceptional and will usually only be permitted if service on the defendant overseas cannot be effected. Service may be effected on the agent if the business is that of the corporation and not solely the personal business of the agent or representative. For example, if the agent is empowered to make contracts on behalf of the company and displays its name on its premises in England, this would possibly contribute to establishing that the 'place of business' is that of the corporation.

SUBMISSION TO THE JURISDICTION

7–011   A person who would not otherwise be subject to the jurisdiction[40] of the court may preclude him or herself by conduct from objecting to the jurisdiction, and thus give the court jurisdiction which, but for his or her submission, it would not possess.[41] The court must be satisfied that the defendant's conduct indicates "an intention on the part of the defendant to have the case tried in England."[42]

This submission may take place in various ways. A person who begins an action as claimant in general gives the court jurisdiction to entertain a counterclaim (classed in the Civil Procedure Rules as a "Part 20 claim") by the

---

[36] CPR r.6.11.
[37] CPR r.6.11.
[38] CPR r.6.12.
[39] CPR r.6.12(4).
[40] The person does not need to be present in the jurisdiction at the time of issue or service of the claim form; he may, for example, have instructed his solicitor to accept service on his behalf.
[41] cf. reg.44/2001. art.26; reg.1215/2012, art.26.
[42] *Future New Developments Ltd v B&S Patente Und Marken GmbH* [2014] EWHC 1874 (IPEC), at [29].

defendant in some related matter, but not an action on an independent ground.[43] If the court considers that justice requires the counterclaim to be dealt with separately, it may so order; and in exercising this power it has in mind, amongst other factors, the connection between the Part 20 claim and the claim made by the claimant.[44]

A defendant who wishes to dispute the court's jurisdiction to try the claim must first file an acknowledgment of service and then make the application, with supporting evidence, for an order by which the court declares that it has no jurisdiction.[45] The mere filing of the acknowledgment of service does not deprive the defendant of any right to dispute the court's jurisdiction,[46] but a defendant who does not make an application within the period prescribed in the Rules is treated as having accepted that the court has jurisdiction to try the claim.[47] There is no submission, however, if the defendant applies and is granted an extension of the time limit pursuant to the court's general case management powers.[48] If the court does not make the declaration that it has no jurisdiction, the original acknowledgment of service ceases to have effect. If the defendant then files a further acknowledgment of service (to avoid a default judgment being given) that is treated as an acceptance that the court has jurisdiction to try the claim.[49] If a claim form has been validly served (including some method agreed in a contract to which the defendant is party) and no acknowledgement of service or defence is filed, the jurisdiction cannot be contested.

It must be emphasised that the principle of submission cannot give the court jurisdiction to entertain proceedings that are beyond the competence or authority of the court, for instance, where the courts of another EU Member State have exclusive jurisdiction. Furthermore, submission only applies to actions in personam: it does not apply, for instance, to petitions for a decree of divorce or nullity of marriage.[50]

SERVICE OUT OF THE JURISDICTION

At common law, if the defendant was not served with the claim form while present in England and did not submit to the jurisdiction, the court had no jurisdiction to entertain an action in personam. The Common Law Procedure Act 1852 modified the position and gave the court a discretionary power to permit service out of the jurisdiction.[51] The power to do so, which as we have seen is a

7–012

---

[43] *South African Republic v Compagnie Franco-Belge du Chemin de Fer du Nord* [1987] 2 Ch. 487; [1898] 1 Ch. 190; *Factories Insurance Co v Anglo-Scottish Insurance Co* (1913) 29 T.L.R. 312; *High Commissioner for India v Ghosh* [1960] 1 Q.B. 134.

[44] CPR rr.3.1 and 20.9.

[45] CPR r.11(1), (2), (4).

[46] CPR r.11(3).

[47] CPR r.11(5).

[48] CPR r.3.1(2)(a); *The Alexandros T* [2013] UKSC 70. Such an application can be made even when the time limit has expired (*Chris Sawyer v Atari Interactive Inc* [2005] EWHC 2351 (Ch)).

[49] CPR r.11(7).

[50] Domicile and Matrimonial Proceedings Act 1973 s.5(2) and (3); below, paras 12–004 and following.

[51] The power may be exercised retrospectively: *Kosa v Nesheim* [2006] EWHC 2710 (Ch).

power to establish jurisdiction, was until 2008 regulated by rules of court. Now, the issue is dealt with in the Civil Procedure Rules and the detailed grounds for permitting service out of the jurisdiction (heads of jurisdiction) are contained in para.3.1 of Practice Direction 6B of the Rules. Some of these heads of jurisdiction have a very long history in the rules of court in England, and many of them are 'connecting factors' internationally recognised as providing a strong enough connection between the forum and the parties, or the forum and the cause of action.

In modern times, service out of the jurisdiction is considered to be an essential feature of international litigation. In *Abela v Baadarani*[52] Lord Sumption, summarised the view of the UK Supreme Court:

> "This characterisation of the jurisdiction to allow service out is traditional, and was originally based on the notion that the service of proceedings abroad was an assertion of sovereign power over the Defendant and a corresponding interference with the sovereignty of the state in which process was served. This is no longer a realistic view of the situation. The adoption in English law of the doctrine of forum non conveniens and the accession by the United Kingdom to a number of conventions regulating the international jurisdiction of national courts, means that in the overwhelming majority of cases where service out is authorised there will have been either a contractual submission to the jurisdiction of the English court or else a substantial connection between the dispute and this country. ... It should no longer be necessary to resort to the kind of muscular presumptions against service out which are implicit in adjectives like "exorbitant". The decision is generally a pragmatic one in the interests of the efficient conduct of litigation in an appropriate forum."[53]

If the English traditional rules are applicable the exercise of jurisdiction in relation to a defendant that is located out of the jurisdiction is discretionary and permission to serve out of the jurisdiction must be sought based on the heads of jurisdiction provided for in para.3.1. of Practice Direction 6B.[54]

There is an essential difference between cases where the defendant is in England and served there with the claim form, or where the defendant submits to the jurisdiction, and the cases which are about to be considered. If the defendant is in the jurisdiction, or submits to the jurisdiction, the claimant may proceed "as of right"; but under r.6.36 the jurisdiction of the court is essentially discretionary, and will only be exercised if England is the most appropriate forum.[55]

---

[52] [2013] UKSC 44; [2013] 1 W.L.R. 2043.

[53] [2013] UKSC 44; [2013] 1 W.L.R. 2043, per Lord Sumption, at [53].

[54] Outside the scope of application of the English traditional rules, a claim form may be served on a defendant out of the jurisdiction without the permission of the court where (a) each claim included in the claim form made against the defendant to be served is a claim which the court has power to determine under the European regime; *and* no proceedings between the parties concerning the same claim are pending in the courts of any other part of the UK or any other Member State; *and* the defendant is domiciled in the UK or in any Member State, or (b) there is jurisdiction under art.24 (exclusive jurisdiction) or art.25 (jurisdiction agreements) of the Brussels I *bis* Regulation (CPR r.6.33(1); *DSG International Sourcing Ltd v Universal Media Corp (Slovakia) SRO* [2011] EWHC 1116 (Comm); [2011] I.L.Pr. 33). A claim form may be also served on a defendant out of the jurisdiction without the permission of the court where each claim made against the defendant to be served is a claim which, under any other enactment, the court has power to determine, although (a) the person against whom the claim is made is not within the jurisdiction; or (b) the facts giving rise to the claim did not occur within the jurisdiction (CPR r.6.33(3)).

[55] *VTB Capital Plc v Nutritek International Corp* [2013] UKSC 5; [2013] 2 A.C. 337, at paras [13], [44], [80] and [190]. See further below.

Before we examine the specific connecting factors (heads of jurisdiction) justifying the exercise of this discretionary power, certain principles of general application must first be considered.

1. Pragmatism in the interests of the efficient conduct of litigation in an appropriate forum. In *Abela v Baadarani*[56] the notion that the service of proceedings abroad was an assertion of sovereign power over the defendant and a corresponding interference with the sovereignty of the State in which process was served, was considered to be out-dated. In the past, it was considered that the court ought to be exceedingly careful before it allowed a claim form to be served on a defendant located outside England because of the apparent interference with the sovereignty of the foreign state concerned.[57] The UK Supreme Court considered in *Abela* that the decision whether to permit service out of the jurisdiction is generally a pragmatic one in the interests of the efficient conduct of litigation in an appropriate forum.[58]

2. Construction of heads of jurisdiction in favour of the defendant. The courts have long held that if there is any doubt in the construction of any of the connection factors enshrined in the heads of jurisdiction now included in the Practice Direction, the doubt ought to be resolved in favour of the defendant.[59]

3. Full and fair disclosure by the claimant of all relevant facts. Since applications for permission are made without notice to the defendant, the claimant must make a full and fair disclosure of all relevant facts.[60]

4. Permission should not be given if the case is within the letter but outside the spirit of the Rule.[61] This is emphasised by a provision in the Rules that the court must not give its permission unless the claimant satisfies it that England is a proper place in which to bring the claim.[62] The court will consider whether England is the forum conveniens,[63] taking into account the nature of the dispute, the legal and practical issues involved, such questions as local knowledge, availability of witnesses and their evidence, and expense.[64]

---

[56] [2013] UKSC 44; [2013] 1 W.L.R. 2043.

[57] *Société Générale de Paris v Dreyfus Bros* (1887) 37 Ch.D. 215.

[58] [2013] UKSC 44; [2013] 1 W.L.R. 2043, See Dickinson (2014) 130 L.Q.R. 197; Collins (2014) 130 L.Q.R. 555; Folkard [2014] L.M.C.L.Q. 492.

[59] *Société Générale de Paris v Dreyfus Bros* (1887) 37 Ch.D. 215.

[60] See, e.g., *Trafalgar Tours v Henry* [1990] 2 Lloyd's Rep. 298.

[61] *Johnson v Taylor Bros* [1920] A.C. 144 at 153; *Rosler v Hilbery* [1925] Ch. 250 at 259–260; *George Monro Ltd v American Cyanamid Corporation* [1944] K.B. 432 at 437 and 442. See also *Conductive Inkjet Technology Ltd v Uni-Pixel Displays Inc* [2013] EWHC 2968 (Ch.), at [59].

[62] CPR r.6.37(3). See r.6.37(4) for special factors when service is to be in Scotland or Northern Ireland.

[63] *Société Générale de Paris v Dreyfus Bros* (1887) 37 Ch.D. 215; *Rosler v Hilbery* [1925] Ch. 250; *Kroch v Rossell* [1937] 1 All E.R. 725.

[64] *Spiliada Maritime Corp v Cansulex Ltd* [1987] A.C. 460, adopting the approach of Lord Wilberforce in *Amin Rasheed Shipping Corp v Kuwait Insurance Co* [1984] A.C. 50 at 72; *Roneleigh Ltd v M.I.I. Exports Inc* [1989] 1 W.L.R. 619; *Metall und Rohstoff AG v Donaldson Lufkin & Jenrette Inc* [1990] Q.B. 391.

5. Interlocutory proceedings on jurisdiction should not become a mini-trial. In *VTB Capital Plc v Nutritek International*[65] Lord Neuberger[66] noted that hearings concerning the issue of appropriate forum should not become a mini-trial, that is, they should not involve masses of documents, long witness statements, detailed analysis of the issues, and long argument.[67] Notwithstanding the foregoing there is an inherent tension surrounding the scale of jurisdiction disputes: on the one hand, jurisdictional disputes are interlocutory, but on the other hand, pragmatically, they influence dramatically the outcome of the dispute on the merits, justifying the parties' attempts to litigate such issues fully, and the risks of doing so before the facts and law are fully established.[68]

Requirements and Standards

7–013   The courts have spelt out carefully the considerations which govern the exercise of the discretion,[69] including the general cautionary point that the court ought to be exceedingly careful before it allows a claim form to be served on a foreigner outside England because of the apparent interference with the sovereignty of the foreign state concerned. In words dating from 1887[70] but repeatedly approved by later courts[71]:

> "[I]t becomes a very serious question … whether this court ought to put a foreigner, who owes no allegiance here, to the inconvenience and annoyance of being brought to contest his rights in this country, and I for one say, most distinctly, that I think this court ought to be exceedingly careful before it allows a writ to be served out of the jurisdiction".

Perhaps this sort of consideration carries less weight with the much greater speed of international travel and the growth of multinational corporations; but the cautionary note is still relevant.[72]

The modern approach of the English court was well summarised by Lord Collins of Mapesbury in *AK Investment CJSC v Kyrgyz Mobil Tel Ltd*,[73] a Privy Council appeal from the Isle of Man:

---

[65] [2013] UKSC 5; [2013] 2 A.C. 337.

[66] At [82]–[83].

[67] The risk of allowing these interlocutory proceedings to determine jurisdiction to become too expensive and time-consuming, is that they may be used as a litigation tactic by a richer party to wear down a poorer party, or by a party with a weak case to prevent, or at least to discourage, a party with a strong case from enforcing its rights.

[68] Rogerson, (2013) 9 J.Priv.Int.L. 387; R Fentiman, *International Commercial Litigation* (2015), pp.309 and following.

[69] *Société Générale de Paris v Dreyfus Bros* (1887) 37 Ch.D. 215; *The Hagen* [1908] P. 189; *Re Schintz* [1926] Ch. 710.

[70] *Société Générale de Paris v Dreyfus Bros* (1885) 29 Ch.D. 239 at 242–243.

[71] *Brownlie v Four Seasons Holdings Inc* [2015] EWCA Civ 665; [2015] C.P. Rep. 40, at [17].

[72] Cf. the decision of the Court of Appeal in *Brownlie v Four Seasons Holdings Inc* [2015] EWCA Civ 665; [2015] C.P. Rep. 40, where the passage from *Société Générale de Paris v Dreyfus Bros* (1885) 29 Ch.D. (at 242–243) was quoted (at [17]) with the approach of the UK Supreme Court in *Abela v Baadarani* [2013] UKSC 44; [2013] 1 W.L.R. 2043, per Lord Sumption, at [53] (see para.7-012, above).

[73] [2011] UKPC 7, reported as *Altimo Holdings and Investment Ltd v Kyrgyz Mobil Tel Ltd* [2012] 1 W.L.R. 1804 at paras [71] and [81]). See also *Global 5000 Ltd v Wadhawan* [2012] EWCA Civ 13.

"On an application for permission to serve a foreign defendant ... out of the jurisdiction, the claimant ... has to satisfy three requirements.[74] First, the claimant must satisfy the court that in relation to the foreign defendant there is a serious issue to be tried on the merits, i.e. a substantial question of fact or law, or both. The current practice in England is that this is the same test as for summary judgment, namely whether there is a real (as opposed to a fanciful) prospect of success. Second, the claimant must satisfy the court that there is a good arguable case that the claim falls within one or more classes of case in which permission to serve out may be given. In this context 'good arguable case' connotes that one side has a much better argument than the other.[75] Third, the claimant must satisfy the court that in all the circumstances [England] is clearly or distinctly the appropriate forum for the trial of the dispute, and that in all the circumstances the court ought to exercise its discretion to permit service of the proceedings out of the jurisdiction ... However, if a question of law arises on an application in connection with service out of the jurisdiction, and the question of law goes to the existence of jurisdiction, the court will normally decide it, rather than treating it as a question of whether there is a good arguable case."[76]

A serious issue to be tried on the merits (real prospect of success)

The Civil Procedure Rules require the claimant to offer evidence stating that he believes that the claim has a reasonable prospect of success against the defendant that is outside of the jurisdiction.[77] It has been sustained that the standard is the same as if the claimant was resisting an application by the defendant for summary judgment.[78]   **7–014**

A good arguable case that the claim falls within one of the heads of jurisdiction

The question before the court in relation to this point is normally decided on affidavits from both sides and without cross-examination; mini-trials on jurisdiction issues are to be discouraged. The court needs to be satisfied—in the context of an interlocutory process—that connecting factors exist which allow the court to exercise jurisdiction.[79] Proceedings may fall within more than one of the headings of jurisdiction provided for in the Civil Procedure Rules.   **7–015**

The established standard is known as the "*Canada Trust* gloss", as it has been drawn from the following passage in the judgment of Waller LJ in *Canada Trust Co v Stolzenberg (No.2)*[80]:

"'Good arguable case' reflects in that context that one side has a much better argument on the material available. It is the concept which the phrase reflects on which it is important to concentrate, i.e. of the court being satisfied or as satisfied as it can be having regard to the limitations which an interlocutory process imposes that factors exist which allow the court to take jurisdiction."

---

[74] *Seaconsar Far East Ltd v Bank Markazi Jomhouri Ilami Iran* [1994] 1 A.C. 438 at 453–457.
[75] See *Canada Trust Co v Stolzenberg (No.2)* [1998] 1 W.L.R. 547 at 555–7 per Waller LJ (affd [2002] 1 A.C. 1); *Bols Distilleries BV v Superior Yacht Services* [2006] UKPC 45; [2007] 1 W.L.R. 12.
[76] *Hutton (EF) & Co (London) Ltd v Mofarrij* [1989] 1 W.L.R. 488 at 495 (CA); *Chellaram v Chellaram (No.2)* [2002] EWHC 632 (Ch); [2002] 3 All E.R. 17 at 36.
[77] CPR r. 6.37(1)(b).
[78] *AK Investment CJSC v Kyrgyz Mobil Tel Limited* [2011] UKPC 7, reported as *Altimo Holdings and Investment Ltd v Kyrgyz Mobil Tel Ltd* [2012] 1 W.L.R. 1804.
[79] CPR r.6.37(1)(b).
[80] [1998] 1 W.L.R. 247.

The court must be satisfied that England is the appropriate forum[81]

7–016   In relation to the determination of England as the appropriate forum in *VTB Capital Plc v Nutriek International Corp*[82] the UK Supreme Court reinforced the applicability of the *Spiliada* test. In the words of Lord Mance, giving the leading judgment on the jurisdiction issue:

> "The ultimate over-arching principle is that stated in the *Spiliada*, and, if a court is not satisfied at the end of the day that England is clearly the appropriate forum, then permission to serve out must be refused or set aside."[83]

The standard is substantially the same as that developed for the use of the power, formerly extensively used, to stay in English proceedings on the ground of forum non conveniens,[84] that England was *not* the appropriate forum. That the test was the same in both types of case was recognised in the leading House of Lords case, *Spiliada Maritime Corp v Cansulex Ltd*.[85] This means that it is legitimate to draw on the forum non conveniens cases in the present context, but this must be done with care. Not only has the scope for pleas of forum non conveniens been drastically reduced since the decision of the CJEU in *Owusu v Jackson*[86] but it has also to be remembered that in r.6.36 cases, unlike those dealing with pleas of forum non conveniens, the burden of proof is on the claimant: the claimant must persuade the court that the case is a proper one for service out of the jurisdiction and that England is clearly the appropriate forum.

In assessing the claimant's arguments, the court will seek to identify the "natural forum", meaning "that with which the action has the most real and substantial connection",[87] and will examine not only factors affecting convenience or expense (such as the availability of witnesses), but also such matters as the law governing the transaction, and the places where the parties reside or carry on business.[88] On the governing law, the courts take the common-sense view that difficult legal issues are best dealt with by judges familiar with them.[89] For example, in *Wright v Deccan Chargers Sporting Ventures Ltd*[90]:

---

[81] CPR r.6.37(1)(b).

[82] [2013] UKSC 5; [2013] 2 A.C. 337, at paras [13], [44], [80] and [190].

[83] [2013] UKSC 5; [2013] 2 A.C. 337, at para [18].

[84] See below, paras 7–031 and following.

[85] [1987] A.C. 460. See for criticism, Arzandeh (2014) 10 J.Priv.Int.L. 89. The *Spiliada* test has been confirmed as 'the test' for determining whether England is the appropriate forum by the UK Supreme Court in *VTB Capital Plc v Nutritek International Corp* [2013] UKSC 5; [2013] 2 A.C. 337.

[86] Case C-281/02 *Owusu v Jackson* [2005] E.C.R I-1383; [2005] Q.B. 801.

[87] A formulation used by Lord Keith in *The Abidin Daver* [1984] A.C. 398 at 415.

[88] e.g., *Chellaram v Chellaram (No.2)* [2002] EWHC 632; [2002] 3 All E.R. 17 (trusts probably governed by Hindu or Bermudan law; defendants domiciled in Bermuda, Gibraltar, Hong Kong, India and Spain; Indian forum more appropriate than English).

[89] e.g., *Smay Investments Ltd v Sachdev* [2003] EWHC 474; [2003] 1 W.L.R. 1973 (dispute over ownership of Indian company best dealt with by Indian courts; *VTB Capital Plc v Nutritek International Corp* [2013] UKSC 5; [2013] 2 A.C. 337; applied in *Navig8 Pte Ltd v Al-Riyadh Co for Vegetable Oil Industry* [2013] EWHC 328 (Comm.); [2013] 2 Lloyd's Rep. 104; *Caresse Navigation Ltd v Office National de L'Electricité* [2013] EWHC 3081 (Comm.); [2014] 1 Lloyd's Rep. 337, aff'd. (but not on this point): [2014] EWCA Civ 1366; [2015] Q.B. 366. For a critical analysis of this approach, see M Hook (2014) 63 I.C.L.Q. 963.

[90] [2011] EWHC 1307 (QB); [2011] I.L.Pr 37.

W had entered into a contract of employment with D, an Indian company. The contract stated that D required W's services in the development of a business model and plan to support an initial public offering of D's stock on the English market. It provided that W would be based initially in England and would travel to India and elsewhere as necessary and that D would establish an office in England for W. The contract also stated that it was to be governed by English law. The contract was terminated. W alleged there had been a breach of contract and sought to serve proceedings in England. D had never established an office in England for W.

It was held that the matters were relatively evenly balanced but marginally favoured English jurisdiction for two reasons: the English courts would be preferable in applying English law (as there were issues in the case that suggested the application of English law would not be straightforward); and D's agreement that W should remain resident in England and that it would establish an office in England.

Nevertheless, the applicability of English law as the governing law to the merits is not determinant in establishing that England is clearly the appropriate forum for the sake of granting permission to serve a defendant out of the jurisdiction. It may be outweighed by other factors, including the location of witnesses and evidence.[91]

It may be relevant that particular courts have special expertise in the relevant type of case. For example, if a city or region is known as the centre of a specialised industrial process, its courts may be more familiar with the types of damage that may be sustained by workers in that industry. In cases involving insurance policies negotiated in accordance with the practices of the London market, the English courts will usually be held to be the appropriate forum.[92] If a court has already dealt with a related aspect of some specialised or very complex litigation, it may well be appropriate that other aspects are dealt with by that court.[93] It is important in complex litigation involving multiple parties to identify where possible a forum in which all the issues can be resolved, and so minimise the risk of inconsistent judgments in different jurisdictions.[94]

Although every case must turn on its own facts, the natural forum for a claim in tort is likely to be held to be the country in which the tort occurred,[95] not least because the relevant evidence is likely to be there. The place of the tort will not always be the natural forum: in a case the apt name of which alone justifies its mention here, *The Forum Craftsman*,[96] the Angolan owners of a Panamanian ship

---

[91] *VTB Capital Plc v Nutritek International Corp* [2013] UKSC 5; [2013] 2 A.C. 337.

[92] e.g., *Lincoln National Life Insurance Co v Employers Reinsurance Corp* [2002] EWHC 28; [2002] Lloyd's Rep I.R. 853. See also *Travelers Casualty and Surety Co of Europe Ltd v Sun Life Assurance Co of Canada (UK) Ltd* [2004] EWHC 1704 (Comm); [2004] Lloyd's Rep. IR 846 (relevance of involvement of regulatory authority in England).

[93] *Spiliada Maritime Corpn v Cansulex Ltd* [1987] A.C. 460, where there is discussion of the so-called "Cambridgeshire factor", the fact that related litigation involving a ship of that name had already been dealt with by the English court.

[94] See, e.g., *JSC BTA Bank v Granton Trade Ltd* [2010] EWHC 2577 (Comm); [2011] 2 All E.R. (Comm) 542.

[95] See *MacShannon v Rockware Glass Ltd* [1978] A.C. 795 (accident in factory in Scotland) and the line of cases following *Cordoba Shipping Co Ltd v National State Bank, Elizabeth, New Jersey, The Albaforth* [1984] 2 Lloyd's Rep 91 (negligent misstatement) and endorsed in *Berezovsky v Michaels* [2000] 1 W.L.R. 1004 (defamation); and *King v Lewis* [2004] EWCA Civ 1329; [2005] I.L.Pr. 16 (internet material originating in New York downloaded in England and so published there).

[96] [1984] 2 Lloyd's Rep. 102.

with a Greek crew sued in respect of damage to cargo as the vessel was about to set sail from Yokohama, Japan; the argument that Japan was the natural forum failed.

If the court gives permission for the service of the claim form out of the jurisdiction, the defendant has the opportunity to challenge the decision by applying for the service to be set aside.[97] The application will then be heard with both parties present, the initial decision having been made only on the submissions of the potential claimant.[98]

Connecting factors: heads of jurisdiction

7–017   The various sub-heads of para.3.1 of the Practice Direction, listing the cases in which permission may be given for service out of the jurisdiction, will now be examined in turn[99].

General grounds

7–018   (1) a claim is made for a remedy against a person domiciled within the jurisdiction.[100]

"Domicile", here and throughout Pt 6 of the Civil Procedure Rules, is to be determined not in accordance with the rules of common law but in accordance with the provisions of the European regime and paras 9 to 12 of Sch.1 to the Civil Jurisdiction and Judgments Order 2001.[101] This means that the test for domicile is the same whichever set of jurisdictional rules applies. If the case falls within the scope of the Brussels I *bis* Regulation, the domicile of the defendant will give the English courts jurisdiction[102] and permission to serve the claim form will *not* be required.[103]

(2) a claim is made for an injunction ordering the defendant to do or refrain from doing an act within the jurisdiction.[104]

The injunction need not be the only relief sought, and it is immaterial whether or not damages are also claimed; but the injunction must be the substantial relief sought: permission will be refused if the claim for an injunction is not made bona fide but merely to bring the case within the sub-head.[105] Permission will also be refused if a foreign court can more conveniently deal with the question,[106] or if

---

[97] CPR Pt 11.
[98] See the discussion on forum non conveniens below, para.7–031 and following.
[99] The 81st Update to the Civil Procedure Rules introduced a number of changes to these sub-heads. The new wording is indicated in italics. The majority of the amendments came into force on 1 October 2015. Furthermore, two new sub-headings (4A) and (21) were introduced.
[100] Practice Direction 6B, 3.1 (1).
[101] CPR r.6.31(i); see above, para.6–008.
[102] See above, para.6–007.
[103] CPR r.6.33(3).
[104] Practice Direction 6B, para.3.1(2).
[105] *De Bernales v New York Herald* [1893] 2 Q.B. 97n.; *Watson v Daily Record* [1907] 1 K.B. 853; contrast *Dunlop Rubber Co Ltd v Dunlop* [1921] 1 A.C. 367.
[106] *Société Générale de Paris v Dreyfus Bros* (1887) 37 Ch.D. 215; *Rosler v Hilbery* [1925] Ch. 250.

there is no real ground to anticipate repetition of the action complained of,[107] or if the injunction cannot be made effective in England.[108]

(3) a claim is made against a person ("the defendant") on whom the claim form has been or will be served and (a) there is between the claimant and the defendant a real issue which it is reasonable for the court to try[109]; and (b) the claimant wishes to serve the claim form on another person who is a necessary or proper party to that claim.[110]

(4) a claim is an additional claim under Pt 20 and the person is a necessary or proper party to the claim or additional claim.[111]

(4a) a claim is made against the defendant in reliance on certain specific sub-heads of jurisdiction[112] and a further claim is made against the same defendant which arises out of the same or closely connected facts[113]

These sub-heads are important, and have given rise to much litigation. The most obvious cases covered are cases where joint debtors or joint tortfeasors are alleged to be liable to the claimant[114]; or where the claimant has alternative claims against two persons, for example a claim against a principal for breach of contract, and against an agent for breach of warranty of authority.[115]

The new general ground introduced in (4a) aims to enable claims which have a close factual relationship to be brought together in one jurisdiction against the defendant. This expansion is justified due to the sheer practical advantages of trying closely related claims against the same defendant to be tried together[116], bearing in mind that permission to serve out the jurisdiction will only be given if the court is also satisfied that England is the appropriate forum for the closely related claim.

The person whom it is sought to serve out of the jurisdiction must be a "necessary or proper" party to the action. These terms are alternative, and a person may be a proper party although he or she is not a necessary party. The question whether B is a proper party to an action against A is simply answered: suppose both A and B had been in England, would they both have been proper parties to the action? If they would, and only one of them, A, is in England, then B is a proper party, and permission may be given to serve B out of the jurisdiction.[117] For instance, if defective goods are manufactured by B abroad,

---

[107] *De Bernales v New York Herald* [1893] 2 Q.B. 97n.; *Watson v Daily Record* [1907] 1 K.B. 853.

[108] *Marshall v Marshall* (1888) 38 Ch.D. 330.

[109] See *Erste Group Bank AG (London) v JSC (VMZ Red October)* [2015] EWCA Civ 379.

[110] Practice Direction 6B, para.3.1(3).

[111] Practice Direction 6B, para.3.1(4).

[112] Practice Direction 6B, para.3.1(4A). The specific sub-heads of jurisdiction are those provided for in paragraphs (2), (6) to (16), (19) or (21) of para.3.1 of Practice Direction 6B.

[113] This new sub-head came into force on 1 October 2015.

[114] *Williams v Cartwright* [1895] 1 Q.B. 142.

[115] *Massey v Heynes* (1888) 21 Q.B.D. 330.

[116] See Civil Procedure Rule Committee, *Gateways for service out of the jurisdiction*, CPR (15) 28, 12 June 2015.

[117] *Massey v Heynes* (1888) 21 Q.B.D. 330 at 338; *The Elton* [1891] P. 265; *Osterreichische Export etc. Co v British Indemnity Co Ltd* [1914] 2 K.B. 747; *The Goldean Mariner* [1990] 2 Lloyd's Rep. 215.

and supplied to A in England, and sold by A to the claimant, the claimant can bring an action for breach of contract against A and in tort against B.[118]

Claims for interim remedies

(5) a claim is made for an interim remedy under s.25(1) of the Civil Jurisdiction and Judgments Act 1982.[119]

7–019   In the past there were technical difficulties concerning applications for a freezing (*Mareva*) injunction in respect of the defendant's assets. Where permission to serve documents was needed, it was formerly sought under a sub-head dealing with injunctions. It was held at one time that this was not possible where the defendant was not otherwise amenable to the jurisdiction and the substantive proceedings had been brought, or were to be brought, in another country.[120] However, this limitation was removed, first in relation to proceedings in other Contracting States to the Brussels and Lugano Conventions,[121] and then in respect of proceedings in any country.[122] The application can now be made under this sub-head, first introduced in 2000.

Claims in relation to contracts

7–020   (6)   a claim is made in respect of a contract where the contract:
   (a)   was made within the jurisdiction;
   (b)   was made by or through an agent trading or residing within the jurisdiction;
   (c)   is governed by English law; or
   (d)   contains a term to the effect that the court shall have jurisdiction to determine any claim in respect of the contract.[123]

There is an initial characterisation issue: is this a "contract" case? It has been held, for example, that the relationship between a company and a director of that company is not a matter of contract.[124] The text of the predecessor provision in the former Order 11 spoke of claims "brought to enforce, rescind, dissolve, annul, or otherwise affect a contract, or to recover damages or obtain other relief in respect of the breach of a contract": the current rule can be no less wide in scope and it has indeed been held that the current formulation is "deliberately wider" than its predecessor.[125] So this sub-head will be available where the claimant seeks a declaration that a contract has been frustrated,[126] and where the claim is

---

[118] *The Manchester Courage* [1973] 1 Lloyd's Rep. 386.
[119] Practice Direction 6B, para.3.1(5).
[120] *The Siskina v Distos Compania Naviera* [1979] A.C. 210; *Mercedes Benz AG v Leiduck* [1996] A.C. 284.
[121] Civil Jurisdiction and Judgments Act 1982 s.25(1).
[122] SI 1997/302, made under ibid., s.25(3).
[123] Practice Direction 6B, para.3.1(6).
[124] *Newtherapeutics Ltd v Katz* [1991] Ch. 226.
[125] *Albon v Naza Motor Trading Sdn Bhd* [2007] EWHC 9 (Ch); [2007] 1 W.L.R. 2489; *Global 5000 Ltd v Wadhawan* [2011] EWHC 853 (Comm); [2011] 2 All E.R. (Comm) 190.
[126] *BP Exploration (Libya) Ltd v Hunt* [1976] 1 W.L.R. 788.

for restitution, the repayment of money paid under a mistake of fact in circumstances related to, but not arising under, a contract.[127] The position was further clarified in *Greene Wood & McLean LLP v Templeton Insurance Ltd*[128]:

> Large numbers of miners brought claims in respect of lung disease and vibration white finger. Their solicitors, G, made an unsuccessful application in the course of the litigation and costs were ordered against the miners. The solicitors accepted liability to pay those costs but brought a claim against T, an insurance company based in the Isle of Man, for contribution. The claim alleged that G and T were liable for the same damage, G under their contract with the miners, T under an After The Event insurance policy taken out in the name of the miners. G argued that their contribution claim arose in respect of a contract (the insurance policy) which was governed by English law. T argued that there was no contractual relationship between G and T, and that the power to permit service out of the jurisdiction applied only where claimant and proposed defendant were parties to the relevant contract.

The Court of Appeal rejected T's argument. To say that, for a claim to be "in respect of a contract", it must be "in respect of a contract between the intended claimant and the intended defendant" would be to add words to the rule which were not there. Since the Contracts (Rights of Third Parties) Act 1999, there were cases in which a third party could sue on a contract made between two persons for his or her benefit; such a third party should be able to rely on the contractual aspects of the rules as to service out of the jurisdiction. The claim in the instant case clearly had a connection with a contract governed by English law, even though it was not a claim brought under the contract. No doubt some connections with contracts were more remote than others; that could be taken into account in considering whether England was the appropriate forum.

This sub-head is very important in practice: its four branches require separate discussion.

(a) Contracts made in England

A contract concluded by postal correspondence is made where the letter of acceptance is posted.[129] Many contracts are now made by "instantaneous" means of communication, telephone, fax or email, in which case the contract is made where the acceptance is communicated to the offeror.[130] In *Brinkibon Ltd v Stahag Stahl und Stahlwaren-handelgesellschaft mbH*[131]:

> The contract concerned the supply of steel bars by S (an Austrian company) to B (an English company acting as agent (though it had not disclosed this fact) for a Swiss company. The steel was to be delivered by sea from Alexandria in Egypt. The contract was not performed after a dispute about the financial arrangements, and B sought to sue in England claiming that the contract was made in England. The acceptance of the terms was by a telex message from London to Vienna. The House of Lords confirmed that the postal communication rules did not apply to instantaneous communications. On the facts, the contract was made in Vienna.

---

[127] *Albon v Naza Motor Trading Sdn Bhd* [2007] EWHC 9 (Ch); [2007] 1 W.L.R. 2489.
[128] [2009] EWCA Civ 65; [2009] 1 W.L.R. 2013.
[129] *Wansborough Paper Co Ltd v Laughland* [1920] W.N. 344; *Benaim v Debono* [1924] A.C. 514 at 520; *Clarke v Harper and Robinson* [1938] N. Ir. 162; *Williams v Society of Lloyd's* [1994] 1 V.R. 274; *Lewis Construction Co Ltd v M Tichauer SA* [1996] V.R. 341.
[130] *Entores Ltd v Miles Far East Corporation* [1955] 2 Q.B. 327; *Surrey (UK) Ltd v Mazandaran Wood & Paper Industries* [2014] EWHC 3165 (Comm.).
[131] [1983] 2 A.C. 34.

The importance of the case lies in some qualifications mentioned by Lord Wilberforce. Indicating that there could be no "universal rule" he suggested facts which might render the communication less than instantaneous. The receiving machine might have a fault; it might be in a different building, or belong to a third party. Although he was speaking about telex machines, now outmoded, the same could be said about fax machines, and similar questions could be asked about email or internet messages sent overnight and read in the morning, perhaps by a businessman in a hotel room far removed from his usual office and even in a different country. Lord Wilberforce referred to "business practice" and that appears to accept that all these cases are to be treated as covered by the "instantaneous" rule.

For a contract to be "made within the jurisdiction" it suffices that it is "substantially made" within the jurisdiction.[132] If a contract is made within the jurisdiction, a variation taking place abroad in the terms of the contract will not deprive the English court of jurisdiction, at least where the core obligations of the contract are untouched.[133]

(b) Contracts made by or through English agents of foreign principals[134]

This includes not only contracts made by agents but also contracts made through agents who have no authority to make contracts, but only to obtain orders and transmit them to the foreign principal for acceptance or rejection.[135] The sub-head applies only where the foreign principal is the intended defendant, and is not available to such a principal as claimant.[136] Rule 6.12 of the Civil Procedure Rules provides an alternative method of service if the conditions laid down in (ii) are satisfied and also two further conditions, namely that the contract was made in England, and that the agent's authority has not been determined and he is still in business relations with his principal. The method is to issue the claim form against the principal and serve it with permission of the court on the agent in England.

(c) Contracts governed by English law

Whether a contract is governed by English law is determined in accordance with the Rome I Regulation,[137] the provisions of which are considered in detail elsewhere in this book.[138] It goes without saying that English judges are especially well qualified to apply the English law of contract, but nonetheless Lord Diplock observed in *Amin Rasheed Shipping Corp v Kuwait Insurance Co*[139] that jurisdiction exercised under this sub-head over a foreign corporation

---

[132] *BP Exploration (Libya) Ltd v Hunt* [1976] 1 W.L.R. 788 at 798.
[133] *Sharab v Al-Saud* [2008] EWHC 1893 (Ch); [2009] 2 Lloyd's Rep 160.
[134] The Rules no longer state, as did the former Order 11, that the agent must be acting "on behalf of a principal trading or residing out of the jurisdiction" but this will still be the case.
[135] *National Mortgage and Agency Co of New Zealand v Gosselin* (1922) 38 T.L.R. 832.
[136] *Union International Insurance Co v Jubilee Insurance Co* [1991] 1 W.L.R. 415.
[137] European Parliament and Council Regulation No 593/2008 of 17 June 2008 on the law applicable to contractual obligations (Rome I), OJ L 177/6, 4.7.2008.
[138] Below, Ch.15.
[139] [1984] A.C. 50.

with no place of business in England was an exorbitant jurisdiction, one which an English court would not recognise as possessed by a foreign court in the absence of some treaty. For that reason, the judicial discretion to grant permission in such cases "should be exercised with circumspection". This part of Lord Diplock's speech was endorsed by the House of Lords in *Spiliada Maritime Corp v Cansulex Ltd*,[140] where it was emphasised that the importance of the English governing law was something which varied greatly depending on the circumstances of the case.

So in *Novus Aviation Ltd v Onur Air Tasimacilik AS*[141] which concerned dealings between Bahamian and Turkish companies, the claimant's reliance on the choice of English law to govern the contract was unavailing: it was described as a simple case, concerning merely the evidential interpretation of one sentence in the minutes of a meeting. There was no important issue of English law. That case may be contrasted with *Stonebridge Underwriting Ltd v Ontario Municipal Insurance Exchange*.[142] In that case the implied choice of English law[143] in a reinsurance contract, placed in London, by London brokers, with a London reinsurer, and incorporating a number of standard London market clauses was of considerable significance in determining that England was the proper place for hearing a dispute under the reinsurance contract; the issues were seen as "particularly suited" for determination by the English Commercial Court, whose habitual business includes the resolution of reinsurance disputes between reassureds and Lloyd's underwriters in accordance with well-developed principles of law and construction.

If the claimant has alternative remedies in contract and tort upon the same facts, he can choose his remedy. Thus, where the claimant was employed abroad under a contract governed by English law, and sustained personal injuries abroad in the course of his employment there, he was allowed to serve the claim form on his employers out of the jurisdiction in an action for breach of an implied term in the contract, even though the facts also gave rise to a claim in tort, for which permission would have been refused because the tort was not committed in England.[144]

(d) Contracts containing a jurisdiction clause selecting the English court

Most cases otherwise under this heading will fall under the European regime,[145] the intra-UK scheme,[146] or the Hague Choice of Court Agreements Convention.[147] In such cases permission to serve out of the jurisdiction is unnecessary. In

---

[140] [1987] A.C. 460. See also *Ilyssia Cia. Naviera SA v Bamaodah, The Elli 2* [1985] 1 Lloyd's Rep. 107 for an explanation (endorsed in *Spiliada*) of related aspects of Lord Diplock's speech.
[141] [2009] EWCA Civ 122; [2009] 1 Lloyd's Rep. 576.
[142] [2010] EWHC 2279 (Comm); [2011] Lloyd's Rep IR 171.
[143] On the relevance of choice of law agreements for the determination of jurisdiction see M Hook, (2014) 63 I.C.L.Q. 963.
[144] *Matthews v Kuwait Bechtel Corporation* [1959] 2 Q.B. 57.
[145] Regulation 1215/2012, art.25; reg.44/2001, art.23; Lugano Convention (2007), art.23.
[146] Civil Jurisdiction and Judgments Act 1982 Sch.4 as substituted by the Civil Jurisdiction Order 2001 (SI 2001/3929), amended by the Civil Jurisdiction and Judgments Regulations 2009 (SI 2009/3131) and further amended in light of the Brussels I Recast by the Civil Jurisdiction and

cases outside the scope of these instruments, where the parties have agreed that the English courts should have jurisdiction permission to serve out of the jurisdiction will normally be granted.[148]

Submission to the jurisdiction of the court may be inferred from the terms of a contract. If one party to a contract gives an address for service within the jurisdiction, service may be effected on the agent as of right.[149] Otherwise, the permission of the court under this sub-head is needed.

(7) a claim is made in respect of a breach of contract committed within the jurisdiction.[150]

For the purposes of this sub-head, it is immaterial where the contract was made or whether, in the language of the former Order 11, "the breach was preceded or accompanied by a breach committed out of the jurisdiction that rendered impossible the performance of so much of the contract as ought to have been performed within the jurisdiction".

A contract may be broken in one of three ways; namely by express repudiation, implied repudiation, or failure to perform.

Breach by express repudiation occurs when one party informs the other that he or she no longer intends to perform the contract. If X who is abroad writes a letter of repudiation to A in England, the breach is not committed in England.[151] On the other hand, if X who is abroad sends an agent to England, or writes to an agent who is in England, instructing the agent to repudiate a contract with A who is in England, and the agent does so, for example by letter posted in England, then the breach is committed in England.[152]

Breach by implied repudiation occurs when one party does an act that is inconsistent with the contract, for instance, when X promises to sell a house to A but sells it to B instead. Although there is no authority on the point, the breach in such a case presumably occurs where the inconsistent act is performed.

The normal form of breach is the failure by one party to perform one or more of his or her obligations under the contract. In such a case it is not necessary that the whole contract was to be performed in England by both parties, but it is necessary that some part of it was to be performed in England and that there has been a breach of that part.[153] It is not sufficient if the contract or part of it might be performed either in England or abroad; it is necessary that the contract or part

Judgments (Amendment) Regulations 2014 (SI 2014/2947) and the Civil Jurisdiction and Judgments (Amendment) (Scotland) Regulations 2015 (SSI 2015/1).
[147] See para.5-017.
[148] However, note the power to stay proceedings brought in England as the contractual forum, *UBS AG v Omni Holding AG* [2000] 1 W.L.R. 916; *Marubeni Hong Kong & South China Ltd v Mongolian Government* [2002] 2 All E.R. (Comm.) 873.
[149] CPR rr.6.3, 6.8.
[150] CPR, r.6.36 and PD 6B, para.3.1 (7).
[151] *Cherry v Thompson* (1872) L.R. 7 Q.B. 573 at 579; *Holland v Bennett* [1902] 1 K.B. 867, both approved by the Privy Council in *Martin v Stout* [1925] A.C. 359 at 368–369; but see *Cooper v Knight* (1901) 17 T.L.R. 299.
[152] *Mutzenbecher v La Aseguradora Espanola* [1906] 1 K.B. 254; *Oppenheimer v Louis Rosenthal & Co AG* [1937] 1 All E.R. 23.
[153] *Rein v Stein* [1892] 1 Q.B. 753.

of it was to be performed in England and not elsewhere.[154] The contract need not contain an express term providing for performance in England[155]: it is enough if the court can gather that this was the intention of the parties by construing the contract in the light of the surrounding circumstances, including the course of dealing between the parties.[156]

In most of the reported cases, the breach complained of was the failure to pay money, a matter in which it is especially difficult to determine the place of performance in the absence of an express term in the contract. "The general rule is that where no place of payment is specified, either expressly or by implication, the debtor must seek out his creditor".[157] But this is only a general rule and, as stated, it only applies where no place of payment is expressed or implied in the contract. It certainly does not mean that a creditor can confer jurisdiction on the English court merely by taking up residence in England after the making of the contract, thus making England the place of performance.[158]

In a contract of employment, wages or salary would normally be payable where the service is to be performed, in the absence of an express or implied term in the contract.[159] But if the employee is employed in only a nominal or consultative capacity, and is free to reside where he likes, his salary may be payable in England, if that is where the employee decides to live.[160] In a contract for services, it may be possible to infer that the fee or commission is payable at the contractor's usual place of business in England, even if the work is to be performed abroad.[161]

In a contract for the sale of goods by a seller in England to a buyer abroad, it will, in the absence of a contractual term to the contrary, be easy to infer that the buyer's obligation was to pay for the goods in England.[162] The same is the case if a principal in England sends goods to an agent abroad to be sold on commission.[163] But it is otherwise if, on the true construction of the contract, the only duty of the foreign agent is to sell the goods and remit the proceeds to England from abroad in a specified manner, because it will be inferred that the agent's duty is at an end when the remittance is made.[164] If a foreign principal appoints an agent in England to sell goods on commission, it is usually inferred that the commission is payable in England.[165]

---

[154] *Bell & Co v Antwerp London and Brazil Line* [1891] 1 Q.B. 103; *The Eider* [1893] P. 119; *Comber v Leyland* [1898] A.C. 524; *Cuban Atlantic Sugar Sales Corporation v Compania de Vapores San Elefterio Lda* [1960] 1 Q.B. 187.

[155] *Reynolds v Coleman* (1887) 36 Ch.D. 453.

[156] *Rein v Stein* [1892] 1 Q.B. 753; *Fry & Co v Raggio* (1891) 40 W.R. 120; *Charles Duval & Co Ltd v Gans* [1904] 2 K.B. 685.

[157] *The Eider* [1893] P. 119 at 136–137, per Bowen LJ.

[158] *Malik v Narodni Banka Ceskoslovenska* [1946] 2 All E.R. 663.

[159] See *Malik v Narodni Banka Ceskoslovenska*, above.

[160] *Vitkovice Horni A Hutni Tezirstvo v Korner* [1951] A.C. 869.

[161] *Thompson v Palmer* [1893] 2 Q.B. 80.

[162] *Robey & Co v Snaefell Mining Co Ltd* (1887) 20 Q.B.D. 152; *Fry & Co v Raggio* (1891) 40 W.R. 120.

[163] *Rein v Stein* [1892] 1 Q.B. 753; *Charles Duval & Co Ltd v Gans* [1904] 2 K.B. 685.

[164] *Comber v Leyland* [1898] A.C. 524, a case "of a somewhat special character" per Stirling LJ in *Charles Duval & Co Ltd v Gans*, above, at p.691.

[165] *Hoerter v Hanover etc. Works* (1893) 10 T.L.R. 103; *International Corporation Ltd v Besser Manufacturing Co* [1950] 1 K.B. 488.

(8) a claim is made for a declaration that no contract exists where, if the contract was found to exist, it would comply with the conditions set out in sub-head (6).[166]

At one time it was doubtful whether an application for service out of the jurisdiction could be made where the claimant sought a declaration that there never was a contract. This is now the subject of the express provision in this sub-head.

Claims in tort

7–021   a claim is made in tort where

(9)

    (a)   damage was sustained, or will be sustained within the jurisdiction; or

    (b)   damage which has been or will be sustained results from an act committed, or likely to be committed, within the jurisdiction.[167]

The language of this sub-head was based on the approach adopted by the then ECJ in interpreting art.5(3) of the Brussels Convention.[168] The analysis of the equivalent provisions of the Brussels I *bis* Regulation is provided elsewhere. This sub-head was recently extended to include in (a) and (b) damage that 'will be' sustained within the jurisdiction.[169][170] As a sub-head of the English traditional rules of jurisdiction, and particularly as a connecting factor enabling in certain circumstances the exercise of jurisdiction over a defendant not present in the jurisdiction, what law is to determine whether the claim is "in tort" as opposed to any other type of action? This is essentially a characterisation exercise, which is appropriately carried out by reference to English law as the law of the forum.[171]

If it is argued that the damage results from an act committed in England and the facts show acts both within and without the jurisdiction, the sub-head will apply if the damage results from substantial and efficacious (as opposed to minor and insignificant) acts of the defendant within the jurisdiction.[172] It seems that the

---

[166] Practice Direction 6A, para.3.1(8).

[167] CPR, r.6.36 and Practice Direction 6B, para.3.1(9). As to the scope of this sub-head see *Fern Computer Consultancy Ltd v Intergraph Cadworx & Analysis Solutions Inc* [2014] EWHC 2908 (Ch.); [2014] Bus. L.R. 1397.

[168] Case 21/76 *Bier BV v Mines de Potasse d'Alsace SA* [1978] Q.B. 708. Note how this history affected the interpretation of this rule by the Court of Appeal in *Brownlie v Four Seasons Holdings Inc* [2015] EWCA Civ 665; [2015] C.P. Rep. 40.

[169] The amendment to this sub-head follows a suggestion of Lord Mance, Chairman of the Lords Chancellor Advisory Committee on Private International Law, for the sake of consistency with new sub-head introduced in paragraph (21). See Civil Procedure Rule Committee, *Gateways for service out of the jurisdiction*, CPR (15) 28, 12 June 2015.

[170] See para.6-021.

[171] *Metall und Rohstoff AG v Donaldson Lufkin & Jenrette Inc* [1990] 1 Q.B. 391 (CA), overruled in *Lonrho Plc v Fayed* [1992] 1 A.C. 448 on other aspects. See also *Vidal-Hall v Google Inc* [2014] EWHC 13 (QB); [2015] EWCA Civ 311; [2015] 3 W.L.R. 409 (CA (Civ Div)).

[172] *Metall und Rohstoff AG v Donaldson Lufkin & Jenrette Inc* [1990] 1 Q.B. 391, 437 (CA).

sub-head will apply to any sort of damage, provided it is significant; the *Dumez France* principle[173] has not been applied in this context.

In the past, in the case of claims relating to a death abroad, the sustaining in England of a loss of financial dependency and the incurring of funeral expenses has constituted "damage" for this purpose.[174] However, in *Brownlie v Four Seasons Holdings Inc*[175] the English Court of Appeal overruled these previous first instance decisions, and adopted a narrow interpretation of "damage" for the purposes of this sub-head of jurisdiction, which does not include consequential losses.

> Sir Ian and Lady Brownlie were involved in a car accident during an excursion in Egypt. Tragically, Sir Ian was killed and Lady Brownlie was injured. The excursion was organised by the concierge of the hotel in Cairo where they were staying. Lady Brownlie instituted proceedings in the English courts in contract and in tort against the Canadian company that runs the hotel. Permission to serve out of the jurisdiction was granted by the court in first instance under para.3.1(9)(a) of the Practice Direction. The Court of Appeal overturned the judge's decision to allow service out of the jurisdiction on the basis that the relevant connecting factor, i.e. damage sustained in the jurisdiction[176] had to be interpreted consistently with art.4 of the Rome II Regulation[177] (on the law applicable to non-contractual obligations). On this narrow interpretation the English courts did not have jurisdiction over Lady Brownlie's tort claims (save in relation to her claim under the Fatal Accidents Act 1976) because the 'damage' had occurred in Egypt.[178] The damage suffered within the jurisdiction was consequential loss only, which was insufficient to found jurisdiction under this sub-head.[179]

This decision, as to the understanding of "damage" as a connecting factor in relation to this provision of the CPR,[180] sits uneasily with the overall approach to service out of the jurisdiction in the English traditional rules.

As we have seen, if there are alternative causes of action in contract and tort on the same facts, the claimant may choose to rely on any of sub-heads (6), (7) or (9).

In relation to defamation cases, attention should be paid to the Defamation Act 2013 s.9 and s.10. It applies to actions for defamation against a person who is not domiciled (a) in the UK; (b) in another Member State; or (c) in a State party to the Lugano Convention.[181] It is provided that the court does not have jurisdiction to hear and determine such an action unless the court is satisfied that, of all the places in which the statement complained of has been published, England is clearly the most appropriate forum in which to bring an action in respect of the

---

[173] See paras 6-023 and following.
[174] *Booth v Phillips* [2004] EWHC 1437. See also *Cooley v Ramsey* [2008] EWHC 129 and *Wink v Croatia Osiguranje DD* [2013] EWHC 1118 (QB) (party injured in an accident abroad but continues to suffer the effects in the jurisdiction). See also *Erste Group Bank AG, London Branch v JSC "VMZ Red October"* [2015] EWCA Civ 379, where the Court of Appeal had already shown reservations on this point ([104]–[105]).
[175] [2015] EWCA Civ 665; [2015] C.P.Rep. 40. See Bergson, (2016) L.Q.R. 42.
[176] CPR r .3.1(6)(a) and (c) and 3.1(9)(a) of PD 6B.
[177] See para 16-012.
[178] The decision has generated criticism. See Bergson, (2016) LQR 132, 42-46.
[179] At [83]–[88].
[180] See at [83] and [85].
[181] Section 9(1).

statement.[182] A range of factors can be considered by the courts in deciding this point, for example, the amount of damage to the claimant's reputation in the jurisdiction compared to elsewhere, the extent to which the publication was targeted at a readership in the jurisdiction; and whether there is reason to think that the claimant would not receive a fair trial in the alternative forum. A court does not have jurisdiction to hear and determine an action for defamation brought against a person who was not the author, editor or publisher of the statement complained of unless the court is satisfied that it is not reasonably practicable for an action to be brought against the author, editor or publisher.[183]

Enforcement of judgments or arbitral awards

7–022 (10) a claim is made to enforce any judgment or arbitral award.[184]

This sub-head enables permission to be granted in a common law action on a foreign judgment or arbitration award against a debtor who remains out of England. The claimant does not have to show that there are assets in England available for execution.[185] This sub-head is all the more necessary now that s.34 of the Civil Jurisdiction and Judgments Act 1982 prevents the claimant from bringing a fresh action in England on the original cause of action.

Claims about property within the jurisdiction

7–023 (11) the subject matter of a claim relates wholly or principally to property within the jurisdiction provided that nothing under this sub-head renders justiciable the title to or the right to possession of immovable property outside England and Wales.[186]

This extended sub-head replaced earlier provisions. The extension has its origin in a proposal put forward by the Trust Law Committee. The new formulation adds flexibility to the sub-head and should allow for a broader coverage[187]. The sub-head expressly preserves the effects of the basic principle of the conflict of laws according to which questions concerning the title to, or the right to possession of, immovable property are to be determined by the *lex situs*. It is not limited to claims relating to the ownership or possession of property, but extends to any claim for relief (whether for damages or otherwise) so long as it is related *wholly or principally* to property located within the jurisdiction.[188] It

---

[182] Section 9(2).

[183] Section 10(1).

[184] CPR, r.6.36 and Practice Direction 6B, para.3.1(10).

[185] *Tasarruf Mevduati Sigorta Fonu v Demirel* [2007] EWCA Civ 799; [2007] 1 W.L.R. 2508; *Habib Bank Ltd v Central Bank of Sudan* [2014] EWHC 2288 (Comm.). Cf. *Linsen International Ltd v Humpuss Sea Transport Pte Ltd* [2011] EWCA Civ 1042.

[186] CPR, r.6.36 and Practice Direction 6B, para.3.1(11).

[187] For example, claims relating to a trust fund which mainly comprises property within the jurisdiction, but also includes some foreign investments. See further Civil Procedure Rule Committee, *Gateways for service out of the jurisdiction*, CPR (15) 28, 12 June 2015.

[188] *Banca Carige SpA v Banco Nacional de Cuba* [2001] 1 W.L.R. 2039.

covers, for example, a claim in an insolvency context that property had been sold at an undervalue, a claim to recover rent due under a lease of land, and a claim for damages for breach of covenant.[189]

Claims about trusts, etc.

Under this heading, the Rules contain five distinct sub-heads:

7–024

(12) a claim is made in respect of a trust which is created by the operation of a statute, or by a written instrument, or created orally and evidenced in writing, and which is governed by the law of England and Wales.

(12a) a claim is made in respect of a trust which is created by the operation of a statute, or by a written instrument, or created orally and evidenced in writing, and which provides that jurisdiction in respect of such a claim shall be conferred upon the courts of England and Wales.[190]

(13) a claim is made for any remedy which might be obtained in proceedings for the administration of the estate of a person who died domiciled within the jurisdiction, or whose estate includes assets within the jurisdiction.[191]

(14) a probate claim or a claim for the rectification of a will.[192]

(15) a claim is made against the defendant as constructive trustee, or as trustee of a resulting trust, where the claim arises out of acts committed or events occurring within the jurisdiction or relates to assets within the jurisdiction.[193]

The predecessor provision of this sub-head was added to fill a lacuna revealed by the decision in *Metall und Rohstoff AG v Donaldson Lufkin & Jenrette Inc*[194] that an action for breach of duty as a constructive trustee could not be regarded as "founded on a tort" and so within the sub-head dealing with claims in tort. It is not necessary to show that all the defendant's acts were committed within the jurisdiction[195]: and it may be that where the defendant did no act in England, some other link will suffice.[196]

---

[189] See *Agnew v Usher* (1884) 14 Q.B.D. 78; *Kaye v Sutherland* (1887) 20 Q.B.D. 147; *Tassell v Hallen* [1892] 1 Q.B. 321; *Official Solicitor v Stype Investments Ltd* [1983] 1 W.L.R. 214; *Banca Carige SpA v Banco Nacional de Cuba* [2001] 1 W.L.R. 2039.

[190] CPR, r. 6.36 and Practice Direction 6B, para.3.1(12) and (12A).There is no requirement that the trust property be situated in England. See *Williams v Central Bank of Nigeria* [2013] EWCA Civ 785. The new formulation of these sub-heads in force since 6 April 2015 was proposed by the Trust Law Committee. See further CPR (15) 15, 6 March 2015, Annex D, *Minutes of the meeting of the Lord Chancellor's Advisory Committee on Private International Law* held on Monday 1 December 2014.

[191] CPR, r.6.36 and Practice Direction 6B, para.3.1(13). The amendments to this sub-heading were introduced on 1 October 2015.

[192] CPR, r.6.36 and Practice Direction 6B, para.3.1(14). The amendments to this sub-heading were introduced on 1 October 2015.

[193] Practice Direction 6A, para.3.1(15).

[194] [1990] Q.B. 391.

[195] *ISC Technologies Ltd v Guerin* [1992] 2 Lloyd's Rep. 430.

[196] *NABB Brothers International Ltd v Lloyds Bank International (Guernsey) Ltd* [2005] EWHC 405 (Ch); [2005] I.L.Pr. 506.

(16) a claim is made for restitution where (a) the defendant's alleged liability arises out of acts committed within the jurisdiction, or[197] (b) the enrichment is obtained within the jurisdiction; or (c) the claim is governed by the law of England and Wales[198]

The proper characterisation of restitution claims has given rise to difficulty under the Regulation rules.[199] This sub-head clarifies the position under the traditional rules.

Claims by HM Revenue and Customs

7–025 (17) a claim is made by the Commissioners for HM Revenue and Customs relating to duties or taxes against a defendant not domiciled in Scotland or Northern Ireland.[200]

Other claims

7–026 Other sub-heads cover claims made by a party to proceedings for an order that the court exercise its power under s.51 of the Senior Courts (formerly Supreme Court) Act 1981 to make a costs order in favour of or against a person who is not a party to those proceedings[201]; certain salvage claims[202]; and claims made under an enactment which allows proceedings to be brought where those proceedings are not covered by any other sub-head.[203]

Claims for breach of confidence or misuse of private information

7–026A (21) a claim is made for breach of confidence or misuse of private information where – (a) detriment was suffered, or will be suffered, within the jurisdiction; or (b) detriment which has been, or will be, suffered results from an act committed, or likely to be committed, within the jurisdiction.[204]

---

[197] Practice Direction 6A, para.3.1(16). The original sub-head covered only this first part, i.e. what currently is sub-paragraph (a) of this sub-head.

[198] Sub-headings 16 (b) and 16 (c) came into force on 1 October 2015.

[199] *Kleinwort Benson Ltd v Glasgow City Council* [1999] 1 A.C. 153; see above, para.6–015.

[200] Practice Direction 6A, para.3.1(17).

[201] CPR, r.6.36 and Practice Direction 6B, para.3.1(18).

[202] CPR, r.6.36 and Practice Direction 6B, para.3.1(19).

[203] CPR, r.6.36 and Practice Direction 6B, para.3.1(20).

[204] CPR, r. 6.36 and Practice Direction 6B, para.3.1(21). This new sub-heading came into force 1 October 2015. It follows from a proposal from Mr. J. Tugendhat and Mr. J. Arnold, *Amendment of CPR Practice Direction 6B paragraph 3.1*, of 28 January 2014, and further recommendation by the Civil Procedure Rules Committee. The need for this new sub-heading came to the fore in *Vidal-Hall v Google Inc* [2014] EWHC 13 (Q.B.), [2014] 1 W.L.R. 4155, although in this case the Court of Appeal [2015] EWCA Civ 311 found that claims for misuse of private information and breach of confidence could fell within sub-head (9) (claims in tort). However, the new sub-heading is welcomed as it provides an independent jurisdictional ground for these two distinct causes of action t protect privacy in English law. See Civil Procedure Rule Committee, *Gateways for service out of the jurisdiction*, CPR (15) 28, 12 June 2015, paras [35]-[47]. See, inter alia, J Folkard, *Privacy and conflicts in the Court of Appeal* (case comment), L.Q.R. 2016 (132) 31.

Effecting Service Abroad

The principles for service on a defendant abroad are well established. English courts will recognise service of process in English proceedings effected abroad by any method allowed in the country where the defendant is to be served, or any applicable international convention.[205] As with service in England, service may be direct, effected on the defendant by any means permitted in the country where service is sought, or it may be done by official channels, most extendedly as provided for in the 1965 Hague Convention on Service Abroad of Judicial and Extrajudicial Documents in Civil or Commercial Matters, or for defendants located within the EU, by the EU Regulation 1393/2007 on the service in the Member States of judicial and extrajudicial documents in civil or commercial matters.[206]

7–027

The 1965 Hague Convention on Service of Documents

The 1965 Hague Convention on service of documents has provided the international community with extensive support on cross-border transmission of judicial and extrajudicial documents and on service on the defendant in the receiving country. The Convention official method is transmission via the designated authority in the States parties to the Convention (Central Authorities).[207] The Convention provides a range of other alternative methods for effecting service, including post[208]; judicial officers in the receiving country at the instance of the claimant[209]; and consular or diplomatic channels.[210]

7–028

The EU Service Regulation

In connection with defendants that need to be served in another Member State of the EU, service in cases where the defendant's address is known,[211] is governed by the EU Service Regulation.[212] The Regulation provides for direct service on the defendant and for the official transmission of documents. Service may be effected by post,[213] by registered letter with acknowledgment of receipt or equivalent, where such direct service is permitted under the law of the receiving

7–029

---

[205] CPR r.6.40.

[206] European Parliament and Council Regulation No.1393/2007 of 13 November 2007 on the service in the Member States of judicial and extrajudicial documents in civil or commercial matters (service of documents), OJ L 324/79, 10.12.2007.

[207] Article 2.

[208] Article 10(a). Note however that several countries have limited this provision by means of a reservation to the international treaty, limiting the scope of this provision to recorded delivery or other means of evidencing that delivery has effectively taken place.

[209] Article 10(c).

[210] Article 8(1), 9.

[211] Article 1.

[212] European Parliament and Council Regulation No 1393/2007 of 13 November 2007 on the service in the Member States of judicial and extrajudicial documents in civil or commercial matters (service of documents), OJ L 324/79, 10.12.2007.

[213] Article 14.

country[214]; or through 'transmitting agencies'[215] and 'receiving agencies',[216] supported by a 'central body'[217] designated in each Member State. The Regulation also provides for service through consular or diplomatic channels.[218]

Alternative methods—where the defendant's location is not known

7–030   As referred to above, the Civil Procedure Rules permits service of the claim form at an alternative place or to an alternative person,[219] usually at the offices of the defendant's lawyers, where other methods are unavailable. However an order of that kind cannot be provided disregarding the Hague Convention.[220] Whether or not service on an alternative place, or to an alternative person, can be justified needs to be decided on the facts. In *Abela v Baadarani*[221] it was held that in deciding whether to make an order to such effect the mere fact that the defendant had learned of the existence and content of the claim form could not in itself constitute enough justification but it was a crucial factor for the court to consider; other relevant factors were whether service through other means had proved impractical and further attempts would lead to unacceptable delay and expense; and whether a defendant had refused to cooperate by disclosing his address. It was held that an order of this kind involves a value judgment by the judge rather than an exercise of discretion.

STEERING A CASE TOWARDS AN APPROPRIATE FORUM

7–031   In international litigation concurrent jurisdiction is the rule rather than the exception. Very often the courts of more than one country will have jurisdiction to entertain a claim under the applicable set of jurisdictional rules.[222] In cases of competing jurisdictions, the different approach adopted in the European regime as compared to the English traditional rules of jurisdiction to steer a case towards an appropriate forum was introduced in the first chapter on jurisdiction of this book. There reference was made to the procedural mechanisms developed in most common law countries which enable the judges to steer a case towards the most appropriate forum, and in the process off-set to some extent the initial advantage enjoyed by a claimant in selecting a forum likely to prove favourable to the claim. So, a court in a common law country typically has an inherent jurisdiction, reinforced in England by statute,[223] to stay an action brought in that country or to

---

[214] Article 15.
[215] Article 2(1).
[216] Article 2 (2).
[217] Article 3.
[218] Articles 12 and 13.
[219] CPR r.6.15.
[220] *Abela v Baadarani* [2013] UKSC 44; [2013] 1 W.L.R. 2043.
[221] *Abela v Baadarani* [2013] UKSC 44; [2013] 1 W.L.R. 2043.
[222] See para 5-004.
[223] Senior Courts (formerly Supreme Court) Act 1981 s.49(3); Civil Jurisdiction and Judgments Act 1982 s.49.

restrain by injunction (an "anti-suit injunction") the institution or continuation of proceedings in a foreign court, whenever it is necessary to do so in order to prevent injustice.[224]

The English courts have in this context an inherently procedural power to order a stay in *lis pendens* scenarios in the exercise of case management.[225] Considerations central to the conflict of laws get intertwined in this sphere with these inherently procedural postulates to the point that it is sometimes difficult to distinguish in the reasoning of decided cases where the exercise of this discretionary powers rests.

In turn, these discretionary powers makes the determination of jurisdiction a very important stage in English litigation practice.[226] Challenges being invoked on the grounds that the availability of a more suitable forum elsewhere means that England is an inappropriate forum for the trial of the case (forum non conveniens); that simultaneous actions are pending in England and in a foreign country between the same parties[227] and involving the same or similar issues (*lis alibi pendens*); or that the parties have entered into a choice of court agreement. This approach to jurisdiction is characteristic of common law countries: the civil law tradition knows of jurisdiction clauses, but deals with cases of *lis alibi pendens* by a mechanistic rule giving priority to the action commenced first, and cannot accept the extensive degree of judicial discretion deployed in forum non conveniens cases. The adoption of the civil law approach in the European regime has greatly limited the use of the common law approach in the English courts.[228]

Forum non conveniens

The power to stay actions on the ground that the forum chosen by the claimant was inappropriate for the trial of the action was devised by the Scottish courts in the nineteenth century. It was much developed by the courts of the US where it is now an essential part of litigation strategy as a means by which the defendant can resist the invocation by the claimant of what are often very widely-drawn (often styled "long-arm") bases of jurisdiction. The English courts eventually adopted a similar set of principles.[229]

7–032

---

[224] See Fawcett, *Declining Jurisdiction in Private International Law* (Oxford: Clarendon Press, 1995); Bell, *Forum Shopping and Venue in International Litigation* (Oxford: Oxford University Press, 2003); Robertson (1987) 103 L.Q.R. 398; Slater, (1988) 104 L.Q.R. 398; Kennett, [1995] C.L.J. 552; Peel, (2001) 117 L.Q.R. 187.

[225] *Isis Investments Ltd v Oscatello Investments Ltd* [2013] EWHC 7 (Ch.) (stay on case management grounds refused).

[226] However, see the caution that appellate courts have in reviewing findings on these issues (*AmTrust Europe Ltd v Trust Risk Group SpA* [2015] EWCA Civ 437; [2015] 2 Lloyd's Rep. 154).

[227] Very exceptionally, the power to stay English proceedings may be exercised where the outcome of the case is intimately bound up with foreign proceedings involving different parties: *Reichhold Norway ASA v Goldman Sachs International* [1999] 2 All E.R. (Comm) 174.

[228] See, particularly, C-281/02 *Owusu v Jackson* [2005] E.C.R. I-1383; [2005] Q.B. 801, discussed below, para.7-033

[229] The development of the doctrine can be traced in a number of landmark cases: *The Atlantic Star* [1974] A.C. 436; *MacShannon v Rockware Glass Ltd* [1978] A.C. 795; and *The Abidin Daver* [1984] A.C. 398.

The practice of the English courts was authoritatively stated by Lord Goff in *Spiliada Maritime Corpn v Cansulex Ltd*.[230] It can be stated as follows:

(a)   The basic principle is that a stay will only be granted on the ground of forum non conveniens where the court is satisfied that there is some other available forum, having competent jurisdiction, which is the appropriate forum for the trial of the action, i.e., in which the case may be tried more suitably for the interests of all the parties and the ends of justice.[231]

   The defendant must show that another forum is "available". This means that the claimant must be able to begin proceedings against the defendant in the other forum as of right, either because the case falls within the jurisdiction regularly exercised by the courts of that country or as a result of a jurisdiction clause. It is not sufficient that an action could be brought in the named country on the basis of an undertaking proffered by the defendant to submit to its jurisdiction.[232]

(b)   The burden of proof is on the defendant to show not only that England is not the natural or appropriate forum, but also that there is another available forum which is clearly or distinctly more appropriate than the English forum.[233]

(c)   In deciding whether there is another forum clearly more appropriate, the court will seek to identify the "natural forum", meaning "that with which the action has the most real and substantial connection",[234] and will examine not only factors affecting convenience or expense (such as availability of witnesses), but also such matters as the law governing the transaction, and the places where the parties reside or carry on business. In cases where the cause of action is governed by English law, the English courts may make their own assessment of the strength of the claim under English law when deciding whether or not to grant a stay.[235]

   Although every case must turn on its own facts, the natural forum for a claim in tort is likely to be held to be the country in which the tort occurred, as illustrated by the facts of the *MacShannon* case[236]:

---

[230] [1987] A.C. 460.

[231] *Spiliada Maritime Corp v Cansulex Ltd* [1987] A.C. 460, at p.476.

[232] *Lubbe v Cape Plc* [1999] I.L.Pr. 113 (claim arising out of operations of defendant's subsidiaries in South Africa; defendant company itself not amenable to South African jurisdiction in absence of undertakings; stay of English action refused).

[233] cf. the approach adopted in Australia, of asking whether the Australian forum chosen by the claimant is "clearly inappropriate" which in effect means examining the choice of that forum for elements of vexation or oppression: *Voth v Manildra Flour Mills Pty Ltd* (1991) 171 C.L.R. 538; *Regie Nationale des Usines Renault SA v Zhang* [2002] HCA 10; (2003) 210 C.L.R. 491. Some American decisions arrive at a similar result by stressing the "deference" to be given to the claimant's choice of forum, especially if it is the claimant's "home forum".

[234] A formulation used by Lord Keith in *The Abidin Daver* [1984] A.C. 398 at 415.

[235] In *Baturina v Chistyakov* [2014] EWCA Civ 1134, [2014] 2 C.L.C. 209, the Court of Appeal held that the court should not export to a foreign jurisdiction, on the supposed footing that it was a clearly more appropriate forum, a claim which was governed by English law and was unsustainable under that law.

[236] [1978] A.C. 795.

M was a Scotsman resident in Scotland. He was injured in an accident at work in a factory in Scotland owned by his employers, a company registered in England. On the advice of the English solicitors to his London-based trade union, he brought his action in England and not in Scotland, because his solicitors believed that he would get higher damages in England and that proceedings in Scotland would take longer to come to trial. But when it was shown that medical and other expert witnesses were equally available in Scotland, and that therefore the comparative cost and inconvenience of a trial in England would be appreciably greater than those of a trial in Scotland, the House of Lords unanimously ordered the English action to be stayed.

(d)   If there is another forum which prima facie is clearly more appropriate, the court will ordinarily grant a stay unless there are circumstances by reason of which justice requires that a stay should not be granted; at this point the burden of proof shifts to the claimant. It may be, for example, that for some reason the claimant could not obtain justice in the foreign country because of the weakness of,[237] or severe delays in,[238] the foreign legal system; the absence in the foreign country of the legal or other specialist assistance required for the fair hearing of the case[239]; or the existence of racial or political prejudice against the claimant.[240]

(e)   The mere fact that the claimant has a legitimate personal or juridical advantage in proceeding in England cannot be decisive. As Lord Goff put it in *Connelly v RTZ Corp Plc*[241]:

"If a clearly more appropriate forum overseas had been identified, generally speaking the plaintiff will have to take that forum as he finds it, even if it is in certain respects less advantageous to him than the English forum. He may, for example, have to accept lower damages, or do without the more generous English system of discovery. The same must apply to the system of court procedure, including the rules of evidence, applicable in the foreign forum."

Effects of the European Regime

There is, in general, no room for the operation of the doctrine of forum non conveniens in the context of the European regime. The European rules allocate jurisdiction and cannot be the subject of any general judicial discretion; it is seen as unnecessary, even unseemly, to argue that of the two or more courts in Member

7–033

---

[237] *889457 Alberta Inc v Katanga Mining Ltd* [2009] I.L.Pr. 14, where in the alternative forum, the Republic of Congo, injustice was 'widespread and endemic' (at para.34). cf. *Ferrexpo AG v Gilson Investments Ltd* [2012] EWHC 721 (Comm.); [2012] 1 Lloyd's Rep. 588 (Ukraine); *Mengiste v Endowment Fund for the Rehabilitation of Tigre* [2013] EWHC 599 (Ch.) (Ethiopia). In the latter case the proceedings were stayed on the proviso that the claimants could reapply in the event that they were not afforded a fair trial in Ethiopia.

[238] *The Jalakrishna* [1983] 2 Lloyd's Rep. 628 (five year delay in India in case of severe personal injuries).

[239] *Connelly v RTZ Corp plc* [1998] A.C. 854 (but note the dissent of Lord Hoffman).

[240] e.g., *Mohammed v Bank of Kuwait* [1996] 1 W.L.R. 1483 (Iraqi citizen claiming arrears of salary for period including that of the Iraqi occupation of Kuwait); *Cherney v Deripaska (No.2)* [2009] EWCA Civ 849; [2010] 2 All E.R. (Comm) 456 (Russia was the natural forum, but the claimant feared that in Russia he would risk assassination or arrest on trumped-up charges, and that the defendant's government connections would prevent a fair trial; England held the appropriate forum); but cf. *Askin v Absa Bank Ltd* [1999] I.L.Pr. 471 (threats of assassination against claimant; stay nonetheless refused).

[241] [1998] A.C. 854 at 872.

States competent to hear a particular case one is more appropriate than another. If an action is brought in England by a claimant domiciled in a Member State against a defendant domiciled in England, the English court clearly has jurisdiction under art.4 of the Brussels I *bis* Regulation, and must exercise it; a plea of forum non conveniens cannot be heard.[242]

For many years after the Brussels Convention, the predecessor of the Regulations, first had legal effect in England, the courts continued to entertain pleas of forum non conveniens in the very common type of case involving an action by a claimant resident and domiciled in, say, New York (or any other country which is not a Member State) and begun by the service of process in England upon a defendant who was at the time of service present and domiciled in England. It will be seen that the English courts will undoubtedly have jurisdiction, by virtue either of the service of the claim form or the general jurisdiction basis of the Regulation. After a number of first-instance decisions to the contrary, the Court of Appeal decided in *Re Harrods (Buenos Aires) Ltd*[243] that in such cases what was then the Brussels Convention did not preclude the application of national law principles, including the forum non conveniens doctrine. The court's view was essentially that the purpose of the Brussels Convention was to set up an intra-Community mandatory system of jurisdiction, and that relations between individual Member States and non-Member States were outside that system. It followed that to consider a plea of forum non conveniens, and to uphold it in the appropriate cases, would be in no way inconsistent with the Convention.

The CJEU eventually rejected the arguments adopted in *Re Harrods (Buenos Aires)* Ltd. It had previously held, in a different context, that the rules in the Brussels I Regulation were "in principle applicable where the defendant has its domicile or seat in a [Member] State, even if the plaintiff is domiciled in a non-member country".[244] The specific issue came before the European Court in *Owusu v Jackson*[245]:

> O, a British national domiciled in the United Kingdom, hired a holiday villa in Jamaica from J, also domiciled in the United Kingdom. O was rendered tetraplegic by an accident while diving from the private beach belonging to the villa. O began proceedings in England, against J for breach of an implied term in their contract, and in tort against several Jamaican companies which were allegedly in breach of duties connected with the safety of the beach. J and several of the other defendants applied for a stay of the English proceedings under the forum non conveniens doctrine, arguing that in all the circumstances the case was more appropriately tried in Jamaica.

---

[242] See *Aiglon Ltd v Gau Shan Co Ltd* [1993] 1 Lloyd's Rep. 164; Case C-288/92 *Custom Made Commercial Ltd v Stawa Metallbau GmbH* [1994] E.C.R. I-2913. See also the reasoning of the ECJ in Case C-159/02 *Turner v Grovit* [2004] E.C.R. I-3565; [2005] 1 A.C. 101, considered below, para.7-037.

[243] [1992] Ch. 72. See Collins, (1990) 106 L.Q.R. 535, the argument in which is adopted by the Court of Appeal. *Re Harrods* was followed in a number of later Court of Appeal cases: *Ace Insurance SA-NV v Zurich Insurance Co* [2001] Lloyd's Rep IR 504; *American Motorists Insurance Co v Cellstar Corp.* [2003] EWCA Civ 206; [2003] Lloyd's Rep IR 295; *Anton Durbeck GmbH v Den Norske Bank ASA* [2003] EWCA Civ 147; [2003] Q.B. 1160 (a case on the Lugano Convention).

[244] Case C-412/98 *Universal Insurance Co v Group Josi Reinsurance Co SA* [2000] E.C.R. I-5925; [2001] Q.B. 68 (a case under the Brussels Convention).

[245] Case C-281/02, [2005] Q.B. 801; [2005] ECR I-1383.

The then ECJ held that the Brussels Convention precluded a court of a Contracting State from declining the jurisdiction conferred on it by what was art.2 of that Convention on the ground that a court of a non-Contracting State would be a more appropriate forum for the trial of the action even if the jurisdiction of no other Contracting State were in issue or the proceedings had no connecting factors to any other Contracting State.

In reaching this conclusion, the Court noted that nothing in the wording of what was then art.2 suggested that its application was subject to the condition that there should be a legal relationship involving a number of Contracting States. The uniform rules of jurisdiction contained in the Convention were not intended to apply only to situations in which there is a real and sufficient link with the working of the internal market, by definition involving a number of Member States. The intention was to eliminate obstacles to the functioning of the internal market derived from disparities between national legislations on the subject. The forum non conveniens doctrine was recognised only in a limited number of Contracting States, and the objective of the Convention was precisely to lay down common rules to the exclusion of derogating national rules. Article 2 was mandatory in nature and, according to its terms, there could be no derogation from the principle it lays down except in the cases expressly provided for by the Convention and no exception on the basis of the forum non conveniens doctrine was provided for. Application of the forum non conveniens doctrine, which allowed the court seised a wide discretion as regards the question whether a foreign court would be a more appropriate forum for the trial of an action, was liable to undermine the predictability of the rules of jurisdiction laid down by the Convention, in particular that of art.2, and consequently to undermine the principle of legal certainty, which was the basis of the Convention.

The court recognised the concerns of the defendants, the negative consequences which would result in practice were the English courts be obliged to try the case, inter alia as regards the expense of the proceedings, the possibility of recovering their costs in England if the claimant's action were dismissed, the logistical difficulties resulting from the geographical distance, the need to assess the merits of the case according to Jamaican standards, the enforceability in Jamaica of a default judgment and the impossibility of enforcing cross-claims against the other defendants. But, said the court, "genuine as those difficulties may be, suffice it to observe that such considerations, which are precisely those which may be taken into account when forum non conveniens is considered, are not such as to call into question the mandatory nature of the fundamental rule of jurisdiction contained in Art.2".

The reference to the ECJ in *Owusu v Jackson*[246] sought a ruling on the position where identical or related proceedings were already pending before a court of a non-Contracting State, where a choice of court clause gave jurisdiction to such a court, or where there was a connection with that state of the same type as those referred to in art.16 of the Convention (now art.24 of the Brussels I *bis* Regulation). The Court refused to deal with these circumstances, which were not raised by the facts of the instant case.

---

[246] Case C-281/02, [2005] Q.B. 801; [2005] ECR I-1383.

In *Ferrexpo AG v Gilson Investments Ltd*[247] the High Court answered positively the question of the "reflexive effect" of the European regime in relation to the courts of a non-Member State. The court held that it was entitled to exercise its discretion to stay a case before it in favour of the courts of a non-Member State in those cases where, had the court been that of a Member State, the provisions of arts 22, 27 or 28 of the Brussels I Regulation (now arts 24, 29 and 30 of the Brussels I *bis* Regulation) would have applied.

> "This case involved the validity of the resolutions of an organ of a Ukrainian company. The provisions on exclusive jurisdiction embodied in art.22(2) or (3) of the Brussels I Regulation would have been applicable had the proceedings been pending in another European Member State. The court understood that the same approach could permissibly be applied to justify the exercise of the court's discretion to decline jurisdiction in favour of the courts of a non-Member State. Moreover, the Ukrainian court was first seised with proceedings involving the same cause of action and between the same parties, and therefore the court had discretion to stay its proceedings, giving reflexive effect to the relevant provisions of the Brussels I Regulation."

Despite the fact that the Brussels I *bis* Regulation deals with litigation in third States in other circumstances,[248] it does not make express provision for the reflexive effect of the Regulation in cases involving non-Member States, in circumstances like those in *Ferrexpo* (exclusive jurisdiction) or pursuant to an exclusive jurisdiction clause under art.25. However, Recital (24) provides that, in applying the new provisions of arts 33 and 34 in cases of *lis pendens* and related actions, the court's assessment of the proper administration of justice may also include "consideration of the question whether the court of the third State has exclusive jurisdiction in the particular case in circumstances where a court of a Member State would have exclusive jurisdiction".[249]

In the case of exclusive jurisdiction clauses in favour of the courts of non-Member States, such clauses may be given effect where the designated court is in a Contracting State to the Hague Convention on Choice of Court Agreements.[250]

When is forum non conveniens still available?

7–034   The forum non conveniens doctrine does remain available in some types of case. One is in intra-UK cases where an English court is invited to hold that a Scottish or Northern Ireland court is a more appropriate forum.[251] Finally, the plea remains available in areas of law, such as succession, outside the scope of the Brussels I *bis* Regulation.[252]

---

[247] [2012] EWHC 721 (Comm.), [2012] 1 Lloyd's Rep. 588. See Smith et al. (2012) 8 J. Priv. Int. L. 389; Goodwin (2013) 129 L.Q.R. 317; Crawford and Carruthers (2013) Edin. L. Rev. 78.
[248] See para.6–068.
[249] Regulation 1215/2012, Rec.(24). See Briggs, *Private International Law in English Courts* (Oxford: Oxford University Press, 2014), paras 3.364–3.371.
[250] See further paras 5-027.
[251] In Scots law, the Civil Jurisdiction and Judgments Act 1982, which entered into force in 1987, has a supplementary provision that specially establishes: "(1) Nothing in Schedule 8 [Civil Jurisdiction in Scotland] shall prevent a court from declining jurisdiction on the ground of forum non conveniens."
[252] e.g., *Dellar v Zivy* [2007] EWHC 2266 (Ch); [2007] I.L.Pr. 868 (interpretation of a will).

Lis alibi pendens

Although intervention on the ground of *lis alibi pendens* has a much longer   **7-035**
history in English law than forum non conveniens, it came to be treated as a
sub-set of the latter (and many of the leading cases in which that latter doctrine
was developed rested also on *lis alibi pendens*).

The court may be asked to stay an action in England, or to enjoin an action
abroad, where the same claimant sues the same defendant in England and abroad
or where the roles of claimant and defendant are reversed in the two countries. It
used to be said that it required a stronger case to induce the court to interfere in
the second situation; surprisingly, the power of the court to interfere in the second
situation was established as early as 1821,[253] but in the first situation not until
1882.[254] At common law, the English court might stay the English proceedings,
or restrain the foreign proceedings by injunction, or require the claimant to elect
which proceedings to pursue.[255]

ANTI-SUIT INJUNCTIONS

In a number of contexts, the courts in England are asked on grounds similar to   **7-036**
those already examined not to stay its own proceedings but to enjoin the
commencement or continuation of proceedings abroad. The English courts have
an equitable jurisdiction to do so, that is, to restrain a party from instituting or
prosecuting proceedings in a foreign court, statutorily recognised in s.37 of the
Senior Courts Act 1981.[256] This is not a case of attempting to dictate to the
foreign court, for "the injunction is not to the court, but to the party".[257] The
effect, nonetheless, is to interfere with proceedings in another jurisdiction, so "the
power should be exercised with great caution".[258]

The applicable principles were restated by the Privy Council in *Société
Nationale Industrielle Aérospatiale v Lee Kui Jak*[259]:

> A fatal helicopter crash in Brunei led to actions being commenced both in Brunei and in Texas
> against the manufacturers (A) and the company responsible for operating and maintaining the
> helicopter (B). It appeared highly likely that the Texas courts would have jurisdiction over A
> but not over B, and were A held liable in Texas, A would have to claim contribution from B in

---

[253] *Bushby v Munday* (1821) 5 Madd. 297; *Beckford v Kemble* (1822) 1 S. & St. 7. See McClean
(1969) 18 I.C.L.Q. 931.
[254] *McHenry v Lewis* (1882) 22 Ch.D. 397.
[255] *The Christianborg* (1885) 10 P.D. 141 at 152–153, per Baggallay L.J.
[256] "[T]he High Court may by order (whether interlocutory or final) grant an injunction or appoint a
receiver in all cases in which it appears to the court to be just and convenient to do so". *AES
Ust-Kamenogorsk Hydropower Plant LLP v Ust-Kamenogorsk Hydropower Plant JSC* [2013] UKSC
35; [2013] 1 W.L.R. 1889.
[257] *Love v Baker* (1665) 1 Cas. in Ch. 67; *Bushby v Munday* (1821) Madd. 297 at 306–307; *Societe
Nationale Industrielle Aerospatiale v Lee Kui Jak* [1987] A.C. 871. For this reason, the use of the term
"anti-suit injunction" has been criticised (see *Turner v Grovit* [2001] UKHL 65; [2002] 1 W.L.R. 107
at 117 per Lord Hobhouse) but the usage is well established.
[258] *Cohen v Rothfield* [1919] 1 K.B. 410 at 413; *Settlement Corpn v Hochschild* [1966] Ch. 10 at 15.
[259] [1987] A.C. 871.

some other forum. Reversing the lower courts in Brunei, the Privy Council held that Brunei was the natural forum and granted an injunction restraining the continuation of the Texas proceedings.

The importance of the decision lies in its examination of the grounds upon which the court should intervene. It had been suggested in earlier cases[260] that the applicable principles corresponded to those elaborated in *Spiliada Maritime Corp v Cansulex Ltd.*[261] Those principles would, however, enable injunctions to be granted too readily, and the Privy Council chose to go back to the language used in earlier cases[262]: foreign proceedings would only be enjoined if they were "vexatious" or "oppressive", and the court would not deprive the claimant of an advantage in the foreign forum of which it would be unjust to deprive him.[263]

Subsequent cases, of which there is an abundance, have refined the tests to be applied. In *Deutsche Bank AG v Highland Crusader Offshore Partners LP*,[264] Toulson LJ reviewed the authorities and set out a summary of the correct approach:

(1)   Under English law the court may restrain a defendant over whom it has personal jurisdiction from instituting or continuing proceedings in a foreign court when it is necessary in the interests of justice so to do.

(2)   It is too narrow to say that such an injunction may be granted only on grounds of vexation or oppression,[265] but, where a matter is justiciable in an English and a foreign court, the party seeking an anti-suit injunction must generally show that proceeding before the foreign court is or would be vexatious or oppressive.

(3)   The courts have refrained from attempting a comprehensive definition of vexation or oppression, but in order to establish that proceeding in a foreign court is or would be vexatious or oppressive on grounds of forum non conveniens, it is generally necessary to show that (a) England is clearly the more appropriate forum (the natural forum), and (b) justice requires that the claimant in the foreign court should be restrained from proceeding there.

(4)   If the English court considers England to be the natural forum and can see no legitimate personal or juridical advantage in the claimant in the foreign proceedings being allowed to pursue them, it does not automatically follow

---

[260] Notably *Castanho v Brown & Root (UK) Ltd* [1981] A.C. 557.

[261] [1987] A.C. 460; see above, para.7–016.

[262] Especially in *St. Pierre v South American Stores (Gath & Chaves) Ltd* [1936] 1 K.B. 382.

[263] See *British Airways Board v Laker Airways Ltd* [1985] A.C. 58, decided before the Aerospatiale case (anti-trust remedies only available in US courts). cf. the related case of *Midland Bank Plc v Laker Airways Ltd* [1986] Q.B. 689.

[264] [2009] EWCA Civ 725; [2010] 1 W.L.R. 1023.

[265] *Stichting Shell Pensioenfonds v Krys* [2014] UKPC 41; [2015] A.C. 616, in which the Board concluded (at [39]) that "where a creditor or member who is amenable to the personal jurisdiction of the Court begins or continues foreign proceedings which will interfere with the statutory trusts over the assets of a company in insolvent liquidation, in principle an injunction will be available to restrain their prosecution irrespective of the nationality or residence of the creditor in question". The grounds for the issue of an injunction in such cases is not that the conduct is vexatious or oppressive, but rather the existence of an equitable jurisdiction to enforce a statutory distribution on insolvency in accordance with its terms.

that an anti-suit injunction should be granted. For that would be to overlook the important restraining influence of considerations of comity.

(5)   An anti-suit injunction always requires caution because by definition it involves interference with the process or potential process of a foreign court. An injunction to enforce an exclusive jurisdiction clause governed by English law is not regarded as a breach of comity, because it merely requires a party to honour his contract. In other cases, the principle of comity requires the court to recognise that, in deciding questions of weight to be attached to different factors, different judges operating under different legal systems with different legal policies may legitimately arrive at different answers, without occasioning a breach of customary international law or manifest injustice, and that in such circumstances it is not for an English court to arrogate to itself the decision how a foreign court should determine the matter. The stronger the connection of the foreign court with the parties and the subject matter of the dispute, the stronger the argument against intervention.

(6)   The prosecution of parallel proceedings in different jurisdictions is undesirable but not necessarily vexatious or oppressive.

(7)   A non-exclusive jurisdiction agreement precludes either party from later arguing that the forum identified is not an appropriate forum on grounds foreseeable at the time of the agreement, for the parties must be taken to have been aware of such matters at the time of the agreement. For that reason an application to stay on forum non conveniens grounds an action brought in England pursuant to an English non-exclusive jurisdiction clause will ordinarily fail unless the factors relied upon were unforeseeable at the time of the agreement.[266] It does not follow that an alternative forum is necessarily inappropriate or inferior.

(8)   The weakness of the foreign claim may be a factor to consider in the exercise of the discretion, where England is the natural forum and foreign proceedings have been brought in an attempt to jeopardise the English proceedings. However, English courts are not in a position to judge the strength of claims before foreign courts, especially where England is not the natural forum.[267]

(9)   The decision whether or not to grant an anti-suit injunction involves an exercise of discretion and the principles governing it contain an element of flexibility.

An attempt was made to extend the availability of anti-suit injunctions in *Airbus Industrie GIE v Patel*[268]:

An air crash in India involved an Airbus 320 manufactured by AI in France and used exclusively on internal Indian flights. The plaintiffs, representing the victims of the crash and

---

[266] cf. the position where there is an exclusive clause: *Donohue v Armco Inc* [2001] UKHL 64; [2002] 1 All E.R. 749.
[267] *Star Reefers Pool Inc v JFC Group Ltd* [2012] EWCA Civ 14; [2012] 1 Lloyd's Rep. 376, at [31] and the authorities there cited; applied in *Vitol Bahrain EC v Nasdec General Trading LLC* [2013] EWHC 3359 (Comm.).
[268] [1999] 1 A.C. 119; see Peel, (1998) 114 L.Q.R. 543.

their estates, commenced an action in Texas. An action in Texas, where liability was strict, was likely to succeed, and there was the added attraction to the plaintiffs of the possible award of punitive damages. An action in India, requiring proof of fault, would probably fail. The Indian courts had granted an anti-suit injunction, but that was not enforceable in England where the plaintiffs were resident. The applicants sought a similar injunction from the English court. The issue was whether an injunction could be granted, despite the fact that there were (and could be) no English proceedings, the natural forum being India.

The House of Lords ruled that in such circumstances an injunction was not available; but the door was not firmly closed. It was recognised that there might be "extreme cases" where the conduct of the foreign State exercising jurisdiction was such as to deprive it of the respect normally required by comity. The refusal of Texas to countenance forum non conveniens applications in personal injury cases was not seen as bringing the case into that extreme category.

Anti-suit injunctions not admissible in the European regime

7–037 The House of Lords in *Airbus Industrie* drew attention to the very different approach of the civil law tradition as expressed in the Brussels and Lugano Conventions. That was made clear in *Turner v Grovit*:

> T was employed as an in-house lawyer by an English company, which was later taken over by H Ltd, a company in the C group of companies. For a period in 1997–1998, T was posted to Madrid, where CSA, another company in the C group, was based, but the English court held that he was still employed by H Ltd. After a dispute, T returned to England and successfully brought a claim against H Ltd in an Employment Tribunal for unfair and wrongful dismissal. Some six months after the commencement of those proceedings, CSA brought a claim against T in the Spanish courts alleging breach of contract.

The English tribunal was the "court first seised" and the Court of Appeal issued an anti-suit injunction restraining the Spanish proceedings on the ground that they were vexatious and had been begun in bad faith. On a reference by the House of Lords, the ECJ emphasised that:

> "[T]he Convention is necessarily based on the trust which the Contracting States accord to one another's legal systems and judicial institutions. It is that mutual trust which has enabled a compulsory system of jurisdiction to be established, which all the courts within the purview of the Convention are required to respect, and as a corollary the waiver by those States of the right to apply their internal rules on recognition and enforcement of foreign judgments in favour of a simplified mechanism for the recognition and enforcement of judgments".[269]

It followed that any injunction prohibiting a claimant from bringing an action in another Convention State had to be seen as constituting interference with the jurisdiction of the foreign court which, as such, was incompatible with the system of the Convention.[270]

---

[269] Case C-159/02, [2005] 1 A.C. 101 at [24].
[270] ibid. at [27].

Anti-suit injunctions and arbitration

Anti-arbitration injunctions

As arbitration is excluded from the scope of the Brussels regime, the Regulation   **7–038**
does not prevent the English court from granting an injunction to restrain arbitral
proceedings abroad, even in another Member State. This power will, however be
exercised only in "exceptional circumstances": it must be shown, as a minimum,
to establish that the applicant's legal or equitable rights have been infringed or
threatened by a continuation of the arbitration, or that its continuation will be
vexatious, oppressive or unconscionable.[271]

Anti-suit injunctions to enforce arbitration agreements

Different considerations apply when the court is asked to exercise its   **7–039**
discretionary powers to issue an anti-suit injunction in support of an arbitration
agreement. In *AES Ust-Kamenogorsk Hydropower Plant LLP v AES Ust-
Kamenogorsk Hydropower Plant JSCI*,[272] where no arbitration had been
commenced, the Court of Appeal held that it was open to the court to consider
whether, and how best, if at all, to protect such a right to arbitrate by way of an
anti-suit injunction.

The scenarios where this remedy is available have been greatly reduced by
virtue of the European regime. In the *West Tankers* case[273] the CJEU held that
even though proceedings to enforce an arbitration agreement via an anti-suit
injunction do not come within the scope of the European regime of jurisdiction[274]
"they may nevertheless have consequences which undermine its effectiveness", if
they prevent a court of another Member State from exercising the jurisdiction that
it has under the regime. Accordingly, the CJEU held that "it is incompatible with
[the original Brussels I Regulation] for a court of a Member State to make an
order to restrain a person from commencing or continuing proceedings before the
courts of another Member State on the ground that such proceedings would be
contrary to an arbitration agreement."[275]

Furthermore, in *Gazprom*[276] the CJEU distinguished the issuing of an anti-suit
injunction from the recognition and enforcement of an arbitral award prohibiting
a party from bringing certain claims before a court of a Member State. The
European court considered that while the anti-suit injunction was contrary to the

---

[271] *Claxton Engineering Services Ltd v TXM Olaj-es Gazkutato Kft* [2010] EWHC 2567 (Comm);
[2011] 2 All E.R. (Comm) 38.
[272] [2011] EWCA Civ 647; [2011] 2 Lloyd's Rep 233.
[273] Case C-185/07 *Allianz SpA and Generali Assicurazioni Generali SpA v West Tankers Inc.*
EU:C:2009:69 [30-31].
[274] See para.6-005.
[275] Case C-185/07, *Allianz SpA and Generali Assicurazioni Generali SpA v West Tankers Inc.* at
[30]–[31].
[276] Case C-536/13 *Gazprom OAO*. See Briggs [2015] L.M.C.L.Q. 284; Hartley (2015) 64 I.C.L.Q.
965; Kajkowska (2015) 74 C.L.J. 412 (Gazprom); and Ojiegbe (2015) 11 J. Priv. Int. L. 267.

general principles of jurisdiction established in the European regime, the recognition and enforcement of such an award did not as such infringed it.[277]

If proceedings on the merits of a dispute are instituted in England in breach of an arbitration agreement, the Arbitration Act 1996 applies.[278] Section 9 of the Act implements art.2 of the New York Convention of 1958.[279] The English courts are required to grant a stay of proceedings if there is a valid[280] arbitration agreement "in writing" "in respect of a matter which under the agreement is to be referred to arbitration".[281]

Anti-suit injunctions to enforce choice of court agreements

7–040   The principles applying in cases which do not attract the provisions of the European regime or the Choice of Court Agreements Convention were fully examined by Lord Bingham in *Donohue v Armco Inc*.[282] He said:

> "If contracting parties agree to give a particular court exclusive jurisdiction to rule on claims between those parties, and a claim falling within the scope of the agreement is made in proceedings in a forum other than that which the parties have agreed, the English court will ordinarily exercise its discretion (whether by granting a stay of proceedings in England, or by restraining the prosecution of proceedings in the non-contractual forum abroad, or by such other procedural order as is appropriate in the circumstances) to secure compliance with the contractual bargain, unless the party suing in the non-contractual forum (the burden being on him) can show strong reasons for suing in that forum".

Intervention would require "strong reasons". Lord Bingham approved a list of some of the matters which could be taken into account that was given by Brandon J in *The Eleftheria*[283]:

> "(a) In what country the evidence on the issues of fact is situated, or more readily available, and the effect of that on the relative convenience and expense of trial as between the English and foreign courts; (b) Whether the law of the foreign court applies and, if so, whether it differs from English law in any material respects; (c) With what country either party is connected, and how closely; (d) Whether the defendants genuinely desire trial in the foreign country, or are only seeking procedural advantages; (e) Whether the plaintiffs would be prejudiced by having to sue in the foreign court because they would—(i) be deprived of security for that claim, (ii) be unable to enforce any judgment obtained, (iii) be faced with a time-bar not applicable in England, or (iv) for political, racial, religious or other reasons be unlikely to get a fair trial."

---

[277] Case C-536/13 *Gazprom OAO* at [36]–[40].

[278] Section 9 of the Act implements art.2 of the United Nation Convention on the Recognition and Enforcement of Foreign Arbitral Awards (New York, 1958).

[279] United Nation Convention on the Recognition and Enforcement of Foreign Arbitral Awards (New York, 1958).

[280] The agreement must not be "null and void, inoperative or incapable of being performed" (Arbitration Act 1996 s.9(4)). The validity of the arbitration agreement is determined according to the applicable law to such agreement. See Parish, (2010) 76 Arbitration 661; see also Fentiman, (2010) 69 C. L. J. 242.

[281] Arbitration Act 1996 s.9(1).

[282] [2001] UKHL 64; [2002] 1 All E.R. 749.

[283] [1970] P. 94. As Lord Bingham recognised, this was a staying rather than an anti-suit injunction case, so the criteria to be applied in considering the listed matters would be different.

Where the English court has power to intervene and the dispute is between two parties only, one party sues in a forum other than that specified in exclusive jurisdiction clause in their contract, and the interests of other parties are not involved, effect will in all probability be given to that clause.[284] However, where the interests of parties other than the parties bound by the exclusive jurisdiction clause are involved, or grounds of claim not the subject of the clause are part of the relevant dispute, there may be a risk of parallel proceedings and inconsistent decisions. In such a case, the English court may well decline to grant an injunction or a stay, as the case may be. This was the situation in *Donohue v Armco Inc.*[285]

> The case concerned dealings between a group of companies and four individuals, and the heart of the case lay in allegations of fraud made by the companies against those four individuals. Mr Donohue was party, with some but not all the companies, to a clause giving exclusive jurisdiction to the English courts, but that clause did not bind all the claimant companies or all the defendants. The companies wished to sue in New York.

This decision gave great weight to the danger of dividing the litigation between different courts.[286] Only the New York courts could hear all the issues in a single composite trial. An anti-suit injunction restraining proceedings in New York was not granted, but the court accepted an undertaking by the claimant companies not to seek multiple or punitive damages in the New York proceedings.[287]

---

[284] See Lord Bingham in *Donohue v Armco Inc* [2001] UKHL 64; [2002] 1 All E.R. 749 at para.[25] citing authorities from England, Australia, Canada and the US.

[285] *Donohue v Armco Inc* [2001] UKHL 64; [2002] 1 All E.R. 749, per Lord Bingham at para.[27].

[286] cf. *Astrazeneca UK Ltd v Albemarle International Corp* [2010] EWHC 1028 (Comm); [2011] 1 All E.R. (Comm) 510 (exclusive jurisdiction clause in favour of the courts of South Carolina in respect of certain claims; court accepted that different claims would have to be heard in different countries).

[287] See further *Bank St Petersburg OJSC v Arkhangelsky* [2014] EWCA Civ 593; [2014] 1 W.L.R. 4360 for the distinction between anti-suit injunctions and anti-enforcement injunctions in this context.

CHAPTER 8

SOVEREIGN AND DIPLOMATIC IMMUNITY

The courts of England are, generally speaking, open to the whole world. In particular, the possession of foreign nationality is no bar to being a claimant or a defendant. It is quite common for English courts to try disputes between foreigners with no connection whatsoever with England. This is because the parties have agreed to litigate in England, attracted no doubt by the high reputation for impartiality which English justice enjoys among those who can afford it.

8–001

There is, however, one class of persons who cannot sue, namely alien enemies, and three classes of persons who cannot as a general rule be sued, namely foreign sovereign States; foreign diplomats; and international organisations and their members. These last will now be discussed.

FOREIGN STATES

At common law, no foreign sovereign State could be sued in the English courts without its consent.[1] The immunity was derived ultimately from the rules of public international law and from the maxim of that law, *par in parem non habet imperium*. These rules of public international law became part of the English common law.[2] In the nineteenth century and for most of the twentieth century the "absolute" rule of immunity prevailed, whereby foreign sovereign states were accorded immunity for all activities, whether governmental or commercial. But the increase in state trading in the twentieth century led a number of states (including the US) to develop what is generally known as the "restrictive" theory of immunity, resting upon a distinction between acts of government, *acta jure imperii,* and acts of a commercial nature, *acta jure gestionis*.[3] Under the restrictive theory, states were immune in respect of acts of government but not in respect of commercial acts. The UK was slow to adopt the restrictive theory, and it was even said that "the English courts accord to foreign States immunity to an extent to which no other State would accord immunity either to this country or to any other State".[4]

8–002

In 1981, however, the House of Lords finally adopted the restrictive theory.[5] The Privy Council had earlier held that a foreign government was not entitled to

---

[1] *Duke of Brunswick v King of Hanover* (1844) 6 Beav. 1; (1848) 2 H.L.C. 1.
[2] *The Cristina* [1938] A.C. 485, 490, per Lord Atkin. See Marasinghe, (1991) 54 M.L.R. 664.
[3] See *Kuwait Airways Corp v Iraqi Airways Co* [1995] 1 W.L.R. 1147.
[4] Cohn, (1958) 34 B.Y.I.L. 260.
[5] *The I Congreso del Partido* [1983] 1 A.C. 244; see Fox, (1982) 98 L.Q.R. 94.

immunity in an action in rem against a ship used for trading purposes,[6] and the Court of Appeal had held, by a majority, that a State was not entitled to immunity in respect of commercial transactions.[7] The judgment of Lord Denning MR in that case was later described as marking "the definitive absorption by the common law of the restrictive theory of sovereign immunity".[8]

Lord Wilberforce sought to define the effect of the new approach in *I Congreso del Partido*[9]:

> "In considering, under the 'restrictive' theory whether state immunity should be granted or not, the court must consider the whole context in which the claim against the state is made, with a view to deciding whether the relevant act(s) upon which the claim is based, should, in that context, be considered as fairly within an area of activity, trading or commercial, or otherwise of a private law character, in which the state has chosen to engage, or whether the relevant act(s) should be considered as having been done outside that area, and within the sphere of governmental or sovereign activity".

The boundary between the two areas is not a fixed one. In *Holland v Lampen-Wolfe*,[10] a professor of international relations at an American university was seconded to teach on a Master's course provided for US military personnel serving at a base in England. She alleged that the defendant, the educational services officer at the base, defamed her in a written report. He pleaded state immunity, arguing that he was acting as an official of the US in an official capacity.

The House of Lords upheld the plea of immunity. As Lord Cooke of Thorndon put it:

> "changing concepts and circumstances may call on occasion for some extension of the field of the doctrine. At the present day, I think, a state may reasonably claim to have welfare and educational responsibilities towards the members of its armed forces. In turn the quality and efficiency of the forces may be strengthened if the state discharges those responsibilities. In their discharge the state may reasonably claim that it should not be subject to interference by other states or their courts".

In 1972 a comprehensive European Convention on State Immunity, severely restricting the scope of the doctrine, was concluded under the auspices of the Council of Europe and came into force in 1976.[11] It prompted legislation in the UK, the State Immunity Act 1978. The United Nations General Assembly adopted a Convention on Jurisdictional Immunities of States and Their Property on 16 December 2004, which adopts similar principles; it is not yet in force.[12]

---

[6] *The Philippine Admiral* [1977] A.C. 373.

[7] *Trendtex Trading Corporation v Central Bank of Nigeria* [1977] Q.B. 529.

[8] *Alcom Ltd v Republic of Colombia* [1984] A.C. 580, per Lord Diplock.

[9] [1983] 1 A.C. 244.

[10] [2000] 1 W.L.R. 1573 (noted Yang, [2001] C.L.J. 17) (where the matter was still governed by the common law owing to the exclusion of cases related to visiting armed forces from Pt I of the State Immunity Act 1978 by s.16 of the Act).

[11] The text of the Convention is printed in Cmnd. 5081. For a commentary, see Sinclair, (1973) 22 I.C.L.Q. 254. The Convention has so far only eight ratifications, including that by the UK.

[12] The UK has signed but not ratified it. Article 30 of the Convention provides that it will enter into force some time after the thirtieth ratification; at the time of writing it has only eleven ratifications. However, it has been considered as customary international law in *Cudak v Lithuania* [2010] E.H.R.R. 15 at paras 63 to 66. See also Gardiner, (2006) 55 I.C.L.Q. 407.

State Immunity Act 1978

The law of sovereign immunity in the UK is now largely regulated by the State Immunity Act 1978, which was designed in part to implement the European Convention, but is worldwide in effect.[13] The Act goes considerably further than the Convention in restricting immunity. It applies to any foreign or Commonwealth State other than the UK, and it applies not only to the state itself but also to the sovereign or other Head of State in his or her public capacity,[14] to the government of the state, and any department of its government.[15]

8–003

There is no express reference to the servants and agents of foreign states, but as the House of Lords held in *Jones v Ministry of the Interior of Saudi Arabia*,[16] there is "a wealth of authority" to show that a foreign state is entitled to claim immunity for its servants as it could if sued itself, though in some cases there could be doubt whether the conduct of an individual, although a servant or agent of the state, had a sufficient connection with the state to entitle it to claim immunity for his conduct.

At common law a difficult question that often arose was whether a state corporation or agency could claim to be an emanation of the foreign state and thus entitled to immunity. The Act deals with this problem through the concept of a "separate entity". A separate entity which is distinct from the executive organs of the foreign government, and is capable of suing and being sued, is not entitled to immunity unless the proceedings relate to something done by it in the exercise of sovereign authority[17] and the circumstances are such that the State would have been immune.[18] It may still be difficult for the courts to determine whether a "separate entity" was acting "in the exercise of sovereign authority".[19]

Provision is made for the application of the Act by Order in Council to the constituent territories of a federal state.[20] The effect of such an Order is that some

---

[13] See generally, Fox and Webb, *The Law of State Immunity*, 3rd edn (Oxford: Oxford University Press, 2013).

[14] Section 20 applies the Diplomatic Privileges Act 1964 (see para.8–012) to Heads of State, and this applies to a Head in both the public and private capacities: *Aziz v Aziz (Sultan of Brunei intervening)* [2007] EWCA Civ 712; [2008] 2 All E.R. 501. A former Head of State continues to enjoy immunity in respect of acts done as part of his official functions as Head of State: *R. v Bow Street Magistrate, Ex p. Pinochet Ungarte (No.3)* [2000] A.C. 147, but not in respect of acts in a private capacity: *Harb v Aziz* [2014] EWHC 1807 (Ch.); [2014] 1 W.L.R. 4473 (alleged settlement with secret wife). Members of the Head of State's family, forming part of his household, are also covered; the scope of this provision is narrowly interpreted: *Apex Global Management Ltd v Fi Call Ltd* [2013] EWCA Civ 642; [2014] 1 W.L.R. 192 (princes related to Head of State not covered). See the Resolution of the *Institut de droit international* on immunities from jurisdiction and execution of Heads of State and Government in international law, (2000–2001) 69 Annuaire de l'Institut 742.

[15] Section 14(1).

[16] [2006] UKHL 26; [2007] 1 A.C. 270. See also *Jones v United Kingdom* (2004) 59 E.H.R.R. 1 and *Belhaj v Straw* [2014] EWCA Civ 1394, [2015] 2 W.L.R. 1105.

[17] Which means an act *iure imperii;* see above, para.8–002 and *Kuwait Airways Corp. v Iraqi Airways Co* [1995] 1 W.L.R. 1147.

[18] Section 14(1) and (2).

[19] See, e.g., *Koo Golden East Mongolia v Bank of Nova Scotia* [2007] EWCA Civ 1443; [2008] Q.B. 717 (central bank of Mongolia a separate entity but acted in bullion transaction in exercise of sovereign authority).

[20] Section 14(5).

or all of the Act's provisions apply to the constituent territory as they apply to a state. The position where no such Order has been made was examined in *Pocket Kings Ltd v Safenames Ltd*[21]:

> A court in the Commonwealth of Kentucky, a state of the US, ordered the transfer to itself of a domain name, deemed to be a 'gambling device' under Kentucky law. Proceedings were begun in England against the Commonwealth of Kentucky seeking a declaration that the court would not recognise or enforce the order.

The court held that the Commonwealth of Kentucky, being one of the constituent territories of the US, was not itself a state for the purposes of s.14(1) of the Act. If it were to be treated as a "separate entity" it would have immunity in respect of "anything done by it in the exercise of sovereign authority" but it was held that this meant the sovereign authority of the entity recognised as a state, here the US. What had been done in Kentucky was an exercise of state and not federal authority; accordingly, the Commonwealth of Kentucky could not claim state immunity under the Act.

Exceptions to the immunity rule

8–004   Section 1 of the Act lays down what is still the general rule, namely that a state is immune from the jurisdiction of the courts of the UK, and that they must give effect to this immunity even though the state does not appear. The next 10 sections lay down exceptions to this general rule. It is important to bear in mind that none of these exceptions (except the first) confers jurisdiction on the English courts which otherwise they would not have: they merely remove an immunity which otherwise would exist.

A state is not immune in the following types of proceedings:

(1)   Proceedings in respect of which the state has submitted to the jurisdiction of the courts of the UK.[22]

At common law, sovereign immunity could be waived by or on behalf of the foreign state, but the doctrine was confined within very narrow limits. Waiver had to take place at the time when the court was asked to exercise jurisdiction[23]; it could not be inferred from a prior contract to submit to the jurisdiction of the court[24] or to arbitration.[25] The Act has made a far-reaching and welcome change by providing that a state may submit after the dispute has arisen, or by a prior written agreement.[26] It will also be deemed to have submitted if it institutes the proceedings, or intervenes or takes any step in the proceedings, unless the intervention was solely for the

---

[21] [2009] EWHC 2529 (Ch); [2010] Ch. 438. See *Bank of Credit and Commerce International (Overseas) Ltd v Price Waterhouse* [1998] Ch. 84 (Ruler of Abu Dhabi); *R. (on the application of HRH Sultan of Pahang) v Secretary of State for the Home Department* [2011] EWCA Civ 616.

[22] Section 2(1).

[23] *Mighell v Sultan of Johore* [1894] 1 Q.B. 149.

[24] *Kahan v Pakistan Federation* [1951] 2 K.B. 1003; *Baccus S.R.L. v Servicio Nacional del Trigo* [1957] 1 Q.B. 438.

[25] *Duff Development Co v Government of Kelantan* [1924] A.C. 797.

[26] Section 2(2).

purpose of claiming immunity, or unless it was in reasonable ignorance of facts entitling it to immunity, and immunity is claimed as soon as reasonably practical.[27] A submission in respect of any proceedings extends to an appeal, but not to a counterclaim unless it arises out of the same legal relationship or facts as the claim.[28] The submission must be in specific terms; a mere statement that a government would waive any right of sovereign immunity, with no reference to the jurisdiction of any country's courts, may not suffice.[29]

The Supreme Court considered a number of related issues in *NML Capital Ltd v Argentina*.[30] An action was brought in England on a New York judgment in favour of a "vulture fund"[31] and against the Republic of Argentina. The bonds issued by Argentina provided that any related judgment would be binding on Argentina and could be enforced in any court to whose jurisdiction Argentina could be subject by a suit upon the judgment. It was held that this constituted a waiver of state immunity applying to the proceedings in England.[32]

A written submission to arbitration by a state is submission to proceedings (including those in relation to enforcement) in the courts of the UK relating to the arbitration, unless contrary provision is made or the arbitration agreement is between states.[33]

(2)   Proceedings relating to a commercial transaction entered into by the state.[34]

This exception is extremely important and is much wider than the corresponding provision in the European Convention. "Commercial transaction" is defined to mean (a) any contract for the supply of goods or services; (b) any loan or other transaction for the provision of finance (and any guarantee or indemnity in respect thereof or of any other financial obligation); and (c) any other transaction or activity (whether of a commercial, industrial, financial, professional or other similar character) into which a state enters otherwise than in the exercise of sovereign authority.[35] But it does not include a contract of employment: that is made a

---

[27] Sections 2(3), (4) and (5).

[28] Section 2(6).

[29] *Svenska Petroleum Exploration AB v Government of the Republic of Lithuania (No.2)* [2006] EWCA Civ 1529; [2007] Q.B. 886.

[30] [2011] UKSC 31; [2011] 2 A.C. 495.

[31] A vulture fund buys at a discount the debts of sovereign states that are in acute financial difficulty then seeks to enforce the debt.

[32] At paras 57–61, 127–130. A similar result was reached in corresponding proceedings in the Brussels Court of Appeal; but French Cour de Cassation, basing itself on customary international law, held that Argentina was immune as waivers of sovereign immunity need not only to be express but also specially drafted as to cover diplomatic assets.

[33] State Immunity Act 1978 s.9. See Fox, (1988) 37 I.C.L.Q. 1, 11–18; *Svenska Petroleum Exploration AB v Government of the Republic of Lithuania (No.2)* [2006] EWCA Civ 1529; [2007] Q.B. 886; *London Steam Ship Owners Mutual Insurance Association Ltd v Kingdom of Spain* [2013] EWHC 3188 (Comm.); [2014] 1 Lloyd's Rep. 309.

[34] Section 3(1)(a). This confirms the decision of the Court of Appeal in *Trendtex Trading Corporation v Central Bank of Nigeria* [1977] Q.B. 529.

[35] Section 3(3). On the phrase "the exercise of sovereign authority" see *Kuwait Airways Corp v Iraqi Airways Co* [1995] 1 W.L.R. 1147 and cf. *Littrell v Government of the United States (No.2)* [1995] 1 W.L.R. 82.

separate exception.[36] In *NML Capital Ltd v Argentina*,[37] the underlying transaction was clearly a "transaction for the provision of finance" but the Supreme Court decided, by a majority, that the exception did not extend to actions to enforce a foreign judgment, even if that judgment was itself based on a commercial transaction.

(3) Proceedings relating to an obligation of the state which by virtue of a contract (whether a commercial transaction or not) falls to be performed wholly or partly in the UK.[38]

This would include contracts made in the exercise of sovereign authority provided they are to be performed here.

(4) Proceedings relating to a contract of employment between the state and an individual where

(a) the contract was made in the UK or

(b) the work is to be wholly or partly performed there.[39]

This exception does not apply if either (a) at the time when the proceedings are brought, the employee is a national of the foreign state, or (b) at the time when the contract was made, the employee was neither a national of nor habitually resident in the UK.[40] But it does apply in each of these cases if the work is for an office, agency or establishment maintained by the state in the UK for commercial purposes, unless the employee was, at the time when the contract was made, habitually resident in the foreign state.[41] Nor does the exception apply to proceedings concerning the employment of members of a diplomatic mission or consular post.[42]

(5) Proceedings in respect of death or personal injury, or damage to or loss of tangible property, caused by an act or omission in the UK.[43]

(6) Proceedings relating to any interest of the state in, or its possession or use of, immovable property in the UK, or any obligation of the state arising therefrom.[44]

(7) Proceedings relating to any interest of the state in movable or immovable property by way of succession, gift or bona vacantia.[45]

The fact that a state claims an interest in any property does not preclude the court from exercising any jurisdiction relating to the estates of deceased persons or persons of unsound mind or to insolvency, the winding up of companies or the administration of trusts.[46]

---

[36] Exception (4), below.
[37] [2011] UKSC 31; [2011] 2 A.C. 495.
[38] Section 3(1)(b).
[39] Section 4(1).
[40] Section 4(2). For the meaning of "national of the United Kingdom" see s.4(5) as amended by British Nationality Act 1981 Sch.7.
[41] Section 4(3). See *Egypt v Gamal-Eldin* [1996] 2 All E.R. 237 (drivers attached to medical office of embassy; not for a "commercial" purpose).
[42] Section 16(1)(a).
[43] Section 5. See *Ogbonna v Republic of Nigeria* (2011) UKEAT/0585/10; [2012] 1 W.L.R. 139 (personal injury includes mental ill-health; available even if consequent on a discrimination claim, and on facts to employee not within the exception as employed in a diplomatic mission).
[44] Section 6(1). See *Intro Properties (UK) Ltd v Sauvel* [1983] Q.B. 1019.
[45] Section 6(2).
[46] ibid.

(8)   Proceedings relating to UK patents, trademarks and similar rights belonging to the state, or to the alleged infringement by the state in the UK of any such rights, including copyright.[47]

(9)   Proceedings relating to the state's membership of a corporate or unincorporated body or a partnership which has members other than states and is incorporated or constituted under the law of the UK or is controlled from or has its principal place of business in the UK.[48]

(10) Actions in rem against a ship belonging to the state, or actions in personam for enforcing a claim in connection with such a ship, if at the time when the cause of action arose the ship was in use or intended for use for commercial purposes.[49]

A similar provision applies to actions in rem against a cargo belonging to the state if both the cargo and the ship were in use or intended for use for commercial purposes, and to actions in personam for enforcing a claim in connection with such a cargo.[50]

(11) Proceedings relating to a state's liability for value added tax, customs duty, agricultural levy, or rates in respect of premises occupied by it for commercial purposes.[51]

Indirect impleading

So far we have assumed (except in exception (10) above) that the question of sovereign immunity arises in proceedings in which the state is named as defendant in an action *in personam*, i.e. direct impleading. But at common law the doctrine of sovereign immunity protected a foreign state not only in direct proceedings against it but also in indirect proceedings against property in its possession or control or in which it claimed an interest. Thus if a foreign state had an interest in property situated in England, whether proprietary, possessory or of some lesser nature, an action which affects its interest would be stayed, even though it was not brought against it personally but was, e.g., an action in rem against a ship[52] or an action in personam against its bailee[53] or agent.[54] The rule was not limited to ownership, and applied to lesser interests which might not merely be not proprietary but not even possessory, so that it applied to property under the control of the foreign state[55] and perhaps also to property in respect of which it had no beneficial interest but only the legal title.[56] These limitations

8–005

---

[47] Section 7.

[48] Section 8.

[49] Section 10(1) and (2). This confirms the decision of the Privy Council in *The Philippine Admiral* [1977] A.C. 373. "Commercial purposes" are defined in s.17(1).

[50] Section 10(4).

[51] Section 11.

[52] *The Parlement Belge* (1880) 5 P.D. 197; *The Jupiter* [1924] P. 236; *The Cristina* [1938] A.C. 485; *The Arantzazu Mendi* [1939] A.C. 256.

[53] *USA and Republic of France v Dollfus Mieg et Cie* [1952] A.C. 582.

[54] *Rahimtoola v Nizam of Hyderabad* [1958] A.C. 379.

[55] *The Cristina* [1938] A.C. 485; *The Arantzazu Mendi* [1939] A.C. 256.

[56] *Rahimtoola v Nizam of Hyderabad* [1958] A.C. 379, at p.403.

were re-affirmed by the Court of Appeal in *Belhaj v Straw*,[57] the court rejecting an argument that indirect impleader extended to any case in which the rights of the state concerned would be obviously affected.

The Act implicitly assumes that these rules of the common law will continue to apply.[58] Moreover, it specifically provides that the court may entertain proceedings against a person other than a state notwithstanding that the proceedings relate to property in its possession or control, or in which it claims an interest, if the state would not have been immune had the proceedings been brought against it, or, in the case where the state merely claims an interest, if the claim is neither admitted nor supported by prima facie evidence.[59]

Enforcement of foreign judgments

8–006   Section 31(1) of the Civil Jurisdiction and Judgments Act 1982 provides that a foreign judgment against a foreign State (other than the UK or the State in which the foreign proceedings were brought) is to be recognised and enforced in England if (and only if) (a) the normal conditions for recognition and enforcement of judgments are fulfilled, and (b) mutatis mutandis the foreign State would not have been immune if the foreign proceedings had been brought in the UK.[60]

Execution

8–007   In general, even if a state is not immune under one of the exceptions, its property is not subject to execution for the enforcement of a judgment or arbitration award.[61] This is subject to two important exceptions: execution is allowed if (a) the state consents in writing, or (b) the property is for the time being in use or intended for use[62] for commercial purposes.[63] A central bank is accorded special treatment under the Act. If (as is likely) it is a "separate entity", its property is immune from execution, even if it is not entitled to immunity from suit; and its property is not regarded as in use or intended for use for commercial purposes.[64] In practice, therefore, the property of a state's central bank will only be liable to execution if it has waived, in writing, its immunity from execution.

---

[57] [2014] EWCA Civ 1394; [2015] 2 W.L.R. 1105.

[58] See ss.2(4)(b), 6 and 10.

[59] Section.6(4). See *Juan Ysmael & Co Inc v Indonesian Government* [1955] A.C. 75; *Rahimtoola v Nizam of Hyderabad* [1958] A.C. 379, at p.410; *Shearson Lehman Bros Inc v Maclaine Watson & Co Ltd* [1988] 1 W.L.R. 16.

[60] See *NML Capital Ltd v Argentina* [2011] UKSC 31; [2011] 2 A.C. 495 (Argentina not entitled to immunity in New York had the 1978 Act's rules applied, because of the "commercial transactions" exception, so not immune from enforcement).

[61] Section 13(2)(b).

[62] And not merely derived from a commercial transaction: *SerVaas Inc v Rafidain Bank* [2012] UKSC 40; [2013] A.C. 595.

[63] Section 13(3) and (4). "Commercial purposes" are defined in s.17(1). See *A. Company Ltd v Republic of X* [1990] 2 Lloyd's Rep. 520; *Continental Tranfert Technique Ltd v Nigeria* [2010] EWHC 780 (Comm) at para.12.

[64] Section 14(4).

Service of process

The Act provides for a method of service on a state by transmission of the claim form through the Foreign and Commonwealth Office to the state's Ministry of Foreign Affairs.[65] A state which appears in proceedings cannot thereafter object that service was not properly effected upon it.[66] Service by transmission of the claim form through the Foreign and Commonwealth Office is not necessary if the state has agreed to a different method of service.[67]   **8–008**

Miscellaneous

Provision may be made by Order in Council to restrict or extend the immunities of a state under the Act. If they exceed those accorded by the law of that state in relation to the UK, they may be restricted. If they are less than those required by any treaty or convention to which that state and the UK are parties, they can be extended.[68]   **8–009**

A certificate from the Secretary of State is conclusive evidence on any question whether any country is a state, whether any territory is a constituent territory of a federal state, or as to the person or persons to be regarded as the head or government of a state.[69]

The scope of the doctrine

The scope of the doctrine of sovereign or state immunity continues to attract controversy. In *Holland v Lampen-Wolfe*,[70] the House of Lords was pressed to declare that the doctrine was inconsistent with art.6 of the European Convention on Human Rights which deals with the right of access to justice. It held that there was no inconsistency, principally because art.6 forbids a Contracting State from denying individuals the benefit of its powers of adjudication and cannot operate to give the courts additional powers of adjudication.   **8–010**

The House was referred to cases then pending before the European Court of Human Rights in which similar issues were being raised. One of those cases, *Al-Adsani v United Kingdom*,[71] which concerned an action against the Kuwaiti

---

[65] Section 12(1); *Kuwait Airways Corp v Iraqi Airways Co* [1995] 1 W.L.R. 1147.
[66] Section 12(3).
[67] Section 12(6).
[68] Section 15.
[69] Section 21(a).
[70] [2000] 1 W.L.R. 1573 (where the matter was still governed by the common law owing to the exclusion of cases related to visiting armed forces from Pt I of the State Immunity Act 1978 by s.16 of the Act); *Jones v Ministry of Interior of the Kingdom of Saudi Arabia (Secretary of State for Constitutional Affairs intervening)* [2006] UKHL 26; [2007] 1 A.C. 270 at [14] and [64]; applied to the immunities of an international organisation in *Entico Corporation Ltd v United Nations Educational Scientific and Cultural Association* [2008] EWHC 531 (Comm.), [2008] 2 All E.R. (Comm.) 97.
[71] (App. No. 35763/97) (2001) 34 E.H.R.R. 273. cf. *R. v Bow Street Metropolitan Stipendiary Magistrate, Ex p. Pinochet Ugarte (No.3)* [2000] A.C. 147, which did not deal with state immunity from civil actions based on allegations of torture.

Government based on allegations of torture, was considered by the Grand Chamber of that court. It was held that art.6 was engaged but that the UK, in enacting the State Immunity Act, was within the "margin of appreciation" that States enjoy to limit Convention rights. The Act pursued a legitimate aim, compliance with international law, and was proportionate. The majority held that, while the prohibition of torture had achieved the status of a peremptory norm in international law, it was unable to discern a firm basis for concluding that, as a matter of international law, a state no longer enjoyed immunity from civil suit in the courts of another state where acts of torture were alleged. This decision was followed in a second House of Lords decision, *Jones v Ministry of the Interior of the Kingdom of Saudi Arabia*.[72]

In *Cudak v Lithuania*,[73] however, the Grand Chamber of the European Court of Human Rights held that there could be circumstances in which a national court's refusal to entertain a case on the ground of state immunity would violate art.6; this was where the national court, in failing to preserve a reasonable relationship of proportionality, had overstepped the margin of appreciation and had impaired the very essence of the applicant's right of access to a court.

FOREIGN DIPLOMATS

8–011   Before 1964, the immunity from suit of foreign ambassadors and members of their staffs was secured by the common law as reinforced by the Diplomatic Privileges Act 1708, which has always been treated as declaratory of the common law. That Act was passed in the following remarkable circumstances[74]:

The Russian ambassador to the Court of St James was arrested and removed from his coach in London for non-payment of a debt of £50. Tsar Peter the Great resented this affront so highly that he demanded that the Sheriff of Middlesex and all others concerned in the arrest should be punished with instant death. But, to the amazement of the Tsar's despotic court, Queen Anne informed him "that she could inflict no punishment upon the meanest of her subjects, unless it was warranted by the law of the land; and therefore she was persuaded that he would not insist upon impossibilities". To appease the wrath of Peter, a Bill was brought into Parliament and duly passed. A copy of this Act, elegantly engrossed and illuminated, accompanied by a letter from the Queen, was then sent to Moscow by ambassador extraordinary.

The Act of 1708 has now been repealed and replaced by the Diplomatic Privileges Act 1964, which gives effect to the Vienna Convention on Diplomatic Relations 1961.[75] Section 1 of the Act provides that the following provisions of the Act shall have effect in substitution for any previous enactment or rule of law;

---

[72] [2006] UKHL 26; [2007] 1 A.C. 270. See Fox, (2006) 2 E.H.R.L.R.; Wright, (2010) 30 O.J.L.S. 143. For a similar outcome in the European Court for Human Rights, see *Jones v United Kingdom* (2014) 59 E.H.R.R. 1.

[73] [2010] E.C.H.R. 15869/02.

[74] *Taylor v Best* (1854) 14 C.B. 487, 491–493.

[75] The full text of the Convention is printed in (1961) 10 I.C.L.Q. 600. For a commentary on the Act and the Convention, see Buckley, (1965–66) 41 B.Y.I.L. 321. See also Brown, (1988) 37 I.C.L.Q. 53.

and s.2 enacts those articles of the Convention which are set out in the First Schedule as part of the law of the UK. Hence, much of the old case law is now only of historical interest.

The most important single change effected by the Convention in the law of the UK is that it abolishes the principle of absolute immunity: diplomatic immunity, even that of the ambassador himself, is now only qualified. The Convention divides persons entitled to diplomatic immunity into three categories[76]:

(1)   "diplomatic agents", namely, the head of the mission and members of his or her diplomatic staff;
(2)   "members of the administrative and technical staff", i.e. persons employed in secretarial, clerical, communications and public relations duties, such as typists, translators, coding clerks and press and cultural representatives; and
(3)   "members of the service staff", namely, members of the staff of the mission in its domestic service, such as cooks, cleaners, porters and chauffeurs. These three classes are each entitled to differing degrees of immunity from civil and criminal jurisdiction.

Foreign consuls

Foreign consuls and members of their staffs are not within the terms of the Vienna Convention on Diplomatic Relations. It appears to be accepted that they are entitled to immunity from suit at common law in respect of their official acts, but not in respect of their private acts.[77] This is confirmed by the Consular Relations Act 1968, which enacts as part of the law of the UK those articles of the Vienna Convention on Consular Relations 1963 which are set out in the First Schedule.[78] Under that Convention, consular officers and consular employees[79] are not amenable to jurisdiction in respect of acts performed in the exercise of consular functions, with some exceptions in civil actions.

8–012

Evidence

If in any proceedings any question arises whether or not any person is entitled to immunity from suit, a certificate issued by or under the authority of the Secretary of State stating any fact relating to that question is conclusive evidence of that fact.[80]

8–013

---

[76] Diplomatic Privileges Act 1964 Sch.1, art.1.
[77] *Engelke v Musman* [1928] A.C. 433, 437–438; Oppenheim, International Law, 8th edn, Vol. I. p.841; Beckett (1944) 21 B.Y.I.L. 34.
[78] Section 1(1). The full text of the Convention is printed in (1964) 13 I.C.L.Q. 1214.
[79] For definitions, see Sch.1, art.1(d) and (e).
[80] Diplomatic Privileges Act 1964 s.4; Consular Relations Act 1968 s.11.

Waiver

8–014   Diplomatic and consular immunity may be waived by the sending state.[81] A waiver by the head or acting head of a diplomatic mission is deemed to be a waiver by that state.[82] Waiver must always be express, except that the initiation of proceedings precludes the claimant from invoking immunity from jurisdiction in respect of any counterclaim directly connected with the principal claim.[83] There is no requirement that waiver must take place in the face of the court, as in waiver of sovereign immunity at common law. Waiver of immunity from jurisdiction in civil or administrative proceedings does not imply waiver of immunity in respect of execution of the judgment, for which a separate waiver is required.[84]

INTERNATIONAL ORGANISATIONS

8–015   The position of international organisations, much more recently arrived on the international scene than sovereigns and their diplomatic representatives, rests on statute rather than common law.[85] The International Organisations Act 1968 empowers the Crown by Order in Council to confer various degrees of immunity from suit and legal process upon any international organisation of which the UK is a member[86]; on representatives to the organisation or representatives on, or members of, any of its organs, committees or sub-committees, on specified high officers of the organisation, and persons employed by or serving as experts or as persons engaged on missions for the organisation[87]; and on specified subordinate officers or servants of the organisation.[88] No such immunity may be conferred on any person as the representative of the UK or as a member of his or her staff.[89]

The Act also empowers the Crown by Order in Council to confer immunity from suit on the judges, registrars or other officers of any international tribunal, on parties to any proceedings before any such tribunal, and their advocates and witnesses[90]; and on representatives of foreign states and their official staffs attending conferences in the UK.[91]

---

[81] Diplomatic Privileges Act 1964 Sch.1, art.32(1); Consular Relations Act 1968 Sch.1, art.45(1). See the curious case of *Fayed v Al-Tajir* [1988] Q.B. 712.

[82] Diplomatic Privileges Act 1964 s.2(3); Consular Relations Act 1968 s.1(5).

[83] Diplomatic Privileges Act 1964 Sch.1, art.32(2) and (3); Consular Relations Act 1968 Sch.1 art.45(2) and (3). See *High Commissioner for India v Ghosh* [1960] 1 Q.B. 134.

[84] Article 32(4) of Sch.1 of the 1964 Act; art.45(4) of Sch.1 of the 1968 Act.

[85] This seems to be clear from some of the issues in the litigation resulting from the collapse of the International Tin Council; see especially *J. H. Rayner (Mincing Lane) Ltd v Dept of Trade and Industry* [1989] Ch. 72, where the C.A. examines, inter alia, the European Community's lack of immunity.

[86] Section (1), (2)(b), and Sch.1, Pt I, para.1. The International Organisations Act 1981 s.2 extends this to international commodity organisations of which the UK is not a member. For the capacity of international organisations of which the UK is not a party to sue as plaintiff, see *Arab Monetary Fund v Hashim (No.3)* [1991] 2 A.C. 114.

[87] Section 1(2)(c), (3), and Sch.1, Pt II, para.9.

[88] Section 1(2)(d), and Sch.1, Pt III, para.14.

[89] Section 1(6)(b).

[90] Section 5(1), (2).

[91] Section 6.

If in any proceedings a question arises whether any person is or is not entitled to any immunity, a certificate issued by or under the authority of the Secretary of State stating any fact relating to that question is conclusive evidence of that fact.[92] Orders in Council have been made under this and earlier Acts conferring immunity from suit on a large number of international organisations and (in most cases) on their representatives, officers and staffs. These organisations range from the United Nations Organisation to the International Coffee, Cocoa and Sugar Organisations. The possibility of waiver of the immunities thereby con-ferred is specifically provided for by these Orders in Council; but the term is not defined.

This type of immunity has been challenged as offending against the right guaranteed by art.6 of the European Convention on Human Rights which deals with the right of access to justice. As in the case of the similar challenge to state immunity,[93] this challenge has failed: the immunity of international organisations reflected generally recognised rules of public international law and could not be regarded as imposing a disproportionate restriction on the right of access to court as embodied in art.6.[94]

---

[92] Section 8. See also *Zoernsch v Waldock* [1964] 1 W.L.R. 675.
[93] See above, paras 8-010.
[94] *Entico Corp Ltd v United Nations Educational Scientific and Cultural Association* [2008] EWHC 531 (Comm.); [2008] 1 Lloyd's Rep. 673.

CHAPTER 9

THE CONDUCT OF INTERNATIONAL LITIGATION

This chapter is concerned with some of the processes involved in a cross-border, **9–001** and so a conflicts, case. It describes an important part of the context within which conflicts issues arise, although of course many cases that raise issues in the conflict of laws do not lead to litigation. Some of the issues are very technical and all that is given here is an outline of what they involve.

SUBSTANCE AND PROCEDURE

There is an important rule, found in all systems of the conflict of laws, that all **9–002** matters of procedure are governed exclusively by the law of the court seised of the case, the *lex fori*. Every legal system has its own ways of dealing with cases, for example in settling which judges sit to hear the case and how far the procedure is oral as opposed to written. It would be quite impracticable to have different kinds of process for cases containing foreign elements and for purely domestic cases. This means that an English court will apply to a case containing foreign elements any rule of English law which, in its view, is procedural, and will refuse to apply any rule of foreign law which, in its view, is procedural. That needs to be balanced by a loyal application of foreign law insofar as it governs the substance of the case as the *lex causae*.[1]

That principle is well established but the line between substance and procedure is a difficult one to draw. It is of course a question of characterisation; and we shall see how controversial that doctrine is.[2] At one time it was possible to say that "English lawyers give the widest possible extension to the meaning of the term 'procedure'".[3] The risk inherent in this approach was that it might well defeat the whole object of the conflict of laws by denying a remedy where one should exist or, conversely, by allowing claims which should be rejected. Academic writing and the development of EU law have done much to change the approach.[4]

In principle, the line between substance and procedure should be drawn with some regard for the reason for drawing it. Cook[5] suggested as a practical test: "How far can the court of the forum go in applying the rules taken from the

---

[1] See *Cox v Ergo Versicherung AG* [2014] UKSC 22; [2014] A.C. 1379 at [12]ff.
[2] Below, para.20–002.
[3] Dicey, 1st edn (1896), p.712.
[4] See Carruthers, (2004) 53 I.C.L.Q. 691.
[5] Cook, *Logical and Legal Bases of the Conflict of Laws* (Cambridge MA: Harvard University Press, 1942), p.166.

foreign system of law without unduly hindering or inconveniencing itself?" Cook also pointed out that the line between substance and procedure may have to be drawn in one place for the purposes of the conflict of laws and in another place in other contexts, e.g., for the purpose of the rule that statutes affecting procedure are, but statutes affecting substance are not, presumed to have retrospective effect. This is not to say that the distinction may not be drawn in the same place for many purposes: it is merely to deny that it must necessarily be drawn in the same place for all purposes.

The primary object of the rule that procedural matters are governed by the *lex fori* is to obviate the inconvenience of conducting the trial of a case containing foreign elements in a manner with which the court is unfamiliar, and which may indeed simply be impracticable given other features of local practice. If, therefore, it is possible to apply a foreign rule, or to refrain from applying an English rule, without running into that sort of difficulty, those rules should not necessarily be characterised as procedural for the purposes of the conflict of laws.

One consequence of European legal developments on English practice has been to shift the balance between substance and procedure at a number of points. The process began with the Rome Convention, which applied the law governing the contract to cover some issues which at common law would be matters of procedure governed by the *lex fori*; the resulting position is maintained in the Rome I Regulation. In the context of non-contractual obligations, there are similar rules in the Rome II Regulation. Their effect is noted at the relevant points in the discussion which follows.

PARTIES

9–003   Earlier editions of this book contained the general proposition that it is for the *lex fori* to determine who are the proper parties to proceedings. Such a general proposition can no longer be sustained, as many issues related to the identity of the proper parties will fall to be decided by reference to some other law.

So, where the issue is whether a potential party has legal personality, the English court will accept the view of the law of the country in which the entity is established. A business association created under Swiss law and having legal personality under that law (though as a partnership it would not have such personality in English law) has been held entitled to sue in England.[6] A rather more surprising example is that of an Indian temple, also held to be a competent claimant.[7]

In many contexts, the question of the identity of the proper parties cannot be distinguished from the underlying question of liability, who is liable to whom, which is clearly governed by the *lex causae*, the law governing the relevant contract, tort or other claim. The Rome II Regulation spells this out in the context of non-contractual obligations: the law applicable under the Regulation governs the determination of persons who may be held liable for acts performed by them[8]; the question whether a right to claim damages or a remedy may be transferred,

---

[6] *Oxnard Financing SA v Rahn* [1998] 1 W.L.R. 1465.
[7] *Bumper Development Corp v Commissioner of Police for the Metropolis* [1991] 1 W.L.R. 1362.
[8] Article 15(a).

including by inheritance[9]; persons entitled to compensation for damage sustained personally[10]; and liability for the acts of another person.[11]

There remain, however, some issues as to the proper parties which are merely procedural and so a matter for the *lex fori*. That law determines who may take steps as an administrator of an estate of a deceased person, foreign-appointed representatives not being recognised for this purpose.[12] A similar question is whether the person sued is the proper defendant to the action. In some foreign systems of law a defendant cannot be sued unless and until some other person has been sued first. For instance, in some foreign systems a creditor cannot sue an individual partner without first suing the firm and exhausting its assets, or cannot sue a surety without first suing the principal debtor. Such rules are in sharp contrast to the rule of English law that any partner may be sued alone for the whole of the partnership debts, and that a surety may be sued without joining the principal debtor. Even under the Rome II Regulation it seems that the question is whether such a rule of foreign law is substantive or procedural. If the *lex causae* regards the defendant as under no liability whatever unless other persons are sued first, the rule is substantive and must be applied in English proceedings; the Regulation governs the determination of persons who may be held liable for acts performed by them.[13] If on the other hand the *lex causae* regards the defendant as liable, but makes the defendant's liability conditional on other persons being sued first, then the rule is procedural and is ignored in English proceedings.[14]

SERVICE OF PROCESS

Where proceedings are commenced in the English courts, it is for English law as the *lex fori* to determine whether there has been good service of the claim form. The law of the country in which service is to be effected cannot, however, be ignored. The law of any state may properly exercise control over actions taking place on its territory. States in the civil law tradition tend to see service of process as an exercise of the judicial power of a state, and are reluctant to permit within their borders an expression of the sovereignty of another state. For example, in Switzerland service on behalf of the claimant of foreign process without the permission of the Swiss authorities is an offence.[15]

9–004

Rule 6.40(4) of the Civil Procedure Rules provides that "Nothing in [the relevant rule, r.6.40(3)] or in any court order authorises or requires any person to

---

[9] Article 15(e).

[10] Article 15(f).

[11] Article 15(g). See Schoeman, [2010] L.M.C.L.Q. 81.

[12] See *Kamouh v Associated Electrical Industries International Ltd* [1980] Q.B. 199 (where the same approach was applied to the administration of an absentee's property).

[13] Article 15(a). See the common law cases of *General Steam Navigation Co v Guillou* (1843) 11 M. & W. 877 and *The Mary Moxham* (1876) 1 P.D. 107.

[14] *General Steam Navigation Co v Guillou*, above; *Bullock v Caird* (1875) L.R. 10 Q.B. 276; *Re Doetsch* [1896] 2 Ch. 836; *Subbotovsky v Waung* [1968] 3 N.S.W.R. 261, affirmed on other grounds, ibid., at p.499. This rule is criticised by Wolff, *Private International Law*, 2nd edn (Oxford: Clarendon Press, 1950), p.240.

[15] *Ferrarini SpA v Magnol Shipping Co Inc, The Sky One* [1988] 1 Lloyd's Rep 238; and see *Bentinck v Bentinck* [2007] EWCA Civ 175; [2007] 2 F.L.R. 1.

do anything which is contrary to the law of the country where the claim form or other document is to be served". If service is effected in a way that contravenes this principle, the English court does have a discretion nonetheless to allow service to stand, but will do so only in "a very strong case", for example where there was an express representation by the defendant that the method of service adopted was lawful.[16] In 'truly exceptional cases' the English court may achieve the same result by dispensing with service.[17]

Official assistance may be available in the service of process, either under a bilateral Civil Procedure Convention between the UK and the country in which service is to be effected, or the Hague Convention on the service abroad of judicial and extra-judicial documents of 1965.[18] Within the EU, Parliament and Council Regulation 1393/2007 of 13 November 2007 deals with the service in the Member States of judicial and extrajudicial documents[19] in civil or commercial matters.[20] It provides a mechanism for service via transmitting and receiving agencies in each Member State and governs whether the method of service is valid and when service took place.[21]

MAREVA OR FREEZING INJUNCTIONS

9–005 A freezing injunction is one restraining a defendant from dealing, or disposing of, or removing from the jurisdiction any or all of his assets to prevent their dissipation. It takes the name by which is commonly known from one of the first cases in which such an injunction was granted, *Mareva Compania Naviera SA v International Bulkcarriers SA*[22] The purpose of the injunction is to prevent a potential defendant from thwarting the claimant's plans by moving assets from one country to another. As part of English procedural law, the power to grant such injunctions applies to many cases where the *lex causae* and the primary jurisdiction is that of a foreign country.

It was once the case that a freezing injunction could not be granted unless the English court had jurisdiction over the merits of the case.[23] This limitation was

---

[16] *Ferrarini SpA v Magnol Shipping Co Inc, The Sky One* [1988] 1 Lloyd's Rep 238.

[17] C.P.R., r. 6.16. See *Phillips v Symes (No.3)* [2008] UKHL 1, *sub nom Phillips v Nussberger* [2008] 1 W.L.R. 180 (essential document omitted by misunderstanding from a bundle of documents served in Switzerland); *Olafsson v Gissurarson (No.2)* [2008] EWCA Civ 152; [2008] 1 W.L.R. 2016 (personal service in Iceland; Icelandic law was not complied with as addressee not asked to sign a receipt for the documents).

[18] See McClean, *International Co-operation in Civil and Commercial Matters*, 3rd edn, (Oxford: Oxford University Press, 2012).

[19] "Extrajudicial documents" include both documents drawn up or certified by a public authority or official and private documents of which the formal transmission to an addressee residing abroad is necessary for the purposes of exercising, proving or safeguarding a right or a claim in civil or commercial law: C-14/08 *Roda Golf & Beach Resort (document drawn up by notary); Case C-223/14 Tecom Mican SL* (letter of demand following unilateral termination of contract).

[20] For text see OJ L 324/79, 10.12.2007. It replaced an earlier Regulation, 1348/2000, which was in turn based on a draft Convention signed in 1997 but never in force.

[21] *Tavoulareas v Tsavliris* [2004] EWCA Civ 48; [2004] 1 Lloyd's Rep 445.

[22] [1975] 2 Lloyd's Rep. 509. For the history, see McClean (1996) 260 Hague *Receuil des cours* 22–35.

[23] *Siskina v Distos Compania Naviera SA* [1979] A.C. 210. See *Mercedes Benz AG v Leiduck* [1996] A.C. 284.

removed by statutory intervention, first by s.25(1) of the Civil Jurisdiction and Judgments Act 1982 which enabled the High Court to grant interim relief where proceedings had been or were to be commenced in a Contracting State to the Brussels or the Lugano Convention. This provision was extended in 1997 to apply to proceedings commenced or to be commenced in any country.[24]

Similarly, it was thought at one time that a freezing injunction was a remedy only available against foreign defendants, perhaps because in such cases the risk of assets being removed was usually greater and more obvious.[25] It was however accepted by the Court of Appeal in 1980 that an injunction could properly be granted even if the defendant was based in England if in the circumstances there was a danger of the assets being removed,[26] and this was put beyond doubt by s.37(3) of the Supreme Court Act 1981.

Again, the Court of Appeal formerly held that an injunction had to be limited to the assets of the defendant within the jurisdiction of the court,[27] but since 1989 the courts have made "worldwide" freezing injunctions.[28] The terms of a worldwide injunction do however provide that it applies only to a limited class of persons outside the jurisdiction and does not, in respect of assets located outside the jurisdiction,

"prevent any third party from complying with what it reasonably believes to be its obligations, contractual or otherwise, under the laws and obligations of the country or state in which those assets are situated or under the proper law of any contract between itself and the Respondent; and any orders of the courts of that country or state, provided that reasonable notice of any application for such an order is given to the Applicant's solicitors".[29]

The Court of Appeal has set out five considerations which the court should bear in mind, when considering the question whether it is inexpedient to make an order[30]:

First, whether the making of the order will interfere with the management of the case in the primary court, e.g. where the order is inconsistent with an order in the primary court or overlaps with it. Second, whether it is the policy in the primary jurisdiction not itself to make worldwide freezing/disclosure orders. Third, whether there is a danger that the orders made will give rise to disharmony or confusion and/or risk of conflicting inconsistent or overlapping orders in other jurisdictions, in particular the courts of the state where the person enjoined resides or where the assets affected are located. If so, then respect for the territorial jurisdiction of that state should discourage the English court from using its unusually wide powers against a foreign defendant. Fourth, whether at the time the order is sought there is likely to be a potential conflict as to jurisdiction, rendering it inappropriate and inexpedient to make a worldwide order. Fifth,

---

[24] SI 1997/302.
[25] This was the explanation offered by Megarry VC in *Barclay-Johnson v Yuill* [1980] 1 W.L.R. 1259.
[26] *Prince Abdul Rahman Bin Turki Al Sudairy v Abu Taha* [1980] 1 W.L.R. 1268.
[27] *Ashtiani v Kashi* [1987] Q.B. 888.
[28] *Babanaft International C SA v Bassatne* [1990] Ch. 13; *Republic of Haiti v Duvalier* [1990] Q.B. 202; *Derby & Co. Ltd v Weldon (No.1)* [1990] Ch. 48.
[29] C.P.R. Practice Direction 25A, Annex, para.20.
[30] *Motorola Credit Corporation v Uzan* [2003] EWCA Civ 752; [2004] 1 W.L.R. 113.

whether, in a case where jurisdiction is resisted and disobedience to be expected, the court will be making an order which it cannot enforce.

A worldwide freezing order will usually contain an undertaking by the party who obtained the order not to seek to enforce it in another jurisdiction without the permission of the court.[31]

EVIDENCE

9–006 "The law of evidence", said Lord Brougham, "is the *lex fori* which governs the courts. Whether a witness is competent or not; whether a certain matter requires to be proved by writing or not; whether certain evidence proves a certain fact or not; that is to be determined by the law of the country where the question arises, and where the court sits to enforce it".[32] On the other hand,

> "it is not everything that appears in a treatise on the law of evidence that is to be classified internationally as adjective law, but only provisions of a technical or procedural character -for instance, rules as to the admissibility of hearsay evidence or what matters may be noticed judicially."[33]

Thus, the *lex causae* generally determines what are the facts in issue;[34] and it may do so by providing that no evidence need, or may, be given as to certain matters, for instance as to compliance, or failure to comply, with certain formalities of a marriage ceremony. Such provisions are substantive.[35] On the other hand the *lex fori* determines how the facts in issue must be proved.

To this last principle there are important exceptions. Article 18 of the Rome I Regulation provides that the law governing a contractual obligation under the Regulation applies to the extent that, in matters of contractual obligations, it contains rules which raise presumptions of law or determine the burden of proof. A contract or an act intended to have legal effect may be proved by any mode of proof recognised by the law of the forum or by any of the laws referred to in art.11 of the Regulation under which that contract or act is formally valid, provided that such mode of proof can be administered by the forum. Similar provisions are found in the Rome II Regulation dealing with non-contractual obligations.[36]

---

[31] For the considerations governing the grant of permission, see *Dadourian Group International Inc v Simms* [2006] EWCA Civ 399; [2006] 1 W.L.R. 2499.

[32] *Bain v Whitehaven and Furness Rly* (1850) 3 H.L.C. 1, 19.

[33] *Mahadervan v Mahadervan* [1964] P. 233, 243, per Simon P.

[34] *The Gaetano and Maria* (1882) 7 P.D. 137.

[35] *Mahadervan v Mahadervan,* above.

[36] Article 22.

Admissibility

Questions as to the admissibility of evidence are decided in accordance with the *lex fori*.[37] Thus a document may be received in evidence by the English court although it is inadmissible by the *lex causae*.[38] Conversely, copies of foreign documents admissible by the *lex causae* are only admissible in England if they comply with English law as to the admissibility of copies.[39]

9–007

A distinction has been drawn between extrinsic evidence adduced to interpret a written document, e.g., a contract, and extrinsic evidence adduced to add to, vary or contradict its terms. The admissibility of the former is a question of interpretation, governed by the law applicable to the contract; the Rome I Regulation affirms this principle in cases to which it applies.[40] The admissibility of the latter is, subject to the exceptions in the Rome I Regulation, a question of evidence governed by the *lex fori*.[41] Thus in *St Pierre v South American Stores Ltd*[42] a question arose as to the meaning of the covenant to pay rent contained in a lease of land in Chile and governed by Chilean law. It was held that evidence of negotiations prior to the contract and of subsequent writings was admissible, although it was inadmissible by English law. On the other hand, in *Korner v Witkowitzer*[43] the plaintiff sued to recover arrears of pension due under a contract governed by Czech law. In order to obtain leave to serve notice of the writ out of the jurisdiction he had to prove that the contract was broken in England. It was held that evidence of an oral agreement whereby the plaintiff was to receive his pension in the country in which he might be living when it accrued was inadmissible, since this would be to vary the terms of the written agreement.

Requirement of written evidence

Section 4 of the Statute of Frauds 1677 provided that "no action shall be brought" on a number of contracts unless the agreement, or some note or memorandum thereof, was in writing. Section 4 now applies only to contracts of guarantee.[44] In the famous (or notorious) case of *Leroux v Brown*[45] it was held that s.4 contained a rule of procedure and therefore prevented the enforcement in England of an oral contract governed by French law which could have been sued upon in France.

9–008

---

[37] *Yates v Thompson* (1835) 3 Cl. & F. 544; *Bain v Whitehaven and Furness Ry.* (1850) 3 H.L.C. 1.

[38] *Bristow v Sequeville* (1850) 5 Exch. 275.

[39] *Brown v Thornton* (1837) 6 Ad. & El. 185. For an exception, see the Evidence (Foreign, Dominion and Colonial Documents) Act 1933, as amended by s.5 of the Oaths and Evidence (Overseas Authorities and Countries) Act 1963 (Orders in Council may provide for admissibility of official and properly authenticated copies of foreign public registers).

[40] Rome I Regulation, art.12(1)(a); (at common law:) *St Pierre v South American Stores Ltd* [1937] 1 All E.R. 206, 209; affd. [1937] 3 All E.R. 349.

[41] *Korner v Witkowitzer* [1950] 2 K.B. 128, 162–163; affirmed *sub nom. Vitkovice v Korner* [1951] A.C. 869.

[42] [1937] 1 All E.R. 206, 209; affd. [1937] 3 All E.R. 349.

[43] [1950] 2 K.B. 128; affd. [1951] A.C. 869.

[44] Law Reform (Enforcement of Contracts) Act 1954 s.1.

[45] (1852) 12 C.B. 801.

Although the decision has never been overruled,[46] it would seem to have been overtaken by the provisions in the Rome I Regulation already referred to. It deserves a mention because it illustrates how *not* to approach the distinction between substance and procedure. To characterise the section as procedural merely because it says "no action shall be brought" is to regard the form of the section as more important than its substance. To characterise it as procedural for the purposes of the conflict of laws, merely because it had previously been characterised as procedural for some purposes of English domestic law, is to lose sight of the purpose of the characterisation.

Witnesses

9–009   Whether a witness is competent or compellable appears to be a matter for the *lex fori*.[47] If the question depends, as it often does, on the matrimonial status of a witness (because for example a spouse may not be a compellable witness to testify against the other spouse), the question of status must be referred to the appropriate *lex causae* before the English rule of evidence can be applied.

Burden of proof

9–010   Subject once again to the far-reaching effect of the provisions in the Rome I and Rome II Regulations, it seems that in English law questions relating to the burden of proof are matters for the *lex fori*.[48] Yet there is much to be said for treating them as substantive, as the outcome of a case can depend on where the burden of proof lies. As Lorenzen says, "the statement that courts should enforce foreign substantive rights but not foreign procedural laws has no justifiable basis if the so-called procedural law would normally affect the outcome of the litigation".[49]

Presumptions

9–011   Presumptions are of three kinds: presumptions of fact, and rebuttable and irrebuttable presumptions of law. Presumptions of fact arise when, on proof of certain basic facts, the trier of fact may, but need not, find the existence of a presumed fact. Presumptions of fact have, strictly speaking, no legal effect at all, and need not be considered here. So far as presumptions of law are concerned, the Rome I and Rome II Regulations provide that in the case of contractual and non-contractual obligations within the scope of the regulations, the law governing the obligation applies to the extent that it contains, in the substantive law as opposed to the law of procedure, rules which raise presumptions of law.[50] No

---

[46] See *Irvani v G. and H. Montage GmbH* [1990] 1 W.L.R. 667 and the cases there discussed; the Statute of Frauds was ultimately held inapplicable on the facts.
[47] *Bain v Whitehaven and Furness Rly* (1850) 3 H.L.C. 1, 19.
[48] *The Roberta* (1937) 58 Ll.L.Rep. 159, 177; *In the Estate of Fuld (No.3)* [1968] P. 675, 696–697.
[49] Lorenzen, op. cit., p.134.
[50] Rome I Regulation, art.18(1); Rome II Regulation, art.22(1).

distinction is drawn between presumptions of law which are rebuttable and those which are irrebuttable; the rule appears to apply to both categories.

That distinction does, however, need to be observed when considering the position at common law. Irrebuttable presumptions of law arise when, on proof of the basic facts, the trier of fact *must* find the presumed fact in any event. An example is the presumption of survivorship contained in s.184 of the Law of Property Act 1925. It is now generally agreed that, even for the purposes of domestic law, irrebuttable presumptions of law are rules of substance, and this is also true for the purposes of the conflict of laws.[51] Rebuttable presumptions of law arise when, on proof of the basic facts, the trier of fact must find the presumed fact unless the contrary is proved. For the purposes of the conflict of laws such presumptions must be divided into those which only apply in certain contexts, and those which apply in all types of case. Examples of the first type are the presumptions of resulting trust, advancement, satisfaction and ademption, and the presumptions contained in s.2 of the Perpetuities and Accumulations Act 1964 to the effect that a female under the age of 12 or over the age of 55 cannot have a child. All these are thought to be so closely connected with the existence of substantive rights that they ought to be characterised as rules of substance.

Examples of the second type of rebuttable presumptions are the presumptions of marriage, legitimacy,[52] and death. It is uncertain whether these presumptions are rules of substance or rules of procedure. In cases involving presumptions of marriage the courts have applied the *lex causae* whenever that law was proved[53]; and the most recent dictum on the subject treats such a presumption as a rule of substance.[54]

Obtaining evidence abroad[55]

In countries in the common law tradition the preparation of a case for trial is the private responsibility of the parties. In contrast to this approach, many civil law countries view the obtaining of evidence as part of the judicial function, and the actions of agents of a foreign court may be seen as offending the sovereignty of the state in its judicial aspect. If evidence is to be obtained in such countries, official intervention will normally be required, though bilateral and multilateral civil procedure conventions may exist to regulate and simplify the procedures.

9–012

English law makes ample provision enabling parties to English proceedings to obtain evidence abroad. The powers given are exercised with the greatest discretion,[56] partly because of the sensitivities of other countries but also to avoid unnecessary expense, delay and inconvenience. The court acts under its general power to order depositions to be taken before an examiner, with appropriate

---

[51] *Re Cohn* [1945] Ch. 5.
[52] Much weakened by s.26 of the Family Law Reform Act 1969.
[53] *Hill v Hibbit* (1871) 25 L.T. 183; *De Thoren v Attorney General* (1876) 1 App.Cas. 686; *Re Shephard* [1904] 1 Ch. 456.
[54] *Mahadervan v Mahadervan* [1964] P. 233, 242.
[55] See McClean, op. cit.
[56] *Settebello Ltd v Banco Totta & Acores* [1985] 1 W.L.R. 1050; *Charman v Charman* [2005] EWCA Civ 1606; [2006] 1 W.L.R. 1053; *Honda Giken Kogyou Kabushiki Kaisha v KJM Superbikes Ltd* [2007] EWCA Civ 313.

disclosure of documents before the examination takes place.[57] The procedure usually adopted involves the issue of a Letter of Request to the judicial authorities of the foreign country asking the foreign court to take the required evidence or arrange for it to be taken.[58] A Letter of Request may ask only for the production of documents without the examination of a witness.[59]

Increasing numbers of countries, including the UK, are parties to the Hague Convention on the Taking of Evidence Abroad in Civil and Commercial Matters 1970, which establishes clear procedures and improves the flow of information between Contracting States. Within the EU, Council Regulation No.1206/2001 of 28 May 2001 on co-operation between the courts of Member States in the taking of evidence in civil and commercial matters provides a procedure designed to ensure the swift production of evidence available in another Member State.

Obtaining evidence in England for use abroad

9–013   There is no objection in English law to the taking of evidence required for use in foreign proceedings without the intervention or permission of an English court or official agency. Such intervention will be required if measures of compulsion are required against an unwilling witness. However, the oath may only be administered in England with lawful authority. A person appointed by a court or other judicial authority of a foreign country does have power to administer oaths in the UK for the purpose of taking evidence in civil proceedings carried on under the law of that foreign country,[60] and a foreign diplomatic agent or consular officer has a general power to administer oaths in accordance with the law of the foreign country concerned.[61]

The High Court may order the taking of evidence in England at the request of a foreign court or tribunal under the Evidence (Proceedings in Other Jurisdictions) Act 1975. Although the Act was passed to enable the UK to ratify the Hague Convention on the Taking of Evidence Abroad in Civil and Commercial Matters 1970, it does not reproduce the provisions of the Convention. The Act is drafted so as to apply to all requests for assistance whether or not made under the Convention.

When an application is made to the High Court under the Act, the court must be satisfied that the evidence is to be obtained for the purposes of civil proceedings which have either been instituted before the requesting court or whose institution before that court is contemplated.[62] In this context "civil proceedings" means "proceedings in any civil or commercial matter".[63] Given that there is in this context no internationally acceptable definition of a "civil or commercial matter", the English court must satisfy itself that the proceedings concern a civil or commercial matter under the laws of both the requesting and

---

[57] CPR r.34.8.
[58] CPR r.34.13.
[59] *Panayiotou v Sony Music Entertainment (UK) Ltd* [1994] Ch. 142; *TCT Mobile Europe SAS v Telefonaktiebolaget LM Ericsson* [2015] EWHC 938 (Pat).
[60] Oaths and Evidence (Overseas Authorities and Countries) Act 1963 s.1.
[61] Consular Relations Act 1968 s.10(1).
[62] Evidence (Proceedings in Other Jurisdictions) Act 1975 s.1(b).
[63] Evidence (Proceedings in Other Jurisdictions) Act 1975 s.9(1).

requested countries.[64] For the purposes of English law, "proceedings in any civil matter" includes all proceedings other than criminal proceedings, and "proceedings in any commercial matter" fall within "proceedings in any civil matter". So far as the law of a requesting country is concerned, reference is to be made to the law and practice of that country, having regard to the manner in which classification is ordinarily made in that country.[65] In English law, fiscal matters are properly within the category of "civil and commercial", and a request by a foreign country for assistance in obtaining evidence to be used in the enforcement of the revenue law of that country in proceedings before the courts of that country, does not constitute direct or indirect enforcement of the revenue law of a foreign State.[66]

The English court may not order any steps to be taken unless they are steps which could be required to be taken by way of obtaining evidence for the purposes of English civil proceedings.[67] Where the foreign court seeks the disclosure of documents, there are clear limitations on what may be ordered. What is sought must be evidence, and not merely information which might suggest a line of enquiry leading to evidence: "fishing expeditions" are not allowed.[68] On a request for oral evidence to be taken, the test is whether there is good reason to believe that the intended witness has knowledge of matters in issue so as to be likely to be able to give evidence relevant to those issues.[69]

The Protection of Trading Interests Act 1980, which was enacted primarily in the context of hostility to the US anti-trust jurisdiction, provides that the English court must refuse to make an order in response to a foreign court's request if it is shown that the request infringes the jurisdiction of the UK or is otherwise prejudicial to the sovereignty of the UK. A certificate signed by or on behalf of the Secretary of State to the effect that the request is such an infringement or is so prejudicial is conclusive.[70]

The Secretary of State may also give directions for prohibiting compliance with certain orders of foreign courts or authorities requiring any person in the UK to produce any commercial document not within the territorial jurisdiction of the foreign country, or to provide commercial information compiled from such documents, or to publish any such document or information.[71] A direction may be given if it appears to the Secretary of State that a requirement infringes the

---

[64] *Re State of Norway's Application (Nos 1 and 2)* [1990] 1 A.C. 723, where the history of UK legislation since the Foreign Tribunals Evidence Act 1857 is examined. See Mann, (1989) 105 L.Q.R. 341.

[65] *Re State of Norway's Application (Nos 1 and 2)* [1990] 1 A.C. 723.

[66] ibid.

[67] Evidence (Proceedings in Other Jurisdictions) Act 1975 s.2(3). See, e.g. *Goncharova v Zolotova* [2015] EWHC 3061 (DNA samples from body of deceased Russian oligarch sent to Russia for use in paternity case).

[68] ibid., s.2(4); *Re State of Norway's Application (Nos 1 and 2)* [1990] 1 A.C. 723.

[69] *First American Corp v Sheikh Zayed Al-Nahyan* [1999] 1 W.L.R. 1154.

[70] Protection of Trading Interests 1980 s.4.

[71] Protection of Trading Interests Act 1980 s.2(1). See *British Airways Board v Laker Airways Ltd* [1985] A.C. 58.

jurisdiction of the UK or is otherwise prejudicial to the sovereignty of the UK, or if compliance with it would be prejudicial to the security or foreign relations of the UK.[72]

NATURE OF THE CLAIMANT'S REMEDY

9–014   At common law, the nature of the remedy is a matter of procedure to be determined by the *lex fori*. Thus if the claimant is by the *lex causae* entitled only to damages but is by English law entitled to specific relief, e.g., specific performance or an injunction, that type of remedy is available in England.[73] Conversely, an English court will not grant specific relief where to do so is contrary to the principles of English law.[74] It is not always easy to distinguish questions of remedy from those of liability. In *Harding v Wealands*[75] provisions in the New South Wales Motor Accident Compensation Act 1999 placing floors and ceilings on compensation for injury were held to go to remedy and so were classed as procedural and irrelevant to claims brought in England. But in *Allen v DePuy International Ltd*[76] the bar in s.317(1) of the New Zealand Accident Compensation Act 2001 on claims for damages where compensation was available under the New Zealand Accidents Compensation Scheme were held substantive as going to liability.

Although an action in England will not fail merely because the claim is unknown to English law, it will fail if English law has no appropriate remedy for giving effect to the plaintiff's alleged foreign right. Thus in *Phrantzes v Argenti*[77]:

> A Greek daughter who had just been married claimed that by Greek law her father was under an obligation to provide her with a dowry. Her claim failed, not because it was unknown to English law, but because by Greek law the amount of the dowry was within the discretion of the court and varied in accordance with the wealth and social position of the father and the number of his children, and with the behaviour of the daughter. The English court therefore had no remedy for giving effect to the Greek claim.

The question is whether English law, as the law of the forum, provides a remedy which harmonises or is "cognate" with the liability according to its nature and extent as fixed by the foreign *lex causae*.[78] In very many cases it will, in the form of damages.

Here again, the principle that the nature of the remedy is a matter for the *lex fori* is affected by the provisions of the Rome I and Rome II Regulations. The law applicable by virtue of the Rome I Regulation governs, within the limits of the

---

[72] Protection of Trading Interests Act 1980 s.2(2).

[73] *Baschet v London Illustrated Standard* [1900] 1 Ch. 73; *Boys v Chaplin* [1971] A.C. 356, 394, per Lord Pearson.

[74] Consider *Warner Brothers Pictures v Nelson* [1937] 1 K.B. 209 where, however, foreign law was not pleaded.

[75] [2006] UKHL 32; [2007] 2 AC 1 (but note the doubt expressed in *Cox v Ergo Versicherung* [2014] A.C. 1379 at [43]).

[76] [2015] EWHC 926.

[77] [1960] 2 Q.B. 19.

[78] *Cox v Ergo Versicherung AG* [2014] UKSC 22; [2014] A.C. 1379 at [21]; *Iraqi Civilians v Ministry of Defence* [2014] EWHC 3686 at [37].

powers conferred on the court by its procedural law,[79] the consequences of breach, including the assessment of damages so far as it is governed by rules of law.[80] The law applicable by virtue of the Rome II Regulation governs the existence, the nature and the assessment of damage or the remedy claimed, and, within the limits of powers conferred on the court by its procedural law, the measures which a court may take to prevent or terminate injury or damage or to ensure the provision of compensation.[81]

Where the Regulations apply, the distinction formerly drawn between remoteness of damage, which has always been treated as a question of substance governed by the *lex causae*, and measure or quantification of damages, seen as a question of procedure governed by the *lex fori*,[82] is inapplicable: the assessment of damages is a matter for the *lex causae*.

Judgments in foreign currency

Prior to 1975 it had been regarded as settled law for nearly 400 years that an English court could not give judgment for the payment of an amount expressed in foreign currency. The reason was that the sheriff could not be expected to know the value of foreign currency (currency-conversion websites not having been invented) and thus could not enforce any money judgment by execution unless it was expressed in pounds sterling. The rule was re-asserted by a unanimous House of Lords in 1961 in *Re United Railways of the Havana and Regla Warehouses*,[83] where Lord Denning declared, "If there is one thing clear in our law, it is that the claim must be made in sterling and the judgment given in sterling. We do not give judgments in dollars any more than the United States courts give judgments in sterling".[84]

9–015

This rule was an unjust rule, because it made an anomalous and unnecessary exception to the principle of "nominalism". If a debt is expressed in foreign currency, both parties expect to measure their rights and obligations in terms of that currency and no other. The creditor should bear the risk of a depreciation of that currency after the date of maturity of the debt; the debtor should bear the risk of its appreciation. Most English judges remained impervious to the injustice of the rule until sterling depreciated in terms of the foreign currency, rather than the other way round as in the earlier cases.

In 1975 the House of Lords in *Miliangos v George Frank (Textiles) Ltd*[85] discarded the rule, overruled its own previous decision in *Re United Railways*, and held that judgment could be given for an amount expressed in foreign currency or the sterling equivalent at the date when the court authorises enforcement of the judgment in terms of sterling.

---

[79] i.e., the forum court is not required to make an order unknown to its legal system.
[80] Rome I Regulation art.12(1)(c) replacing the Rome Convention art.10(1)(c).
[81] Rome II Regulation art.15(c),(d).
[82] *Boys v Chaplin* [1971] A.C. 356 (where the House of Lords had to determine the proper characterisation of rules as to recoverable heads of damage, and held that they went to substance).
[83] [1961] A.C. 1007.
[84] At pp.1068–1069.
[85] [1976] A.C. 443.

The action was by a Swiss seller against an English buyer for the price of goods sold. The price was quoted in Swiss francs and Swiss law was the proper law of the contract. The sterling equivalent of the price was £42,000 in 1971 when payment was due and (owing to the depreciation of the pound) £60,000 in 1974 at the date of the hearing. The House of Lords held that the Swiss seller was entitled to the larger sum.

As a precedent, the decision in the *Miliangos* case was expressly confined to claims for a liquidated debt expressed in foreign currency in cases where the proper law of the contract was that of a foreign country and where the money of account and payment was that of that country or possibly of some third country outside the UK. The House of Lords declined to review the whole field of the law regarding foreign currency obligations, leaving it open to future discussion whether the same rule should apply to claims for damages for breach of contract or for tort. But a spate of cases rapidly clarified the scope of the decision. It is now clear that the court can give judgment for payment of an amount in foreign currency as damages for breach of contract[86] or for tort.[87] It can also do so on making an award under s.1(3) of the Law Reform (Frustrated Contracts) Act 1943 for the restoration of a valuable benefit to the claimant.[88] It has also been held that the principle of *Miliangos* applies even though the contract is governed by English law.[89] But there must of course be some foreign element. In the case of a liquidated debt, it is presumably sufficient if the debt was expressed in foreign currency. In the case of damages for breach of contract or for tort, the test adopted by the House of Lords is that damages can be awarded in a foreign currency if that was the currency in which the loss was effectively felt or borne by the person suffering it, having regard to the currency in which he or she generally operates or with which he or she has the closest connection.[90] In the case of restitution for unjust enrichment, the award will be made in the currency in which the defendant's benefit can be most fairly and appropriately valued.[91]

STATUTES OF LIMITATION

9–016   The common law distinguishes two kinds of statutes of limitation: those which merely bar a remedy and those which extinguish a right.[92] This common law rule was well-established, although it has been subjected to searching judicial criticism, doubting whether the distinction between "right" and "remedy" provided an acceptable basis on which to proceed.[93] Statutes of the former kind are procedural, while statutes of the latter kind are substantive. In general, the

---

[86] *Jean Kraut A/B v Albany Fabrics Ltd* [1977] Q.B. 182; *Services Europe Atlantique Sud v Stockholm Rederiaktiebolag Svea* [1979] A.C. 685.

[87] *The Despina R* [1979] A.C. 685.

[88] *BP Exploration Co (Libya) Ltd v Hunt (No.2)* [1979] 1 W.L.R. 783, 840–841.

[89] *Barclays Bank International Ltd v Levin Brothers (Bradford) Ltd* [1977] Q.B. 270; *Services Europe Atlantique Sud v Stockholm Rederiaktiebolag Svea* [1979] A.C. 685.

[90] *The Despina R* [1979] A.C. 685; *Services Europe Atlantique Sud v Stockholm Rederiaktiebolag Svea* [1979] A.C. 685.

[91] *BP Exploration Co (Libya) Ltd v Hunt (No.2)* [1979] 1 W.L.R. 783.

[92] *Phillips v Eyre* (1870) L.R. 6 Q.B. 1, 29; *Black-Clawson Ltd v Papierwerke Waldhof-Aschaffenberg AG* [1975] A.C. 591, 630.

[93] See the dissenting judgments in *McKain v R. W. Miller & Co (South Australia) Pty Ltd* (1991) 174 C.L.R. 1.

English law as to limitation of actions has been regarded as procedural,[94] but ss.3(2), 17 and 25(3) of the Limitation Act 1980 are probably substantive since they expressly extinguish the title of the former owner. Sometimes a statute creates an entirely new right of action unknown to the common law and at the same time imposes a shorter period of limitation than that applicable under the general law. An example is the Civil Liability (Contribution) Act 1978: where a person becomes entitled to a right to recover contribution under s.1 of that Act, the limitation period is two years.[95] There is Scottish, Australian and American authority in favour of the view that such special periods of limitation are substantive, even if they are contained in a different statute from that which creates the right.[96]

At common law, the English courts used the same distinction between right and remedy in characterising foreign statutes of limitation, with results which were far from happy. The Foreign Limitation Periods Act 1984, based on recommendations by the Law Commission,[97] adopts the general principle, subject to an exception based on public policy where the court finds that there would be "undue hardship" to a person who is or might be a party,[98] that the limitation rules of the *lex causae* are to be applied in actions in England. English limitation rules are not to be applied unless English law is the *lex causae* or one of two *leges causae* governing the matter.[99] The applicable provisions of the foreign *lex causae* are defined to include both procedural and substantive rules with respect to a limitation period.[100] English law as the *lex fori* does, however, determine whether, and the time at which, proceedings have been commenced,[101] and so whether the proceedings were commenced within the time limit.

Under the Rome I Regulation, the applicable law governs the various ways of extinguishing obligations, and prescription and limitation of actions[102]; under the Rome II Regulation a fuller provision to similar effect subjects to the applicable law the manner in which an obligation may be extinguished and rules of prescription and limitation, including rules relating to the commencement, interruption and suspension of a period of prescription or limitation.[103] These provisions achieve the same result as the Foreign Limitation Periods Act 1984. In each case application of the governing law may be refused if its application would be manifestly contrary to English public policy[104]; this, it is submitted, is a stricter test than that applied under the 1984 Act.

---

[94] *Williams v Jones* (1811) 13 East 439; *Ruckmaboye v Mottichund* (1851) 8 Moo.P.C. 4.
[95] Limitation Act 1980 s.10.
[96] For a comparative study, see Harder, (2011) 60 I.C.L.Q. 659.
[97] Law Com. No. 114 (1982).
[98] 1984 Act s.2. See *The Komninos S* [1990] 1 Lloyd's Rep. 541; *Harley v Smith* [2010] EWCA Civ 78.
[99] Section 1(1)(2). Foreign torts were, until the coming into force of Pt III of the Private International Law (Miscellaneous Provisions) Act 1995, an example of the "two *leges causae*" situation.
[100] Foreign Limitation Periods Act 1984 s.4.
[101] Foreign Limitation Periods Act 1984 s.1(3).
[102] Rome I Regulation art.12(1)(d).
[103] Rome II Regulation art.15(h). See SI 2008/2986.
[104] Rome I Regulation art.21; Rome II Regulation art.26.

CHAPTER 10

RECOGNITION AND ENFORCEMENT OF FOREIGN JUDGMENTS

It is sometimes easier to obtain a judgment than to enforce it. A claimant who, for **10–001** example, successfully sues in Japan for breach of contract or for tort and is awarded damages may discover that the defendant has removed all his or her assets to England. The judgment cannot be enforced in Japan, because there are no assets there. The officers charged with the enforcement of judgments in the English legal system will not act on a Japanese judgment. The Japanese officials cannot act in England. What is the claimant to do? This chapter seeks to answer that question and deal with the sometimes difficult issues surrounding the recognition and enforcement of foreign judgments.[1]

There is an important distinction between the recognition of a judgment as one entitled to be given some weight in the court of the forum and the enforcement of that judgment. A court must recognise every foreign judgment which it enforces, but it need not enforce every foreign judgment which it recognises. Some foreign judgments do not lend themselves to enforcement, but only to recognition. Examples are a judgment dismissing a claim (unless it orders the unsuccessful claimant to pay costs, as it frequently does); or a declaratory judgment; or a decree of divorce or nullity.[2] But there may be orders ancillary to such decrees which, because they order the payment of money, are capable of enforcement: for example orders dealing with the financial consequences of divorce or orders as to costs.

This chapter is divided into two parts: the first deals with the modern rules as to the recognition and enforcement of judgments given in Member States of the EU, principally to be found in the Brussels I *bis* Regulation[3]; the second deals with the much older and more complex rules, derived partly from common law and partly from statute, as to judgments from other countries.

---

[1] See, generally, Read, *Recognition and Enforcement of Foreign Judgments* (Cambridge MA: Harvard University Press, 1938); Patchett, *Recognition of Commercial Judgments and Awards in the Commonwealth* (London: Butterworths, 1984).

[2] For the recognition in England of foreign decrees of divorce and nullity, see Chapter 12. This chapter is concerned only with foreign judgments in personam.

[3] European Parliament and Council Regulation 1215/2012 on jurisdiction and the recognition and enforcement of judgments in civil and commercial matters, [2012] OJ L 351, 20.12.2012, p. 1. This applies to legal proceedings instituted on or after 10 January 2015, art.66(1); proceedings instituted before that date remain governed by Council Regulation No.44/2001 of 22 December 2000 on the recognition and enforcement of judgments in civil and commercial matters. See generally, Chapter 6.

RECOGNITION AND ENFORCEMENT WITHIN THE EUROPEAN UNION

The Brussels I *bis* Regulation

10–002   The jurisdictional provisions of the Brussels I *bis* Regulation were discussed in Chapter 6. For reasons of clarity of exposition, the provisions of the Regulation on jurisdiction and on the recognition and enforcement of judgments are dealt with in different chapters, but it cannot be stressed too strongly that the Regulation is one and indivisible and must be considered as a whole.

The Regulation's rules on jurisdiction provide ample guarantees for the defendant: as a general rule the defendant can only be sued in the courts of his or her domicile[4]; if the defendant does not enter an appearance the court itself must declare of its own motion that it has no jurisdiction, unless its jurisdiction is derived from the provisions of the Regulation[5]; the court must stay the proceedings unless satisfied that the defendant had an opportunity to be heard.[6] The strictness of these provisions has its counterpart in the extreme liberality of the provisions on recognition and enforcement, which are designed to allow judgments given in one Member State to run freely throughout the EU. The principles on which the Regulation is based seek to minimise the obstacles to the recognition and enforcement of judgments; in the context of enforcement, the Brussels I *bis* Regulation took the application of these principles further than its predecessor Regulation. As a general rule, a court of a Member State in which enforcement is sought may not investigate the jurisdiction of the court in another Member State which gave the judgment: it is for the original court to determine that it has jurisdiction and that determination cannot, in general, be questioned in another Member State at the recognition and enforcement stage.

The provisions on recognition and enforcement, which form Ch.III of the Regulation, apply only to judgments within the scope of the Regulation as defined in art.1.[7] Subject to that, "judgment" means any judgment given by a court or tribunal of a Member State, whatever the judgment may be called, including a decree, order, decision or writ of execution, as well as the determination of costs or expenses by an officer of the court[8]; and not only money judgments but also, for example, injunctions and orders for specific performance. Provisional or protective orders are included; though not if they are granted without notice to the defendant.[9]

It is important to note that under the Regulation the enforcement procedures apply to all judgments within its scope, whether or not they are against persons domiciled in a Member State and whether or not the original court assumed jurisdiction on a ground set out in the Regulation or a ground to be found in its

---

[4]   Article 4.
[5]   Article 28(1).
[6]   Article 28(2).
[7]   See above, para.6-002.
[8]   Article 2(a). A judgment includes its *ratio decidendi*: Case C-456/11 *Gothaer Allgemeine Versicherung AG v Samskip GmbH* [2013] Q.B. 458 (Belgium could decline jurisdiction on account of choice of court clause; that judgment could not be recognised as such in another Member State, but holding as to validity of the clause was to be recognised there).
[9]   Article 2(b).

national law. So, an English judgment against a New York resident where the jurisdiction of the English court was based on the temporary presence of the defendant in England is enforceable in France; and a French judgment against a New York resident where the jurisdiction of the French court was based on the French nationality of the claimant under art.14 of the French Civil Code is enforceable in England. It is immaterial that the grounds for jurisdiction are "exorbitant", and that their use is prohibited as against defendants domiciled in a Member State by art.5(2). Article 59 of the Brussels Convention allowed a Contracting State to enter into a binding agreement with a non-Contracting State that it will not recognise judgments given in other Contracting States on exorbitant grounds against defendants domiciled or habitually resident in that non-Contracting State. The UK took advantage of this provision to make agreements with Canada[10] and Australia.[11] The effect of those agreements is preserved under the Brussels I *bis* Regulation,[12] but no new agreements may be made.

Recognition

Article 36(1) of the Regulation provides simply that "a judgment given in a Member State shall be recognised in the other Member States without any special procedure being required". In fact, art.37 does contain some minimal procedural requirements: the party wishing to invoke in one Member State a judgment given in another Member State must produce a copy of the judgment "which satisfies the conditions necessary to establish its authenticity"[13] and a certificate setting out basic details about the judgment issued by the court of origin under art.53.[14] Any interested party may apply for a decision that there are no grounds for refusal of recognition[15]; equally, any interested party may apply for a refusal of recognition.[16]   **10–003**

The court or authority before which a judgment given in another Member State is invoked may suspend the proceedings, in whole or in part, if the judgment is challenged in the Member State of origin; or if an application has been submitted for a decision that there are no grounds for refusal of recognition or for a decision that the recognition is to be refused on the basis of one of those grounds.[17]

---

[10] By an Exchange of Notes of 7 November 1994 and 17 February 1995, published in the UK as Cmnd. 2894. For UK legislative provision, see Reciprocal Enforcement of Foreign Judgments (Canada) Order 1987, SI 1987/468, as amended by SI 1995/2708.
[11] See Reciprocal Enforcement of Foreign Judgments (Australia) Order 1994, SI 1994/1901 and *New Cap Reinsurance Corp Ltd (In Liquidation) v Grant* [2011] EWCA Civ 971.
[12] Article 72.
[13] For translation requirements, se art.37(2).
[14] The form is set out in Annex I.
[15] Article 36(2). See also art.36(3) which removes any doubt as to the jurisdiction of a court to determine any incidental question of recognition.
[16] Article 45(1). For the procedure, see art.47ff and CPR Pt 74.
[17] Article 38.

Grounds on which recognition may be refused

10–004   Recognition may be refused on certain limited grounds set out in art.45. They are as follows:

(1)   recognition is manifestly contrary to public policy in the Member State addressed.

The case-law establishes that this ground is to be relied upon only in exceptional circumstances[18]; the word "manifestly", which was not in the equivalent Brussels Convention provision, was included to emphasise this point. To safeguard the ready recognition of judgments, the Regulation must be interpreted so as to set limits on the use which may be made of national understandings of public policy. The European Court has held that they can be used to deny recognition only where recognition or enforcement would be at variance to an unacceptable degree with the legal order of the state in which enforcement is sought; a manifest breach of a rule of law regarded as essential in the legal order of that state or of a right recognised as being fundamental within that legal order.[19] A judgment will be recognised even if the defendant was debarred from defending,[20] and even fraud in obtaining the judgment may not attract the defence, at least if there is a remedy in the foreign court.[21]

(2)   where the judgment was given in default of appearance, if the defendant was not served with the document which instituted the proceedings or with an equivalent document in sufficient time to enable him to arrange for his defence, unless the defendant failed to commence proceedings to challenge the judgment when it was possible for him to do so.

The notion of "default of appearance" has a European autonomous meaning and may be rather larger in scope than in the law of some Member States.[22] It is not enough simply to show that the defendant was aware of the proceedings; "service" must be understood in a way consonant with art.30 of the Brussels I Regulation itself[23] and with other Regulations, notably what is now Regulation 1393/2007 on the service in the Member States of judicial and extrajudicial documents in civil or commercial matters.[24] The final clause means that a defendant who becomes aware of the proceedings in a particular Member State or the ensuing judgment and decides not to take steps open to him or her in that state is debarred from alleging that there was no service or no opportunity to arrange a defence. If

---

[18] Case C–78/95 *Hendrickman v Magenta Dock & Verlag GmbH* [1996] E.C.R. I–4943. For the growing importance of human rights in assessing public policy, see Oster (2015) 11 J.Priv.Int.L. 542.

[19] Case C–7/98 *Krombach v Bamberski* [2000] E.C.R. I–1935.

[20] Case C–394 *Gambazzi v Daimler Chrysler Canada Inc* [2009] E.C.R. I-2563.

[21] *Interdesco SA v Nullifire Ltd* [1992] 1 Lloyd's Rep. 180.

[22] Case C–78/95 *Hendrickman v Magenta Dock & Verlag GmbH* [1996] E.C.R. I–4943 (assertion by defendant that the lawyer who appeared for him was not authorised to do so: held "in default of appearance" for purposes of the Brussels Convention though not under the national law of the forum).

[23] See para.4–064.

[24] *Tavoulareas v Tsavliris (No.2)* [2006] EWCA Civ 1772; [2007] 1 W.L.R. 470.

a defendant does seek to challenge a default judgment and fails in the challenge after a full hearing, the default nature of the original judgment can no longer be relied upon.[25]

(3)   if the judgment is irreconcilable with a judgment given in a dispute between the same parties in the Member State addressed.

(4)   if the judgment is irreconcilable with an earlier judgment given in another Member State or a third State involving the same cause of action and between the same parties, provided that the earlier judgment fulfils the conditions necessary for its recognition in the Member State addressed.

In this context, "irreconcilable" means having mutually exclusive consequences.[26]

(5)   If the judgment conflicts with the provisions of arts 10 to 16 (insurance), 17 to 19 (consumer contracts) or 20 to 23 (individual contracts of employment), where the policy-holder, the insured, the beneficiary of the insurance contract, the consumer or the employee was the defendant[27]; or conflicts with art.24 (exclusive jurisdiction).[28]

Other issues going to recognition

The court in which recognition is sought may not review the merits of the judgment.[29] Nor can it question the jurisdiction of the court which gave the judgment, and may not apply the test of public policy to rules relating to jurisdiction.[30] But even in these cases, the court in which enforcement is sought is bound by the findings of fact on which the court of origin based its jurisdiction.[31] However, the court in which enforcement is sought is not bound by the findings of the original court as to whether the case is within the scope of the Regulation.[32]   **10–005**

Enforcement

It is in this context that the Brussels I *bis* Regulation made the greatest changes, by abolishing the previous requirement of a declaration of enforceability in the Member State addressed under the *exequatur* procedure, once a feature common to States in the civil law tradition. The general provision in the Regulation is now that a judgment given in a Member State which is enforceable in that Member State shall be enforceable in the other Member States without any declaration of enforceability being required.[33] An enforceable judgment carries with it by operation of law the power to proceed to any protective measures which exist   **10–006**

---

[25] Case C-420/07 *Apostolides v Orams* [2009] E.C.R. I-3571.
[26] e.g. Case 145/86 *Hoffman v Krieg* [1988] E.C.R. 645 (maintenance order inconsistent with divorce granted in State of intended enforcement).
[27] Article 45(1)(e)(i).
[28] Article 45(1)(e)(ii).
[29] Article 52.
[30] Article 45(3).
[31] Article 45(2).
[32] Case 29/76 *LTU v Eurocontrol* [1976] E.C.R. 1541.
[33] Article 39(1).

under the law of the Member State addressed.[34] It is enforceable in the Member State addressed under the same conditions as a judgment given in the Member State addressed.[35]

The procedure for the enforcement of judgments given in another Member State is governed by the law of the Member State addressed, subject to the provisions of the Regulation itself.[36] For the purposes of enforcement, the applicant must provide the competent enforcement authority with a copy of the judgment which satisfies the conditions necessary to establish its authenticity; and the certificate issued under art.53, in this case certifying that the judgment is enforceable[37] and containing an extract of the judgment as well as, where appropriate, relevant information on the recoverable costs of the proceedings and the calculation of interest.[38] The certificate must be served on the person against whom the enforcement is sought prior to the first enforcement measure, together with the judgment, if that has not already been served on that person.[39]

Refusal of enforcement

10–007 On the application of the person against whom enforcement is sought, enforcement may be refused on the grounds in art.45, already set out, on which recognition may be refused; or on the grounds for refusal or of suspension of enforcement under the law of the Member State addressed in so far as they are not incompatible with the art.45 grounds.[40] Either party may appeal against a decision to refuse, or to decline to refuse, enforcement, with the possibility of a further appeal.[41] A court considering an application for refusal of enforcement—an appeal—may stay the proceedings if an "ordinary appeal" has been lodged against the judgment in the Member State of origin or if the time for such an appeal has not yet expired. Where the judgment was given in the UK (or in Ireland or Cyprus) where the category of "ordinary appeal" has no meaning, any form of appeal available in the Member State of origin is to be treated as an ordinary appeal.[42]

---

[34] Article 40.

[35] Article 41(1).

[36] Article 41(1).

[37] The competent authority in the Member State addressed must, on the application of the person against whom enforcement is sought, suspend the enforcement proceedings where the enforceability of the judgment is suspended in the Member State of origin: art.44(2).

[38] Article 42(1). For the rather different requirements where the judgment is one ordering provisional, including protective, measures, see art.42(2); for translation requirements, see art.42(3),(4).

[39] Article 43(1). For translation requirements, see art.43(2); art.43 does not apply to the enforcement of a protective measure in a judgment or where the person seeking enforcement proceeds to protective measures under the law of the State addressed under art.40: art.43(3).

[40] Articles 41(2), 46. See art.47 for the procedure for applying for refusal of enforcement; a decision on the application must be reached "without delay": art.48.

[41] Articles 49, 50.

[42] Article 51.

European enforcement order

Steps were taken in 2004 to simplify enforcement procedures in respect of judgments in uncontested claims.[43] A claim is regarded as uncontested if: **10–008**

(a)   the debtor has expressly agreed to it by admission or by means of a settlement which has been approved by a court or concluded before a court in the course of proceedings; or

(b)   the debtor has never objected to it, in compliance with the relevant procedural requirements under the law of the Member State of origin, in the course of the court proceedings; or

(c)   the debtor has not appeared or been represented at a court hearing regarding that claim after having initially objected to the claim in the course of the court proceedings, provided that such conduct amounts to a tacit admission of the claim or of the facts alleged by the creditor under the law of the Member State of origin; or

(d)   the debtor has expressly agreed to it in an authentic instrument.[44]

In these cases the requirement of *exequatur*, that is the need for a declaration of enforceability, is abolished and the judgment is to be recognised and enforced in other Member States without any possibility of the judgment-debtor opposing its recognition.[45] However, a judgment can only be certified as a European Enforcement Order if the debtor is entitled, under the law of the Member State of origin, to apply for a review of the judgment in certain specified cases.[46]

European order for payment

International litigation, outside the area of family law, is typically between corporations and involves large sums of money. That is certainly true of the reported cases cited in this book. It tends to conceal the great volume of relatively low-value cross-border business. Unpaid bills are a major problem to small and medium enterprises and late payment of sums which are clearly due can drive small traders into insolvency. To address this problem the EU established a European order for payment procedure available in every Member State (except Denmark) by adopting Regulation 1896/2006 of the European Parliament and of the Council of 12 December 2006 creating a European order for payment procedure.[47]   **10–009**

The declared purpose of the Regulation is to simplify, speed up and reduce the costs of litigation in cross-border cases concerning uncontested pecuniary claims, and to permit the free circulation of European orders for payment throughout the

---

[43] European Parliament and Council Regulation 805/2004 of 21 April 2004 creating a European Enforcement Order for uncontested claims (O.J. L 143/15, 30.4.2004) as amended by Regulation 1869/2005 (O.J. L 300/6, 17.11.2005) and Regulation 1103/2008 (O.J. L 304/80, 14.11.2008).
[44] Article 3(1).
[45] Article 5.
[46] See art.19 and Case C-300/14 *Imtech Marine Belgium NV v Radio Hellenic SA* (CJEU, December 2015).
[47] For text, see O.J. L 399/1, 30.12.2006.

Member States by laying down minimum standards, compliance with which renders unnecessary any intermediate proceedings in the Member State of enforcement prior to recognition and enforcement.[48] It therefore lays down a harmonised procedure, as an alternative to whatever other procedures may be available under national law.[49] It applies when at least one of the parties is, when the application is submitted, domiciled or habitually resident in a Member State other than the Member State of the court seised.[50]

An application for a European order for payment is made using a standard form prescribed in the Regulation. It gives full details of the claim and a description of evidence supporting it.[51] The court to which application is made is required to examine, as soon as possible and on the basis of the application form, whether the requirements of the Regulation are met and whether the claim appears to be well founded. The Regulation states that this examination "may take the form of an automated procedure", and a judge will not usually be involved.[52] If need be, the applicant may be given an opportunity to complete or rectify an application.[53] At no stage in the procedure is legal representation required.[54]

If the application is in order, the court must issue, as soon as possible and normally within 30 days of the lodging of the application, a European order for payment in a prescribed standard form, which is accompanied by a copy of the application form. The order presents the defendant a choice between paying to the claimant the amount stated in the order and opposing the order by lodging with the court of origin a statement of opposition, to be sent within 30 days of service of the order on him, failing which the order becomes enforceable.[55] There is another standard form for opposition to the order; the defendant does not have to specify any reasons.[56] A statement of opposition has the effect of transferring the proceedings to be dealt with in accordance with the rules of ordinary civil procedure unless the claimant has explicitly requested that the proceedings be terminated in that event.[57]

If no statement of opposition has been lodged with the court of origin, that court must without delay declare the European order for payment enforceable and

---

[48] Article 1(1).
[49] See art.1(2).
[50] Article 3. Domicile is determined under arts 62 and 63 of the Brussels I *bis* Regulation (Regulation No.1215/2012 on jurisdiction and the recognition and enforcement of judgments in civil and commercial matters). Jurisdiction is governed by the rules in that Regulation; but if the claim relates to a contract concluded by a person, the consumer, for a purpose which can be regarded as being outside his trade or profession, and if the defendant is the consumer, only the courts in the Member State in which the defendant is domiciled have jurisdiction. See arts 3(2) and 6.
[51] Article 7.
[52] Article 8, and see Recital (16).
[53] Article 9.
[54] Article 24.
[55] Article 12; for rules as to service of the order, see arts 13–15.
[56] Article 16.
[57] Article 17.

send the enforceable European order for payment to the claimant.[58] It is enforced under the same conditions as an enforceable decision issued in the Member State of enforcement.[59]

European small claims procedure

The process of developing harmonised claims procedures within the EU was taken further with the adoption of Regulation 861/2007 of the European Parliament and of the Council of 11 July 2007 establishing a European Small Claims Procedure, applying from 1 January 2009 in all Member States except Denmark.[60] It is intended to simplify and speed up litigation concerning small claims in cross-border cases, and to reduce costs; the new procedure is available to litigants as an alternative to the procedures existing under national law.[61] It applies where the value of a claim does not exceed €2,000.[62] The definition of a cross-border case and the rules as to jurisdiction are the same as in the European order for payment procedure.[63]

    10–010

The European Small Claims Procedure is a written procedure. The court will hold an oral hearing if it considers it to be necessary or if a party so requests; it may refuse a request for an oral hearing if it considers that an oral hearing is obviously not necessary for the fair conduct of the proceedings.[64] The procedure is begun by the lodging of a prescribed standard form of claim, which includes a description of evidence supporting the claim and is accompanied, where appropriate, by any relevant supporting documents. A copy of the claim form, completed or rectified if necessary, is served, with its supporting documents and an answer form, on the defendant; these documents must be dispatched within 14 days of the receipt of a properly filled in claim form. The defendant must submit a response within 30 days of service of the claim form and answer form, by filling in the answer form and sending it, with any relevant supporting documents, to the court. Within 14 days of receipt of the response from the defendant, the court must send a copy, together with any relevant supporting documents, to the claimant.[65]

The court has 30 days after the receipt of the final document within which to give judgment, to request further information, to take evidence (and the court, not the parties, decides what evidence is required), or to summon the parties to an oral hearing to be held within 30 days of the summons. The court must give the judgment either within 30 days of any oral hearing or after having received all

---

[58] Article 18.

[59] Article 21; note the translation requirements. There are very limited grounds on which enforcement may be refused: art.22.

[60] For text, see O.J. L 199/1, 31.7.2007. There are minor amendments in Commission Regulation 936/2012 of 4 October 2012 (O.J. L 283/1, 16.10.2012) and Council Regulation 517/2013 of 13 May 2013 (O.J. L 158/1, 10.6.2013).

[61] Article 1.

[62] Article 2(1).

[63] Article 3.

[64] Article 5. The hearing (and the taking of any evidence) may be by video conference or other communications technology: arts 8, 9.

[65] See art.5 generally; the procedure allows for counterclaims.

information necessary for giving the judgment.[66] Legal representation is not mandatory.[67] A judgment given in a Member State in the European Small Claims Procedure is to be recognised and enforced in another Member State without the need for a declaration of enforceability and without any possibility of opposing its recognition.[68]

In the small claims procedure choice of law issues can arise, but the low value of the claim and the simplicity of the issues will almost always mean that they are effectively ignored. Even if they are raised, the applicable law is very likely to be that of a Member State.

Mediation directive

10–011   Various forms of mediation, in commercial and in family cases, are an increasingly common feature of civil procedure in many countries. In 2008 the EU adopted a Directive dealing with mediation in cross-border disputes,[69] to be transposed into national law by 21 May 2011.[70] Its declared aim is to facilitate access to alternative dispute resolution and to promote the amicable settlement of disputes by encouraging the use of mediation and by ensuring a balanced relationship between mediation and judicial proceedings.[71] "Mediation" is defined as "a structured process, however named or referred to, whereby two or more parties to a dispute attempt by themselves, on a voluntary basis, to reach an agreement on the settlement of their dispute with the assistance of a mediator".[72] Mediation initiated by the parties or suggested or ordered by a court or prescribed by the law of a Member State is included, as is mediation conducted by a judge who is *not* responsible for any judicial proceedings concerning the dispute in question.[73]

The effect of the Directive is limited to cross-border disputes, defined as those in which at least one of the parties is domiciled[74] or habitually resident in a Member State[75] other than that of any other party on the date on which the parties agree to use mediation after the dispute has arisen, or mediation is ordered by a court, or an obligation to use mediation arises under national law, or the court invites the parties to use mediation.[76]

Member States must ensure that parties who choose mediation in an attempt to settle a dispute are not subsequently prevented from initiating judicial

---

[66] Article 7.
[67] Article 10.
[68] Article 20(1).
[69] European Parliament and Council Directive 2008/52/EC of 21 May 2008 on certain aspects of mediation in civil and commercial matters, O.J. No. L 136/3, 24.05.2008.
[70] Article 12(1).
[71] Article 1.
[72] Article 3. Member States are to take certain steps to ensure the quality of mediation services: art.4; for confidentiality of mediation, see art.7.
[73] ibid.
[74] Domicile is determined in accordance with arts 62 and 63 of the Brussels I *bis* Regulation; see para.6–007, above: Directive, art.2(3).
[75] Denmark is not included in the term 'Member State" for the purposes of the Directive.
[76] Article 2(1).

proceedings or arbitration in relation to that dispute by the expiry of limitation or prescription periods during the mediation process.[77]

Member States must ensure that it is possible for the parties, or for one of them with the explicit consent of the others, to request that the content of a written agreement resulting from mediation be made enforceable. The content of such an agreement is to be made enforceable unless, in the case in question, either the content of that agreement is contrary to the law of the Member State where the request is made or the law of that Member State does not provide for its enforceability.[78] The outcome, a judgment or decision or an authentic instrument, will be enforceable under the Brussels I Regulation.

JUDGMENTS RENDERED OUTSIDE THE MEMBER STATES

Where the judgment was given in a State outside the EU, the recognition and enforcement of foreign judgments rest on common law developments with some statutory interventions.

10–012

English courts have recognised and enforced foreign judgments from the seventeenth century onwards.[79] It was at one time supposed that the basis of this enforcement was to be found in the doctrine of comity,[80] and a healthy fear that if foreign judgments were not enforced in England, English judgments would not be enforced abroad.[81] But later this theory was superseded by what is called the doctrine of obligation,[82] the best-known formulation of which is that of Blackburn J in *Schibsby v Westenholz*[83]:

> "We think that . . . the true principle on which the judgments of foreign tribunals are enforced in England is . . . that the judgment of a court of competent jurisdiction over the defendant imposes a duty or obligation on the defendant to pay the sum for which judgment is given, which the courts in this country are bound to enforce".

This was re-affirmed as "a purely theoretical and historical basis for the enforcement of foreign judgments at common law" in *Rubin v Eurofinance SA*.[84]

Whatever the theoretical basis of the rules in this area, the English courts came to recognise the conclusiveness of foreign judgments, first those in favour of defendants[85] and then those in favour of claimants.[86]

At one time, it was always open to a claimant who had obtained a foreign judgment to sue all over again in England relying on the original cause of action.

---

[77] Article 8.

[78] Article 6(1).

[79] See Sack in *Law, a Century of Progress, 1835–1935* (1937), Vol. 3, pp.342, 382–384.

[80] On the decline, fall, but apparent survival of the notion of comity, see Collins, in Fawcett (ed), *Reform and Development of Private International Law* (Oxford: Oxford University Press, 2002) at 89–110.

[81] See *Roach v Garvan* (1748) 1 Ves. Sen. 157, 159; *Wright v Simpson* (1802) 6 Ves. 714, 730; *Alves v Bunbury* (1814) 4 Camp. 28.

[82] See per Parke B in *Russell v Smyth* (1842) 9 M. & W. 810, 819 and *Williams v Jones* (1845) 13 M. & W. 628, 633.

[83] (1870) L.R. 6 Q.B. 155, 159. See Ho, (1997) 46 I.C.L.Q. 443.

[84] [2012] UKSC 46; [2013] 1 A.C. 236 at [9].

[85] *Ricardo v Garcias* (1845) 12 Cl. & F. 368.

[86] *Godard v Gray* (1870) L.R. 6 Q.B. 139. cf. *Castrique v Imrie* (1870) L.R. 4 H.L. 414.

The Civil Jurisdiction and Judgments Act 1982[87] ended this possibility, so that a foreign judgment, like an English judgment, extinguished the original cause of action which is said to merge in the judgment-debt. The avenues now open to the judgment-creditor are to bring an action in England on the judgment-debt, or, where the relevant statutes apply, to register the foreign judgment in the High Court. Something will be said about each of these methods of proceeding, before a consideration of the principles followed by the English courts: they are largely, but not wholly, the same whichever method is used.

Action on the judgment-debt at common law

10–013   At common law, a judgment creditor seeking to enforce a foreign judgment in England may bring an action on the foreign judgment.[88] A creditor can apply for summary judgment under Pt 24 of the Civil Procedure Rules on the ground that the defendant has no real prospect of successfully defending the claim; and if the application is successful, the defendant will not be allowed to defend at all. The speed and simplicity of this procedure, coupled with the tendency of English judges narrowly to circumscribe the defences that may be pleaded to an action on a foreign judgment, mean that foreign judgments are in practice enforceable in England much more easily than they are in many civil law countries, where enforcement is easy in theory but difficult in practice because of the tendency of the courts to enlarge the scope of the defence that enforcement would be contrary to *ordre public* or public policy.[89] Thus it came about that foreign judgments are more easily enforceable in England than are English judgments in some foreign countries.[90]

Enforcement by registration under statute

10–014   A foreign judgment under which a sum of money is payable may be enforceable in England under statute by a slightly more direct process of registration. The two most important statutes are the Administration of Justice Act 1920, and the Foreign Judgments (Reciprocal Enforcement) Act 1933.

Part II of the Administration of Justice Act 1920 provides for the enforcement of judgments of superior courts in the UK by registration in designated Commonwealth countries and, conversely, for the enforcement of judgments of superior courts of those Commonwealth countries by registration in the UK. The Act has been applied by Order in Council to numerous countries of the Commonwealth. Registration is discretionary and not as of right, since it can be refused unless the registering court "in all the circumstances of the case ... thinks it just and convenient that the judgment should be enforced in the UK".[91]

---

[87] Section 34.

[88] This does not apply in the context of insolvency, where special rules apply: *Rubin v Eurofinance SA* [2010] EWCA Civ 895; [2011] Ch. 133 (under appeal to the Supreme Court).

[89] See Gutteridge, (1932) 13 B.Y.I.L. 49; Graupner, (1963) 12 I.C.L.Q. 367.

[90] See the Report of the Foreign Judgments (Reciprocal Enforcement) Committee, Cmd.4213 (1932), paras 2, 9, 10, 14.

[91] Section 9(1).

Moreover, registration may not be ordered if the original court acted without jurisdiction (though no attempt is made to elucidate the meaning of this term), or if the defendant establishes any of a limited number of defences which are very similar to those available at common law.[92]

The Foreign Judgments (Reciprocal Enforcement) Act 1933 provides for the reciprocal enforcement by registration of judgments of courts in the UK on the one hand, and judgments of courts in politically foreign countries, and also in countries of the Commonwealth outside the UK, on the other (the reason for including Commonwealth judgments was the intention that the regime of the 1933 Act would gradually replace that of the 1920 Act). The 1933 Act is much more important than that of 1920. This is because the 1933 Act is drafted in much more detail, and contains specific rules on when foreign courts are deemed to have jurisdiction for the purposes of the Act, and on what defences the defendant may set up in opposition to an application to register a foreign judgment. These rules are modelled very closely on those of the common law. Registration of a judgment under the Act is available as of right instead of merely at discretion as under the Act of 1920.

Sections 18 and 19 of the State Immunity Act 1978 provide for the recognition (but not the enforcement) of judgments rendered against the UK in states which are parties to the European Convention on State Immunity.

Relationship of common law and statute

The Acts of 1920 and 1933 are of limited geographical application and the judgments of very many foreign countries are outside their scope. There thus remains a considerable area within which enforcement of a foreign judgment at common law is the only process possible. The provisions of the Act of 1933 were deliberately framed so as to reproduce the rules of the common law as closely as possible,[93] though, as the Foreign Judgments (Reciprocal Enforcement) Committee conceded, it was found desirable to make one or two very slight departures from the common law in order to secure international agreements which would be more likely to operate satisfactorily in practice.[94] The question therefore arises whether the provisions of the Act as to the jurisdiction of foreign courts, and as to the scope of the defences, can legitimately be invoked by a court which is asked to enforce a foreign judgment at common law, even though the Act has not been extended by Order in Council to the foreign country in question. After some fluctuation of opinion among judges of first instance, it was laid down by the Court of Appeal that "one cannot ascertain what the common law is by arguing backwards from the provisions of the Act".[95]

10–015

---

[92] Section 9(2).
[93] Report of the Foreign Judgments (Reciprocal Enforcement) Committee, Cmd.4213 (1932), paras 2, 16, 18 and Annex V, para.7.
[94] ibid., Annex V, para.7.
[95] *Henry v Geoprosco International Ltd* [1976] Q.B. 726, 751.

Jurisdiction of the foreign court

10–016 The most fundamental of all requirements for the recognition or enforcement of foreign judgments in England (whether at common law or under the 1920 or 1933 Acts) is that the foreign court should have had jurisdiction according to the English rules of the conflict of laws. These are "indirect jurisdiction rules", and there is no reason for them to mirror the ("direct jurisdiction") rules governing the jurisdiction of the English courts.

Where there is uniformity of direct jurisdiction rules, as within the EU, there is no need for a separate set of indirect jurisdiction rules: it is enough that the judgment was given by a court in a Member State. The ill-fated Judgments Project of the Hague Conference on Private International Law set out to achieve the same result on a global scale.[96] Where, however, national laws differ widely as to rules of direct jurisdiction, a court asked to recognise and enforce a foreign judgment has to have some criteria for determining whether the assumption of jurisdiction by the foreign court was proper. In a famous leading case[97]:

> The claimant brought an action in England on a judgment of a court in the island of Tobago. The defendant had never been in the island, nor had he submitted to its jurisdiction. There had been a substituted service, valid by the law of Tobago, effected by nailing a copy of the writ to the courthouse door. Lord Ellenborough refused to enforce the judgment. He said: 'Can the island of Tobago pass a law to bind the rights of the whole world? Would the world submit to such an assumed jurisdiction?'

Where jurisdiction exists

The defendant's residence or presence in the foreign country

10–017 In *Emanuel v Symon*[98] Buckley LJ set out a list of circumstances in which a foreign court would be regarded as having jurisdiction. One was "where [the defendant] was resident in the foreign country when the action began". It is natural for the claimant to sue in the defendant's home country, and it is well settled that the residence of the defendant is a sufficient basis for recognition.[99]

International practice is coming to speak of *habitual* residence, preferred in the discussions during the Hague Judgments Project, or domicile, as in the EU instruments. However, it was the term "residence" that was used by Buckley LJ in *Emanuel v Symon*, and the same word is to be found in the Foreign Judgments (Reciprocal Enforcement) Act 1933, under which a foreign court is deemed to have had jurisdiction if "the judgment debtor, being a defendant in the original

---

[96] See McClean, in Fawcett (ed), *Reform and Development of Private International Law* (Oxford: Oxford University Press, 2002) at 255–271; Barcelo and Clermont (eds), *A Global Law of Jurisdiction and Judgments: Lessons from The Hague* (2002).

[97] *Buchanan v Rucker* (1809) 9 East 192. cf. *Sirdar Gurdyal Singh v Rajah of Faridkote* [1894] A.C. 670, 683–684, *per* Lord Selborne.

[98] [1908] 1 K.B. 302, 309. cf. *Schibsby v Westenholz* (1870) L.R. 6 Q.B. 155, 161; *Rousillon v Rousillon* (1880) 14 Ch.D. 351, 371.

[99] *Schibsby v Westenholz* (1870) L.R. 6 Q.B. 155, 161. *Actor sequitur forum rei* is the time-honoured maxim.

court, was at the time when the proceedings were instituted resident in, or being a body corporate had its principal place of business in, the country of that court".[100]

Residence has no precise definition: in most cases, it imports physical presence; but the two can be separated, so that the defendant is physically present in the foreign country but cannot be said to be resident there, or is a resident but was not physically present at the relevant time. The English courts have taken the view that at common law temporary residence and even mere presence in the foreign country suffices,[101] a rule which mirrors the extensive claims made for the jurisdiction of the English courts. As a matter of principle, it is not clear that the bases upon which the English courts take jurisdiction (especially as the doctrine of forum non conveniens moderated their effect) should be translated unchanged into bases for the recognition of the jurisdiction of a foreign court. However the Court of Appeal in *Adams v Cape Industries Plc*[102] held that:

> "the voluntary presence of an individual in a foreign country, whether permanent or temporary and whether or not accompanied by residence, is sufficient to give the courts of that country territorial jurisdiction over him under our rules of private international law".

That case involved a corporate defendant, and the Court of Appeal sought to clarify the, necessarily artificial, concept of the presence of a corporation. It held that the English court was likely to treat a corporation as present in a country only if either (a) it had established and maintained at its own expense a fixed place of business of its own in that country and for more than a minimal period of time had carried on its own business there by its servants or agents, or (b) a representative of the corporation had for more than a minimal period of time been carrying on the corporation's business (not the representative's own business) at or from some fixed place of business in that country. The mere presence there of a representative of the corporation would not suffice.[103] Nor would it be sufficient if the corporation had a representative resident there who had authority to elicit orders from customers but not to make contracts on its behalf.[104]

None of this is affected by the appearance of internet trading. The fact that a company has a website accessible in a particular country and can and does accept orders placed via the website does not make it present there.[105] As the Court of Appeal observed:

> "It is true that the Internet and its uses take us into a new world, and that its existence as it were in the ether (but based on servers physically located in the real world) has in general presented novel difficulties to the law and to regulators. It is also true that a website can be both wonderfully expressive and can also, subject to change and removal, be found repeatedly at its web address. The question, however, is whether for current purposes the Internet or a website

---

[100] Section 4(2)(a)(iv).
[101] See for early authority see *Carrick v Hancock* (1895) 12 T.L.R. 59 where, however, the defendant had submitted to the jurisdiction of the foreign court. The presence basis was endorsed in *Rubin v Eurofinance SA* [2012] UKSC 46; [2013] 1 A.C. 236 at [10].
[102] [1990] Ch. 433.
[103] *Littauer Glove Corporation v F. W. Millington Ltd* (1928) 44 T.L.R. 746.
[104] *Vogel v R. A. Kohnstamm Ltd* [1973] 1 Q.B. 133. cf. *Sfeir & Co v National Insurance Co of New Zealand Ltd* [1964] 1 Lloyd's Rep. 330, a case on the Administration of Justice Act 1920.
[105] *Lucasfilm Ltd v Ainsworth* [2009] EWCA Civ 1328; [2010] Ch. 503; the point was not raised in the Supreme Court.

are fundamentally different from other matters which have enabled business persons to present themselves and their products where they are not themselves present: such as advertisements, salesmen, the post, telephone, telex and the like. We do not believe so . . . On the contrary, it might be said that the sheer omnipresence of the Internet would suggest that it does not easily create, outside the jurisdiction or jurisdictions in which its website owners are on established principle already to be found, that presence, partaking in some sense of allegiance, which has been recognised by our jurisprudence and rules of private international law as a necessary ingredient in the enforceability of foreign judgments".[106]

The Foreign Judgments (Reciprocal Enforcement) Act 1933 requires that the corporation must have its principal place of business (and not merely carry on business) in the foreign country.[107] The Act also provides that the foreign court is deemed to have jurisdiction for the purposes of the Act if the defendant (not necessarily a corporation) had an office or place of business in the foreign country and the proceedings were in respect of a transaction effected through or at that office or place.[108] There does not appear to be any authority for this basis of jurisdiction at common law; but the Foreign Judgments (Reciprocal Enforcement) Committee regarded it as a rational extension of the common law rules.[109]

Submission

10–018   The differences in legal procedure between different legal traditions are such that the notion of "submission" may not have the same meaning everywhere. In *Rubin v Eurofinance SA*,[110] Lord Collins of Mapesbury emphasised that:

"The characterisation of whether there has been a submission for the purposes of the enforcement of foreign judgments in England depends on English law. The court will not simply consider whether the steps taken abroad would have amounted to a submission in English proceedings. The international context requires a broader approach. Nor does it follow from the fact that the foreign court would have regarded steps taken in the foreign proceedings as a submission that the English court will so regard them. Conversely, it does not necessarily follow that because the foreign court would not regard the steps as a submission that they will not be so regarded by the English court as a submission for the purposes of the enforcement of a judgment of the foreign court. The question whether there has been a submission is to be inferred from all the facts."

Submission to the jurisdiction of a foreign court can take place in various ways. In the language of the 1933 Act, they are where:

(i)   the judgment debtor, being a defendant in the original court, submitted to the jurisdiction of that court by voluntarily appearing in the proceedings; or

(ii)   the judgment debtor was the claimant in, or counter-claimed in, the proceedings in the original court; or

(iii)   the judgment debtor, being a defendant in the original court, had before the commencement of the proceedings agreed, in respect of the subject matter

---

[106] At paras 193–194.
[107] Section 4(2)(a)(iv).
[108] Section 4(2)(a)(v).
[109] Cmd. 4213 (1932), Annex V, para.8.
[110] [2012] UKSC 46; [2013] 1 A.C. 236 at [161].

of the proceedings, to submit to the jurisdiction of that court (or to the jurisdiction of the courts of the relevant country).

The most obvious example is actually case (ii), where the claimant invokes the jurisdiction and thereby is rendered liable to a judgment for the defendant in respect of a counterclaim, cross-action or costs.[111]

A more frequent situation is that of case (i), that in which the defendant voluntarily appears in, or takes part in, the foreign proceedings. By that action the defendant becomes subject to the foreign court's jurisdiction, both for the original claim and also for any others the original claimant may add in accordance with the procedural rules of the foreign forum.[112]

A defendant may, however, appear in the foreign proceedings solely to contest the jurisdiction. In those circumstances, it would be perverse to interpret the defendant's action as a submission to the very jurisdiction he or she actively repudiates. The courts showed themselves surprisingly reluctant to accept this glimpse of the obvious, and it was only as a result of the Civil Jurisdiction and Judgments Act 1982 that rationality was introduced into this corner of the law.[113] Section 33 of that Act provides that the defendant shall not be regarded as having submitted to the jurisdiction of an overseas court if he appeared (a) to contest the jurisdiction of the court; (b) to ask the court to dismiss or stay the proceedings on the ground that the dispute should be submitted to arbitration,[114] or to the determination of the courts of another country; or (c) to protect or obtain the release of property seized or threatened with seizure in the proceedings.

In some legal systems, an appearance to contest the jurisdiction must be accompanied by an appearance on the merits, although this can sometimes be merely pro forma, without substantive argument. Despite earlier authority to the contrary,[115] it is thought that such an appearance when unaccompanied by any positive act addressing the merits will not amount to submission.[116]

Another example of submission is case (iii), where a contract provides that all disputes between the parties shall be referred to the exclusive jurisdiction of a foreign tribunal. In such a case the foreign court is deemed to have jurisdiction over the parties.[117] An agreement to submit may also take the form of an agreement to accept service of process at a designated address. But English courts have stopped short of inferring an agreement to submit from a mere general provision in the foreign law (and not in a statute specifically referring to the

---

[111] *Schibsby v Westenholz* (1870) L.R. 6 Q.B. 155, 161; Foreign Judgments (Reciprocal Enforcement) Act 1933 s.4(2)(a)(ii).

[112] *Murthy v Sivajothi* [1999] 1 W.L.R. 467.

[113] There was an earlier provision, Foreign Judgments (Reciprocal Enforcement) Act 1933 s.4(2)(a)(i), of limited scope.

[114] See *Tracomin SA v Sudan Oil Seeds Co Ltd* [1983] 1 W.L.R. 662, 1026.

[115] *Boissiere & Co v Brockner* (1889) 6 T.L.R. 85.

[116] *Marc Rich & Co AG v Soc Italiana Impianti PA (No.2)* [1992] 1 Lloyd's Rep. 624. cf. Case 150/80 *Elefanten Schuh GmbH v Jacqmain* [1981] E.C.R. 1671 (a case on submission under art.18 of the Brussels Convention).

[117] *Feyerick v Hubbard* (1902) 71 L.J.K.B. 509; *Jeannot v Fuerst* (1909) 25 T.L.R. 424; Foreign Judgments (Reciprocal Enforcement) Act 1933 s.4(2)(a)(iii).

particular company) that the shareholder must "elect a domicile" for the service of process,[118] unless the defendant does in fact elect such a domicile.[119]

As a general rule, an agreement to submit to the jurisdiction of a foreign court must be express: it cannot be implied.[120] If the parties agree, expressly or by implication, that their contract shall be governed by a particular foreign law, it does not follow that they agree to submit to the jurisdiction of the courts which apply it.[121] Nor can any such agreement be implied from the fact that the cause of action arose in a foreign country, nor from the additional fact that the defendant was present there when the cause of action arose.[122]

Where jurisdiction does not exist

10–019   The provisions of the Foreign Judgments (Reciprocal Enforcement) Act 1933 as to the jurisdiction of the foreign court are exclusive. That is to say, no judgment can be registered under the Act unless the jurisdiction of the foreign court can be brought under one of the five heads of s.4(2)(a).[123] But the rules of common law as to jurisdiction are not necessarily exclusive, and it has sometimes been suggested that other bases of jurisdiction, often relied on by foreign courts, might be available in England. It seems reasonably clear that this is not the case.

So, it is not sufficient that the judgment-debtor possessed property in the foreign country; this is relied upon in Scotland, but has been rejected in England.[124] Nor is it sufficient that the defendant was present in the foreign country at the time when the cause of action arose[125]; nor that the defendant was domiciled there.[126] There is a long chain of dicta extending from 1828 to 1948 suggesting that the courts of a country might have jurisdiction over a defendant who was a national of that country.[127] But there is no actual decision to this effect. On the contrary, nationality as a basis of jurisdiction has more recently been doubted by three High Court judges,[128] and definitely rejected by the Irish

---

[118] *Copin v Adamson* (1874) L.R. 9 Ex. 345 (the second replication). The point was reserved in the Court of Appeal: see 1 Ex.D. 17, 19.

[119] *Vallée v Dumergue* (1849) 4 Exch. 290.

[120] *Sirdar Gurdyal Singh v Rajah of Faridkote* [1894] A.C. 670; *Emanuel v Symon* [1908] 1 K.B. 302; *Vogel v R. A. Kohnstamm Ltd* [1973] 1 Q.B. 133; *Adams v Cape Industries Plc* [1990] Ch. 433 (a point not taken on appeal), not following dicta in *Blohn v Desser* [1962] 2 Q.B. 116, 123, and in *Sfeir & Co v National Insurance Co of New Zealand Ltd* [1964] 1 Lloyd's Rep. 330, 339–340.

[121] *Dunbee Ltd v Gilman & Co Ltd* [1968] 2 Lloyd's Rep. 394.

[122] *Sirdar Gurdyal Singh v Rajah of Faridkote* [1894] A.C. 670; *Emanuel v Symon* [1908] 1 K.B. 302.

[123] *Société Co-opérative Sidmetal v Titan International Ltd* [1966] 1 Q.B. 828.

[124] *Emanuel v Symon* [1908] 1 K.B. 302.

[125] *Sirdar Gurdyal Singh v Rajah of Faridkote* [1894] A.C. 670; *Emanuel v Symon* [1908] 1 K.B. 302.

[126] For early dicta to the contrary, see *Turnbull v Walker* (1892) 67 L.T. 767, 769; *Emanuel v Symon* [1908] 1 K.B. 302, 308, 314; *Jaffer v Williams* (1908) 25 T.L.R. 12, 13; *Gavin Gibson & Co v Gibson* [1913] 3 K.B. 379, 385.

[127] *Douglas v Forrest* (1828) 4 Bing. 686; *Schibsby v Westenholz* (1870) L.R. 6 Q.B. 155, 161; *Rousillon v Rousillon* (1880) 14 Ch.D. 351, 371; *Emanuel v Symon* [1908] 1 K.B. 302, 309; *Gavin Gibson & Co v Gibson* [1913] 3 K.B. 379, 388; *Harris v Taylor* [1915] 2 K.B. 580, 591; *Forsyth v Forsyth* [1948] P. 125, 132.

[128] *Blohn v Desser* [1962] 2 Q.B. 116, 123, per Diplock J.; *Rossano v Manufacturers Life Insurance Co Ltd* [1963] 2 Q.B. 352, 382–383, per McNair J; *Vogel v R. A. Kohnstamm Ltd* [1973] 1 Q.B. 133, 141, per Ashworth J.

High Court.[129] It cannot, therefore, safely be relied upon today. It is obviously inappropriate when the defendant is a British citizen or an American citizen, since in neither case does the political unit (or state) coincide with the law district (or country).

A question which requires more discussion is whether the jurisdiction of the foreign court would be recognised if the situation were such that, mutatis mutandis, the English court might have assumed jurisdiction, e.g. under the Civil Procedure Rules.[130] The answer is "no". In *Schibsby v Westenholz*,[131] the claimant brought an action in England on a French judgment. The defendant was not in France when the writ was issued (it was served on him in England), nor did he appear or submit to the jurisdiction. It was argued that as the English court would have power to order service out of the jurisdiction on similar facts, it should enforce the French judgment. In rejecting this argument, Blackburn J said:

"If the principle on which foreign judgments were enforced was that which is loosely called 'comity', we could hardly decline to enforce a foreign judgment given in France against a resident in Great Britain under circumstances hardly, if at all, distinguishable from those under which we, *mutatis mutandis*, might give judgment against a resident in France; but it is quite different if the principle be that which we have just laid down [i.e. the doctrine of obligation, quoted earlier in this chapter[132]]".

This refusal to include in rules governing recognition a principle found in the English jurisdiction rules may seem surprising. It is, however, clear that English courts do not concede jurisdiction in personam to foreign courts merely because English courts would, in converse circumstances, have power to order service out of the jurisdiction.[133] This means, of course, that in actions in personam English courts claim a wider jurisdiction than they concede to foreign courts.

Defences

The most usual defence pleaded to an action on a foreign judgment at common law is that the foreign court had no jurisdiction to give the judgment according to the recognition rules just examined. Several other defences are available. In considering these defences, it should be borne in mind that, unless otherwise stated, they may be pleaded as a defence to an action on the judgment at common law, or used as grounds for refusing to register the judgment under the Administration of Justice Act 1920 or for setting aside the registration of the judgment under the Foreign Judgments (Reciprocal Enforcement) Act 1933.

10–020

---

[129] *Rainford v Newell-Roberts* [1962] I.R. 95.
[130] Above, para.7–012.
[131] (1870) L.R. 6 Q.B. 155, 159 followed in *Turnbull v Walker* (1892) 67 L.T. 767.
[132] Above, para.10–010.
[133] *Re Trepca Mines Ltd* [1960] 1 W.L.R. 1273, 1280–1282; *Société Co-opérative Sidmetal v Titan International Ltd* [1966] 1 Q.B. 828; in *Rubin v Eurofinance SA* [2012] UKSC 46; [2013] 1 A.C. 236 at [127].

Jurisdiction contrary to a jurisdiction agreement between the parties

10–021   Section 32 of the Civil Jurisdiction and Judgments Act 1982 provides that a judgment given by a court of an overseas country cannot be recognised or enforced in the UK if (a) the bringing of the proceedings in the foreign court was contrary to a valid agreement under which the dispute was to be settled otherwise than by proceedings in the courts of that country; and (b) the judgment debtor did not agree to the bringing of those proceedings, counterclaim or otherwise submit to the jurisdiction of that court.[134] The latter condition means that jurisdiction based on submission is unaffected by s.32.

Fraud

10–022   It is settled that a foreign judgment, like any other, can be impeached for fraud.[135] Such fraud may be either fraud on the part of the court, for example where the judge deliberately made a false decision because of a personal interest in the outcome; or fraud on the part of the successful party in, for example, suppressing evidence or producing forged or perjured evidence; or fraud on the part of both court and party, as where one party bribes the court.

The difficult question is whether a foreign judgment can be impeached for fraud if, in order to prove the fraud, it is necessary to reopen the merits which have already been decided by the foreign court. Two principles are here in conflict: the principle that foreign judgments are impeachable for fraud, and the principle that the merits cannot be reopened. No English judgment can be impeached for fraud in the absence of fresh evidence: if the former principle prevails, and it is now clear that it does, a foreign judgment is more susceptible to impeachment as no fresh evidence need be presented.

The leading case is *Abouloff v Oppenheimer & Co*[136] where Lord Coleridge CJ said:

> "where a judgment has been obtained by the fraud of a party to a suit in a foreign country, he cannot prevent the question of fraud from being litigated in the courts of this country, when he seeks to enforce the judgment so obtained. The justice of that proposition is obvious: if it were not so, we should have to disregard a well-established rule of law that no man shall take advantage of his own wrong".

The principle was reaffirmed by the House of Lords in *Owens Bank Ltd v Bracco*.[137] In that case:

> the claimant bank claimed to have lent nine million Swiss francs to the defendant, who received the money in cash against signed documents typed on the notepaper of a Geneva hotel. Bracco resisted a claim in the courts of Saint Vincent for the capital lent and interest, denying that he had ever entered into the transaction. The bank succeeded, and sought to

---

[134] There was a similar provision (now repealed as redundant) in s.4(3)(b) of the Foreign Judgments (Reciprocal Enforcement) Act 1933, but no authority at common law.

[135] This does not apply to cases under the Brussels I or Brussels I *bis* Regulations, which have no defence of fraud; see para.10–004 for the public policy ground under the Regulation which may include some cases of fraud.

[136] (1882) 10 Q.B.D. 295, 300, followed in *Vadala v Lawes* (1890) 25 Q.B.D. 310.

[137] [1992] 2 A.C. 443. See also *Jet Holdings Inc v Patel* [1990] 1 Q.B. 335.

register the judgment in England under the Administration of Justice Act 1920, to be met by an argument based on the bank's alleged fraud in making the claim.

Lord Bridge reviewed the cases which, although they have been criticised by academic writers, provided a consistent line of authority for the availability of the defence of fraud in such circumstances. They included four decisions of the Court of Appeal[138]; and there could have been added another Court of Appeal decision in which these cases had been regarded as authoritative but distinguished because the very issue of fraud had been addressed in a separate action in the courts of the foreign country concerned.[139]

Lord Bridge recognised that as a matter of policy there might be a strong case to be made, in the changed circumstances of the 1990s, for giving to foreign judgments the same finality accorded to English judgments. But both the Administration of Justice Act 1920,[140] applicable to the instant case, and the Foreign Judgments (Reciprocal Enforcement) Act 1933[141] provided for impeachment of the foreign judgment for fraud, and to alter the common law rule would produce such anomalies as to put that possibility out of the question.[142]

In a later Privy Council case, giving rise to similar issues, *Owens Bank Ltd v Etoile Commerciale SA*,[143] Lord Templeman said that "Their Lordships do not regard the decision in *Aboulof's* case with enthusiasm, especially in its application to countries whose judgments the UK has agreed to register and enforce. In these cases the salutary rule which favours finality in litigation seems more appropriate", but the old rule was not directly in issue.

Contrary to public policy

A foreign judgment can be impeached if its enforcement or recognition in England would be contrary to public policy[144]: but there are very few reported cases in which such a plea has been successful.

In *Re Macartney*,[145] a Maltese judgment ordering the personal representatives of a deceased putative father to pay perpetual maintenance to the mother of his illegitimate child was refused enforcement in England on three grounds: (1) it was contrary to public policy to enforce an affiliation order not limited to the child's minority;[146] (2) the cause of action, a posthumous affiliation order, was unknown to English domestic law; and (3) the judgment was not final and conclusive, because the Maltese court could vary the amount of the payments.[147]

10–023

---

[138] *Aboulof v Oppenheimer* (1882) 10 Q.B.D. 295; *Vadala v Lawes* (1890) 25 Q.B.D. 310; *Syal v Heyward* [1948] 2 K.B. 443; and *Jet Holdings Inc v Patel* [1990] 1 Q.B. 335.
[139] *House of Spring Gardens Ltd v Waite* [1991] 1 Q.B. 241.
[140] Section 9(2)(d).
[141] Section 4(1)(a)(iv).
[142] For criticism, see Collier, [1992] C.L.J. 441.
[143] [1995] 1 W.L.R. 44 (P.C.).
[144] See Administration of Justice Act 1920 s.9(2)(f); Foreign Judgments (Reciprocal Enforce-ment) Act 1933 s.4(1)(a)(v). For public policy generally, see above, Ch.4.
[145] [1921] 1 Ch. 522.
[146] The notion was that it was undesirable that the illegitimate daughter should spend her whole life in idleness basking in the Mediterranean sunshine, while father toiled in cloudy England to support her.
[147] See below, paras 10–030 and 13–026.

The third ground by itself would have been sufficient to dispose of the case. Under the second ground, the court relied heavily on an American case[148] in which a French judgment awarding maintenance to a French son-in-law against his American father-in-law and mother-in-law was refused enforcement in the United States.

This American case and *Re Macartney* were disapproved or distinguished in two later cases, one Canadian, the other English. In *Burchell v Burchell*,[149] an Ontario court enforced a judgment of an Ohio divorce court ordering a wife to make a lump-sum payment to her husband, although by the law of Ontario a wife was not bound to support her husband. In *Phrantzes v Argenti*[150] (which was not a case on a foreign judgment), Lord Parker CJ refused to enforce a claim by a Greek daughter against her father for the provision of a dowry on her marriage as required by Greek law. His ground for doing so was not that the cause of action was unknown to English domestic law, but that English law had no remedy for awarding a dowry, the amount of which in Greek law was within the discretion of the court and varied in accordance with the wealth and social position of the father and the number of his children. Given that in some cases an English court may entertain a claim on a cause of action unknown to English domestic law, there seems no good reason, despite what was said in *Re Macartney*, for refusing to enforce a foreign judgment based on such a cause of action. It is not contrary to public policy to enforce a foreign judgment for what in England would be called exemplary damages.[151]

On the other hand, the Supreme Court of the Republic of Ireland has refused to enforce an English order for costs which was ancillary to a divorce decree.[152] The grounds of this decision were partly that the cause of action was unknown to the law of the Republic (where divorce was not then allowed), and partly that to enforce an order ancillary to a divorce decree was contrary to Irish public policy.

Contrary to natural justice

10–024 At common law, a foreign judgment can be impeached on the ground that the proceedings were opposed to natural justice; but the limits of this defence are even vaguer than those of public policy, and reported cases in which it has been successfully raised are rarer still. The proceedings are not opposed to natural justice merely because the judgment is manifestly wrong,[153] merely because the court admitted evidence which is inadmissible in England,[154] or did not admit evidence which is admissible in England,[155] for the admissibility of evidence is a matter of procedure and so governed by the *lex fori*.[156]

---

[148] *De Brimont v Penniman* (1873) 10 Blatchford Circuit Court Reports 436.

[149] [1926] 2 D.L.R. 595.

[150] [1960] 2 Q.B. 19, 31–34.

[151] *S.A. Consortium General Textiles v Sun and Sand Agencies Ltd* [1978] Q.B. 279, 300.

[152] *Mayo-Perrott v Mayo-Perrott* [1958] I.R. 336.

[153] *Godard v Gray* (1870) L.R. 6 Q.B. 139; *Castrique v Imrie* (1870) L.R. 4 H.L. 414; *Robinson v Fenner* [1913] 3 K.B. 835, 842.

[154] *De Cosse Brissac v Rathbone* (1861) 6 H. & N. 301 (the sixth plea).

[155] *Scarpetta v Lowenfeld* (1911) 27 T.L.R. 509; *Robinson v Fenner*, above.

[156] See above, para.9–006.

In *Adams v Cape Industries Plc*[157]:

> a default judgment was entered by a US court in a complex case in which some two hundred claimants claimed in respect of injury caused by exposure to asbestos. Damages were fixed, in effect, by counsel for the claimants after the judge had indicated, without hearing any evidence, that the average recovery should be at a given level and that individual claimants should be allocated to one of a number of broad categories; there was no judicial assessment of damages.

The Court of Appeal held that the concept of procedural natural justice was not limited to cases in which the defendant receives no notice[158] or is given no adequate opportunity to make a defence[159]; it extended to any circumstances which would constitute a breach of the English court's understanding of "substantial justice". Absence of a judicial determination of damages was such a breach.

It can be argued that reliance on the alleged breach of substantial justice should be excluded if the defendant took, or could have taken, the point in the foreign court. In *Adams v Cape Industries*, Scott J at first instance regarded the possibility of appeal from, or collateral attack on, the judgment in the courts of the foreign country as immaterial. The Court of Appeal, by analogy with the fraud cases, held that the availability of remedies in the foreign country was indeed immaterial in cases where the defendant received no notice or was not given an adequate opportunity to make a defence; but in other cases it would be wrong in principle to ignore the possibility that there was a fair opportunity for remedy in the foreign country. What weight was to be given to that factor would depend on a number of matters: how far the defendant had known of the procedural defects and whether in all the circumstances it was reasonable to expect use to be made of the foreign remedy. On the particular facts, however, the defendants had no knowledge of (or reasonable means of knowing) the facts which could have prompted them to make an application for the foreign remedy, and were accordingly not precluded from relying on the ground of natural justice.

Neither the Administration of Justice Act 1920 nor the Foreign Judgments (Reciprocal Enforcement) Act 1933 mentions the defence that the proceedings were opposed to natural justice. Instead, the former Act provides that no judgment may be registered thereunder if the defendant was not duly served with the process of the court and did not appear[160]; and the latter Act provides that the registration of a judgment must be set aside if the defendant did not receive notice of the proceedings in sufficient time to enable him to defend them and he did not appear.[161]

Article 6 of the European Convention for the Protection of Human Rights and Fundamental Freedoms protects the right to a fair trial. The House of Lords held

---

[157] [1990] Ch. 433.

[158] But note that "it is not contrary to natural justice that a man who has agreed to receive a particular mode of notification of legal proceedings should be bound by a judgment in which that particular mode of notification has been followed, even though he may not have had actual notice of them": *Vallée v Dumergue* (1849) 4 Exch. 290 at p.303, per Alderson B.

[159] cf. the position under the Brussels I Regulation: para.10–004, above.

[160] Section 9(2)(c).

[161] Section 4(1)(a)(iii).

in *Government of the United States of America v Montgomery (No.2).*[162] that non-compliance with art.6 was a ground for refusing recognition or enforcement in the UK of a judgment obtained in another State, whether or not the latter is an adherent to the Convention.[163] This was applied in *Merchant International Co Ltd v Natsionalna Aktsionerna Kompaniya Naftogaz Ukrayiny*[164]:

> A judgment had been obtained in Ukraine and the successful claimant obtained an English judgment by a common law action on the judgment-debt. The foreign judgment was later set aside by the Supreme Commercial Court of Ukraine. Normally this would have destroyed the basis for the English judgment, but the English court held that the proceedings before the Ukrainian Supreme Commercial Court did not meet the standard required by art.6. Accordingly, the judgment of that court would be ignored and an application to set aside the English judgment was dismissed.

Judgments for multiple damages

10–025 Section 5 of the Protection of Trading Interests Act 1980 prohibits the enforcement in the UK of judgments for multiple damages or any judgment specified by the Secretary of State as concerned with the prohibition of restrictive trade practices. Section 6 goes much further and gives UK citizens, corporations incorporated in the UK, and persons carrying on business in the UK against whom multiple damages have been awarded, the right to recover so much of the damages as exceeds the sum assessed by the foreign court as compensation for the loss or damage sustained.[165] This section also contains the unusual provision that proceedings under it may be brought notwithstanding that the claimant in the foreign proceedings is not within the jurisdiction of the UK court. These two sections are aimed primarily at the tendency of American courts to interpret US anti-trust legislation in such a way as to infringe the sovereignty of the UK and other states.

What are not defences

10–026 The above sub-heading is somewhat more dogmatic than the cases warrant. It is certain that the first matter about to be discussed is not itself a defence; but there is more doubt as to the status of the second.

Errors of fact or law

10–027 It is no defence that the foreign judgment is manifestly wrong either on the facts or on the law.[166] The merits cannot be reopened in England. But, as we have seen, this rule does not apply if it is alleged that the judgment was obtained by fraud.

---

[162] [2004] UKHL 37; [2004] 4 All E.R. 289.
[163] See Fawcett, (2007) 56 I.C.L.Q. 1.
[164] [2012] EWCA Civ 196; [2012] 1 W.L.R.3036.
[165] See *Lewis v Eliades* [2003] EWCA Civ 1758; [2004] 1 W.L.R. 692, noted Briggs, (2003) 74 B.Y.B.I.L. 549; Kellman, (2004) 53 I.C.L.Q. 1025 (compensatory element enforceable).
[166] *Godard v Gray* (1870) L.R. 6 Q.B. 139; *Castrique v Imrie* (1870) L.R. 4 H.L. 414.

In *Godard v Gray*,[167] it was held to be no defence that the foreign court, purporting to apply English domestic law, made an obvious mistake in doing so. It would seem to follow that it is no defence that the foreign court applied its own domestic law when according to English rules of the conflict of laws it should have applied English domestic law.

This finality of foreign judgments (subject to the grounds for impeachment already examined) is a form of estoppel *per rem judicatem*. The applicability of that doctrine, and in particular of issue estoppel, to foreign judgments has been recognised in two decisions of the House of Lords.[168] To attract this doctrine the decision must be a final and conclusive decision on the merits of a court of competent jurisdiction.

Lack of internal competence

Is it a defence that, though the foreign court had jurisdiction in the sense of the English rules of the conflict of laws, it lacked competence in the sense of its own domestic law? This is a difficult question, and the authorities are in a state of some confusion.   **10–028**

In *Vanquelin v Bouard*,[169] the defendant was sued in England on a French judgment in respect of a bill of exchange. The French court had jurisdiction according to the English rules of the conflict of laws; and the subject matter of the action (bills of exchange) was within its internal competence. But the defendant pleaded that this particular French court had no internal competence over him because he was not a trader. This plea was held bad.

On the other hand, in *Castrique v Imrie*,[170] a case on a foreign judgment in rem, Blackburn J regarded it as material "whether the sovereign authority of that state has conferred on the court jurisdiction to decide as to the disposition of the thing, and the court has acted within its jurisdiction". This could be taken to mean that a foreign judgment in rem, in order to be recognised in England, must have been pronounced by a court having internal competence as well as international jurisdiction. Further, in *Papadopoulos v Papadopoulos*,[171] one reason for refusing to recognise a Cypriot decree of nullity was that the Cypriot court had no internal competence to annul a marriage under the Order in Council which established it. And in *Adams v Adams*,[172] a Rhodesian divorce was not recognised because the judge who pronounced it had not taken the oath of allegiance and the judicial oath in the prescribed form.

In *Macalpine v Macalpine*,[173] there was some discussion whether fraud rendered a Wyoming decree of divorce void or merely voidable. It is believed that this distinction furnishes the key to the problem here discussed. If the foreign

---

[167] (1870) L.R. 6 Q.B. 139.
[168] *Carl Zeiss Stiftung v Rayner & Keeler Ltd (No.2)* [1967] 1 A.C. 853; *The Sennar (No.2)* [1985] 1 W.L.R. 490.
[169] (1863) 15 C.B. (n.s.) 341; approved in *Pemberton v Hughes* [1899] 1 Ch. 781, 791.
[170] (1870) L.R. 4 H.L. 414, 429. Blackburn J.'s statement was approved by Lord Chelmsford at p.488.
[171] [1930] P. 55.
[172] [1971] P. 188.
[173] [1958] P. 35, 41, 45; cf. *Merker v Merker* [1963] P. 283, 297–299.

judgment is merely irregular, i.e. valid until set aside, it will be held valid in England unless and until it is set aside in the foreign country.[174] If, on the other hand, the foreign judgment is a complete nullity by the law of the foreign country, then it will be held invalid in England. A foreign judgment is, of course, much more likely to be irregular than void. Hence lack of internal competence is in practice hardly ever a good defence.

Enforcement

10–029   A foreign judgment can be enforced in England by action at common law or, in cases to which they apply, by registration under the Administration of Justice Act 1920, or the Foreign Judgments (Reciprocal Enforcement) Act 1933.

At common law

10–030   A foreign judgment in personam, given by a court having jurisdiction according to English rules of the conflict of laws, may be enforced by action in England, provided (a) it is for a debt, or definite sum of money, (b) it is not a judgment for taxes or penalties, and (c) it is "final and conclusive".

The judgment must be for a debt, or definite[175] sum of money (including damages and costs[176]), and not, for example, a judgment ordering the defendant specifically to perform a contract.[177]

It must not be for taxes[178] or penalties.[179] It is well settled that an English court will not entertain an action for the enforcement, either directly or indirectly, of a foreign penal or revenue law.[180] Hence it will not enforce, either directly or indirectly, a foreign judgment ordering the payment of taxes or penalties. However, if the foreign judgment imposes a fine on the defendant and also orders the defendant to pay compensation to the injured party (called the *partie civile* in French proceedings), the latter part of the judgment can be severed from the former and enforced in England. Thus in *Raulin v Fischer*[181]:

> D, a young American lady, while recklessly galloping her horse in the Bois de Boulogne, Paris, ran into P, an elderly French colonel, and seriously injured him. D was prosecuted for her criminal negligence by the French authorities, and P intervened in the proceedings and claimed damages from D as allowed by French law. The court convicted D, fined her 100 francs, and ordered her to pay 15,000 francs to P by way of damages, and also costs. It was held that P could recover the sterling equivalent of the damages and costs in England.

---

[174] See, to this effect, *S.A. Consortium General Textiles v Sun and Sand Agencies Ltd* [1978] Q.B. 279, 279, 307.

[175] See *Sadler v Robins* (1808) 1 Camp. 253.

[176] *Russell v Smyth* (1842) 9 M. & W. 810.

[177] The restriction of the common law recognition rule to money judgments has been abandoned in Canada (*Pro Swing Inc v Elite Golf Inc* (2006) SCC 52) and seems to have been doubted by the Privy Council (on appeal from the Isle of Man) in *Pattni v Ali* [2007] 2 A.C. 85. See the Jersey case of *Brunei Investment Agency v Fidelis Nominees Ltd* [2008] JRC 152.

[178] *Government of India v Taylor* [1955] A.C. 491, 514; *Rossano v Manufacturers Life Insurance Co Ltd* [1963] 2 Q.B. 352, 376–378. See Stoel, (1967) 16 I.C.L.Q. 663.

[179] *Huntington v Attrill* [1893] A.C. 150.

[180] See above, Ch.4.

[181] [1911] 2 K.B. 93.

The judgment must be "final and conclusive" in the court which rendered it.[182] "It must be shown that in the court by which it was pronounced, it conclusively, finally and for ever established the existence of the debt of which it is sought to be made conclusive evidence in this country, so as to make it res judicata between the parties".[183] So a summary judgment in which only a limited number of defences can be pleaded, and which is liable to be upset by the unsuccessful party in plenary proceedings where all defences may be set up, is not final and conclusive. However, at common law a foreign judgment may be final and conclusive even though it is subject to an appeal, and even though an appeal is actually pending in the foreign country where it was given.[184] But in a proper case, a stay of execution would no doubt be ordered pending a possible appeal. A default judgment will be regarded as final and conclusive, even though there may be a possibility of it being later set aside.[185]

The requirement that the foreign judgment must be final and conclusive usually makes it impossible to enforce a foreign maintenance order in England at common law, because the foreign court usually has power to vary the amount of the payments.[186] If, however, the foreign court has power to vary the amount of future payments, but not that of past payments, then an action may be brought in England to recover the arrears.[187] And as we shall see,[188] provision is made by statute for the reciprocal enforcement in one part of the UK of maintenance orders made in another part, and for the reciprocal enforcement in England of maintenance orders made in the Commonwealth overseas and certain foreign countries and vice versa.

Under the Administration of Justice Act 1920

Where Pt II of this Act has been extended by Order in Council to any part of the Commonwealth outside the UK, a judgment creditor who has obtained a judgment in a superior court in that part of the Commonwealth may, if a sum of money is payable under the judgment, apply to the High Court in England or Northern Ireland or to the Court of Session in Scotland at any time within 12 months of the date of the judgment to have the judgment registered in that court; and the court may order the judgment to be registered accordingly,[189] in which case the judgment will be of the same force and effect as if it were a judgment of the court in which it is registered.[190]   **10–031**

Registration of a judgment under the Act is not as of right, but discretionary: the Act provides that the court may order the judgment to be registered if the court thinks it just and convenient that the judgment should be enforced in the

---

[182] *Nouvion v Freeman* (1889) 15 App. Cas. 1; *Blohn v Desser* [1962] 2 Q.B. 116.
[183] *Nouvion v Freeman* (1889) 15 App. Cas. 1, 9, per Lord Herschell.
[184] *Scott v Pilkington* (1862) 2 B. & S. 11; *Colt Industries Inc v Sarlie (No.2)* [1966] 1 W.L.R. 1287.
[185] *Vanquelin v Bouard* (1863) 15 C.B. (n.s.) 341.
[186] *Harrop v Harrop* [1920] 3 K.B. 386; *Re Macartney* [1921] 1 Ch. 522. The rule is criticised by Grodecki, (1959) 8 I.C.L.Q. 18, 32–40.
[187] *Beatty v Beatty* [1924] 1 K.B. 807.
[188] Below, para.13–024 ff.
[189] Section 9(1).
[190] Section 9(3)(a).

UK.[191] Moreover, registration may not be ordered if the original court acted without jurisdiction, or if the defendant establishes any one of a limited number of defences.[192] These accord very closely with those available at common law, except that no judgment can be registered if the judgment debtor satisfies the court either that an appeal is pending, or that he is entitled and intends to appeal against the judgment.[193]

The judgment creditor remains free to bring an action on the foreign judgment in the ordinary way; but in that instance will usually not be awarded costs.[194]

Under the Foreign Judgments (Reciprocal Enforcement) Act 1933

10–032 When Pt I of this Act has been extended by Order in Council to any foreign country outside the UK, a judgment creditor under a judgment to which the Act applies may apply to the High Court in England or Northern Ireland or to the Court of Session in Scotland at any time within six years of the date of the judgment to have the judgment registered in that court, and on any such application the court must (not may) order the judgment to be registered.[195] A registered judgment has the same force and effect as if it had been a judgment originally given in the registering court.[196] The Act applies to any judgment of a court (not necessarily a superior court) of a country to which Pt I extends if it is final and conclusive as between the parties thereto, and there is payable thereunder a sum of money, not being a sum payable in respect of taxes or in respect of a fine or other penalty.[197] As at common law, a judgment is deemed to be final and conclusive notwithstanding that an appeal is pending against it.[198] But the court has a discretionary power to set aside the registration of a judgment on such terms as it thinks fit, if the defendant satisfies the court that an appeal is pending, or that he is entitled and intends to appeal.[199]

Registration must be set aside if the original court had no jurisdiction, or if the defendant establishes any one of a limited number of defences which accord very closely with those available at common law.[200] Registration may be set aside if the matter in dispute had, before the foreign judgment was given, been the subject of a final and conclusive judgment by a court having jurisdiction in the matter.[201] For instance, if a claimant sues a defendant in Switzerland and in Austria, and both courts have jurisdiction, and the Swiss court dismisses the action, but the

---

[191] Section 9(1).
[192] Section 9(2).
[193] Section 9(2)(e).
[194] Section 9(5).
[195] Sections 2(1), 12(a), 13(a).
[196] Section 2(2). Hence a stay of execution will not be ordered merely because an English action is pending between the same parties and raising similar issues: *Wagner v Laubscher Bros & Co* [1970] 2 Q.B. 313.
[197] Section 1(2), as amended by Civil Jurisdiction and Judgments Act 1982 Sch.10, para.1. A sum payable by way of exemplary damages is not a penalty: *S.A. Consortium General Textiles v Sun and Sand Agencies Ltd* [1978] Q.B. 279, 299–300, 305–306.
[198] Section 1(3).
[199] Section 5.
[200] Section 4(1)(a).
[201] Section 4(1)(b).

Austrian court gives judgment for the claimant, the English court may set aside the registration of the Austrian judgment.

Unlike the Administration of Justice Act 1920, the Act of 1933 prevents the judgment creditor from bringing an action in England on the foreign judgment,[202] and from suing on the original cause of action.[203]

Recognition as a defence

A foreign judgment in personam in favour of the defendant given by a court having jurisdiction may be relied upon for defensive purposes by the defendant if the claimant sues in England on the original cause of action. A foreign judgment in favour of the defendant is a conclusive answer to an action in England on the original cause of action.[204] The judgment must be "final and conclusive" in the court which rendered it.[205] This last requirement applies when the judgment is relied upon as a defence, just as it does when the claimant seeks to enforce it.[206] The foreign judgment is not a defence if the action was brought against a different party[207]; nor is it a defence unless it was given on the merits.

10–033

Section 3 of the Foreign Limitation Periods Act 1984 provides that where a court of a foreign country has determined any matter by reference to the law relating to limitation of that or any other country (including England), the court shall be deemed to have determined that matter on its merits.

Reciprocal enforcement within the United Kingdom

The reciprocal enforcement of judgments within the UK now depends on s.18 and Schs 6 and 7 of the Civil Jurisdiction and Judgments Act 1982, which apply equally to money and non-money judgments. Thus under the 1982 Act injunctions and orders for specific performance granted or made in one part of the UK are enforceable in other parts. Section 18 does not apply to judgments in proceedings other than civil proceedings, nor to maintenance orders or orders concerning the legal capacity of an individual, including judicial separation, guardianship and custody, nor to judgments in bankruptcy, the winding up of companies, or the administration of the estate of a deceased person.[208]

10–034

Enforcement is by way of registration in the court in which enforcement is sought of a certificate granted by the court which gave the judgment. Registration (even of certificates of judgments of inferior courts) is in superior courts only, i.e. the High Court in England or Northern Ireland, or the Court of Session in

---

[202] Section 6.
[203] Civil Jurisdiction and Judgments Act 1982 s.34.
[204] *Ricardo v Garcias* (1845) 12 Cl. & F. 368; *Jacobson v Frachon* (1927) 138 L.T. 386. cf. Foreign Judgments (Reciprocal Enforcement) Act 1933 s.8.
[205] *Plummer v Woodburne* (1825) 4 B. & C. 625; *Frayes v Worms* (1861) 10 C.B. (n.s.) 149; *Carl Zeiss Stiftung v Rayner & Keeler Ltd (No.2)* [1967] 1 A.C. 853.
[206] Above, para.10–030.
[207] *Carl Zeiss Stiftung v Rayner & Keeler Ltd (No.2)* [1967] 1 A.C. 853, 910–911, 928–929, 936–937, 944–946. See *The Sennar (No.2)* [1985] 1 W.L.R. 490.
[208] Section 18(3), (5) and (6).

Scotland. Sch.6 contains the procedure for enforcement of certificates of money judgments, and Sch.7 for enforcement of certificates of non-money judgments. Registration of a certificate must be set aside if the registration was contrary to the provisions of the Schedules, and may be set aside if the registering court is satisfied that the matter in dispute had previously been the subject of a judgment by another court having jurisdiction in the matter.[209] It is not a ground for setting registration aside that the original court had no jurisdiction over the defendant, or that the judgment was obtained by fraud, or that its enforcement would be contrary to public policy, or that the proceedings were opposed to natural justice.

The judgment may not be enforced except by registration under Schs 6 or 7.[210] Section 19 contains provisions for the recognition, as opposed to enforcement, of judgments to which s.18 applies.

FOREIGN ARBITRAL AWARDS

10–035 International commercial arbitration is of enormous practical importance, and is a subject in its own right. Here we can examine only a limited topic: the enforcement of foreign arbitral awards. The issues are similar to those already considered, in the context of the enforcement of foreign judgments, but the answers are different as "arbitration" is excluded from the Brussels I *bis* Regulation (and from the Lugano Convention).[211] This means that a foreign arbitral award cannot be enforced under the Regulation or Convention; but if a foreign judgment has been obtained on the basis of the award it can be enforced under the usual rules relating to foreign judgments.

Foreign arbitral awards can be enforced in England in various ways. First, they can be enforced by action at common law; this mode of enforcement is always an option. Second, they can be enforced under the terms of international conventions, the earlier Geneva Convention for the Execution of Foreign Arbitral Awards of 1927, given effect by the Arbitration Act 1950 and not further considered here, and the much more important New York Convention on the Recognition and Enforcement of Foreign Arbitral Awards of 1958, given effect by the Arbitration Act 1996. Arbitration awards made in countries of the Commonwealth outside the UK to which Pt II of the Administration of Justice Act 1920 extends, or in countries to which Pt I of the Foreign Judgments (Reciprocal Enforcement) Act 1933 extends, can be enforced in England as if they were judgments, i.e. by registration,[212] and arbitration awards made in one part of the UK can be enforced in other parts by registration under the Civil Jurisdiction and Judgments Act 1982.

It is important, in reading what follows, to bear in mind that an arbitration clause in a contract is treated as if it were a separate contract. In English law, s.7 of the Arbitration Act 1996 provides:

---

[209] Schedule 6 para.10; Sch.7 para.9.
[210] Section 18(8).
[211] See above, Ch.6.
[212] Certain arbitration awards made in pursuance of a contract for the international carriage of goods can also be enforced by registration under this Act: Carriage of Goods by Road Act 1965, ss.4(1), 7(1). See also the Arbitration (International Investment Disputes) Act 1966.

"Unless otherwise agreed by the parties, an arbitration agreement which forms or was intended to form part of another agreement (whether or not in writing) shall not be regarded as invalid, non-existent or ineffective because that other agreement is invalid, or did not come into existence or has become ineffective, and it shall for that purpose be treated as a distinct agreement."

As Lord Hoffman explained in *Fiona Trust & Holding Corp v Privalov*[213]:

"The invalidity or rescission of the main contract does not necessarily entail the invalidity or rescission of the arbitration agreement. The arbitration agreement must be treated as a "distinct agreement" and can be void or voidable only on grounds which relate directly to the arbitration agreement. Of course there may be cases in which the ground upon which the main agreement is invalid is identical with the ground upon which the arbitration agreement is invalid. For example, if the main agreement and the arbitration agreement are contained in the same document and one of the parties claims that he never agreed to anything in the document and that his signature was forged, that will be an attack on the validity of the arbitration agreement. But the ground of attack is not that the main agreement was invalid. It is that the signature to the arbitration agreement, as a "distinct agreement", was forged. . . . On the other hand, if . . . the allegation is that the agent exceeded his authority by entering into a main agreement in terms which were not authorised or for improper reasons, that is not necessarily an attack on the arbitration agreement. It would have to be shown that whatever the terms of the main agreement or the reasons for which the agent concluded it, he would have had no authority to enter into an arbitration agreement."

At common law

In the eyes of an English court, the jurisdiction of the arbitrators is derived from the agreement of the parties to arbitrate. Such an agreement may assume one of two forms, in that it may submit present or future disputes to arbitration. A contract may contain an arbitration clause by which the parties agree that if disputes arise under the contract they shall be referred to arbitration. Or parties may agree to submit a particular dispute between them (which need not necessarily stem from a contract) to the decision of a particular arbitrator.

10–036

The enforcement of foreign arbitral awards sometimes raises even more delicate questions than does the enforcement of foreign judgments. Moreover, the enforcement of foreign awards may be required more frequently than the enforcement of foreign judgments. This is because actions in personam are usually brought in the country where the defendant resides and keeps his or her assets, so that the need for enforcement elsewhere is the exception rather than the rule. But there is an increasing tendency for contracts between commercial parties from different countries to provide for arbitration in a third or "neutral" country, where neither resides or keeps assets, in which case the need for enforcement is the rule rather than the exception. On the other hand, parties may perhaps be more inclined to obey the award of a tribunal of their own choice than they are to obey the decision of a court.

Although English courts have enforced foreign judgments from the seventeenth century onwards, it is only since 1927[214] (so far as one can judge from reported cases) that they have enforced foreign arbitral awards, and so authority is relatively scanty. This is no doubt because arbitration is so ancient and

---

[213] [2007] UKHL 40; [2008] 1 Lloyd's Rep. 254.
[214] *Norske Atlas Insurance Co Ltd v London General Insurance Co Ltd* (1927) 43 T.L.R. 541.

well-developed an institution in England that for many years most disputes that had any connection with England, and many that had none,[215] were referred to arbitration in England, and so the enforcement of the award in England was a purely domestic matter.

Conditions for enforcement

10–037 A foreign arbitration award can be enforced by action in England at common law if (1) the parties submitted to the arbitration by an agreement which is valid by its governing law, and (2) the award is valid and final according to the law which governs the arbitration proceedings.

The validity, interpretation, and effect of the agreement to arbitrate are governed by the proper law of the agreement. The Rome I Regulation does not apply to arbitration agreements, so the common law rules as to the proper law of a contract remain applicable. This means that if there is an express choice of law in respect of the arbitration agreement, the chosen law will govern. The choice of the place where the arbitration is to be conducted (its "seat") may be treated as an implied choice of the governing law.[216] This is so even if the contract of which the arbitration clause forms part is governed by some other law.[217] Where there is neither an express nor an implied choice of law by the parties, regard must be had to all the circumstances in deciding with which law the agreement is most closely connected.

The parties can not only choose the law which governs their agreement to arbitrate but also the law which governs the arbitration proceedings. Normally the parties' choice of the place where the arbitration is to be conducted, its seat, will be accompanied by, or will imply, the choice of the law of that place as the law to govern the procedure. It is possible, however, for the parties to agree that state A shall be the seat of the arbitration but that the procedure shall be that of state B. In such a case, the parties' choice of procedural law will be respected but only subject to any mandatory provisions of the law of state A. In the absence of any choice by the parties, the law of the seat of the arbitration will govern the procedure.

If England is the seat of the arbitration, the provisions of the Arbitration Act 1996 will determine such issues as how the arbitrators are to be appointed, whether an arbitrator may be appointed by the court, whether the authority of an arbitrator can be revoked, what law the arbitrators are to apply, and whether they can decide *ex aequo et bono*.[218] The scheme of the Act, which cannot be examined in detail here, is to set out some provisions which are mandatory,

---

[215] For a striking and well-known example, see *Gilbert v Burnstine*, (1931) 255 N.Y. 348, 174 N.E. 706, where the New York Court of Appeals enforced an English award made in pursuance of an arbitration clause in a contract made and to be performed in New York between two residents of that state. See also Kerr J, (1978) 41 M.L.R. 1, 5–6.

[216] *Hamlyn v Talisker Distillery* [1894] A.C. 202.

[217] *Deutsche Schachtbau v Shell International Petroleum Ltd* [1990] 1 A.C. 295 (a CA judgment, revd on other grounds at p.329).

[218] On the law to be applied in English arbitrations, see Arbitration Act 1996 s.46.

applying notwithstanding any contrary agreement by the parties, and those which are non-mandatory, applying in the absence of any special agreement by the parties.

Finality of the award

To be enforceable in England, the award must be final and binding on the parties in the English sense, i.e. it must fulfil one of the conditions for the enforcement of foreign judgments in personam.[219] Whether the award is final in the English sense depends on the law governing the arbitration proceedings. The question to be answered is:

> "Has it become final, as we understand that phrase, in the country in which it was made? Of course the question whether it is final in [that country] will depend no doubt upon [the foreign] law, but the [foreign] law is directed to showing whether it is final as that word is understood in English".[220]

10–038

These remarks were made in a case where the award was enforced under Pt II of the Arbitration Act 1950, but it is thought that they are equally applicable to the enforcement of awards at common law.

Mode of enforcement

In order to enforce an arbitration award in England it is necessary to obtain an enforcement title from a court. A claimant seeking to enforce an English award can choose either to bring an action on the award or to apply for leave to enforce it under s.66 of the Arbitration Act 1996. This summary procedure is also available for the enforcement of a foreign award; but it should only be used where the validity of the award or the right to proceed upon it is "reasonably clear".[221]

10–039

An award may be expressed in foreign currency, and such an award can be enforced under s.66.[222] Whether enforced by action or under s.66, it must be converted into sterling before it can be enforced in England by any process of execution. The date for conversion will be the date when the court authorises enforcement of the judgment or when leave to enforce the award in sterling under s.66 is given.[223]

A foreign arbitration award may be enforced in England whether or not the law governing the arbitration proceedings requires a judgment or order of the

---

[219] See above, para.10-030.

[220] *Union Nationale des Coopératives Agricoles v Catterall* [1959] 2 Q.B. 44, 53, per Lord Evershed MR.

[221] *Re Boks & Co and Peters, Rushton & Co Ltd* [1919] 1 K.B. 491; but see *Middlemiss and Gould v Hartlepool Corporation* [1972] 1 W.L.R. 1643, 1647. In *Union Nationale des Coopératives Agricoles v Catterall* [1959] 2 Q.B. 44, 52, this test was adopted and applied to the enforcement of a foreign award under Pt II of the Arbitration Act 1950.

[222] *Jugoslavenska Oceanska Plovidba v Castle Investment Co* [1974] Q.B. 272. See above, para.19–014.

[223] *Miliangos v George Frank (Textiles) Ltd* [1976] A.C. 443, 469, per Lord Wilberforce.

foreign court to make the award enforceable.[224] Provided the award is final in the English sense, it can be enforced in England even though by the law governing the arbitration proceedings it is not enforceable in the foreign country until a judgment of a court has been obtained. If the English court insisted on a foreign judgment in order to make the award enforceable in England, it would not be enforcing the award but the judgment, and the foreign award as such would be deprived of all effect in England. All doubts concerning this important principle were dispelled by the decision of the Court of Appeal in *Union Nationale des Coopératives Agricoles v Catterall*.[225] That case was decided under Pt II of the Arbitration Act 1950, but it is thought that the principle applies equally to enforcement at common law.

However, if the party in whose favour a foreign award is made does obtain a judgment on it in the country where it was rendered, that judgment can be enforced in England in accordance with the principles on which foreign judgments are enforced.[226] By submitting to arbitration in a foreign country, the parties also submit to the jurisdiction of the foreign court which declares the award enforceable.[227]

Recognition as defence

10–040   The conditions under which a foreign arbitration award may be enforced in England at common law apply also to its recognition as a defence to an action on the original cause of action. A valid English award duly made in pursuance of a valid agreement to arbitrate is a defence to an action on the original cause of action, and there seems no reason for the same not to be true of a foreign award.

Defences to actions on foreign awards

10–041   There is very little authority on the grounds on which a foreign award can be challenged in England, notwithstanding that it was made in accordance with a valid agreement to arbitrate, and is valid and final according to the law governing the arbitration proceedings. But it can hardly be supposed that foreign arbitration awards will be more readily enforced or recognised in England than are foreign judgments. Hence the existence of the following grounds of challenge can probably be taken for granted:

(a)   that under the agreement to arbitrate the arbitrators had no jurisdiction to make the award[228];

---

[224] *Union Nationale des Coopératives Agricoles v Catterall* [1959] 2 Q.B. 44. The decision to the contrary in *Merrifield Ziegler & Co v Liverpool Cotton Association* (1911) 105 L.T. 97 should not now be followed: *Dalmia Dairy Industries Ltd v National Bank of Pakistan* [1978] 2 Lloyd's Rep. 223, 249.

[225] [1959] 2 Q.B. 44.

[226] *East India Trading Co Inc v Carmel Exporters and Importers Ltd* [1952] 2 Q.B. 439.

[227] *International Alltex Corporation v Lawler Creations Ltd* [1965] I.R. 264.

[228] See *Kianta Osakeyhtio v Britain and Overseas Trading Co Ltd* [1953] 2 Lloyd's Rep. 569; [1954] 1 Lloyd's Rep. 247; *Dalmia Dairy Industries Ltd v National Bank of Pakistan* [1978] 2 Lloyd's Rep. 223.

(b)   that the award was obtained by fraud[229];

(c)   that the enforcement or recognition of the award would be contrary to English public policy in the limited sense in which that concept is deployed in conflicts cases[230] and;

(d)   that the proceedings in which the award was obtained were opposed to natural justice.

Under the New York Convention

Efforts to promote the international enforcement and recognition of commercial arbitration awards have on a number of occasions been made by means of multilateral international conventions. The UK is a party to the Protocol on Arbitration Clauses 1923, and to the Geneva Convention on the Execution of Foreign Arbitral Awards 1927 which has been almost entirely replaced by the New York Convention 1958. Part II of the Arbitration Act 1950 (repealing and replacing earlier legislation) enacts the Protocol of 1923 as supplemented by the Convention of 1927 as part of the law of the UK. Part III of the Arbitration Act 1996 replaces earlier provisions in the Arbitration Act 1975 which was passed to enable the UK to accede to the New York Convention on the Recognition and Enforcement of Foreign Arbitral Awards of 1958.[231]

10–042

The New York Convention applies to an award made in a State, other than the UK, which is a party to the Convention.[232] The claimant seeking enforcement merely has to produce the original award or a certified copy of it, the original arbitration agreement or a certified copy of it, and (where the award or agreement is in a foreign language) a certified translation.[233] Section 101 of the Arbitration Act 1996 provides that "A New York Convention award may, by leave of the court, be enforced in the same manner as a judgment or order of the court to the same effect ... Where leave is so given, judgment may be entered in terms of the award." As Gross J explained in *Norsk Hydro ASA v State Property Fund of Ukraine*[234]:

> "There is an important policy interest, reflected in this country's treaty obligations, in ensuring the effective and speedy enforcement of such international arbitration awards; the corollary, however, is that the task of the enforcing court should be as 'mechanistic' as possible. Save in connection with the threshold requirements for enforcement and the exhaustive grounds on which enforcement of a New York Convention award may be refused ..., the enforcing court is neither entitled nor bound to go behind the award in question, explore the reasoning of the arbitration tribunal or second-guess its intentions."

---

[229] See *Oppenheim & Co v Mahomed Haneef* [1922] 1 A.C. 482, 487; *Westacre Investments Inc v Jugoimport-SDPR Holding Co Ltd* [1999] 3 All E.R. 864 (refusing to extend to foreign arbitral awards the rule in *Abouloff v Oppenheimer & Co* (1882) 10 Q.B.D. 295, above para.10–022).

[230] See *Dalmia Dairy Industries Ltd v National Bank of Pakistan*, above; cf. *Westacre Investments Inc v Jugoimport-SDPR Holding Co Ltd*, above (contract for purchase of personal influence contrary to domestic English public policy but not in international sense).

[231] For the text of the Convention, see Fifth Report of the Private International Law Committee, Cmnd. 1515 (1961).

[232] Arbitration Act 1996 s.100(1).

[233] Arbitration Act 1996 s.102.

[234] [2002] EWHC 2120 (Comm.), [2009] Bus.L.R. 558 (judgment naming parties other than those in the award set aside).

The burden is then on the defendant resisting enforcement to prove any of the following substantive circumstances under which the court may refuse enforcement:

(a) that a party to the arbitration agreement was (under the law applicable to him or her) under some incapacity;

(b) that the arbitration agreement was not valid under the law to which the parties subjected it, or, failing any indication thereon, under the law of the country where the award was made[235];

(c) that he or she was not given proper notice of the appointment of the arbitrator or of the arbitration proceedings or was otherwise unable to present his or her case;

(d) that the award deals with a difference not contemplated by or not falling within the terms of the submission to arbitration or contains decisions on matters beyond the scope of the submission to arbitration (unless they can be separated);

(e) that the composition of the arbitral authority or the arbitral procedure was not in accordance with the agreement of the parties, or, failing such agreement, with the law of the country where the arbitration took place; or

(f) that the award has not yet become binding on the parties, or has been set aside or suspended by a competent authority of the country in which, or under the law of which, it was made.[236]

The courts will only refuse that in a clear case where the grounds were met, asking whether there was a real prospect of successfully establishing the ground alleged and assessing the material before it critically.[237] If the defendant proves any of these defences, the court retains a discretion nonetheless to enforce the award but will only do so in rare cases, where for example there has been some agreement to the contrary.[238]

Recognition or enforcement of an award may also be refused if the award is in respect of a matter which is not capable of settlement by arbitration, or if it would

[235] See *Dallah Real Estate and Tourism Holding Co v Ministry of Religious Affairs of the Government of Pakistan* [2010] UKSC 46; [2011] 1 A.C. 763. *Renvoi* is inapplicable, but an English court will nonetheless recognise that a foreign court might apply different principles in an international as opposed to a purely domestic case: ibid., at para [125].

[236] Arbitration Act 1996 s.103(2), (4).

[237] *Honeywell International Middle East Ltd v Meydan Group LLC* [2014] EWHC 1344 (TCC); [2014] 2 Lloyd's Rep. 133.

[238] *Kanoria v Guinness* [2006] EWCA Civ 222; [2006] 1 Lloyd's Rep.701. The discretion must be exercised so as to give effect to the purposes of the Convention; where there was no valid arbitration agreement, a refusal of recognition will almost inevitably follow: *Dallah Real Estate and Tourism Holding Co v Ministry of Religious Affairs of the Government of Pakistan* [2010] UKSC 46; [2011] 1 A.C. 763.

be contrary to public policy to recognise or enforce the award.[239] Recognition or enforcement may not be refused except in the cases mentioned above.[240]

A party who has obtained a Convention award may, if he or she chooses, enforce it either by action or by an application for leave to enforce the award summarily under s.66 of the Arbitration Act 1996.[241] The award may also be relied upon as a defence to an action on the original cause of action.[242]

Awards made in other parts of the United Kingdom

For the purposes of s.18 of the Civil Jurisdiction and Judgments Act 1982, which provides for the reciprocal enforcement of judgments within the UK,[243] "judgment" is defined so as to include an arbitration award which has become enforceable in the part of the UK in which it was given in the same manner as a judgment given by a court of law in that part.[244] The Act thus provides machinery for the reciprocal enforcement of such awards within the UK. Such awards made in Scotland or Northern Ireland can be enforced in England under Sch.6 of the Act (if they order payment of a sum of money) or under Sch.7 (if they order any relief or remedy not requiring payment of a sum of money). But registration under these Schedules is not the only way in which such awards can be enforced. They can also be enforced in England at the option of the claimant under the summary procedure of s.66 of the Arbitration Act 1996 or by action at common law.[245] But, for some obscure reason, the provisions of s.19 as to recognition as opposed to enforcement do not apply to arbitration awards.

10–043

Awards recognised or enforced under foreign judgments legislation

As we have seen,[246] the Administration of Justice Act 1920 provides for the direct enforcement in the UK of judgments of superior courts of other Commonwealth countries to which the Act has been extended by Order in Council. The Act defines a judgment so as to include an arbitration award if the award has, in pursuance of the law in force in the place where it was made, become enforceable in the same manner as a judgment given by a court in that place.[247] The claimant remains free to bring an action on the award at common law, but in that case may not be awarded costs.[248]

10–044

---

[239] Arbitration Act 1996 s.103(3); *Westacre Investments Inc v Jugoimport-SDPR Holding Co Ltd* [2000] 1 Q.B. 288 and *Omnium de Traitement et de Valorisation SA v Hilmarton Ltd* [1999] 2 Lloyd's Rep. 222 (both dealing with illegality of the contract); *Kanoria v Guinness* [2006] EWCA Civ 222; [2006] 1 Lloyd's Rep.701 (party not given proper notice of case to be met); Case C-126/97 *Eco Swiss China Time Ltd v Benetton International NV* [1999] E.C.R. I–3055 (relevance of EU public policy).
[240] Arbitration Act 1996 s.103(1).
[241] Arbitration Act 1996 s.101(2).
[242] Arbitration Act 1996 s.101(1).
[243] See above, para.10–034.
[244] Section 18(2)(e).
[245] Section 18(8).
[246] Above, para.10–031.
[247] Administration of Justice Act 1920 s.12(1).
[248] Administration of Justice Act 1920 s.9(5).

The Foreign Judgments (Reciprocal Enforcement) Act 1933 also provides[249] that the provisions of the Act, except ss1(5) and 6, apply to an arbitration award which has become enforceable in the same manner as a judgment in the place where it was made. The effect of the exception for s.6 is that such an award can be enforced at the option of the claimant either by registration under the Act or under the summary procedure of s.66 of the Arbitration Act 1996 or by action at common law.

---

[249] Section 10A, added by Civil Jurisdiction and Judgments Act 1982 Sch.10, para.4.

CHAPTER 11

MARRIAGE

Marriage is known to every culture and every legal system. If the concept of **11–001**
marriage were the same everywhere, it would scarcely merit attention in a book
on the conflict of laws. In fact, marriage varies enormously from country to
country, and has varied over time, and the conflicts issues these variations create
are of especial interest.

In 1866 the future Lord Penzance could say with complete confidence that
"marriage is the voluntary union for life of one man and one woman to the
exclusion of all others".[1] Since 2013 marriage in England, as in a growing
number of other countries, may be between two men or between two women.[2]
Scotland followed suit in 2014[3] but same-sex marriage is still unknown in
Northern Ireland. In some cultures and legal systems a man may have several
wives. In fewer, but still a surprisingly large number of, cultures a woman may
have several husbands, though that practice is seldom recognised in formal legal
provisions. Many countries have a form of legal relationship between couples,
such as the civil partnership found in all parts of the UK, which is not marriage
but creates rights and responsibilities almost identical to those of marriage. In
some legal systems, the fact of living together for some time may create legal
rights and obligations even when the couple concerned have deliberately chosen
not to marry.

Given that the very nature of marriage varies so, it is not at all surprising that
the legal rules as to its creation or dissolution are equally varied. The minimum
age for marriage is set at different ages or, in some systems of customary law, is
unregulated or defined by reference to puberty. The prohibitions on marriage to a
close relative, by blood or marriage, the rules of "consanguinity and affinity",
also vary and in England have become more liberal over time. In some countries,
including England, a marriage may be created by a wholly religious ceremony; in
others, a civil ceremony is essential even if the parties may choose to follow it
with a religious service. In many systems of customary law the payment of a
"bride-price" and the formal delivery of the bride to her intended husband are all
that is required by way of ceremony. The one feature that seems to be found in all
societies—party, feast, reception or wedding breakfast—may be enjoyable, and
expensive, but has no legal significance.

As will become clearer in the next chapter, there is similar variety in the ways
in which a marriage may be dissolved. At one extreme, a court or other authority

---

[1] *Hyde v Hyde* (1866) L.R. 1 P. & M. 130, 133.
[2] Marriage (Same Sex Couples) Act 2013.
[3] Marriage and Civil Partnership (Scotland) Act 2014.

has to examine whether there are legally-recognised reasons for it to decree the ending of the marriage. At the other, a marriage may be ended by consent, by the unilateral act of one party, or the return of the wife and the bride-price to her family.

All this variety and the increasing numbers of people who migrate from one country to another have an obvious result. Many couples who married in State A, complying with all its legal requirements, will later live in State B, a State with different requirements which their marriage does not meet. Very often this does not matter at all: a marriage in a Church of England parish church, entirely valid in English law, does not satisfy the requirements of domestic French law, but no-one suggests that an English couple marrying in that way cease to be married if they move to live in France. But sometimes it matters a great deal: if the parties to a same-sex marriage in England were to move to a country in which homosexuality is unacceptable, and perhaps even criminal, they could not expect to be treated there as a validly married couple. One of the purposes of this chapter is to examine where, in less extreme cases, the differences in legal requirements matter so as to affect the treatment in English law of a supposed marriage elsewhere.

So far, we have concentrated on the place of the marriage, the country in which it is created. That is unfortunately an over-simplification of the issues we have to examine. An example may make this clear. H, a married man born and bred in England and so domiciled there, announces his conversion to Islam, travels to a country in which Islamic law is in force, and returns with three additional wives. Most English people, considering that example, would say, "Surely he cannot get away with that"; and their reaction would reflect the actual legal position. The reason is that the law is not simply "territorial", applying in particular areas of the Earth's surface; it is also "personal" so that individuals, wherever they may travel, carry with them some elements of their "personal law" and remain bound by its obligations and restrictions.

A final preliminary observation. There is much force in the proposition that if two people go to the trouble of getting married, observing all the relevant rules of the local law, they should be able to rely on its continuing validity wherever they may come to live. Nonetheless, there must be circumstances in which this cannot be the case. Differences in the laws as to marriage and divorce may create what is sometimes known as a "limping marriage", where H and W are a married couple in one country but not in another. Or, even more awkwardly, where H is married to W1 in one country but to W2 in another. The parties may be unaware of the legal position, or be unembarrassed by it, but it may cause very real difficulties in determining property rights and when the death of one party leads to rival claims to inheritance.

THE APPLICABLE RULES

As Lincoln J observed,[4] "Ideally, the conflict rules relating to the status of **11–002** married and divorced persons should be simple and easily understood". Unfortunately the relevant English conflict of laws rules do not live up to this ideal. The Law Commission for long entertained hopes of clarifying and simplifying the rules. Its consideration of the matter was suspended for more than a decade in the hope that work under the auspices of the Hague Conference on Private International Law might produce rules which would be internationally agreed. The relative failure of that work[5] led the Law Commission to publish its own Working Paper in 1985.[6] After consultation, however, the Commission reported, with a humility not always displayed by law reform agencies, that the law was still developing and that it was better, for the time being at least, to leave the process in the hands of the judges.[7]

The original English rule was that the validity of a marriage always depended on the law of the place of celebration *(lex loci celebrationis)*; that remains the rule generally followed in the United States. However, in 1861 the House of Lords in *Brook v Brook*[8] recognised and applied in the context of marriage the distinction, noted above, between rules that are properly territorial and rules that are personal. The House limited the application of the law of the place of celebration to questions concerning the formalities required to bring the marriage into being. That law was held to be inapplicable to questions as to the capacity of the parties to enter into the marriage, which were held to be governed by the law of each party's antenuptial domicile.

The facts of *Brook v Brook* may puzzle the modern reader and the outcome was disastrous for the family concerned. A man and woman, both British subjects domiciled in England, went through a ceremony of marriage during a temporary visit to Denmark. By Danish law, the law of the place of celebration, the marriage was valid. However by English law, as it then stood, a man might not legally marry his deceased wife's sister; that was the relationship between the parties. The House of Lords held that this was a question of capacity to enter the marriage and was governed by English law, the law of the parties' domicile. The marriage was therefore void. In fact, the husband, the wife, and one of the infant children of the marriage had died within a few days of each other in an epidemic of cholera. As the marriage was void, the children were declared illegitimate, and therefore the dead child's one-fifth share of the family property passed to the Crown as bona vacantia and not to his natural brothers and sisters.

The simple distinction between formalities and capacity drawn in *Brook v Brook* is not an adequate basis on which to examine the modern law. The consent of the parties, always an essential ingredient of a valid marriage, is a distinct

---

[4] *Lawrence v Lawrence* [1985] 1 All E.R. 506, 509.
[5] The Hague Convention on Celebration and Recognition of the Validity of Marriages 1978 was much criticised and the UK has not ratified it. Only Australia, Luxembourg and The Netherlands have done so.
[6] Working Paper No.89 (1985).
[7] *Choice of Law Rules in Marriage* (Law Com. No. 165, 1987). Choice of law rules were introduced in Scotland: Family Law (Scotland) Act 2006 s.38.
[8] (1861) 9 H.L.C. 193.

issue. For reasons that are not entirely clear, the question whether and to what extent polygamous marriages can be recognised has attracted an extraordinary amount of attention in England. The matter is further complicated by the distinction drawn in many national legal systems between marriages that are void and so open to attack at any time, even after the death of the parties, by any person, and those that are voidable and that can be set aside only in nullity proceedings brought by one of the parties. In English domestic law the court may make orders as to financial relief in favour of one or other party whether the marriage is void or voidable, but the courts have recognised that some events are so far removed from a valid marriage that it would be inappropriate to hold either party entitled to such relief; such events are styled "non-marriages". We need, therefore, to consider the English conflict rules as to marriage under four headings: formalities, capacity, consent of the parties, and polygamy; and to say something about "non-marriages" and civil partnerships.

FORMALITIES OF MARRIAGE

11–003 The term "formalities" includes such questions as whether a civil ceremony, or any ceremony at all, is required, the number of witnesses necessary, the permitted hours during which marriages can be celebrated, whether publication of banns or some other form of advanced notification is necessary, and so on.

It has been settled law since 1752[9] that the formalities of marriage are governed by the law of the place of celebration. It is sufficient to comply with the formalities prescribed by that law; and as a general rule it is also necessary so to do.

The leading case is *Berthiaume v Dastous*,[10] where two Roman Catholics domiciled in Quebec were married in France in a Roman Catholic church. Owing to the carelessness of the priest who married them, there was no civil ceremony as required by French law. The Privy Council held that the marriage was void; and Lord Dunedin, describing the question as one better settled than any other in international law, said[11]:

> "If a marriage is good by the laws of the country where it is effected, it is good all the world over, no matter whether the proceeding or ceremony which constituted marriage according to the law of the place would or would not constitute marriage in the country of the domicile of one or other of the spouses. If the so-called marriage is no marriage in the place where it is celebrated, there is no marriage anywhere, although the ceremony or proceeding if conducted in the place of the parties' domicile would be considered a good marriage".

So well-established is the principle that compliance with the local form is sufficient, that it applies even though the marriage, originally invalid by the local law, has been subsequently validated by retrospective legislation in the country of the place of celebration, and even though the legislation does not take effect until

---

[9] *Scrimshire v Scrimshire* (1752) 2 Hagg. Con. 395; *Dalrymple v Dalrymple* (1811) 2 Hagg. Con. 54; *Simonin v Mallac* (1860) 2 Sw. & Tr. 67; *Berthiaume v Dastous* [1930] A.C. 79; *Apt v Apt* [1948] P. 83; *Kenward v Kenward* [1951] P. 124; *McCabe v McCabe* [1994] 1 F.L.R. 410.
[10] [1930] A.C. 79.
[11] ibid., at 83.

after the parties have acquired an English domicile. Thus, in *Starkowski v Attorney General*[12] two Roman Catholics domiciled in Poland were married without any civil ceremony in a Roman Catholic church in Austria in May 1945. At that time Austrian law did not recognise marriages without a civil ceremony; but a few weeks later a law was passed in Austria retrospectively validating such marriages if they were duly registered. By some oversight the marriage in question was not registered until 1949, by which time the parties had acquired an English domicile, and separated. In 1950, the wife married another man in England. The House of Lords held that the Austrian marriage was valid and therefore the English ceremony was bigamous and void. Their Lordships expressly left open the question what the position would have been if the English ceremony had preceded the registration of the Austrian marriage. It is thought that, in that case, the English ceremony would be held valid and the Austrian marriage void, because foreign retrospective legislation would hardly be held to invalidate a valid marriage celebrated in the country of the parties' domicile. There is Canadian authority which indirectly supports this view.[13]

For the law of the place of celebration to be complied with, it is, of course, necessary to know where the marriage is celebrated. It is sometimes assumed, incorrectly, that an embassy or consulate forms part of the territory of the sending State. In fact a marriage in such a building must comply with the formalities required by the law of the State in which it is situated; the fact that it may be regarded as valid under the law of the sending State is immaterial.[14] Other facts present greater difficulty[15] and with certain cultures accepting marriage by telephone,[16] it may soon be necessary for the English courts to consider the place of celebration of marriage by a variety of electronic means.

Scope of the rule

Marriages by proxy

Under some systems of law a marriage may be celebrated by proxy, one or both parties being represented at the ceremony by other persons whom they have duly authorised to make the necessary declarations. The law of the place of the ceremony governs, even if one or both of the parties are in another country. In *Apt v Apt*,[17] the Court of Appeal upheld a marriage celebrated by proxy in Argentina between a man domiciled and resident there and a woman domiciled and resident in England, since it appeared that proxy marriages were valid by Argentine law.[18]

11–004

---

[12] [1954] A.C. 155.

[13] *Ambrose v Ambrose* (1961) 25 D.L.R. (2d) 1. See below, para.20–037.

[14] *Dukali v Lamrani (Attorney General intervening)* [2012] EWHC 1748 (Fam.); [2012] 2 F.L.R. 1099 (Moroccan civil ceremony in London consulate), following in this respect a dictum in *Radwan v Radwan* [1973] Fam. 24.

[15] See para.11–009 for cases of marriages on board ships.

[16] *KC v City of Westminster Social and Community Services Dept* [2008] EWCA Civ 198; [2008] 2 F.C.R. 146. See also the unsatisfactory Scottish case of *MRA v NRK* [2011] CSOH 101.

[17] [1948] P. 83.

[18] In *Apt v Apt* the Court of Appeal distinguished between the fact of consent and the method of giving consent; the acceptability of proxies went to the latter and was an aspect of formalities.

A more extreme set of facts presented themselves in *McCabe v McCabe*.[19]

> A man domiciled in the Republic of Ireland and a woman domiciled in Ghana were living together in England. They agreed to marry according to the tribal custom of the Akan, a people living in Ghana. The man provided a bottle of gin and some money (as '*aseda*'), which were taken to Ghana where a ceremony was held. Neither the man nor the woman was present at the ceremony, nor was either of them represented by proxy.

The Court of Appeal held that the couple were validly married, finding on the basis of expert evidence that the ceremony constituted a valid marriage under Akan customary law.[20] It does not seem to have been argued whether the place of celebration was Ghana (where, according to one expert witness, no ceremony was necessary at all) or England, the place where the couple gave their consent.

Parental consent

11–005 The most controversial question is whether lack of parental consent relates to formalities of marriage or to capacity to marry. The answer appears to be that it relates to the formalities, whether the requirement is imposed by English law or foreign law, and in the latter case no matter how stringently the requirement is expressed. However, the cases have been much criticised.

English law requires the consent of the "appropriate person" to the marriage of a person below the age of 18; this will normally be a parent with parental responsibility for that person or his or her guardian.[21] There is some historical justification for treating this requirement as a formality. It was first imposed by Lord Hardwicke's Marriage Act of 1753. That Act also dealt with licences and publication of banns, matters which no one doubts are formalities. The Act applied to England only and not to Scotland. Hence the practice arose of eloping English couples marrying without parental consent and without formal ceremony at Gretna Green, just across the border in Scotland. The validity of such marriages was established in a series of eighteenth-century cases[22] which were decided at a time when English courts did not distinguish between the formalities of marriage and capacity to marry, but referred both aspects to the law of the place of celebration. When that distinction was introduced in 1861, the Gretna Green cases were explained away as having turned on the formalities of marriage.[23]

Of course it did not follow from this that foreign requirements of parental consent could also be treated as formalities. In *Simonin v Mallac*,[24] the English court was dealing with the more stringent rules of French law, which expressly

---

[19] [1994] 1 F.L.R. 410.

[20] The evidence was that the only (formal?) requirement of an Akan marriage was the consent of the parties and of their families, with some degree of publicity; even the *"aseda"* was not essential.

[21] Marriage Act 1949 s.3 (as amended by the Family Law Reform Act 1987 Sch.2, para.9). There are detailed provisions as to the identity of the appropriate person in a case involving adoption or where a special guardianship order, care order, child arrangements order, or placement order is in force. "Parental consent" is convenient shorthand.

[22] The leading case is *Compton v Bearcroft* (1769) 2 Hagg. Con. 444n.

[23] *Brook v Brook* (1861) 9 H.L.C. 193, 215, 228–229, 236.

[24] (1860) 2 Sw. & Tr. 67.

applied to the marriages of Frenchmen and Frenchwomen, no matter where celebrated; non-compliance rendered the marriage voidable at the instance of the party who needed parental consent, or of his or her parents. Yet these rules were treated as inapplicable to a marriage between French persons celebrated in England. In that case a Frenchman aged 29 married a Frenchwoman aged 22 in England. The marriage was valid by English domestic law, but voidable by French law because neither party had obtained the consent of his or her parents as required by what was then art.151 of the French Civil Code. Although the marriage was annulled in France,[25] the country of the parties' domicile, it was held valid in England. The ground of the decision was that the validity of marriage generally is governed by the law of the place of celebration, but it was subsequently explained as having turned on formalities.[26] The court intimated[27] that art.148 of the French Civil Code, which imposed an absolute and not merely a qualified prohibition on marriages without parental consent, might receive a different interpretation.

However, the suggested distinction was ignored in *Ogden v Ogden*,[28] where a domiciled Frenchman aged 19 married in England a domiciled Englishwoman without the consent of his parents as required by art.148 which provided that a son who had not attained the age of 25 years could not contract marriage without the consent of his parents. The parties lived together in England for a few months, after which the husband returned to France, leaving the wife in England, and obtained a nullity decree from the French court on the ground of lack of parental consent. The Court of Appeal held that nevertheless the marriage was valid in England, because (among other reasons) the requirement of parental consent was a formality.[29] Although heavily criticised, *Ogden v Ogden* has since been followed in Scotland[30] and England.[31]

Renvoi

There is some reason to believe that if the marriage is formally invalid by the domestic law of the place of celebration, but formally valid by the system of law referred to by its conflict rules, the marriage would be held valid in England under the doctrine of *renvoi*.[32] In *Taczanowska v Taczanowski*,[33] two Polish

11–006

---

[25] The French nullity decree would now be recognised in England, but was not under the then English rules for the recognition of foreign decrees.

[26] *Brook v Brook* (1861) 9 H.L.C. 193, 218; *Sottomayor v De Barros (No.1)* (1877) 3 P.D. 1, 7.

[27] At p.77.

[28] [1908] P. 46. This case affords a striking example of characterisation in accordance with the *lex fori;* see below, para.20-006.

[29] At pp.57, 75. The other reasons relate to capacity to marry and are considered below, para.11–015. The consequences of this decision were extremely awkward for the English woman, for both parties had remarried on the strength of the French nullity decree, but she was left married to a man who by the law of his domicile was not only not her husband but was the husband of someone else. She could not as the law then stood divorce her husband in England, since he was domiciled in France; nor was the French nullity decree recognised in England.

[30] *Bliersbach v McEwen*, 1959 S.C. 43.

[31] *Lodge v Lodge* (1963) 107 S.J. 437.

[32] For *renvoi*, see below, para.20–011. In Working Paper No.89 (1985), para.2.39, the Law Commission favoured the use of *renvoi* in this context; commentators were divided in their response.

nationals domiciled in Poland were married in Italy in a form which did not constitute a valid marriage by Italian domestic law. There was evidence that the Italian courts would recognise a marriage celebrated in Italy in accordance with the forms prescribed by the law of the parties' common nationality. But the marriage was not formally valid by Polish domestic law, and so it was not held valid in England on this ground (it was held valid on another ground which is discussed later[34]). It seems a safe deduction that it would have been held valid if it had been valid by Polish domestic law. Otherwise there would have been no point in admitting and discussing the evidence of the Italian conflict rule.

Exceptions to the rule

11–007   There is no exception to the proposition that a marriage, formally valid by the law of the place of celebration, is formally valid in England. But there are two statutory and some, less secure, common law exceptions to the converse proposition that a marriage which is formally invalid by the law of the place of celebration is also formally invalid in England.

Consular and forces marriages

11–008   The statutory exceptions involve consular marriages and forces marriages, the subject of special rules in Sch.6 to the Marriage (Same Sex Couples) Act 2013 (the Schedule applying to marriages generally, not only to same-sex marriages) and Orders made under it.

A consular marriage is one conducted in the premises of a British consulate abroad by an authorised registration officer, usually an officer in the consular service; at least one of the people proposing to marry must be a UK national. The Consular Marriages and Marriages under Foreign Law (No.2) Order 2014[35] sets out detailed requirements as to such matters as notice of intended marriage, consents, and the oath each party must swear. The form of the ceremony is not specified save that at some point the parties must each state or indicate that they know of no legal impediment to their marriage and that they take one another as wedded wife or husband. The parties must be eligible to marry each other in whichever of England and Scotland they select as the part of the UK relevant to their marriage; a same sex couple is eligible. A consular marriage is valid in law as if the marriage had been solemnised in the relevant part of the UK with a due observance of all forms required by the law of that part.

The extent to which consular marriages form an exception to the application of the law of the place of celebration, that is of the country in which the consulate is situated, is limited by some important provisions. It must be the case that the authorities of that country had notified the Secretary of State in writing that there was no objection to such marriages taking place there[36]; only certain countries have indicated that there is no objection to same-sex marriages. There are two

---

[33] [1957] P. 301, 305, 318.
[34] Below, para.11–010.
[35] SI 2014/3265.
[36] 2013 Act Sch.6, para.1(2)(c); 2014 Order, art.2.

further matters, each requiring the registration officer to make a difficult judgment. The registration officer must be satisfied that "insufficient facilities" exist for the parties to enter into a marriage under the law of country concerned[37]; and is not required to allow two people to marry each other if in the registration officer's opinion a marriage between them would be inconsistent with international law or the comity of nations.[38]

Forces marriages are regulated by the Overseas Marriage (Armed Forces) Order 2014,[39] which contains detailed provisions as to notice of intended marriage to the commanding officer of one of the parties, the necessary certificate by the commanding officer, consents to the marriage, and its solemnisation. A forces marriage may take place in any country outside the UK, but in the case of same-sex marriages only in those countries which have notified the Secretary of State in writing that there is no objection to such marriages taking place.[40] At least one of the people proposing to marry must be a member of HM Forces serving in the country in which it is proposed that they marry, or a civilian subject to service discipline who is employed in that country, or a child of any such person whose home is with that person in that country.[41] The parties must be eligible to marry each other whichever part of the UK they nominate[42]; a same sex couple is eligible where that is England or Scotland, but not if it is Northern Ireland.[43] A forces marriage must be conducted by an "authorised person", a chaplain serving in any of HM Forces in the relevant country[44] or a person authorised by the local commanding officer of any of HM Forces in that country.[45] Such a forces marriage is valid in law as if the marriage had been solemnised in the relevant part of the UK with a due observance of all forms required by the law of the relevant part of the UK.[46]

Use of the local form impossible

There may be insuperable difficulties in using the local form. Quite how **11–009** frequently such cases can arise in modern circumstances is open to question. The standard examples are of "desert islands" with no marriage procedures, and such islands may well exist only in the imagination; and while there may be states which insist on marriage in accordance with the rites of a single religious creed,

---

[37] 2013 Act Sch.6, para.1(2)(d).

[38] 2013 Act Sch.6, para.2; either party may appeal in writing to the Secretary of State against a refusal on this ground: 2014 Order art.13.

[39] SI 2014/1108.

[40] 2014 Order, art.5.

[41] 2013 Act Sch.6, para.8(2)(a); see para.8(3) for cases in which a child is treated as a child of the family. The 2014 Order art.10 has a list of relevant civilian functions.

[42] 2013 Act Sch.6, para.8(2)(b); 2014 Order art.4.

[43] The parties' choice is untrammelled; there is nothing to stop an Irish Guardsman from Belfast who wishes to marry a same-sex partner from selecting England or Scotland as the relevant part.

[44] But note the prohibition in the case of the marriage of a same sex couple of the use of the rites of certain churches including the Church of England and the Church in Wales (2013 Act Sch.6, para.9; 2014 Order, art.12; and see the Marriage of Same Sex Couples (Use of Armed Forces' Chapels Regulations 2014 SI 2014/815)).

[45] 2013 Act Sch.6, para.12(2).

[46] 2013 Act (Sch.6, paras 10 and 11.

which might be unacceptable to the parties, the notion of "insuperable difficulty" interpreted strictly might also involve an examination of the question as to whether the parties could travel to a neighbouring and more accommodating jurisdiction; and, in the light of modern social values, whether they should simply have waited until they could. However, it is thought that an English court would not be so accommodating of modern social ideas as was the Australian Family Court which excused compliance with the law of the Thai place of celebration because registration of the marriage would oblige the wife to take her husband's surname.[47]

Some of the marriages which have been held valid under this principle are not real exceptions to the general rule that the law of the place of celebration must be complied with. For their validity depended on the principle that the English common law, or so much of it as is applicable in the circumstances, applies to British subjects in a settled colony and also in some other colonies and places where Britain once exercised extra-territorial jurisdiction.[48] Hence this law becomes, by a fiction of law, part of the law of the place of celebration itself.[49]

If the principle does apply, a marriage will be formally valid if it is celebrated in accordance with the requirements of English common law. This means English law as it stood before Lord Hardwicke's Marriage Act 1753; the formalities introduced by that Act could not be operative outside England. So the marriage need not be celebrated in church, and no licence or publication of banns or witnesses are necessary: it is sufficient if the parties take each other as husband and wife.[50] At one time it was supposed that it was essential to the validity of an English common law marriage that it should be celebrated in the presence of an episcopally ordained clergyman. But the two decisions of the House of Lords[51] which laid down this rule have since been confined to marriages celebrated in England or Ireland[52]; and of course the principle under consideration could hardly apply to such a marriage, for ample facilities are provided for civil marriages in both countries, with or without such religious ceremony as the parties see fit to adopt. Hence a common law marriage celebrated abroad may be valid if celebrated before a minster of religion who is not episcopally ordained,[53] or before a layperson,[54] or (presumably) with no "officiant" of any sort, and merely the presence of others who could testify to what had taken place should the marriage need to be proved.

---

[47] *Nygh and Kasey* [2010] FamCA 145.
[48] *Catterall v Catterall* (1847) 1 Rob. Ecc. 580 (New South Wales); *Wolfenden v Wolfenden* [1946] P. 61 (China, in which the British sovereign had extra-territorial rights and had established a system of courts); *Penhas v Tan Soo Eng* [1953] A.C. 304 (Singapore).
[49] *Taczanowska v Taczanowski* [1957] P. 301, 328, 329.
[50] However, for an analysis of the existence and effects of this type of pre 1753 'marriage', see Probert [2008] C.F.L.Q. 1.
[51] *R. v Millis* (1844) 10 Cl. & F. 534; *Beamish v Beamish* (1861) 9 H.L.C. 274. These two decisions have been much criticised: see Pollock and Maitland, *History of English Law*, Vol. 2, pp.370–372; Lord Hodson, (1958) 7 I.C.L.Q. 205, 208–209; *Merker v Merker* [1963] P. 283, 294, per Sir Jocelyn Simon P.
[52] *Wolfenden v Wolfenden* [1946] P. 61; approved by the Court of Appeal in *Apt v Apt* [1948] P. 83, 86, and by the Privy Council in *Penhas v Tan Soo Eng* [1953] A.C. 304, 319.
[53] *Wolfenden v Wolfenden* [1946] P. 61.
[54] *Penhas v Tan Soo Eng* [1953] A.C. 304.

There is no English authority on the validity of marriages celebrated in merchant ships on the high seas.[55] It is thought that such a marriage would be held valid if celebrated in accordance with the formalities prescribed by the law of the ship's port of registration; and that, if this was English law, it would suffice if the parties took each other for husband and wife, provided the court was satisfied that it was impracticable for them to wait until the ship reached a port where a consular marriage was possible or sufficient facilities were available either by the local law. There would be no such element of emergency if the ship was lying in a foreign port, unless there was an insuperable difficulty in marrying ashore. However, a marriage celebrated in a British warship lying off Cyprus has been upheld.[56] The parties were British subjects domiciled in England, the husband was an army officer, and the ceremony was performed by the ship's chaplain in the presence of the captain, though without banns or licence. It is clear from the reported argument that English common law was relied on; there was at the time no legislation as to forces marriages.

Marriages in countries under belligerent occupation

During the concluding weeks of the Second World War and its immediate aftermath, many thousands of marriages were celebrated in Germany and Italy between Roman Catholics or Jews domiciled in Poland and other Eastern European countries. These marriages were not valid by the local law, either because there was no civil ceremony or because some formality required by the local law was omitted. The validity of these marriages has been tested in a number of cases, and they have been held valid if they were celebrated in the form required by English common law and the husband was a member of belligerent occupying forces,[57] or of forces associated with them,[58] or (perhaps) of an organised body of escaped prisoners of war.[59] The status of the wife seems to have been treated as immaterial.[60] The leading case is the test case of *Taczanowska v Taczanowski*,[61] where the Court of Appeal upheld the validity of a marriage celebrated in 1946 in an Italian church by a Roman Catholic priest serving as a Polish Army chaplain; the husband was an officer of the Polish forces serving with the British Army in Italy and the wife a Polish civilian. The marriage was formally invalid by Italian law and also by Polish law. There was no insuperable difficulty in complying with the local law and the marriage did not qualify as a Forces marriage as the priest was not a chaplain acting under the orders of the British Commander-in-Chief. The main ground of the decision appears to have been that, as the husband was not in Italy from choice but under the orders of his military superiors, he was exempt from the operation of the local law unless he submitted to it of his own volition. Widely construed, this could

11–010

---

[55] See Goddard, [2002] L.M.C.L.Q. 498 for a detailed consideration of marriages at sea.
[56] *Culling v Culling* [1896] P. 116.
[57] *Taczanowska v Taczanowski* [1957] P. 301.
[58] *Preston v Preston* [1963] P. 411.
[59] *Merker v Merker* [1963] P. 283, 295.
[60] *Taczanowska v Taczanowski*, above; *Preston v Preston*, above, at pp.425, 430.
[61] [1957] P. 301. According to contemporary press reports, this was a test case involving the validity of some 3,000–4,000 similar marriages.

have been taken to include ordinary civilians who are present in a country from necessity and not from choice. But it is now clear that the principle does not extend to them.[62]

The decision in *Taczanowska v Taczanowski* has been followed[63] and distinguished[64] and has been heavily criticised by academic writers.[65] It is indeed a remarkable proposition that a marriage celebrated in a foreign country between persons domiciled in another foreign country who have never visited England in their lives, and may never do so, can derive formal validity from compliance with the requirements of English domestic law as it existed 200 years before the marriage. It cannot be supposed that such parties ever intended to submit to English common law.[66] If the law of the place of celebration is inapplicable for any reason, it would seem more sensible to refer the formal validity of the marriage to the law of the parties' domicile, but this suggestion has found no favour with the courts.[67] It should be noted that these decisions belong to a very different social era, and the validity of such marriages today may be viewed more restrictively.

"Non-marriages"

11–011   A failure to comply with every detail of the prescribed formalities will not necessarily invalidate a marriage. So far as marriages in England are concerned, the Marriage Act 1949 does not prescribe the form and content of the ceremony beyond requiring it to include to the parties' statements (or answers to questions) indicating the absence of any lawful impediment and of taking one another as husband and wife[68]; but a marriage is void if the parties "knowingly and wilfully intermarry" in breach of certain listed requirements[69]; other legal systems may draw a similar distinction between breaches of the formal requirements which do and do not render the marriage void).

---

[62] *Preston v Preston* [1963] P. 411, 426–427, 434–435, disapproving *Kochanski v Kochanska* [1958] P. 147, where the principle was extended to the marriage of inmates of a Polish displaced persons' camp in Germany; but in *Preston v Preston*, above, the same camp was held to be a military one.

[63] *Kochanski v Kochanska* [1958] P. 147; *Merker v Merker* [1963] P. 283; *Preston v Preston* [1963] P. 141, 411. It is a pity that the husband's conduct in this last case was so reprehensible that the Court of Appeal refused him leave to appeal to the House of Lords.

[64] *Lazarewicz v Lazarewicz* [1962] P. 171.

[65] Mendes da Costa, (1958) 7 I.C.L.Q. 217, 226–235; Andrews, (1959) 22 M.L.R. 396, 403–407.

[66] In an Irish case, *Hassan v Minister for Justice, Equality & Law Reform* [2013] IESC 8, Fennelly J doubted whether the common-law marriage argument could be relied upon where the marriage was "conducted in a jurisdiction having no connection with the common law and where neither of the parties is alleged ever to have been a subject of the common law in Ireland or anywhere else".

[67] *Taczanowska v Taczanowski*, above, at pp.326, 331; *Preston v Preston* [1963] P. 141, at 152–153.

[68] Marriage Act 1949 s.44 as amended by the Immigration and Asylum Act 1999 Sch.14, para.23 and the Marriage (Same Sex Couples) Act 2013 Sch.7, para.11.

[69] Marriage Act 1949 s.49 as amended by the Immigration and Asylum Act 1999 Sch.14, para.27 and the Marriage Act 1994 Sch, para.3. *A v A (Attorney General intervening)* [2012] EWHC 2219 (Fam.); [2013] Fam. 51 (Muslim ceremony conducted by an imam in a mosque registered for the solemnisation of marriages and in the presence of an authorised person, the imam telling the parties that they had done all that was required to enter a marriage; breach of listed formalities (no notice given to, or certificate obtained from, the registrar) but parties not knowingly acting in breach.

A void marriage may be the subject of a nullity decree with ancillary financial provisions, but the courts have identified a category of "non-marriages" where no decree will be granted and no financial provision ordered.[70] It would be inappropriate to order financial provision between the parties if the only ceremony in which they took part is found to have been in the nature of a betrothal or engagement ceremony and not a marriage.[71] An event more nearly approximating to a marriage ceremony was considered in *Hudson v Leigh*[72]:

> H and W became engaged but could not agree on the nature of the marriage ceremony. Eventually they agreed that a minister of religion would conduct a religious ceremony in South Africa to be followed by a civil ceremony in England. The religious ceremony, based on a marriage service but omitting phrases referring to 'husband' and 'wife', was not held in a church and the parties and the minister agreed that the parties were not seeking to be married at law until the civil ceremony. After the religious ceremony, the parties' relationship broke down; the proposed civil ceremony never took place. This was a 'non-marriage' rather than a void marriage; no ancillary financial relief was available to W.

So far as ceremonies taking place in England are concerned, it has been held that the central issue in considering whether what occurred was a "non-marriage" was whether what took place was sufficiently within the 1949 Act for the marriage to be capable of being a valid marriage under English law; was the marriage "of the kind" permitted by English law or "in a form known to and recognised by our law as capable of producing, when there performed, a valid marriage"? Was it a ceremony which "as a ceremony, would be sufficient to constitute a valid marriage"?[73] The parties' intentions are plainly relevant, especially where, as in *Hudson v Leigh*, the parties did not intend to create a valid marriage, or where they realised that for some reason they would not be able to do so[74]; but the parties' belief or intent that a ceremony would be valid cannot serve to convert something which would otherwise have been a "non-marriage" into a (void) marriage.[75]

CAPACITY TO MARRY

Capacity to marry (sometimes referred to as the essential validity of the marriage) concerns whether the parties to the marriage are legally able to contract a marriage, as opposed to *how* the marriage should be celebrated. Traditionally, this rubric includes the impediments of the prohibited degrees of consanguinity and affinity and lack of age; but there seems no reason for it not also to include the   **11–012**

---

[70] On the concept of "non-marriage" generally, see Probert (2013) 25 Ch.F.L.Q. 314.

[71] *Alfonso-Brown v Milwood* [2006] EWHC 642 (Fam.); [2007] 2 F.L.R. 265 (event in Ghana found to be an engagement ceremony); *Al-Saedy v Musawi* [2010] EWHC 3293 (Fam.); [2011] 2 F.L.R. 287 (family gathering in England; event denied by one party, described as a "religious agreement" by the other)

[72] [2009] EWHC 1306 (Fam.); [2009] 2 F.L.R. 1129.

[73] *A v A (Attorney General intervening)* [2012] EWHC 2219 (Fam.), [2013] Fam. 51.

[74] *Galloway v Goldstein* [2012] EWHC 60 (Fam.); [2012] Fam. 129, a ceremony which conformed to all the requirements of the Marriage Act a "non-marriage" as the parties had validly married one another in the USA and arranged the second, English, ceremony by false representations to the registrar knowing that it would have no legal effect.

[75] *El Gamal v Al-Maktoum* [2012] 2 F.L.R. 387 (Muslim ceremony in a private flat).

impediments of lack of parental consent, in so far as that is not treated as a mere formality; previous marriage; and physical incapacity: in short, all impediments to marriage, other than formal ones, which have already been considered, and lack of consent of parties, which is discussed later. This has the advantage of avoiding a multiplicity of categories: but it should be borne in mind that the social and policy reasons for the various impediments are not always the same, and that this may possibly justify the application of different conflict rules.

The rival theories

11–013   It is now well-established, though with a number of exceptions,[76] that capacity to marry is governed by the law of each party's antenuptial domicile: the "dual domicile" theory. In other words, a marriage is invalid if it fails to satisfy the requirements as to capacity in the law of the country or countries in which the parties are domiciled at the time of their marriage.

The courts still refer back to what has become a rather tired argument between rival views as to the rule which should govern capacity to marry.[77] The views are associated with two leading writers, Dicey and Cheshire. Dicey argued for what has become the established view, arguing that the community to which each party belongs is interested in his or her status. Cheshire argued that that the community to which the parties belong *after* their marriage is more interested in their status than the communities to which they belonged before. This led him to formulate a theory, virtually abandoned by recent editors of his book, known as the "intended matrimonial home" theory. If the parties at the time of the marriage intended to establish their home in a certain country and that they did in fact establish it there within a reasonable time, the law of that country would govern the issue of capacity. Very serious practical difficulties are likely to arise if the validity of a marriage has to remain in suspense while we wait and see (for an unspecified period) whether or not the parties implement their (unexpressed) intention to settle in another country; this is especially true if interests in property depend on the validity of a marriage, as, for instance, where a widow's pension ceases on her remarriage. To reduce this element of uncertainty, Cheshire's approach included a presumption that capacity to marry was to be governed by the law of the husband's domicile at the time of the marriage, a presumption rebuttable if the parties were shown to have acted on their intention to settle in a new country. The

---

[76] The exceptions all involve the application for certain purposes of English law: the application of the Royal Marriages Act 1772 (or, when it is brought into force, the Succession to the Crown Act 2013) to the marriages of certain members of the Royal Family; the probable additional application of English law to marriages in England of persons domiciled abroad (see para.11–006); an exception derived from *Sottomayor v De Barros (No.2)* (1879) 5 P.D. 94 (see para.11–015); cases in which a foreign incapacity is seen in the eyes of English law to be penal or discriminatory (see para.11–022); certain cases of re-marriage after a foreign divorce or nullity decree (see para.11–020); and certain cases in which a civil partnership is converted into a same-sex marriage (see para.11–026)

[77] For other views, see Hartley, (1972) 35 M.L.R. 571 (a marriage should be valid if it complies with the law of the domicile of either party); Jaffey, (1978) 41 M.L.R. 38 (different rules suggested for different impediments); Fentiman, [1985] C.L.J. 256 (the law with the most significant relationship to the spouses and the marriage). See also Murphy, (2000) 49 I.C.L.Q. 643 for a consideration of cultural factors.

selection of the husband's domicile, ignoring that of the wife, is a very old-fashioned one, not compatible with modern ideas of sex equality. It is true that an incapacity imposed by the law of the wife's antenuptial domicile would invalidate the marriage according to Dicey, but would not generally invalidate it according to Cheshire. So, as a general rule, rather more marriages would be valid under Cheshire's theory than under Dicey's; but this is not invariably the case.[78]

Both theories make use of the concept of domicile. As our earlier examination of the concept of domicile made clear, it does not always identify a country with which an individual has a continuing and close connection, the community to which he or she can be said to belong. Dicey and Cheshire were both writing before habitual residence began to feature prominently in conflicts rules. Habitual residence for a prescribed period might, in this as in some other contexts, be a better alternative to domicile; though the number of cases in which the validity of a marriage would actually be affected by any such change is almost certainly very small indeed.

The two main theories, together with a number of other possibilities, were fully canvassed by the Law Commission in its 1985 Working Paper; the arguments against the intended matrimonial home theory were adjudged "more cogent" than those in its favour,[79] and the Commission's provisional view was that the dual domicile test be adopted to govern all issues of legal capacity.[80] The ensuing consultations showed a substantial majority in favour of this view but, as we have seen, it was decided to take no legislative action.[81] The issue therefore remains a matter for the courts,[82] and it is to the case law that we must now turn. We shall see that (apart from physical incapacity) with one exception[83] the cases strongly support Dicey's view, and that the more recent ones[84] expressly approve it.

Consanguinity and affinity

The English domestic law background

In the nineteenth century, the prohibited degrees of consanguinity or affinity in English law were, as a general rule, stricter than those of neighbouring European **11–014**

---

[78] A case in point is *Schwebel v Ungar* (1964) 48 D.L.R. (2d) 644; below, para.11–021. There the validity of the marriage could only be sustained by an exclusive reference to the law of the wife's antenuptial domicile.

[79] Working Paper, para.3.35.

[80] Working Paper, para.3.36.

[81] *Choice of Law Rules in Marriage* (Law Com. No.165), para.2.6 (1987).

[82] Although an alternative reference test was rejected by the Law Commission's Working Paper No.89, para.3.37, Wall LJ expressed the view in *KC v City of Westminster Social and Community Services Dept* [2008] EWCA Civ 198; [2008] 2 F.C.R. 146, at para.90 that: "... departures from the dual domicile rule designed to uphold the principle of marriage may be appropriate when the marriage in question is one which, on grounds of public policy, the courts will think it right to uphold."

[83] *Sottomayor v De Barros (No.2)* (1879) 5 P.D. 94; below, para.11–021.

[84] *Padolecchia v Padolecchia* [1968] P. 314, 336; *R. v Brentwood Marriage Registrar* [1968] 2 Q.B. 956, 968; *Szechter v Szechter* [1971] P. 286, 295B. See however *Radwan v Radwan (No 2)* [1973] Fam. 35, discussed below, para.11–034.

countries. For example, in English law a man could not marry his deceased wife's sister, nor a woman her deceased husband's brother, while in many European countries such marriages were valid. Until Lord Lyndhurst's Marriage Act of 1835, a marriage within the prohibited degrees was only voidable and so was treated as valid unless the parties themselves chose to challenge its validity. After the 1835 Act such marriages were void, and if the marriage was void the children were illegitimate. If after the death of the parties a dispute arose as to succession rights, any claimant could assert that the marriage was void and so deny the children their expected inheritance. It therefore became the practice for English couples within the English prohibited degrees to marry during a temporary visit to some European country where the marriage was valid. Just as English couples in the eighteenth century managed to escape from the provisions of Lord Hardwicke's Marriage Act 1753 as to formalities by marrying in Scotland, so their successors hoped to escape from the rigours of Lord Lyndhurst's Marriage Act 1835 by marrying in a suitable European country.

This practice was brought to an abrupt halt by the decision of the House of Lords in *Brook v Brook*,[85] the facts of which have already been given.[86] That decision contributed to political pressure to relax domestic English law as to the prohibited degrees. Although no progress was made for almost 50 years, legislation has since effected repeated reforms.[87] The combined effect of these reforms was greatly to reduce the discrepancy between English law and the laws of neighbouring European countries, and thus to reduce the practical importance of the English conflict rules about to be discussed. However, these rules still have some importance because, for example, a marriage between uncle and niece is void by English law but valid by the laws of many other countries, while on the other hand a marriage between first cousins is valid in English law but invalid by the laws of some Catholic countries and in about half the States of the USA.

The conflict of laws

11–015   In *Brook v Brook*,[88] the House of Lords finally established that a distinction must be drawn between the formalities of marriage, governed by the law of the place of celebration, and capacity to marry, governed by the law of each party's antenuptial domicile. In that case both parties were domiciled in England. At about the same time it was held in *Mette v Mette*[89] that a marriage in Frankfurt

---

[85] (1861) 9 H.L.C. 193.
[86] Para 11–002.
[87] See the Deceased Wife's Sister's Marriage Act 1907; the Deceased Brother's Widow's Marriage Act 1921; the Marriage (Prohibited Degrees of Relationship) Act 1931 (a man and his deceased wife's niece or aunt, or between a woman and her deceased husband's nephew or uncle); the Marriage (Enabling) Act 1960 (a man and his divorced wife's sister, niece or aunt, or between a woman and her divorced husband's brother, nephew or uncle); the Marriage (Prohibited Degrees of Relationship) Act 1986 (certain marriages between step-parent and step-child); and, after a decision of the European Court of Human Rights in *B v United Kingdom* (2006) 42 E.H.R.R. 11; [2006] 1 F.L.R. 35, the Marriage Act 1949 (Remedial) Order 2007, SI 2007/438 (the marriage of a person to the parent of his former spouse and the marriage of a person to the former spouse of his child).
[88] (1861) 9 H.L.C. 193. cf. *Re De Wilton* [1900] 2 Ch. 481, to the same effect.
[89] (1859) 1 Sw. & Tr. 416. The ratio decidendi was "There can be no valid contract unless each was competent to contract with the other" (p.423).

between a man domiciled in England and a woman domiciled in Frankfurt was void because they were within the prohibited degrees of English law, although the marriage was valid by the law of Frankfurt. It was subsequently held in *Re Paine*[90] that a marriage in Germany between a man domiciled in Germany and a woman domiciled in England was void because they were within the prohibited degrees of English law, although the marriage was valid by the law of Germany.

In *Sottomayor v De Barros (No.1)*,[91] two first cousins supposedly domiciled in Portugal married in England. The marriage was valid by English law, but invalid by the law of Portugal, under which first cousins could not marry without papal dispensation. The parties were very young—the boy was aged 16 and the girl 14½. The marriage was one of convenience only, arranged for them by their parents; and though they lived together in the same house in England for six years, the marriage was never consummated. The girl then petitioned for a decree of nullity on the ground of consanguinity. The suit was undefended, but the Queen's Proctor intervened and alleged[92] (inter alia) that the parties were domiciled in England and not in Portugal; that they intended at the time of the marriage to live together in England and did so live for six years; and that the validity of the marriage was to be determined by English domestic law. What proved to be an inconvenient course was taken of ordering that the question of law should be argued before the questions of fact. On the assumption, then, that the parties were both domiciled in Portugal at the time of the marriage, the Court of Appeal held that the marriage was void, because "as in other contracts, so in that of marriage, personal capacity must depend on the law of the domicile".[93] This seems a clear decision against the law of the intended matrimonial home.

The case was then remitted to the Divorce Division for the questions of fact to be determined. When it appeared that the husband's domicile at the time of the marriage was not in Portugal but in England, Sir James Hannen P pronounced the marriage valid[94] in reliance on a dictum in the judgment of the Court of Appeal that "Our opinion on this appeal is confined to the case where both the contracting parties are, at the time of their marriage, domiciled in a country the laws of which prohibit their marriage".[95] The judgment of Hannen P seems to be based on the theory that capacity to marry is governed by the law of the place of celebration, which is, to put it mildly, difficult to reconcile with *Brook v Brook* and *Sottomayor v De Barros (No.1)*.

There is obvious difficulty in reconciling this decision with the other cases, and especially with *Mette v Mette*[96] and *Re Paine*.[97] Of the various attempts at reconciliation, the most significant are (a) that an incapacity imposed by English law is more important than an incapacity imposed by foreign law; and (b) that an incapacity imposed by the law of the husband's domicile is more important than

---

[90] [1940] Ch. 46. It is perhaps unfortunate that Cheshire's book (first published in 1935) was not cited to the court in this case.

[91] (1877) 3 P.D. 1.

[92] See the report of the case in the court below: 2 P.D. 81, 82.

[93] (1877) 3 P.D. 1, 5.

[94] *Sottomayor v De Barros (No.2)* (1879) 5 P.D. 94.

[95] (1877) 3 P.D. 1, 6–7.

[96] (1859) 1 Sw. & Tr. 416.

[97] [1940] Ch. 46.

an incapacity imposed by the law of the wife's domicile. Neither of these is satisfactory. Dicey found it necessary to make an exception to his general rule that capacity to marry is governed by the law of each party's antenuptial domicile, which exception he formulated as follows:

> "The validity of a marriage celebrated in England between persons of whom the one has an English, and the other a foreign, domicile is not affected by any incapacity which, though existing under the law of such foreign domicile, does not exist under the law of England".[98]

This exception is admittedly illogical, though it can be said to have a practical advantage in that it reduces the risk of a void marriage due to the ignorance of the provisions of the relevant foreign law by officiating clergy or registrars. The exception has been approved by the Court of Appeal,[99] and until *Sottomayor v De Barros (No.2)* is overruled, it must be taken to represent the law. But, as we shall see,[100] its scope is reduced by the Marriage (Enabling) Act 1960.

If the marriage is celebrated abroad and is valid by the law of each party's domicile, it will be held valid in England though the parties were within the prohibited degrees of English law.[101] At any rate this is true if the parties are not so closely related that intercourse between them would be incestuous by English criminal law.[102] On this ground, marriages celebrated in Italy between a woman and her deceased husband's brother,[103] and in Egypt between an uncle and niece,[104] have been held valid, even though the parties were within the prohibited degrees of English law.

Section 1 of the Marriage (Enabling) Act 1960 permits a marriage between a man and his former wife's sister, aunt or niece, or between a woman and her former husband's brother, uncle or nephew. Section 1(3) of the Act provides that the section does not validate a marriage if either party is at the time of the marriage domiciled in a country under whose law there cannot be a valid marriage between the parties. Hence the section implicitly accepts Dicey's view on capacity to marry and rejects that of Cheshire. The reference to "either party" means that neither Cheshire's intended matrimonial home theory nor Dicey's exception based on *Sottomayor v De Barros (No.2)*[105] can apply to any marriage mentioned in s.1, if one party was domiciled in England at the time of the marriage.

Relevance of the law of the place of celebration

11–016   Must the parties have capacity to marry by the law of the place of celebration as well as by the laws of their antenuptial domiciles? There is singularly little authority on this question. On principle it would seem that if the marriage is

---

[98]   See now Dicey, Morris & Collins, *The Conflict of Laws*, 15th edn (London: Sweet and Maxwell, 2012), exception 4 to Rule 72.

[99]   *Ogden v Ogden* [1908] P. 46, 74–77.

[100]   Below.

[101]   *Re Bozzellis Settlement* [1902] 1 Ch. 751; *Cheni v Cheni* [1965] P. 85.

[102]   *Cheni v Cheni* [1965] P. 85, 97.

[103]   *Re Bozzellis Settlement* [1902] 1 Ch. 751.

[104]   *Cheni v Cheni* [1965] P. 85.

[105]   (1879) 5 P.D. 94. See North (1980) I *Recueil des Cours* 57–65.

celebrated in England, the answer must be yes, because the English court could hardly disregard its own law on such a vital matter and hold valid a marriage which that law prohibited, even if it was valid by the law of the parties' domicile.[106] If the marriage is celebrated abroad, the question is more difficult.[107] There is no English authority,[108] but there is one early Australian case and one modern Canadian case, in each of which the marriage was held valid, despite the lack of capacity by the law of the place of celebration. In *Will of Swan*,[109] it was held that a will had been revoked by the testator's marriage in Scotland to his deceased wife's niece. The marriage was void by Scots law, but voidable in his lifetime by the Victorian law of his domicile, since Lord Lyndhurst's Marriage Act 1835 had not then been adopted in Victoria. Similarly, in *Reed v Reed*,[110] two first cousins domiciled in British Columbia wished to marry. The girl, who was aged 18, was unable to obtain the consent of her parents as required by the law of British Columbia. So the parties were married in the state of Washington, where such consent was not required. But unknown to them, first cousins were incapable of marriage by the law of Washington, though they were capable by the law of British Columbia. The marriage was held valid.

Lack of age

Section 2 of the Marriage Act 1949 (re-enacting the Age of Marriage Act 1929) provides that a marriage between persons either of whom is under the age of 16 is void. In other systems, the minimum age for marriage may be higher or lower. There is only one reported English case in which the law governing this impediment has been considered. In *Pugh v Pugh*,[111] a marriage was celebrated in Austria between a British officer domiciled in England but stationed in Austria, and a girl of 15 domiciled in Hungary. Four years later the parties came to England in accordance with their antenuptial intention, but parted almost at once. The marriage was valid by Austrian and Hungarian law, but it was held void. It therefore appears that no marriage is valid if either party is under 16, if either party (not necessarily the party under age) is domiciled in England. The law is different in Scotland, where s.1(1) of the Marriage (Scotland) Act 1977 provides that "no person domiciled in Scotland may marry before he attains the age of 16."

11–017

---

[106] In Scotland, there is a statutory rule that the law of Scotland prevails in such a case; see Family Law (Scotland) Act 2006 s.38(3).

[107] The Law Commission examined this matter in its Working Paper No.89 (1985), paras 3.40–3.44; after receiving divided views in response, the Commission's view was that the law of the place of celebration, where it was not the forum, should be ignored: Law Com. No.165, para.2.6 (1987).

[108] But see *Breen v Breen* [1964] P. 144, where, in the different context of bigamy, Karminski J was prepared to hold that incapacity by the law of the place of celebration was fatal to the validity of a marriage.

[109] (1871) 2 V.R. (I.E. & M.) 47.

[110] (1969) 6 D.L.R. (3d) 617.

[111] [1951] P. 482, cited, without disapproval, in *Re X (Children) (Parental Order)* [2008] EWHC 3030 (Fam.); [2009] Fam. 71. cf. *Mohamed v Knott* [1969] 1 Q.B. 1, where the girl was only 13, but the marriage was held valid because it was valid by the law of each party's antenuptial domicile. The Domicile and Matrimonial Proceedings Act 1973 s.3(1), assumes that parties may be validly married under foreign law below the age of 16: see above, para.3–026.

The court in *Pugh v Pugh* relied on *Brook v Brook*[112] and on the other cases on the prohibited degrees which have already been considered: this seems sufficient justification for treating lack of age as coming under capacity to marry.

It is thought that a marriage celebrated in England will be held void if one party was under sixteen, regardless of the domicile of the parties: and there is a dictum to this effect in *Pugh v Pugh*.[113] This is, indeed, the case in Scotland, where s.1(2) of the Marriage (Scotland) Act 1977 states that "A marriage solemnised in Scotland between persons either of whom is under the age of 16 shall be void".

Lack of parental consent

11–018   As we have seen, English courts seem committed to the view that lack of parental consent, whether imposed by English or by foreign law, and no matter how stringently the requirement is expressed, is a mere formality and therefore incapable of invalidating a marriage celebrated in England. In *Ogden v Ogden*,[114] however, the facts of which have already been stated, this was not the only ground of the decision. Other grounds were (a) that capacity to marry is governed by the law of the place of celebration and not by the law of the parties' domicile[115]; and (b) that a marriage celebrated in England between a person domiciled in England and a person domiciled abroad is not invalidated by any incapacity which, though existing under the foreign law, does not exist in English law.[116] The first of these grounds is manifestly inconsistent with the decisions of the House of Lords in *Brook v Brook*[117] and of the Court of Appeal in *Sottomayor v De Barros (No.1)*.[118] The second reflects the illogical exception to the general rule on capacity to marry which was introduced by *Sottomayor v De Barros (No.2)*.[119]

These two additional grounds leave open the possibility that a foreign requirement of parental consent may one day be characterised as relating to capacity to marry and not to the formalities of marriage.

The decision in *Ogden v Ogden* can be defended on policy grounds. It is a strong thing to hold that a marriage, celebrated in England and valid by English law, is invalid because of its failure to comply with foreign law. Of course the decision left the woman in an unfortunate position, and for this reason it has been described as "grotesque from the social point of view."[120] But it was really

---

[112] (1861) 9 H.L.C. 193.
[113] [1951] P. 482, 491–492. The possible scope of the English statute is discussed by Beckett, (1934) 15 B.Y.I.L. 46, 64–65, and Morris, (1946) 62 L.Q.R. 170–171.
[114] [1908] P. 46.
[115] At pp.58–62.
[116] At pp.75–77.
[117] (1861) 9 H.L.C. 193.
[118] (1877) 3 P.D. 1.
[119] (1879) 5 P.D. 94.
[120] Falconbridge, *Selected Essays on the Conflict of Laws*, 2nd edn (Toronto: Canada Law Book, 1954), p.74.

fortuitous that she had remarried: the decision might not have seemed so grotesque if she had been seeking to uphold the marriage, e.g. by claiming maintenance from her French husband.

Previous marriage

It is submitted with some confidence that this impediment may properly be included under the heading of capacity to marry. There is high authority for placing it under this rubric[121]; nor does it seem an abuse of language to say that a monogamously married man or woman has no capacity to contract a second marriage until the first is dissolved.   **11–019**

If this is correct, the authority of the House of Lords may be cited for the proposition that capacity to marry is governed by the law of each party's antenuptial domicile and not by the law of the husband's domicile or that of the intended matrimonial home. In *Shaw v Gould*,[122] a man and a woman, both domiciled in England, married there and separated soon afterwards. The marriage was dissolved by the Court of Session in Scotland, and the woman then married a domiciled Scotsman and lived with him in Scotland. The divorce was not recognised in England because the first husband never lost his English domicile of origin. The House of Lords held that the second marriage was void, although it was valid by the law of the second husband's domicile and by the law of the intended matrimonial home. Lord Cranworth said: "If the first marriage here was not dissolved there could not have been a second marriage. Till the first was dissolved there was no capacity to contract a second."[123] It is submitted that this type of case demonstrates the impossibility of accepting any other view than that capacity to marry is governed by the law of each party's antenuptial domicile.

Again, in *Padolecchia v Padolecchia*[124] a man domiciled in Italy was divorced from his first wife in Mexico. This divorce was not recognised in Italy. He went to live in Denmark and, during a one-day visit to England, went through a ceremony of marriage with a woman domiciled in Denmark. They both returned to Denmark to live, and later the man (still domiciled in Italy) petitioned the English court for a decree of nullity on the ground of his own bigamy. Sir Jocelyn Simon P held that since the Mexican divorce was not recognised in Italy, the man had no capacity to marry by the law of his domicile; and he expressly approved the Rule in Dicey and Morris's treatise stating the dual domicile test.[125] He declined to consider the possibility that the marriage might be valid by the law of the intended matrimonial home. This decision is thus a strong authority in favour of the orthodox view.

Three situations need to be discussed in greater detail. The first is where the remarriage of a person whose marriage has been validly dissolved or annulled has

---

[121] See, e.g., *Conway v Beazley* (1831) 3 Hagg. Ecc. 639, 647, 652, per Dr. Lushington; *Brook v Brook* (1861) 9 H.L.C. 193, 211–212, per Lord Campbell; *Shaw v Gould* (1868) L.R. 3 H.L. 55, 71, per Lord Cranworth; *Padolecchia v Padolecchia* [1968] P. 314, 336, per Sir Jocelyn Simon P.; *Wicken v Wicken* [1999] Fam. 224.

[122] (1868) L.R. 3 H.L. 55.

[123] At p.71.

[124] [1968] P. 314.

[125] At p.336.

been held invalid. The second is where the remarriage has been held valid notwithstanding an invalid decree of divorce. The third is where the law of the country where a divorce was granted imposes some restriction on the right of a divorced person to remarry.

Remarriage after valid foreign divorce or nullity decree

11–020 It was at one time clear, but inconvenient, law that a person whose divorce decree in State A was entitled to recognition in England might be unable to remarry here if the law of his or her domicile, State B, refused recognition to the same decree[126]; in effect, the choice of law rules as to capacity to marry prevailed over those on the recognition of foreign decrees.[127] That particular type of case was dealt with by legislation in 1971,[128] in a provision limited to foreign divorces (as opposed to nullity decrees[129]) and to remarriage in England (and not elsewhere[130]).

The matter is now governed by s.50 of the Family Law Act 1986.[131] Where a divorce or annulment is granted, or is entitled to recognition, in any part of the UK, the fact that it may not be recognised elsewhere does not preclude either party to the marriage from forming a subsequent marriage or civil partnership in that part of the UK or cause the subsequent marriage or civil partnership of either party (wherever it takes place) to be treated as invalid in that part.

Remarriage after void foreign divorce

11–021 The converse situation arose in the Canadian case of *Schwebel v Ungar*.[132] A husband and wife, both Jews, were domiciled in Hungary. They decided to emigrate to Israel. While en route to Israel they were divorced by a Jewish ghet (or extra-judicial divorce) in Italy. They then separately acquired domiciles of choice in Israel. The wife married a man domiciled in Ontario during a temporary visit to that province. The ghet was ineffective to dissolve the marriage by the law of Hungary (where they were domiciled at the time of the ghet) but was effective to do so by the law of Israel (where they were domiciled at the time of the remarriage). It was not recognised as a valid divorce in Ontario, since the parties were not domiciled in Israel when it was delivered. Nevertheless, the remarriage was held valid, because immediately prior to the remarriage the wife's status by the law of her domicile was that of a single woman.

---

[126] *R. v Brentford Marriage Registrar* [1968] 2 Q.B. 956.
[127] This is an example of the "incidental question'; see para.20–010.
[128] Recognition of Divorces and Legal Separations Act 1971 s.7 (since repealed).
[129] See *Perrini v Perrini* [1979] Fam. 84.
[130] See *Lawrence v Lawrence* [1985] Fam. 134.
[131] As amended by the Civil Partnership Act 2004 Sch. 27 para.125.
[132] (1963) 42 D.L.R. (2d) 622 (Ontario Court of Appeal); (1964) 48 D.L.R. (2d) 644 (Supreme Court of Canada); discussed by Lysyk (1965) 43 Can. Bar Rev. 363; approved by Simon P in *Padolecchia v Padolecchia* [1968] P. 314, 339. The case is another example of the incidental question: see below, para.20–010.

Restrictions on the remarriage of divorced persons

Such restrictions are imposed for three main reasons: first, to punish the 'guilty party'; second, to safeguard the unsuccessful party's right to appeal; and third, to prevent disputes about the paternity of children subsequently born to the woman.[133]

11–022

In *Scott v Attorney General*,[134] a husband obtained a divorce in Cape Colony, where he was domiciled, on the ground of his wife's adultery. By the law of the Cape, a person divorced for adultery was prohibited from remarrying so long as the injured party remained unmarried. After the divorce the wife came to England and married the co-respondent, who was domiciled in England. It was held that her remarriage was valid, because after the divorce she was a single woman and therefore free to acquire an English domicile separate from that of her first husband. But in the later case of *Warter v Warter*,[135] the same judge (Sir James Hannen P) explained *Scott v Attorney General* on the different ground that the prohibition on remarriage attached only to the guilty party and could therefore be disregarded in England because it was penal, i.e. discriminatory. The implication is that the remarriage in England would have been held valid even if the wife had remained domiciled in Cape Colony.

In *Warter v Warter*, a husband, domiciled in England but resident in India, divorced his wife in India for adultery.[136] She married in England a man domiciled in England less than six months after the decree absolute. Section 57 of the Indian Divorce Act 1869 provided that it should be lawful for the parties to remarry when six months from the date of the decree absolute had expired and no appeal had been presented, but not sooner. It was held that the remarriage was invalid.

The result of these two cases appears to be that if the restriction on remarriage imposed by the foreign law is an integral part of the proceedings by which alone both parties can be released from their incapacity to contract a fresh marriage, it will receive effect in England; but if the restriction on remarriage is imposed on one party only, it will be disregarded as penal.

Physical incapacity

In English domestic law, a marriage (other than one between persons of the same sex[137]) is voidable if one of the parties is incapable of consummating it,[138] or if it has not been consummated owing to the wilful refusal of the respondent to

11–023

---

[133] See Hartley, (1967) 16 I.C.L.Q. 680, 694–699. As to the third reason, see *Lundgren v O'Brien (No.2)* [1921] V.L.R. 361.

[134] (1886) 11 P.D. 128.

[135] (1890) 15 P.D. 152, 155. The decision in *Warter v Warter* was followed in *Miller v Teale* (1954) 92 C.L.R. 406 (High Court of Australia) and *Hellens v Densmore* (1957) 10 D.L.R. (2d) 561 (Supreme Court of Canada), but distinguished in *Buckle v Buckle* [1956] P. 181.

[136] At that time it was supposed that the Indian courts had jurisdiction to grant divorces to persons domiciled in England and resident in India.

[137] Matrimonial Causes Act 1973 s.12(2) inserted by the Marriage (Same Sex Couples) Act 2013 Sch.4, para.4.

[138] Matrimonial Causes Act 1973 s.12(1)(a) (a rule of great antiquity).

consummate it.[139] Wilful refusal is more likely than impotence to produce problems in the conflict of laws, because impotence renders a marriage invalid nearly everywhere, whereas wilful refusal is sometimes a ground for nullity, as in England, sometimes a ground for divorce, as in Canada, and is sometimes not an independent ground for relief at all, as in Scotland and Australia.

English courts have always applied English domestic law when deciding whether to grant divorces. Until 1947, it was assumed that the same applied to the annulment of marriages on the grounds of impotence and wilful refusal: and it may well be that this is still the law. For example, in two cases decided in 1944,[140] marriages were annulled on the ground of the wife's wilful refusal to consummate, although in each case the husband was domiciled abroad and there was no evidence that by the law of his domicile this was a ground for annulment. In neither case was foreign law pleaded.

In 1947, in *Robert v Robert*,[141] the possible application of foreign law to this question was considered for the first time. The marriage was celebrated in Guernsey, between parties domiciled there; and Barnard J held that the question as to whether it should be annulled for wilful refusal to consummate must be decided by the law of Guernsey, either because "wilful refusal to consummate a marriage . . . must be considered as a defect in marriage, an error in the quality of the respondent" (a matter for the law of the place of celebration)[142] or else because a question of capacity was involved, with the result that the law of the parties' domicile must be applied in accordance with the decision in *Sottomayor v De Barros (No.1)*.[143] But *Robert v Robert* is not a very impressive authority for the application of foreign law: not only did the law of the place of celebration and the law of the parties' domicile coincide, but also no difference was shown to exist between the law of Guernsey and the law of England. Moreover, *Robert v Robert* was overruled in *De Reneville v De Reneville*[144] on the question of jurisdiction, although it was not expressly dissented from on the question of choice of law.[145]

In *Ponticelli v Ponticelli*,[146] Sachs J held that English law, which was the *lex fori* and the law of the husband's domicile, and not Italian law, which was the law of the place of celebration and the law of the wife's antenuptial domicile, determined the question of wilful refusal to consummate. Had it been necessary to choose between the law of the husband's domicile and the *lex fori*, he would have preferred the former.

---

[139] ibid., s.12(b). This was first made a ground for nullity by s.7 of the Matrimonial Causes Act 1937.
[140] *Easterbrook v Easterbrook* [1944] P. 10; *Hutter v Hutter* [1944] P. 95.
[141] [1947] P. 164.
[142] At pp.167–168. There is some difficulty in accepting Barnard J's view that wilful refusal as a ground for nullity depends upon error, for there is no requirement in s.13(3) of the Matrimonial Causes Act 1973 or its predecessors that the petitioner was at the time of the marriage ignorant of the facts alleged. Moreover, as we shall see (below, para.11–028) the effect of mistake is not a matter for the law of the place of celebration.
[143] (1877) 3 P.D. 1; above, para.11–015.
[144] [1948] P. 100, 118.
[145] Much the same can be said of the Northern Ireland case of *Addison v Addison* [1955] N.Ir. 1, 30, overruled on the jurisdictional issue in *Ross Smith v Ross Smith* [1963] A.C. 280, 307, 312, 348.
[146] [1958] P. 204, following *Way v Way* [1950] P. 71 (below, para.11–028), and not following *Robert v Robert* [1947] P. 164, above.

On the other hand, in *Ross Smith v Ross Smith*[147] the House of Lords held that the English court had no jurisdiction to annul a marriage for wilful refusal to consummate merely because it had been celebrated in England. Lord Reid and Lord Morris[148] both gave as one of their reasons for declining jurisdiction the undesirability of granting relief on grounds unknown to the law of the parties' domicile. This could be taken to imply that, had jurisdiction been held to exist, the *lex fori* would have been applied.[149]

In this confusing state of the authorities, it is very much an open question as to what law governs impotence and wilful refusal. It has been plausibly suggested[150] that the applicable law should be the law of the petitioner's domicile at the date of the marriage, on the ground that if the petitioner has no ground of complaint under his or her personal law, he or she ought not to be granted a decree. Certainly it seems that reliance on the law of the husband's domicile as such cannot survive s.1 of the Domicile and Matrimonial Proceedings Act 1973 which as we have seen, provides that a wife can have a domicile different from that of her husband.

There is however no reported case in which the court has applied a foreign law which differed from English domestic law. So far as wilful refusal is concerned, the whole problem would admit of a simple and rational solution if wilful refusal were dealt with in the context of divorce rather than nullity. It is hard to justify the existence of wilful refusal as a ground for nullity, because it is necessarily a post-matrimonial matter.

Although a decree annulling a voidable marriage formerly declared the marriage to be and to have been absolutely void to all intents and purposes, nevertheless it seems that if the *lex fori* is applicable, it must be applied as it is at the date of the trial, and not as it was at the date of the marriage. For marriages have been annulled for wilful refusal to consummate even though they were celebrated before 1938,[151] when this first became a ground for annulment in English law.

Same-sex marriages and civil partnerships

English law now provides for same-sex couples two forms of legal relationship, civil partnership and marriage.   **11–024**

Civil partnerships

The Civil Partnership Act 2004 provides for the registration of civil partnerships   **11–025**
by same-sex partners over the age of 16 who are not already married or a party to

---

[147] [1963] A.C. 280.

[148] At p.306 and pp.313, 322 respectively.

[149] In *Magnier v Magnier* (1968) 112 S.J. 233, a marriage was annulled for wilful refusal without reference to the law of the husband's domicile: but foreign law was not pleaded.

[150] Bishop, (1978) 41 M.L.R. 512.

[151] *Cowen v Cowen* [1946] P. 36, overruled in *Baxter v Baxter* [1948] A.C. 274, but not on this point: see at p.282; *Dredge v Dredge* [1947] 1 All E.R. 29; but in none of these cases was the point argued. None of them had anything to do with the conflict of laws. cf. *De Reneville v De Reneville* [1948] P. 100, where the marriage was celebrated in 1935.

a civil partnership, who are not within the prohibited degrees of relationship,[152] and who have both resided in England for at least seven days before giving notice of their intended registration.[153]

The 2004 Act provides for recognition in England and Wales of "overseas relationships" registered outside the UK between persons of the same sex,[154] either as "specified relationships" (a defined list of partnerships listed in Sch.20)[155] or under the "general conditions".[156] The general conditions are that, under the law of the country of registration including its conflict of laws rules,[157] the parties are not already in such a relationship or married, the relationship is of indeterminate duration, and the parties are treated as a couple for general or specified purposes or treated as married.

As is the case with marriage, there are conflict rules as to the law governing formalities and capacity.[158] The formalities are those of the place of registration, a rule corresponding to that applying to marriages. The capacity of the parties to enter the partnership[159] is governed, not by the antenuptial domicile of the parties as in the case of marriage, but by the law of the country of registration. That latter rule is qualified in two ways. The reference to the law of the place of registration includes its conflict rules, which may well refer to the law of the domicile or nationality of the parties. In a case in which one party is domiciled in England at the time of registration, neither party must be under the age of 16 or within the prohibited degrees of affinity.[160] If all these criteria are fulfilled, the relationship will be recognised subject to an exception that it would be manifestly contrary to public policy to recognise one or both parties' capacity under the relevant law to enter into such a relationship.[161]

How a civil partnership registered in England will be regarded in another country depends on the law of that country. For example, in *Hincks v Gallardo*[162] the Ontario Court of Appeal held that a civil partnership registered in England was a "marriage" for the purposes of the Civil Marriage Act and the Divorce Act of Canada.

Same-sex marriage

11–026   Until the law was changed by the Marriage (Same Sex Couples) Act 2013, a marriage between persons of the same sex was impossible in the eyes of English law. Any purported same-sex marriage was void, though after 2004 certain marriages in a country the law of which permitted same-sex marriage would be

---

[152] Section 3(1). Parental consent is required for persons under the age of 18, s.4. The prohibited degrees are defined in Sch.1, para.1.

[153] Section 8(1)(b). Provision is made for the registration of a civil partnership at a British Consulate overseas (s.210) and for armed forces personnel serving abroad (s.211).

[154] Section 216(1).

[155] Section 213.

[156] Section 214.

[157] Section 54(10).

[158] Section 215.

[159] And presumably any issue as to consent, not specifically mentioned in the legislation.

[160] Section 217(2).

[161] Section 218. The provisions contained in s.54(7) and (8) deal with void and voidable partnerships.

[162] (2014) 120 OR (3d) 721.

recognised in England as civil partnerships.[163] The 2013 Act extended marriage to same-sex couples. It is now the case that in the law of England, marriage has the same effect in relation to same sex couples as it has in relation to opposite sex couples, and English law (including all legislation including that enacted before the date of the 2013 Act[164]) has effect accordingly.[165]

Under the Marriage (Same Sex Couples) Act 2013, the parties to civil partnerships registered in England (and certain civil partnerships registered at British consulates or by armed forces personnel) may convert the civil partnership into a marriage.[166] In the case of a civil partnership registered in England, there is no requirement that the parties should have capacity under the law of their domiciles. It is therefore possible for a civil partnership to be converted into a valid marriage despite the fact that at the date of the registration of the partnership (which is the date from which the marriage will be treated as having subsisted)[167] the parties lacked capacity to marry under the law of their domiciles.

Transsexual cases

Under the Gender Recognition Act 2004 a person born into one gender may acquire the opposite gender.[168] The grant of a full gender recognition certificate means that the person's gender becomes for all purposes the acquired gender.[169] It appears that there is no requirement for an applicant for a certificate to be domiciled, habitually resident, resident or a national of the UK, but certain conditions in the Act, such as the reports required from registered medical practitioners, may make it practically necessary to have at least a limited residential connection with a part of the UK. If a person's gender is changed under the law of an "approved country" outside the UK,[170] a full gender recognition certificate may be obtained in the UK,[171] but until such a certificate is obtained the foreign gender change has no effect in the UK.[172] Two questions

11–027

---

[163] See *Wilkinson v Kitzinger (No.2)* [2006] EWHC 2022 (Fam); [2007] 1 F.L.R. 295

[164] Sch.3 to the 2013 Act sets out detailed rules as to the effect on the interpretation of legislation.

[165] Marriage (Same Sex Couples) Act 2013 s.11(1)(2); this is subject to certain qualifications and to any contrary provision made by statutory instrument. See the Marriage (Same Sex Couples) Act 2013 (Consequential and Contrary Provisions and Scotland) Order 2014, SI 2014/560: in addition to listing a number of specific enactments, the Order provides that s.11(1) and (2) do not apply to EU instruments nor to the common law rights to the titles of Queen Consort or Princess of Wales or to any peerage. A same-sex marriage in England will be treated in Northern Ireland as a civil partnership: s.10(3) and Sch.2, para.2.

[166] Section 9 and see the Marriage of Same Sex Couples (Conversion of Civil Partnership) Regulations 2014, SI 2014/3181.

[167] Civil Partnership Act 2004 s.9(6)(b).

[168] The Act was passed following judgments of the European Court of Human Rights in *Goodwin v United Kingdom* (2002) 35 E.H.R.R. 18 and of the House of Lords in *Bellinger v Bellinger* [2003] UKHL 21; [2003] 2 A.C. 467.

[169] Section 9; but the grant of the certificate does not affect things done, or events occurring, before the certificate is issued: s.9(2).

[170] For the list of approved countries, see SI 2011/1630.

[171] Sections 1(1)(b), 2(2), 3(5).

[172] Section 21(1).

arise: the effect of a legally-recognised change of gender on (a) capacity to enter a marriage, and (b) an existing marriage.

A person to whom a full gender recognition certificate has been issued is free to marry in the acquired gender. Before the Marriage (Same Sex Couples) Act 2013, this was the only way in which such a person could marry someone of his or her original gender. The Act not only removed that limitation but also means that a marriage abroad after a foreign gender change but before the grant in the UK of a full gender recognition certificate will be recognised in England as valid, despite the fact that under the law of the foreign country the relevant party will be regarded as marrying in the acquired gender and in England as doing so in the original gender.

The change of gender by a party to an existing marriage may prompt the other party to seek to end the marriage.[173] The grant of an interim gender recognition certificate to one party to the marriage renders the marriage voidable. If both parties wish the marriage to continue despite the change in gender and there is evidence of this in the form of a statutory declaration, a full gender recognition certificate may be issued and the marriage continues unaffected by the change of gender. This applies equally to marriages celebrated abroad.[174]

CONSENT OF THE PARTIES

11–028 Marriage is a voluntary union; there can be no valid marriage unless each party consents to marry the other. The question of consent is often a question of fact, but sometimes it may be a question of law. Of course the laws of foreign countries may differ widely from English law, on for instance, the effect of fraud; the distinction between mistake as to the identity of the other party and mistake as to attributes, or between mistake as to the nature of the ceremony and mistake as to its effects; and whether duress or fear must emanate from the other party or can be extraneous.

In English law it was formerly a disputed question as to whether lack of consent rendered a marriage void or voidable. The question is set at rest (insofar as marriages taking place after 31 July 1971, are concerned) by s.12(c) of the Matrimonial Causes Act 1973, which provides that a marriage shall be voidable if either party did not consent to it, whether in consequence of duress, mistake, unsoundness of mind or otherwise. In addition to these common law instances of lack of consent, there are three situations where by statute a marriage is voidable on this ground. The first is where, at the time of the marriage, either party, though capable of giving a valid consent, was suffering from mental disorder within the meaning of the Mental Health Act 1983 of such a kind or to such an extent as to be unfit for marriage.[175] The second is where the respondent was at the time of

---

[173] In certain circumstances, a party to a marriage discovering that the other party had changed gender before the marriage may have the marriage annulled: Matrimonial Causes Act 1973 s.12(1)(h) as inserted by Gender Recognition Act 2004 Sch.4, para.5.

[174] See the changes to the Gender Recognition Act 2004 made by Sch.5 to the Marriage (Same Sex Couples) Act 2013.

[175] Matrimonial Causes Act 1973 s.12(d). See, for example, *KC v City of Westminster Social and Community Services Dept* [2008] EWCA Civ 198; [2008] 2 F.C.R. 146.

the marriage suffering from venereal disease in a communicable form. The third is where the respondent was at the time of the marriage pregnant by some person other than the petitioner.[176] In the second and third cases it is provided that the court shall not grant a decree of nullity unless it is satisfied that the petitioner was at the time of the marriage ignorant of the facts alleged[177] and this is why they are properly characterised as instances of lack of consent. They are cases of mistake as to the attributes of the other party—a kind of mistake which was inoperative at common law.

The issue of forced marriages, whereby an adult female or a child is taken abroad without their consent for the purposes of marriage,[178] is now the subject of pre-emptive legislation rather than purely being subject to the remedy of nullity under the Matrimonial Causes Act s.12(c). Part 4A of the Family Law Act 1996, as inserted by the Forced Marriage (Civil Protection) Act 2007 gives jurisdiction to the High Court or a county court to make a forced marriage protection order.[179] The order may contain any prohibitions, restrictions or requirements necessary to either prevent the marriage taking place or to protect the victim of a forced marriage, and the terms of an order may relate to conduct outside England and Wales. The protection orders may be made in any family proceedings including the High Court's inherent jurisdiction.[180]

There are a few reported cases which suggest, but do not conclusively answer, the question of what system of law governs the requirement of consent. In *Apt v Apt*,[181] where it was held that the validity of proxy marriages was a question of formalities, the Court of Appeal drew a distinction between the method of giving consent and the fact of consent. This observation enabled Hodson J in *Way v Way*[182] to hold that "questions of consent are to be dealt with by reference to the personal law of the parties rather than by reference to the law of the place where the contract was made." But this case is not a clear-cut authority because no difference was shown to exist between English law (which was the law of the husband's domicile) and Russian law (which was the law of the wife's domicile and also the law of the place of celebration). It was followed in *Szechter v Szechter*,[183] where a Polish professor divorced his wife and married his secretary in order to rescue her from prison and enable her to escape to the West; and Sir Jocelyn Simon P applied Polish law as the law of each party's antenuptial domicile. But this case also is not a clear-cut authority because the law of the parties' domicile and the law of the place of celebration coincided, and because, before pronouncing a decree, the learned President held that the marriage was also invalid by English domestic law.

---

[176] Section 12(e) and (f).
[177] Matrimonial Causes Act 1973 s.13(3).
[178] See, generally, Gaffney-Rhys [2008] I.F.L. 26.
[179] A forced marriage is one that has been entered into without the person's free and full consent, Family Law Act s.64A(4).
[180] Family Law Act 1996 s.63C.
[181] [1948] P. 83, 88.
[182] [1950] P. 71, 78. His judgment was reversed by the Court of Appeal, *sub nom Kenward v Kenward* [1951] P. 124, but not on this point. Sir Raymond Evershed MR at p.133 was prepared to assume that Hodson J's view on the law governing consent was correct.
[183] [1971] P. 286.

On the other hand, the law of the place of celebration was applied in *Parojcic v Parojcic*[184]; but the decision would have been the same if the law of each party's antenuptial domicile had been applied, because they had lost their Yugoslav domicile of origin and acquired an English domicile of choice before their marriage in England. More recently, Singer J in *Alfonso-Brown v Milwood*[185] seems to have applied the law of the placement of celebration, Ghanaian customary law, to the question of consent to enter into a marriage instead of what the respondent understood to be an engagement; however, the legal point as to what law governed the giving of consent was not discussed. Moreover, it so happens that in all the reported cases,[186] English domestic law has been applied, either alone or cumulatively with the law of the domicile as in *Szechter v Szechter*,[187] even where the marriage was celebrated abroad and both parties were domiciled abroad at the time of their marriage.[188] However, this may have been because there was no evidence, or insufficient evidence, of the foreign law.

It cannot be said, therefore, that the question is finally settled in England. But it is submitted that the best rule is that no marriage is valid if by the law of either party's domicile he or she does not consent to marry the other. This approach was adopted in the instructive Canadian case of *Grewal v Kaur*.[189] In that case, H was domiciled in Ontario, W in India; it was found that W, unknown to H, married only to obtain immigration status in Canada; was H's consent vitiated by W's fraud? Van Rensburg J held that the issue of the consent of the parties was governed by the dual domicile rule; he rejected the alternative of the law of the intended matrimonial home. Taking the approach that reference should be made exclusively to the law of the domicile of the party whose consent was in issue, he applied the law of Ontario. By that law it was not vitiated, and the marriage was therefore valid; a divorce was granted on other grounds.

It may be that the rule in *Sottomayor v De Barros (No.2)*[190] applies to consent of parties as it applies to capacity to marry.[191]

---

[184] [1958] 1 W.L.R. 1280; criticised by Webb, (1959) 22 M.L.R. 198.

[185] [2006] EWHC 642 (Fam); [2006] 2 F.L.R. 265 at para.53.

[186] See, in addition to the cases cited above, *Cooper v Crane* [1891] P. 369; *Valier v Valier* (1925) 133 L.T. 830; *Hussein v Hussein* [1938] P. 159 (in each of which the marriage was celebrated in England); and *Mehta v Mehta* [1945] 2 All E.R. 690; *Silver v Silver* [1955] 2 All E.R. 614; *Kassim v Kassim* [1962] P. 224 (in each of which the marriage was celebrated abroad). See also *Di Mento v Visalli* [1973] 2 N.S.W.L.R. 199 (a dramatic tale of the sacrifice of a young girl on the altar of family pride, calculated to bring tears to the eyes; its jurisprudential qualities are less marked).

[187] [1971] P. 286.

[188] *H. v H.* [1954] P. 258, discussed by Woodhouse, (1954) 3 I.C.L.Q. 454; *Buckland v Buckland* [1968] P. 296.

[189] [2011] O.J. No 1413 (Ont. Superior Ct).

[190] (1879) 5 P.D. 94; above, para.11–015.

[191] *Vervaeke v Smith* [1981] Fam. 77. The House of Lords made no comment on this proposition: [1983] 1 A.C. 145.

POLYGAMOUS MARRIAGES

Even if the marriage complies with the law of the place of celebration as regards formalities and with the law of each party's antenuptial domicile as regards capacity to marry and consent of the parties, it will, for certain limited purposes only, not be regarded as a valid marriage in England if it is polygamous. Some systems of law, especially those following Islamic principles, allow a man to have several wives; fewer systems allow a woman more than one husband.[192] The importance of this topic is now much reduced because the former hostility of English law[193] to polygamous marriages has largely disappeared.

11–029

It is not often that an undefended divorce case becomes a leading case, not only in England but wherever the common law prevails: but such has been the fate of *Hyde v Hyde*.[194]

> The petitioner was an Englishman by birth, and in 1847, when he was about 16 years old, he joined a congregation of the Church of Jesus Christ of Latter Day Saints (the Mormons) in London. In London he met the respondent and her family, all of whom were Mormons, and became engaged to her. In 1850, the respondent emigrated to Salt Lake City, in the Territory of Utah, in the United States, and in 1853 the petitioner joined her there. They were married in 1853, the marriage being celebrated by Brigham Young, the president of the Mormon church, and governor of the territory. They lived together in Utah until 1856, when the petitioner went on a mission to the Sandwich Islands (now called Hawaii), leaving the respondent in Utah. On his arrival in the islands, he renounced the Mormon faith and preached against it. A sentence of excommunication was pronounced against him in Utah in December 1856 and his wife was declared free to marry again, which she did in 1859 or 1860. In 1857 the petitioner resumed his domicile in England, where he became the minister of a dissenting chapel at Derby. He petitioned for divorce on the ground of his wife's adultery.

Lord Penzance refused to adjudicate on the petition on the ground that "marriage, as understood in Christendom, may for this purpose be defined as the voluntary union for life of one man and one woman to the exclusion of all others,"[195] and that this Mormon marriage was no marriage which the English Divorce Court could recognise, because there was evidence that polygamy was a part of the Mormon doctrine, and was the common custom in Utah. "It is obvious," he said, "that the matrimonial law of this country is adapted to the Christian marriage, and is wholly inapplicable to polygamy".[196] He pointed out that to divorce a husband at the suit of his first wife on the ground of his bigamy and adultery with the second, or to annul the second marriage on the ground that it was bigamous, would be "creating conjugal duties, not enforcing them, and furnishing remedies when there was no offence."[197]

---

[192] The former is technically polygyny, the latter polyandry. The history can be traced in the voluminous literature. See Fitzpatrick, (1900) 2 Jo.Comp.Leg. (2nd series) 359; Beckett, (1932) 48 L.Q.R. 341; Morris, (1953) 66.

[193] Harv.L.Rev. 961; Sinclair, (1954) 31 B.Y.I.L. 248; Mendes da Costa, (1966) 44 Can. Bar Rev. 293; Hartley, (1969) 32 M.L.R. 155; Poulter, (1976) 25 I.C.L.Q. 475; Jaffey, (1978) 41 M.L.R. 38; Shah, (2003) 52 I.C.L.Q. 369.

[194] (1866) L.R. 1 P. & M. 130.

[195] At p.133.

[196] At p.135. cf. *Baindail v Baindail* [1946] P. 122, 125, per Lord Greene MR. This could be regarded as the first example of a "non-marriage"; see para.11–001.

[197] At pp 135, 136–137.

At the end of his judgment Lord Penzance made the following important reservation[198]:

> "This court does not profess to decide upon the rights of succession or legitimacy which it might be proper to accord to the issue of polygamous unions, or upon the rights or obligations in relation to third persons which people living under the sanction of such unions may have created for themselves. All that is intended to be here decided is that as between each other they are not entitled to the remedies, the adjudication, or the relief of the matrimonial law of England".

What is a polygamous marriage?

11–030 In the modern law, we have to distinguish between three different questions:

(a) Is the marriage in question monogamous or polygamous?
(b) If it is polygamous, is it a valid marriage?
(c) What effect is to be given in England to a valid polygamous marriage?

Is the marriage monogamous or polygamous?

Marriages in England

11–031 English domestic law makes no provision for polygamous marriages, and it follows that a marriage celebrated in England can only be monogamous.[199] Hence, if a Muslim domiciled, e.g., in Kuwait, goes through a ceremony of marriage in an English register office, he contracts a monogamous marriage. If a civil ceremony in an English register office is followed by a religious ceremony in Islamic form, the religious ceremony does not supersede or invalidate the prior civil ceremony and is not registered as a marriage in any marriage register book.[200] The only marriage is that created by the register office ceremony, necessarily monogamous. If there is a combined religious and civil ceremony in a Muslim mosque registered under s.41 of the Marriage Act 1949, the resulting marriage will again be monogamous. A "marriage" celebrated in England in accordance with polygamous forms and without any civil ceremony as required by English law is simply invalid, and that is true whatever the domicile of the parties.[201]

---

[198] At p.138.
[199] *Chetti v Chetti* [1909] P. 67; *R. v Hammersmith Marriage Registrar* [1917] 1 K.B. 634; *Srini Vasan v Srini Vasan* [1946] P. 67; *Baindail v Baindail* [1946] P. 122; *Maher v Maher* [1951] P. 342; *Ohochuku v Ohochuku* [1960] 1 W.L.R. 183; *Russ v Russ* [1964] P. 315; *Qureshi v Qureshi* [1972] Fam. 173.
[200] Marriage Act 1949 s.46(2) as amended by Marriage Act 1983.
[201] However, in *A-M v A-M* [2001] 2 F.L.R. 6, the wife was entitled to the benefit of a presumption of marriage based on a long cohabitation coupled with a reputation of marriage, even where the original ceremony had taken place in polygamous Islamic form. Hughes J found that there was no evidence to rebut the presumption that the parties had subsequently contracted a valid polygamous marriage in an Islamic country at a time when they were domiciled in Islamic countries. The contortions involved in this case underline the difficulties and discrimination in this area of law; see Shah, (2002) 52 I.C.L.Q. 369.

Marriages elsewhere

In considering whether a marriage elsewhere is monogamous or polygamous, the **11–032** first reference is to the effect of the ceremony according to the law of the place of celebration. If that law regards the marriage as monogamous, that is an end to the matter. Or, to adopt a more sophisticated statement, it is for the law of the place of celebration to determine the nature and incidents of the union and then for English law to decide whether the union is a monogamous or polygamous marriage.[202] Adopting this approach, Japanese marriages[203] have been treated as monogamous, and so has a composite ceremony at Singapore in mixed Chinese and Jewish form.[204] If a country has provision for both polygamous and monogamous marriages, as was formerly the case in India, the parties' choice of form of ceremony will determine the nature of the marriage. The question which has to be asked is "What are the terms under which the parties enter into the marriage? Is it to the exclusion of other marriage partners or not?" If the husband may take other wives, the marriage is potentially polygamous even if the husband intends never to take further wives and never in fact does so.[205] (The marriage in *Hyde v Hyde* was not actually but only potentially polygamous because the petitioner never married more than one wife.)

If the marriage is prima facie polygamous, it is necessary to take into account the personal law of the parties. That this is the case was established in the important case of *Hussain v Hussain* in 1983.[206] This involved a marriage in Pakistan, the law of which permitted polygamy, between two Muslims, a man domiciled in England and a woman domiciled in Pakistan. It was argued that this must be a polygamous marriage, and so void under s.11(d) of the Matrimonial Causes Act 1973 which, as it then stood, provided that an actually or potentially polygamous marriage entered into outside England after July 31, 1971 by a person domiciled in England was void. The Court of Appeal recognised that the acceptance of this argument would have repercussions for the Muslim community in this country which would be "widespread and profound", since many Muslim men domiciled in England return to the country of their birth to find a bride. It therefore held that a marriage is not potentially polygamous, even though celebrated in polygamous form, if neither spouse can under his or her personal law take another spouse during the subsistence of the marriage. In the instant case, the man could not lawfully take another wife under English law and the woman could not lawfully take another husband under the law of Pakistan. Had the woman been domiciled in England and the man in Pakistan, the decision would have been different, for then by the law of his domicile the man could take further wives.

It is important to understand what *Hussain v Hussain* did and did not decide. It did not change (indeed it proceeded on the basis of) the position that someone

---

[202] *Lee v Lau* [1967] P. 14.

[203] *Brinkley v Attorney General* (1890) 15 P.D. 76.

[204] *Penhas v Tan Soo Eng* [1953] A.C. 304.

[205] *Hyde v Hyde* (1866) L.R. 1 P. & M. 130; *Sowa v Sowa* [1961] P. 70. If the husband is not allowed to take more than one wife, but may have concubines, a marriage celebrated under such a law is polygamous, at any rate if concubinage is a status recognised by that law: *Lee v Lau* [1967] P. 14.

[206] [1983] Fam. 26. See Schuz, (1983) 46 M.L.R. 653.

domiciled in England could not enter a polygamous marriage. It did decide that in the circumstances identified in the judgment, the marriage was a *monogamous* marriage, notwithstanding the law of the place of celebration; and this meant that the marriage did not fall within s.11(d) which applied only to actually or potentially polygamous marriages. This ingenuity was, however, accompanied by an element of injustice: it operated to the benefit of Muslim men domiciled in England but not of Muslim women so domiciled. Legislation was plainly necessary to eliminate this discrimination.

Sections 5 to 8 of the Private International Law (Miscellaneous Provisions) Act 1995 are the result, based on the recommendations of the Law Commission in a report published ten years earlier.[207] Section 5(1) provides that:

> "A marriage entered into outside England and Wales between persons neither of whom is already married is not void under English law on the ground that it was entered into under a law which permits polygamy and that either party is domiciled in England and Wales".

Section 11 of the Matrimonial Causes Act 1973 was amended[208] so that it now provides that, for the purpose of s.11(d), a marriage is not polygamous if, at its inception, neither party has any spouse additional to the other.

The result of these new provisions is that where the man or the woman is, or both parties are, domiciled in England, a marriage which would otherwise be potentially (as opposed to actually) polygamous is treated as a monogamous marriage.

Change in the nature of the marriage

11–033   It was at one time supposed that the monogamous or polygamous character of the marriage had to be determined once and for all at its inception.[209] But now it is clear that a potentially polygamous marriage may become monogamous by reason of subsequent events. This may happen if, for instance, the parties (being domiciled in a country the law of which has both polygamous and monogamous marriages) change their religion from one which permits polygamy to one which does not[210]; or if the husband changes his domicile from a country whose law permits polygamy to a country (such as England) whose law does not[211]; or if the law under which the marriage is celebrated subsequently prohibits polygamy[212]; or (under some systems of law) if a child is born.[213] It was originally thought that a polygamous marriage could become a monogamous marriage if the parties, having gone through a polygamous ceremony in a country whose law permits polygamy, subsequently went through a monogamous ceremony in England.[214]

---

[207] *Capacity to Contract a Polygamous Marriage and Related Issues* (Law Com. No.146).

[208] Private International Law (Miscellaneous Provisions) Act 1995 Sch.1, para.2(2).

[209] *Hyde v Hyde* (1866) L.R. 1 P. & M. 130; *Mehta v Mehta* [1945] 2 All E.R. 690.

[210] *The Sinha Peerage Claim* (1939) 171 Lords' Journals 350; [1946] 1 All E.R. 348n., as explained in *Cheni v Cheni* [1965] P. 85, 90–91, and in *Parkasho v Singh* [1968] P. 233, 243, 253.

[211] *Ali v Ali* [1968] P. 564; *R. v Sagoo* [1975] Q.B. 885. It is otherwise if the wife changes her domicile: *Onobrauche v Onobrauche* (1978) 122 S.J. 210.

[212] *Parkasho v Singh* [1968] P. 233; *R. v Sagoo* [1975] Q.B. 885.

[213] *Cheni v Cheni* [1965] P. 85.

[214] *Ohochuku v Ohochuku* [1960] 1 W.L.R. 183.

However, in 1968[215] it was pointed out that if the polygamous marriage was valid, it is difficult to see how the registrar succeeded in marrying the parties again in England; and in *Mark v Mark*[216] the Court of Appeal assumed this not to be so; per Thorpe J: "Given that the prior polygamous marriage was recognised in this jurisdiction as a valid marriage, the . . . [Register] Office ceremony was a nullity".[217]

In all these cases of conversion, the marriage was only potentially polygamous; but there seems no reason for the principle not to be equally effective in converting an actually polygamous marriage into a monogamous one, after the number of wives has been reduced to one by death or divorce.

There is no English authority on the converse problem, namely, when does a monogamous marriage become polygamous.[218] The answer may be that the marriage has, so to speak, the benefit of the doubt: if it is monogamous at its inception, it remains monogamous although a change of religion or of domicile may entitle the husband to take another wife; if it is polygamous at its inception, it may become monogamous by reason of a change of religion, of domicile, or of law before the happening of the events which give rise to the proceedings.[219] Since a marriage celebrated in England between parties whose personal law permits polygamy is a monogamous marriage, it is difficult to see how a change of religion or of domicile could convert such a marriage into a polygamous one.

Is the marriage, though polygamous, a valid marriage?

Whether a marriage is monogamous or polygamous in form, it will be a valid marriage only if the usual rules are satisfied as to the formal requirements of the law of the place of celebration and those as to the capacity and consent of the parties. Capacity to marry is, as we have seen,[220] governed by the law of each party's antenuptial domicile. Hence it seems to follow that a man or woman whose personal law does not permit polygamy has no capacity to contract a valid polygamous marriage.[221] This was an essential assumption in *Hussain v Hussain*.[222]

Some doubt was created by the surprising decision of Cumming-Bruce J in *Radwan v Radwan (No.2)* where the law of the intended matrimonial home was

11–034

---

[215] *Ali v Ali* [1968] P. 564, 578.

[216] [2004] EWCA Civ 168.

[217] ibid., at para.7.

[218] The case of *Attorney General of Ceylon v Reid* [1965] A.C. 720 was concerned solely with the law of Ceylon (now Sri Lanka); and in *Nabi v Heaton* [1983] 1 W.L.R. 626 the Court of Appeal presumed a second polygamous marriage to be valid without discussing the position of the first monogamous marriage, and Vinelott J at first instance declined to express an opinion [1981] 1 W.L.R. 1052.

[219] See Simon P in *Cheni v Cheni* [1965] P. 85, 90.

[220] Above, para.11–012.

[221] *Re Bethell* (1887) 38 Ch.D. 220; *Risk v Risk* [1951] P. 50; *Ali v Ali* [1968] P. 564; *Crowe v Kader* [1968] W.A.R. 122; *contra*, *Kenward v Kenward* [1951] P. 124, 145, per Denning LJ; *Radwan v Radwan (No.2)* [1973] Fam. 35. "Personal law" is preferred to "domicile" because in many eastern countries the personal law is often a religious law. Hence a domiciled Englishman or Englishwoman who acquired a domicile of choice in, e.g., India, Pakistan or Sri Lanka could not contract a valid polygamous marriage without a change of religion.

[222] [1983] Fam. 26.

applied to govern the capacity of a woman domiciled in England and so uphold an actually polygamous marriage between her a man domiciled in Egypt at the Egyptian Consulate-General in Paris. The decision was the subject of heavy criticism by academic commentators,[223] and it is submitted that it was wrongly decided. It is inconsistent with the tenor of the argument in the later Court of Appeal case of *Hussain v Hussain* and with the repeated references to domicile in the relevant provisions of the Private International Law (Miscellaneous Provisions) Act 1995

Domicile in England

11–035 The effect of the Private International Law (Miscellaneous Provisions) Act 1995 is, as we have seen, that a person domiciled in England has capacity to enter a marriage under a law that permits polygamy if, but only if, neither party is already married. The fact of domicile in England cannot render it void on any ground relating to polygamy; though of course the marriage might be held void on some other basis such as age or affinity. An actually, as opposed to a potentially polygamous marriage entered into by a person domiciled in England will be void.

Domicile abroad

11–036 The relevant provisions of the Private International Law (Miscellaneous Provisions) Act 1995 do not affect the determination of the validity of a marriage by reference to the law of another country (i.e., other than England) to the extent that it falls to be determined under the rules of private international law. If neither party is domiciled in England, the law of each party's antenuptial domicile determines their capacity to enter the marriage. So, if a man and a woman both domiciled in Pakistan marry there, the marriage will be a valid polygamous marriage. If they are, or one party is, domiciled in a country the domestic law of which has no provision allowing polygamy, the validity of their marriage in polygamous form in Pakistan will depend on whether the law of that country regards them as having capacity to enter that marriage.[224] In the Canadian case of *Azam v Jan*[225] the court, having determined that it would no longer follow the decision in *Hyde v Hyde* that there could be no jurisdiction over a polygamous marriage, applied the dual domicile test and as the husband was found to have a domicile in Alberta the law of which did not allow its domiciliaries to marry polygamously, his second and actually polygamous marriage in Pakistan was void.

---

[223] Karsten, (1973) 36 M.L.R. 291; Pearl, [1973] C.L.J. 43; Wade, (1973) 22 I.C.L.Q. 571. It was defended by Jaffey, (1978) 41 M.L.R. 38.
[224] Private International Law (Miscellaneous Provisions) Act 1995 s.5(2).
[225] (2013) 362 DLR (4th) 111 (Alta).

Effect of valid polygamous marriages in England

We come now to the important question: to what extent will English law **11–037** recognise a valid polygamous marriage? It must be borne in mind that we are dealing with marriages that are both polygamous and valid, e.g. a marriage celebrated in Pakistan between Muslims domiciled there.

The present law can be summarised by saying that a polygamous marriage will be recognised in England as a valid marriage, even if it is actually polygamous, unless there is some strong reason to the contrary.[226] In spite of Lord Penzance's emphatic statement in *Hyde v Hyde*[227] that his decision was limited to the question of matrimonial relief, there was for many years a tendency to assume that all polygamous marriages were wholly unrecognised by English law. However, since 1939[228] it has become clear that they are recognised for many purposes. We shall now consider some typical situations.

Whether a bar to a subsequent monogamous marriage

A valid polygamous marriage will be recognised to the extent that it constitutes a **11–038** bar to a subsequent monogamous marriage in England, and so entitles the second "wife" (or the husband) to a decree of nullity on the ground of bigamy.[229] Otherwise the husband would be validly married to his first wife in the country where he married her and to his second wife in England—a situation that would encourage rather than discourage polygamy.

Matrimonial proceedings

The rule in *Hyde v Hyde*,[230] that the parties to a polygamous marriage were not **11–039** entitled to the remedies, the adjudication, or the relief of the matrimonial law of England, was abolished (on the recommendation of the Law Commission)[231] by s.1 of the Matrimonial Proceedings (Polygamous Marriages) Act 1972, now re-enacted as s.47 of the Matrimonial Causes Act 1973, which provides that English courts are not precluded from granting matrimonial relief or making a declaration concerning the validity of a marriage by reason only that the marriage was entered into under a law that permits polygamy. This applies whether the marriage is potentially or actually polygamous; in the latter case, rules of court may require notice of the proceedings to be served on any other spouse, and may give him or her the right to be heard.[232]

---

[226] See Winn J in *Shahnaz v Rizwan* [1965] 1 Q.B. 390, 397 and Lord Parker CJ in *Mohamed v Knott* [1969] 1 Q.B. 1, 13–14.

[227] (1866) L.R. 1 P. & M. 130, 138; quoted above, para.11–029.

[228] *The Sinha Peerage Claim* (1939) 171 Lords' Journals 350; [1946] 1 All E.R. 348n., is usually considered to mark the turning point.

[229] *Srini Vasan v Srini Vasan* [1946] P. 67; *Baindail v Baindail* [1946] P. 122; *Hashmi v Hashmi* [1972] Fam. 36; see Hartley, (1969) 16 I.C.L.Q. 680, 691–694.

[230] (1866) L.R. 1 P. & M. 130.

[231] See Law Com. No.42 (1971).

[232] s.47(4), (as substituted by Private International Law (Miscellaneous Provisions) Act 1995 Sch.1, para.2(3)(b). See the Family Proceedings Rules, Practice Direction 7C (Polygamous Marriages).

"Matrimonial relief" is widely defined[233] so as to include decrees of divorce, nullity of marriage, judicial separation, presumption of death and dissolution of marriage, divorce and separation orders under the Matrimonial Causes Act 1973, and orders for financial provision under s.27 of the 1973 Act, the variation of maintenance agreements, ancillary relief, and orders under Pt I of the Domestic Proceedings and Magistrates' Courts Act 1978. A "declaration concerning the validity of a marriage" is defined[234] to mean any declaration under Pt III of the Family Law Act 1986[235] involving a determination as to the validity of a marriage.

This enactment does not mean that a polygamously married wife could obtain a divorce on the ground of her husband's adultery with another wife, because adultery involves sexual intercourse with a person other than one's spouse. Since ex hypothesi both the marriages are valid and the other wife is a "spouse", the husband cannot commit adultery with her.[236] Nor does it mean that a later wife could get a decree of nullity on the ground of bigamy, because her marriage is ex hypothesi valid.

Criminal law: bigamy

11–040 The question whether a valid polygamous marriage is a sufficient first marriage to support an indictment for bigamy was expressly left open in *Baindail v Baindail*.[237] It has subsequently been held not to be sufficient.[238] However, there seems no reason why a polygamously married man should not be convicted of perjury under s.3 of the Perjury Act 1911 if he obtained a certificate for an English marriage ceremony by falsely stating that he was an unmarried man and that he knew of no impediment to his marriage. (The maximum penalty for this offence is the same as that for bigamy.) It is one thing for a polygamist to marry two wives, and quite another thing for him to pose as an unmarried man.

Legitimacy of and succession by children

11–041 "It cannot, I think, be doubted now", said Lord Maugham, delivering the opinion of the Committee of Privileges of the House of Lords in *The Sinha Peerage Claim*,[239] "(notwithstanding some earlier *dicta* by eminent judges[240]) that a Hindu marriage between persons domiciled in India[241] is recognised by our courts, that

---

[233] 1973 Act s.47(2).
[234] 1973 Act s.47(3).
[235] Below, para.12–007.
[236] *Onobrauche v Onobrauche* (1978) 122 S.J. 210.
[237] [1946] P. 122 at p.130.
[238] *R. v Sarwan Singh* [1962] 3 All E.R. 612 (a decision of Quarter Sessions). This case was overruled in *R. v Sagoo* [1975] Q.B. 885, but only on the ground that the marriage had become monogamous under the principles stated above, para.11–033. The principle of the decision was not doubted.
[239] (1939) 171 Lords' Journals 350; [1946] 1 All E.R. 348n. cf. *Baindail v Baindail* [1946] P. 122, 127, per Lord Greene MR.
[240] The reference is apparently to the decision of Stirling J in *Re Bethell* (1887) 38 Ch.D. 220, which is usually explained away on the ground that the husband was domiciled in England and therefore lacked capacity to contract a valid polygamous marriage.
[241] The Hindu Marriage Act 1955 abolished polygamy among Hindus in India.

the issue are legitimate, and that such issue can succeed to property in this country, with a possible exception which will be referred to later." Provided the marriages are valid by the law of the place of celebration and by the personal law of the parties, it is immaterial that the husband married more than one wife or that the succession is governed by English law. Thus, in *Bamgbose v Daniel*,[242] children of no fewer than nine polygamous marriages celebrated in Nigeria between persons there domiciled were held entitled to succeed to their father's property on his death intestate, although by a Nigerian Marriage Ordinance of 1884 the property was distributable in accordance with the English Statute of Distribution 1670. Similarly, each of the seven (or possibly eight) wives of a husband dying intestate domiciled in Ghana was held in *Official Solicitor v Yemoh*[243] to be a 'spouse' for the purposes of the Administration of Estates Act 1925. The "possible exception" referred to by Lord Maugham in *The Sinha Peerage Claim* is the right to succeed as heir to real estate in England (which after 1925 is restricted to succession to entailed property and one or two other exceptional cases[244]). This exception was considered necessary because it was thought that difficulties might arise if there was a contest between the first-born son of the second wife and the later-born son of the first wife, each claiming to be the heir.

Succession by wives

It seems that the surviving wife of a polygamous marriage could succeed to the husband's property on his death intestate, whether he married one wife or several, and whether he died domiciled in a country whose law permits polygamy or in England. In *Coleman v Shang*[245] the widow of a potentially polygamous marriage celebrated in Ghana between parties domiciled there was held entitled to a grant of letters of administration to the husband's estate on his death intestate, although by a Ghana Marriage Ordinance of 1884 two-thirds of the property was distributable in accordance with the English Statute of Distribution 1670. Therefore, the word "wife" in that statute (and presumably the word "spouse" in the Administration of Estates Act 1925) is wide enough to cover the wife of a polygamous marriage, at any rate if there is only one.

11–042

In *Re Sehota*,[246] one of two surviving widows of a polygamous marriage was held to be a "wife" within the meaning of s.1(1)(a) of the Inheritance (Provision for Family and Dependants) Act 1975 and as such entitled to apply for financial provision under that Act. Moreover, the Privy Council has, without apparent difficulty, adopted the practice, in dealing with the estates of deceased Chinese who died domiciled in Malaysia, of assigning the one-third share of the widow under the Statute of Distribution equally between the several widows.[247] And

---

[242] [1955] A.C. 107.
[243] [2010] EWHC 3727 (Ch); [2011] 1 W.L.R. 1450.
[244] Law of Property Act 1925 s.131, (as amended by Trusts of Land and Appointment of Trustees Act 1996 Sch.3, para.4(14)); s.132; Administration of Estates Act 1925 s.51(2).
[245] [1961] A.C. 481; cf. *Baindail v Baindail* [1946] P. 122, 127, per Lord Greene MR.
[246] [1978] 1 W.L.R. 1506.
[247] *Cheang Thye Phin v Tan Ah Loy* [1920] A.C. 369; cf. *The Six Widows Case* (1908) 12 Straits Settlements L.R. 120.

there is Canadian and Zimbabwe authority for the proposition that gifts by will to a surviving wife attract succession duty at the lower rate applicable to a spouse, even if there is more than one wife.[248]

Social security legislation

11–043 The legislation governing social security benefits and allowances and tax credits deals expressly with the rights of those who have married under a law which allows polygamy. Many Acts contain regulation-making powers and the regulations provide that a polygamous marriage is to be treated as having the same consequences as a monogamous marriage for any day, but only for any day, throughout which it is in fact monogamous.

Miscellaneous cases

11–044 The Divisional Court has recognised a potentially polygamous marriage celebrated in Nigeria between a man and a girl of thirteen domiciled there, and revoked a "fit person" order made in respect of the girl (on the basis that she was "exposed to moral danger") under the Children and Young Persons Act 1933.[249] The Privy Council has held that a husband and wife whose marriage is potentially polygamous cannot be guilty of a criminal conspiracy.[250] The wife of a potentially polygamous marriage has been allowed to assert a contractual claim against her husband for "deferred dower" under a marriage contract governed by Muslim law.[251] There is American authority for the proposition that the surviving spouse of a valid polygamous marriage can recover workmen's compensation for the death of her husband in an accident arising in the course of his employment.[252] If this case is followed in England, it would mean that the surviving spouse of a valid polygamous marriage would rank as a dependant under the Fatal Accidents Act 1976 (as amended) and could recover damages for the tortiously-inflicted death of her husband. In the law of immigration, the word "wife" includes each of two or more wives for the purposes of deportation,[253] and there are severe limitations on the extent to which a polygamous wife may exercise a right of abode in the UK if another wife of the same husband is already in the UK.[254] The summary remedy provided by s.17 of the Married Women's Property Act 1882 (as amended) applies to the spouses of a valid polygamous marriage.[255] Part IV of the Family Law Act 1996 (Family Homes and Domestic Violence) applies as between parties to a polygamous marriage.[256] A man who

---

[248] *Yew v Attorney General for British Columbia* [1924] 1 D.L.R. 1166; *Estate Mehta v Acting Master*, 1958 (4) S.A. 252. In the latter case there was only one wife, but reliance on this fact was expressly disclaimed (at p.262).

[249] *Mohamed v Knott* [1969] 1 Q.B. 1.

[250] *Mawji v The Queen* [1957] A.C. 126.

[251] *Shahnaz v Rizwan* [1965] 1 Q.B. 390; *Qureshi v Qureshi* [1972] Fam. 173.

[252] *Royal v Cudahy Packing Co*, 195 Iowa 759, 190 N.W. 427 (1922).

[253] Immigration Act 1971 s.5(4).

[254] Immigration Act 1988 s.2.

[255] *Chaudhry v Chaudhry* [1976] Fam. 148.

[256] Section 63(5); a similar rule applied under the predecessor Matrimonial Homes Act 1983.

maintains his wife under a polygamous marriage is entitled to a deduction of tax under ss.257A and 257AB of the Income and Corporation Taxes Act 1988, even if there is more than one wife.[257]

Thus, a great deal of water has flowed under the bridge since 1866, when Lord Penzance denied matrimonial relief to the unfortunate Mr Hyde. It is now clear that English law does recognise valid polygamous marriages unless there is some strong reason to the contrary. The previous pages have shown that this reason has to be very strong indeed before recognition will be denied.

---

[257] *Nabi v Heaton* [1981] 1 W.L.R. 1052; appeal allowed by consent [1983] 1 W.L.R. 626.

CHAPTER 12

ENDING MARRIAGES

Not every marriage succeeds; one or both parties may decide to end the **12–001** relationship. Legal systems have to recognise and respond to that, though the responses are remarkably varied.

Some legal systems treat the ending of a marriage as entirely a matter for the parties, though there may be some requirement of registration to ensure that the State's civil status records are updated. In some systems of Islamic law, the ending of a marriage is entirely a matter for one party, the husband, who can divorce his wife by uttering a prescribed form of words.[1] Other States seek to control or limit the circumstances in which a marriage may be ended: an application may have to be made, by one or both parties, for a court order or decree, which may only be granted on proof of certain facts; or there may be a waiting period in which the parties are required to use the services of a mediator.

The process of ending a marriage will commonly lead to a divorce, a dissolution of the legal relationship created by the marriage. There are other possibilities. In many systems, some defect in the marriage may lead to its annulment. The parties are free thereafter to regard themselves for most purposes as never having been married; though pragmatism may triumph over strict logic in that the law may continue to recognise some legal consequences of the annulled marriage, for example by regarding any children as legitimate. Again many systems provide for the case in which parties to a marriage decide to live apart permanently without actually obtaining a divorce: the parties may obtain a judicial or legal separation (confusingly referred to in the older cases as divorce *a mensa et thoro* (from bed and board)) in which issues as their property rights and the future of any children may be resolved.

Those issues, as to financial matters and as to the children of the marriage, are often the most difficult aspects of marital breakdown. There is material in the two following chapters relevant to those issues. Here we are concerned with the conflict of laws aspects of the court procedures and alternative processes for ending the marriage. Where court proceedings are involved they are often referred to as matrimonial causes, a term which also includes proceedings for proceedings for the presumption of death and dissolution of marriage, or for a declaration as to status.

---

[1] The *talak* divorce, discussed below.

JURISDICTION

12–002 Before 1858 jurisdiction in England over matrimonial causes (except divorce) was vested in the ecclesiastical courts. Their jurisdiction depended on the residence of the respondent within the relevant diocese. They had no power to dissolve a marriage; that could only be done by private Act of Parliament. In 1857 the Matrimonial Causes Act introduced judicial divorce and transferred the matrimonial jurisdiction to the secular courts.

The Act contained no rules as to jurisdiction in divorce. After a long period of uncertainty, the Privy Council held in *Le Mesurier v Le Mesurier*[2] that the only court which had jurisdiction to dissolve a marriage was the court of the common domicile of the parties. As the domicile of the wife during marriage was at common law the same as that of her husband, an Englishwoman whose husband had, or acquired, a foreign domicile would not have access to the divorce jurisdiction of the English courts. Legislation in 1937 and 1949[3] mitigated this hardship, but substantial reform came only with the reform of the law of domicile to allow married women an independent domicile.

The Domicile and Matrimonial Proceedings Act 1973 created a new set of jurisdictional principles applying to divorce and (with slight modifications) to other matrimonial causes.[4] The English court had jurisdiction if either party was domiciled in England on the date on which proceedings were instituted or had been habitually resident in England for at least 12 months on that date. These rules applied until the coming into force of a European Regulation on 1 March 2001.[5] That Regulation was later revised, though with no changes of substance so far as matrimonial matters were concerned.

The governing rules

12–003 Jurisdiction in respect of most matrimonial causes is now governed by Council Regulation No.2201/2003[6] (commonly known as the Brussels IIa Regulation) which came into force on 1 March 2005.[7] The Regulation contains a set of rules applicable in all Member States except Denmark but allows national law to apply in certain cases. It provides a uniform set of jurisdictional rules and almost

---

[2] [1895] A.C. 517, 540.

[3] Matrimonial Causes Act 1937 s.13 (deserted wives whose husbands had been domiciled in England) and Law Reform (Miscellaneous Provisions) Act 1949 s.1 (wives ordinarily resident for three years in England).

[4] For the background to this Act, see Law Com. No.48 (1972).

[5] Council Regulation No.1347/2000 of 29 May 2000 on jurisdiction and the recognition and enforcement of judgments in matrimonial matters and in matters of parental responsibility for children of both spouses, referred to as the "Brussels II Regulation". For text see [2000] O.J. L160/19. The Regulation was based on a draft Convention, agreed in 1998 but never brought into force.

[6] Council Regulation No.2201/2003 of 27 November 2003 concerning jurisdiction and the recognition and enforcement of judgments in matrimonial matters and the matters of parental responsibility, repealing Regulation No.1347/2000. For text see [2003] O.J. L 338/1.

[7] See generally McEleavy, (2004) 53 I.C.L.Q. 605; Boele-Woelki and González Beilfuss (eds.), *Brussels IIbis: Its impact and application in the Member States* (Antwerp: European Family Law Series No.14, Intersentia). For a critique of the original Brussels II Convention and ensuing Regulation see: Karsten, [1998] I.F.L. 75; and Mostyn, [2001] Fam. Law 359.

automatic recognition of matrimonial judgments throughout the EU. It applies, whatever the nature of the court or tribunal, in civil matters relating to divorce, legal separation or marriage annulment as long as the matter is not excluded by art.1(3).[8] As Recital (8) makes clear, the Regulation applies "only to the dissolution of matrimonial ties and should not deal with issues such as the grounds for divorce, property consequences of the marriage or any other ancillary measure". It is treated in English law as applicable only to marriages between a man and a woman.[9]

Grounds of jurisdiction The Regulation bases jurisdiction primarily on habitual residence, deploying this connecting factor in a variety of ways, but also preserves jurisdiction based, so far as the UK and Ireland are concerned, on the common domicile of the parties—the traditional rule established in *Le Mesurier v Le Mesurier*,[10] and for other Member States on the common nationality of the parties—a feature of the traditional approach of many civil law States.

Article 3 of the Regulation contains a list of grounds on which the courts of a Member State have jurisdiction in divorce, legal separation and marriage annulment. Jurisdiction is given to the courts of the Member State:

> "(a)   in whose territory:
> (i)   the spouses are habitually resident, or
> (ii)   the spouses were last habitually resident, insofar as one of them still resides there, or
> (iii) the respondent is habitually resident, or
> (iv)   in the event of a joint application, either of the spouses is habitually resident, or
> (v)   the applicant is habitually resident if he or she resided there for at least a year immediately before the application was made,[11] or
> (vi)   the applicant is habitually resident if he or she resided there for at least six months immediately before the application was made and is either a national of the Member State in question or, in the case of the United Kingdom and Ireland, has his or her "domicile"[12] there;
> (b)   of the nationality of both spouses or, in the case of the UK and Ireland, of the "domicile" of both spouses."

Additionally, where proceedings are pending in a court on the basis of art.3, that same court will also have jurisdiction to examine a counterclaim coming within the scope of the Regulation[13]; and where a court of a Member State has granted a legal separation, that court also has jurisdiction to convert the legal separation into divorce.[14] Article 20 allows for provisional, including protective, measures to be taken in urgent cases even if the courts of another Member State have jurisdiction under the Regulation as to the substance of the matter, but this provisional jurisdiction ceases to apply when the court of the Member State

---

[8] Article 1; art.1(3) excludes maintenance obligations and trusts or succession. Recital (10) also explains that the Regulation does not apply to matters of social security, asylum and immigration.

[9] Domicile and Matrimonial Proceedings Act 1973 s.5(1) as amended by the Marriage (Same Sex Couples) Act 2013, Sch.4, para.6(1). For same-sex relationships, see para.12–006, below.

[10] [1895] A.C. 517, 540.

[11] As in *Sulaiman v Juffali* [2002] 1 F.L.R. 479, a case under the Brussels II Regulation.

[12] Domicile is declared to have the same meaning as it has under the legal systems of the UK and Ireland: art.3(2).

[13] Article 4.

[14] Article 5.

having jurisdiction under the Regulation takes the measures it considers appropriate.[15] The situation where the parties seek to begin proceedings in two different states is considered below.

Perceived problems with these rules   Before we look in more detail at particular features of these rules, it should be noted that the European Commission has repeatedly recognised that the rules are not entirely satisfactory. In the very month the Regulation came into force, March 2005, the Commission issued a consultation paper,[16] which was followed in July 2006 by a Proposal for a replacement Regulation. That proposal failed to garner sufficient support for it to be taken further. The eventual outcome was limited to applicable law, and then only between certain Member States, not including the UK.[17] In a 2014 report on the application of the Brussels IIa Regulation,[18] the Commission spelt out several perceived difficulties in relation to jurisdiction in matrimonial causes. First, the non-hierarchical grounds of jurisdiction set out in the Regulation in conjunction with the absence of harmonised choice of law rules in the entire EU seemed to offer a potential incentive for a spouse to rush to court to apply for divorce proceedings before the other spouse did, to ensure that the law applied in the divorce proceedings would safeguard his or her own interests. This was seen as undesirable as it might result in the application of a law to which the defendant did not feel closely connected or which failed to take into account his or her interests. It could also hinder efforts at reconciliation and mediation. Secondly, the Regulation does not provide for choice of court agreements and the Commission considered that limited party autonomy in this sphere could be particularly useful in cases of divorce by mutual consent.

Habitual residence   The primary connecting factor of habitual residence is not defined in the Regulation. The Hague Conference has repeatedly declared the term a question of fact, but courts in England and many other countries have developed various legal criteria for the establishment of habitual residence depending on the nature of the claim under consideration. In the context of art.3 of the Brussels IIa Regulation, habitual residence is to be given a European autonomous definition derived from the Borrás report on the preceding Brussels II Convention, from decisions of the European Court in other contexts,[19] and by

---

[15] European Parliament and Council Regulation 606/2013 of 12 June 2013 on mutual recognition of protection measures in civil matters ([2013] O.J. L181/4) does not apply to protection measures falling within the scope of the Brussels IIa Regulation: art.2(3).

[16] COM(2005)82 final.

[17] See para.12–012.

[18] COM(2014) 225 final, p.5.

[19] In Case C–523/07 *A (Applicant)* (*sub nom Re A (Area of Freedom, Security and Justice* [2009] 2 F.L.R. 1) at [38], the European Court indicated that decisions on the meaning of habitual residence in one area of EU law could not always be transposed so as to apply in another area (in the instant case the question of the habitual residence of a child). That case was distinguished in *Z v Z (Divorce: Jurisdiction)* [2009] EWHC 2626 (Fam.); [2010] 1 F.L.R. 694, where the context was art.3 of Brussels II *bis* rather than art.8.

the French Cour de Cassation.[20] The meaning derived from these authorities is that a person is habitually resident in the place which is the habitual centre of his or her interests. The interests to be weighed, the importance of which will vary from case to case, may include employment, educational, emotional, personal and family interests, a balancing exercise more difficult than the assessment undertaken by the English courts in considering habitual residence in other contexts. In this context, a person may only have one habitual residence.[21] The test is an objective one, the stated intentions of the parties being merely one factor in the assessment.[22]

The text of the fifth and sixth indents of art.3(1) of the Regulation use both "habitual residence" and "residence". The courts are divided as to whether in this context the latter term is to be interpreted as meaning habitual residence. In *Munro v Munro*[23] Bennett J thought it should be so interpreted, relying essentially on the dominant role given to habitual residence in art.3 as stressed in the Borrás report on the equivalent material in the earlier draft Convention. In *Marinos v Marinos*[24] Munby J took a different view, believing that the authors of the Regulation had deliberately distinguished between the two concepts, so that for the period of six or 12 months only residence simpliciter need be established. In neither case was a resolution of this issue essential. In *V v V (Divorce: Jurisdiction)*,[25] where the issue was only lightly argued, Peter Jackson J. favoured the *Marinos* view. In *Tan v Choy*[26] Aikens LJ identified three possible readings of the fifth indent, without having to decide which was correct:

> "First, it could mean that the person seeking to found jurisdiction has to be 'habitually resident' in the territory concerned at the date the proceedings are started and he also has to have 'resided' there for at least a year before the relevant proceedings are started. Secondly, it could mean that the person seeking to found jurisdiction has simply to have been 'habitually resident' for one year prior to the start of the proceedings. Thirdly, it could mean that the person seeking to found jurisdiction has to establish that he/she is 'habitually resident' at the time the proceedings are started and that this fact is proved by establishing that he/she has 'resided' in that territory for at least a year immediately before the proceedings were started ('... application was made')."

The domicile basis.   Article 3(b) of the Regulation gives jurisdiction on the basis of the common nationality, or in the case of the UK and Ireland, the

---

[20] *L-K v K (No.2)* [2006] EWHC 3280 (Fam.); [2007] 2 F.L.R. 729; *Marinos v Marinos* [2007] EWHC 2047 (Fam.); [2007] 2 F.L.R. 1018; *Munro v Munro* [2007] EWHC 3315 (Fam.); [2007] 1 F.L.R. 1613.

[21] *Marinos v Marinos* [2007] EWHC 2047 (Fam.); [2007] 2 F.L.R. 1018 (not following *Armstrong v Armstrong* [2003] EWHC 777 (Fam.); [2003] 2 F.L.R. 375); *Munro v Munro* [2007] EWHC 3315 (Fam.); [2007] 1 F.L.R. 1613. See Lamont (2007) 3 J.Priv.Int.L. 261.

[22] *Z v Z (Divorce: Jurisdiction)* [2009] EWHC 2626 (Fam.); [2010] 1 FLR 694; *V v V (Divorce: Jurisdiction)* [2011] EWHC 1190 (Fam.), [2011] 2 F.L.R. 778.

[23] [2007] EWHC 3315 (Fam.); [2007] 1 F.L.R. 1613 at [45] to [53].

[24] [2007] EWHC 2047 (Fam.); [2007] 2 F.L.R. 1018 at [45] to [49].

[25] [2011] EWHC 1190 (Fam.); [2011] 2 F.L.R. 778 at [41] to [47].

[26] [2014] EWCA Civ 251; [2015] 1 F.L.R. 492.

common domicile of the spouses. In the case of the two named states, only domicile may be relied upon; nationality is irrelevant.[27]

Exclusivity of the rules   In many cases the rules just considered are exclusive: no other jurisdictional rules can be relied upon. So, a spouse who is either habitually resident or a national of a Member State, or has his or her domicile in the UK or Ireland, may only be sued in accordance with the rules in arts 3 to 5 of the Regulation[28]; and only where none of the connecting factors in those provisions point to a Member State may a spouse be sued according to the traditional rules found in the national law of the forum State.[29] It follows that where the respondent is a national of a Member State but habitually resident in a non-Member State (and not domiciled in the UK or Ireland), and the applicant cannot satisfy one of the jurisdictional criteria in arts 3 to 5, no Member State will have jurisdiction to grant a divorce, legal separation or annulment.[30] It may be, of course, that the non-Member State will have jurisdiction, a matter governed by its national law.

Residual jurisdiction   Where the jurisdictional rules of arts 3 to 5 are not exclusive and no court of a Member State has jurisdiction under those rules,[31] jurisdiction may be exercised in accordance with the national law of the Member State before which the proceedings are begun.[32] The scope of national law is indeed extended by the Regulation: as against a respondent who is not habitually resident and is not a national of a Member State (or not domiciled in the UK or Ireland), any national of a Member State who is habitually resident within the territory of another Member State may, like the nationals of that State, avail him- or herself of the rules of jurisdiction applicable in that State.[33] The effect of these provisions is that as against such respondents, pre-existing national bases of jurisdiction remain in force and are available to nationals of other Member States, the resulting judgments having the benefit of the recognition provisions of the Regulation. This has rightly been described by one commentator as "a very unprincipled grab for excessive matrimonial jurisdiction."[34]

---

[27] *Re N (Jurisdiction)* [2007] EWHC 1274 (Fam.); [2007] 2 F.L.R. 1196. Where nationality is relevant and the parties are both dual nationals of the same two Member States, the parties may invoke the jurisdiction of either State: C–168/08 *Hadadi v Hadadi* [2009] E.C.R. I–6871.

[28] Article 6. A pre-nuptial agreement including a clause that the parties will only litigate in a particular State has no effect; *C v C (Divorce: Jurisdiction)* [2005] EWCA Civ. 68; (2005) 149 S.J.L.B. 113 although the point was not expressly argued.

[29] Article 7; Case 68/07 *Lopez v Lizazo* [2007] E.C.R. I–10403; [2008] Fam. 21. See below for the English traditional rules.

[30] This was one of the problems that the rejected 2006 Proposal for a replacement Regulation aimed to remedy.

[31] Emphasised in Case 68/07 *Lopez v Lizazo* [2007] E.C.R. I–10403; [2008] Fam. 21. See Kruger and Samyn, (2016) 12 J.Priv.Int.L 132 at 140, suggesting that the residual jurisdiction under the national law rules be replaced by a *forum necessitatis* prescribed by the Regulation.

[32] Article 7(1).

[33] Article 7(2).

[34] Beaumont, in evidence to a House of Lords committee: H.L. Paper 19, Session 1997–98.

The traditional rules in English law

Divorce and judicial separation

Where the provisions of arts 6 and 7 of the Regulation allow for residual **12–004** jurisdiction under the domestic laws of each Member State, s.5(2) of the Domicile and Matrimonial Proceedings Act 1973[35] provides that English courts have jurisdiction to entertain proceedings for divorce and judicial separation if (and, subject to s.5(5) considered below, only if):

(a)   the court has jurisdiction under the Brussels IIa Regulation; or
(b)   no court of a Contracting State has jurisdiction under the Brussels IIa Regulation and either of the parties to the marriage is domiciled in England and Wales on the date when proceedings are begun.

Thus the residual jurisdiction under the traditional rules will only arise if the respondent is not habitually resident in a Member State, is not a national of a Member State other than the UK and Ireland, and is not domiciled in the UK or Ireland, but the applicant is domiciled in England.

Section 5(5) of the Act is, on first reading, a complex provision, but is the counterpart under the traditional rules to art.4 of the Regulation regarding counterclaims. The basic idea is that once the English court is properly exercising jurisdiction over a marriage, it retains that jurisdiction even if the nature of the relief sought changes. Section 5(5) provides that the court has jurisdiction to entertain proceedings for divorce, judicial separation or nullity of marriage, notwithstanding that the jurisdictional requirements of the section are not (when those particular decrees are sought) satisfied, if they are begun at a time when proceedings which the court has jurisdiction to entertain[36] are pending in respect of the same marriage for divorce, judicial separation or nullity of marriage. This subsection contemplates (a) supplemental petitions by the petitioner for the same relief on a different ground, or for a different form of relief, and (b) cross-petitions by the respondent. The court will have jurisdiction to entertain the supplemental or cross-petition, even though the applicant is not domiciled in England, provided it had jurisdiction to entertain the original petition and that petition is still pending.

The exercise of the English courts' jurisdiction in proceedings for divorce is subject to rules requiring or enabling the court to stay those proceedings in certain circumstances. These rules are considered later in this chapter.

---

[35] As substituted by the European Communities (Matrimonial Jurisdiction and Judgments) Regulations 2001, SI 2001/310. Note that the definition of "Council Regulation" in s.5(1A) has been amended by the European Communities (Jurisdiction and Judgments in Matrimonial and Parental Responsibility Matters) Regulations 2005, SI 2005/265.
[36] By virtue of s.5(2),(3) or (5).

Nullity of marriage

12–005 Before 1974 the jurisdiction of the English courts to entertain petitions for nullity of marriage was one of the most vexed and difficult questions in the whole of the English conflict of laws. An enormous simplification of the law was effected by the Domicile and Matrimonial Proceedings Act 1973.[37] Section 5(3) of the Act[38] provides that English courts have jurisdiction to entertain such petitions[39] if (and, subject to s.5(5), only if):

> "(a) the court has jurisdiction under the Brussels IIa Regulation; or
> (b) no court of a Contracting State has jurisdiction under the Brussels IIa Regulation and either of the parties to the marriage:
> (i) is domiciled in England and Wales on the date when the proceedings are begun; or
> (ii) died before that date and either was at death domiciled in England and Wales or had been habitually resident in England and Wales throughout the period of one year ending with the date of death."

Subsection (b)(ii) is intended to cover the rare but still theoretically possible case where a person with sufficient interest petitions for a decree that a marriage is void after the death of one or both of the parties thereto. In theory, that can be done during the lives of the parties.

The provisions of s.5(5) of the 1973 Act on jurisdiction to entertain supplemental or cross-petitions apply to nullity of marriage as they apply to divorce and judicial separation. There is therefore no need to repeat here the earlier discussion.

The exercise of the English courts' jurisdiction in proceedings for nullity of marriage is subject to rules enabling the court to stay those proceedings in certain circumstances. These rules are considered later in this chapter.

Same-sex relationships

12–006 An increasing number of legal systems, in both EU and non-EU States, now provide for marriages or civil partnerships (or both) between couples of the same sex. On the assumption that the Brussels IIa Regulation does not apply to such relationships, provision has been made to give the English courts jurisdiction.[40]

The Civil Partnership Act 2004 makes provision for the English court to make dissolution, separation or nullity orders. The design of the Act is such that some of the grounds on which jurisdiction may be taken, grounds similar to those in art.3(a) of the Brussels IIa Regulation, are prescribed by Regulations and others

---

[37] Implementing the recommendations of the Law Commission: Law Com. No.48 (1972), paras 49–62.

[38] As substituted by the European Communities (Matrimonial Jurisdiction and Judgments) Regulations 2001, SI 2001/310.

[39] The bases for jurisdiction are the same whether the marriage is alleged to be void or voidable.

[40] See Woelke [2004] I.F.L. 111 (doubting the wisdom of extending the comprehensive régime of jurisdictional rules in matrimonial matters to civil partnerships) and Kruger and Samyn, (2016) 12 J.Priv.Int.L 132 at 135ff (examining the arguments for interpreting the regulation as applicable to same-sex marriages).

by the Act itself. So far as dissolution and annulment are concerned the English courts have jurisdiction under the Civil Partnership (Jurisdiction and Recognition of Judgments) Regulations 2005[41] where:

(a) both civil partners are habitually resident in England;
(b) both civil partners were last habitually resident in England and one of the civil partners continues to reside there;
(c) the respondent is habitually resident in England;
(d) the petitioner is habitually resident in England and has resided there for at least one year immediately preceding the presentation of the petition; or
(e) the petitioner is domiciled and habitually resident in England and has resided there for at least six months immediately preceding the presentation of the petition.

Section 221 of the Act provides that where no court has jurisdiction under the 2005 Regulations, there is jurisdiction to make a dissolution order if either party is domiciled in England on the date the proceedings are begun and the parties are registered as civil partners of each other in England, and it appears to the court to be in the interests of justice to assume jurisdiction in the case.[42] Similarly, if no court has jurisdiction under the 2005 Regulations the English court will have jurisdiction to grant a nullity order, where either party is domiciled in England on the date when the proceedings are begun, or died domiciled or habitually resident for one year in England and the parties are registered as civil partners of each other in England, and it appears to the court to be in the interests of justice to assume jurisdiction in the case.[43] Additionally, where proceedings are pending and the court has jurisdiction in respect of one of the orders, the court may also take jurisdiction to make a different type of order even if jurisdiction was not exercisable at that time.[44]

The Marriage (Same Sex Couples) Act 2013 made similar, but not identical, provision in respect of same sex marriages. Provision is made in the Marriage (Same Sex Couples) (Jurisdiction and Recognition of Judgments) Regulations 2014[45] for jurisdiction on grounds corresponding to those in the equivalent civil partnership Regulations and also where both spouses are domiciled in England. The 2004 Act inserted a new Sch.A1 to the Domicile and Matrimonial Proceedings Act 1973 which contains provisions corresponding to those in s.221 of the Civil Partnership Act 2004 dealing with cases in which there is no jurisdiction under the 2014 Regulations and with the making of different orders from that originally sought.

---

[41] SI 2005/3334.
[42] Section 221(1).
[43] Section 221(2).
[44] Section 221(3).
[45] SI 2014/543.

Declarations as to status

12–007 Declarations as to status are not covered by the Brussels IIa Regulation. Accordingly, jurisdiction is governed by English law. Declarations as to status can be important as the procedural method of testing whether a foreign divorce or other matrimonial decree is entitled to recognition. Pt III of the Family Law Act 1986,[46] implementing a report of the Law Commission,[47] enacted a comprehensive code of statutory rules as to declarations of status.[48] It applies to five types of declarations as to marital status specified in s.55(1) of the 1986 Act. These are declarations (a) that a marriage was at its inception a valid marriage; (b) that a marriage subsisted on a date specified in the application; (c) that a marriage did not subsist on a date so specified; (d) that the validity of a divorce, annulment or legal separation obtained in any country outside England in respect of a marriage is entitled to recognition in England; and (e) that the validity of a divorce, annulment or legal separation so obtained in respect of a marriage is not entitled to recognition in England. No court may make a declaration that a marriage was at its inception void[49]; such an allegation must be made in a petition for a decree of nullity of marriage.[50]

There is jurisdiction to make such a declaration if, and only if, either of the parties to the marriage concerned is domiciled in England on the date of the application, or was habitually resident in England throughout the period of one year ending with that date, or died before that date and either was at death domiciled in England, or had been habitually resident in England throughout the period of one year ending with the date of death.[51] The domicile and habitual residence of an applicant who is not a party to the marriage is immaterial; the court must, however, refuse to hear an application made by such a person if it considers that he or she does not have a sufficient interest in the determination of the application.[52]

The manner in which the court is to exercise its jurisdiction is dealt with in s.58(1) of the 1986 Act. Where the proposition to be declared is proved to the satisfaction of the court, the court must make the declaration unless to do so would be manifestly contrary to public policy. The Law Commission indicated that the reference to the court being satisfied was intended to make clear that the standard of proof is high and that the evidence must be clear and convincing.[53] It may be doubted whether the statutory words actually convey that meaning.

---

[46] For a critique of the Family Law Act 1986, see Lowe, (2002) 32 Fam. Law 39.

[47] Declarations in Family Matters, Law Com. No.132 (1984).

[48] The inherent jurisdiction of the High Court formerly relied on as a basis for making certain types of declarations as to status is excluded: Family Law Act 1986 s.58(4).

[49] Family Law Act 1986, s.58(5)(a); *A Local Authority v X* [2013] EWHC 3274 (Fam.); [2014] 2 F.L.R. 123 (distinguishing "non-marriage" cases as to which see para.11–011, above). *Toy v Chan* [2014] EWCA Civ 251; [2015] 1 F.L.R. 492.

[50] See, for example, *KC v City of Westminster Social and Community Services Dept* [2008] EWCA Civ. 198; [2008] 2 F.C.R. 146; *XCC v AA* [2012] EWHC 2183 (COP); [2013] 2 All E.R. 988.

[51] Family Law Act 1986 s.55(2). These jurisdictional rules correspond to those which governed jurisdiction to grant a decree of nullity of marriage before the European Regulations were adopted. See below for jurisdiction in respect of same-sex relationships.

[52] Family Law Act 1986 s.55(3).

[53] Law Com. No.132, para.3.57, n.265.

Same-sex relationships. The Civil Partnership Act 2004 provides that any person with sufficient interest may apply to the English court for a declaration of validity or otherwise of a civil partnership, or the validity or otherwise of the dissolution of a civil partnership.[54] However, the court may make such a declaration if, and only if, either of the partners is domiciled in England and Wales on the date of the application, or has been habitually resident throughout the period of one year ending with that date, or died domiciled or habitually resident for one year in England and Wales, and the two people concerned are civil partners of each other and it appears to the court to be in the interests of justice to assume jurisdiction.[55]

The Marriage (Same Sex Couples) Act 2013 made similar provision in respect of same sex marriages. In the case of a same-sex marriage, the English courts may make declarations (a) as to the validity of the marriage, (b) as to the subsistence of the marriage, or (c) as to the validity of a divorce, annulment or judicial separation obtained outside England in respect of such a marriage.[56] There is jurisdiction if, and only if, either of the parties to the marriage to which the application relates is domiciled in England on the date of the application, or has been habitually resident in England throughout the period of one year ending with that date, or died before that date and either was at death domiciled in England or had been habitually resident in England throughout the period of one year ending with the date of death, or the two people concerned married each other under the law of England and it appears to the court to be in the interests of justice to assume jurisdiction in the case.[57]

Other types of declaration. Despite the existence of this statutory code, other declarations relating to the validity of marriage are possible under the inherent jurisdiction of the High Court. So, declarations that an adult lacked capacity to enter a marriage on account of a mental condition have been made in a number of cases[58]; a declaration that the marriage was not recognised as a valid marriage in the jurisdiction of England and Wales (used in cases of forced marriages abroad)[59]; or that there never has been a marriage between the parties, when any ceremony or event involving the parties can be regarded as within the "non-marriage" category.[60]

---

[54] Civil Partnership Act 2004 s.58.

[55] Civil Partnership Act 2004 s.224.

[56] Domicile and Matrimonial Proceedings Act 1973 Sch.A1, para.6 as inserted by Marriage (Same Sex Couples) Act 2013 Sch.4, para.8

[57] Domicile and Matrimonial Proceedings Act 1973 Sch.A1, para.4 as inserted by Marriage (Same Sex Couples) Act 2013 Sch.4, para.8.

[58] *X City Council v MB* [2006] EWHC 168 (Fam.); [2006] 2 F.L.R. 968; *Local Authority X v MM* [2007] EWHC 2003 (Fam.); [2009] 1 F.L.R. 443; *Ealing LBC v S* [2008] EWHC 636 (Fam.), sub nom *Re K* [2008] 2 F.L.R. 720; *XCC v AA* [2012] EWHC 2183 (COP); [2013] 2 All E.R. 988.

[59] *SH v NB* [2009] EWHC 3274 (Fam); [2010] 1 F.L.R. 1927; *Re P (Forced Marriage)* [2010] EWHC 3467 (Fam); [2011] 1 F.L.R. 2060.

[60] *Hudson v Leigh* [2009] EWHC 1306 (Fam.); [2009] 2 F.L.R. 1129; *B v I (Forced Marriage)* [2010] 1 F.L.R. 1721. For "non-marriages" see para.11–011, above.

STAYING OF MATRIMONIAL PROCEEDINGS

12–008   As a result of the many and various grounds of jurisdiction available for divorce, legal separation and nullity, it is quite possible that the parties may each start proceedings relating to the same matrimonial matters in the courts of different countries. The effect of the rules governing any possible stay of the English proceedings has been much reduced by the Brussels IIa Regulation.

The Regulation provisions

12–009   The Brussels IIa Regulation, following the model first found in the 1968 Brussels Convention on jurisdiction and the recognition and enforcement of judgments in civil and commercial matters (now replaced by the Brussels I *bis* Regulation), adopts a civil law approach to the question of *litispendence,* the existence of two (or more) proceedings in relation to the same matter in different countries.

Article 19 provides that, where proceedings relating to divorce, legal separation or marriage annulment between the same parties are brought before courts of different Member States,[61] the court second seised must of its own motion stay its proceedings until such time as the jurisdiction of the court first seised is established.[62] Where the jurisdiction of the court first seised is established, the court second seised must decline jurisdiction in favour of that court. In that case, the party who brought the relevant action before the court second seised may bring that action before the court first seised.[63] For this purpose, a court is seised (a) at the time when the document instituting the proceedings or an equivalent document is lodged with the court, provided that the applicant has not subsequently failed to take the steps he or she was required to take to have service effected on the respondent; or (b) if the document has to be served before being lodged with the court, at the time when it is received by the authority responsible for service, provided that the applicant has not subsequently failed to take the steps he or she was required to take to have the document lodged with the court.[64] "Lodge" in this context means that the documentation was filed and proceeded with in a manner accepted by the court and which led to the issue of a petition by the proceedings by the court.[65] Proceedings are

---

[61] In contrast to the position in civil and commercial matters, the two sets of proceedings need not have the same cause of action: Case C 489/14 *A v B* (CJEU, 6 October 2015) (proceedings for judicial separation in one State; divorce petition in the other).
[62] art.19(1). See *Leman-Klemmers v Klemmers* [2007] EWCA Civ 919; [2008] 1 F.L.R. 692 (English court first seised); *Re N (Jurisdiction)* [2007] EWHC 1274 (Fam.); [2007] 2 F.L.R. 1196 (French court first seised). cf. *Bentinck v Bentinck* [2007] EWCA Civ 175; [2007] 2 F.L.R. 1, decided under the Lugano Convention 1988. It was held in *Jefferson v O'Connor* [2014] EWCA Civ 38; [2014] 2 F.L.R. 759 that the effect of art.19 could not be defeated by an agreement between the parties or by estoppel.
[63] Article 19(3).
[64] Article 16.
[65] See *L-K v L-K (No.3)* [2006] EWHC 3281 (Fam.); [2007] 2 F.L.R. 741 (where failure to produce marriage certificate did not prevent there being a sufficient "lodging" in the English court).

continuing in another jurisdiction when they have been commenced there and have not been dismissed[66] and have not lapsed as a result of inaction by the applicant.[67]

Whether preliminary proceedings are proceedings relating to a divorce, legal separation or marriage annulment, is a matter for the characterisation of the court seised of those preliminary proceedings, and a court potentially second seised should ascertain the decision of the court potentially first seised by direct judicial cooperation.[68]

Although it could be argued that the absolute nature of the *lis pendens* rule serves to promote a race to litigate in the country perceived to give the applicant a particular advantage and in *L-K v L-K (No.3)*[69] Singer J described the "first past the post" régime as arbitrary and as having the potential to be unfair to one party or the other, it must be remembered that the jurisdictional rules do provide for a real connection between the applicant and the forum. A spouse who wishes to avail him- or herself of the jurisdiction of a Member State to which the respondent has no connection has to have been habitually resident in that state for one year, or for six months if also a national of that state (or domiciled in that state in the case of the UK and Ireland), thereby limiting the race to court to situations in which the marriage has true connections to more than one Member State.[70] It may, however, be doubted whether any sort of race to court is desirable in the context of matrimonial disputes, especially in the light of the promotion of mediation as a family dispute solving mechanism.[71]

English law

Obligatory stays

Paragraph 8 of Sch.1 to the 1973 Act contains provisions obliging the English courts in certain circumstances to stay proceedings where other proceedings in respect of the same marriage[72] are pending in a "related jurisdiction". Related

12–010

---

[66] See *C v S (Divorce: Seisin and Jurisdiction)* [2010] EWHC 2676 (Fam.); [2011] 2 F.L.R. 19 (where the foreign court had rejected the petition before it and was held no longer seised).

[67] Case C 489/14 *A v B* (CJEU, 6 October 2015).

[68] *Chorley v Chorley* [2005] EWCA Civ 68; [2005] 1 W.L.R. 1469, per Thorpe LJ at para.44. The case involved a French judicial hearing designed to enable the possibility of reconciliation to be explored and seen as distinct from possible divorce proceedings.

[69] [2006] EWHC 3281 (Fam.); [2007] 2 F.L.R. 741.

[70] See generally Truex, [2001] Fam. Law 233; Mostyn, [2001] Fam. Law 359.

[71] See, for example, Directive 2008/52/EC on certain aspects of mediation in civil and commercial matters; and see the earlier report *Parental Separation: Children's Needs and Parents' Responsibilities: Next Steps. Report of the Responses to Consultation and Agenda for Action*, Cm 6452 (2005), which stated at p.11: "The Government does not mean to make mediation compulsory but will strongly promote its use."

[72] Similar rules apply in cases involving civil partnerships: see the Family Proceedings (Civil Partnership: Staying of Proceedings) Rules 2010, SI 2010/2986. the rules in the text apply in same sex marriage cases: Domicile and Matrimonial Proceedings Act 1973 s.5(6) as amended by Marriage (Same Sex Couples) Act 2013 Sch.4, para.6(4); and Domicile and Matrimonial Proceedings Act 1973 Sch.1 para.2, as amended by Marriage (Same Sex Couples) Act 2013 Sch.4 para.9.

jurisdictions are those within the British Isles.[73] They include Scotland and Northern Ireland;[74] but Guernsey, Jersey and the Isle of Man, not Member States, are also "related jurisdictions": if the English court has jurisdiction under art.7, the rules as to obligatory stays would be applicable.

Paragraph 8 provides that where before the beginning of the trial or first trial in any proceedings for divorce which are continuing in an English court it appears to the court:

(a)   that proceedings for divorce or nullity of marriage in respect of that marriage are continuing in another jurisdiction in the British Isles; and

(b)   that the parties to the marriage have resided together after its celebration; and

(c)   that the place where they resided together when the proceedings in the English court were begun, or last resided together before those proceedings were begun, is in that other jurisdiction; and

(d)   that either of the parties was habitually resident in that jurisdiction throughout the year ending with the date on which they last resided together before the date on which the proceedings in the English court were begun,

the English court must order the proceedings to be stayed. The object of this provision was to give jurisdictional priority to the country most closely connected with the marriage, that is to say to the country to which the marriage may be said to "belong".[75]

Discretionary stays

12–011   Paragraph 9 of Sch.1 to the Domicile and Matrimonial Proceedings Act 1973 makes provision for matrimonial proceedings in an English court to be stayed in favour of the court of another country in certain situations.[76]

Where before the beginning of the trial or first trial in any matrimonial proceedings, other than proceedings governed by the Brussels IIa Regulation, which are continuing in the court, it appears to the court:

(a)   that any proceedings in respect of the marriage in question, or capable of affecting its validity or subsistence, are continuing in another jurisdiction; and

---

[73] Schedule 1, para.3(2).

[74] It is unclear whether the Regulation allows the continued application of the rules as to obligatory stays in cases involving other proceedings in those countries, art.19 giving priority to the court first seised speaks of the "courts of different Member States" but the effect of art.66 may be that the courts in England and Scotland are to be treated as if they were courts in different Member States.

[75] Law Com. No.48 (1972), para.85.

[76] Similar provisions exist for civil partnerships: Family Proceedings (Civil Partnership: Staying of Proceedings) Rules 2005/2921.

(b)   that the balance of fairness (including convenience) as between the parties to the marriage is such that it is appropriate for the proceedings in that other jurisdiction to be disposed of before further steps are taken in the proceedings in the court,

the English court may, if it thinks fit, order that the proceedings before it be stayed.[77]

Paragraph 9 now applies only to proceedings other than those governed by the Brussels IIa Regulation.[78] The meaning of this exclusion was not wholly clear, for cases in which jurisdiction is taken under national law can be regarded as governed by the provision as to "residual jurisdiction" under art.7 of the Regulation. However in *Mittal v Mittal*[79] the Court of Appeal interpreted the exclusion as limited to cases in which the Regulation "tells the court how to deal with the application"; in cases under art.7 national law governs. The intention appears to be that para.9 should continue to apply where that residual jurisdiction is invoked.[80]

The question of the application in this context of the decision in *Owusu v Jackson*[81] (which in the context of the Brussels I Regulation precluded the English courts from using the notion forum non conveniens to stay proceedings) was squarely faced for the first time in *JKN v JCN*.[82] The court held that *Owusu v Jackson* did not apply to cases governed by the Brussels IIa Regulation, for a number of reasons. *Owusu v Jackson* did not address the position that arises under the Domicile and Matrimonial Proceedings Act 1973 where by definition there are concurrent proceedings. *Owusu v Jackson* should be limited to cases under the Brussels I and Brussels I *bis* Regulations, essentially civil and commercial cases, and not extended so as to apply to the Brussels IIa Regulation dealing with family law. Article 2 of the Brussels I Regulation (art.4 of the Brussels I *bis* Regulation) had been described as "mandatory" by the European Court, but under art.3 of the Brussels IIa Regulation there was no corresponding obligation: art.3 envisaged a multiplicity of Member States having concurrent jurisdiction, art.2 of the Brussels I Regulation envisaged only one. This reasoning was endorsed by the Court of Appeal in *Mittal v Mittal*.[83]

The discretionary power in para.9 may be exercised on the court's own motion as well as on the application of a party to the marriage. In considering the balance of fairness and convenience, the court must have regard to all factors appearing to

---

[77] Domicile and Matrimonial Proceedings Act 1973 Sch.1, para.9 as amended by the European Communities (Matrimonial Jurisdiction and Judgments) Regulations 2001, SI 2001/310. See *Mytton v Mytton* (1977) 7 Fam. Law 244; *Shemshadfard v Shemshadfard* [1981] 1 All E.R. 726; *Thyssen-Bornemisza v Thyssen-Bornemisza* [1986] Fam. 1; *S v S (Matrimonial Proceedings: Appropriate Forum)* [1997] 1 W.L.R. 1200. For the discharge of stays, and the effect of a stay on powers to make orders as to financial and other ancillary matters, see Domicile and Matrimonial Proceedings Act 1973 Sch.1, paras 10 and 11.

[78] See SI 2001/310, reg.4.

[79] [2013] EWCA Civ 1255; [2014] 2 F.C.R. 208.

[80] *JKN v JCN* [2010] EWHC 843 (Fam.); [2011] 1 F.L.R. 826.

[81] Case 281/02 [2005] E.C.R. I–1383; [2005] Q.B. 801.

[82] [2010] EWHC 843 (Fam.); [2011] 1 F.L.R. 826.

[83] [2013] EWCA Civ 1255; [2014] 2 F.C.R. 208, followed on this point in *Toy v Chan* [2014] EWCA Civ 251; [2015] 1 F.L.R. 492.

be relevant, including the convenience of witnesses and any delay or expense which may result from the proceedings being stayed, or not being stayed. The court will exercise its discretion on the same basis as in forum non conveniens cases, using the principles set out in *Spiliada Maritime Corp. v Cansulex Ltd.*[84] That this was the correct approach was established in the House of Lords in *De Dampierre v De Dampierre*,[85] a case which illustrates the operation of the rules on discretionary stays.

> H was a French aristocrat whose family estates produced cognac. He married W, also a French national, in France in 1977. They moved to England in 1979, where their only son was born in 1982. In 1985, W took the child to New York and the marriage broke down. H began divorce proceedings in France in May 1985; W petitioned for divorce in England in July 1985, and H sought a stay of the English proceedings. Although unsuccessful in the lower courts, H succeeded in the House of Lords.

The decision in the lower courts was based on the fact that a maintenance order would be made in favour of W in the English proceedings, but that under French law a finding that she was responsible for the failure of the marriage would lead to a denial of any such order. The House of Lords, following the *Spiliada* approach, held that the financial advantage W might gain from proceeding in England was only one factor. Given the tenuous nature of her links with England, it was logical and not unfair to allow the litigation between the parties, both of whom were French and who had married in France, to be conducted in the courts of that country.[86]

The English court has power, which will be very sparingly exercised, to grant an interim injunction restraining the continuance of foreign matrimonial proceedings.[87] The principles applicable are again those developed in non-matrimonial cases, i.e., those in *S.N.I. Aerospatiale v Lee Kui Jak.*[88]

CHOICE OF LAW

Divorce

12–012   The question of choice of law has never been prominent in the English rules of the conflict of laws relating to divorce, which has always been treated as primarily a jurisdictional question.[89] English courts when deciding whether to recognise foreign divorces have never examined the grounds on which the decree was granted in order to see whether they were sufficient by English domestic law.

---

[84] [1987] A.C. 460; see above, para.7–031.
[85] [1988] A.C. 92. Were the facts to recur, the outcome would now be different: the French proceedings, being in another Member State, would have priority under art.19.
[86] For other illustrations, see *R v R (Divorce: Stay of Proceedings)* [1994] 2 F.L.R. 1036 (stay refused); *T v T (Jurisdiction: Forum Conveniens)* [1995] 2 F.L.R. 660 (stay granted); *Otobo v Otobo* [2002] EWCA Civ 949; [2003] 1 F.L.R. 192 (stay refused); *Ella v Ella* [2007] EWCA Civ 99; [2007] 2 F.L.R. 35 (stay granted, relevance of pre-nuptial agreement).
[87] e.g., *Hemain v Hemain* [1988] 2 F.L.R. 388.
[88] [1987] A.C. 871; see above, para.7–036.
[89] For academic discussions, see Carruthers (2012) 61 I.C.L.Q. 881; Shakargy (2013) 9 J.Priv.Int.L. 499.

On the other hand, when English courts have themselves assumed jurisdiction, they have never applied any other law than that of England. In marked contrast, courts on the continent of Europe have, since the beginning of this century, often applied foreign law, usually the law of the parties' nationality. This has sometimes involved them in very complicated problems, especially when the parties are of different nationalities.

The civil law approach is well illustrated by Council Regulation 1259/2010 of 20 December 2010 implementing enhanced co-operation in the area of the law applicable to divorce and legal separation.[90] This sets out uniform applicable law rules for divorce and legal separation for the 14 participating Member States, not including the UK. The Regulation introduces an element of party autonomy, with the parties being able to designate the applicable law, subject to certain safeguards, from a list of options: (a) the law of the State of the spouses' habitual residence at the time of conclusion of the agreement; (b) the law of the State of the spouses' last habitual residence if one of them still resides there at the time of conclusion of the agreement; (c) the law of the State of nationality of one of the spouses at the time of conclusion of the agreement; and (d) the law of the forum.[91] In the absence of a choice by the parties, a "cascade" of possibly applicable laws is established. Divorce and legal separation would be subject to the law of the State: (a) where the spouses are habitually resident at the time the court is seised; or, failing that, (b) where the spouses were last habitually resident, provided that the period of residence did not end more than one year before the court was seised, in so far as one of the spouses still resides in that State at the time the court is seised; or, failing that, (c) of which both spouses are nationals at the time the court is seised; or, failing that, (d) where the court is seised.[92] Where the law applicable under these rules makes no provision for divorce or does not grant one of the spouses equal access to divorce or legal separation on grounds of their sex, the law of the forum is to apply.[93]

In English law, the only possible alternative to the *lex fori* would be the law of the domicile. No difference between them could exist before 1938, because English courts did not exercise jurisdiction unless the parties were domiciled in England. When this did become possible, the Court of Appeal assumed without discussion that nevertheless English law was still applicable,[94] and this was confirmed by a legislative provision last enacted as s.46(2) of the Matrimonial Causes Act 1973.[95] This provided that in any proceedings in which the court had jurisdiction by virtue of that section, the issues should be determined in accordance with the law which would be applicable thereto if both parties were domiciled in England at the time of the proceedings, i.e., English law. This

---

[90] [2010] O.J. L343, p. 10. For the discussions which led to the UK's decision not to participate the account given by Thorpe LJ in *Radmacher v Granatino* [2009] EWCA Civ 649; [2009] 2 F.C.R. 645 at [6] to [9].
[91] Article 5. For provisions as to the formal and essential validity of the agreement, see arts 6 and 7.
[92] Article 8.
[93] Article 10.
[94] *Zanelli v Zanelli* (1948) 64 T.L.R. 556.
[95] Re-enacting earlier legislation going back to the Law Reform (Miscellaneous Provisions) Act 1949.

subsection was repealed in 1973, but this was not intended to alter the law.[96] Hence, if a spouse habitually resident in England but domiciled abroad wishes to obtain a divorce on a ground recognised by the law of his or her domicile but not by English law, the English court cannot assist. To require English courts to dissolve marriages on exotic foreign grounds would be distasteful to the judges and unacceptable to public opinion. Conversely, if the English court can grant a divorce under the terms of the 1973 Act, it is immaterial that the law of the domicile has no comparable ground of divorce. This approach can, of course, cause problems where the law of the parties' domicile does not recognise the divorce, but this has been held to be irrelevant.[97]

Separation

12–013 Unlike divorce *a vinculo matrimonii* (dissolving the marriage bond), judicial or legal separation was a remedy granted by the ecclesiastical courts before 1858. Its principal effect was (and is) to entitle the petitioner to live apart from the respondent, but not to dissolve their marriage nor enable either party to remarry. It is little used today; the remedy is sought chiefly by persons who have religious scruples about divorce. It has never been doubted that the English courts will apply English domestic law and no other, even if the parties are domiciled abroad.

Nullity of marriage

12–014 The question of what law governs the validity of a marriage was considered in the previous chapter. It was there pointed out that the formal validity of a marriage is governed (in general) by the law of the place of celebration, and capacity to marry (in general) by the law of each party's antenuptial domicile. There is more doubt about physical incapacity, which may be governed by the *lex fori* or possibly by the law of the petitioner's domicile, and consent of parties, which may be governed by the law of each party's antenuptial domicile or possibly by the *lex fori*. There is no need to repeat the former discussion of these matters in this chapter. But something should be said on the question of whether a marriage could be annulled in England on some ground unknown to English law.

The grounds on which a marriage is void or voidable in English law are clearly set out in ss.11 and 12 respectively of the Matrimonial Causes Act 1973 as amended, and the bars to relief in the case of voidable marriages in s.13. Section 14(1) provides that where, apart from the Act, any matter affecting the validity of a marriage would under the rules of private international law fall to be determined by reference to the law of a foreign country, nothing in ss.11, 12 or 13(1) shall preclude the determination of that matter by that foreign law, or require the application to the marriage of the grounds or bar to relief there mentioned. This subsection seems to leave open the question with which we are concerned.

---

[96] Law Com. No.48, para.103–108.
[97] *Kapur v Kapur* [1984] F.L.R. 920; *Otobo v Otobo* [2002] EWCA Civ 949; [2003] 1 F.L.R. 192.

Of course a marriage could be annulled for failure to comply with the formalities prescribed by the law of the place of celebration, however much those formalities might differ from those of English domestic law.[98] And a marriage could be annulled if the parties were within the prohibited degrees of the law of their antenuptial domicile, even though they might have capacity to marry by English domestic law.[99] But could a marriage be annulled in England on some ground quite unknown to English domestic law, e.g., lack of parental consent[100] or mistake as to the attributes of the other spouse?[101] In the former case, it is possible that the English court might fall back on tradition, characterise the impediment as a formality, and treat it as immaterial if the marriage was celebrated in England[102] or Scotland[103] but as invalidating the marriage if it was celebrated in the country by whose law the requirement of parental consent was imposed. But, as we have seen,[104] there are grave objections to this course. In the latter case, the impediment could not by any stretch of the imagination be characterised as a formality, and the court would be squarely faced with the question whether a marriage could be annulled on some ground unknown to English law. There is no English authority on this question. All that can be said is that there is no reported case in which a marriage has been annulled on any such ground.

In *Vervaeke v Smith*,[105] the House of Lords refused to recognise a foreign decree annulling a marriage celebrated in England on the ground (unknown to English law) that it was a mock marriage. The implication is that the English court would not annul a marriage on such a ground.

RECOGNITION OF DIVORCES, SEPARATIONS AND ANNULMENTS

The simple statement in *Le Mesurier v Le Mesurier*[106] that domicile was the true test of jurisdiction did not exhaust the issues surrounding divorce. Many other countries, notably those in the civil law tradition, proceeded on a quite different basis, for example that of nationality. A failure on the parts of the courts of one country to recognise the decrees granted in another country creates a "limping marriage" valid in some parts of the world but invalid or dissolved elsewhere, with inconvenient consequences for the parties. The liberalisation of the bases on which jurisdiction could be assumed, a feature not only of English law but of that of many other countries in recent decades, requires a corresponding liberalisation

12–015

---

[98] See, e.g. *Berthiaume v Dastous* [1930] A.C. 79 (marriage in church without civil ceremony); *Asaad v Kurter* [2013] EWHC 3852 (Fam.); [2014] 2 F.L.R. 833 (church marriage in Syria; failure to register the marriage with civil authorities and to obtain authorities' consent to marriage involving a foreign national).

[99] *Sottomayor v De Barros (No.1)* (1877) 3 P.D. 1 (first cousins).

[100] See *Ogden v Ogden* [1908] P. 46 (French law).

[101] See *Mitford v Mitford* [1923] P. 130 (German law).

[102] *Simonin v Mallac* (1860) 2 Sw. & Tr. 67; *Ogden v Ogden*, [1908] P. 46.

[103] *Lodge v Lodge* (1963) 107 S.J. 437.

[104] Above, para.11–018.

[105] [1983] 1 A.C. 145. See also *R. (on the application of Baiai) v Secretary of State for the Home Department* [2008] UKHL 53; [2009] 1 A.C. 287 re-affirming the rule of public policy that a "sham" marriage is still a valid marriage in English law.

[106] [1895] A.C. 517, 540.

of the rules governing the recognition of foreign decrees if the limping marriage syndrome is to be kept within bounds. Recognition cannot, however, be wholly automatic: the English courts need not accept every assertion of jurisdiction by a foreign court. Balancing these considerations makes for a certain necessary complexity in the law.

The law on the recognition and enforcement of decrees granted outside England and Wales depends in the first instance on where the decree was granted, and sometimes on the type of decree under consideration in the English court.

Decrees granted in other European Union Member States

12–016 Although the Brussels IIa Regulation[107] contains detailed rules as to jurisdiction in matrimonial causes, its most important role is ensuring the proper working of the internal market in the area of the free movement of persons by providing for the mutual recognition and enforcement of divorce, legal separation and marriage annulment throughout the EU.[108] The Regulation does not apply to same-sex marriages, but in England there is legislation dealing with such cases.[109]

Article 21(1) provides that a judgment given in a Member State must be recognised in the other Member States without any special procedure being required, a judgment being one for divorce, legal separation or marriage annulment whatever the judgment may be called, including a decree, order or decision.[110] However, this automatic recognition is subject to the fact that any interested party may apply for a decision that the judgment not be recognised.[111] The grounds for non-recognition are limited to those listed in art.22:

(a) that recognition is manifestly contrary to the public policy of the Member State in which recognition is sought;

(b) where the judgment was given in default of appearance, that the respondent was not served with the document which instituted the proceedings, or not so served in sufficient time to enable him or her to arrange a defence; unless the respondent accepted the judgment unequivocally;

(c) that the judgment is irreconcilable with a judgment in proceedings between the same parties in the Member State in which recognition is sought; or

(d) that the judgment is irreconcilable with an earlier judgment given between the same parties in another Member State,

or in a non-Member State where the judgment is entitled to recognition in the Member State in which recognition is sought.

In practice, the availability of the public policy ground is extremely limited: neither the jurisdiction of the Member State granting the decree which is the subject of recognition[112] nor the substance of that decision[113] may be reviewed,

---

107 See generally McEleavy, (2004) 53 I.C.L.Q. 605, at p.633ff.
108 With the exception of Denmark.
109 See para.12–040, below.
110 Article 2.
111 Article 21(3).
112 Article 24.

and recognition may not be refused because the decree was granted on a basis unknown to the law of the recognising State.[114] This means that the public policy ground will be available only in extreme situations as the European jurisprudence under the Brussels I Regulation[115] demonstrates:

"Recourse to the public-policy clause ... can be envisaged only where recognition or enforcement of the judgment delivered in another Contracting State would be at variance to an unacceptable degree with the legal order of the State in which enforcement is sought inasmuch as it infringes a fundamental principle ... the infringement would have to constitute a manifest breach of a rule of law regarded as essential in the legal order of the State in which enforcement is sought or of a right recognised as being fundamental within that legal order".[116]

The second ground for refusal, relating to default of appearance of the respondent, is qualified by references to cases in which the respondent has accepted the judgment unequivocally. So, where the respondent has acted subsequently in such a way as to rely on that judgment, such as remarrying, the ground will not be available. This ground is mirrored in the non-recognition provisions of the Family Law Act 1986.[117]

The last two grounds deal with irreconcilable judgments. There is no requirement that the judgments contain the same cause of action so once the marriage has been ended in one particular way, e.g., by annulment, a court may not recognise an alternative termination, e.g., a divorce. The ground is extended to earlier decrees of non-Member States as long as they fulfil the conditions necessary for recognition in the recognising state. However, since there are no provisions for a stay of proceedings in the courts of a Member State when the courts of a non-Member State are already seised, it is possible that irreconcilable judgments will be pronounced in the courts of a Member State and a non-Member State. The Regulation provides no answer to the resulting problem, but the spirit of the Regulation suggests that the judgment of the Member State would be preferred.

Decrees granted in the British Isles

The automatic recognition throughout the UK of decrees of divorce granted under the law of any part of the British Isles was first provided for, on the recommendation of the English and Scottish Law Commissions,[118] in the Recognition of Divorces and Legal Separations Act 1971. The Family Law Act 1986 extended the earlier provisions to nullity decrees and s.44(2) now provides for the automatic recognition throughout the UK of divorces, annulments and

12–017

---

[113] Article 26.
[114] Article 25.
[115] See para.10–004, above.
[116] Case C–7/98 *Krombach v Bamberski* [2000] E.C.R. I-1935 at para.37.
[117] See below para.12–034.
[118] Law Com. No.34 (Scot. Law Com. No.16) (1970), para.51.

judicial separations granted at any time by a court of civil jurisdiction in any part of the British Isles, including the Channel Islands and the Isle of Man.[119]

Such decrees cannot be questioned in England on any ground of lack of jurisdiction. Recognition may, however, be refused in the discretion of the court in limited circumstances examined below.[120]

The provisions in the Family Law Act 1986 as to the recognition or non-recognition of the validity of a decree granted elsewhere in the British Isles apply in relation to any time before the coming into effect of those provisions as well as in relation to any later time, but not so as to affect any property to which any person became entitled before that date,[121] or to affect the recognition of the validity of the decree if that matter had been decided by any competent court in the British Isles before that date.[122] In the latter case, the policy of the Act is not to disturb the position reached as a result of litigation.

Certain extra-judicial divorces granted in the British Isles before 1 January 1974 and recognised as valid under the common law rules applicable before that date remain entitled to recognition in England. The relevant pre-1974 recognition rule is that in *Armitage v Attorney General*,[123] under which divorces recognised as valid under the law of the spouses' common domicile were recognised in England,[124] subject to a residual discretion not to recognise if justice so required.[125]

Apart from those exceptional cases, s.44(1) of the Family Law Act 1986 provides that no divorce or annulment obtained in any part of the British Isles shall be regarded as effective in England unless granted by a court of civil jurisdiction. It is no longer possible for parties seeking a divorce to resort to the various ecclesiastical courts, such as that of the Greek Orthodox Church or the court of the Chief Rabbi.[126] So far as annulments are concerned, this provision was new but stated what had been the position at common law. A nullity decree pronounced by a Roman Catholic diocesan tribunal has never had any effect on the civil, as opposed to the ecclesiastical, status of the parties.[127]

Decrees granted elsewhere[128]

12–018   In the period before 1972, English judges developed a number of rules for the recognition of foreign divorces. Over time, the rules became more and more liberal; in all of them, the basis on which the foreign court assumed

---

[119] This seems to apply to same-sex marriages as in other cases; there has been no specific legislation dealing with the point.

[120] Below, para.12–031.

[121] 4 April 1988.

[122] Family Law Act 1986 s.52(2).

[123] [1906] P. 135.

[124] See *Har-Shefi v Har-Shefi (No.2)* [1953] P. 220; *Qureshi v Qureshi* [1972] Fam. 173.

[125] *Qureshi v Qureshi* [1972] Fam. 173, 201.

[126] See *Solovyev v Solovyeva* [2014] EWFC 1546; [2015] 1 F.L.R. 734 (divorce in Russian consulate in London "obtained in" England and so not entitled to recognition).

[127] cf. *Di Rollo v Di Rollo*, 1959 S.C. 75, 79.

[128] i.e., outside the EU with the exception of Denmark.

jurisdiction,[129] and the grounds on which it pronounced a divorce,[130] were both equally irrelevant. The rules became not only more liberal but also more technical and often unpredictable in effect. Fresh legislative intervention was plainly required, and a model came to hand in 1968, when the Hague Conference on Private International Law produced a Convention on the recognition of divorces and legal separations.[131] The provisions of this Convention were originally implemented by the Recognition of Divorces and Legal Separations Act 1971 now replaced by more liberal provisions in the Family Law Act 1986. The Family Law Act 1986 provides in s.45 that an overseas divorce or legal separation must be recognised in the UK if, and only if, it is entitled to recognition under the Act or some other statutory provisions.[132] The effect of this important provision is retrospectively to abolish for all purposes the common law recognition rules and also to preclude the courts from developing further judge-made rules of recognition.

Requirements for recognition

The Family Law Act 1986, though in almost all respects a distinct improvement on the legislation it replaced, makes use of a troublesome distinction between divorces "obtained by means of judicial or other proceedings" and other divorces. The nature of this distinction between "proceedings" and "non-proceedings" divorces is more conveniently explored in a later context[133]; the rules now to be examined are those applicable to "proceedings" divorces, which are by far the most common. Such a divorce (or legal separation) obtained in a country outside the British Isles is entitled to recognition in England if (a) it is effective under the law of that country[134]; and (b) at the date of the commencement of the proceedings,[135] either party to the marriage was habitually resident or domiciled in, or was a national of that country.[136]

12–019

(i) Effective

The first requirement is that the divorce or separation must have been effective under the law of the foreign country in which it was obtained. A foreign divorce may of course be effective for some purposes but not for others: thus it may be effective to restore the spouses to the status of single persons, but ineffective to

12–020

---

[129] *Robinson-Scott v Robinson-Scott* [1958] P. 71, 88; *Indyka v Indyka* [1969] 1 A.C. 33, 66.

[130] *Bater v Bater* [1906] P. 209; *Wood v Wood* [1957] P. 254; *Indyka v Indyka* [1969] 1 A.C. 33.

[131] For the text of the Convention and comment thereon by Anton, see (1969) 18 I.C.L.Q. 620–643, 657–664. The text and a commentary also appear in Law Com. No.34 (Scot. Law Com. No.16) (1970).

[132] These other statutory provisions, such as the Indian and Colonial Divorce Jurisdiction Act 1926 are of very limited importance. An argument that the Foreign Judgments (Reciprocal Enforcement) Act 1933 was relevant in the context of the recognition of overseas divorces was rejected, it is submitted rightly, in *Maples v Maples* [1988] Fam. 14 (not following dicta to the contrary in *Vervaeke v Smith* [1981] Fam. 77 at 125–126).

[133] See below, para.12–025.

[134] Family Law Act 1986 ss.46(1)(a).

[135] Section 46(3)(a).

[136] Section 46(1)(b).

destroy the wife's right to maintenance from her husband. Presumably "effective" here means (in the case of a divorce) effective to dissolve the marriage. The divorce or separation would presumably not be effective if, e.g., the foreign court had no internal competence under its own law to grant it[137]; or if the foreign decree is not final until a specified period of time has elapsed, or until a decree absolute is pronounced, or while an appeal is pending. A divorce will be recognised as "effective" if the substantive rules of the foreign law have been followed; questions of proof which may arise, for example as to whether a letter of divorce had actually been delivered, are matters for English law.[138] "Effective" has been held to imply a less rigorous standard than "valid": it can mean a decree which, although invalid per se in the granting state, is none the less to be treated as valid by virtue of some supervening legal decision or equitable principle such as estoppel.[139] The requirement that the divorce or separation must have been effective under the law of the foreign country has important implications for the recognition in England of divorces granted in federal states where divorce is a matter for State as opposed to federal law, e.g., the US. This matter is considered below.[140]

(ii)   Personal connecting factors

12–021   If the divorce or separation is in this sense effective, its recognition depends upon the existence at the date of the commencement of the proceedings of one of the specified links between one or both parties and the country in which it was obtained, i.e. habitual residence,[141] domicile, or nationality. For this purpose, "domicile" has two alternative meanings.[142] The first is that the party concerned was domiciled in the relevant foreign country under the normal rules as to domicile in English law. The second is domicile according to the law of the relevant foreign country "in family matters"; this last phrase ensures that if a country has differing concepts of domicile, as has England since the Civil Jurisdiction and Judgments Act 1982, it is that concept relevant to family law which will be used.

If there are cross-proceedings for divorce or separation, it is sufficient if the jurisdictional tests were satisfied at the date of commencement of either the original proceedings or the cross-proceedings, and it is immaterial which of them led to the decree. The decree must in other respects be entitled to recognition, e.g. it must be effective under the law of the country in which it is granted.[143]

In some countries, a legal separation can be converted into a divorce after a prescribed period, e.g., one year. The Act provides that in such a case if the original legal separation was entitled to recognition and is converted in the

---

[137] See *Adams v Adams* [1971] P. 188, where a Southern Rhodesian divorce was refused recognition in England because the judge who pronounced it had not taken the oath of allegiance or the judicial oath in the prescribed form.

[138] *Wicken v Wicken* [1999] Fam. 224; *K v R* [2007] EWHC 2945 (Fam).

[139] *Kellman v Kellman* [2000] 1 F.L.R. 785 ("mail order" decree in Guam).

[140] See para.12–028.

[141] As to the meaning of habitual residence, see above, para.3–004.

[142] Family Law Act 1986 s.46(5).

[143] Section 47(1).

country in which it was obtained into a divorce effective under the law of that country, it will be recognised in England. It is immaterial that the spouses had lost the habitual residence, domicile or nationality of that country between the date of the original decree and its conversion into a divorce.[144]

(iii) Findings of jurisdictional fact

If the foreign court makes a finding of fact, including a finding that either spouse was habitually resident or domiciled under the law of the foreign country, or a national of the foreign country, whether expressly or by implication, on the basis of which jurisdiction was assumed, that finding is conclusive evidence of that fact if both spouses took part in the proceedings, and in any other case is sufficient proof of that fact unless the contrary is shown.[145] If the proceedings are judicial in character, appearance in the proceedings is treated as taking part therein.[146]

12–022

(iv) Retrospective application

In its application to overseas divorces and legal separations the Family Law Act 1986, like its predecessor, is retrospective. It applies to the recognition of divorces and legal separations obtained before or after the date of commencement of Pt II of the Act; and in the case of a decree obtained before that date it requires recognition in relation to any time before that date as well as in relation to any subsequent time.[147] There are two exceptions to this: s.52(2) provides that the provisions of Pt II of the Act do not affect any property to which any person became entitled before the date of commencement of that Part, or affect the recognition of the validity of the decree if that matter had been decided by any competent court in the British Isles before that date. In the latter case, that court decision will be followed.

12–023

(v) Federal and other composite states

Special considerations arise where a divorce or legal separation is obtained in a federal or composite state in which the different territorial units have different systems of law in respect of matrimonial causes. The matter is complicated by the fact that while there is little difficulty in identifying the habitual residence or domicile of a party by reference to a particular territory or province, nationality is essentially a matter for the political state, the federation: one can speak of Australian citizenship but not of Tasmanian citizenship.

Accordingly, special provisions are contained in s.49 of the Family Law Act 1986. These provisions distinguish between cases in which recognition depends upon the habitual residence or domicile of a party and those in which the nationality criterion is used. Where the recognition of the decree depends upon

12–024

---

[144] Section 47(2).
[145] Section 47(1)(2). See *Torok v Torok* [1973] 1 W.L.R. 1066. But the Act does not require the recognition of any finding of fault made by the foreign court: s.51(5).
[146] Section 48(3).
[147] Section 52.

habitual residence or domicile, s.46 of the Act[148] has effect as if each territory were a separate country. If, for example, a divorce is obtained in Nevada, it will be entitled to recognition if one party to the marriage is habitually resident or domiciled in Nevada[149] and the divorce is effective under the law of Nevada.[150] Where the divorce can be recognised only on the basis of nationality, a decree pronounced in any territorial unit of the state granting that nationality will be capable of recognition but only if the decree is effective throughout that state.[151] Were it possible to grant a divorce in Nevada to a US citizen, neither party being habitually resident or domiciled in Nevada, the decree would be recognised in England only if it would be recognised in the other States of the Union. An ex parte divorce obtained in one state of the US on the basis of the plaintiff's alleged domicile in the state is prima facie entitled to full faith and credit in the other states[152] but any other state may find that the plaintiff was not really domiciled in the divorce state and deny recognition on that ground.[153] A decree dissolving a same-sex union may similarly be denied recognition in some other states.

The difficulties discussed above do not arise in relation to every federal state, but only those in which divorce (or the relevant matrimonial remedy) is a provincial rather than a federal matter. In both Australia and Canada, for example, divorce is now a federal matter and s.49 of the Act does not apply.

Recognition of non-proceedings divorces

12–025 Some religious laws provide for divorce by the act of one party to a marriage (usually the husband) or of both parties. In Islamic law the process is called a *talak* and in Jewish law a *ghet*. In Jewish law a *ghet* is a form of divorce by mutual consent, expressed in a document prepared on the instructions of the husband, approved by a rabbinical court, and delivered to the wife before witnesses.[154] The court proceedings are "in no sense a judicial investigation."[155] In the Islamic law in force in Kashmir,[156] the Gulf States,[157] the Sudan and some other Islamic countries, the husband can divorce his wife by unilateral declaration, saying "I divorce you" three times. No reasons need be given, the presence of the wife is not necessary, and in some countries no notice need be given to her.[158] In Lebanon, registration is mandatory[159]; in Egypt the divorce is

---

[148] And s.47(2) which deals with the conversion of a legal separation into a divorce.
[149] Satisfying s.46(1)(b)(i) or (ii).
[150] Satisfying s.46(1)(a).
[151] Section 46(1)(a) as adapted by s.49(3)(a). A corresponding adaptation is made in s.47(2), the case of the conversion of legal separation into divorce.
[152] *Williams v North Carolina (No. 1).*, 317 U.S. 287 (1942).
[153] *Williams v North Carolina (No. 2)*, 325 U.S. 226 (1945).
[154] See Berkovits, (1988) 104 L.Q.R. 60.
[155] *Har-Shefi v Har-Shefi (No.2)* [1953] P. 220, 222.
[156] e.g., *Chaudhary v Chaudhary* [1985] Fam. 19.
[157] e.g., *Zaal v Zaal* (1983) 4 F.L.R. 284 (Dubai); *Z v Z (Financial Provision: Overseas Divorce)* [1992] 2 F.L.R. 291 (Bahrain).
[158] e.g., Lebanon, *El Fadl v El Fadl* [2000] 1 F.L.R. 175; and Saudi Arabia, *Sulaiman v Juffali* [2002] 1 F.L.R. 479.
[159] *El Fadl v El Fadl* [2000] 1 F.L.R. 175.

usually registered with a court, though this is not essential for its validity[160]; in Saudi Arabia registration is not strictly mandatory but is a practical necessity.[161] Under the Pakistani Muslim Family Laws Ordinance 1961, the effect of the *talak* is suspended for 90 days to allow conciliation proceedings to take place before an arbitration council on which the wife is represented.[162] These conciliation proceedings may take place either in Pakistan or in a Pakistani embassy abroad.

After early doubts, it became clear that such divorces could be recognised in England,[163] and this was held to be the case even where the *ghet* was obtained or the *talak* was delivered in England,[164] provided that the parties were domiciled in a country (e.g., Israel or Pakistan) the laws of which permit such a method. The reason was that if the grounds for divorce are immaterial, so should the method be.

This reasoning remains largely unaffected by the modern legislation, subject to the important qualification that extra-judicial divorces may no longer be obtained in England. Extra-judicial divorces may be recognised under the Family Law Act 1986, but, as has already been observed, s.46 of that Act draws a distinction between overseas divorces "obtained by means of proceedings" and those "obtained otherwise than by means of proceedings." Extra-judicial divorces may fall into either category and unfortunately the distinction between the two categories, a matter on which the Act departed from the recommendations of the Law Commission,[165] is unclear. "Proceedings" is defined in the Family Law Act 1986[166] to mean "judicial or other proceedings". The latter phrase appears in the Hague Convention and was also used in s.2 of the Recognition of Divorces and Legal Separations Act 1971.[167]

In *Quazi v Quazi*[168] the House of Lords considered the interpretation of the phrase "other proceedings" in s.2 of the 1971 Act. The House held that a Pakistani *talak* effective under the Pakistan Muslim Family Laws Ordinance 1961, which requires notification to the chairman of an arbitration council and postpones the coming into effect of the *talak* until the expiry of a 90-day period during which a reconciliation might be brought about, was within the phrase. It was not essential to the notion of "proceedings" that there be some state body having power to prevent the parties from dissolving their marriage as of right.[169] Lord Fraser expressed the view that the only limitation on the scope of "proceedings" was that they should be officially recognised and legally effective in that country.[170] Lord Scarman referred to "proceedings" as "any act or acts,

---

[160] See the expert evidence given in *Russ v Russ* [1963] P. 87, 95; [1964] P. 315, 321–322.
[161] *H v S (Recognition of Overseas Divorce)* [2012] 2 F.L.R. 157.
[162] See *Quazi v Quazi* [1980] A.C. 744.
[163] *Sasson v Sasson* [1924] A.C. 10-07 (P.C.); *Har-Shefi Har-Shefi (No.1)* [1953] P. 200; *Russ v Russ* [1964] P. 315; *Qureshi v Qureshi* [1972] Fam. 173; *Quazi v Quazi* [1980] A.C. 744.
[164] *Har-Shefi v Har-Shefi (No.2)* [1953] P. 200; *Qureshi v Qureshi* [1972] Fam. 173.
[165] See Law Com. No.137 (1984), para.6.11 and Young (1987) 7 Legal Studies 78.
[166] Section 54(1).
[167] The term "proceedings" was also used in two other closely-related statutory provisions, s.6 of the 1971 Act as substituted by the Domicile and Matrimonial Proceedings Act 1973, and s.16 of the latter Act. These provisions are now repealed but are discussed in the cases cited in the text.
[168] [1980] A.C. 744.
[169] [1980] A.C. 744, 814, 823 rejecting the view of the Court of Appeal on this point.
[170] *Quazi v Quazi* [1980] A.C. 744, at p.814.

officially recognised as leading to divorce in the country where the divorce was obtained".[171] The Law Commission, following Lord Scarman's approach, recommended that "judicial or other proceedings" should include acts which constitute the means by which a divorce may be obtained in a country and which are done in compliance with the law of that country[172] but this recommendation was not implemented in the Family Law Act 1986 nor was the same approach taken in later cases.

The Court of Appeal in *Chaudhary v Chaudhary*[173] interpreted the speeches in *Quazi v Quazi* as requiring the phrase "judicial or other proceedings" to be read as indicating a narrower category of divorces than all divorces obtained by any means whatever which are effective by the law of the country in which the divorce is obtained. This interpretation is based on the dubious ground that the House of Lords, while differing from the Court of Appeal, did not expressly dissent from a passage to that effect in the judgment of Ormrod LJ.[174] It was therefore possible to hold in *Chaudhary v Chaudhary*[175] that a "bare" *talak*, requiring nothing more than the making of a declaration by the husband, was not within the phrase "other proceedings" in s.2. Other forms of divorce by the private agreement of the parties would seem to be in the same position.[176]

The Family Law Act 1986 contains no direct guidance on the meaning of the phrase "judicial or other proceedings". Implicitly, however, it rejects the more liberal approach of Lords Fraser and Scarman, for effectiveness under the law of the country in which the divorce was obtained is a prerequisite to the recognition of any divorce whether or not obtained by means of proceedings, and cannot be a criterion for distinction between the two categories. A Jewish *ghet*, which involves the active participation of members of the rabbinical court, has been held to be "obtained by means of proceedings"[177]; the Japanese *kyogi rikon* divorce contained sufficient state regulation for the divorce to be a proceedings divorce[178]; the same would seem to apply to a foreign divorce obtained by a legislative or administrative process.[179] The position therefore is that Jewish *ghets*, Pakistani *talaks*[180] and Japanese *kyogi rikon* divorces fall to be treated as "proceedings" divorces,[181] and so under the rules already examined, but "bare" *talaks* and similar divorces can only be recognised under the more stringent rules now to be examined applicable to "non-proceedings" divorces.

---

[171] *Quazi v Quazi* [1980] A.C. 744, at p.824.

[172] Law Com. No.137, p.122.

[173] [1985] Fam. 19.

[174] *Quazi v Quazi* [1980] A.C. 744, 788, in the Court of Appeal.

[175] [1985] Fam. 19, resolving a conflict of judicial opinion revealed in *Sharif v Sharif* (1980) 10 Fam. Law 216 and *Zaal v Zaal* (1983) 4 F.L.R. 284.

[176] e.g. Thai divorces of this type, as in *Ratanachai v Ratanachai*, The Times, 4 June 4 1960, and *Varanand v Varanand* (1964) 108 S.J. 693; *Chaudhary v Chaudhary* [1985] Fam. 19, 42.

[177] *Berkovits v Grinberg* [1995] Fam. 142.

[178] *H v H (Validity of Japanese Divorce)* [2006] EWHC 2989 (Fam.); [2007] 1 F.L.R. 1318.

[179] *Manning v Manning* [1958] P. 112.

[180] *H v H (Talaq Divorce)* [2007] EWHC 2945 (Fam.); [2008] 2 F.L.R. 857.

[181] See also *NP v KRP (Recognition of Foreign Divorce)* [2013] EWHC 694 (Fam.); [2014] 2 F.L.R. 1 (Indian "*panchayat*" divorce, where involvement of community members essential).

Requirements for recognition of non-proceedings divorces

Such a divorce or legal separation, provided it is obtained in a country outside the British Isles, will be entitled to recognition in England if (a) it is effective under the law of that country[182]; and (b) on the date of which it was obtained[183] either each party to the marriage was domiciled in that country[184] or either party to the marriage was domiciled in that country and the other party was domiciled in a country under whose law the decree is recognised as valid.[185] However, recognition will not be extended to such a divorce or separation where either party to the marriage was habitually resident in the UK throughout the period of one year immediately preceding the date on which it was obtained.[186] This last provision is designed to prevent easy circumvention of the rule that no extra-judicial divorce can be obtained in England; an English resident obtaining such a divorce on a short trip abroad will find that it will not be recognised.

12–026

The country in which a divorce is obtained

Where a divorce is in the form of a court decree, there is no difficulty in identifying the country in which it is obtained. Extra-judicial divorces may not be so easily located, and can present the problem of the "transnational divorce". A "bare" *talak* would seem to be located where the husband speaks the required formula.[187] It was held in a case decided under the Recognition of Divorces and Legal Separations Act 1971[188] that if a *talak* is of the Pakistani variety, and so within *Quazi v Quazi,* it can only be recognised in England if the entirety of the relevant proceedings takes place in Pakistan. It was held that it is not possible to treat as an overseas divorce a *talak* pronounced by the husband in England even if it is then communicated to the wife and the appropriate procedures as to an arbitration council are completed in Pakistan. The principle of this decision was held applicable under the rather different language of the Family Law Act 1986 in a case involving a *ghet*.[189] The court held that the writing of the *ghet* and its delivery to the wife were each steps in the proceedings by which the dissolution of the marriage was obtained. As they had occurred in different countries, and as "proceedings" was held to be a concept territorial in nature, relating to the jurisdiction of a particular judicial authority within a specific geographical location, it was impossible to recognise a divorce as having been obtained in the country in which the *ghet* was delivered. The court recognised the strong policy considerations against the conclusion it felt bound to adopt: a wealthy man might find it easier to travel to the country in which his wife was living, to complete the

12–027

---

[182] Family Law Act 1986 s.46(2)(a).
[183] Section 46(3)(b).
[184] Section 46(2)(b)(i).
[185] Section 46(2)(b)(ii). For this purpose, domicile means domicile as understood in English law or the law of the relevant foreign country in family matters; see above, para.12–019.
[186] Section 46(2)(c).
[187] *Sulaiman v Juffali* [2002] 1 F.L.R. 479.
[188] *R. v Secretary of State for the Home Department, Ex p. Fatima* [1986] A.C. 527.
[189] *Berkovits v Grinberg* [1995] Fam. 142. See McClean, (1996) 112 L.Q.R. 230.

whole process there, than a poorer man to whom the transnational procedure operated, with great care, by Beth Dins in different countries was attractive.

In Jewish law there are serious consequences for a woman who re-marries without a *ghet* having been delivered in respect of her first marriage, and that requires the co-operation of the first husband. In a number of cases in which the husband refused to co-operate, the courts refused to make a secular divorce decree absolute[190]; the matter has now been put on a statutory footing by s.10A of the Matrimonial Causes Act 1973, inserted by the Divorce (Religious Marriages) Act 2002. Where the parties married in accordance with the usages of the Jews (or any other religious usages prescribed by statutory instrument) and the parties must co-operate if the marriage is to be dissolved in accordance with those usages, the court may order that the secular divorce decree may not be made absolute until both parties declare that steps have been taken to dissolve the marriage in accordance with those usages.

Federal and composite states

12–028   The requirements as to the recognition of "non-proceedings" divorces are adapted to the case of federal and composite states by s.49(4) of the 1986 Act. Each territory within such a State is treated for this purpose as a separate country.

Nullity decrees

12–029   Until the coming into force of Pt II of the Family Law Act 1986, the recognition of foreign nullity decrees was governed by common law rules which were as unsatisfactory in content as they were uncertain in scope; happily they are no longer of any relevance. On the recommendation of the English and Scottish Law Commissions, the 1986 Act provided a comprehensive statutory scheme which would include divorces and legal separations as well as annulments. The provisions of the 1986 Act applying to nullity decrees are retrospective: they apply to annulments granted or obtained before the date of commencement of these provisions as well as after that date,[191] so that it is no longer necessary to refer to the former common law rules. In their application to any time before the commencement date, however, the provisions do not affect any property to which any person became entitled before that date or affect the recognition of an annulment if that matter had been decided by any competent court in the British Isles before that date.[192]

Requirements for recognition

12–030   Here, as in the context of overseas divorces, the Act distinguishes between annulments obtained by means of judicial or other proceedings and "non-proceedings" annulments; but it is difficult to imagine actual cases which could

---

[190] *O v O (Jurisdiction; Jewish Divorce)* [2000] 2 F.L.R. 147.
[191] Family Law Act 1986 s.52.
[192] Section 52(2).

fall within the latter category. An overseas annulment obtained by means of proceedings is entitled to recognition in England if (a) it is effective under the law of that country[193]; and (b) either at the date of the commencement of the proceedings,[194] either party to the marriage was habitually resident or domiciled in, was a national of that country[195] or at the earlier date of the death of a party to the marriage, that party was habitually resident or domiciled in, or a national of, that country.[196]

It will be seen that, when compared with the rules as to overseas divorces and legal separations, there is here additional material to deal with the cases, which cannot arise in the divorce context, where nullity proceedings concern a marriage, a party to which is already dead. In such cases the connecting factors of habitual residence, domicile and nationality are taken as regards that party by reference to the date of the death rather than the date of the commencement of the proceedings.

The provisions of the Family Law Act 1986 as to cases of cross-proceedings,[197] the proof of facts relevant to recognition,[198] and the application of the recognition rules to decrees granted in federal and composite states,[199] all of which have been examined above, apply equally in the present context.

Grounds upon which recognition may be withheld

A divorce, annulment or judicial separation entitled to recognition under the principles examined thus far may in certain circumstances be refused recognition in England. At common law, the circumstances in which foreign decrees would be refused recognition were confined within narrow limits for fear of creating uncertainty in an area in which certainty was greatly to be desired. The Family Law Act 1986, building on earlier provisions in the Recognition of Divorces and Legal Separations Act 1971 and (in part) upon the recommendations of the Law Commissions,[200] sets out a clear set of grounds for non-recognition. They can be compared with those in art.22 of the Brussels IIa Regulation[201]; but unlike the grounds in the Regulation, all are discretionary; and all may be invoked not only by a party to the marriage but also by third parties, e.g., a second spouse or a person interested in property on the ground that the decree is invalid in England.[202]

12–031

---

[193] Section 46(1)(a).
[194] Section 46(3)(a).
[195] Section 46(1)(b). For this purpose, domicile means domicile as understood in English law or the law of the relevant foreign country in family matters; see above, para.12–019.
[196] Section 46(1)(b), (4).
[197] Section 57(1).
[198] Section 48.
[199] Section 49.
[200] Law Com. No.137 (1984), paras 4.6–4.10, 6.62–6.68.
[201] See para.12–016, above.
[202] See *Pemberton v Hughes* [1899] 1 Ch. 781.

(a)   Irreconcilable judgments

12–032   A divorce, legal separation or annulment may be refused recognition if it was granted at a time when it was irreconcilable with a previous decision given or entitled to recognition in England as to the subsistence or validity of the marriage of the parties.[203] So far as nullity is concerned this rule adopts the principle established by the House of Lords in *Vervaeke v Smith*[204] where a foreign decree annulling a marriage for lack of consent was refused recognition in England because it was inconsistent with a prior English decision refusing to annul the same marriage on substantially the same grounds.

(b)   No subsisting marriage

12–033   This ground applies to divorces or judicial separations, but not to annulments. A divorce or legal separation may be refused recognition in England if it was granted at a time when, according to English law (including the English rules of the conflict of laws) there was no subsisting marriage between the parties.[205] In some cases the facts will come within both grounds (a) and (b), e.g., where a nullity decree pronounced in one jurisdiction and entitled to recognition in England is followed by a divorce decree in respect of the same marriage granted in another jurisdiction: that divorce decree will be both inconsistent with the earlier decision (for a divorce decree can only be made where there is a subsisting marriage to dissolve) and granted at a time when English law considered there to be no subsisting marriage. Ground (b) will, however, cover cases in which an English court would treat the marriage purportedly dissolved by a foreign divorce decree as void ab initio (e.g. because under the English rules of the conflict of laws one party lacked capacity to marry) but no nullity decree has ever been pronounced.[206]

(c)   Want of notice

12–034   An overseas divorce, annulment or judicial separation obtained by means of judicial or other proceedings may be refused recognition in England on the ground of want of proper notice of the proceedings to a party to the marriage, that is without such steps having been taken for giving notice of the proceedings to a party to the marriage[207] as, having regard to the nature of the proceedings and all the circumstances, should reasonably have been taken.[208] This ground has long been familiar to English judges; and since non-recognition on this ground is discretionary under the Act, some guidance may still be derived from the case law before the Act. It was at one time supposed that a foreign divorce could never be recognised in England if the respondent had insufficient notice of the proceedings

---

[203] Family Law Act 1986 s.51(1). See Law Com. No.137 (1984), para.6.66.
[204] [1983] 1 A.C. 145.
[205] Family Law Act 1986 s.51(2).
[206] See Law Com. No.137 (1984), paras 6.64–6.66.
[207] Not limited to the respondent spouse as was the predecessor provision: Recognition of Divorces and Legal Separations Act 1971 s.8(2)(a)(i) (repealed).
[208] Family Law Act 1986 s.51(3)(a)(i).

to enable him or her to defend them.[209] But in each of the cases which appear to support this extreme proposition, the main ground for refusing recognition was that the parties were not domiciled in the country where the divorce was granted.[210] Under the Act the question is one of reasonableness, and involves an examination of the extent to which the respondent was actually prejudiced.[211] In the usual case, notice of the commencement of proceedings will suffice, but there may be special circumstances in which more is required.[212] Recognition is most likely to be refused if the want of notice is combined with fraud, as where the petitioner falsely tells the foreign court that he or she does not know the respondent's address.[213] On the other hand, recognition will not necessarily be obtained by proof that the petitioner complied with local procedure; that procedure may itself be unreasonable or contrary to natural justice.[214]

(d)   Want of opportunity to take part

An overseas divorce, annulment or judicial separation obtained by means of judicial or other proceedings may be refused recognition in England if it was obtained without a party to the marriage having been given (for any reason other than lack of notice) such opportunity to take part in the proceedings as, having regard to the nature of the proceedings and all the circumstances, he should reasonably have been given.[215] There are very few reported cases in which a party to foreign matrimonial proceedings, while receiving notice of the proceedings, was denied an opportunity to take part. In *Newmarch v Newmarch*,[216] failure by the wife's Australian solicitors to file an answer to the husband's petition as instructed, so that the suit went undefended, was treated as a ground for not recognising the decree under this head: but, in all the circumstances which included the fact that the petition could not have been successfully opposed, the decree was recognised. In *Mitford v Mitford*,[217] a German nullity decree was recognised in England, although the English respondent could not be personally heard because of war conditions. In two cases, a German court granted a divorce although the respondent was resident in

12–035

---

[209] *Shaw v Att-Gen* (1870) L.R. 2 P. & D. 156; *Rudd v Rudd* [1924] P. 72; *Scott v Scott*, 1937 S.L.T. 632. Although see *Hornett v Hornett* [1972] P 255 where, even though the husband had not received notice, the French divorce was recognised since no injustice would be caused.

[210] See, to this effect, *Maher v Maher* [1951] P. 342, 344–345.

[211] *Sabbagh v Sabbagh* [1985] F.L.R. 29; *D v D* [1994] 1 F.L.R. 38; *El Fadl v El Fadl* [2000] 1 F.L.R. 175.

[212] *Ashoor v Layass* (sub nom *A v L (overseas divorce)*) [2010] EWHC 460 (Fam);[2010] 2 FLR 1418.

[213] *Sabbagh v Sabbagh* [1985] F.L.R. 29 (compliance with foreign procedure not sufficient; but as no prejudice to respondent in all circumstances, decree recognised). cf. cases where decrees were recognised after compliance with foreign rules as to substituted service or dispensing with service: *Macalpine v Macalpine* [1958] P. 35. The court refused to recognise the Nigerian divorce in *Duhur-Johnson v Duhur-Johnson* [2005] 2 F.L.R. 1042 since the husband only provided the wife's Nigerian address knowing that she was living in England at the time.

[214] *Boettcher v Boettcher* [1949] W.N. 83; *Igra v Igra* [1951] P. 404; *Arnold v Arnold* [1957] P. 237; *Wood v Wood* [1957] P. 254, 296; *Hornett v Hornett* [1971] P. 255.

[215] Family Law Act 1986, s.51(3)(a)(ii), 54(1).

[216] [1978] Fam. 79. cf. *Hack v Hack* (1976) 6 Fam. Law 177; *Joyce v Joyce* [1979] Fam. 93.

[217] [1923] P. 130.

England and could not be personally heard for the same reason: but in each case he received no notice of the proceedings.[218] In *Ashoor v Layass*,[219] divorce proceedings had been begun by the wife in England and by the husband in Egypt. The husband was restrained by a *Hemain* injunction from taking further steps in the Egyptian court but, having obtained an adjournment of the English proceedings on spurious grounds, and despite the injunction, obtained an Egyptian divorce decree. The wife was deprived of the opportunity to take part in the Egyptian proceedings in which she could have raised issues of substance as well as the position reached in England.

The Act is concerned not only with the existence of an opportunity to take part but also with its quality. The court will consider whether, in all the circumstances, the party was given the opportunity to take an effective part in the proceedings, and a relevant question is whether he had the financial means to obtain appropriate legal representation. So, in *Joyce v Joyce,*[220] a husband who was in arrears in respect of payments to his wife under a maintenance order petitioned for divorce in Quebec; the wife was unable to afford to travel to Quebec, and could obtain no legal aid from either the English or the Quebec authorities. Despite the husband's remarriage, the divorce was refused recognition in England.

This ground applies to certain extra-judicial divorces, *ghets* and Pakistani *talaks*, which are obtained by "judicial or other proceedings" for the purposes of the Family Law Act 1986. The "nature of the proceedings" is a relevant consideration in deciding whether the steps taken to give notice of the proceedings were reasonable and whether the opportunity to take part in the proceedings was reasonable.[221] The English court will not require in relation to such proceedings precisely the length and form of notice and the opportunity to take part which would be appropriate to proceedings in an ordinary court of civil jurisdiction; the appropriate test would appear to be whether a party was prejudiced by conduct which, given the approach of the legal system under which the divorce was obtained, must be categorised as unreasonable. Compliance with the strict procedures required in the case of a *ghet* will fully protect the interests of the parties, and it is submitted that the Pakistani legislation will be similarly regarded. Little guidance can be found in case law, for the issue has been discussed in the context of "bare" *talaks*[222] to which the present ground does not apply.

---

[218] *Igra v Igra* [1951] P. 404; *Re Meyer* [1971] P. 298.

[219] *sub nom A v L (overseas divorce)* [2010] EWHC 460 (Fam), [2010] 2 FLR 1418. cf. *Golubovich v Golubovich* [2010] EWCA Civ 810; [2011] Fam. 88: the fact that a foreign decree was obtained in breach of a *Hemain* injunction issued by the English court will not in itself justify refusal of recognition on public policy grounds.

[220] [1979] Fam. 93. See also *Mamdani v Mamdani* [1984] F.L.R. 699; *Sabbagh v Sabbagh* [1985] F.L.R. 29.

[221] Family Law Act 1986 s.51(3)(a)(i) and (ii).

[222] See *Maher v Maher* [1951] P. 342, 345; *Zaal v Zaal* (1983) 4 F.L.R. 284, 288–9; *Chaudhary v Chaudhary* [1985] Fam. 19, 48.

(e) Want of documentation in non-proceedings cases

An overseas divorce, annulment or judicial separation obtained otherwise than by means of judicial or other proceedings may be refused recognition in England on the ground of the absence of an official document certifying (a) its effectiveness under the law of the country in which it was obtained; or (b) where relevant,[223] that it is recognised as valid in another country in which either party was domiciled.[224] An "official" document is one issued by a person or body appointed or recognised for the purpose under the relevant law.[225] These provisions as to documentary proof are unusual (and were not recommended by the Law Commission); it is not clear what policy is served by requiring a particular form of proof. The absence of the necessary certificate is in any event only a discretionary ground for the refusal of recognition.[226]

12–036

(f) Recognition contrary to public policy

An overseas divorce, annulment or judicial separation may be refused recognition in England if its recognition would be manifestly contrary to public policy.[227] In *Kendall v Kendall*,[228] the wife was deceived by the husband's lawyers into applying for a divorce which she did not want in a language which she did not understand. It was held that recognition would be refused in England on the ground of public policy. This appears to be the only reported case in which a foreign divorce has been refused recognition solely on this ground. It was thought at one time that the public policy ground might be successfully invoked where a husband ordinarily resident in England obtained a divorce abroad (perhaps a *talak*, where the wife would have few if any procedural rights) in an attempt to avoid financial or other consequences attaching to a divorce obtained in England. It is now recognised that the enactment of Pt III of the Matrimonial and Family Proceedings Act 1984[229] prevents there being any public policy issue so far as financial consequences are concerned.[230] The recent case law evidences a very restrictive approach to the ground of public policy: in *Kellman v Kellman* it was held that "manifestly contrary to public policy" is "a very high hurdle to clear"[231]; in *Emin v Yeldag*[232] a divorce granted by a court of Northern Cyprus was entitled to recognition even though that state was not recognised by the UK

12–037

---

[223] See Family Law Act 1986 s.46(2)(b)(ii) and above, para.12–026.
[224] Sections 51(3)(b), (4), 54(1).
[225] Section 51(4).
[226] In the case of federal or composite states, it would appear to have been the intention of the draftsman to provide that these provisions were to have effect as if each territory in such a state were a separate country; s.49(4) refers in this context to s.52(3)(4) when s.51(3)(4) is plainly intended.
[227] Section 51(3)(*c*).
[228] [1977] Fam. 208. See also *Joyce v Joyce* [1979] Fam. 93. cf. *Eroglu v Eroglu* [1994] 2 F.L.R. 287 where the public policy ground was not available, both parties having joined in a deception practised on the foreign court.
[229] See below, para.13–023.
[230] *Chaudhary v Chaudhary* [1985] Fam. 19; *Tahir v Tahir*, 1993 S.L.T. 194.
[231] [2000] 1 F.L.R. 785 at p.798E.
[232] [2002] 1 F.L.R. 956. See, however, the earlier case of *B v B (Divorce: Northern Cyprus)* [2000] 2 F.L.R. 707 where the opposite result was reached.

government; and in *Golubovich v Golubovich*[233] it was said that to refuse recognition of a divorce decree pronounced by the court in another jurisdiction within the Council of Europe, in the absence of any breach of natural justice, must be regarded as truly exceptional.

Other grounds not available

12–038 These are the only grounds on which the court has discretionary power to refuse recognition to an otherwise valid foreign divorce. The fact that it was obtained by fraud, or without the petitioner's consent, is not such a ground. At common law, it was doubtful whether a foreign divorce could be impeached on the ground that it was obtained by fraud: under the Act, a divorce obtained by fraud might in some circumstances be refused recognition in England on the ground that recognition would be manifestly contrary to public policy.

Same-sex relationships

Civil partnerships

12–039 The Civil Partnership (Jurisdiction and Recognition of Judgments) Regulations[234] contain provisions, in Pt 2, corresponding to the Brussels IIa Regulation for the dissolution or annulment of a civil partnership or the legal separation of civil partners, pronounced by a court of a Member State,[235] however termed by that State. Any interested party may apply for recognition or such recognition may arise as incidental issue to other proceedings.[236] Regulation 8 on the grounds for refusal of recognition is, however, curious. Even though the instrument purports to apply the Brussels IIa Regulation provisions to the recognition of dissolution or annulment of civil partnerships, the grounds for refusal of recognition mirror the grounds under the Family Law Act 1986, which apply to non-EU matrimonial judgments.

An order granted in one part of the UK will not be recognised in another part unless it has been obtained from a court of civil jurisdiction.[237] Recognition in the other part of the UK may only be refused where the judgment is irreconcilable with a judgment of that other part, or of a judgment that is entitled to recognition in that other part,[238] or where according to the law of that part there was no subsisting civil partnership.[239]

Recognition of overseas orders is governed by ss.235–237 of the Civil Partnership Act 2004.[240] Since the grounds for recognition and refusal of recognition mirror the provisions in the Family Law Act 1986 for the recognition

---

[233] [2010] EWCA Civ 810; [2011] Fam. 88.
[234] SI 2005/3334.
[235] It is interesting to note the Regulation lists all Member States *including* Denmark.
[236] Regulation 7.
[237] Section 233(1).
[238] Section 233(3).
[239] Section 233(4).
[240] As supplemented by SI 2005/3104.

of overseas matrimonial decrees in that they distinguish orders made by way of proceedings and orders otherwise than by way of proceedings, and provide for grounds on which recognition may be refused, it is not necessary to repeat the earlier examination of these provisions.

Same-sex marriages

Provision is made in Pt 3 of the Marriage (Same Sex Couples) (Jurisdiction and Recognition of Judgments) Regulations 2014,[241] as to the recognition of the divorce, legal separation or annulment of a marriage of same sex couple in another Member State of the EU. The Regulations are similar to those applying to civil partnership cases. A decision will not be recognised if it was obtained on a date before 13 March 2014 (the date on which same sex couples were enabled to marry in England) unless at the date of the judgment the marriage would have been treated under English law as a subsisting civil partnership.[242]   **12–040**

Foreign declarations

No statutory provision is made for the recognition in England of foreign declarations as to status, e.g. that the parties were validly married. It is thought unlikely that an English court would regard such a declaration as binding. In *Al-Saeedy v Musawi*[243] such a declaration was tendered but in an attempt to prove that a ceremony had in fact taken place. It was disregarded as the party obtaining the decree had misled the foreign court as to the respondent's whereabouts so that he had no notice of the application.   **12–041**

PRESUMPTION OF DEATH AND DISSOLUTION OF MARRIAGE

Jurisdiction of the English courts

Proceedings for presumption of death and dissolution of marriage were first introduced into English law by s.8 of the Matrimonial Causes Act 1937 and are now regulated by the Presumption of Death Act 2013. The relief provided is not primarily or in essence dissolution of marriage. Its object is to enable the petitioner to obtain a declaration as to the death of a missing person who is thought to have died, or has not been known to be alive for a period of at least seven years. But a safeguard is added to guard against the awkward situation which would otherwise arise if the presumption turned out to be wrong. This safeguard takes the form of joining to the decree of presumption of death a decree of dissolution. But this is merely ancillary to the former decree and does not alter   **12–042**

---

[241] SI 2014/543. See also the Marriage (Same Sex Couples) Act 2013 Sch.2, para.4 on the recognition of order made in Scotland and Northern Ireland in respect of an English same-sex marriage treated there as a civil partnership (which is no longer the case in Scotland).
[242] Regulation 5.
[243] [2010] EWHC 3293 (Fam); [2011] 2 F.L.R. 287.

its essential character.[244] The subject receives separate treatment here not because it is particularly important but because of the clear doctrinal distinction drawn in *Wall v Wall*[245] between ordinary divorce decrees and decrees of presumption of death and dissolution of marriage.

Section 1 of the Presumption of Death Act 2013 provides that the High Court has jurisdiction to make the declaration if (and only if) (a) the missing person was domiciled in England on the day on which he or she was last known to be alive; (b) the missing person had been habitually resident in England throughout the period of one year ending with that day; or (c) if the application is made by the spouse or civil partner of the missing person and (i) the applicant is domiciled in England on the day on which the application is made, or (ii) the applicant has been habitually resident in England and Wales throughout the period of one year ending with that day. In the case of a party to a same-sex marriage or a civil partnership, there is an additional basis for jurisdiction, that the two people concerned married each other under the law of England, or registered as civil partners of each other in England, and it appears to the court to be in the interests of justice to assume jurisdiction in the case.[246] However, the court must refuse to hear an application if it is made by someone other than the missing person's spouse, civil partner, parent, child or sibling, and the court considers that the applicant does not have a sufficient interest in the determination of the application.[247]

Choice of law

12–043   Section 19(5) of the Matrimonial Causes Act 1973 (re-enacting earlier legislation) provided that the issues should be determined in accordance with the law which would be applicable if both parties to the marriage were domiciled in England at the time of the proceedings, i.e., English law. This subsection has now been repealed, but this was not intended to alter the law.[248]

Recognition of foreign decrees

12–044   English courts are not bound to treat as conclusive a decree of presumption of death made by a foreign court, even a court of the domicile,[249] unless it is accompanied by an order vesting the deceased's property in someone, e.g. an administrator,[250] or (perhaps) by a decree of dissolution of marriage. But they will probably do so in order to avoid a limping marriage if the foreign court is

---

[244] For the strange consequences which sometimes ensue, see *Deacock v Deacock* [1958] P. 230, where a wife who was judicially presumed to be dead was subsequently awarded maintenance.
[245] [1950] P. 112.
[246] See (for same sex marriage cases) Domicile and Matrimonial Proceedings Act 1973 Sch.A1, para.3 as inserted by Marriage (Same Sex Couples) Act 2013 Sch.4, para.8; and (for civil partnership cases) Civil Partnership Act 2013 s.222 as amended by Presumption of Death Act 2013 Sch.2, para.3.
[247] Presumption of Death Act 2013 s.1(5).
[248] See Law Com. No.48 (1972), para.108.
[249] *In the Goods of Wolf* [1948] P. 66.
[250] *In the Goods of Spenceley* [1892] P. 255; *In the Goods of Schulhof* [1948] P. 66; *In the Goods of Dowds* [1948] P. 256.

that of the domicile, or if (mutatis mutandis) the English court would have had jurisdiction in the circumstances. Thus in *Szemik v Gryla*[251] the husband and wife were Polish nationals domiciled in Poland where they married in 1936. In 1947 the wife obtained a declaration from a Polish court that the husband died in 1942 and she remarried in 1953. By Polish law the declaration entitled the wife to remarry and her remarriage dissolved her first marriage. In fact the husband was not dead but was living in England where he had acquired an English domicile in 1946. Scarman J recognised the Polish declaration and remarriage as having dissolved the first marriage.

---

[251] (1965) 109 S.J. 175.

CHAPTER 13

FINANCE AND PROPERTY DURING AND AFTER MARRIAGE

This chapter deals with two matters that have traditionally, and in previous **13-001**
editions of this book, been treated separately.

In many legal systems, the marriage of two persons has an effect on their
property rights and in a book written in a civil law country, the reader would find
a chapter dealing with "matrimonial property régimes". To the bewilderment of
some civil lawyers, England has no such régime, or rather, none in the civilian
sense. Since the Married Women's Property Act 1882, marriage as such has had
no effect in English law on the property of the spouses. Both parties remain
separately entitled to the property owned by them at the time of the marriage or
acquired afterwards, unless they choose to regulate their property rights by a
marriage contract or settlement. A marriage contract for this purpose means an
agreement regulating the property rights of the parties during their marriage; in
practice, very few English couples enter into such a contract. On the death of a
party, any such agreement will of course determine what property forms part of
the deceased's estate.

When a marriage ends, by divorce or annulment, or there is a judicial
separation, the courts in many countries, including England, may make orders as
to the property of the parties and as to payments, in a lump sum or by way of
periodical payments, by one party for the maintenance of the other (and of any
children). In a legal system under which the parties' property rights are governed
by a matrimonial property régime, the régime itself or a pre-nuptial agreement
made under it may preclude any further court orders; or, at the very least, will
provide the necessary starting point for any decisions as to the future.

The position in English law was formerly that while a marriage contract or
settlement would govern the respective property rights of the parties during their
marriage, pre-nuptial or post-nuptial agreements purporting to deal with the
financial and property consequences of any future divorce or separation were
contrary to public policy. In the leading case of *Granatino v Radmacher*,[1] the
Supreme Court swept away the old public policy rule, but emphasised that it was

---

[1] *Granatino v Radmacher* [2010] UKSC 42; [2011] 1 A.C. 534. There is a growing body of case law,
including *Kremen v Agrest (financial remedy: non-disclosure: post-nuptial agreement)* [2012] EWHC
45 (Fam.); [2012] 2 F.C.R. 472 (where agreement in Israeli on facts give no weight); *B v S (Financial
Remedy: Marital Property Régime)* [2012] EWHC 265 (Fam.); [2012] 2 F.L.R. 502 (emphasising the
difference between a negotiated pre-nuptial agreement which specifically contemplates divorce and
which seeks to restrict or influence the exercise of discretion to which the law gives access, and an
agreement made in a civil jurisdiction which adopts a particular marital property régime); *SA v PA
(Premarital Agreement: Compensation)* [2014] EWHC 392 (Fam.); [2014] 2 F.L.R 1028 (Dutch
agreement); *Y v Y (Financial Remedy: Marriage Contract)* [2014] EWHC 292. (Fam.) (French
contrat de mariage selecting the régime of *séparation de biens*).

still for the court to determine the appropriate ancillary relief when a marriage came to an end. The court could give some weight to a pre-nuptial agreement and would make an order in terms similar to those of the agreement when, but only when, it was fair to do so. It was for English law to govern the exercise of this discretion, even if there were a pre-nuptial agreement governed by some other law.

This chapter therefore deals with the English conflict of law rules dealing first with the property rights of the parties during marriage, and then with the financial relief that may follow divorce, annulment or separation.

PROPERTY RIGHTS DURING MARRIAGE

13–002   Although under English law, both parties to a marriage[2] remain separately entitled to the property owned by them at the time of the marriage or acquired afterwards, unless they choose to regulate their property rights by a marriage contract or settlement, the position is very different in many continental European countries, in nine states in the US,[3] and under the Roman-Dutch law applied in South Africa. There, a system of community of property exists under which marriage has the effect of vesting the property, owned by either spouse at the time of the marriage or acquired during its subsistence, in both of them jointly; and pre-nuptial contracts may have binding effect on divorce.

There are many different systems of community property,[4] but for present purposes they may be divided into three main types: full (or universal) community, community of gains (acquests), and community of chattels and gains. In full community, which exists in the Netherlands and South Africa, the community extends to all movables and to immovables[5] acquired during the marriage, and the husband has wide powers of administration over the property; there is a tendency in modern law, however, to restrict them. In community of gains, which applies now in Spain, in some of the US, in many Eastern European countries, and—since 1965 in a very attenuated form—in France, the community is confined to property acquired during the marriage otherwise than by gift or inheritance. The husband usually has powers of administration, but the wife may have power to deal with her earnings or her separate property. The mixed form, the community of gains and chattels, comprises all chattels whether owned at the time of the marriage or acquired during its subsistence, but only such land as the spouses acquired during the subsistence of the marriage through work or thrift. It does not apply to land held by either spouse at the time of the marriage or acquired during its subsistence through inheritance or gift. This is the classic

---

[2] So far as English law is concerned, the statements in this chapter as to the conflict of laws rules relating to the effect of marriage on property rights apply also in respect of civil partnerships.

[3] Arizona, California, Idaho, Louisiana, Nevada, New Mexico, Texas, Washington, and Wisconsin: see Darie, (1993) 42 I.C.L.Q. 855.

[4] Law Com. Working Paper No. 42, Family Property Law (1971); Rheinstein and Glendon, Int. Ency. Comp.L., Vol.4, Ch.4; Marsh, *Marital Property in the Conflict of Laws* (University of Washington, Seattle, 1952).

[5] The distinction between movables and immovables is fully examined in Ch.17; "immovables" in practice usually means land; "movables" other property such as shares, bank account balances, and chattels.

form of community under the original French Civil Code of 1804 but has been abolished not only in France itself but also in countries such as Belgium and Luxembourg where the 1804 Code formerly applied. "Deferred community" or "participation", which exists in the Scandinavian countries, Germany, Quebec and elsewhere, is a system of separation of property: no assets are held as joint assets during the marriage, but when the marriage is dissolved, either by death or divorce, the law provides for each spouse (or the estate of a deceased spouse) to receive a specified share of their combined assets or in the increase in those assets during the marriage.

Nearly all systems of community property régime allow the spouses to contract out of the system if they so desire, and in most systems, the failure of the spouses to do so means that they become subject to the standard community régime provided by law. The effect of this often is that the spouses adopt the standard régime by a kind of tacit consent.

In the conflict of laws, the effect of marriage on the property of the spouses differs in accordance with whether there is or is not a marriage contract or settlement between them.[6] Most of the English cases are concerned with the former (and less frequently encountered) situation, and English authority on the latter is sparse. The law on this whole topic is in an unsatisfactory state, the case law lacking coherence and a number of issues remaining unresolved.

WHERE THERE IS NO MARRIAGE CONTRACT OR SETTLEMENT

A hundred years ago, the rule applying in this type of case was seen as wholly unproblematic:

13–003

> "It is not necessary to cite authorities to show that it is now settled that, according to international law as understood and administered in England, the effect of marriage on the movable property of spouses depends (in the absence of any contract) on the domicile of the husband in the English sense."[7]

Today, however, this is one area of the conflict of laws where it is difficult to state the position with any certainty.

One element in the current uncertainty concerns the parties' freedom of choice: the scope in this context of "party autonomy". It is argued in the current edition of *Dicey, Morris and Collins* that "if the parties to a marriage are entitled to regulate their matrimonial régime directly by contract [that is, a marriage contract or settlement stating the respective property rights of the parties], it would be strange if they were unable to do so by making a contract to determine the governing law". And that "if they are entitled to choose the governing law by means of an express contract, why should they not be entitled to do so by means of an implied contract?"[8] The courts have not endorsed, or indeed even considered, these arguments, and it is not at all clear how one would discern an

---

[6] The validity of this distinction is denied by Goldberg, (1970) 19 I.C.L.Q. 557.
[7] *Re Martin* [1900] P. 211, 233, per Lindley MR. This was accepted as correct by the Court of Appeal in *Slutsker v Heron Investments Ltd* [2014] EWCA Civ 430; [2014] 1 F.L.R. 1115.
[8] Dicey, Morris and Collins, *The Conflict of Laws,* 15th edn (London: Sweet & Maxwell, 2012), para.28–019.

"implied contract" selecting the governing law. Where the parties have not entered into a marriage contract or settlement to govern their property rights, they may well have given no thought at all to the matter and it would be wrong to find any implied contract. So, even if the arguments advanced in *Dicey, Morris and Collins* are seen as persuasive, there must still be a rule that can be applied in the absence of choice by the parties.

So far as movables are concerned, there is general agreement that the governing law (whether it applies in the absence of or regardless of choice by the parties) is the law of the "matrimonial domicile". There is much less certainty in the case of immovables, considered separately below.[9] Even in the case of movables, there is uncertainty about the meaning of "matrimonial domicile". Before 1956 there was a difference of opinion on that point between Dicey and Cheshire. Cheshire's view, which was consistent with his theory on the law governing capacity to marry, was that it meant the intended matrimonial home, the domicile which the husband and wife intended to acquire and did acquire within a reasonable time after the marriage. If, for instance, a man domiciled in England married a woman domiciled in South Africa, and the husband and wife flew to South Africa immediately after the ceremony, intending to make it their matrimonial home, Cheshire would say that South Africa, not England, was their matrimonial domicile, and that South African law should determine the effect of their marriage on their movable property. But, as Dicey pointed out, there was no conclusive English authority in favour of this view, and there were practical difficulties in its application. What if the husband and wife did not fly to South Africa until a month, or a year, after the ceremony? Where was the line to be drawn? Were the rights of the spouses to remain in suspense until they actually acquired a new domicile in pursuance of their pre-matrimonial intention? Dicey concluded that the safer rule to adopt was that the matrimonial domicile meant the husband's domicile at the time of the marriage, except perhaps in a clear case where the domicile is changed very shortly after the marriage.

In 1956, in *Re Egerton's Will Trusts*,[10] Roxburgh J considered the rival views and preferred that of Dicey. Since the change of domicile in that case did not take place until two years after the marriage, the judge's observations about the effect of an immediate change of domicile were (as he pointed out) obiter. Nevertheless he made it clear that the law of the intended matrimonial domicile could apply only in very special circumstances, for example where the change of domicile followed immediately on the marriage and the spouses were at that time without means.[11]

After that decision, it was again regarded as settled law that it was the law of the husband's domicile at the time of the marriage which governed its effect on the movable property of the spouses. The selection of the husband's rather than the wife's domicile was then entirely natural, for at common law the wife acquired the husband's domicile as a direct result of the marriage. The abolition

---

[9] See para.13–010.
[10] [1956] Ch. 593.
[11] At pp.604–605. See the similar decision by the Appellate Division of the Supreme Court of South Africa in *Estate Frankel v The Master,* 1950 (1) S.A. 220, after an elaborate argument in which counsel cited cases from all over the world and the opinions of jurists from the sixteenth century onwards.

of that rule by the Domicile and Matrimonial Proceedings Act 1973 raised questions that were not previously relevant. If, for example, a woman domiciled in State A marries a man domiciled in State B (each retaining those domiciles after the marriage); the woman brings to the marriage considerable property, mostly in the form of investments in companies established in State A, but the man has only very limited savings; and the matrimonial home is, at least initially, established in State A, there seems little merit in applying the law of the husband's domicile to determine the matrimonial property régime.

It would be consistent with *Re Egerton's Will Trusts* to interpret the term "matrimonial domicile" as being *in the usual case* the domicile of the husband. It is not possible to be very clear as to the circumstances that would justify a departure from this presumption, but the example just used suggests some factors that might be relevant. A different approach, giving more weight to the expressed or implied intentions of the parties, or making an objective assess-ment of the country with which the issue had the closest and most real connection,[12] would be a more radical break with past orthodoxy. All that can be said is that, despite the long tradition of applying the law of the husband's domicile, further development of the law is possible and indeed overdue.

Change in the matrimonial domicile

What happens if the matrimonial domicile (however defined) changes during the marriage? It is a disputed question whether such a change of domicile alters the governing law. The prevailing doctrine in mainland Europe and in South Africa is the doctrine of *immutability*, according to which the rights of the spouses "are regulated once and for all by the law of the domicile of marriage".[13] In the US, on the other hand, the prevailing doctrine is the doctrine of *mutability*, according to which the rights of the spouses to after-acquired movables are regulated by the law of the domicile at the time of acquisition.[14]

13–004

English law is not yet committed either to the doctrine of mutability or to the doctrine of immutability.[15] In *Lashley v Hog*,[16] the House of Lords held (on appeal from the Court of Session) that a change of domicile from England to Scotland carried with it the application of Scots law. A different decision was reached, also by the House of Lords, in *De Nicols v Curlier*.[17]

> H and W, French citizens domiciled in France, married there without a marriage contract. There was evidence that by French law the effect was the same as if they had made an express contract incorporating the system of community of goods. At the time of the marriage they had no means whatever, but nine years later they immigrated to England with joint savings of £400, and acquired an English domicile. They set up a small restaurant called the Café Royal

---

[12] Hartley in Fawcett (ed.), *Reform and Development of Private International Law* (Oxford: Oxford University Press, 2002), p.226, uses the term "the centre of gravity of the marriage", presumably at the time of the marriage.

[13] *Brown v Brown*, 1921 A.D. 478, 482.

[14] Restatement, s.258. If, however, the after-acquired movables represent property acquired under an earlier matrimonial property régime, that régime will apply, so mutability is heavily qualified.

[15] See Hartley in Fawcett (ed), op. cit., pp.219–224.

[16] (1804) 4 Paton 581; analysed by Goldberg, (1970) 19 I.C.L.Q. 557, 580–584.

[17] [1900] A.C. 21.

in Regent Street, London, which prospered exceedingly. H died having by his will given all his real and personal estate on trust for sale and to hold the proceeds on trust for W for life, and then for his daughter and her husband and children. He left about £600,000 worth of property in England and about £100,000 worth of wine in France.

Had English law governed, H's estate would comprise all the property but W would take the life interest under the will. Dissatisfied with the provision made for her by H's will, W claimed that despite the change of domicile and the provisions of the will she was entitled to one-half of the property under the system of community of goods. It was arranged that the argument should be confined in the first instance to the effect of the change of domicile on the testator's movables only. The House of Lords held that W was entitled to the half-share she had claimed.

The House of Lords evidently regarded *Lashley v Hog* as an embarrassing rather than a helpful decision. They distinguished it on two grounds: (1) in *De Nicols v Curlier* the effect of marriage without an express contract was assumed to be that an implied contract was imposed on the parties by French law, whereas there was no such contract in *Lashley v Hog*[18]; and (2) in *Lashley v Hog* the question was not one of matrimonial property law at all but of the law of succession.[19] If the first ground of distinction is the one to be preferred, it means that *De Nicols v Curlier* belongs exclusively to the next section of this chapter, and that we are left with *Lashley v Hog* as our only authority on mutability versus immutability. The first ground of distinction was adopted by the majority of their Lordships, but some eminent writers have preferred the second.[20] It is therefore an open question as to whether an English court will apply the doctrine of mutability or immutability in the event of a change of domicile, and in the absence of a contract express or implied.

The doctrine of immutability does not produce satisfactory results if the spouses are forced to change their domicile by political or economic pressure. It does not seem reasonable that refugees, who have acquired a domicile of choice in England or elsewhere after their marriage, should continue to be governed for the rest of their lives by the law of their matrimonial domicile, perhaps the one country in the world which they will never revisit. Moreover, the doctrine of immutability may give rise to difficult questions of characterisation, and may require the court to draw delicate distinctions between questions of matrimonial property law and questions of the law of succession. Take, for example, a case in which the husband and wife were married while domiciled in France and were subject to the French system of community, and the husband died intestate domiciled in England. French law would (if the doctrine of immutability were applied) determine how much of the common movable property of the spouses belonged to the husband at the time of his death. English law, as the law

---

[18] ibid., per Lord Macnaghten at pp.34, 36; per Lord Shand at p.37; per Lord Brampton at p.44.

[19] ibid., per Lord Halsbury at p.29; per Lord Morris at p.36.

[20] Westlake, *Private International Law*, 7th edn (London: Sweet & Maxwell, 1925), p.74; Foote, *Private International Law*, 5th edn (London: Sweet & Maxwell, 1925), p.355; Falconbridge, *Selected Essays on the Conflict of Laws* (Toronto: Canada Law Book Co, 1954) p.106; cf. Mann, (1954) 31 B.Y.I.L. 217, 224–226. This view was taken by a US court which held that *De Nicols v Curlier* was authority for the application of mutability in English law: *Estate of Charnia v Shulman*, 608 F. 3d 67 (1st Cir, 2010).

governing succession to movables, would determine what proportion of the husband's movables passed to the wife by reason of his intestacy.[21] The result might be to give the wife a much larger share than she would have got if either French law alone or English law alone had governed the property rights of the spouses from the time of the marriage. Under English law, she would have acquired no rights in her husband's movables by reason of the marriage, but only by reason of his death intestate; under French law, she would have had no rights on his death intestate except to her share of the community property. In the converse case of a change of domicile from England to France, she might get nothing.[22]

Claims by third parties

It is arguable that the subtle questions surrounding the use of the matrimonial domicile test are inappropriate in cases in which the dispute is not primarily about the relative rights of the parties to a marriage but about the claims of third parties, for example on the bankruptcy of one of the spouses. In such a case, the creditors will seek to enforce their claims against any property vested in the bankrupt spouse, but excluding property that spouse holds as trustee as opposed to beneficially. The question is whether the interests of the other spouse under some matrimonial property régimes also defeat the creditors. Hartley has suggested[23] that for this purpose the respective rights of the spouses should be governed not by the otherwise applicable matrimonial property régimes but by the *lex situs* of the property, both movable and immovable. Although Hartley claims that this approach is the only way in which justice can be done to the parties, it seems that the underlying policy question is one of priorities: are the other spouses' claims to be preferred to or subordinated to those of third parties? The courts have yet to address such issues.

13–005

WHERE THERE IS A MARRIAGE CONTRACT OR SETTLEMENT

If there is a marriage contract or settlement, the terms of the contract (assuming it to be valid) govern the rights of the husband and wife to all property within its terms which are then owned or subsequently acquired, notwithstanding any subsequent change of domicile. Whether any particular property, for example after-acquired property, is within its terms is a question of construction of the contract.

13–006

---

[21] See *Beaudoin v Trudel* [1937] 1 D.L.R. 216.
[22] See Lipstein, (1972) 135 *Recueil des Cours,* 209; Kahn-Freund, (1974) 143 *Recueil des Cours,* 377–380.
[23] In Fawcett (ed), *Reform and Development of Private International Law* (2002) at pp.232–234.

Formal validity

13–007   A marriage settlement will be formally valid if it complies with the formalities prescribed by either the law of the place where it was executed[24] or the proper law.[25]

Essential validity and interpretation

13–008   The essential validity, interpretation and effect of the marriage contract or settlement are governed by its proper law.[26] The search for the proper law of a marriage contract or settlement is generically similar to the search, under the common law rules formerly applying, for the proper law of an ordinary commercial contract. Because of the nature of the subject matter, the weight to be given to the various factors is different. In the absence of an express selection of the proper law by the parties, the most important single factor is undoubtedly the matrimonial domicile, though perhaps it is putting the matter too strongly to say that there is a presumption in favour of this law. Subject to what has been said above, the matrimonial domicile means the husband's domicile at the time of the marriage.[27]

Other factors which may have to be considered, and which frequently point to some other law, are: the fact that the settled property belonged to the wife or her family, and that her domicile before or after the marriage was different from the husband's[28]; the language and legal style of the settlement;[29] the fact that its provisions are invalid by the law of the matrimonial domicile[30]; the place of management of the trust[31]; the place of residence of the trustees[32]; the place of investment of the securities.[33] Since the last two factors may change, the relevant time for giving effect to them is the date of the settlement.[34]

The case of *Duke of Marlborough v Attorney General*[35] illustrates the application of the law of the matrimonial domicile:

> H, the ninth Duke of Marlborough, who was domiciled in England, married W, the daughter of a wealthy New Yorker. A marriage settlement in English language and form was made whereby W's father settled US $2.5 million and covenanted that his executors would settle a further US $2.5 million after his death. The settlement comprised included no English property

---

[24] *Guepratte v Young* (1851) 4 De G. & Sm. 217.

[25] *Van Grutten v Digby* (1862) 31 Beav. 561; *Viditz v O'Hagan* [1899] 2 Ch. 569; *Re Bankes* [1902] 2 Ch. 333.

[26] The Rome I Regulation does not apply to contractual obligations relating to rights in property arising out of a matrimonial relationship: see above, para.6–005.

[27] See para.13–003.

[28] *Van Grutten v Digby* (1862) 31 Beav. 561; *Re Megret* [1901] 1 Ch. 547; *Re Bankes* [1902] 2 Ch. 333; *Re Fitzgerald* [1904] 1 Ch. 573; *Re Mackenzie* [1911] 1 Ch. 578.

[29] *Re Megret*, above; *Re Bankes*, above; *Re Fitzgerald*, above; *Re Mackenzie*, above; *Re Hewitts Settlement* [1915] 1 Ch. 228.

[30] *Re Bankes*, above; *Re Fitzgerald*, above.

[31] *Re Cloncurry's Estate* [1932] I.R. 687.

[32] *Van Grutten v Digby*, above; *Re Megret*, above; *Re Cloncurry's Estate*, above.

[33] ibid.

[34] *Re Hewitt's Settlement*, above; *Duke of Marlborough v Attorney General* [1945] Ch. 78.

[35] Above; criticised by Morris, (1945) 61 L.Q.R. 223.

at all. (Evidently it is an expensive business to marry an English Duke.) The settled property was and remained invested in American securities. One trustee was English and the other American. The settlement contained ancillary clauses which were meaningless (but not invalid) by New York law. The question was whether or not English estate duty was payable on the death of H. The Court of Appeal held that the proper law of the settlement was English law and that estate duty was payable.

The case of *Re Bankes*,[36] which is typical of many others, illustrates the application of some other law:

> H, domiciled in Italy, married W, domiciled in England. A marriage settlement in English language and form was made whereby property belonging to W, which was invested in English securities, was vested in English trustees. By Italian law the settlement was invalid (a) because it was not executed before a notary (a question of form) and (b) because it altered Italian rules of succession (a question of essential validity). It was held that the proper law of the settlement was English law, and that it was valid.

There can be no doubt that the parties are free to choose the proper law by an express clause in the settlement, at any rate if the transaction has a substantial connection with the selected law.[37] "As a general rule the law of the matrimonial domicile is applicable to a contract in consideration of marriage. But this is not an absolute rule. It yields to an express stipulation that some other law shall apply".[38]

Capacity to make a marriage contract or settlement

The question as to which law governs capacity to make a marriage settlement is rather more difficult. On principle, capacity should be governed by the proper law of the settlement. That is the law which at common law governed capacity to make a commercial contract, and there seems no reason for a different principle to be applied here. It is sometimes said, however, that capacity to make a marriage settlement is governed, not by the proper law (which as we have seen is usually but not necessarily the law of the matrimonial domicile), but by the law of the domicile of the party alleged to be incapable. According to this view, the capacity of an English girl under 18 years of age to make an antenuptial settlement prior to her marriage with a domiciled foreigner would be governed by English law. The three cases usually cited for this proposition are *Re Cooke's Trusts*,[39] *Cooper v Cooper*[40] and *Viditz v O'Hagan*.[41] It is submitted that, properly considered, these cases lay down no such proposition but, on the contrary, decide that capacity is governed by the proper law.[42]

    In *Re Cooke's Trusts*:

13–009

---

[36] [1902] 2 Ch. 333.
[37] *Montgomery v Zari*, 1918 S.C. (H.L.) 128.
[38] *Re Fitzgerald* [1904] 1 Ch. 573, 587.
[39] (1887) 56 L.T. 737.
[40] (1888) 13 App.Cas. 88.
[41] [1900] 2 Ch. 87.
[42] See Morris, (1938) 54 L.Q.R. 78.

> a domiciled English woman aged under 21 made a notarial contract in French form prior to her marriage with a domiciled Frenchman. She died domiciled in New South Wales having by her will given all her property to X. Her children attacked her will on the ground that the contract gave them vested rights in her property.

Stirling J rejected their claim on the ground that her capacity to make the contract was governed by English law as the law of her antenuptial domicile and that by English law the contract was "void". But the value of this case as an authority is impaired by the erroneous assumption made by the court as to English domestic law. In English domestic law (and the law of Ireland is the same), marriage settlements made by minors are not void but voidable in the sense that they are binding on the minor unless the minor repudiates them within a reasonable time after attaining the age of majority.

In *Cooper v Cooper*,[43]

> a domiciled Irish girl aged under 21 married a domiciled Scotsman in Dublin. By an antenuptial contract made in Scottish form, the husband covenanted to pay her a small annuity if she survived him and the wife accepted this in full satisfaction of her rights as a Scottish widow. 36 years later the husband died domiciled in Scotland and the wife claimed to repudiate the contract.

The House of Lords held that she was entitled to do so. It is true that Lord Halsbury and Lord Macnaghten gave as their reason for this conclusion that the wife was an infant by Irish law when she made the contract. But it is impossible to accept these statements at their face value. For Lord Halsbury said that by Irish law an infant's marriage settlement contracts are "void",[44] and Lord Macnaghten said that Mrs Cooper's contract was "voidable" in the sense that it was binding on her until she repudiated it, which she had elected to do.[45] Yet in *Edwards v Carter*[46] (which was not a case on the conflict of laws), the House of Lords held that a minor's marriage settlement contract was neither void, nor voidable whenever the minor chose to repudiate it, but voidable only within a reasonable time after the minor had attained his majority. The House of Lords further held that it was too late for the minor to repudiate when he attained the age of 26, yet Mrs Cooper was allowed to repudiate at the age of 54. It is plain that there is a direct inconsistency between *Cooper v Cooper* and *Edwards v Carter* which cannot be reconciled, unless we assume that Scots law as the law of the matrimonial domicile as well as Irish law as the law of the wife's antenuptial domicile exerted an influence on the decision in the former case. The true position would appear to be that by Irish law the contract was voidable for a short time only, but by Scots law it was voidable for ever, because any ratification by Mrs Cooper would have been revocable as a donation between husband and wife.[47] Therefore she had never had capacity to make a binding contract.

In *Viditz v O'Hagan*[48] the Court of Appeal expressly adopted this view of *Cooper v Cooper*. The facts were that:

---

[43] (1888) 13 App.Cas. 88.
[44] At p.99.
[45] At pp.107–108.
[46] [1893] A.C. 360.
[47] See per Lord Watson at p.106.
[48] [1900] 2 Ch. 87.

a domiciled Irish girl aged under 21 married a domiciled Austrian. She made an antenuptial settlement in English form, settling her property on the usual trusts of an English marriage settlement. 29 years later the husband and wife, still domiciled in Austria, purported to revoke the settlement by a notarial act made in Austria in Austrian form. By Austrian law such revocation was valid notwithstanding the birth of children.

It was held that the revocation was valid, because the wife never possessed capacity to make an irrevocable settlement either before or after her marriage. Two passages from Lord Lindley's judgment are instructive. Speaking of the case before him, he said[49]:

"By the Austrian law she was unable to ratify or confirm this contract; she could always repudiate it, but could never ratify it, i.e. deprive herself of the right to repudiate it. This was the case in *Cooper v Cooper,* but it was not so in *Edwards v Carter.*"

And speaking of *Cooper v Cooper* he said[50]:

"In that case a lady did succeed in repudiating a marriage settlement made when she was an infant after the lapse of much more than a reasonable time, if you shut out of consideration the change of her domicile between the execution of the settlement and the repudiation."

The clear inference from the concluding words in this passage is that in Lord Lindley's view the House of Lords in *Cooper v Cooper* did not "shut out of consideration" the law of Scotland. If so, *Cooper v Cooper* is no authority for the proposition that capacity to make a marriage settlement is governed by the law of the domicile of the party alleged to be incapable. It is therefore submitted that such capacity is governed by the proper law of the contract, which means, in this connection, the system of law with which the contract is most closely connected, and not the law intended by the parties. As Lord Macnaghten said in *Cooper v Cooper*,[51] "it is difficult to suppose that Mrs Cooper could confer capacity on herself by contemplating a different country as the place where the contract was to be fulfilled".

The lowering of the age of majority in English law from 21 to 18[52] has of course reduced the practical significance of the problem here discussed.

IMMOVABLES

The account thus far distinguishes between cases in which there is or is not a marriage contract or settlement. The subject of immovables has been reserved until this point because the reasoning in some of the few relevant cases seems to ignore that distinction.   **13–010**

The strongest authority on the effect of marriage on the immovable property of the spouses seems to be *Welch v Tennent*[53] in which it was held that the law of the country in which the land is situated, the *lex situs*, governed. In that case, a

---

[49] At p.96.
[50] At p.98.
[51] (1888) 13 App. Cas. 88, 108.
[52] Family Law Reform Act 1969 s.1(1).
[53] [1891] A.C. 639.

husband and wife were married in 1877 (i.e., before the Married Women's Property Act 1882). They were domiciled in Scotland. The wife owned land in England, which she sold with her husband's concurrence, and the proceeds of sale were paid to him. The parties then separated and the wife took proceedings in the Scottish courts asking for a declaration that she was entitled to the proceeds under Scottish law. The Scottish courts agreed but the House of Lords reversed the decision, and held that English law applied and that the proceeds of sale belonged to the husband. Strictly, this is a decision on the conflict of laws rules of Scotland and that gives English courts some room for manoeuvre if they wish to take a different view.

A considerable number of people now own land in two or more countries, and a rule under which each piece of property is subject to a different legal régime is inconvenient and can produce unexpected and even unfair results. There is a strong case, on policy grounds, for applying a single system of law, and that of the matrimonial domicile is the obvious candidate.

This view gathers some support from a decision of Stirling J in *Chiwell v Carlyon*.[54] At the time of their marriage the parties were domiciled in South Africa, the husband acquired land in Cornwall. The question was whether this land was subject to the South African system of community. Stirling J sent a case for the opinion of the Supreme Court of Cape Colony under the British Law Ascertainment Act 1859. In other words, he decided that the rights of the spouses in the English land were governed by South African law. The South African court gave an opinion that by South African law the English land was held in community, whether or not the spouses had acquired an English domicile. Stirling J then gave judgment in accordance with this opinion.

A similar conclusion was reached by Kekewich J in the later case of *De Nichols v Curlier (No.2)*.[55] The facts of the earlier decision in that case, dealing with the movable property, have already been given.[56] When the summons came on for further argument as to the effect of the change of domicile on the testator's immovables in England, Kekewich J held in *Re De Nicols (No.2)*[57] that the wife was also entitled to one half of the immovables. The judge's reasoning was that under French law the parties were deemed to have entered into a contract as to their matrimonial property régime. This was therefore a case in which there was a marriage contract, the terms of which determined the outcome.

The reasoning is very unsatisfactory. If the law was as it was supposed to be in *Welch v Tennent*, the content of French law would be irrelevant. Equally if French law applied as the law of the matrimonial domicile, it would make no difference whether the community régime applied by operation of law, by the tacit consent of the parties, or by virtue of some sort of implied contract.

The matter was reviewed most recently by Underhill J in his first-instance decision in *Slutsker v Heron Investments Ltd*.[58] One question in case concerned

---

[54] (1897) 14 S.C. 61. The case is unreported in England.
[55] [1990] 2 Ch 410.
[56] See para.13–004.
[57] [1900] 2 Ch. 410. For a full critique of aspects of Kekewich J's reasoning in distinguishing *Lashley v Hog*, see Hartley in Fawcett (ed), *Reform and Development of Private International Law* (2002) at pp.221–224.
[58] [2012] EWHC 2539 (Ch.).

the relevance of Russian law, as that of the matrimonial domicile, to dealings with property in London. The judge noted a New South Wales case, *Murakami v Wiryadi*,[59] in which the court broadly followed *De Nicols v Curlier (No.2)* but applied the law of the matrimonial domicile not on the basis of an implied contract but on that of the reasonable expectations of the parties. Underhill J followed *De Nicols v Curlier (No.2)* in preference to *Welch v Tennant*. The Court of Appeal was content to decide the case on that basis, leaving open for further discussion the debate as between the law of the matrimonial domicile and the *lex situs*.

In *Re De Nicols (No.2)* and *Chiwell v Carlyon*, it was clear that the French and South African systems of community included land situated outside France and South Africa respectively. In *Callwood v Callwood*,[60] there was no evidence that, under the law of the Danish West Indian island where the parties were domiciled, the Danish system of community extended to land situated outside the island. Consequently it was held that when the husband acquired land in the British Virgin Islands, it was not subject to community.

There is very little authority on the essential validity and interpretation of a marriage settlement comprising immovables. In *Re Pearse's Settlement*,[61] an English marriage settlement contained a covenant by the wife to settle her after-acquired property. She acquired land in Jersey. By the law of Jersey no trusts of land were permitted and all transfers thereof had to be for value. It was held that the land in Jersey was not caught by the covenant.

INTERNATIONAL AND EUROPEAN DEVELOPMENTS

Hague Convention

In 1978, the Hague Conference on Private International Law agreed a Convention on the Law Applicable to Matrimonial Property Régimes. Only three states ratified the Convention. The primary rule was that the matrimonial property regime was governed by the internal law designated by the spouses before marriage, chosen from a restricted list: the law of any state of which either spouse was a national at the time of designation; the law of the state in which either spouse had his or her habitual residence at the time of designation; and the law of the first state where one of the spouses established a new habitual residence after marriage. The spouses could also designate, with respect only to immovables, the law of the place where the immovables were situated.[62] They might also provide that any immovables which may subsequently be acquired were to be governed by the law of the place where such immovables were situated. In the absence of any choice by the spouses, and with certain exceptions, the applicable law would

13–011

---

[59] [2010] NSWCA 7; (2010) 268 A.L.R. 377.
[60] [1960] A.C. 659; criticised by Unger (1967) 83 L.Q.R. 427, 440–441.
[61] [1909] 1 Ch. 304.
[62] Article 3.

be that of the state in which both spouses establish their first habitual residence after marriage.[63] The spouses could change the governing law during their marriage.[64]

Proposed European Union Regulation

13–012 In March 2011, the Commission published a proposal for a Council Regulation on jurisdiction, applicable law and the recognition and enforcement of decisions in matters of matrimonial property régimes.[65] This builds upon the Hague Convention but, as its title indicates, has a much wider scope. In June 2011 it was announced that the UK did not propose to opt in to this Proposal and it became clear in 2014 that the necessary consensus had not yet been achieved for the Regulation to be adopted.

FINANCIAL PROVISION

13–013 Given that English law has no matrimonial property régime in the civil law sense, the English courts have extensive powers to deal with the property and financial affairs of the parties to a marriage. The power of an English divorce court to make "financial provision" includes the making of orders not only for periodical payments but also orders for lump sum provision, property adjustment orders, pension sharing orders and pension compensation sharing orders.[66] Under s.27 of the Matrimonial Causes Act 1973,[67] the court also has power to order either party to the marriage to make periodical payments (secured or unsecured) or pay a lump sum to the other or for the benefit of a child of the family on the ground that he has failed to provide reasonable maintenance for the applicant or has failed to provide, or to make a proper contribution towards, reasonable maintenance for any child of the family. This power is exercisable although no proceedings for divorce, separation or nullity of marriage are in train.

The conflict of laws rules governing the exercise of these powers and the international enforcement of orders are largely governed by two instruments: the Council Regulation 4/2009 of 18 December 2008 on jurisdiction, applicable law, recognition and enforcement of decisions and co-operation in matters relating to maintenance obligations, 'the Maintenance Regulation'[68]; and the Hague Convention of 23 November 2007 on the International Recovery of Child Support and Other Forms of Family Maintenance.[69]

---

[63] Article 4.

[64] Article 6.

[65] COM(2011) 126 final.

[66] Matrimonial Causes Act 1973 ss.21, 21A (as inserted by Welfare Reform and Pensions Act 1999 Sch.3, para.2), 21B and 21C (as inserted by Pensions Act 2008 Sch.6, para.2).

[67] As amended by s.63 of the Domestic Proceedings and Magistrates' Court Act 1978.

[68] [2009] O.J. L7, p.1. The Lugano Convention, art.5(2) deals with jurisdiction in "maintenance" where it applies.

[69] For a detailed study of these instruments, see Walker, *Maintenance and Child Support in Private International Law* (Oxford: Hart Publishing, 2015). For a collection of papers on wider aspects of the topic, see Beaumont et al (eds), *The Recovery of Maintenance in the EU and Worldwide* (Oxford: Hart Publishing, 2015).

The nature of the powers of the English courts gives rise to a particular question as to the scope of application of the Maintenance Regulation. It applies to all maintenance obligations arising from a family relationship, parentage, marriage or affinity. "Maintenance obligation" is interpreted autonomously.[70] The European Court in *De Cavel v De Cavel (No.1)* distinguished, for the purposes of the Brussels I Regulation which then governed maintenance, between "propri-etary legal relationships between spouses resulting directly from the matrimonial relationship or the dissolution thereof" and "proprietary legal relations existing between them which have no connection with the marriage."[71] The question seems to be whether the rights in issue existed by virtue of the marriage or its dissolution, or independently; it is not correct to treat "maintenance" as an umbrella term for any financial award which was made in order to provide for the respective needs and resources of the parties.[72] The language in the Maintenance Regulation, "maintenance obligations arising from a family relationship" seems to reflect the same distinction.

The matter was made a little clearer in the later decision in *Van den Boogaard v Laumen*.[73] This concerned an order of the English High Court that the husband transfer to the wife the matrimonial home and a painting and pay the wife a lump sum of £355,000. Periodical payments were to be made on an interim basis until the other parts of the order were complied with. Enforcement of the order was sought in the Netherlands under the Maintenance Regulation. The CJEU noted that English courts had the task of regulating, in a single decision, the matrimonial relationships and maintenance obligations arising from dissolution of a marriage. The court from which leave to enforce is sought had to distinguish between those aspects of the decision which relate to rights in property arising out of a matrimonial relationship and those which relate to maintenance, having regard in each particular case to the specific aim of the decision rendered.[74] The court rules that a decision rendered in divorce proceedings ordering payment of a lump sum and transfer of ownership in certain property by one party to his or her former spouse must be regarded as relating to maintenance if its purpose is to ensure the former spouse's maintenance. It will be otherwise if payments represent solely the money value of the divided property.[75] A foreign court may not be given much help by the nature of the English order or the full judgment: the purpose of the various parts of the award may not be specified, and judges may use other notions such as that of "compensation"[76] which sit ill with the distinction drawn in *Van den Boogaard v Laumen*.

---

[70] See Recital (11) and art.1. Succession is excluded: art.1(3)(f); see Case C-404/14 *Matoušková v Martinus* [2015] I.L.Pr. 897.

[71] Case 143/78, [1979] E.C.R. 1055, at p.1066.

[72] *JKN v JCN* [2010] EWHC 843 (Fam.); [2011] 1 F.L.R. 826.

[73] Case C-220/95 *Van den Boogaard v Laumen* [1997] E.C.R. I-1147; [1998] Q.B. 759. See Schlosser, paras 93-5.

[74] Judgment, para.21.

[75] See *Moore v Moore* [2007] EWCA Civ 361; [2007] 2 FLR 339, and Walker, *Maintenance and Child Support in Private International Law* (2015) pp.41-416.

[76] e.g. *Miller v Miller*; *McFarlane v McFarlane* [2006] UKHL 24; [2006] 2 A.C. 618.

Jurisdiction of the English courts: the Maintenance Regulation

13–014   The jurisdiction of the English courts is largely, but not wholly, governed by the Maintenance Regulation.

Ancillary relief

13–015   A court exercising this jurisdiction will make an order for periodical payments by a husband even though he is domiciled and resident abroad and has no assets in England.[77] It will vary a settlement which comprises property situated abroad and is governed by foreign law and the trustees of which reside abroad.[78] It will order a settlement of a party's English property, although he is domiciled and resident abroad.[79] But it will decline to exercise its powers in cases where any order that it might make would be wholly ineffective.[80]

The principal jurisdictional rules

13–016   The Maintenance Regulation provides that in matters relating to maintenance obligations in Member States, jurisdiction is to lie with:

(a)   the court for the place where the defendant is habitually resident[81]; or

(b)   the court for the place where the creditor is habitually resident[82]; or

   The language "the court for the place . . ." means that the relevant provisions concern both international and local jurisdiction. A German rule, under which a cross-border maintenance claim was within the jurisdiction of the local court which sat at the seat of the regional court, rather than the court at the local place of residence, was held to be prima facie inconsistent with the Maintenance Regulation. Such a "centralisation" rule would only be justified where it helped to achieve the objective of a proper administration of justice and protected the interests of maintenance creditors while promoting the effective recovery of such claims, which was, however, a matter for the national courts to determine.[83]

(c)   the court which, according to its own law, has jurisdiction to entertain proceedings concerning the status of a person if the matter relating to maintenance is ancillary to those proceedings, unless that jurisdiction is based solely on the nationality (domicile in the case of the UK and Ireland) of one of the parties[84]; or

---

[77] *Cammell v Cammell* [1965] P. 467.

[78] *Nunneley v Nunneley* (1890) 15 P.D. 186; *Forsyth v Forsyth* [1891] P. 363.

[79] *Hunter v Hunter and Waddington* [1962] P. 1.

[80] *Tallack v Tallack* [1927] P. 211; *Goff v Goff* [1934] P. 107; *Wyler v Lyons* [1963] P. 274.

[81] Article 3(a).

[82] Article 3(b).

[83] Joined Cases C–400/13 *Sanders v Verhaegan* and C–408/13 *Huber v Huber* (CJEU, 18 December 2014).

[84] Article 3(c).

This preserves the wide powers of the English courts under the Matrimonial Causes Act 1973 to make financial provision and property adjustment orders in favour of a party to a marriage or a child of the family.

(d)   the court which, according to its own law, has jurisdiction to entertain proceedings concerning parental responsibility if the matter relating to maintenance is ancillary to those proceedings, unless that jurisdiction is based solely on the nationality (domicile in the case of the UK and Ireland) of one of the parties.[85]

Party autonomy

The Maintenance Regulation adopts the principle of party autonomy, the parties being able to agree that certain courts chosen from a prescribed list are to have jurisdiction to settle any disputes in matters relating to a maintenance obligation which have arisen or which may arise between them. The agreement must be in writing, or by a communication by electronic means which provides a durable record of the agreement.[86] The parties may select: **13–017**

(a)   a court or the courts of a Member State in which one of the parties is habitually resident;

(b)   a court or the courts of a Member State of which one of the parties has the nationality (in which one of the parties is domiciled in the case of the UK and Ireland);

(c)   in the case of maintenance obligations between spouses or former spouses:
   (i)   the court which has jurisdiction to settle their dispute in matrimonial matters; or
   (ii)   a court or the courts of the Member State which was the Member State of the spouses' last common habitual residence for a period of at least one year.[87]

The relevant connecting factors have to be satisfied at the time the choice of court agreement is concluded or at the time the court is seised. The jurisdiction conferred by such an agreement is exclusive unless the parties have agreed otherwise.[88] As between the different parts of the UK, these choice of court provisions apply as if "part of the United Kingdom" replaced the term "Member State".[89]

---

[85] Article 3(d). See Case C–184/14 *A v B* (CJEU, 16 July 2015) (if courts in two different Member States have jurisdiction under (c) and (d), a maintenance issue relating to a child will be dealt with by the court having jurisdiction under (d)).

[86] Article 4(2).

[87] Articles 2(3), 4(1). An agreement of this sort may not be made in the case of a dispute relating to a maintenance obligation towards a child under the age of 18: art.4(3). For cases in which the chosen court is in a State party to the Lugano Convention which is not also a Member State, see art.4(4).

[88] Article 4(1).

[89] Civil Jurisdiction and Judgments (Maintenance) Regulations 2011, SI 2011/1484, Sch.6, para.5.

Jurisdiction based on appearance

13–018 Apart from jurisdiction derived from other provisions of the Regulation, a court of a Member State before which a defendant enters an appearance has jurisdiction. This rule does not apply where appearance was entered to contest the jurisdiction.[90]

"Subsidiary jurisdiction"

13–019 Where no court of a Member State has jurisdiction under the above rules, and no court of a State party to the Lugano Convention which is not a Member State has jurisdiction pursuant to the provisions of that Convention, the courts of the Member State of the common nationality of the parties have jurisdiction.[91] In the case of the UK and Ireland, common domicile is substituted for common nationality; and a case in which the parties are domiciled in different territorial units of the same Member State amounts to common domicile in that Member State.[92] Where the parties are domiciled in different parts of the UK, the courts of either part may exercise jurisdiction under this provision.[93]

The forum necessitatis

13–020 The Regulation also introduces a *forum necessitatis*. Where no court of a Member State has jurisdiction pursuant to any of the above rules, the courts of a Member State may, on an exceptional basis, hear the case if proceedings cannot reasonably be brought or conducted or would be impossible in a third State with which the dispute is closely connected. The dispute must have a 'sufficient connection', not further defined, with the Member State of the court seised[94]; in the UK this must be with the part of the UK in which the court seised is located.[95]

Special rule for debtor's application for modifiation

13–021 The Regulation contains a provision inspired by, and referring to, the Hague Convention of 23 November 2007 on the International Recovery of Child Support and Other Forms of Family Maintenance, which provides for close co-operation between Contracting States especially in the context of child support, and also deals with the enforcement of decisions.

Where a decision is given in a Member State or a Contracting State to the Hague Convention in which the creditor is habitually resident, proceedings to modify the decision or to have a new decision given cannot be brought by the debtor in any other Member State as long as the creditor remains habitually resident in the State in which the decision was given. This prohibition does not

---

[90] Article 5; for application between the parts of the UK, see SI 2011/1484, Sch.6, para.6.
[91] Article 6.
[92] Article 2(3).
[93] SI 2011/1484, Sch.6, para.7.
[94] Article 8.
[95] SI 2011/1484, Sch.6, para.8.

apply in certain cases: (a) where the parties have agreed (in accordance with art.4) to the jurisdiction of the courts of that other Member State; (b) where the creditor submits to the jurisdiction of the courts of that other Member State; (c) where the competent authority in the Hague Convention Contracting State of origin cannot, or refuses to, exercise jurisdiction to modify the decision or give a new decision; or (d) where the decision given in the Hague Convention Contracting State of origin cannot be recognised or declared enforceable in the Member State where proceedings to modify the decision or to have a new decision given are contemplated.[96] This provision applies as between different parts of the UK, so that where a decision is given in a part of the UK where the creditor is habitually resident, proceedings to modify the decision or to have a new decision given cannot be brought by the debtor in any other part of the UK as long as the creditor remains habitually resident in the part of the UK in which the decision was given, unless the parties have the courts of that other part of the UK or the creditor submits to the jurisdiction of the courts of that other part.[97]

Other provisions

There are special rules as to the service of process when the defendant is habitually resident in a State other than the Member State where the action is brought and does not enter an appearance.[98] Application may be made to the courts of a Member State for such provisional, including protective, measures, as may be available under the law of that State even if the courts of another Member State have jurisdiction under the Maintenance Regulation to the substance of the matter.[99] The exercise of jurisdiction is subject to rules as to *lis pendens* and related actions.[100]

13–022

The Maintenance Regulation contains in Ch.VII (arts 49 to 63) detailed provisions, largely modelled on those in the Hague Convention of 2007, establishing a network of Central Authorities to facilitate the obtaining and enforcement of decisions as to maintenance. Chapter IV (arts 44 to 47) of the Regulation contain provisions as to legal aid.[101] The Regulation gives parties who are involved in a dispute covered by this Regulation a qualified right to effective access to justice in another Member State, including enforcement and appeal or review procedures.

After a foreign decree

The English courts formerly had no jurisdiction to make an order for financial provision where the main decree was granted by a foreign court. The liberality of the English rules for the recognition of foreign decrees coupled with the restrictive approach of some foreign courts in considering financial provision produced cases of serious hardship to wives and children. Remedial legislation

13–023

---

[96] Article 8.
[97] SI 2011/1484, Sch.6, para.9.
[98] Article 11. For the position as between different parts of the UK, see SI 2011/1484, Sch.6, para.11.
[99] Article 14. For the position as between different parts of the UK, see SI 2011/1484, Sch.6, para.14.
[100] Articles 12 and 13.
[101] Very few non-EU States are as yet parties to the Convention.

based on recommendations by the Law Commission[102] was enacted as Pt III of the Matrimonial and Family Proceedings Act 1984. This is, however, now subject to the Maintenance regulation. If an application or part of an application relates to a matter within the scope of the Maintenance Regulation, the jurisdictional rules in the 1984 Act are replaced by those in the Regulation (or of the Lugano Convention where it applies). If there has been a decision as to maintenance in Member State under the Maintenance Regulation (or in a Contracting State to the Lugano Convention), any application under Pt III of the 1984 Act so far as it related to matters falling within the scope of the Regulation or Convention would constitute an attempt to vary that order.[103]

The general effect of these provisions is to enable the English courts to exercise, after a foreign decree,[104] the full range of powers to make financial provision or property adjustment orders, including consent orders and orders for the transfer of tenancies, and to prevent or set aside transactions designed to defeat applications for financial relief.[105] The powers are only available if the marriage has been dissolved or annulled, or the parties to a marriage legally separated, by means of judicial or other proceedings in an overseas country and the decree is entitled to recognition in England.[106] In addition, there are a number of important qualifications affecting the exercise of this jurisdiction.

The first is the existence of a "filter mechanism". No application for an order for financial relief after a foreign decree may be made unless the applicant has first obtained the leave of the court, and leave may not be granted unless the court considers that there is substantial ground for the making of such an order,[107] and that the enforcement mechanisms in the foreign jurisdiction have been exhausted.[108] The applicant must satisfy the court that there are substantial grounds upon which the court could be invited to exercise its powers under s.12. Where the question of financial provision is currently before a court in the foreign country in which the decree was pronounced, the court will have to consider whether England is an appropriate forum.[109] The principal object of the filter mechanism is to prevent wholly unmeritorious claims being pursued to oppress or blackmail a former spouse. The Supreme Court has held that the threshold is not high, but is higher than "serious issue to be tried" or "good arguable case" found in other contexts. It is perhaps best expressed by saying that

---

[102] *Financial Relief after Foreign Divorce*, Law Com. No. 117 (1982).

[103] It is thought that such a foreign order would not preclude an application for some other form of financial provision, e.g., a property adjustment order, under Part III. See *Agbaje v Agbaje* [2010] UKSC 13; [2010] 1 A.C. 628 at [55]–[57] where the issues were raised but not resolved.

[104] Even if granted before the 1984 Act: *Chebaro v Chebaro* [1987] Fam. 127.

[105] Matrimonial and Family Proceedings Act 1984 ss.17, 19, 22–24 and 34, as amended.

[106] Section 12(1).

[107] Section 13(1); *N. v N. (Foreign Divorce: Financial Relief)* [1997] 1 F.L.R. 900; *M v M* [2014] EWHC 925 (Fam.); [2015] 1 F.L.R. 465 (fact that foreign court uses a different methodology to value pensions insufficient). The applicant for leave must make full disclosure of the material facts: *W v W (Financial Provision)* [1989] 1 F.L.R. 22.

[108] *Jordan v Jordan* [2000] 1 W.L.R. 210.

[109] *Holmes v Holmes* [1989] Fam. 47; *M. v M. (Financial Provision after Foreign Divorce)* [1994] 1 F.L.R. 399; *Hewitson v Hewitson* [1995] Fam. 100. The principles developed in *Spiliada Maritime Corp v Cansulex Ltd.* [1987] A.C. 460 and applied in a matrimonial causes context in *De Dampierre v De Dampierre* [1988] A.C. 92 (see above, para.12–010) will be applied in considering the forum conveniens aspect.

in this context "substantial" means "solid".[110] It is not necessary for the applicant to show the existence of hardship, nor that there was injustice as a result of whatever position emerged from the foreign proceedings: these are factors to be considered in exercising the jurisdiction and not preconditions on its exercise.[111]

Leave may be granted subject to such conditions as the court thinks fit[112]; for example, the applicant may be required to give an undertaking not to enforce any order made by a foreign court or to have any such order discharged.

The second is that the parties must have a genuine connection with England; the jurisdiction is not available to those who are "birds of passage".[113] The jurisdictional requirements which reflect this policy are that the applicant must show that at one of two relevant dates, that of the initial application for the leave of the court or that on which the decree of divorce, nullity of marriage or legal separation took effect in the foreign country, either party was domiciled[114] in England or had been habitually resident there throughout the period of one year ending on that date.[115] Alternatively, it must be shown that either or both parties had, at the date of the application for leave, a beneficial interest in possession in a dwelling-house[116] situated in England which was at some time during the marriage a matrimonial home of the parties to the marriage[117]; where this is the only basis for jurisdiction the powers of the court are limited to the making of orders affecting an interest in the dwelling-house or as to lump sum payments, limited in amount to the value of that interest, to a party to the marriage or for the benefit of a child of the family.[118]

Even if the jurisdictional requirements are satisfied, the court is required, before making an order, to consider whether England is the appropriate venue.[119] If the court is not satisfied that it would be appropriate for such an order to be made by a court in England, it must dismiss the application. Factors are specified to which the court must in particular have regard:

(i) the connection which the parties to the marriage have with England, with the foreign country in which the divorce, annulment or legal separation was granted, and with any other country;

(ii) any financial benefits received or likely to be received, in consequence of the foreign decree, by virtue of any agreement or the operation of the law of any foreign country, or under a foreign order for the making of payments or the transfer of property;

---

[110] *Agbaje v Agbaje* [2010] UKSC 13; [2010] 1 A.C. 628 at [33].
[111] *Jordan v Jordan* [2000] 1 W.L.R. 210 (CA); *Agbaje v Agbaje* [2010] UKSC 13; [2010] 1 A.C. 628 at [60]–[61].
[112] Matrimonial and Family Proceedings Act 1984 s.13(3).
[113] Law Com. No. 117, para.2.9.
[114] In the traditional family law sense.
[115] Matrimonial and Family Proceedings Act 1984 s.15(1)(a)(b).
[116] Defined, s.27.
[117] Section 15(1)(c).
[118] Section 20.
[119] Section 16.

(iii)   any right which the applicant has, or has had, to apply for financial relief from the respondent under the law of any foreign country, and if the applicant has omitted to exercise that right, the reason for that omission[120];

(iv)   the availability in England of any property in respect of which an order in favour of the applicant could be made;

(v)   the extent to which any order is likely to be enforceable; and

(vi)   the length of time which has elapsed since the date of the foreign decree.[121]

Although many of the factors to be considered have much in common with those which would be relevant in a forum non conveniens enquiry, the issue is not one of forum non conveniens. Section 16 does not require the court to determine the only appropriate forum where the case may be tried more suitably for the interests of the parties and the ends of justice; no choice between jurisdictions is involved.[122]

Maintenance orders in the family court "REMO"

13–024   Special provisions are made for maintenance orders to be made by a combined operation involving the family court in England and corresponding courts in certain Commonwealth countries; this is often referred to as the REMO system, the acronym referring to the reciprocal enforcement of maintenance orders. The arrangements governing the process are not affected by the Maintenance Regulation (or the Lugano Convention).

If the respondent resides in any part of the Commonwealth to which the Maintenance Orders (Facilities for Enforcement) Act 1920 has been extended by Order in Council,[123] machinery is provided by the Act whereby an applicant wife or other dependant resident in England can get a provisional maintenance order[124] from the family court in England, which will be enforceable against the respondent if and when it is confirmed by a court in the country where he resides. It is immaterial that the applicant's cause for complaint did not arise in England.[125] The Act also provides reciprocal machinery whereby a provisional order made in the absence of the husband in a country to which the Act extends may be confirmed by the family court in England if the husband resides there and has been served with a summons. Thus there are two hearings, one in the absence of the husband, and the other in the absence of the wife. The husband may raise

---

[120] The fact that the party seeking relief might have claimed in the foreign proceedings, though significant, is not to be treated as determinative: *Moore v Moore* [2007] EWCA Civ 361; [2007] 2 F.L.R. 339.

[121] *Lamagni v Lamagni* [1995] 2 F.L.R. 452 (delay of some 13 years due to lawyers' errors); *M v L* [2003] EWHC 328 (Fam.); [2003] 2 F.L.R. 425 (after 33 years of voluntary contributions).

[122] *Agbaje v Agbaje* [2010] UKSC 13; [2010] 1 A.C. 628 at [50]; see also the discussion of "comity" at [51]–[54]. See also *Traversa v Freddi* [2009] EWHC 2101 (Fam.); [2010] 1 F.L.R. 324.

[123] The Act has been extended to a large number of Commonwealth countries: see the Maintenance Orders (Facilities for Enforcement) Order 1959/377, as amended.

[124] A "maintenance order" is defined by s.10 of the Act as an order (other than an affiliation order) for the periodical payments of sums of money towards the maintenance of the wife or other dependants of the person against whom the order is made. "Dependants" are defined to mean such persons as he is liable to maintain according to the law in force where the order was made.

[125] *Collister v Collister* [1972] 1 W.L.R. 54.

any defence that he might have raised in the original proceedings, but no other defence. It is entirely within the discretion of the court whether to confirm the order with or without modifications, or refuse to confirm it, or remit the case to the court which made the order for the purpose of taking further evidence. This machinery is sometimes known as the "shuttlecock" procedure.[126] Of course the machinery is defective, in that the wife at the first hearing cannot be cross-examined on behalf of the husband, and the husband at the second hearing cannot be cross-examined on behalf of the wife. But it is better than no machinery at all.

Part I of the Maintenance Orders (Reciprocal Enforcement) Act 1972 as amended, which is intended ultimately to replace the Act of 1920,[127] makes similar and more elaborate provision for the reciprocal enforcement of maintenance orders, not confined to cases where the defendant is resident in any part of the Commonwealth. Pt I of the Act differs from the Act of 1920 in several respects, of which the following are the most important:

(1)   It applies to Scotland as well as to England and Northern Ireland.
(2)   It can be extended to any country outside the UK which is prepared to grant reciprocal treatment to UK orders (called in the Act a "reciprocating country"[128]) and not merely to any part of the Commonwealth outside the UK.
(3)   It defines a maintenance order so as to include an affiliation order,[129] which the Act of 1920 did not.
(4)   The "shuttlecock" procedure applies to orders varying or revoking maintenance orders.[130] The provisions of the Act of 1920 in this respect were found to be defective.[131]
(5)   It defines a maintenance order so as to include an order for the payment of a lump sum,[132] which the Act of 1920 did not.

Since the general scheme of Pt I of the Act is the same as that of the Act of 1920, there is no need to give a detailed exegesis here.

Part II of the Maintenance Orders (Reciprocal Enforcement) Act 1972 gives effect to the New York Convention on the Recovery of Maintenance Abroad 1956, negotiated under the aegis of the United Nations.[133] It provides a procedure under which there is only one hearing, in the country where the defendant resides. The Convention is tersely drafted and this has given rise to considerable differences in interpretation, reducing its effectiveness.

---

[126] See *Pilcher v Pilcher* [1955] P. 318, 330.
[127] See s.22(2)(a), which repeals the Act of 1920. This subsection is not yet in force.
[128] Section 1. The countries which have been designated as "reciprocating countries" (usually with a restricted definition of "maintenance orders") are listed in statutory instruments. Modified versions are applied to those Hague Convention countries which are not EU Member States (it now applies only to Australia, Switzerland and Turkey); and to the US).
[129] Section 21.
[130] Sections.5, 9.
[131] See *Pilcher v Pilcher* [1955] P. 318.
[132] Section 21(1)(a), as amended by Civil Jurisdiction and Judgments Act 1982 Sch.11, para.4.
[133] A modified version of Pt II of the Act applies to the US: SI 2007/2006.

Choice of law

13–025   Under the 1920 and 1972 Acts, there are some exceptional situations in which an English court has to apply the law of a reciprocating country. In all other cases, the English court will apply its own domestic law. This principle was re-affirmed by the Supreme Court in *Granatino v Radmacher*.[134] Although the court cited without disapproval an earlier case[135] in which it was said that there could be "a sideways look at foreign law as part of the discretionary analysis required by [English] substantive law", the Supreme Court emphasised that the weight to be given to a pre-nuptial contract governed by German law was entirely matter for English domestic law.

The Hague Conference on Private International Law adopted in November 2007 a Protocol on the Law Applicable to Maintenance Obligations.[136] The Protocol is essentially a revision of earlier Hague Conventions of 1956 and 1973, which had attracted support entirely from States in the civil law tradition. Article 15 of the Maintenance Regulation provides that the law applicable to maintenance obligations is to be determined in accordance with the Protocol in those Member States bound by the Hague Protocol. The UK is not, and will not be, so bound.

Enforcement of foreign maintenance orders

Common law

13–026   A foreign maintenance order for periodical payments ranks at common law as a foreign judgment in personam. If, as is usually the case, the foreign court has power to vary the amount of the payments, the foreign order cannot be enforced in England at common law, because it is not "final and conclusive".[137] However, if the foreign court has power to vary the amount of future payments, but not that of past payments, then the arrears may be recovered in England by an action on the foreign judgment.[138]

This is the position at common law, and it usually prevents the enforcement of foreign maintenance orders in England. But the common law has been radically altered by the Maintenance Regulation and by statutes which provide for the reciprocal enforcement of maintenance orders within the UK, and also between England (and Northern Ireland) and countries of the Commonwealth overseas, and between the UK and designated countries overseas.

---

[134] [2010] UKSC 42; [2011] A.C. 534.
[135] *C v C (Ancillary Relief: Nuptial Settlement)* [2004] EWHC 742 (Fam.); [2005] Fam. 250.
[136] See Bonomi, (2008) 10 Yb.P.I.L. 333.
[137] *Harrop v Harrop* [1920] 3 K.B. 386; *Re Macartney* [1921] 1 Ch. 522; *Cartwright v Cartwright* [2002] EWCA Civ. 931; [2002] 2 F.L.R. 610. The rule is criticised by Grodecki (1959) 8 I.C.L.Q. 18, 32–40; but it is well established. The rule is not followed in Ireland: *McC v McC* [1994] 1 I.R.L.M. 101 (Irish High Ct.).
[138] *Beatty v Beatty* [1924] 1 K.B. 807.

Orders made in Member States

The Maintenance Regulation contains provisions as to recognition and enforcement of maintenance decisions.[139] Many provisions of the Regulation are very similar to those of the Hague Convention on the International Recovery of Child Support and Other Forms of Family Maintenance, though the Regulation deals, as the Hague Convention does not, with jurisdiction as well as recognition and enforcement. The Hague Convention was designed to take account of important developments in the field (notably the move in countries such as Australia and the UK from court-based to administrative, formula-driven maintenance systems), to meet the specific needs of the US which has a very large amount of "traffic" in this area, and to replace the United Nations Convention on the Recovery Abroad of Maintenance of 1956, the provisions of which have proved unsatisfactorily vague.[140] Subject to some transitional provisions,[141] the Maintenance Regulation applies only to proceedings instituted, to court settlements approved or concluded, and to authentic instruments established after 18 June 2011. **13–027**

Different rules as to recognition and enforcement apply depending on the source of the decision. The rules in s.1 (arts 17 to 22) of Ch.IV of the Regulation applying to decisions given in a Member State bound by the Hague Protocol of 23 November 2007 on the law applicable to maintenance obligations. Section 2 (arts 23 to 38) applies to decisions given in a Member State not bound by that Protocol; apart from the UK, the only Member State not bound by the Hague Protocol is Denmark.[142]

Section 3 (arts 39 to 43) of the Regulation contains provisions applying whatever the origin of a decision. So, the procedure for the enforcement of decisions given in another Member State is to be governed by the law of the Member State of enforcement. A decision given in a Member State which is enforceable in the Member State of enforcement must be enforced there under the same conditions as a decision given in that Member State of enforcement.[143] Under no circumstances may a decision given in a Member State be reviewed as to its substance in the Member State in which recognition, enforceability or enforcement is sought.[144] Recovery of any costs incurred in the application of the Regulation is not to take precedence over the recovery of maintenance.[145]

---

[139] "Decision" is defined (art.2(1)) as a decision in matters relating to maintenance obligations given by a court of a Member State, whatever the decision may be called, including a decree, order, judgment or writ of execution, as well as a decision by an officer of the court determining the costs or expenses.

[140] The Convention entered into force on 1 January 2013; the UK and other EU Member States became bound by it on 1 August 2014.

[141] Articles 75, 76.

[142] For the recognition and enforcement of maintenance decisions from Denmark (and to certain cases under the transitional provisions in art.75(2)(a) and (b)), see SI 2011/1484, Sch.1, Part 3.

[143] Article 41(1).

[144] Article 42. Under art.19, a defendant who did not enter an appearance in the Member State of origin has the right to apply for a review of the decision before the competent court of that Member State in certain circumstances.

[145] Article 43.

A decision given in a Member State other than Denmark will be recognised in England without any special procedure being required and without any possibility of opposing its recognition.[146] Such a decision which is enforceable in the Member State of origin is enforceable in England without the need for any declaration of enforceability.[147]

Jurisdiction in relation to applications for enforcement of such a maintenance decision lies with the courts for the part of the UK in which (a) the person against whom enforcement is sought is resident, or (b) assets belonging to that person and which are susceptible to enforcement are situated or held.[148] In England, application is to be made to the family court. The claimant must provide the court with: (a) a copy of the decision which satisfies the conditions necessary to establish its authenticity; (b) what is referred to as an "extract from the decision" (actually a detailed form prescribed in Annex I to the Regulation setting out all relevant details) completed by the court of origin; (c) where appropriate, a document showing the amount of any arrears and the date such amount was calculated; (d) where necessary, a transliteration or a translation of the "extract of the decision". The court may require the claimant to provide a translation of the decision itself if, but only if, the enforcement of the decision is challenged.[149]

An enforceable decision carries with it by operation of law the power to proceed to any protective measures available in English law.[150] For the purposes of the enforcement of a relation to its enforcement the same powers, and proceedings for or with respect to its enforcement may be taken, as if the decision had originally been made by the enforcing court.[151]

The recognition and enforcement of a decision under the Maintenance Regulation does not in any way imply the recognition of the family relationship, parentage, marriage or affinity underlying the maintenance obligation which gave rise to the decision.[152]

By virtue of art.48, court settlements and authentic instruments which are enforceable in the Member State of origin are to be recognised and enforced in other Member States in the same way as decisions.[153]

Orders from other parts of the United Kingdom

13–028   Under Pt II of the Maintenance Orders Act 1950, a maintenance order made in one part of the UK may be registered in a court in another part of the UK if the person liable to make the payments resides there and it is convenient that the order should be enforceable there.[154] The registration of the order is therefore within the discretion of the court; but this discretion vests in the court which

---

[146] Article 17(1).
[147] Article 17(2).
[148] SI 2011/1484, Sch.1, para.4(3) as amended by SI 2012/2814, Sch.5, para.8.
[149] Article 20.
[150] Article 18.
[151] SI 2011/1484, Sch.1, para.4(4). For limited powers to refuse or suspend enforcement, see art.21; SI 2011/1484, Sch.1, para.4(10).
[152] Article 22.
[153] For the definitions of "court settlements" and "authentic instruments", see art.2(2),(3). See SI 2011/1484, Sch.3.
[154] Sections 16(1), 17(2).

made the order and not in the court which is asked to register it.[155] An order so registered in a court in any part of the UK may be enforced in that part of the UK in all respects as if it had been made by that court and as if that court had had jurisdiction to make it.[156] When a maintenance order is registered in the family court in England, that court may vary the rate of the payments under the order on an application by either party but no such variation may impose on the person liable to make payments under the maintenance order a liability to make payments in excess of the maximum rate (if any) authorised by the law for the time being in force in the part of the UK in which the maintenance order was made,[157] and this power may not be exercised where the maintenance creditor remains habitually resident in the part of the UK in which the order was made.[158]

REMO arrangements

Under s.1 of the Maintenance Orders (Facilities for Enforcement) Act 1920, a maintenance order made in a country to which the Act extends may be registered in England or Northern Ireland. Section 2 provides reciprocal machinery whereby a maintenance order made in England or Northern Ireland may be registered in a country to which the Act extends. When an order has been registered, it has the same force and effect as if it had been an order originally obtained in the court in which it is registered. The court has no discretion to refuse to register an order, nor has the husband any right to be heard to show cause against the registration, or to appeal against it. Pt I of the Maintenance Orders (Reciprocal Enforcement) Act 1972 makes similar but more elaborate provision for the registration in the UK of maintenance orders made in reciprocating countries and vice versa.

13–029

---

[155] Section 17(2), (4).

[156] Section 18(1).

[157] Section 21(1) (as amended by Domestic Proceedings and Magistrates' Courts Act 1978 Sch.2, para.(14)) and (4).

[158] Section 21(1ZA) as inserted by SI 2011/1484, reg.9, Sch.7, para.1(1), (3)(b).

CHAPTER 14

CHILDREN

As students of family law will know all too well, the English law dealing with children has become very complex. Disputes about a child's future can be bitter, and there is an enormous amount of litigation in the family court and the High Court. Unfortunately, there is a similar complexity in the relevant rules of the conflict of laws. They are found principally in two distinct instruments, an EU instrument usually referred to as the Brussels IIa Regulation[1] and a Hague Convention of 1996.[2] The inter-relationship of the two depends essentially on the habitual residence of the child. If the child is habitually resident in an EU Member State, the Regulation applies[3]; if the child is habitually resident in a non-EU Convention Contracting State, the Convention will apply.[4]

14–001

JURISDICTION OF THE ENGLISH COURT

The Brussels IIa Regulation

Scope

The Brussels IIa Regulation provides uniform jurisdictional rules for the attribution, exercise, delegation, restriction or termination of parental responsibility,[5] and almost automatic recognition of judgments throughout the EU.[6] Unlike its predecessor, which was limited to children of both spouses on the occasion of matrimonial proceedings, the Brussels IIa Regulation covers all decisions on

14–002

---

[1] Council Regulation No.2201/2003 of 27 November 2003 concerning jurisdiction and the recognition and enforcement of judgments in matrimonial matters and the matters of parental responsibility, repealing Regulation No.1347/2000. See Dutta and Schulz, (2014) 10 J.Priv.Int.L. 1. The relevant provisions of English domestic law are amended by the European Communities (Jurisdiction and Judgments in Matrimonial and Parental Responsibility Matters) Regulations 2005, SI 2005/265.
[2] Hague Convention of 19 October 1996 on Jurisdiction, Applicable Law, Recognition, Enforcement and Co-operation in respect of Parental Responsibility and Measures for the Protection of Children.
[3] See Brussels IIa Regulation, art.61 and the Convention, art.52.
[4] For the case in which a child is habitually resident in a State in neither category, see para.14–027.
[5] Article 1(1)(b). Parental responsibility is defined in art.2 as all rights and duties relating to the person or the property of a child which are given to a natural or legal person by judgment, by operation of law or by an agreement having legal effect, including rights of custody and rights of access.
[6] With the exception of Denmark.

parental responsibility, including measures for the protection of the child,[7] independent of any link with matrimonial proceedings, in order to ensure equality for all children.[8] The Regulation does not, however, apply to the establishment or contesting of a parent-child relationship, adoption, a child's name, emancipation, maintenance, trusts or succession, or criminal offences committed by children,[9] although it does apply to a public law decision to take a child into care.[10] With regard to the child's property, the Regulation only applies to measures for the protection of the child:[11] measures concerned with the child's property but not concerned with the protection of the child continue to be governed by the Brussels I (and now Brussels I *bis*) Regulation.[12]

Principal jurisdictional rule

14–003   Article 8 establishes the primary jurisdictional rule in matters of parental responsibility, giving jurisdiction to the Member State in which the child is habitually resident at the time the court is seised.[13] The meaning of "habitual residence" has been fully examined in an earlier chapter.[14] Briefly, a child will be habitually resident for this purpose in the place which reflects some degree of integration by the child in a social and family environment. The duration, regularity, conditions and reasons for the stay on the territory of a Member State and the family's move to that State, the child's nationality, the place and conditions of attendance at school, linguistic knowledge and the family and social relationships of the child in that State must be taken into consideration.[15]

This primary rule is supplemented by three additional grounds for jurisdiction, and is subject to two special rules. Provision is made for cases of *lis pendens*, and there exists a residual jurisdiction rule allowing the application of national law. The Regulation also deals with provisional or protective measures. These matters will be dealt with in turn.

---

[7] Normally thought of as public law measures in English law, but included in the Regulation under the concept of broadly defined "civil matters".

[8] Recital (5). There is no maximum age for a child in the Regulation; this is a matter for the internal law of each Member State.

[9] Article 1(3).

[10] Case C-435/06 *C (A Child)* [2007] E.C.R. I-10141; [2008] Fam. 27. This applies even if the child is placed for education and therapy in a Member State other than that of its habitual residence: Case C-92/12 PPU *Health Service Executive v SC* [2012] 2 F.L.R. 1040.

[11] Article 1(2)(e).

[12] Recital (9). For the Brussels I and Brussels I *bis* Regulations, see Ch.6.

[13] The definition of when a court is seised is found in art.16: when the document instituting the proceedings is lodged with the court, provided that the applicant has not subsequently failed to take the steps required to have service effected on the respondent.

[14] See para.3–004.

[15] Case C-497/10 *Mercredi v Chaffe* [2012] Fam 22; Case C-523/07 *Proceedings brought by A* [2009] 2 E.C.R. I-2805; *A v A (Children: Habitual Residence)* [2013] UKSC 60; [2014] A.C. 1; *Re R (Children)* [2015] UKSC 35; [2016] A.C. 76; *Re R (Children)* [2015] UKSC 35; [2016] A.C. 76.

Prorogation of jurisdiction

One additional ground, or set of grounds, for jurisdiction is established by art.12 under the heading "prorogation of jurisdiction", though more is required than a simple choice of court by the parties. The courts of a Member State exercising jurisdiction in matrimonial proceedings under art.3 of the Regulation[16] also have jurisdiction for matters relating to parental responsibility where at least one of the spouses has parental responsibility for the child and the jurisdiction has been accepted[17] expressly or otherwise unequivocally by the spouses and any other holders of parental responsibility, and is in the superior interests of the child.[18] The courts of a Member State also have jurisdiction in matters relating to parental responsibility where the child has a substantial connection with that Member State (in particular because someone with parental responsibility is habitually resident in that State, or the child is a national of that State) and the jurisdiction has been accepted expressly or otherwise unequivocally by all the parties to the proceedings, and is in the best interests of the child.[19] In neither case is it essential that the child be resident in a Member State.[20]

14–004

The expression "accepted expressly or otherwise unequivocally" has been considered in a number of cases. Where someone initiates proceedings in a particular court, acceptance of jurisdiction will be readily inferred,[21] but not if the first step taken in those proceedings is to challenge the jurisdiction of the court.[22]

---

[16] See para.12–003, above.

[17] That is, jurisdiction over parental responsibility rather than over the matrimonial proceedings: *Bush v Bush* [2008] EWCA Civ 865; [2008] 2 F.L.R. 1437. Members of the Supreme Court expressed different views in *Re I (A Child) (Contact Application: Jurisdiction)* [2009] UKSC 10; [2010] 1 A.C. 319 as to the time (whether before or after the court becoming seised) at which agreement had to be expressed; but once given, agreement could not be withdrawn; the CJEU held in Case C-656/13 *L v M* [2015] Fam. 173 that the agreement must be at the latest at the time when the document instituting the proceedings or an equivalent document is lodged with the court chosen. Acceptance cannot be limited to certain aspects of responsibility: *AP v TD* [2010] EWHC 2040 (Fam.); [2011] 1 F.L.R. 1851.

[18] Article 12(1); *Butt v Butt* [2010] EWHC 1989 (Fam); [2011] 1 F.L.R. 54. *The Practice Guide for the application of the new Brussels II Regulation* (published by the European Commission in consultation with the European Judicial Network), p.17, makes it clear that the drafters did not intend there to be any distinction between the term "superior" and "best" interests of the child; and in fact other language versions use identical wording in arts 12(1)(b) and 12(3)(b); this has been accepted in *Bush v Bush* [2008] EWCA Civ 865; [2008] 2 F.C.R. 139 and in *Re I (A Child) (Contact Application: Jurisdiction)* [2009] UKSC 10; [2010] 1 A.C. 319. For the termination of jurisdiction when a final judgment is given or the proceedings end for some other reason, see art.12(2).

[19] Article 12(3). cf. *Re A (children) (removal outside jurisdiction: habitual residence)* [2011] EWCA Civ 265; [2011] 1 F.L.R. 2025; *H v H* [2011] EWCA Civ 796. art.12(4) adds that it will be deemed to be in the child's interest for the Member State to have jurisdiction under the provisions of the Article where the child is habitually resident in a State that is not a Contracting State to the Hague Convention of 1996, if it is found impossible to hold proceedings in the State of the child's habitual residence.

[20] *Re I (A Child) (Contact Application: Jurisdiction)* [2009] UKSC 10; [2010] 1 A.C. 319 (child in Pakistan).

[21] *Re C (A Child) (Jurisdiction and Enforcement of Orders relating to Child)* [2012] EWHC 907 (Fam.); [2012] 2 F.L.R. 1191.

[22] Case C-656/13 *L v M* [2015] Fam. 173. cf. Case C-215/15 *Gogova v Iliev* (failure of court-appointed lawyer to contest jurisdiction not acceptance by the parties).

Jurisdiction based on the child's presence

14–005   It is not always easy or even possible to determine the habitual residence of a child. The Brussels IIa Regulation addresses this difficulty by providing that where the child's habitual residence cannot be established and jurisdiction cannot be founded on art.12, then the courts of the Member State in which the child is present have jurisdiction.[23]

Provisional and protective measures

14–006   Article 20(1) of the Brussels IIa Regulation provides that in urgent cases its provisions do not prevent the courts of a Member State from taking such provisional, including protective, measures in respect of persons or assets in that State as may be available under the law of that Member State, even if, under the Regulation, the court of another Member State has jurisdiction as to the substance of the matter. Courts may be tempted to abuse this power in order to secure a final outcome which they judge desirable, but it has been held repeatedly that the provision is to be interpreted strictly and used only exceptionally.[24] The child must be protected from harm but the court must act so as to assist the foreign court in its task of making the final decision.[25]

Qualifications on the general rule: transfer to a more appropriate forum

14–007   Forum non conveniens in the traditional common law sense is all but outlawed by the Brussels I Regulation[26] and (less certainly) by the Brussels IIa Regulation so far as it deals with matrimonial proceedings. However, the Brussels IIa Regulation in its provisions on matters of parental responsibility enables a court with jurisdiction to stay its proceedings either in whole or in part in favour of a more appropriate court. Article 15 contains detailed provisions under which a court may stay its proceedings, or request the court of another Member State to take jurisdiction, if the child has a particular connection with that other Member State, a court in that Member State would be better placed to hear the case (or a specific part of it), and the use of the power would be in the best interests of the child.[27] A court in one Member State may request a court in another Member State to exercise this power, so for example an English court may invite a Dutch court seised of a case to exercise its power under art.15 and transfer the case to

---

[23] Article 13. e.g., *London Borough of Lambeth v JO* [2014] EWHC 3597 (Fam.) (child integrated into family and social life in both England and Nigeria).

[24] Case C-523/07 *Proceedings brought by A* [2009] 2 E.C.R. I-2805; Case C-403/09 PPU *Detiček v Sgueglia* [2009] E.C.R. I-12193; [2010] Fam. 104. On difficulties caused by the latter case in treating "persons" as including the parents as well as the child, see Kruger and Samyn, (2016) 12 J.Priv.Int.L. 132 at 149.

[25] *Re S (Care; Jurisdiction)* [2008] EWHC 3013 (Fam.); [2009] 2 F.L.R. 550.

[26] See para.7–033.

[27] Article 15(1); *Re D (A Child) (Transfer of Proceedings)* [2014] EWCA 152; [2014] 2 F.L.R. 1372; *Re J (Brussels II Revised: Article 15)* [2015] EWCA Civ 1112.

England.[28] The child is to be considered to have a particular connection to a Member State for this purpose if that Member State: (a) has become the habitual residence of the child after the original court was seised; or (b) is the former habitual residence of the child; or (c) is the place of the child's nationality; or (d) is the habitual residence of a holder of parental responsibility; or (e) is the place where property of the child is located and the case concerns measures for the protection of the child relating to the administration, conservation or disposal of this property.[29] In order to determine whether there is a better forum in which to hear the case, the courts may co-operate either directly or through the Central Authorities.[30]

Although to an English lawyer this seems to be a form of forum non conveniens, the case law governing practice under that doctrine is inapplicable: as the Court of Appeal has held that "the construction of article 15 must be uniform throughout the courts of the member states. It cannot be dominated by a domestic law approach in cases brought under the domestic jurisdiction".[31]

Qualifications on the general rule: continuing jurisdiction in certain access cases

Once the court of a Member State is seised under the primary rule, it may continue to have jurisdiction, even after a change in the child's habitual residence, for certain limited purposes connected with access rights. Where the proceedings as to parental responsibility in one Member State have led to a judgment on access rights, and the child acquires a new habitual residence by moving lawfully to another Member State, art.9 permits the courts of the former habitual residence to continue to exercise jurisdiction for a three-month period[32] for the purpose of modifying the judgment on access rights. The courts of the child's new habitual residence do not have jurisdiction in this period, during which the holder of access rights, who will normally be still habitually resident in the Member State of origin, can apply to the same court for a variation when those access rights can no longer be exercised. However, art.9 does not apply if the holder of access rights has accepted the jurisdiction of the new court by participating in proceedings before that court without contesting its jurisdiction.[33] It is important to stress that this provision only relates to access rights; it does not prevent the courts of the new Member State from deciding other matters as long as the proceedings in the first court have become final and not subject to appeal.[34]

14–008

---

[28] The facts of *B v B (Brussels II Revised: Article 15)* [2008] EWHC 2965 (Fam.); [2009] 1 F.L.R. 517.

[29] Article 15(3).

[30] Article 15(6).

[31] *Re T (A Child) (Care Proceedings: Request to Assume Jurisdiction)* [2013] EWCA Civ 895; [2014] Fam. 130.

[32] Calculated from the date the child physically moves from the Member State of origin; *Practice Guide*, p.14.

[33] Article 9(2).

[34] Articles 17 and 19; *A v A (Jurisdiction: Brussels II)* [2002] 1 F.L.R. 1042, a case under the repealed Regulation 1347/2000.

However, it has been pointed out[35] that this provision is not without its problems since it appears to assume that the child will acquire a new habitual residence immediately on moving from one Member State to another. In English law the concept requires a period of time to have passed before the courts will find that a new habitual residence has been acquired. During the intervening period the court of the Member State of origin will not have jurisdiction under art.9 since the child will not be habitually resident anywhere. Presumably, then, during this time it will be the courts of the child's future habitual residence that will have jurisdiction under art.13 on the grounds of the child's presence, defeating the purpose of maintaining jurisdiction with the court originally seised to vary the original order during a short period of time.

Lis pendens

14–009   Where two sets of proceedings are initiated in the courts of different Member States, art.19 establishes the familiar rule of *lis pendens*. Where the proceedings for parental responsibility in different Member States relate to the same child and the same cause of action, the court second seised must stay its proceedings in favour of the court first seised until such time as the court first seised establishes its jurisdiction, at which time the court second seised will decline jurisdiction,[36] unless the court first seised stays its proceedings on the forum non conveniens grounds described in art.15.

Residual jurisdiction

14–010   If no court of a Member State has jurisdiction under arts 8 to 13, then jurisdiction is to be determined in each Member State by the laws of that State,[37] and those decisions will also be recognised and enforceable in other Member States pursuant to the rules of the Regulation.[38] This type of jurisdiction also applies as between different parts of the UK. This was an assumption made in drafting the European Communities (Jurisdiction and Judgments in Matrimonial and Parental Responsibility Matters) Regulations 2005,[39] and it has been accepted by the courts.[40]

The Hague Convention of 1996

14–011   The Hague Convention of 19 October 1996 on Jurisdiction, Applicable Law, Recognition, Enforcement and Co-operation in respect of Parental Responsibility and Measures for the Protection of Children has similarities to the EU provisions

---

[35] McEleavy, (2004) 53 I.C.L.Q. 503 at 508.

[36] Article 19(2) and (3). See Case 296/10 *Purrucker v Pérez* [2011] Fam. 312 (test where court first seised deals with provisional measures only).

[37] Article 14. For the English rules, see para.14–019.

[38] Articles 21, 28; *Practice Guide*, p.18.

[39] SI 2005/265.

[40] *Re W-B (Family Jurisdiction: Appropriate Jurisdiction within the UK)* [2012] EWCA Civ 592; [2013] 1 F.L.R. 394; *Re PC (Brussels IIR: Jurisdiction within the UK)* [2013] EWHC 2336 (Fam.); [2014] 1 F.L.R. 605.

but also some significant differences which produce unwelcome complication. For ease of comparison what follows uses, as appropriate, the same sub-headings used for the EU Regulation.

Scope

The Convention defines "parental responsibility" as including "parental authority, or any analogous relationship of authority determining the rights, powers and responsibilities of parents, guardians or other legal representatives in relation to the person or the property of the child".[41] Provision is made for a system of Central Authorities in each Contracting State with duties designed to facilitate international co-operation.[42]

14–012

Principal jurisdictional rule

Article 5 of the Convention gives jurisdiction to the state of the child's habitual residence, the same rule as is found in the Brussels IIa Regulation. The two instruments diverge in dealing with the qualifications on this general rule.

14–013

Prorogation of jurisdiction

The courts of a Contracting State exercising jurisdiction to decide upon an application for divorce or legal separation of the parents of a child habitually resident in another Contracting State, or for annulment of their marriage, have jurisdiction if, at the time of commencement of the proceedings, one of his or her parents habitually resides in that State and one of them has parental responsibility in relation to the child, and the jurisdiction has been accepted by the parents, as well as by any other person who has parental responsibility in relation to the child, and is in the best interests of the child.[43] It will be seen that, in contrast to the position under the Brussels IIa Regulation, this provision is limited to cases in which there are matrimonial proceedings, though the jurisdictional basis for those proceedings is not limited to those set out in art.3 of Brussels IIa.

14–014

Jurisdiction based on the presence of the child

Under the Convention, jurisdiction based on the presence of the child may be exercised not only where the child's habitual residence cannot be established, but also in the case of refugee children and children who, due to disturbances occurring in their country, are internationally displaced.[44]

14–015

---

[41] Article 1(2). Articles 3 and 4 set out in detail what is included and what excluded; the language is different but resulting scope seems the same as under the EU Regulation.
[42] Articles 29 to 39.
[43] Article 10.
[44] Article 6 described as creating a *forum necessitatis* in *Re NH (1996 Child Protection Convention: Habitual Residence)* [2015] EWHC 2299 (Fam.).

Provisional, including and protective, measures

14–016   There are some fairly elaborate provisions in the Convention as to protective and other provisional measures. In all cases of urgency, the authorities of any Contracting State in whose territory the child or property belonging to the child is present have jurisdiction to take any necessary measures of protection.[45] The Explanatory Report gives examples: if it is necessary to ensure the representation of a child who is away from his or her habitual residence and who must undergo an urgent surgical operation, or it is necessary to make a rapid sale of perishable goods belonging to the child.[46] Subject to art.7, the authorities of a Contracting State in whose territory the child or property belonging to the child is present have jurisdiction to take measures of a provisional character for the protection of the person or property of the child which have a territorial effect limited to the State in question, in so far as such measures are not incompatible with measures already taken by authorities which have jurisdiction under arts 5 to 10.[47] All these measures lapse when the necessary steps have been taken by the authorities of the state of habitual residence.

Qualifications on the general rule: transfer to a more appropriate forum

14–017   Where the authority of a Contracting State having jurisdiction considers that the authority of another Contracting State would be better placed in the particular case to assess the best interests of the child, it may either request that other authority, directly or with the assistance of the Central Authority of its State, to assume jurisdiction, or suspend consideration of the case and invite the parties to introduce such a request before the authority of that other State. However, the Contracting States which may be approached in this way are limited. They are those of which the child is a national, in which property of the child is located, whose authorities are seised of an application for divorce or legal separation of the child's parents, or for annulment of their marriage, or with which the child has a substantial connection. The authority addressed may assume jurisdiction if it considers that this is in the child's best interests.[48] As in the EU Regulation, the initiative may be taken by a Contracting State qualified to take a transfer.[49]

Qualifications on the general rule: continuing jurisdiction in certain cases

14–018   In case of wrongful removal or retention of the child (defined as in the Hague Abduction Convention), the authorities of the Contracting State in which the child was habitually resident immediately before the removal or retention keep their jurisdiction until the child has acquired a habitual residence in another State, and *either* each person, institution or other body having rights of custody has

---

[45] Article 11.
[46] Paragraph 68.
[47] Article 12.
[48] Article 8.
[49] Article 9.

acquiesced in the removal or retention *or* the child has resided in that other state for a period of at least one year after the person, institution or other body having rights of custody has or should have had knowledge of the whereabouts of the child, no request for return lodged within that period is still pending, and the child is settled in his or her new environment.[50] It will be seen that this provision speaks of the child acquiring a habitual residence in "another state", not necessarily a Contracting State. If that other state is in fact another Contracting State, then so long as the authorities of the Contracting State first mentioned retains jurisdiction, the authorities of the Contracting State to which the child has been removed or in which he or she has been retained can take only such urgent measures as are necessary for the protection of the person or property of the child.[51]

The rules in English law

If no court of a Member State has jurisdiction pursuant to arts 8 to 13 of Regulation 2201/2003,[52] and the Hague Convention does not apply, the traditional rules of English law will govern jurisdiction. The same is true in intra-UK cases. **14–019**

Inherent jurisdiction

Traditionally, the sovereign as *parens patriae* is interested in the welfare of his or her minor subjects who because of tender years are incapable of looking after themselves. The duty to protect their interests was delegated to the Lord Chancellor, from whom it passed first to the Court of Chancery and then to the High Court. This is the origin of the inherent jurisdiction as to children. It is usually invoked by making the child a ward of court. Under it, the court has very extensive powers in relation to the child: it can, for example, restrain him (more usually her) from marrying without the court's consent, prevent him from leaving the country, or send him abroad to be looked after by a foreign guardian. Anyone who disregards an order of the court made in the inherent jurisdiction is liable to severe penalties for contempt of court. **14–020**

The English courts still retain this inherent jurisdiction, although it is now very limited in scope. The English court has jurisdiction if the child concerned is a British citizen, even though the child is not present or habitually resident in England.[53] This may have felt entirely appropriate in the days of Empire but it can now seem exorbitant. The courts have never entirely ruled out reliance on this basis for jurisdiction and the Supreme Court re-affirmed its continued existence in 2013, but also emphasised that its use should be truly exceptional.[54]

---

[50] Article 7(1).
[51] Article 7(3).
[52] See Brussels IIa Regulation, art.14 and Family Law Act 1986 s.2(1)(b).
[53] *Hope v Hope* (1854) 4 D.M. & G. 328; *Re Willoughby* (1885) 30 Ch.D. 324; *Harben v Harben* [1957] 1 W.L.R. 261.
[54] *A v A (Children: Habitual Residence)* [2013] UKSC 60; [2014] A.C. 1 at [59]ff *Re B (A Child) (Inherent Jurisdiction)* [2015] EWCA Civ cf. *Al Habtoor v Fotheringham* [2001] EWCA Civ 186

The High Court will also have jurisdiction in respect of a child if the child is present, or ordinarily or habitually resident, in England, even though the child is domiciled abroad and owns no property in England and even though guardians have already been appointed for the child by the courts of his or her domicile.[55] This basis of jurisdiction was re-affirmed by the House of Lords in *Re S (A Minor) (Custody: Habitual Residence)*[56]:

> S was the child of a Moroccan father and an Irish mother; the parents were not married. The day after the death of the mother in an English hospital, S was taken to Ireland by his maternal grandmother and an aunt. The next day, the father made S a ward of the English court. It was found as a matter of fact that the mother was habitually resident in England at the time of her death. S was therefore also habitually resident in England at that time.

The House of Lords held that the English courts had jurisdiction on the basis of the habitual residence of S, which continued despite the death of his mother, at the time the inherent jurisdiction was invoked. The House approved an earlier decision of the Court of Appeal[57] that the English courts had jurisdiction over a child (in that case, a stateless child) on the basis of its presence in England. In *Re S*, the child was an Irish citizen, but the House of Lords held that the English courts could exercise their jurisdiction even though, by the time of the order, the child had been removed from England and was now living in the country of its nationality. The courts have rejected domicile as an alternative basis for jurisdiction. In *Re P (GE) (An Infant)*[58] Russell LJ said that "the whole trend of English authority on the parental jurisdiction of the Crown over infants bases the jurisdiction on protection as a corollary of allegiance in some shape or form. Domicile is an artificial concept which may well involve no possible connection with allegiance".

The Children Act 1989 and "section 8 orders"

14–021   Section 8 of the Children Act 1989 provides for the making of what are known as "section 8" orders: child arrangement orders, prohibited steps orders and specific issue orders. The rules as to jurisdiction to grant s.8 orders are contained in Pt I of the Family Law Act 1986. English courts have jurisdiction to make such orders in four cases:

(a)   in the course of proceedings for divorce, nullity of marriage or judicial separation ("the divorce basis");

(b)   where the child was habitually resident in England ("the habitual residence basis");

(CA); [2001] 1 F.L.R. 951. See *Re B (A Child) (Inherent Jurisdiction)* [2015] EWCA Civ 886 at [45] where the court listed words used to describe the kind of circumstances in which it might be used: "only under extraordinary circumstances", "the rarest possible thing", "very unusual", "really exceptional", "dire and exceptional", and "at the very extreme end of the spectrum."

[55] *Johnstone v Beattie* (1843) 10 Cl. & F. 42; *Stuart v Marquis of Bute* (1861) 9 H.L.C. 440; *Nugent v Vetzera* (1866) L.R. 2 Eq. 704; *Re D.* [1943] Ch. 305; *J v C* [1970] A.C. 688, 720.

[56] [1998] A.C. 750.

[57] *Re P (G.E.) (An Infant)* [1965] Ch. 568.

[58] [1965] Ch. 568, 592. cf. Lord Denning MR at p.583.

(c)   where the child was in England and the immediate intervention of the court was required for the child's protection ("the emergency basis"); and

(d)   where the child was in England and was not habitually resident in any UK country ("the residual presence basis").[59]

To avoid conflicts of jurisdiction within the UK, priority would be given to jurisdiction on the divorce basis as against the habitual residence and residual presence bases. The emergency basis would always be available but would be capable of being superseded by the exercise of jurisdiction on that or any other basis in another UK country.[60] The crucial date for determining priority is that of the application. So, for example, the court of the country of the child's habitual residence to which an application for an order has been made retains jurisdiction to consider that application even if divorce proceedings are later commenced in another part of the UK.[61] An order made by a court in any one part of the UK in reliance on these principles supersedes any earlier order made by any other such court.[62]

Power to stay proceedings

The English courts have a broad power to stay proceedings when the matter is being or could more appropriately be litigated in the court of another country.[63] The courts apply principles similar to those developed in the case of matrimonial proceedings in *De Dampierre v De Dampierre*.[64] An illustration is provided by *M v B (Child: Jurisdiction)*[65]:   **14–022**

> Both parents were US citizens and the child was born in Texas. They came to England only because of the father's posting as part of his duties in the US Air Force. The parents separated, father and child returning to the US. The mother commenced proceedings in England at a time when the child was with her under agreed shared custody arrangements, but took no steps to take those proceedings forward. The father began proceedings in a US court. The court recognised that whatever forum dealt with the matter, one parent would face inconvenience and expense. The English proceedings were stayed: the case was essentially about an American family and was best dealt with there.

It has been held that in these cases the welfare of the child is important but not paramount.[66]

---

[59] Law Com. No. 138 (1985), paras 4.1–4.92.
[60] ibid., paras 4–91–4–115.
[61] *Dorward v Dorward*, 1994 S.C.L.R. 928.
[62] Family Law Act 1986 s.6(1)(2) (as amended by Children Act 1989 Sch.13, para.62).
[63] Family Law Act 1986 s.5(2) as amended.
[64] [1988] A.C. 92; see para.12–011. See also *Re D (Stay of Children Act Proceedings)* [2003] EWHC 565 (Fam); [2003] 2 F.L.R 1159.
[65] [1994] 2 F.L.R. 819.
[66] *Re S (Residence Order: Forum Conveniens)* [1995] 1 F.L.R. 314; *M v M (Stay of Proceedings: Return of Children)* [2005] EWHC 1159 (Fam.); [2006] 1 F.L.R. 138.

Removal of child from England

14–023   Where an order under the Children Act 1989 dealing with the residence of a child is in force, no person may remove the child from the UK without either the written consent of every person who has parental responsibility for the child or the leave of the court.[67] This does not prevent the removal of a child, for a period of less than one month, by the person in whose favour the order is made.[68] A court making an order may grant leave for the removal of the child from the jurisdiction, and may do so generally or for specified purposes[69] such as a holiday to get to know other members of the child's family.[70]

The principles to be applied when considering whether to grant permission for a child to be permanently removed from the jurisdiction were for many years those contained in the Court of Appeal's judgments in *Payne v Payne*.[71] However, in *DF v N B-F*[72] Ryder LJ observed that

> "in the decade or more since *Payne* it would seem odd indeed for this court to use guidance which out of the context which was intended is redolent with gender based assumptions as to the role and relationships of parents with a child. Likewise, the absence of any emphasis on the child's wishes and feelings or to take the question one step back, the child's participation in the decision making process, is stark. The questions identified in *Payne* may or may not be relevant on the facts of an individual case and the court will be better placed if it concentrates not on assumptions or preconceptions but on the statutory welfare question which is before it".

The leading case is now the Court of Appeal's decision in *MK v CK*.[73] In that case Black LJ emphasised that "the principle—the only authentic principle—that runs through the entire line of relocation authorities is that the welfare of the child is the court's paramount consideration. Everything that is considered by the court in reaching its determination is put into the balance with a view to measuring its impact on the child". The "welfare checklist" in s.1(3) of the Children Act 1989[74] is a useful guide. Where the foreign country is one the legal system of which might not respect the rights of the parent remaining in England, great care will be

---

[67] Children Act 1989 s.13(1).

[68] Section 13(2).

[69] Section 13(3).

[70] *Re S (Leave to Remove from Jurisdiction: Securing Return from Holiday)* [2001] 2 F.L.R. 507, in which it was held that a child has rights under the European Convention on Human Rights to know both sides of its family.

[71] [2001] EWCA Civ 166; [2001] 2 F.L.R. 1052; for criticism, see Hayes, (2006) 18 C.F.L.Q. 351.

[72] [2015] EWCA Civ 882 at [18].

[73] [2011] EWCA Civ 293; [2011] 3 F.C.R. 111, See also *Re F (A Child) (Relocation)* [2012] EWCA Civ 1364; [2013] 1 F.L.R. 645 where the majority judgments in *MK v CK* are preferred to those of Thorpe LJ.

[74] "...[A] court shall have regard in particular to (a) the ascertainable wishes and feelings of the child concerned (considered in the light of his age and understanding); (b) his physical, emotional and educational needs; (c) the likely effect on him of any change in his circumstances; (d) his age, sex, background and any characteristics of his which the court considers relevant; (e) any harm which he has suffered or is at risk of suffering; (f) how capable each of his parents, and any other person in relation to whom the court considers the question to be relevant, is of meeting his needs; (g) the range of powers available to the court under this Act in the proceedings in question."

taken before the court gives permission.[75] In cases involving countries following Islamic principles, the courts have sometimes required a notarised agreement to return the child backed by an order of the courts of the foreign country,[76] or a sworn declaration before a Sharia judge[77]; in the absence of such safeguards, permission may be refused.[78]

An order restricting the removal from the jurisdiction of a child who is still under 16 has effect in each part of the UK other than the part in which it was made, as if it had been made by the appropriate court in that other part. If it prohibits the removal of a child to a particular part, e.g., England, it has the effect in England of prohibiting the further removal of the child from England except to a place to which he or she could be moved consistently with the order.[79]

CHOICE OF LAW

Traditionally, an English court seeking to resolve issues concerning children applies English domestic law. This is qualified where an international convention so requires. Although the Brussels IIa Regulation contains no choice of law rules, the 1996 Hague Convention does. Article 15 provides that in exercising their jurisdiction under the Convention, the authorities of the Contracting States are to apply their own law. The implementing legislation in England applies the same rule when the court takes jurisdiction under the Regulation.[80] As the Explanatory Report to the Convention observes,[81] the principal argument which can be made in support of this rule is that it facilitates the task of the authority which has taken jurisdiction since it will thus apply the law which it knows best. To require the authority exercising jurisdiction in all circumstances that it apply the law of the state of the child's habitual residence would have uselessly complicated the protection of the child. However, in so far as the protection of the person or the property of the child requires, the authority seised of the case may exceptionally apply or take into consideration the law of another State with which the situation has a substantial connection.[82]

14–024

The attribution or extinction of parental responsibility by operation of law, without the intervention of a judicial or administrative authority, is governed by the law of the State of the habitual residence of the child.[83] A change in the child's habitual residence does not affect existing parental responsibility but the

---

[75] In the case of a country not party to the Hague Abduction Convention, expert evidence of the foreign law may be insisted upon: *Re M (Removal from Jurisdiction: Adjournment)* [2010] EWCA Civ 888; [2011] 1 F.L.R. 1943 (proposed holiday in Cameroon).
[76] *Re T (Staying Contact in Non-Convention Country)* [1999] 1 F.L.R. 262.
[77] *Re A (Security for Return to Jurisdiction)* [1999] 2 F.L.R. 1.
[78] As in *Re K (A Minor) (Removal from the Jurisdiction: Practice)* [1999] 2 F.L.R. 1084.
[79] Family Law Act 1986 s.36.
[80] Parental Responsibility and Measures for the Protection of Children (International Obligations) (England and Wales and Northern Ireland) Regulations 2010, SI 2010/1898, reg.7.
[81] Paragraph 86.
[82] Convention art.15(2).
[83] Article 16(1).

law of the State of the new habitual residence may give parental responsibility by operation of law to a person who does not already have such responsibility.[84]

Similarly, the exercise of parental responsibility is governed by the law of the State of the child's habitual residence; if the child's habitual residence changes, it is governed by the law of the State of the new habitual residence.[85]

EFFECT OF FOREIGN ORDERS IN ENGLAND

European Union orders

14–025   The Brussels IIa Regulation provides that any judgment given by the courts of a Member State of the EU[86] is to be recognised in the other Member States without any special procedure being required.[87] Any interested party may apply for recognition and enforcement in one Member State of a judgment on parental responsibility given by the courts of another Member State.[88]

Article 23 lists the grounds under which a court must refuse to recognise a judgment given in another Member State: if it is manifestly contrary to public policy taking into account the best interests of the child[89]; if it was given, except in cases of urgency, without the child having been given the opportunity to be heard, in violation of fundamental principles of procedure of the Member State in which recognition is sought[90]; if it was given in default of appearance of a party who was not served with the initiating document or not served in time to arrange a defence unless that person has accepted the judgment unequivocally[91]; if a person with parental responsibility had not been given the opportunity to be heard; if it is irreconcilable with another judgment; or if art.56 had not been complied with where the court places a child in another Member State. The jurisdiction of the court of the Member State of origin may not be reviewed,[92] and under no circumstances may a judgment be reviewed as to its substance.[93]

In order for a judgment of another Member State to be enforced in a part of the UK, it must be an enforceable judgment in the Member State of origin and registered for enforcement in the relevant part of the UK.[94] The grounds for

---

[84] Article 16(2)(3).

[85] Article 17.

[86] Except Denmark.

[87] Article 21(1).

[88] Article 21(3).

[89] *Re L (A Child) (Recognition of Foreign Order)* [2012] EWCA Civ 1157; [2013] Fam. 94: this ground is a very narrow one and set the bar very high. A high onus rested on a parent who sought to reopen welfare issues and a foreign judgment would not be subverted save in the most exceptional of circumstances; a high degree of disparity was required between the effects of the order if enforced and the child's welfare interests.

[90] See, e.g., *Re D (Recognition and Enforcement of Romanian Order)* [2014] EWHC 2756 (Fam.); [2015] 1 F.L.R. 1272, where the next two grounds were also made out.

[91] See *MD v CT (parental responsibility: recognition and enforcement of foreign judgment)* [2014] EWHC 871 (Fam.); [2015] 1 F.L.R 213.

[92] Article 24. See Case C-195/08 PPU *Inga Rinau* [2008] E.C.R. I-5271; [2009] Fam. 51.

[93] Article 26.

[94] Article 28(2).

refusal of enforcement are the same as for refusal of recognition.[95] The grounds remain the same, but their application may differ: in a case under the original Brussels II Regulation, a court found that, since it was possible for facts to change between the two stages, what was not manifestly contrary to public policy at recognition stage could be so at enforcement stage.[96]

The Brussels IIa Regulation dispenses with this procedure in two types of cases: the return of a child following an abduction[97] and the recognition and enforcement of access rights. One of the main concerns of the Regulation is to ensure that the child continues to benefit from access to the non-custodial parent even where they live in different Member States. Therefore, holders of access rights may enforce them directly on production of a certificate issued by the court of origin.[98] Rights of access include in particular the right to take a child to a place other than his or her habitual residence for a limited period of time.[99] The *Practice Guide* makes it clear that access rights are a matter for national law and, therefore, may be held by the non-custodial parent, or other family members such as grandparents.[100]

Orders from Contracting States to the 1996 Hague Convention

Similarly, art.23 of the Hague Convention of 1996 provides that the measures taken by the authorities of a Contracting State shall be recognised by operation of law in all other Contracting States. **14–026**

Recognition may however be refused if the relevant authority did not have jurisdiction under the rules in Ch.II of the Convention; if the measure was taken, except in a case of urgency, in the context of a judicial or administrative proceeding, without the child having been provided the opportunity to be heard, in violation of fundamental principles of procedure of the requested State[101]; on the request of any person claiming that the measure infringes his or her parental responsibility, if such measure was taken, except in a case of urgency, without such person having been given an opportunity to be heard; if such recognition is manifestly contrary to public policy of the requested State, taking into account the best interests of the child; if the measure is incompatible with a later measure taken in the non-Contracting State of the habitual residence of the child, where this later measure fulfils the requirements for recognition in the requested State; or if in the case of the proposed transfer of the child to foster or institutional care in another state, the special procedure in art.33 of the Convention was not followed.

---

[95] Article 31(2).
[96] *X v Y* [2003] EWHC 2974 (Fam.); [2004] 1 F.L.R. 582.
[97] See below para.14–039.
[98] Article 41.
[99] Article 2(10).
[100] At p.24.
[101] See *G v G* [2014] EWHC 4182 (Fam.) (Russian order refused recognition).

Orders from other states

14-027   An order made by a court in a State which is neither a Member State of the EU nor a Contracting State to the Hague Convention does not prevent the English court from making such orders with respect to the child as, having regard to the child's welfare, it thinks fit.[102] A striking illustration of this principle is afforded by *McKee v McKee*,[103] decided by the Privy Council:

> A husband and wife, American citizens resident in the US, separated and agreed that neither should remove their minor son out of the US without the written consent of the other. In 1945, in divorce proceedings in California, custody of the boy was awarded to the mother, and the father was allowed access. At that time the boy was living with the father under a previous custody order of the Californian court. On Christmas Eve 1946, when he heard that his last appeal against the custody order had failed, the father, in breach of his agreement and without the knowledge or consent of the mother, took the boy to Ontario and settled with him there. The mother then began habeas corpus proceedings in Ontario. In 1947, after a hearing lasting 11 days, the Ontario judge awarded the custody of the boy to the father. His decision was affirmed by a majority of the Ontario Court of Appeal, reversed by a majority of the Supreme Court of Canada, but restored by the Privy Council.

The entire process of litigation in *McKee v McKee* took many years, itself a matter for concern; and the end result did not produce clarity in the law. All that was decided was that a foreign order did not prevent the courts of Ontario from reviewing the matter, applying their understanding of the welfare of the child; but it was left open to the court to do so by way of a full review of the merits or in a more summary fashion, returning the child promptly where that seemed best.

In declining to be bound by foreign orders, English courts are prompted by two considerations. The first is that an order by its nature is not final and is at all times subject to review by the court that made it. The second is that under the Children Act 1989 the welfare of the child is the first and paramount consideration.

This has been interpreted to apply not only to domestic English cases, but also to cases involving a previous order made by a foreign court. This approach has disadvantages: it can create uncertainty, and so instability, in the life of a child, and it can encourage litigation as a parent, denied custody by a foreign court, seeks a more favourable decision in England. A different approach is gaining support in international conventions and EU law, and the Family Law Act 1986 provides for the recognition in each part of the UK of orders made in any other part of the UK and for machinery for their registration and enforcement.[104] In cases not covered by these provisions, the weight to be given in England to a foreign order must depend on the circumstances of the case. An order made very recently, where no relevant change of circumstances is being alleged, will carry great weight.[105] Its persuasive effect is diminished by the passage of time and by a significant change in circumstances, for example the removal of the child to

---

[102] *J v C* [1970] A.C. 668, 700 per Lord Guest; *Re B's Settlement* [1940] Ch. 54; *McKee v McKee* [1951] A.C. 352; *Re Kernot* [1965] Ch. 217; *Re T (an Infant)* [1969] 1 W.L.R. 1608; *Re R. (Minors)* (1981) 2 F.L.R. 416.
[103] [1951] A.C. 352.
[104] Section 25 (as amended).
[105] *McKee v McKee* [1951] A.C. 352, 364; *Re H (Infants)* [1966] 1 W.L.R. 381, 399.

another country.[106] The effect of the foreign order will be weakest when it was made many years ago and has since been modified by consent and the child has nearly attained majority and so can make a personal decision as to with which parent he or she wishes to live.[107]

INTERNATIONAL CHILD ABDUCTION

The courts treat international abduction[108] (or "kidnapping") cases as a special category, or at least one in which the special circumstances have a strong influence on the manner in which the welfare principle is to be applied. In many cases the kidnapping is in defiance of a custody order made by a foreign court,[109] but the same principles apply to any unilateral kidnapping of a child by one parent from the other. **14–028**

The time factor is particularly important in kidnapping cases: a full consideration of the merits of the case may take a long time, since much of the evidence may have to come from abroad, and during that time the child may develop roots in England, a fact which will strengthen the claim of the kidnapper and threaten a grave injustice to the innocent parent. To minimise this risk, the English courts have been prepared to make orders for the peremptory return of a kidnapped child without making a full examination of the merits of the dispute.[110] Decisions of the European Court of Human Rights, made in the context of the Hague Abduction Convention and considered below,[111] placed for a while a question mark against that practice, which however continues to be followed.

Judicial statements as to how this power to make a peremptory order should be exercised reveal a number of shifts of emphasis. At one time it was held that a peremptory order should not be made unless the court was satisfied beyond reasonable doubt that to do so would inflict serious harm on the child, but following the emphatic assertion of the welfare of the child as the first and paramount consideration by the House of Lords in *J v C*,[112] the Court of Appeal held that the principles to be applied in considering the making of a peremptory order were exactly the same as in all other decisions relating to the welfare of children.[113] The courts take into account the psychological damage to the child caused by a sudden removal from a familiar environment, at a time when his or her family life was disrupted; but also the risk of harm to the child if he or she were returned. For a period of time, the Court of Appeal held that decisions in

---

[106] *Re T (An Infant)* [1969] 1 W.L.R. 1608.

[107] ibid.

[108] See generally Lowe, Everall and Nicholls, *International Movement of Children* (Bristol: Jordan Publishing Ltd, 2004).

[109] For a case concerning contempt of court proceedings where a father defied the English court's order to return the child to England, see: *Re A (A Child)* [2008] EWCA Civ 1138.

[110] *Re H (Infants)* [1966] 1 W.L.R. 381; *Re E (D) (An Infant)* [1967] Ch. 287, 761; *Re C (Minors)* [1978] Fam. 105. That the court does have the power to return the child immediately without a full examination of the merits was confirmed by the House of Lords in *Re J (A Child) (Custody Rights: Jurisdiction)* [2005] UKHL 40; [2006] 1 A.C. 80.

[111] See para.14–038.

[112] [1970] A.C. 688 (not an abduction case).

[113] *Re L (Minors)* [1974] 1 W.L.R. 250; *Re C (Minors)* [1978] Fam. 105; *Re R (Minors)* (1981) 2 F.L.R. 416.

international abduction cases should reflect the principles of the Hague Convention on the Civil Aspects of Child Abduction, even if the foreign country concerned were not a party to the Convention.[114] The normal result of applying those principles was that the child must be returned to the country of habitual residence; but subsequently the courts have now recognised that where the country concerned is not a Convention country, each decision must be based on the welfare principle.[115] Baroness Hale in the House of Lords case *Re J (A Child) (Custody Rights: Jurisdiction)*, confirming the paramountcy of the welfare of the individual child, stated that "[t]he most one can say, in my view, is that the judge may find it convenient to start from the proposition that it is likely to be better for a child to return to his home country for any disputes about his future to be decided there. A case against his doing so has to be made. But the weight to be given to that proposition will vary enormously from case to case."[116]

The courts will always consider the desirability of hearing the views of the child or children concerned, to give effect to the principles expressed in art.12 of the United Nations Convention on the Rights of the Child 1989 and art.24 of the Charter of Fundamental Rights of the EU.[117]

In exercising this discretion, the English court will examine whether the courts of the country to which a child may be returned would apply the welfare principle. Differently constituted Courts of Appeal have taken opposite approaches when considering the welfare of a child from a very different legal system. In *Re JA (Child Abduction: Non-Convention Country)*,[118] Ward LJ held that it was an abdication of responsibility and an abnegation of the duty of the English court to surrender the determination of the child's future to a foreign court whose regime may be inimical to the child's welfare. On that other hand, Thorpe LJ in *Osman v Elasha (Abduction: Non-Convention Country)*[119] was of the opinion that "[w]hat constitutes the welfare of the child must be subject to the cultural background and expectations of the jurisdiction striving to achieve it." The House of Lords, preferring the approach taken by Ward LJ, has confirmed[120] that differences between legal systems cannot be irrelevant but that their relevance will depend on the facts of each individual case.[121] If the foreign court must follow the father's wishes rather than approach the mother's application

---

[114] *G v G* [1991] 2 F.L.R. 506 (decided in May 1989); *Re F (A Minor) (Abduction: Custody Rights)* [1991] Fam. 25; *Re S (Minors) (Abduction)* [1993] 1 F.C.R. 789; *Re S (Minors) (Abduction)* [1994] 1 F.L.R. 6; *Re M (Abduction: Non-Convention Country)* [1995] 1 F.L.R. 89.

[115] *D v D (Child Abduction)* [1994] 1 F.L.R. 137; *Re P (A Minor) (Abduction: Non-Convention Country)* [1997] Fam. 45; *Re JA (Child Abduction: Non-Convention Country)* [1998] 1 F.L.R 231; *B v El-B (Abduction: Sharia Law: Welfare of Child)* [2003] 1 F.L.R. 811; McClean and Beevers (1995) 7 Ch. & F.L.Q. 128; *Re J (a Child)* [2005] UKHL 40.

[116] [2005] UKHL 40; [2006] 1 A.C. 80, at para.32.

[117] *Re S (A Child) (Abduction: Hearing the Child)* [2014] EWCA Civ 1557; [2015] Fam. 263.

[118] [1998] 1 F.L.R. 231.

[119] [2000] Fam 62. See also *Al Habtoor v Fotheringham:* [2001] EWCA Civ 186; [2001] 1 F.L.R. 951; *Re S (Child Abduction: Asylum Appeal)* [2002] EWHC 816; [2002] 2 F.L.R. 437; *B v El-B (Abduction: Sharia Law: Welfare of Child)* [2003] 1 F.L.R. 811; Beevers, [2003/4] *Contemporary Issues in Law* 302.

[120] *Re J (A Child) (Custody Rights: Jurisdiction)* [2005] UKHL 40; [2006] 1 A.C. 80.

[121] See, for example, *Re H (Abduction: Dominica: Corporal Punishment)* [2006] EWHC 199 (Fam.); [2006] 2 F.L.R. 314 where the country concerned condoned treating children with physical violence.

with an open mind, then the English court must consider whether it is in the interests of the child for the dispute to be heard in the foreign court.

In cases where the abductor argues that, on return, the children would be taken from her or she would be subject to criminal proceedings, the courts have attempted to safeguard the best interests of the child and the rights of the returning parent by requiring certain undertakings to be put in place before the return is effected.[122] In *Re S (Child Abduction: Asylum Appeal)*[123] two children were returned to India even though their mother was appealing against a refusal of asylum decision on the grounds that she was being persecuted by the father. Bennett J accepted the father's undertakings that he would not institute any criminal proceedings against the mother, nor remove the children from the mother's care, would provide financially for her and the children, and undertake not to molest them.[124] Although accepting that the undertakings were not enforceable, the judge said: "[t]hey provide, in my judgment, if adhered to, proper and adequate protection and support, including financial support for the mother and the children."[125] Although the courts are conscious of the fact that undertakings are not enforceable,[126] and research has shown that they are often broken,[127] they are still probably the best way of safeguarding the children's and returning parent's interests in the circumstances.

International instruments

The Child Abduction and Custody Act 1985 gives the force of law in the UK to two international conventions concluded in 1980. The first is the Luxembourg Convention, a product of the Council of Europe; it is essentially a convention for the enforcement of custody orders. The second, the Hague Child Abduction Convention, drawn up by the Hague Conference on Private International Law, has as its main object the return of a child abducted across national boundaries to the State of its habitual residence. Each convention seeks to protect existing rights of custody and to discourage the international abduction of children in breach of those rights. In consequence, where a child so abducted is to be found in England and one of the conventions applies, the powers of the English courts to review the merits and to form their own judgment as to what best serves the welfare of the child are largely eliminated. The Brussels IIa Regulation takes precedence over both these Conventions in its sphere of operation,[128] in effect replacing the rules of the Luxembourg Convention and supplementing the Hague Convention within the EU.

14–029

---

[122] *Re Z (Abduction: Non-Convention Country)* [1999] 1 F.L.R. 1270; *Re S (Child Abduction: Asylum Appeal)* [2002] EWHC 816; [2002] 2 F.L.R. 437; *Re H (Child Abduction: Mother's Asylum)* [2003] EWHC 1820 (Fam); [2003] 2 F.L.R. 1105.
[123] [2002] EWHC 816; [2002] 2 F.L.R. 437.
[124] ibid. at para.71.
[125] ibid. at para.92.
[126] *Re JA (Child Abduction: Non-Convention Country* [1998] 1 F.L.R. 231 at p.244C; *W and W v H (Child Abduction: Surrogacy) (No.2)* [2002] 2 FLR 252. cf *U v U* [2010] EWHC 1179 (Fam.); [2011] 1 F.L.R. 354 where the undertakings were thought enforceable.
[127] McClean, [1997] C.F.L.Q. 387. See also Beevers [2003/4] C.I.L. 303.
[128] Brussels IIa Regulation, art.60(d).

In January 2003, the President of the Family Division and the Chief Justice of Pakistan signed a UK–Pakistan Protocol[129] in an attempt to protect children from the harmful effects of child abduction. Although the courts have started to apply the protocol in UK–Pakistan cases,[130] the legal effect of the document is unclear.[131]

The European (Luxembourg) Convention

14–030   A European Convention on Recognition and Enforcement of Decisions Concerning Custody of Children and on the Restoration of Custody of Children was prepared under the auspices of the Council of Europe and signed in Luxembourg on 20 May 1980.[132] The 1985 Act gives effect to the provisions of the Convention dealing with the recognition and enforcement of decisions,[133] with certain omissions,[134] but not those dealing with abduction where the provisions of the later Hague Convention are preferred. The adoption of successive European Regulations and the expansion of the EU means that the Convention now has very limited effect, and it is not examined further here.

The Hague Child Abduction Convention

14–031   A Convention on the Civil Aspects of International Child Abduction was prepared under the auspices of the Hague Conference on Private International Law and signed on 25 October 1980.[135] Part I of the Child Abduction and Custody Act 1985 gives effect to this Convention, which deals with custody rights arising in another Contracting State by operation of law or by reason of an agreement having legal effect as well with custody decisions of judicial or administrative authorities.[136] The Convention deals with cases of wrongful removal or retention of a child in breach of rights of custody, and operates on the basis of a semi-automatic return of the child to the country of his or her habitual residence. The effective operation of the Convention relies heavily on a system of Central Authorities established in each Contracting State. The Convention is much used and has given rise to a great mass of case law, most decisions turning on the

---

[129] [2003] Fam Law 199; "Guidance from the President's Office—Implementation of the UK–Pakistan Judicial Protocol on Child Contact and Abduction" (2004) 34 Fam L.J. 609.

[130] *A v A* (Unreported, 2 February 2004); Binns, (2004) 34 Fam L.J. 359. For an example of circumstances in which the Protocol will not apply see *Re H (Child Abduction: Mothers Asylum)* [2003] EWHC 1820 (Fam); [2003] 2 F.L.R. 11-05.

[131] See Young, (2003) 66 M.L.R. 823.

[132] For full text, see Cmnd. 8155 (1981); a partial text forms Sch.2 to the Child Abduction and Custody Act 1985. For commentary, see Jones (1980) 30 I.C.L.Q. 467.

[133] Child Abduction and Custody Act 1985 s.12.

[134] Article 8 of the original text of the Convention is omitted and arts 9 and 10 are modified in consequence of a reservation made by the UK under art.17; see Child Abduction and Custody Act 1985 s.12(2).

[135] For detailed analysis of the Convention see: Beaumont and McEleavy, *The Hague Convention on International Child Abduction* (Oxford; Oxford University Press, 1999); Lowe, Everall and Nicholls, op. cit.; Trimmings, *Child Abduction within the European Union* (Oxford: Hart Publishing, 2013); Schuz, *The Hague Child Abduction Convention: A Critical Analysis* (Oxford: Hart Publishing, 2013).

[136] Convention, art.3.

particular facts; only a few illustrative cases can be cited here. As Black LJ has well observed: "It may be thought paradoxical that a summary procedure such as this should have generated the quantity of jurisprudence that the 1980 Convention has. Over the years there have been many technical and sophisticated legal arguments about how its terms should be interpreted and a significant number of appeals. Technicality of this sort gets in the way of the objectives of the Convention".[137] As Baroness Hale and Lord Walker explained in *Re E (children) (international abduction)*[138]:

> "The first object of the Convention is to deter either parent (or indeed anyone else) from taking the law into their own hands and pre-empting the result of any dispute between them about the future upbringing of their children. If an abduction does take place, the next object is to restore the children as soon as possible to their home country, so that any dispute can be determined there. The left-behind parent should not be put to the trouble and expense of coming to the requested state in order for factual disputes to be resolved there. The abducting parent should not gain an unfair advantage by having that dispute determined in the place to which she has come. And there almost always is a factual dispute, if not about the primary care of the children, then certainly about where they should live, and in cases where domestic abuse is alleged, about whether those allegations are well-founded. Factual disputes of this nature are likely to be better able to be resolved in the country where the family had its home."

The procedure under the convention is that the Central Authority of the state to which the child has been wrongfully removed, or in which it is wrongfully retained, on receiving an application for the return of the child either directly from a person, institution or body concerned or from another Central Authority,[139] must take or cause to be taken all appropriate measures in order to obtain the voluntary return of the child; failing an amicable settlement it must initiate,[140] or facilitate the institution of, proceedings with a view to obtaining an order for the return of the child. The competent authorities are to act expeditiously[141] in such proceedings, and where there has been wrongful removal[142] or retention must order the return of the child forthwith, unless certain grounds for refusal are made out.[143] Where one of these grounds is made out, the court's consideration of the child's future is guided by the welfare test, taking into account the overall purpose and structure of the Convention.[144] The policy of the

---

[137] *Re M (Children) (Child's Objections)* [2015] EWCA Civ 26; [2016] Fam.1, at [12]–[13]. Black LJ endorsed the observation of Wilson LJ that could apply to the whole of our subject: "Nowadays not all law can be simple law; but the best law remains simple law.": *Re P-J (Children)* [2009] EWCA Civ 588; [2010] 1 W.L.R. 1237.

[138] [2011] UKSC 27; [2012] 1 A.C. 144, at para.[8].

[139] Although an application can be made to the court directly, *HA v MB* [2007] EWHC 2016 (Fam.) at para.21.

[140] For the conflict between the two aims of speedy return and amicable settlement see Armstrong, (2002) 51 I.C.L.Q. 427.

[141] Indeed damages have been awarded by the European Court of Human Rights where the delay was excessive, *Deak v Romania and the United Kingdom* [2008] E.C.H.R. 19055/05; [2008] 2 F.C.R. 303.

[142] The High Court has the power to make a declaration that the removal or retention of a child in another country is wrongful; Convention art.15; Child Abduction and Custody Act s.8; *Re L (Children) (Abduction Declaration)* [2001] 2 F.C.R. 1; *Re G (child Abduction) (Unmarried Father: Rights of Custody)* [2002] EWHC 2219 (Fam); [2003] 1 W.L.R. 493.

[143] Convention arts 7–12.

[144] The principles to be applied in undertaking that discretion were spelt out by the House of Lords in *Re M (Children) (Abduction: Rights of Custody)* [2007] UKHL 55; [2008] 1 A.C. 1288.

Convention is to secure the swift return of the child. A heavy burden therefore rests upon an abducting parent who seeks to invoke one of the grounds for refusal. We must now examine some of the terms used in the convention.

Rights of custody

14–032
The phrase "rights of custody" has a Convention meaning which will not necessarily coincide with the meaning of that term in the domestic law of either of the countries concerned, but draws its definition from the definitions, structure and purposes of the Convention. The rights include rights relating to the care of the person of the child and, in particular, the right to determine the child's place of residence.[145] This last phrase will include, for example, the right of a parent who does not have custody of a child to give or refuse consent to the removal of the child from the jurisdiction by the custodian parent,[146] but not a mere right to be consulted and to express views.[147]

The rights of custody may be attributed to a person, an institution, or any body,[148] either jointly or alone. They must exist under the law of the state in which the child was habitually resident immediately before the removal or retention where those rights were actually exercised at the time of removal or retention (or would have been but for the removal or retention).[149] The reference to rights held jointly is important: in most countries parents will be joint custodians of the child in the absence of any order or agreement to the contrary, and either will be able to take steps under the Convention in respect of wrongful removal or retention of the child by the other.

Article 3 of the Convention provides, therefore, that for the removal or retention to be wrongful, it should be in breach of rights of custody that exist under the law of the child's habitual residence immediately before the abduction. The term "law of habitual residence", however, includes that country's rules of private international law[150] and it may be that the rights of custody ultimately fall

---

[145] Convention art.5.

[146] *C v C (Abduction: Rights of Custody)* [1989] 1 W.L.R. 654; *Re P (a child) (abduction: acquiescence)* [2004] EWCA Civ 971; [2005] Fam. 85; *Re F (Children) (Abduction: Rights of Custody)* [2008] EWHC 272 (Fam.); [2008] Fam. 75; *Re D (A Child) (Abduction: Rights of Custody)* [2006] UKHL 51; [2007] 1 A.C. 619. See *Neulinger v Switzerland* [2009] ECHR 41615/07; [2011] 1 F.L.R. 122 (Grand Chamber) at paras 65–74.

[147] *Re V-B (Abduction: Custody Rights)* [1999] 2 F.L.R. 192; *Re D (A Child) (Abduction: Rights of Custody)* [2006] UKHL 51; [2007] 1 A.C. 619.

[148] This term will include a court in cases where the child has been made a ward of court *(Re J (Abduction: Ward of Court)* [1989] Fam. 85) and cases in which the court is currently seised of a custody dispute concerning the child *(B v B (Child Abduction: Custody Rights)* [1993] Fam. 32; *Re H (Child Abduction: Rights of Custody)* [2000] 2 All E.R. 1); but not cases of the mere issue of proceedings for a residence order, where there had been no service on the other party, *Re C (child abduction) (unmarried father: rights of custody)* [2002] EWHC 2219 (Fam); [2003] 1 W.L.R. 493.

[149] Convention art.3. See also art.13(a). These rights are not suspended even though a parent in temporarily incapable of exercising full day-to-day rights because of being in prison; *Re A (Rights of Custody: Abduction: Imprisonment)* [2004] 1 F.L.R. 1.

[150] Perez-Vera, "Explanatory Report of the Hague Convention on the Civil Aspects of International Child Abduction" *Actes et Documents of the XIVe Session*, Volume III, 1982, 426 at para.70.

to be decided by the law of another country to which the child is connected by some other means such as nationality.[151]

In English law a person with "parental responsibility" in the terms of the Children Act 1989 is a person with "rights of custody" for the purposes of the Convention, for "parental responsibility" includes the right to determine where the child shall live. It would seem to follow that where an unmarried father has no parental responsibility (or its equivalent under the law of the relevant foreign country) the removal of the child by the mother cannot be wrongful, even if the father has had joint de facto custody.[152] However, where the child was not in the care of the custodial parent immediately before the abduction because that parent had entrusted the child to the other parent or a family member, the English courts have developed a species of "inchoate rights" so that the carer's rights are protected rights for the purposes of the Convention. The development of this notion was reviewed by the Supreme Court in *Re K (A Child)*.[153] Baroness Hale defined the category of those entitled under this doctrine:

> "(a) They must be undertaking the responsibilities, and thus enjoying the concomitant rights and powers, entailed in the primary care of the child. ... (b) They must not be sharing those responsibilities with the person or persons having a legally recognised right to determine where the child shall live and how he shall be brought up. They would not then have the rights normally associated with looking after the child. (c) That person or persons must have either abandoned the child or delegated his primary care to them. (d) There must be some form of legal or official recognition of their position in the country of habitual residence. This is to distinguish those whose care of the child is lawful from those whose care is not lawful. Examples might be the payment of state child-related benefits or parental maintenance for the child. And (e) there must be every reason to believe that, were they to seek the protection of the courts of that country, the status quo would be preserved for the time being, so that the long term future of the child could be determined in those courts in accordance with his best interests, and not by the pre-emptive strike of abduction".

It will be seen that the courts have not yet reached the point where the unmarried father who is jointly caring for his child can rely on that de facto custody to give him rights of custody to be protected.[154]

Wrongful removal and wrongful retention

The Convention refers to "wrongful removal" or "wrongful retention", meaning in each case removal or retention out of the jurisdiction of the courts of the state of the child's habitual residence.[155] The contrast between the two phrases is between an act of removal which at once breaches custody rights, and a keeping of the child which only breaches those rights when it is continued beyond the limits of lawfulness in terms of time; a typical example of wrongful retention

14–033

---

[151] *Re JB (Child Abduction) (Rights of custody: Spain)* [2003] EWHC 2130; [2004] 1 F.L.R 796; cf. Beevers & Pérez-Milla [2007] J.P.I.L. 1 and see *Kennedy v Kennedy* [2009] EWCA Civ 986; [2010] 1 F.L.R. 782.

[152] *Re J (A Minor) (Abduction: Custody Rights)* [1990] 2 A.C. 562.

[153] [2014] UKSC 29; [2014] A.C. 1401 (which concerned the rights of a grandmother).

[154] For criticism of this situation see: *Hunter v Murrow (Abduction: Rights of Custody)* [2005] EWCA Civ 976; [2005] 2 F.L.R. 1119; Beevers [2006] C.F.L.Q. 499.

[155] *Re H (Abduction: Custody Rights)* [1991] 2 A.C. 476.

occurs when a child is not returned after an agreed period of access.[156] In each case the removal or retention is an event which occurs once and for all on a specific occasion; "removal" and "retention" are mutually exclusive concepts, and it is impossible for them to overlap, or for either of them to follow the other in the same case.[157] For the purposes of the Convention, "retention" is not a continuing state of affairs, but something which occurs when the child should have been returned to his or her custodians, or when the person with rights of custody refuses to agree to an extension of the child's stay in a place other than that of his or her habitual residence.[158] "Retention" does not necessarily entail physical restraint of any sort; the act of applying for a court order preventing the return of the child may amount to wrongful retention,[159] as may a firm decision not to return the child even if made before the expiry of the period for which it had been agreed that the child should remain with the abducting parent.[160]

Grounds for refusing return:

(i) Non-exercise of rights, consent or acquiescence

14–034 The first ground for refusal is that the person, institution or body concerned was not actually exercising the custody rights at the time of removal or retention, or had consented to or subsequently acquiesced in the removal or retention.[161] In the structure of the Convention text, "consent"[162] is something which occurs at or before the time of removal or retention, in contrast to subsequent acquiescence.[163] Consent will occasionally be express[164] but is more often inferred from the dealings between the parties. That may include dealings some time before the removal or retention, but the question is always what was the position at the time of the removal or retention.[165] Apparent consent obtained by deception will be disregarded.[166]

---

[156] ibid.

[157] *Re H (Abduction: Custody Rights)* [1991] 2 A.C. 476; *Re S (A Minor) (Abduction)* [1991] 2 F.L.R. 1.

[158] Difficult questions can arise when the removal of a child has taken place in accordance with a court judgment which (as is the case under some legal systems) was provisionally enforceable but was later overturned by a court judgment fixing the child's residence at the home of the left-behind parent; the failure then to return the child is wrongful retention: Case C-376/14 PPU *C v M* [2015] 1 F.L.R. 1.

[159] *Re B (Minors) (Abduction) (No.2)* [1993] 1 F.L.R. 993; *Re AZ (A Minor) (Abduction: Acquiescence)* [1993] 1 F.L.R. 682.

[160] *Re S (Minors) (Child Abduction: Wrongful Retention)* [1994] Fam. 70.

[161] Convention art.13(a).

[162] For a detailed consideration of "consent" see *Re P (A child) (abduction: acquiescence)* [2004] EWCA Civ 971; [2005] 2 W.L.R. 201.

[163] *Re C (Abduction: Consent)* [1996] 1 F.L.R. 414; *Re M (Abduction) (Consent: Acquiescence)* [1999] 1 F.L.R. 171; *Re H (children) (abduction: children's objections)* [2004] EWHC 2111 (Fam).

[164] *A v T (Abduction: Consent)* [2011] EWHC 3882 (Fam.); [2012] 2 F.L.R. 1333 (written agreement).

[165] Compare *Zenel v Haddow*, 1993 S.C. 612 and *Re P-J (Children) (Abduction: Habitual Residence: Consent)* [2009] EWCA Civ 588; [2010] 1 W.L.R. 1237.

[166] *Re B (A Minor) (Abduction)* [1994] 2 F.L.R. 249; *Re O (Abduction: Consent and Acquiescence)* [1997] 1 F.L.R. 924; *Re L (Abduction: Future Consent)* [2007] EWHC 2181 (Fam.); [2008] 1 F.L.R. 914.

"Acquiescence" refers to a subjective state of mind of the wronged parent in which he or she has accepted, "gone along with" the abduction. It is a pure question of fact, and the court seeks to infer the parent's actual subjective state of mind from outward and visible acts and statements; the burden of proof is on the abducting parent. The court will be slow to infer an intention to acquiesce from attempts to effect reconciliation or to reach an agreed voluntary return of the abducted child.[167] If, however, the wronged parent so conducts himself (for example, by signing an agreement as to the child's future or taking part in proceedings in the country to which the child has been abducted to resolve its long-term future) as to lead the abducting parent to believe that no return is to be insisted upon, the wronged parent cannot be heard to say that his or her actual intention was all along to claim the summary return of the child.[168] Acquiescence may also be based on the conditional agreement for the children to live in another jurisdiction as long as satisfactory contact is established.[169] Express words will not amount to acquiescence where they are spoken without knowledge of the possibility of the rights being enforced; but awareness in general terms will suffice, and there is no need to show that the party concerned was aware of, for example, the expeditious and effective enforcement machinery provided by the Convention.[170]

In *Re A (Minors) (Abduction: Custody Rights)*[171] a letter from a father in Australia saying that his child's removal to England was illegal but that he would not insist on his rights was held to constitute acquiescence despite its retraction when the father learned of the existence of the Hague Convention. The courts have retreated somewhat from that rigorous approach[172]; acquiescence for a very short period may be disregarded if it is clearly withdrawn before the abducting parent has done anything in reliance upon it.[173] Where inactivity, in the sense of failure to make an application for the return of the child for a period of time, is relied upon as amounting to acquiescence, the court will pay some attention to the

---

[167] *Re H (Minors) (Acquiescence)* [1998] A.C. 72 (rejecting the distinction drawn between "active" and passive" acquiescence in *Re A (Minors) (Abduction: Custody Rights)* [1992] Fam. 106). See McClean, (1997) 9 Ch.&F.L.Q. 387. For the effect of without prejudice negotiations, see *P v P (Abduction: Acquiescence)* [1998] 2 F.L.R. 835. The withdrawal of Hague Convention proceedings to facilitate negotiation will not give rise to acquiescence: *Re G (Children) (Abduction: Withdrawal of Proceedings, Acquiescence and Habitual Residence)*, [2007] EWHC 2807; [2008] 2 F.L.R. 351.

[168] *Re H (Minors) (Acquiescence)* [1998] A.C. 72, citing as an example *Re AZ (A Minor) (Abduction: Acquiescence)* [1993] 1 F.L.R. 682; *Re D (Abduction: Acquiescence)* [1998] 2 F.L.R. 335.

[169] *T v T* [2008] EWHC 1169 (Fam.); [2008] 2 F.L.R 972.

[170] *Re A (Minors) (Abduction: Custody Rights)* [1992] Fam. 106; *Re AZ (A Minor) (Abduction: Acquiescence)* [1993] 1 F.L.R. 682; *Re B (Abduction: Acquiescence)* [1999] 2 F.L.R. 818.

[171] [1992] Fam. 106; note dissent by Balcombe LJ.

[172] See *Re S (A Minor) (Abduction)* [1991] 2 F.L.R. 1 (child removed; custodial parent demanded not return but access; held no acquiescence in removal); *Re A (Minors) (Abduction)* [1991] 2 F.L.R. 241 ("emollient statements" to abducting parent inconsistent with conduct; expeditious application for return; acquiescence not made out); *Re I (Abduction: Acquiescence)* [1999] 1 F.L.R. 778 (negotiations not to be equated with acquiescence).

[173] *Re R (Minors: Child Abduction)* [1995] 1 F.L.R. 716. Compare *Re CT (A Minor) (Abduction)* [1992] 2 F.C.R. 92 (parent invoked Convention; later indicated would not press for return; acquiescence established) with *Re B (Minors) (Abduction) (No.2)* [1993] 1 F.L.R. 993 (consent by applicant to procedural steps in respect of custody proceedings in country in which child retained held not to be acquiescence when application for return made on same day).

subjective motives and reasons of the party concerned.[174] It will, for example, take into account the fact that the applicant had initially received erroneous legal advice,[175] and will examine whether in all the circumstances the failure promptly to commence proceedings does point to an acceptance of the situation.[176]

(ii) Grave risk of physical or psychological harm; intolerable situations

14–035   The second ground of refusal, and the one most commonly relied on in practice, is that there is a grave risk that the child's return would expose him or her to physical or psychological harm or otherwise place the child in an intolerable situation.[177] There may be special reasons why a child should not live in a particular country or undergo a change of residence,[178] but matters are seldom that straightforward.

In recent years, the majority of international child abductions have been by the child's primary carer, usually its mother; there is often a history of domestic violence.[179] In such cases, this ground of refusal becomes of even more than usual importance. The violence may not have been directed at the child, so it may not appear to be a case in which there is a grave risk that return would expose the child to physical harm, so the court faces the more difficult issues of "psychological harm" and that of placing the child in an "intolerable situation".

It is sometimes said that art.13(b) is to be restrictively interpreted, but the Supreme Court has said that there is no need for the article to be 'narrowly construed', as by its very terms, it is of restricted application. The court ruled that the words of art.13 are quite plain and need no further elaboration or 'gloss'.[180]

The English courts have taken a rather strict line when faced with allegations of domestic violence where the child has been the bystander, insisting that the grave risk of harm must be to the child and not just to the returning parent,[181] and

---

[174] *H v H (Abduction: Acquiescence)* [1996] 2 F.L.R. 570.

[175] *Re S (Minors) (Abduction: Acquiescence)* [1994] 1 F.L.R. 819. See also *Re R (Minors) (Abduction)* [1994] 1 F.L.R. 190 (four-month delay while awaiting outcome of proceedings in foreign court held not to amount to acquiescence); *Re H (children) (abduction: children's objections)* [2004] EWHC 2111 (Fam) where a 12-month delay was not held to be acquiescence in the circumstances; likewise an 18-month delay in *M v M* [2007] EWHC 1820 (Fam.); [2007] Fam. Law 888 (although the case was overturned by the House of Lords on other grounds: *Re M (Children) (Abduction: Rights of Custody)* [2007] UKHL 55; [2008] 1 A.C. 1288).

[176] *Re K (Abduction: Child's Objections)* [1995] 1 F.L.R. 977 (inactivity for six to seven months held on facts not to amount to acquiescence); *H v H (Abduction: Acquiescence)* [1996] 2 F.L.R. 570 (delay of five months, during which other proceedings, not involving a demand for the immediate return of the child, pursued; acquiescence established); *Re M (Abduction: Acquiescence)* [1996] 1 F.L.R. 315 (delay of 14 months; acquiescence made out) *Re B. (Abduction: Acquiescence)* [1999] 2 F.L.R. 818 (proceedings taken for contact, and only when that proved difficult was Convention invoked; acquiescence established).

[177] Article 13(b).

[178] e.g., *B v B (Abduction: Child with Learning Difficulties)* [2011] EWHC 2300 (Fam.); [2012] 1 F.L.R. 881; *K v D* [2014] EWHC 3188 (Fam.) (involvement of criminal gang; but ground not made out).

[179] Lowe and Perry, (1999) 48 I.C.L.Q. 127; see *Re E (children) (international abduction)* [2011] UKSC 27; [2012] 1 A.C. 144, at [7].

[180] *Re E (Children) (International Abduction)* [2011] UKSC 27; [2012] 1 A.C. 144, at [31].

[181] *K v K (child abduction)* [1998] 3 F.C.R. 207; *Re W (Abduction: Domestic Violence)* [2004] EWHC 1247; [2004] 2 F.L.R. 499.

that parents should take their problems to the courts,[182] and seek the protection of the authorities,[183] of habitual residence rather than abduct their children. Moreover, requested authorities should trust in the capability of requesting states to protect the children on return, and where situations are particularly problematic, courts should insist on undertakings[184] that make a return feasible.[185]

The courts have recognised that some psychological harm to the child may be inherent in the very conflict which is before the court or might normally be expected to occur on the transfer of a child from one parent to another; the Convention envisages more substantial harm, a severe degree of harm hinted at by the later reference to the child being "otherwise... in an *intolerable situation*".[186] There must be "clear and compelling evidence of the grave risk of harm or other intolerability which must be measured as substantial and not trivial".[187]

The Supreme Court has commented on the working of art.13 and especially art.13(b).[188] It emphasised that the burden of proof, on the ordinary balance of probabilities, lies with whoever opposes the child's return. There are, however, limitations involved in the summary nature of the Hague Convention process; it is rarely appropriate to hear oral evidence which could be tested in cross-examination. The risk to the child must be "grave", and not merely "real". Although the words "physical or psychological harm" are not qualified, they gain colour from the phrase "an intolerable situation". Every child had to put up with a certain amount of rough and tumble, discomfort and distress; it was part of growing up. But there were some things which it was not reasonable to expect a child to tolerate including, of course, physical or psychological abuse or neglect of the child him- or herself, and also exposure to the harmful effects of seeing and hearing the physical or psychological abuse of his or her own parent. Article 13(b) is looking to the future: the situation as it would be if the child were to be returned forthwith to the home country. That situation depended crucially on the protective measures which could be put in place to secure that the child would not be called upon to face an intolerable situation when he or she gets home. The appropriate protective measures and their efficacy would obviously vary from case to case and from country to country.

Where there have been allegations of a risk of harm, the courts have adopted the practice in a number of cases of requiring the applicant, before return will be ordered, to accept conditions or to give undertakings, for example as to the maintenance and accommodation of the child and the abducting parent after their

---

[182] *N v N (Abduction: art.13 Defence)* [1995] 1 F.L.R. 107.

[183] *TB v JB (Abduction: Grave Risk of Harm)* [2001] 2 F.L.R. 515.

[184] See below.

[185] *N v N (Abduction: art.13 Defence)* [1995] 1 F.L.R. 107; *K v K (child abduction)* [1998] 3 F.C.R. 207; *Re H (Abduction: Grave Risk)* [2003] EWCA Civ 355; [2003] 2 F.L.R 141; *Re W (Abduction: Domestic Violence)* [2004] EWHC 1247; [2004] 2 F.L.R. 499.

[186] *Re A (A Minor) (Abduction)* [1988] 1 F.L.R. 365; *C v C (Abduction: Rights of Custody)* [1989] 1 W.L.R. 654, 664; *Re N (Minors) (Abduction)* [1991] 1 F.L.R. 413; *B v B (Abduction: Custody Rights)* [1993] Fam. 32.

[187] *Re C (Abduction: Grave Risk of Psychological Harm)* [1999] 1 F.L.R. 1145.

[188] *Re E (children) (international abduction)* [2011] UKSC 27; [2012] 1 A.C. 144, at [32]ff.

return.[189] Undertakings of this sort may have a clear tactical advantage to the parent seeking the return of the child, for they may effectively undermine any argument that the return of the child would expose it to a grave risk of harm.[190] It is not in itself an objection to this practice that the undertakings will be unenforceable,[191] but the court may investigate the likely attitude of the foreign court to the undertakings as part of its assessment of the risk of harm to the child if return is ordered.[192] Where the other country concerned is a party to the Hague Convention on Parental Responsibility and Child Protection 1996, undertakings, or more securely court orders based on them, will be enforceable as "measures of protection" within art.11 of that Convention.[193] There are, however, dangers in the practice of accepting undertakings of this sort. The practice can come close to qualifying the clear duty of the court to order the child's return; and the court "must be careful not to usurp or be thought to usurp the functions of the court of habitual residence".[194]

(iii)   The child's objections to return

14–036   A third ground for refusal in this type of case is that the child objects to being returned and has attained an age and a degree of maturity at which it is appropriate to take account of his or her views.[195] The child's age and maturity are first assessed; if it is judged appropriate to take the child's views into account, the court must then decide what weight to give to them in the light of the return

---

[189] For examples of terms which may be agreed, see *Re W (Abduction: Domestic Violence)* [2004] EWHC 1247; [2004] 2 F.L.R. 499. For a case where undertakings were not considered sufficient to protect the child, see: *Re M (A Child)* [2007] EWCA Civ 260; [2007] 3 F.C.R. 631.

[190] See the Australian case of *McOwan v McOwan* (1994) FLC 92–451 (M had taken the child to England, claiming that F was a violent alcoholic, who failed to support his family; F undertook to provide home for sole use of M and the child, and to allow issues to be raised in proceedings already pending before the Australian Family Court; on M's return to Australia, F reneged on his promises on both counts); *Re J (children) (abduction: child's objections to return)* [2004] EWCA Civ 428; [2004] 2 F.L.R. 64 where previous undertakings had been breached.

[191] In *Re E (children) (international abduction)* [2011] UKSC 27; [2012] 1 A.C. 144, at [37] the Supreme Court urged the Hague Conference to consider whether machinery could be put in place to ensure that protective measures identified by the court in the requested state could be enforceable in the requesting state, for a temporary period at least, before the child was returned.

[192] *Re O (Child Abduction: Undertakings)* [1994] 2 F.L.R. 349.

[193] *Re Y (A Child) (Abduction: Undertakings Given for Return of Child)* [2013] EWCA Civ 129; [2013] 2 F.L.R. 649.

[194] *Re M (Abduction: Undertakings)* [1995] 1 F.L.R. 1021; *Re K (Abduction: Psychological Harm)* [1995] 2 F.L.R. 550; McClean, (1997) 9 Ch.&F.L.Q. 387. See *Re J (A Child)* [2015] UKSC 70; [2015] 3 W.L.R. 1827, per Baroness Hale at [34]: "[T]he art.11 jurisdiction should not be used so as to interfere in issues that are more properly dealt with in the home country. It is a secondary, and not the primary, jurisdiction. Thus it is one thing to use the art.11 jurisdiction in support of the home country, for example, by facilitating a return there after a wrongful removal. It is quite another thing to set up the art.11 jurisdiction in opposition to that of the home country."

[195] Convention, art.13(2); *Re S (A Minor) (Abduction: Custody Rights)* [1993] Fam. 242; *Re J (children) (abduction: child's objections to return)* [2004] EWCA Civ 428; [2004] 2 F.L.R. 64; *Re H (children) (abduction: children's objections)* [2004] EWHC 2111. See generally, McEleavy [2008] I.C.L.Q. 230.

policy of the Hague Convention other facts of the case,[196] and bearing in mind the possibility that the child could have been coached by the abducting parent.[197] The court will ask whether the child is actually voicing an objection, as opposed to a preference.[198] There is no minimum age stipulation; each child will be looked at as an individual; so in *Re R (Child Abduction: Acquiescence)*[199] siblings of seven and a half and six were judged to be mature enough that their objections gave the court discretion as to their return,[200] as was a girl of six in *Re M (A Child) (Abduction: Child's Objections)*.[201] Practice in other countries as to a minimum age varies considerably.

Cases involving two or more siblings can present special problems. A rigorous approach to the application of the Convention in such cases has been adopted in a Canadian case.[202] In that case, the return of one child, a spina bifida sufferer, was refused but a step-sister returned despite evidence that the first child was suicidal at the thought of their separation. The court took the view that art.13 had to be applied to each child separately. Even on that approach, however, it may be possible to find that the return of one child without his or her sibling would place one or other in an intolerable situation, and English courts have reached such a conclusion.[203] However, in *Re HB (Abduction: Children's Objections)*[204] a finding that only one child strongly objected to being returned meant that both children were ordered to return on the grounds it is not usually advisable to separate siblings who are close in age and in their relationship to each other.

The issue as to whether a child should be made a party to the proceedings with separate legal representation was discussed in the judgment of Baroness Hale in *Re M (Children) (Abduction: Rights of Custody)*.[205] To order separate representation in all cases would send the wrong messages to children since they should not be given an exaggerated impression of the relevance and importance of their views, but it would not send the wrong messages to so order in settlement cases under art.12,[206] cases where the views of the child are particularly important. The question the judge should consider is whether separate representation would add enough to the understanding of the case to justify the intrusion, expense and delay that may result.

---

[196] *Re S (Minors) (Abduction: Acquiescence)* [1994] 1 F.L.R. 819 (describing the three-stage approach: were the objections made out, was the child of an age and maturity, should the discretion not to return be exercised; an older child being returned against his wishes.)

[197] *Re P (Abduction: Minor's Views)* [1998] 2 F.L.R. 825; *Re K (1980 Convention: Lithuania)*[2015] EWCA Civ 720.

[198] *Re M (Children) (Child's Objections)* [2015] EWCA Civ 26; [2016] Fam. 1, at [38].

[199] [1995] 1 F.L.R. 716; where despite the objections, their return was ordered.

[200] [2007] EWCA Civ 260; [2007] 2 F.L.R. 72.

[201] [2015] EWCA Civ 26; [2016] Fam. 1.

[202] *Chalkley v Chalkley* (1995) 10 R.F.L. (4th) 442 (Man. C.A.); the Supreme Court of Canada refused leave to appeal: (1995) 11 R.F.L (4th) 376.

[203] *B v K (Child Abduction)* [1993] 1 F.C.R. 382 (disapproved but not on this point, *Re M (A Minor) (Child Abduction)* [1994] 1 F.L.R. 390).

[204] [1997] 1 F.L.R. 392 (order later set aside for other reasons: [1998] 1 F.L.R. 422); cf. *Re W (Minors)* [2010] EWCA Civ 520.

[205] [2007] UKHL 55; [2008] 1 A.C. 1288 at [57], endorsed as superseding earlier cases in *C v C* [2008] EWHC 517 (Fam.); [2008] 2 F.L.R. 6.

[206] See below at para.14–037.

(iv)   Additional ground after 12 months

14–037   Where an application for the return of a child is made after the passage of one year from the date of the wrongful removal or retention, return may also be refused if it is demonstrated that the child is now settled in his or her new environment.[207] The policy behind this rule is that in such cases, the major objective of the Convention, a swift return to the country of origin, cannot be met. As Baroness Hale put it,[208] "These are no longer 'hot pursuit' cases. By definition, for whatever reason, the pursuit did not begin until long after the trail had gone cold." "Settled" is to be given its natural meaning, which includes an examination of the existing facts demonstrating the establishment of the child in a community and an environment,[209] and a consideration of the perceived stability of the position into the future. The "new" features of the situation are to be examined: they will include place, home, school, friends, activities and opportunities, but not as such the continuing relationship with the abducting parent.[210] It is not enough for the courts to consider only the physical characteristics of the settlement, but must also take into account the emotional and psychological elements.[211] A long delay in the proceedings will not of itself excuse compliance with the Convention but it may mean that its provisions designed to protect the best interests of the child by a return to the country of habitual residence would be rendered completely unworkable.[212] It is in this type of case that the views of the children concerned are of particular importance.[213]

Effect on the Hague practice of the European Convention on Human Rights

14–038   The emphasis on a swift return of the child to the more appropriate venue to resolve the underlying issues faced an unexpected challenge from the Grand Chamber of the European Court of Human Rights in *Neulinger v Switzerland*.[214] A mother removed the child from Israel to Switzerland. There was a history of difficulties between the parents, with Israeli social services finding that the father created a hostile environment at home, an atmosphere of verbal aggression and threats that terrorised the mother, such that maintaining a common home was harmful to the child. The father's application for the return of the child under the

---

[207] Convention art.12.

[208] [2007] UKHL 55; [2008] 1 A.C. 1288 at [47].

[209] The meaning of these terms are considered in *Re C (A Child) (Child Abduction: Settlement)* [2006] EWHC 1229 (Fam.); [2006] 2 F.L.R. 797.

[210] *Re N (Minors) (Abduction)* [1991] 1 F.L.R. 413 (where an inoperative fax machine in the Lord Chancellor's Department took the case over the 12-month limit).

[211] *Cannon v Cannon* [2004] EWCA Civ 1330; [2005] 1 W.L.R. 32, where the mother abducted the child and managed to evade the authorities seeking her and the child for four years; the court held that where the parent engages in concealment and subterfuge it will be difficult for her to demonstrate that the child is settled.

[212] *Re D (A Child)(Abduction: Rights of Custody)* [2006] UKHL 51; [2007] 1 A.C. 619 at paras 4–5, where a child had been living in England for more than half his life.

[213] See above at para.14–034; *Re M (Children) (Abduction: Rights of Custody)* [2007] UKHL 55; [2008] 1 A.C. 1288; cf. Schuz [2008] C.F.L.Q. 64.

[214] [2010] ECHR 41615/07; [2011] 1 F.L.R. 122. See Walker, (2010) 6 J.Priv.I.L. 649.

Hague Convention was rejected under art.13(b), the Swiss court finding that there was a grave risk that return would expose the child to physical or psychological harm, but the Swiss Federal Court ultimately allowed an appeal by the father, holding that art.13(b) was not satisfied. The father made an application, which he later withdrew, for enforcement of the return order and was no longer in contact with the Swiss authorities.

On an application by the mother the European Court of Human Rights considered art.8 of the European Convention which protects the right to respect for an individual's private and family life. There is to be no interference by a public authority with the exercise of this right except such as is in accordance with the law and is necessary in a democratic society in the interests of national security, public safety or the economic well-being of the country, for the prevention of disorder or crime, for the protection of health or morals, or for the protection of the rights and freedoms of others.

The Grand Chamber held that the decisive issue was whether a fair balance between the competing interests at stake—those of the child, of the two parents, and of public order—had been struck, within the margin of appreciation afforded to States in such matters, bearing in mind, however, that the child's best interests must be the primary consideration. There was held to a broad consensus in support of the idea that in all decisions concerning children, their best interests must be paramount. The child's interest comprised two limbs. On the one hand, it dictated that the child's ties with his or her family must be maintained, except in cases where the family has proved particularly unfit. It followed that family ties might only be severed in very exceptional circumstances and that everything must be done to preserve personal relations and, if and when appropriate, to 'rebuild' the family. On the other hand, it was clearly also in the child's interest to ensure his or her development in a sound environment, and a parent cannot be entitled under art.8 to have such measures taken as would harm the child's health and development. This philosophy was declared to be inherent in the Hague Convention. The judgment of the Grand Chamber then contains a crucial passage:

> "138. It follows from Art.8 that a child's return cannot be ordered automatically or mechanically when the Hague Convention is applicable. The child's best interests, from a personal development perspective, will depend on a variety of individual circumstances, in particular his age and level of maturity, the presence or absence of his parents and his environment and experiences . . . . For that reason, those best interests must be assessed in each individual case . . .
>
> 139. In addition, the Court must ensure that the decision-making process leading to the adoption of the impugned measures by the domestic court was fair and allowed those concerned to present their case fully . . . To that end the Court must ascertain whether the domestic courts conducted an in-depth examination of the entire family situation and of a whole series of factors, in particular of a factual, emotional, psychological, material and medical nature, and made a balanced and reasonable assessment of the respective interests of each person, with a constant concern for determining what the best solution would be for the abducted child in the context of an application for his return to his country of origin."

The effect of *Neulinger* was examined by the Supreme Court in *Re E (children) (international abduction)*[215]. Baroness Hale and Lord Walker in a joint judgment noted that *Neulinger* had been greeted with "concern, nay even

---

[215] [2011] UKSC 27; [2012] 1 A.C. 144.

consternation" in some quarters, because of its possible impact upon the application of the Hague Convention. After the *Neulinger* ruling had been reiterated by a Chamber of the European Court of Human Rights in *X v Latvia*,[216] the Supreme Court again recorded its unhappiness: "to conduct an in-depth examination of the sort described ... would be entirely inappropriate".[217]

Fortunately, the Grand Chamber beat something of a retreat.[218] It observed that its judgment in Neulinger to which "may and has indeed been read as suggesting that the domestic courts were required to conduct an in-depth examination of the entire family situation and of a whole series of factors". This was not to be taken to "set out any principle for the application of the Hague Convention by the domestic courts". The Court considered that

"a harmonious interpretation of the European Convention and the Hague Convention can be achieved provided that the following two conditions are observed. First, the factors capable of constituting an exception to the child's immediate return in application of arts 12, 13 and 20 of the said Convention, particularly where they are raised by one of the parties to the proceedings, must genuinely be taken into account by the requested court. That court must then make a decision that is sufficiently reasoned on this point, in order to enable the Court to verify that those questions have been effectively examined. Secondly, these factors must be evaluated in the light of art.8 of the Convention. In consequence, the Court considers that art.8 of the Convention imposes on the domestic authorities a particular procedural obligation in this respect: when assessing an application for a child's return, the courts must not only consider arguable allegations of a 'grave risk' for the child in the event of return, but must also make a ruling giving specific reasons in the light of the circumstances of the case. ... Furthermore, as the Preamble to the Hague Convention provides for children's return 'to the State of their habitual residence', the courts must satisfy themselves that adequate safeguards are convincingly provided in that country, and, in the event of a known risk, that tangible protection measures are put in place".

The Brussels IIa Regulation and child abduction

14–039   In an attempt to further deter parental child abduction within the EU, the Brussels IIa Regulation provides that the Hague Child Abduction Convention will continue to be applicable but as supplemented by certain provisions that take precedence over the Convention[219] in cases of child abduction.[220]

Continuing jurisdiction of the State of habitual residence

The Regulation provides that where a child was habitually resident in a Member State immediately before a wrongful removal or retention,[221] the courts of that

---

[216] [2012] 1 F.L.R. 860.
[217] *Re S (A Child) (Abduction: Rights of Custody)* [2012] UKSC 10; [2012] 2 A.C. 257 (in the postscript to the judgment).
[218] (2014) 59 E.H.R.R. 3 at [104]–[108].
[219] Regulation art.60(e).
[220] For detailed explanation and criticism, see: McEleavy, [2005] J.P.I.L. 5; Lowe, [2004] I.F.L.J. 205; McEleavy, (2004) 53 I.C.L.Q. 503, asserting that the inclusion of these provisions is controversial since an equal number of States opposed European legislative intervention; Lowe, Everall & Nicholls, *The new Brussels II Regulation: a supplement to international movement of children* (Bristol: Jordan Publishing Ltd, 2005); Lowe [2007] I.F.L. 182.
[221] Defined in art.2(11) of the Regulation in similar but not identical terms to art.3 of the Convention; for an examination of the differences, held not determinative, see *Re K (A Child)* [2014] UKSC 29;

Member State will continue to have jurisdiction over the child until the child has acquired a habitual residence in another Member State and certain further requirements are met. It will be sufficient if every person, institution or other body having rights of custody has acquiesced in the removal or retention. Otherwise the child must have resided in that other Member State for a period of at least one year after the person, institution or other body having rights of custody has had or should have had knowledge of the whereabouts of the child and the child is settled in his or her new environment and at least one of the following conditions is met: (i) within that period of one year no request for return has been lodged before the competent authorities of the Member State where the child has been removed or is being retained; (ii) a request for return lodged by the holder of rights of custody has been withdrawn and no new request has been lodged within the one year time limit; (iii) a case before the court in the Member State where the child was habitually resident immediately before the wrongful removal or retention has been closed pursuant to art.11(7) (where no submissions have been made to challenge a non-return order made in the other Member State); (iv) a judgment on custody[222] that does not entail the return of the child has been issued by the courts of the Member State where the child was habitually resident immediately before the wrongful removal or retention.[223] There is jurisdiction under this provision even if the child is in a non-EU State.[224] It has been held that this continuing jurisdiction allows the court of origin to determine contact for the non-custodial parent or deal with matters under the Children Act 1989 or the inherent jurisdiction even if it does not order the child's return.[225]

Further provisions as to applications for return

When an application to the authority of a Member State is made by a person, institution or other body having rights of custody seeking the return of a child to its Member State of habitual residence under the Hague Child Abduction Convention, art.11 of the Regulation sets out various supplementary and qualifying provisions. When applying arts 12 and 13 of the Convention (grounds for refusing return) the court must ensure that the child is given the opportunity to be heard unless this is inappropriate for reasons of age or maturity.[226] The court to which an application for return is made must act expeditiously and issue its

14–040

[2014] A.C. 1401. See, however, Case 400/10 PPU *McB v E* (whether a child's removal is wrongful for the purposes of applying the Regulation is entirely dependent on the existence of rights of custody, conferred by the relevant national law.

[222] A final order, not merely an interim one: Case C-211/10 PPU *Povse v Alpago* [2010] 2 F.L.R. 1343.

[223] Article 10.

[224] *A v A (Children) (Habitual Residence)* [2013] UKSC 60; [2014] A.C. 1; *Re H (Children) (Jurisdiction: Habitual Residence)* [2014] EWCA Civ 1101; [2015] 1 W.L.R. 863.

[225] *HA v MB (Brussels II Revised: Article 11(7) Application)* [2007] EWHC 2016 (Fam.); [2008] 1 F.L.R. 289.

[226] Article 11(2). Failure to hear the child will lead to a rehearing being ordered: *Re F* [2007] EWCA Civ 468; [2007] 2 F.L.R. 697.

judgment within six weeks from application except in exceptional circumstances,[227] a timescale that includes any appeal the original decision.[228]

A court cannot refuse to return a child unless the applicant has been given an opportunity to be heard,[229] nor on the basis of art.13(b) of the Convention (grave risk of physical or psychological harm, or placing the child in an intolerable situation) if it is established that adequate arrangements have been made to secure the protection of the child after return.[230] This ground-breaking provision reinforces the principles of the immediate return of the child by minimising the application of the art.13(b) defences. This means that even though the court of refuge believes the child to be in grave risk of danger if returned, the discretion not to return is removed if it can be established that there are adequate protective measures in place in the Member State of habitual residence.[231] It is questionable whether the concept of judicial comity and mutual trust has been taken one step too far. It is one thing for a State to have sophisticated protective mechanisms in place but quite another for a violent parent to comply with them.[232]

Non-return cases

14–041   Where the court of the Member State to which the child has been abducted issues a non-return order pursuant to art.13 of the Convention,[233] that court must immediately transmit a copy of the order and all the relevant documents to the court or Central Authority of the Member State of the child's habitual residence.[234] The court or Central Authority of habitual residence will then notify the parties and invite them to make submissions to that court regarding custody of the child within three months of the date of notification.[235] If no submission is made within the three month period, the case will be considered closed. This provision precludes the Member State of refuge from assuming jurisdiction for substantive custody arrangements as soon as the non-return order is granted. Most importantly, the court of the child's habitual residence may make an order requiring the child to be returned, an order which is enforceable via the fast track system contained in art.42 of the Regulation, without the need for a declaration of

---

[227] Article 11(3); see *Re K (Rights of Custody: Spain)* [2009] EWHC 1066 (Fam.); [2010] 1 F.L.R. 57.

[228] The *Practice Guide* at p.33 makes it clear that six weeks is a strict deadline and one possibility of adhering to the six weeks is for national law to preclude the possibility of an appeal.

[229] Article 11(5). For a discussion as to possible methods of hearing the child, see *Re D (A Child) (Abduction: Rights of Custody)* [2006] UKHL 51; [2007] 1 A.C. 619 at para.60.

[230] Article 11(4). However, see *Re D (A Child) (Abduction: Rights of Custody)* [2006] UKHL 51; [2007] 1 A.C. 619 at para.52 where adherence to this provision would have turned the Regulation into an instrument of harm itself.

[231] For a very difficult case under art.11(4) coupled with the potential for an art.11(8) order (see below), see *K v K* [2007] EWCA Civ 533; [2007] 2 F.L.R. 996.

[232] For example, in 2003 a father applied under the Convention for the return of his children from Spain (SAP Baleares of 23 April 2003). The Spanish court found that the father had been imprisoned for domestic violence and was subject to an English non-molestation order, but that on release from prison he had gone to the mother's address and kicked down the front door, threatening the mother and children.

[233] Not under art.12.

[234] Article 11(6).

[235] Article 11(7).

enforceability and without any possibility of opposing its recognition.[236] So the court of the child's habitual residence before the abduction has the final say. Such "trumping" orders seem out of line with the mutual trust and respect that the Regulation endeavours to engender between the authorities of Member States.[237]

Where the English court is considering making an order for return despite the non-return order in the state of refuge, it is exercising a welfare jurisdiction, the best interest of the child are paramount and a peremptory order can be made in appropriate circumstances.[238]

However, in this context issues arise similar to those in *Neulinger*, considered earlier. In *Šneersone v Italy*,[239] a boy was wrongfully removed by his mother from Italy to Latvia. The Latvian court considered evidence from a psychologist that severance of contact between the child and his mother could negatively affect the child's development and could even create neurotic problems and illnesses; it also received an assurance from the Italian Central Authority that if any of the circumstances mentioned in art.13(b) of the Hague Convention arose, Italy would be able to activate a wide-ranging child protection network which could ensure that the boy and his father received psychological help. The court refused to order the child's return, relying on art.13(b). The Latvian court noted art.11(4) of the Brussels IIa Regulation, precluding a return if it were established that adequate arrangements had been made to secure the protection of the child after his return; it held that as the mother could not afford to return to Italy, the arrangements would not protect the child from psychological harm.

The father applied to the Italian courts for an order under art.11 of the Regulation, proposing detailed arrangements which the court found satisfactory; it made the requested return order. The mother applied to the European Court of Human Rights alleging breach of art.8 of the European Convention. In the light of evidence that the child was suffering psychological stress and anxiety in connection with his potential return to Italy, the court held that the Italian court's order constituted an interference with the applicants' right to respect for family life. Such interference would be allowed where it was "necessary in a democratic society" within the meaning of art.8(2) of the European Convention. It noted that the Italian court had failed to address the risks that had been identified by the Latvian authorities, viewed the arrangements accepted by the Italian court as inadequate, and noted further that the Italian courts had not considered any alternative solutions for ensuring contact between the son and his father. The court concluded that the interference with the applicants' right to respect for their family life was not "necessary in a democratic society" and that art.8 had been violated.

---

[236] Article 11(8). Practical experience is that such an order is very seldom effective.

[237] McEleavy, (2004) 53 I.C.L.Q. 503; for an alternative view, see Lowe; [2004] I.F.L.J. 205 at p.215.

[238] *M v T (Abduction: Brussels II Revised, Art 11(7))* [2010] EWHC 1479 (Fam); [2010] 2 FLR 1685; *D v N* [2011] EWHC 471 (Fam.); [2011] 2 F.L.R. 464; *AF v T (Brussels II Revised; Art 11(7) Application* [2011] EWHC 1315 (Fam.); [2011] 2 F.L.R. 891.

[239] [2011] ECHR 14737/09. See also *Raban v Romania* [2011] ECHR 25437/08 (not a Hague Convention case).

STATUS: LEGITIMACY AND LEGITIMATION

14–042 Legitimacy is the status which a legitimate child acquires at the time of his or her birth. Legitimation means that a child who is illegitimate at the time of birth becomes legitimate by reason of subsequent events.

Legitimacy

14–043 It was once the case that the birth of a child to an unmarried woman was seen as, and in practice often was, disastrous for both child and mother. A single parent may still suffer social and financial disadvantages, but very large numbers of children are born to couples living together in a permanent relationship but not married. The fact that such children may be technically illegitimate bothers no-one, even if the point occurs to anyone. As a matter of law, since the Family Law Reform Act 1987, the marital status of a person's parents at the time of his or her birth is of almost no relevance if the child is claiming to succeed to property under an English deed or will or intestacy. It might be thought that the whole question of legitimacy could be ignored in a modern textbook. But succession is not the only context in which the issue can arise.[240] It will be recalled that the domicile of dependency of a child depends on whether the child is legitimate or illegitimate; the status may be relevant under a particular deed or will if restrictive words are used; legitimacy may be relevant in immigration contexts; and the issue of legitimacy may be raised specifically in an action for a declaration as to status. That the issue is a live one can be seen from the attention paid to it in recent legislation on civil partnerships, same-sex marriages and assisted reproduction.[241]

There is also the situation in which the succession is governed by foreign law. This is the classic case of the incidental question,[242] much discussed by the jurists: should the legitimacy of the child be determined by the conflict rules of the forum, or by the conflict rules of the foreign *lex successionis* (the law governing questions of succession)? There is no English authority on this question. One may hazard the guess that English courts would probably permit the foreign *lex successionis* to determine not only what classes of children were entitled to succeed, but also (if legitimacy were a necessary qualification under the foreign law) whether any individual was or was not legitimate, and what law governed that question.[243]

Recognition of the status

14–044 Here we are confronted not by the familiar question, what is the English conflict rule, but by a more fundamental question: is there an English conflict rule at all?

---

[240] For this reason the view of Welsh, (1947) 63 L.Q.R. 65, that the sole question is one of construction of words like "children" or "issue" in deeds, wills and statutes, cannot be accepted.

[241] Family Law Reform Act 1987 s.1, Legitimacy Act 1976 s.2A and Family Law Act 1986 s.56 all as inserted or amended by the Human Fertilisation and Embryology Act 2008 Sch.6 and SI 2014/560.

[242] See below, para.20–010.

[243] See *Baindail v Baindail* [1946] P. 122, 127.

According to the first and oldest answer, a child is legitimate if (and only if) he or she is born or conceived in lawful wedlock, within a marriage which is valid by English rules of the conflict of laws. Until 1959, this was the traditional test of legitimacy in English domestic law, and the theory under discussion projects that test into the conflict of laws.[244] It follows from this approach that English law has no conflict rule for legitimacy, only a conflict rule for the validity of marriage.[245] This is supported by all the English reported cases before 1947, including two in the House of Lords.

In *Brook v Brook*[246]:

> a man and a woman, both domiciled in England, went through a ceremony of marriage in Denmark and immediately afterwards returned to England. The marriage was valid by Danish law but void by English domestic law because the woman was the sister of the man's deceased wife. A child of the marriage died intestate and unmarried, domiciled in England.

The House of Lords held that the marriage was void, that the child was illegitimate, and that his brothers and sisters could not succeed to his property, which went to the Crown as bona vacantia. The validity of the marriage was the only question discussed by the House of Lords.

In the famous case of *Shaw v Gould*[247]:

> a testator domiciled in England devised land in England on trust for the sons lawfully begotten of his great-niece Elizabeth Hickson, and bequeathed movables on trust for her children. Elizabeth, while domiciled in England, and aged 16, was induced by the fraud of Thomas Buxton (also domiciled in England) to go through a ceremony of marriage with him. The marriage was valid by English law, and at that time could only have been dissolved by private Act of Parliament; but it was never consummated, and Buxton was sent to prison for fraud. Some years later, Elizabeth fell in love with a law student, one John Shaw, who was a student member of Gray's Inn. Her still-subsisting marriage with Buxton was of course an impediment to their union. So Buxton was persuaded to go to Scotland and stay there for 40 days so that Elizabeth could divorce him in the Court of Session. After the divorce Elizabeth married John Shaw, who was now domiciled in Scotland, lived with him in Scotland and had children by him.

The House of Lords held that these children were illegitimate, and could take neither the land nor the movables under the testator's will. The reason was that the marriage of their parents was void, because the Scottish divorce could not be recognised in England, since Buxton (and therefore Elizabeth) was domiciled in England.

It is the case that according to some systems of law, including now English domestic law, a child may be legitimate even though his parents were not, and could not be, validly married. This is the doctrine of "putative marriage", invented by the canon lawyers in order to preserve the legitimacy of the children when they multiplied the grounds on which a marriage could be annulled. From

---

[244] The common law presumption that a child born to a woman during her marriage is also the child of her husband is set aside in the case of same-sex couples: Marriage (Same Sex Couples) Act 2013 s.11 and Sch.4, para.2.

[245] For the validity of marriage, see above, Ch.11.

[246] (1861) 9 H.L.C. 193. See also *Re Paine* [1940] Ch. 46, another deceased wife's sister case where only the wife was domiciled in England.

[247] (1868) L.R. 3 H.L. 55.

the canon law it passed into the law of most continental European countries, and a variation of it was first enacted in England in 1959. The current provision, s.1(1) of the 1976 Act[248] provides that the child of a void marriage[249] shall be treated as the legitimate child of his parents, if at the time of the insemination resulting in the birth or, where there was no such insemination, the child's conception (or at the time of the celebration of the marriage if later[250]) both or either of his parents reasonably believed that the marriage was valid. This applies notwithstanding that the belief that the marriage was valid was due to a mistake as to law.[251] This enactment is retrospective as to status but not as to rights of succession.[252] Section 28 of the Family Law Reform Act 1987 developed the law further, inserting a new sub-section providing for a rebuttable presumption that one of the parties to a void marriage did reasonably believe at the relevant time that the marriage was valid.[253] Section 1(2) of the Legitimacy Act 1976 now provides that the section only applies where the father of the child was domiciled in England at the time of the birth; or, if he died before the birth, was so domiciled immediately before his death; or, if a woman is treated as the female parent of a child by virtue of s.42 or 43 of the Human Fertilisation and Embryology Act 2008, that female parent was domiciled in England and Wales at the time of the birth, or if she died before the birth, was so domiciled immediately before her death.[254]

Given this development, the approach based on *Shaw v Gould* cannot be expressed as a simple rule that the child must be born or conceived in lawful wedlock: the rule must be stated so as to include cases in which the parents are deemed to have been in lawful wedlock as a result of the statutory rules just set out.

Law can never be divorced from its social context, and the social attitude to questions of legitimacy has changed utterly since the 1860s when the House of Lords addressed the matter. Down to 1947 there appears to be no reported English case in which a child not born or conceived in lawful wedlock was held to be legitimate. But in *Re Bischoffsheim*[255] Romer J adopted a new approach, in the following proposition:

"Where succession to personal property depends on the legitimacy of the claimant, the status of legitimacy conferred on him by his domicile of origin (i.e. the domicile of his parents at his birth) will be recognised by our courts, and if that legitimacy be established, the validity of his parents' marriage should not be entertained as a relevant subject for investigation."

---

[248] As amended by the Family Law Reform Act 1987 ss.28(1), 34(5).
[249] Whether born before or after the commencement of the Act. But not a child born before the parents entered into the void marriage: *Re Spence* [1990] Ch. 652.
[250] Or of the conversion of a civil partnership into a marriage: Legitimacy Act 1976 s.1(5) as inserted by SI 2014/3168.
[251] Legitimacy Act 1976 s.1(3) as inserted by Family Law Reform Act 1987 s.28(2) and amended by SI 2014/560. For children born by artificial insemination with the semen of a man other than the mother's husband, see Family Law Reform Act 1987 s.27.
[252] Legitimacy Act 1976 s.11(1) and Sch.1, paras 3, 4(1).
[253] Legitimacy Act 1976 s.1(4) as inserted by Family Law Reform Act 1987 s.28(2). This presumption applies only in relation to a child born after 4 April 1988, the date of the coming into force of that section.
[254] Legitimacy Act 1976 s.1(2) as amended by SI 2014/560.
[255] [1948] Ch. 79, 92; approved by the Privy Council in *Bamgbose v Daniel* [1955] A.C. 107, 120.

In that case a testator, presumably domiciled in England, gave a share of residue to the children of his granddaughter, Nesta. In 1917, Nesta, whose domicile of origin was England, was married in New York to the brother of her first husband, and in 1920 she had a son, Richard. The marriage was valid by the law of New York, but void by English domestic law. Romer J was unable to hold that Nesta and her second husband had acquired a New York domicile by 1917, when they were married, but he did decide that they had acquired a New York domicile by 1920, when Richard was born: and he held that Richard was entitled to share with Nesta's children by her first marriage in the testator's residuary estate.

This decision seems difficult to reconcile with earlier authority,[256] and with *Shaw v Gould* itself. The facts involved two parents with the same domicile; if their domiciles differed, then the case would be caught in a vicious circle: a child's domicile of origin is that of its father if the child is legitimate and that of his mother if illegitimate; and the legitimacy of the child cannot depend on the law of its domicile of origin if that depends on its legitimacy. There were previous dicta favouring reliance on the child's domicile of origin[257]; they were all delivered in cases on legitimation by subsequent marriage, not legitimacy itself.

The question arose again in *Green v Alexander*[258]:

> The 13th Duke of Manchester went through a ceremony of marriage in California with a woman domiciled in that State in May 1993, a week before the birth of the couple's son; a daughter was born in 1999. His Grace had not mentioned the fact that he was still married to another woman, whom he had married in Australia, so the Californian marriage was void for bigamy. The children were held to be legitimate.

The second wife of course thought her marriage valid, so that the doctrine of putative marriage in the Legitimacy Act 1959 would have applied, provided the Duke was domiciled in England at the relevant time. That issue was not resolved, but the court noted that by the domestic law of all possible domiciles (England, Australia and California) the children would be legitimate. The court considered that the children were legitimate without reliance on that doctrine. *Re Bischoffsheim* was followed; and the dicta in the legitimation case of *Re Goodman's Trusts*[259] were held to be equally applicable to legitimacy.

There was the difficult question of *Shaw v Gould*. Floyd J noted that that case merely addressed the question of the recognition of the Scottish divorce. He asserted, incorrectly, that it was decided at a time when a marriage in England was not dissoluble by a court order but required an Act of Parliament; hence the concentration on the question whether a Scottish court could do what an English court could not. He also stated, with an equally fine disregard for history, that the notion of legitimacy as a status, capable of recognition in private international law, "is now, but was not at the time of that decision, well established". He held that *Shaw v Gould* must "now be regarded as a case very closely confined to its

---

[256] *Re Paine* [1940] Ch.46, which was not cited.
[257] *Birtwhistle v Vardill* (1835) 2 Cl. & F. 571, 573–574; *Re Don's Estate* (1857) 4 Drew. 194, 197; *Re Goodman's Trusts* (1881) 17 Ch.D. 266, 291, 292; *Re Andros* (1883) 24 Ch.D. 637, 638.
[258] [2011] EWHC 1856 (Ch).
[259] (1881) 17 Ch.D. 266.

own particular facts, and as deciding only a question concerned with the recognition of a divorce, an issue which would not arise now". In applying the rule that legitimacy depended on the domicile of both parents, the judge added that that rule might be too restrictive; that presumably suggests that the domicile of one parent might suffice, but the remark is not explained.

Although the judgments in both *Re Bischoffsheim* and *Green v Alexander* can be regarded as flawed, the notion of identifying a number of bases upon which legitimacy can be established is welcome in policy terms. As matters now stand, the position seems to be that a child is legitimate in England if born or conceived in lawful wedlock, or during a putative marriage, or he or she is legitimate by the law of the domicile of each parent at the time of the child's birth.

Declarations of parentage or legitimacy

14–045   Under s.55A of the Family Law Act 1986[260] the English courts have jurisdiction to grant a declaration of parentage if, and only if, either of the persons named in the application (that is, the claimed parent and child) is domiciled in England on the date of the application or was habitually resident in England throughout the period of one year ending with that date, or was so connected to England at the date of death.[261] If the applicant is not the child, one of the parents of the child,[262] the Secretary of State or the person with care,[263] then the court will only hear the application if the applicant has sufficient personal interest in the determination of the application.[264] The court may also refuse to hear the application if it considers that it would not be in the best interests of the child.[265]

Similarly, under s.56 of the 1986 Act,[266] the court has jurisdiction to grant a declaration of legitimacy if the applicant (*not* the child) is domiciled in England on the date of the application or was habitually resident in England throughout the period of one year ending with that date. The declaration may take the form that the applicant is the legitimate child of its parents (a declaration of legitimacy); or that the applicant has or has not become a legitimated person (a declaration of legitimation).[267] This statutory declaration is exclusive; it is not possible to invoke the inherent jurisdiction of the High Court.[268]

Questions relating to the parentage or legitimacy of a person may, of course, arise in proceedings other than an application for a declaration, for example in a succession case. The courts decide such questions whenever they arise as between the parties to the proceedings, whether the person whose parentage or

---

[260] As inserted by the Child Support, Pensions and Social Security Act 2000 Sch.9, para.1. See *M v W (Declaration of Parentage)* [2006] EWHC 2341 (Fam.); [2007] 2 F.L.R. 270 for a consideration of the issues that apply in deciding whether to grant such an application.

[261] Section 55A(2).

[262] Section 55A(4).

[263] See Child Support Act 1991 s.27 as substituted by the Child Support, Pensions and Social Security Act 2000 s.83(5), Sch 8, paras 11, 13.

[264] Family Law Act 1986 s.55A(3).

[265] Section 55A(5).

[266] As substituted by Family Law Reform Act 1987 s.22 and amended by the Human Fertilisation and Embryology Act 2008 Sch.6.

[267] Family Law Act 1986 s.56(1)(2) as substituted by Family Law Reform Act 1987 s.22.

[268] Family Law Act 1986 s.58(4).

legitimacy is in question is alive or dead,[269] and whether or not that person is a party to the proceedings. But such decisions do not bind anyone except the parties or those claiming under them, and they do not declare that the person in question is or was legitimate for all purposes, but only for the particular purpose in question.[270]

Legitimation

The law on this subject is needlessly complicated because there are two conflict rules for the recognition of foreign legitimations, a rule of common law and a statutory rule contained in s.3 of the Legitimacy Act 1976.

14–046

Legitimation in English domestic law

Section 2 of the Legitimacy Act 1976,[271] provides that where the mother and father of an illegitimate person marry or have married one another,[272] the marriage shall, if the father was or is at the date of the marriage domiciled in England, render that person, if living, legitimate from 1 January 1927, or from the date of the marriage, whichever last happens. So, a child is now legitimated by subsequent marriage in English domestic law; but, if the marriage was celebrated before 1927, only from 1 January 1927. If the marriage was celebrated before that date, there is nothing in the section which requires that the father should be domiciled in England, or even alive, on 1 January 1927.

14–047

Statutory recognition of foreign legitimations

Section 3(1) of the Act of 1976[273] deals with the recognition of foreign legitimations. It provides that where the mother and father of an illegitimate person marry one another and the father of the illegitimate person is not at the time of the marriage domiciled in England and Wales but is domiciled in a country by the law of which the illegitimate person became legitimated by virtue of such subsequent marriage, that person, if living, shall in England and Wales be recognised as having been so legitimated from 1 January 1927, or from the date of the marriage, whichever last happens, notwithstanding that, at the time of the child's birth, the father was domiciled in a country the law of which did not

14–048

---

[269] *Brook v Brook* (1861) 9 H.L.C. 193.

[270] *Skinner v Carter* [1948] Ch. 387.

[271] Re-enacting s.1(1) of the Legitimacy Act 1926. Provisions dealing with civil partnership cases were inserted by the Human Fertilisation and Embryology Act 2008 Sch.6, and the provision was amended to take into account same-sex marriages by SI 2014/560.

[272] Whether before or after 1 January 1927 (the commencement date of the 1926 Act). Technically, s.2 of the 1976 Act only applies to marriages celebrated after its commence-ment (22 August 1976): but the rights of children legitimated by s.1 of the 1926 Act are preserved by Sch.1, para.1(1) to the 1976 Act.

[273] Re-enacting s.8(1) of the Legitimacy Act 1926; as amended by SI 2014/560. Similar provision is now made to deal with cases in which the female parent in terms of the Human Fertilisation and Embryology Act 2008 subsequently marries or enters into a civil partnership with the child's mother: s.1(2) as inserted by the 2008 Act s.56, Sch.6, Pt 1, para.17 and as amended by SI 2014/560.

permit legitimation by subsequent marriage.[274] It has been held in Australia that, under s.90 of the Marriage Act 1961 (which was closely modelled on s.8(1) of the English Act of 1926), it is not necessary for the marriage to legitimate the child immediately. Effect will be given to a later change in the law of the foreign country which legitimates the child by virtue of the marriage, even if the father is no longer domiciled in the foreign country at the date of the subsequent change in its law.[275]

Even before the 1926 Act introduced the concept of legitimation into English domestic law, the courts had been prepared to recognise legitimations under foreign law. The intention was, no doubt, that the new statutory rule as to the recognition of foreign legitimations would replace the previously existing common law rule altogether. But the courts have held that it still continues to exist side by side with the new statutory rule. It may still be necessary to fall back on it in some cases where it is necessary to show legitimation at a date before 1976. The section only applies to legitimation by subsequent marriage; the common law rule, as we shall see,[276] applies also to other modes of legitimation.

The common law rule: legitimation by subsequent marriage

14–049   In a rule developed long before 1926, the English courts recognise foreign legitimations if the father was domiciled both at the time of the child's birth and at the time of the subsequent marriage in a country the law of which recognised legitimation by subsequent marriage.[277] The place of the child's birth, the place of celebration of the marriage, and the domicile of the mother are all irrelevant. All that matters is the domicile of the father on the two critical dates. If the father was domiciled in England at the time of the child's birth[278] or at the time of the subsequent marriage,[279] the child was not recognised as having been legitimated. It will be seen that the main difference between the statutory rule and the older common law rule is that the latter refers to *two* dates, including the date of the child's birth which is irrelevant under the statutory rule. The common law rule of double reference was based on the argument that "the domicile at birth must give a capacity to the child of being made legitimate; but then the domicile at the time of the marriage, which gives the status, must be domicile in a country which attributes to marriage that effect".[280]

The requirement that the father must be domiciled in a country whose law recognises legitimation by subsequent marriage at the time of the child's birth as well as at the time of the subsequent marriage rests (apart from dicta) on two

---

[274] Whether before or after 1 January 1927. Technically, s.3 of the 1976 Act only applies to marriages celebrated after its commencement (22 August 1976); but the rights of children recognised as legitimated by s.8 of the 1926 Act are preserved by Sch.1, para.1(1) to the 1976 Act.

[275] *Heron v National Trustees Executors and Agency Co of Australasia Ltd* [1976] V.R. 733.

[276] Below, para.14–050 ff.

[277] *Goodman v Goodman* (1862) 3 Giff. 643; *Skottowe v Young* (1871) L.R. 11 Eq. 474; *Re Goodman's Trusts* (1881) 17 Ch.D. 266; *Re Andros* (1883) 24 Ch.D. 637; *Re Grey's Trusts* [1892] 3 Ch. 88; *Re Askew* [1930] 2 Ch. 259; *Re Hurll* [1952] Ch. 722.

[278] *Re Wright's Trusts* (1856) 2 K. & J. 595.

[279] *Re Grove* (1888) 40 Ch.D. 216.

[280] *Re Grove* (1888) 40 Ch.D. 216, at p.238.

cases only, *Re Wright's Trusts*[281] and *Re Luck's Settlement*.[282] The former was decided at a time when the English courts were still disinclined to allow foreign-legitimated children to succeed to property under English wills; and it is surprising that the majority of the Court of Appeal did not take the opportunity of overruling it in *Re Luck's Settlement*. Instead, they extended it to a case of legitimation, not by subsequent marriage, but by parental recognition. They held that the child of a father who was domiciled in England at the time of the child's birth, but in California at the time of the parental recognition, was not recognised in England as having been legitimated, and could not take as a "child" under an English marriage settlement and will, although by Californian law the effect of the parental recognition was to render the child legitimate as from the date of its birth.

In that case, owing to the rule against perpetuities, it was necessary for the child to prove that the legitimation was retrospective. In such a case there may perhaps be some justification for looking to the law of the father's domicile at the time of the child's birth. There can be no such justification if, as in the normal case, it is not necessary to prove that the legitimation is retrospective. The majority of the Court of Appeal pointed out that legitimation affects the status of the father as well as the status of the child; and they refused to allow a foreign law retrospectively to alter the status of a father who, at the time of the child's birth, was domiciled in England. But this reasoning has subsequently been weakened by the decision of the House of Lords in *Starkowski v Attorney General*,[283] where they held that foreign law can retrospectively alter the status of a person domiciled in England.

The decision of the Court of Appeal is also weakened by the vigorous dissenting judgment of Scott LJ, who confessed that:

> "the very idea of attributing to a newly born child, to *alius nullius*, a sort of latent capacity for legitimation at the hands of the natural father to whom he is denied any legal relation, seems to me an even more absurd legal fiction, and even less convincing, than the mythical contract of marriage supposed by the canonists to have been entered into at the moment of procreation".[284]

He could "see no warrant for applying a rule, originating in the special reasons for the doctrine of legitimation by subsequent marriage, and justified by various legal fictions invented to support it, to the simple and straightforward case of a direct command of legitimation by the statute law of the father's domicile".[285]

Legitimation by parental recognition

Re Luck's Settlement is the only reported case in which the English court has had to consider the effect of legitimation otherwise than by subsequent marriage. In

14–050

---

[281] (1856) 2 K. & J. 595.
[282] [1940] Ch. 864.
[283] [1954] A.C. 155; above, para.11–003. In that case Lord Tucker at pp.175–176 and Lord Cohen at pp.180–181 attempted to distinguish *Re Luck's Settlement*, but on very slender grounds.
[284] [1940] Ch. 864, 912.
[285] ibid. at pp.912–913.

that case, counsel for the appellant conceded[286] that if the father had been domiciled in California at the time of the child's birth as well as at the time of the parental recognition, the child would have been recognised in England as having been legitimated. The majority of the Court of Appeal made no comment on this concession; but they did cite with approval[287] Dicey's view[288] that in such a case the child would be recognised in England as legitimate. Moreover, s.10(1) of the Legitimacy Act 1976 assumes that the common law rule is not limited to legitimation by subsequent marriage.

Legitimation by foreign statute

14–051 Statutes very similar to s.2 of the Legitimacy Act 1976 are in force in other countries, e.g., Northern Ireland.[289] What, then, is the position if the English court is asked to recognise the legitimation under one of these statutes of a person whose father was dead, or no longer domiciled in the country in question, on the date when the statute came into operation, the marriage having taken place earlier? The Legitimacy Acts 1926 and 1976 do not in terms answer this question, and one may therefore be thrown back on the rule of common law. Unfortunately the common law rule for legitimation by subsequent marriage is not well adapted to this situation.

The English courts have not yet been confronted by a case of this sort, but it has arisen in the Republic of Ireland and also in Australia and New Zealand with reference to children legitimated by the English Act of 1926. The Australian and New Zealand courts apparently recognise the legitimation of the child only if the father was domiciled in England on three critical dates, the date of the child's birth, the date of the subsequent marriage, and the coming into operation of the Act on 1 January 1927.[290] On the other hand, the Irish court has recognised the legitimation when the father was domiciled in England at the date of the child's birth and at the date of the subsequent marriage, even though he was dead on 1 January 1927.[291] The view of the Irish court seems preferable to that of the Australasian courts, and it is to be hoped that it will be followed in England. It seems unduly onerous to force the child to prove that his father was domiciled in the country in question at three critical dates; and of course it is an impossible task if the father was dead when the Act came into operation. It seems much better to apply the law of the country where the father was domiciled at the date of the child's birth and at the date of the subsequent marriage, as that law stands at the date of the proceedings in England. This would do much to prevent a person being held legitimate in one country and illegitimate in another. This was

---

[286] ibid. at pp.871–872.

[287] ibid. at p.884.

[288] 3rd edn, p.532.

[289] Legitimacy Act (Northern Ireland) 1928 as amended. The status of illegitimacy was abolished in Scotland by the Family Law (Scotland) Act 2006 s.21.

[290] Re Williams [1936] V.L.R. 223; Re Davey [1937] N.Z.L.R. 56; Re Pritchard (1940) 40 S.R.N.S.W. 443; Re James [1942] V.L.R. 12; Thompson v Thompson (1951) 51 S.R.N.S.W. 102; In the Estate of Taylor [1964–65] N.S.W.R. 695; Re Beatty [1919] V.L.R. 81 (decided with reference to a New York statute of 1895).

[291] Re Hagerbaum [1933] I.R. 198.

in effect the test applied by the Irish court and by the Supreme Court of Victoria in the most recent Australian case on the subject.[292]

Declarations of legitimation

The English courts have jurisdiction to grant a declaration that the applicant has or has not become a legitimated person if (and only if) the applicant is domiciled in England on the date of the application or was habitually resident in England throughout the period of one ending with that date.[293] The expression "legitimated person" means a person legitimated by the Legitimacy Act 1976 (or by Legitimacy Act 1926) or recognised as legitimated at common law.[294] The applicant may also seek a declaration that he or she has not become a legitimated person[295]; this form of declaration was first introduced in 1987 and is designed to deal particularly with cases where there is uncertainty as to the effect of an alleged legitimation as a result of formal acknowledgement or governmental act in a foreign country.[296] This statutory jurisdiction is exclusive; it is not possible to seek such a declaration by invoking the inherent jurisdiction of the High Court.[297]

14–052

It will be seen that the jurisdictional requirements are the same as those applying to declarations as to legitimacy.[298]

ADOPTION

Adoption may give rise to complicated problems in the conflict of laws, because the laws of different countries differ widely as to the objects that adoption should serve, the methods by which it is effected, the requirements necessary for adoption (especially the age of the adopter and of the adopted person), and the effects of adoption (especially in the matter of succession). In England, adoption can only be effected by court order after a judicial inquiry directed mainly to ensuring that it will be for the welfare of the child. In some foreign systems, adoption can be effected by agreement between the parties, sometimes with and sometimes without judicial approval, or even by religious ceremony. In many foreign systems the adoption of adults is possible.

14–053

It was not until the Adoption of Children Act 1926 that English law made any provision for adoption, and not until the Adoption Act 1950 that an adopted child acquired rights of succession as a child of its adoptive parents and not of its natural parents. Adoption is now governed by the Adoption and Children Act 2002, which also implements the Hague Convention on Intercountry Adoption.

---

[292] *Heron v National Trustees Executors and Agency Co of Australasia Ltd* [1976] V.R. 733, which (unlike the Australian cases cited above) was decided under s.90(1) of the Australian Marriage Act 1961; the earlier cases were accepted as stating the position at common law.
[293] Family Law Act 1986 s.56(2)(3) (as substituted by Family Law Reform Act 1987 s.22).
[294] Family Law Act s.56(5) (as substituted by Family Law Reform Act 1987 s.22).
[295] Family Law Act 1986 s.56(2)(b) (as substituted by Family Law Reform Act 1987 s.22).
[296] Law Com. No. 132 (1984), para.3.14.
[297] Family Law Act 1986 s.58(4).
[298] See above, para.14–045.

The effect of an English adoption order is to vest parental responsibility for the child in the adopters.[299] This in effect transfers to the adopters all the rights and duties which by law the mother and father have in relation to a legitimate child and its property.

Jurisdiction to make an adoption order

14–054   The Adoption and Children Act 2002 sets out in detail the requirements to be met before an English adoption order can be made. An application to adopt may be made by a couple[300] or by one person if the applicant or one of the couple is domiciled in a part of the British Islands or has been habitually resident in a part of the British Islands for at least one year prior to the date of application.[301]

There is no jurisdictional requirement that the child must be domiciled or even resident in England.[302] However, s.42 states that an adoption order may not be made unless that child has had a home with the applicant(s) for between 10 weeks and three years depending on the category of applicant(s), and the adoption agency must have had sufficient opportunity to see the child with the adoptive parent(s) in their home.[303]

Similar provisions existed under the previous governing statute, the Adoption Act 1976, and it was held in *Re Y (Minors) (Adoption: Jurisdiction)*[304] that the requirement that the agency have sufficient opportunity to see the child in the adoptive home was mandatory and the "home" therefore must be in the area of the local authority to which the applicant was required to give notice of the intent to adopt. However, in *Re S.L. (Adoption: Home in Jurisdiction)*[305] Mumby J distinguished the facts of *Re Y* and held that although the child had to have a home with the applicants in the area of a particular local authority at the time of giving notice (to allow sufficient opportunity for the agency to see the child with the adoptive parents in their home), this did not mean that the "home" had to be the one and only home that the child had with the adopters for the required period of time immediately prior to the making of the adoption order, the two tests having different statutory purposes.[306] So, in *Re S.L.*, the fact that the applicant moved from England to Scotland part way through the required one year period prior to the adoption was not fatal to the jurisdiction of the court to grant an adoption order.

---

[299] Adoption and Children Act 2002 s.46(1).

[300] The definition of a couple is a married couple, two people who are civil partners of each other, or two people (whether of different sexes or the same sex) living as partners in an enduring family relationship: s.144(4) as amended by Civil Partnership Act 2004 s.79.

[301] Adoption and Children Act 2002 s.49.

[302] The Brussels IIa Regulation does not apply to decisions on adoption, measures preparatory to adoption, or the annulment or revocation of adoption: art.1(3)(b). For the meaning of "measures preparatory to adoption", see *Re CB (A Child)* [2015] EWCA Civ 888 and *Re N (Children) (Adoption: Jurisdiction)* [2015] EWCA Civ 1112.

[303] Adoption and Children Act 2002 s.42(7).

[304] [1985] Fam. 136.

[305] [2004] EWHC 1283 (Fam); [2005] 1 F.L.R. 118.

[306] *Re SL (Adoption: Home in Jurisdiction)* [2004] EWHC 1283 (Fam); [2005] 1 F.L.R. 118.

Convention adoptions

The Hague Convention of 29 May 1993 on Protection of Children and Co-operation in respect of Intercountry Adoption[307] is implemented in the UK by the Adoption and Children Act 2002, and the Adoptions with a Foreign Element Regulations 2005.[308]   **14–055**

The Convention applies where a child[309] who is habitually resident in one Contracting State ("the State of origin") has been, is being, or is to be moved to another Contracting State ("the receiving State") either after his or her adoption in the State of origin by spouses or a person habitually resident in the receiving State, or for the purposes of such an adoption in the receiving State or in the State of origin.[310] It only applies to adoptions that create a permanent parent-child relationship.[311]

The connecting factor employed in this Convention to identify the child and the adoptive parents with a Contracting State is that of habitual residence[312] rather than nationality or domicile. This connecting factor is not without its problems in the area of adoption. A child may well be habitually resident in a Contracting State but a national of a State where adoption is considered to be contrary to domestic law,[313] and a subsequent adoption may lead to a difference in the recognition of the child's status depending on the law of the State addressed. Considerations of this possibility and how it affects the adoption process, however, fall to be dealt with both under the principle of the best interests of the child, and the requirement that if the state of origin is satisfied that a child is adoptable, it must "give due consideration to the child's upbringing and to his or her ethnic, religious and cultural background."[314]

The Convention requires that each Contracting State designate a Central Authority to discharge the duties which are imposed by the Convention upon such authorities[315] but allows Central Authorities to delegate much of the actual workload to public authorities or other accredited bodies.[316] In the respective countries reports are prepared on the eligibility of the adoptive parents and on the

---

[307] cf. Parra-Aranguren, *Explanatory Report to the Convention of May 29, 1993 on protection of Children and Co-operation in respect of Intercountry Adoptions;* Van Loon, [1993] VII *Recueil des Cours*, 195; Murphy, *International Dimensions in Family Law* (Manchester: Manchester University Press, 2005), Ch.7.

[308] SI 2005/392 as amended by SI 2009/2563.

[309] The Convention ceases to apply if the child reaches the age of 18 before the agreement of all parties has been obtained; art.3.

[310] Article 2(1).

[311] Article 2(2); i.e., full adoptions as opposed to simple adoptions which do not extinguish all ties to the biological family.

[312] Article 2. See *Greenwich LBC v S* [2007] EWHC 820; [2007] 2 F.L.R. 154 for a discussion of when a child being placed for intercountry adoption gains a new habitual residence. For a general discussion of the term "habitual residence", see para.2–004.

[313] Most Islamic countries fall into this category. However, see Beevers and Ebrahimi, [2002] I.F.L.166.

[314] Article 16(b).

[315] Article 6. For England the Central Authority is the Secretary of State; for Wales, the National Assembly for Wales; SI 2005/392, reg.2.

[316] Intercountry Adoption Convention art.9.

child.[317] The Central Authority of the state of origin has the responsibility of considering these two reports and determining if the proposed intercountry adoption is indeed in the best interests of the child. Once the decision has been made to proceed with the intercountry adoption and the necessary consents have been obtained, the child may only be entrusted to the prospective adoptive parents if both Central Authorities and the adoptive parents agree to the adoption and that the Central Authority of the Receiving State has determined that the child will be authorised to enter and reside permanently in that state.[318]

Adoptions may be made in England as 'convention adoptions' when the procedure set out in the Convention has been followed.[319]

Choice of law

14-056   When deciding whether or not to grant an adoption order, the English court will apply the *lex fori* as contained in the detailed provisions of the 2002 Act.[320] This was held to be the law in *Re B(S) (An Infant)*[321] and the correctness of that decision was emphatically re-affirmed by the Court of Appeal in 2015,[322] though it was recognised the foreign law could be an important factor to be taken into account in considering the *welfare* of the child; the court is required to have regard to the child's background.[323] It is, therefore, always possible that a child may be considered the child of the adoptive parents in England but the child of its biological parents in the child's country of origin. However, as more and more states ratify the Hague Convention of 1993 on Intercountry Adoption, such cases will decrease.

As the English courts have recognised, there is some concern in other States at the, relatively unusual, power under English law to allow adoption without the consent of the natural parent, and even of a foreign parent, a practice castigated by its critics as "forced adoption".[324]

Bringing children into the UK

14-057   The relevant provisions of the 2002 Act, supplemented by the Children and Adoption Act 2006 and by regulations,[325] restrict the conditions under which a child who is habitually resident in country outside the British Islands can be brought in to the UK either for the purpose of adoption, or subsequent to an

---

[317] Article 16(1).

[318] Article 17, together with art.5.

[319] The relevant legislation, described as 'a legal minefield', is examined in *Re M (A Child) (Adoption: Placement outside Jurisdiction)* [2010] EWHC 1694 (Fam.); [2011] Fam. 110.

[320] *Re N (Children) (Adoption: Jurisdiction)* [2015] EWCA Civ 1112 at [91].

[321] [1968] Ch. 204.

[322] *Re N (Children) (Adoption: Jurisdiction)* [2015] EWCA Civ 1112 at [102].

[323] Section 1 of the Act provides an extensive checklist of considerations to which the court and the adoption agency must have regard.

[324] *Re E (Brussels II Revised: Vienna Convention: Reporting Restrictions)* [2014] EWHC 6 (Fam); [2014] 2 FLR 151, at [13] to [15]; *Re D (A Child)* [2014] EWHC 3388 (Fam), at [35]; *Re N (Children) (Adoption: Jurisdiction)* [2015] EWCA Civ 1112 at [8] to [11].

[325] Adoptions with a Foreign Element Regulations 2005, SI 2005/392.

external adoption otherwise than a Convention adoption.[326] Failure to comply with the prescribed conditions is a criminal offence which carries penalties of up to one year in prison.[327] Further restrictions on bringing in children from a particular country for the purposes of adoption may also be imposed by the Secretary of State on the grounds of public policy, including where that country is a Convention country.[328]

Taking children abroad for adoption

Where prospective adoptive parents, who are not domiciled or habitually resident in England and Wales,[329] intend to adopt a child under the law of another country outside the British Islands, the High Court may make an order giving them parental responsibility for that child.[330]

14–058

A child may not be taken out of the jurisdiction "for the purpose of adoption" unless such an order has been made.[331] This does not apply where a child is sent by a local authority to live outside the jurisdiction with the approval of the court.[332] The power to give such approval is not available where a local authority is placing a child for adoption with prospective adopters (para.19(9)) but where a child is sent abroad in circumstances in which adoption is one option being considered, this will not amount to being "placed for adoption".[333]

However, an order giving prospective adopters parental responsibility may not be made unless the child has had a home with the prospective adoptive parent, or in the case of adoption by a couple, both of them, at all times during the preceding 10 weeks.[334] The requirement has been criticised as placing too great a burden on prospective adopters from overseas; there is power[335] to vary or disapply the requirement, notably in the case of adoptions by natural relatives, but the power has not been exercised. However, the courts have interpreted the requirement in ways which assist potential adopters. In *Re G (A Child) (Adoption: Placement outside Jurisdiction)*,[336] the prospective adopters were family members resident in the US; the adoptive mother spent 10 weeks with the child in England, but the adoptive father could only spend three weeks. The Court

---

[326] See *MN (India) v Entry Clearance Officer (New Delhi)* [2008] EWCA Civ 38; [2008] 2 F.L.R. 87 for a discussion of the four different ways for a child to be granted clearance to enter the UK for the purposes of adoption, none of which were fulfilled in this case.

[327] Adoption and Children Act 2002 s.83(8).

[328] Children and Adoption Act 2006, ss.9–12; Adoptions with a Foreign Element (Special Restrictions on Adoptions from Abroad) Regulations 2008, SI 2008/1807; special restrictions have been imposed for Cambodia (SI 2008/1808), Guatemala (SI 2008/1809), Haiti (SI 2010/2265) and Nepal (SI 2010/951).

[329] Adoption and Children Act 2002 s.84(2).

[330] ibid. s.84(1).

[331] ibid. s.85(1)(2); anyone arranging to remove a child without first being granted parental responsibility is guilty of an offence under s.85(4).

[332] Under Children Act 1989 Sch.2, para.19.

[333] ibid. para.19(9); *C v M* [2008] EWHC 332 (Fam), approved in *Re A (A Child) (Adoption: Assessment Abroad)* [2009] EWCA Civ 41; [2010] Fam. 9.

[334] ibid. s.84(4). The Adoptions with a Foreign Element Regulations 2005, SI 2005/392, reg.10, contains further requirements which must be fulfilled prior to removal.

[335] Adoption and Children Act 2002 s.86.

[336] [2008] EWCA Civ 105; [2008] Fam 97.

of Appeal held that this was sufficient in the circumstances to satisfy the purposes of the Act. It was later held that the 10-week period need not be within the jurisdiction. In *Re G (A Child) (Adoption: Placement outside Jurisdiction)*, the Court of Appeal had said that the purpose of this requirement was to ensure that a relationship should begin to establish between the child and the potential adopters and for the authorities to have an opportunity to assess the suitability of those potential adoptive parents, but in *Re A (A Child) (Adoption: Assessment Abroad)*[337] it held that there was no reason for those opportunities for assessment to be in England.

Recognition of foreign adoptions

Adoptions in the British Isles

14–059   There never has been any doubt that adoption orders made in Scotland would be recognised in England without question, and this is now expressly enacted.[338] It is also expressly provided that adoption orders made in Northern Ireland, the Channel Islands and the Isle of Man shall be recognised in England and Scotland.[339]

Overseas adoptions

14–060   Provisions dating from 1968, now contained in s.87 of the Adoption and Children Act 2002, empower the Secretary of State to specify as "overseas adoptions" any adoption effected under the law of any country outside the British Islands. The intention was to recognise adoptions made in countries whose adoption law is broadly similar to our own, and they are specified by Order.[340] They include most of the Commonwealth (exceptions include Jamaica, Nigeria and Malaysia), all EU Member States except Croatia, Turkey, Israel, South Africa, China, the US and Vietnam. Under this Order, there need be no juristic link of any kind, such as domicile, between the adopters and the country where the adoption was made. The only qualifications are that the adoption must have been effected under statutory law and not under common law or customary law; that the adopted person had not attained the age of 18 and had not been married; and that recognition must not be contrary to public policy. Subject to this, recognition is automatic.[341]

Convention adoptions

14–061   Section 66 of the Adoption and Children Act 2002, implementing art.23 of the Convention, provides for the recognition of adoptions under the Hague

---

[337] *Re A (A Child) (Adoption: Assessment Abroad)* [2009] EWCA Civ 41; [2010] Fam. 9.
[338] Adoption and Children Act 2002 s.105.
[339] Section 106 of the 2002 Act for Northern Ireland, and s.108 of the 2002 Act and regulations made under this section in respect of the Channel Islands and the Isle of Man.
[340] See SI 2013/1801.
[341] Adoption and Children Act 2002 ss.66 and 67.

Convention of 1993. Although the Convention covers only adoptions that create a permanent parent-child relationship,[342] it does provide for such adoptions (called in some systems of law "simple adoptions") which do not sever the legal relationship between the child and its natural parents, to be converted into full adoptions by the law of the Contracting State.[343] The 1999 Act establishes a procedure under which the High Court can direct that a Convention adoption should be recognised in England as having more limited effects on the status of the child than a full adoption, so for example enabling the child to succeed to the estate of its natural parent.[344]

Other adoptions

The recognition in England of other adoptions, that is adoptions other than those **14-062** made in the British Isles and other than "overseas" or "Convention" adoptions, still depends on the common law. So many adoptions have been specified as "overseas adoptions" that there is little geographical scope left for the common law to operate in, but it will still apply to adoptions made, e.g., in certain Middle Eastern countries other than Turkey and Israel; Pakistan, Japan and a few Central and South American countries. It will also apply to adoptions made in countries designated in the "overseas adoptions" context where the adoptions were effected under the customary or common law of countries, or involved the adoption of adults.

The majority of the Court of Appeal in *Re Valentine's Settlement*[345] laid it down, in the words of Lord Denning MR, that at common law "the courts of this country will only recognise an adoption in another country if the adopting parents are domiciled there and the child is ordinarily resident there".[346] Danckwerts LJ agreed with the Master of the Rolls, except that he was "not sure" whether the ordinary residence of the child was a requirement for recognition. In that case, the Court of Appeal refused to recognise two South African adoption orders made in respect of two children who were assumed to be resident and domiciled in South Africa, because the applicants were domiciled in what was then Southern Rhodesia (now Zimbabwe).

However, the law of adoption has developed since 1965. It is now possible for a married woman to have a domicile separate from that of her husband. In 1965 the English courts might not themselves make an adoption order unless the applicants were resident and domiciled in England, whereas under the 2002 Act the domicile of one applicant suffices. These developments persuaded Hedley J in *Re R (A Child) (Recognition of Indian Adoption)*[347] to adopt a new approach. He interpreted *Re Valentine's Settlement* as deciding that the English courts would

---

[342] Article 2(2).
[343] Articles 26, 27.
[344] Adoption and Children Act 2002 s.88.
[345] [1965] Ch. 831, 843, 846. Earlier cases are *Re Wilson* [1954] Ch. 733; *Re Wilby* [1956] P. 174; and *Re Marshall* [1957] Ch. 507.
[346] At that time the residence of the child in England was one of the jurisdictional requirements for adoption. This is no longer so. Hence it seems unlikely that the ordinary residence of the child in the foreign country will continue to be necessary for the recognition of foreign adoptions at common law.
[347] [2012] EWHC 2956 (Fam.); [2013] 1 F.L.R. 1487.

recognise an order affecting status where (and only where) the conditions exist which would permit a domestic court to make such an order. That test was satisfied: the husband was domiciled in India (and both parents and the child were habitually resident there).

Discretion and public policy

14–063 In *Re Valentine's Settlement*, Lord Denning MR entered one caveat[348]: the foreign adoption should not be recognised if recognition would be contrary to public policy. There will be some circumstances in which it would be intolerable to recognise a foreign adoption, or to give full effect to it. If, to take an improbable but striking example, the law of a foreign country allowed a bachelor of 50 to adopt a spinster of 17, an English court might hesitate to give the custody of the girl to her adoptive parent; but that might be no reason for not allowing her to succeed to his property as his "child" on his death.

Much more probable are issues which are more to do with judicial discretion than public policy. In *A Council v M*[349] Peter Jackson J put the public policy issue in context; he summarised the case law as establishing that an application for the recognition at common law of a foreign adoption must satisfy a number of specific criteria: the order must have been lawfully obtained in the foreign jurisdiction; the concept of adoption in that jurisdiction must substantially conform to that in England; the adoption process that was undertaken must have been substantially the same as would have applied in England at the time; there must be no public policy consideration militating against recognition; and recognition must be in the best interests of the child.

It may be that these principles are too broadly stated. The fact that the adopted person was over the age of 18, or that the adoption was not made by court order,[350] should not prevent recognition. A system of law which is prepared to recognise polygamous marriages and extra-judicial divorces should not be too squeamish about recognising foreign adoptions. The recognition in England of "overseas adoptions" may be refused on the ground of public policy[351]; but of course the recognition of adoptions made elsewhere in the British Isles may not.

Declarations as to foreign adoptions

14–064 Provision was made in the Family Law Act 1986 for declarations as to the validity of foreign adoptions.[352] Such a declaration may be sought only by an applicant whose status as an adopted child of any person depends on whether the child has been adopted by that person by either a Convention adoption, an overseas adoption as defined in the Adoption and Children Act 2002, or by an adoption recognised by the law of England and Wales and effected under the law

---

[348] [1965] Ch. 831 at p.842. cf. Salmon LJ at p.854.
[349] [2013] EWHC 1501 (Fam.); [2014] 1 F.L.R. 881 at [61].
[350] Adoption and Children Act 2002 s.66(1)(e) assumes that a foreign adoption can be recognised at common law although not made by court order.
[351] Adoption and Children Act 2002 s.89.
[352] Family Law Act 1986 s.57, as amended by the Adoption and Children Act 2002 Sch.3, para.49.

of any country outside the British Islands. The declaration that the applicant is or is not the adopted child of a named person by virtue of such an adoption determines the position of the applicant for the purposes of s.67 of the 2002 Act which deals with the status conferred by adoption.

The jurisdictional rules correspond to those applying to other declarations in family matters. So English courts have jurisdiction if (and only if) the applicant is domiciled in England on the date of the application or was habitually resident in England throughout the period of one year ending with that date.[353]

---

[353] Family Law Act 1986 s.57(3).

CHAPTER 15

CONTRACTUAL OBLIGATIONS

There is an appreciable difference in texture between the rules of the conflict of laws dealing with matters of family law and those, about to be examined, in the field of international contracts. This is no accident but the product of significant differences between the underlying topics.

15–001

Contracts are almost infinitely varied. It is unlikely that a mechanical choice of law rule that is appropriate for a contract to sell land would be equally appropriate for a contract of employment, or a contract for the carriage of goods by sea. The problems that may arise are very numerous, as may be seen by looking at the table of contents of any book on the domestic law of contract. These potential problems are exacerbated in international contracts. It is unlikely that a choice of law rule will be equally appropriate for certain kinds of consumer contracts as much as it would be for international business-to-business transactions. The appropriate rules need to determine the applicable law in relation to a variety of questions such as offer and acceptance, capacity of the parties, formalities, illegality, performance, and damages for breach of contract, amongst others.

All of this has the effect, in almost every legal system, of leading to choice of law rules as to contractual obligations which are characterised by flexibility, and by sensitivity both to the particular circumstances of the contract and to the nature of the issue that has arisen between the parties. This was very clearly so in the English case law which followed the approach of the common law. The civil law approach, with its emphasis on legal certainty, is reflected in the Rome Convention[1] and the Rome I Regulation on the Law Applicable to Contractual Obligations[2]; however, as we shall see, the EU legislation retains many elements of flexibility.

This chapter deals with the ascertainment of the law applicable to contractual obligations to determine the law governing the material validity, formal validity, interpretation and performance of contracts. Even though it deals primarily with the Rome I Regulation that applies to contracts concluded after 17 December 2009,[3] it also examines the Rome Convention of 1980, the provisions of which

---

[1] Rome Convention on the Law Applicable to Contractual Obligations 1980; for text see OJ C 334/1, 30 December 2005.
[2] European Parliament and Council Regulation No 593/2008 of 17 June 2008 on the law applicable to contractual obligations (Rome I), OJ L 177/6, July 4, 2008.
[3] Regulation art.28.

apply to contracts made on or before that date.[4] The Convention will still be relied on in contractual disputes for a number of years, and the interpretative case law on the provisions of the Rome Convention[5] will continue to be useful. Notwithstanding the importance and predominance of these European instruments, the chapter begins by offering an overview of the traditional solution in the English common law; this may remain applicable in the English courts only where the issues at stake are outside the scope of application of the Rome I Regulation.

THE ENGLISH COMMON LAW APPROACH

15–002   In England, the flexible rule that until 1991 governed most issues was known as the "proper law of the contract". In speaking of it, Lord Wright explained[6]:

> "English law in deciding these matters has refused to treat as conclusive, rigid or arbitrary criteria such as *lex loci contractus* [the law of the place in which the contract was made] or *lex loci solutionis* [the law of the place of performance], and has treated the matter as depending on the intention of the parties to be ascertained in each case on a consideration of the terms of the contract, the situation of the parties, and generally on all the surrounding facts. It may be that the parties have in terms in their agreement expressed what law they intend to govern, and in that case *prima facie* their intention will be effectuated by the court. But in most cases they do not do so. The parties may not have thought of the matter at all. Then the court has to impute an intention, or to determine for the parties what is the proper law which, as just and reasonable persons, they ought [to] or would have intended if they had thought about the question when they made the contract."

In the common law approach developed by nineteenth century English judges, the "proper law of the contract" was the system of law by reference to which the contract was made: the law chosen by the parties, or that with which the transaction had its closest and most real connection.[7]

Party autonomy

15–003   The power of the parties to select the law which is to govern their contract, the principle of "party autonomy", can be seen as the conflict of laws aspect of freedom of contract or of the market autonomy. In so far as parties are free to enter into whatever contractual bargains they think fit, that freedom is not

---

[4] For the thinking of the Commission which led to the adoption of the Regulation, see its Green Paper on the conversion of the Convention into a Community instrument and its modernisation, COM/2002/0654 final.

[5] The first reference for a preliminary ruling of the CJEU on the interpretation of the Convention was made in Case C-133/08 *Intercontainer Interfrigo SC v Balkenende Oosthuizen BV* [2009] ECR I-9687.

[6] *Mount Albert Borough Council v Australasian Temperance and General Assurance Society* [1938] A.C. 224 at 240. For the development of this approach and the importance formerly given to the law of the places of contracting and performance, see McClean, De Conflictu Legum (2000) 282 Hague *Recueil des cours*, Ch.V; Nygh, Autonomy in International Contracts (Oxford: Clarendon Press, 1999).

[7] See *Bonython v Commonwealth of Australia* [1951] A.C. 201, per Lord Simonds at 209. More recently, see *Merck KGaA v Merck Sharp & Dohme Corp* [2014] EWHC 3867 (Ch.).

complete unless they can chose the law by reference to which their agreement will be construed.[8] In practical terms, by an express selection of the proper law, the parties relieved the court of the difficult task of ascertaining it when the facts were nicely balanced between two systems of law. To allow them to do so injected some certainty into the common law approach, which was otherwise open to the criticism that it could take a law-suit to determine what law governed. But the principle of party autonomy took root even in the rather different soil of civil law countries, so that by 1980 when it was enshrined in the Rome Convention, it was already part of the law of all the then Member States of the European Community.[9]

Absence of choice by the parties

In the absence of choice, express or implied, by the parties, the courts determined the proper law by identifying the system of law with which the transaction had its closest and most real connection.[10] In this inquiry:

15–004

> "many matters have to be taken into consideration. Of these the principal are the place of contracting, the place of performance, the places of residence or business of the parties respectively, and the nature and subject matter of the contract".[11]

The Assunzione[12] is an instructive illustration of the difficulties inherent in such an open-textured approach: the facts were so nicely balanced between French and Italian law that the Court of Appeal had to use a very delicate pair of scales in order to determine the proper law.

> "The contract was one for the carriage of wheat from Dunkirk to Venice on board an Italian ship. The charterers were an organisation of French grain merchants. The wheat was shipped under an exchange agreement between the French and Italian governments, but the Italian shipowners did not know this. The contract was negotiated by correspondence between brokers in France and brokers in Italy. It was formally concluded in Paris in the English language and in an English standard form. Freight and demurrage were payable in Italian currency in Italy."

It was held unanimously that Italian law was the proper law of the contract. The decisive factor was that both parties had contractual obligations to perform in Italy.

The common law rules here outlined remain in force in many Commonwealth countries. As pointed out in the introduction to this chapter, in England they

---

[8] For possible limitations at common law on the freedom to choose the governing law, see *Vita Food Products Inc v Unus Shipping Co* [1939] A.C. 277.
[9] See the official Explanatory Report on the Convention, the Giuliano and Lagarde report, [1980] O.J. C 283 at pp.15–16.
[10] cf. the notion of the "centre of gravity" of a contract: *Auten v Auten*, 124 N.E.2d 99 (N.Y. C.As, 1954), a notion sometimes also used in European cases: Bundesgerichtshof, 7 May 1969 (VIII ZR 142/68, DB 1969, 1053); Case C-280/90 *Hacker v Euro-Relais GmbH* [1992] E.C.R. I-1111, Opinion of Advocate General Darmon, para.33; Case C-133/08 *Intercontainer Interfrigo SC v Balkenende Oosthuizen BV* [2009] ECR I-9687, Opinion of Advocate General Bot.
[11] *Re United Railways of the Havana and Regla Warehouses Ltd* [1960] Ch. 52 at 91.
[12] [1954] P. 150.

almost wholly gave way first to the provisions of the Rome Convention on the Law Applicable to Contractual Obligations 1980, given effect by the Contracts (Applicable Law) Act 1990, and later to those of the Rome I Regulation, European Parliament and Council Regulation No.593/2008 of 17 June 2008 on the law applicable to contractual obligations[13]. The abandonment of the common law rules was not universally popular. A distinguished commentator wrote as the 1990 Act was coming into force:

> "The Act replaces one of the great achievements of the English judiciary during the last 140 years or so, an achievement which produced an effective private international law of contracts, was recognised and followed in practically the whole world and has not at any time or anywhere led to dissatisfaction or to a demand for reform".[14]

THE EUROPEAN INSTRUMENTS: THE ROME CONVENTION AND THE ROME I REGULATION[15]

15–005 The Rome I Regulation applies to contracts concluded after 17 December 2009.[16] It is a revision[17] of the Rome Convention of 1980, the provisions of which apply to contracts made on or before that date.[18] The Regulation is designed to be consistent both with the European regime on jurisdiction and with the Rome II Regulation.[19] Therefore, the European Court has referred to the Rome Convention when interpreting the European jurisdiction instruments and it has also referred to the jurisdiction case law to interpret the European instruments on applicable law to contractual and non-contractual obligations.[20] It is necessary, in what follows, to deal at times with both the Convention and the Regulation: the Convention will still be relied on in contract disputes for a number of years, and the interpretive case law of the European Court of Justice (ECJ) subsequently renamed as Court of Justice of the European Union (CJEU) on the provisions of

---

[13] O.J. L 177/6, 4.7.2008.

[14] Mann, (1991) 107 L.Q.R. 353.

[15] See Plender and Wilderspin, *The European Private International Law of Obligations,* 3rd edn (London: Sweet & Maxwell, 2009); Ferrari and Leible (eds.), *Rome I Regulation* (Munich: Sellier, 2009); Bělohlávek, *Rome Convention/Rome I Regulation* (Huntington, NJ: Juris, 2010).

[16] Regulation art.28.

[17] The UK played a full part in the negotiations pursuant to the adoption of the Rome I Regulation but initially chose not to be bound by it; as the final text met most of the UK's concerns, it then agreed to opt into the Regulation. See *Rome I—Should the UK opt in?* Consultation Paper CP05/08. See also Ruiz Abou-Nigm, "Rome I: Evolution or Status Quo?" in Fernandez Arroyo and Gonzalez Martin (eds), *Tendencias y relaciones del derecho internacional privado americano actual (Jornadas de la ASADIP 2008)* (Porrua, Mexico 2010) 553.

[18] For the thinking of the Commission which led to the adoption of the Regulation, see its Green Paper on the conversion of the Convention into a Community instrument and its modernisation, COM/2002/0654 final.

[19] European Parliament and Council Regulation No 864/2007 of 11 July 2007 on the law applicable to non-contractual obligations (Rome II) (as to which see Ch.16, below): Rome I Regulation, Recital (7).

[20] e.g., Case C–190/11 *Mühlleitner v Yusufi* [2012] I.L.Pr. 859, at [8]–[9]; Case C–508/12 *Vapenik v Thurner* [2014] 1 W.L.R. 2486, at [29]. See also Crawford and Carruthers (2014) 63 I.C.L.Q. 1.

the Rome Convention[21] will continue to be useful since much of the text of the Rome I Regulation is in fact simply taken over from the Rome Convention.

Interpretation

An explanatory report on the Rome Convention by Professors Mario Giuliano and Paul Lagarde was published in the *Official Journal*,[22] and the Contracts (Applicable Law) Act 1990 enables this to be considered in interpreting the Convention. There is provision in an appended Protocol giving the CJEU jurisdiction to rule on the interpretation of the Convention,[23] and any question of interpretation which is not referred to the CJEU must be determined in accordance with the principles laid down by, and any relevant decision of, the CJEU.[24] The Court is able to rule on the interpretation of the Rome I Regulation under the usual rules applying to European legislation.[25] Where the language of the Convention is carried over into the Regulation, decisions on the Convention are naturally relied on also in relation to the Regulation.[26]

15–006

Material scope of application

The rules of the Rome Convention are declared to apply to "contractual obligations in any situation involving a choice between the laws of different countries".[27] A "choice" exists, in effect, whenever there is a foreign element which might lead to the application of a particular law; it may, for example, be the residence of a party to the contract, the place of performance, or the fact that the parties have chosen a particular law as applicable.[28]

15–007

Article 1 of the Regulation provides:

> "(1)   This Regulation shall apply, in situations involving a conflict of laws, to contractual obligations in civil and commercial matters."

"In situations involving a conflict of laws"

The purpose of this wording is to make clear that the Regulation applies also in situations where there is no other internationalisation factor but a choice of law agreed by the parties selecting a foreign law as the applicable law. Putting it in

15–008

---

[21] The first reference for a preliminary ruling of the CJEU on the interpretation of the Convention was made in Case C-133/08 *Intercontainer Interfrigo SC v Balkenende Oosthuizen BV* [2009] ECR I-9687.

[22] [1980] O.J. C283.

[23] See Sch.3 of the 1990 Act and O.J. C334/1, 30 December 2005.

[24] Contracts (Applicable Law) Act 1990 s.3(1).

[25] Treaty of the European Union (TEU) art.19(3)(b) and Treaty on the Functioning of the European Union (TFEU) art.267. See also the Recommendations of the CJEU to national courts and tribunals in relation to the initiation of preliminary ruling proceedings, [2012] O.J. C 338/1.

[26] This has been referred to as the principle of continuity of interpretation, see Crawford and Carruthers, (2014) 63 I.C.L.Q. 1.

[27] Convention art.1(1).

[28] See Giuliano-Lagarde report, p.10.

another way, it is possible for the Rome I Regulation to apply to a contract that except for the choice of law clause is only connected with a single country.[29] In that sense, if a contract is solely connected with England, that is, both parties are residents in England, they conclude a contract in England, and the contract is to be performed in England; that contract would be subject to the provisions of the Rome I Regulation if the parties decided to include a choice of law clause in the contract selecting the law of any other county as the applicable law.

"Contractual obligations": European autonomous interpretation

15–009   The European Court has been asked to shed light in relation to the European autonomous interpretation of the terms "contractual obligations" on many occasions,[30] in relation to the boundary between, for example, contractual and tortious obligations[31]; or in relation to the word "obligations". The meaning of "contractual obligations" in the Rome I Regulation needs to be interpreted consistently with the concept of "matters related to a contract" in the Brussels I *bis* Regulation.[32] As analysed in a previous chapter,[33] the notion of "contract" is not identical in every legal system, with different understandings of the boundary between contract and tort or property law. For this reason, "contractual obligations" in the European system of private international law, including the instruments regulating jurisdiction as well as choice of law, is given an autonomous meaning, independent of the categories in national legal systems. It is among what has become quite a long list of terms that must be given a "European" meaning, not tied to the understanding of any one legal system. The rationale behind this "European autonomous interpretation" is the aim to attain uniformity in the interpretation of European conflict of laws rules in the European area of justice.

The concept has been interpreted as covering matters having their basis in an agreement,[34] where there is a direct relationship between the parties, and where there was real consensus. Cases where there was no obligation freely entered into by one party to another are excluded.[35] That may suggest that benefits conferred

---

[29] This becomes clearer when read in conjunction with art.3(3) of the Regulation.

[30] e.g. Case C–543/10 *Refcomp SpA v Axa Corporate Solutions Assurance* SA [2013] 1 Lloyd's Rep. 449; Case C–419/11 *Èeská spoøitelna, as v Feichter* [2013] I.L.Pr. 375; Case C–548/12 *Brogsitter v Fabrication de Montres Normandes EURL* [2014] Q.B. 753; Case C–147/12 *Östergötlands Fastigheter AB v Koot* [2015] Q.B. 20; Case C–548/12 *Brogsitter v Fabrication de Montres Normandes EURL* [2014] Q.B. 753; Case C–375/13 *Kolassa v Barclays Bank plc* [2015] I.L.Pr. 245.

[31] See Czepelak, (2011) 7 J.Priv.Int.L. 393. See, e.g., inter alia, case C–475/14 *AAS Gjensidige Baltic v UAB DK PZU Lietuva*, 17 October 2014; Case C-548/12 *Brogsitter v Fabrication de Montres Normandes EURL and another* [2014] Q.B. 753.

[32] European Parliament and Council Regulation 1215/2012 on jurisdiction and the recognition and enforcement of judgments in civil and commercial matters, [2012] OJ L 351/1, December 20, 2012.

[33] See para.6-015ff.

[34] Case 9/87 *Arcado Sprl v Haviland SA* [1988] E.C.R. 1539 (agency dispute involving allegations of bad faith held contractual); Case 334/00 *Fonderie Officine Meccaniche Tacconi SpA v Heinrich Wagner Sinto Maschinenfabrik GmbH* [2002] E.C.R. I-7357.

[35] Case 26/91 *Ste Handte et Cie GmbH v Traitements Mecano-Chimiques des Surfaces* [1992] E.C.R. I-3967; Case C–543/10 *Refcomp SpA v Axa Corporate Solutions Assurance* SA [2013] 1 Lloyd's Rep. 449; Case 419/11 *Ceska Sporitelna AS v Gerald Feichter* [2013] I.L.Pr. 22; Case C–419/11 *Èeská spoøitelna AS v Feichter* [2013] I.L.Pr. 375; Case C–519/12 *OTP Bank Nyilvánosan Mûködõ*

on others, as third party beneficiaries or as sub-purchasers, under some national legal systems, will not be treated as "contractual obligations". However, the Court of Appeal held in *WPP Holdings Italy Srl v Benatti*,[36] that where two contracting parties confer a benefit on a stranger to the contract, intending that the stranger may enforce the benefit in his own right, the claim by the stranger under the Contracts (Rights of Third Parties) Act 1999 was a contractual matter for the purposes of the European regime of jurisdiction.

In legal systems such as English law where it is possible for the claimant in certain circumstances to initiate proceedings alternatively or concurrently in contract and in tort, all the consensual aspects of this claim seem to be governed by the Rome I Regulation for the purposes of determining its applicable law.

"Civil and commercial matters": *European autonomous interpretation*

This concept also has the same meaning in relation to all the conflict-of-laws instruments in the area of freedom, security and justice in the European Union. In that sense, the case law discussed in relation to this concept in the field of jurisdiction, in relation to art.1 of the Brussels I *bis* Regulation,[37] results applicable also to the interpretation of art.1(1) of the Rome I Regulation.

15–010

Excluded matters

Article 1(2) of both the Rome Convention and the Rome I Regulation expressly excludes certain matters from the scope of application of the European choice of law rules in contractual obligations. The list of exclusions is such that in English law some matters of contract, notably arbitration agreements, remain governed by the common law rules.[38]

15–011

Most of the exclusions are stated in absolute terms:

(1)   what might be described by way of shorthand as family law obligations; the language differs as between the Convention and the Regulation. The Convention speaks of:

> "contractual obligations relating to wills and succession, rights in property arising out of a matrimonial relationship, and rights and duties arising out of a family relationship, including maintenance obligations in respect of illegitimate children."

and the Regulation, more elaborate at this point, has two relevant exclusions:

Reszvénytársaság v Hochtief Solutions AG, 17 October 2013; Case C–548/12 *Brogsitter v Fabrication de Montres Normandes EURL* [2014] Q.B. 753; Case 375/13 *Kolassa v Barclays Bank Plc* [2015] C.E.C. 753; [2015] I.L.Pr. 14; Case 147/12 *OFAB, Ostergotlands Fastigheter AB v Koot* [2015] Q.B. 20. See also Joined Cases C-359/14 and C-475/14 *ERGO Insurance SE v If P&C Insurance AS*; *AAS Gjensidige Baltic v UAB DK PZU Lietuva* (CJEU 21 January 2016).
[36] [2007] EWCA Civ 263; [2007] 1 W.L.R. 2316.
[37] See para.6–006.
[38] See, e.g., *Haugesund Kommune v Depfa ACS Bank* [2010] EWCA Civ 579; [2011] 1 All E.R. 190 (legal capacity of companies).

"(b) obligations arising out of family relationships[39] and relationships deemed by the law applicable to such relationships to have comparable effects,[40] including maintenance obligations;

(c) obligations arising out of matrimonial property regimes, property regimes of relationships deemed by the law applicable to such relationships to have comparable effects to marriage, and wills and succession."

(2) obligations arising under bills of exchange, cheques and promissory notes and other negotiable instruments to the extent that the obligations under such other negotiable instruments arise out of their negotiable character; here the text is unchanged in the Regulation,[41] the Recitals to which specify that bills of lading are included to the extent that the obligations under the bill of lading arise out of its negotiable character.[42]

(3) arbitration agreements[43] and agreements on the choice of court[44];

(4) company law issues,[45] i.e., questions governed by the law of companies and other bodies, corporate or unincorporated, such as the creation, by registration or otherwise, legal capacity, internal organisation or winding up of companies and other bodies, corporate or unincorporated and the personal liability of officers and members as such for the obligations of the company or body[46];

(5) the question as to whether an agent is able to bind a principal, or an organ to bind a company or body, corporate or unincorporated, to a third party;

(6) the constitution of trusts and the relationship between settlors, trustees and beneficiaries; and

(7) in the Regulation only, obligations arising out of dealings prior to the conclusion of a contract: the Recitals explain that these obligations are covered by art.12 of the Rome II Regulation[47]; and

---

[39] "Family relationships" covers parentage, marriage, affinity and collateral relatives: Regulation, Recital (8).

[40] The "comparable effects" provisions are to be interpreted in accordance with the law of the Member State seised of the case: Regulation, Recital (8).

[41] See Garcimartín Alférez, (2009) 5 J.Priv.Int.L.85 on the question of whether certain types of financial instruments that are regarded as negotiable instruments are within this exclusion or not.

[42] Regulation, Recital (9).

[43] See Arzandeh and Hill, (2009) 5 J.Priv.Int.L. 425; and Yüksel, (2011) 7 J.Priv.Int.L. 149. On the relevance of the choice of law on the main contract to govern the law applicable to the arbitration agreement see *Sulamérica Cia Nacional de Seguros SA v Enesa Engenharia SA* [2012] EWCA Civ 638; [2013] 1 W.L.R. 102; *Arsanovia Ltd v Cruz City 1 Mauritius Holding* [2012] EWHC 3702 (Comm.); [2013] 2 All E.R. 1; *Habas Sinai Ve Tibbi Gazlar Istihsal Endustrisi AS v VSC Steel Co Ltd* [2013] EWHC 4071 (Comm.); [2014] 1 Lloyd's Rep. 479.

[44] For jurisdiction clauses (i.e. "agreements on the choice of court"), see above, paras 6–054 and 7–011.

[45] For proposed further harmonisation of conflict of laws rules on the law applicable to companies, see *The Stockholm Programme—An open and secure Europe serving and protecting the citizens* (O.J. C115/1, 4.5.2010) and its implementing Action Plan (COM (2010) 171 final).

[46] See *Haugesund Kommune v Depfa ACS Bank* [2010] EWCA Civ 579; [2011] 1 All E.R. 190. See Case C–483/14 *KA Finanz AG v Sparkassen Versicherung AG Vienna Insurance Group* (pending). For the scope of this exclusion, see e.g. *Integral Petroleum SA v SCU-Finanz AG* [2015] EWCA Civ 144.

[47] Regulation, Recital (10).

(8)   certain contracts of insurance; the Regulation has more elaborate provisions as to insurance, which are considered below,[48] covering risks situated (in the understanding of the *lex fori*) in the territories of the Member States.
       Two other exclusions are expressed in more qualified terms:

(9)   questions involving the status or legal capacity of natural persons, without prejudice to one provision which forms art.11 of the Convention and art.13 of the Regulation[49];

(10)   evidence and procedure, without prejudice to another specific provision, which forms art.14 of the Convention and art.18 of the Regulation.[50]

Territorial scope of application: universality

The Rome I Regulation applies whenever the courts of the Member States are asked to determine the applicable law to contractual obligations in civil and commercial matters. Countries whose law may be made applicable are not limited to Member States (or to Contracting States to the Convention); it is expressly provided that a law specified by the Convention or Regulation must be applied whether or not it is the law of such a state.[51] So the rules apply where the countries relevant to a contractual dispute are, for example, England, New Zealand and Ontario.   **15–012**

The applicable law needs to be the law of a State

Under the Convention, the law chosen had to be the law of a state: the contract could not be governed by the customs of international trade (often referred to as the *lex mercatoria*),[52] nor by the rules of an international convention, nor by the rules of Sharia law.[53] The position is not changed under the Regulation so far as the applicable law is concerned, but Recital (13) states that the Regulation does not preclude parties from incorporating by reference into their contract a non-State body of law or an international convention. This means that the terms   **15–013**

---

[48] See below, paras 15–039. Excluded from the Regulation by art.1(2) are insurance contracts arising out of operations carried out by organisations other than undertakings referred to in art.2 of Directive 2002/83/EC concerning life assurance the object of which is to provide benefits for employed or self-employed persons belonging to an undertaking or group of undertakings, or to a trade or group of trades, in the event of death or survival or of discontinuance or curtailment of activity, or of sickness related to work or accidents at work.

[49] See below, paras 15-051 and following.

[50] See paras 9-006 and following.

[51] Convention, art.2; Regulation, art.2.

[52] The Commission's Proposal (COM(2005) 650, para.3.2.) provided for the possibility of choosing non-national rules of law such as the Unidroit Principles of International Commercial Contracts, the Principles of European Contract Law, or the European Common Frame of Reference, but not the *lex mercatoria* or the like, as these concepts were not sufficiently precise. The European Parliament asked for the deletion of references to non-national systems of law in the interests of legal certainty.

[53] *Shamil Bank of Bahrain EC v Beximco Pharmaceuticals Ltd* [2004] EWCA Civ 19; [2004] 1 W.L.R. 1784 (clause reading "Subject to the principles of Glorious Sharia'a, this agreement shall be governed by and construed in accordance with the laws of England" treated as choice of English law); *Halpern v Halpern* [2007] EWCA Civ 291; [2007] 2 Lloyd's Rep. 56; *Musawi v RE International (UK) Ltd* [2007] EWHC 2981 (Ch); [2008] 1 All E.R. (Comm) 607; *Dubai Islamic Bank PJSC Energy Holding BSC* [2013] EWHC 3186 (Comm.).

of such a body of law or convention may become part of the text of the contract, but issues arising will be a matter for the applicable law (governing law) of some state.[54]

In the case of federal or composite states in which each territorial unit (such as Ontario) has its own rules of law in respect of contractual obligations, each territorial unit is treated as a "country" for the purposes of the Convention and the Regulation.[55]

A federal or composite state is not bound to apply the Convention or Regulation to conflicts solely between the laws of different units within that state.[56] The UK is, of course, such a state. Section 2(2) of the 1990 Act provides that the Convention rules are to apply in the case of conflicts between the laws of different parts of the UK. It would have made for needless complexity to retain the common law rules for cases involving, say, a choice only between England and Scotland, but to apply the Convention if the choice of Dutch law were perceived as available on the same facts. A similar provision is made in relation to the Regulation, with an express exclusion of insurance contracts.[57]

DETERMINING THE GOVERNING LAW

15–014 The heart of both the Rome I Regulation and its predecessor the Rome Convention is to be found in arts 3 and 4. Article 3 embodies the principle of "party autonomy", giving the parties freedom to select the law which is to govern the contract. As the Giuliano-Lagarde Report observes, this simply reaffirms a rule embodied in the private international law of all the then Member States of the Community.[58] The recitals to the Regulation affirm the principle that "The parties' freedom to choose the applicable law should be one of the cornerstones of the system of conflict-of-law rules in matters of contractual obligations".[59] The applicable law needs to be determined from the time of conclusion of the contract; that is, even though it is possible for the governing law to change through the lifetime of the contract, as it is explained below,[60] the contract needs to have a governing law from the outset.[61]

---

[54] cf. Inter-American Convention on the Law Applicable to International Contracts (Mexico 1994) (CIDIP-V). art.7(1) allowing the choice of any law, including a non-national system of law such as the Unidroit Principles. On the comparison between the Inter-American Convention and the Rome I Regulation see Albornoz, (2010) 6 J.Priv.Int.L. 23.

[55] Convention, art.19(1); Regulation, art.22(1).

[56] Convention, art.19(2); Regulation, art.22(2).

[57] See Law Applicable to Contractual Obligations (England and Wales and Northern Ireland) Regulations 2009 (SI 2009/3064) reg.5. In relation to Rome I Regulation, art.7 on insurance contracts, see the Financial Services and Markets Act 2000 (Law Applicable to Contracts of Insurance) Regulations 2009 (SI 2009/3075).

[58] Report, p.15.

[59] Regulation, Recital (11). See, e.g. case also Case C–184/12 *United Antwerp Maritime Agencies NV (Unamar) v Navigation Maritime Bulgare* [2014] 1 Lloyd's Rep. 161, at [49].

[60] See para.15–021.

[61] *Mauritius Commercial Bank Ltd v Hestia Holdings Ltd* [2013] EWHC 1328 (Comm.); R Fentiman, International Commercial Litigation, 2nd edn (Oxford: Oxford University Press, 2015) p.194.

Article 4 provides a set of rules for determining the governing law in the absence of a choice by the parties; it is at this point that there is the most significant divergence between Convention and Regulation.

Exclusion of *renvoi*

There is in principle no room for the doctrine of *renvoi*[62] in the context of the Regulation or the Convention.   **15–015**

Article 20 of the Regulation provides:

> "The application of the law of any country specified by this Regulation means the application of the rules of law in force in that country other than its rules of private international law, unless provided otherwise in this Regulation."[63]

Article 3: the law chosen by the parties

Article 3(1) of the Regulation provides that a contract is to be governed by the law chosen by the parties. The choice must be express or clearly demonstrated (at this point the Convention has "demonstrated with reasonable certainty") by the terms of the contract or the circumstances of the case.   **15–016**

Express and implicit (clearly demonstrated) choice

The inclusion of a choice of law clause is such an everyday matter in international contracts that its absence could take one straight to the rules in art.4 as to the position where there is an absence of choice. That would be to ignore commercial realities. Not every international commercial contract receives the attention of lawyers (still less of skilled lawyers). It is quite possible for an express choice of law to be omitted, while the terms of the contract (by their reference to related transactions,[64] or to a recognised standard form or the practices of a particular market,[65] or as to arbitration) can quite properly be interpreted as pointing clearly to the parties' assumption that the law of a particular country will govern.[66] Where there has been an established course of dealing between the parties, fresh contracts may be entered into quite informally: "Could you send us more of the same, please?" Legal rules must in these matters reflect commercial realities and expectations; hence the reference above to "the   **15–017**

---

[62] See below, paras 20–011 and following.

[63] cf. Convention, art.15.

[64] e.g., *FR Lürssen Werft GmbH & Co KG v Halle* [2010] EWCA Civ 587; [2011] 1 Lloyd's Rep. 265.

[65] e.g., the presumption that a re-insurance policy is governed by the same law as the related insurance policy; see *Wasa International Insurance Co v Lexington Insurance Co* [2009] UKHL 40; [2010] 1 A.C. 180.

[66] See the Giuliano-Lagarde report, at p.17.

circumstances of the case". The test of whether an implicit choice can be established must be objective: it is not possible to consider the unspoken thoughts of the parties.[67]

Difficult questions can be asked about the situation in which words in the contract may or may not amount to an express choice of law. The important question is whether art.3(1) has been satisfied; if it is, nothing turns on whether the choice was express or not. The "boundary question" is one of an essentially factual nature: have the parties clearly demonstrated a choice of applicable law? Only if the answer is "no" will art.4 apply. The need for a *clear* demonstration of such a choice may be seen as stricter than the Convention's requirement of demonstration "with reasonable certainty"; the European Commission, commenting on practice under the Convention, observed that "the German and English courts, perhaps under the influence of a slightly more flexible form of words, and under the influence of their previous solutions, are less strict about discerning a tacit choice than their European counterparts".[68] The wording in the Regulation seeks to eliminate these variations in practice.

It is this factual question, with attention being paid not only to the contract as a whole but to all the circumstances of the case, that enables the courts to examine the practical realities just referred to: relevant trade practices, the use of standard forms developed in particular countries where there is special expertise but used worldwide,[69] and the previous course of dealings between the parties. So, in the Convention case of *Egon Oldendorff v Libera Corp (No.2)*[70] there was no choice of law clause in a contract between German and Japanese companies, but their use of a well-known English standard form of charterparty and the presence of a clause specifying arbitration in England was held to demonstrate the choice of English law as the applicable law.

In *Aquavita International SA v Ashapura Minechem Ltd*[71] a letter of guarantee ancillary to a contract of affreightment was considered to be governed by implicitly by the same law as the contract of affreightment, which was English law. It was held that it "would be very surprising, and ... commercially unattractive, if the parties had intended that a guarantee in relation to such contracts would be governed by a different system of law".[72] All other contracts between the parties included an express choice of English law.[73]

---

[67] e.g., *Lawlor v Sandvik Mining and Construction Mobile Crushers and Screens Ltd* [2013] EWCA Civ 365; [2013] 2 Lloyd's Rep. 98.

[68] Green paper, para.3.2.4.2. The similarity between the Convention and the English common law approach was stressed by Mance LJ in *American Motorists Insurance Co v Cellstar Corp* [2003] EWCA Civ 206; [2003] I.L.Pr. 370.

[69] The expertise of the London insurance market is one example: *Gan Insurance Co Ltd v Tai Ping Insurance Co Ltd* [1999] 2 All E.R. (Comm) 54.

[70] [1996] 1 Lloyd's Rep. 380.

[71] *Aquavita International SA v Ashapura Minechem Ltd* [2015] EWHC 2807 (QB).

[72] ibid. at [101](iii).

[73] See also *Cox v Ergo Versicherung AG* [2014] UKSC 22; [2014] A.C. 1379.

Is it possible to infer parallelism[74] between the choice of forum and the choice of law?

Recital (12) to the Regulation declares that an agreement between the parties to **15–018** confer on one or more courts or tribunals of a Member State exclusive jurisdiction to determine disputes under the contract should be one of the factors to be taken into account in determining whether a choice of law has been clearly demonstrated. This reflects long-standing English practice, and the only puzzling feature is the limitation to courts in Member States. In practice, a selection of the courts of New York as having exclusive jurisdiction is just as significant as the choice of the courts of France or Germany. The choice of a particular court is usually supported by very different reasons from those which support a choice of law, so it cannot be automatically inferred from a choice of court that the parties chose the *lex fori* to govern their contract.[75] This is not to say that choice of the *lex fori* might not be a sensible and cost-effective choice, but it should be an informed and deliberate one by the parties. In some scenarios, the parties will agree on the jurisdiction of the courts in a "neutral" country because they wish to avoid proceedings before the courts in the country of the eventual counter-party. In these cases, the choice of forum is not necessarily connected to the choice of law and a presumption in favour of the parallelism between choice of court and choice of law would not lead to an appropriate law to govern the contract.

A common problem, in this as in other areas of the law of contract, is the use by the parties of standard conditions which are mutually inconsistent. There will be no express choice of law within art.3 unless the court can find a consensus between the parties, and the use of inconsistent terms,[76] or the clear rejection of a proffered choice of law clause,[77] indicates a lack of consensus.

Depéçage

By their choice, the parties can select the law applicable to the whole or a part **15–019** only of the contract.[78] This allows *depéçage*, a splitting of the contract between different legal systems. This can be done by reference to different duties of performance or, presumably, different numbered clauses. But there may be problem cases in which the two chosen laws cannot logically be reconciled in their application to a particular situation, for example, repudiation for

---

[74] The parallelism criterion is also known in some Latin American countries as the 'Asser criterion', attributing this solution to TMC Asser in *Elements de Droit International Privé ou du Conflit des Lois*, Paris 1884, p.158 [71].

[75] This presumption was rejected by the House of Lords in *Compagnie d'Armement Maritime SA v Compagnie Tunisienne de Navigation SA* [1971] AC 572 at 596.

[76] See *Iran Continental Shelf Oil Co v IRI International Corp* [2002] C.L.C. 372 (reversed [2002] EWCA Civ 1024, but not on this point).

[77] As in *Land Rover Exports Ltd v Samcrete Egypt Engineers and Contractors SAE* [2001] EWCA Civ 2019; [2002] C.L.C. 533 (choice of law clause in draft agreement crossed out by one party).

[78] Convention, art.3(1); Regulation, art.3(1). This is to be distinguished from an arrangement under which the parties agree that the law applicable depends upon stated circumstances (the law of State A on one contingency, of State B on another); such "floating" choice of law clauses appear perfectly valid.

non-performance[79]; in such a case there can be no effective choice by the parties, and the court would have to rely on art.4.

Altering the choice by the parties

15–020 It is possible for the parties to change the governing law, either by altering their own expressed choice or by making a choice where previously they had not done so.[80] However, any variation by the parties of the law to be applied made after the conclusion of the contract will not prejudice its formal validity (that is, where the contract was formally valid at its inception under the Convention or Regulation rules,[81] any additional formal requirements of the new governing law will be ignored) or adversely affect the rights of third parties.

Changes in the substantive law governing the contract

15–021 The freedom to alter the selection allowed to the parties needs to be distinguished from the changes that may affect the law applicable to contractual obligations in the selected or in the otherwise applicable law. The selection does not remain "frozen" as to the substantive contents of that law at the time of conclusion of the contract. The applicable law is a "living law" and must be applied as it is when the contract is to be performed and not as it was when the contract was made.[82] Thus, legislation passed in the country of the applicable law may have the effect of modifying or discharging the contractual obligation, e.g. by reducing the rate of interest[83] or declaring a gold value clause invalid.[84]

Ample freedom of choice and mandatory rules

15–022 There is no requirement that the chosen law need have any real connection with the parties or the subject matter of their contract.[85] That this is so is apparent from art.3 of both the Regulation and the Convention. However art.3(3) qualifies this

---

[79] An example in the Giuliano-Lagarde Report, p.17.
[80] Convention, art.3(2); Regulation, art.3(2). See *ISS Machinery Services Ltd v Aeolian Shipping SA, The Aeolian* [2001] EWCA Civ 1162; [2001] 2 Lloyd's Rep. 641 (Rome Convention; successive contracts dealing with supply and then provision of spare parts for machine governed by different laws; no evidence that choice of law in second contract intended to change law governing the first contract); See also *Mauritius Commercial Bank Ltd v Hestia Holdings Ltd* [2013] EWHC 1328 (Comm.); [2013] 2 Lloyd's Rep. 121, at [19]–[30]) (Rome I Regulation; original contract governed by the law of Mauritius, replaced by a contract governed by English law; held that no policy of English law was opposed to the parties agreeing to change the governing law of their contract; contrarily, there was a strong countervailing policy that they should be permitted to do so, which was to be found in the principle of freedom of contract). See also *Apcoa Parking Holdings GmbH* [2014] EWHC 3849 (Ch); Rome I Regulation, change to English law).
[81] These are in art.9 of the Convention and art.11 of the Regulation; see above, para.13–034.
[82] *Re Helbert Wagg & Co Ltd's Claim* [1956] Ch. 323 at 341; *Rossano v Manufacturers Life Insurance Co* [1963] 2 Q.B. 352 at 362.
[83] *Barcelo v Electrolytic Zinc Co of Australasia Ltd* (1932) 48 C.L.R. 391.
[84] *R. v International Trustee for the Protection of Bondholders A/G* [1937] A.C. 500.
[85] cf. the issue at common law in *Vita Food Products Inc v Unus Shipping Co Ltd* [1939] A.C. 277.

complete freedom of choice for cases where, except for the choice of law clause, the contract is in fact domestic.[86] The provision is more elegantly drafted in the Regulation, where it reads:

> "Where all other elements relevant to the situation at the time of the choice are located in a country other than the country whose law has been chosen, the choice of the parties shall not prejudice the application of provisions of the law of that other country which cannot be derogated from by agreement."[87]

In the Convention text the provisions which cannot be derogated from by agreement are described as "mandatory rules". Such rules may serve many purposes. They may relate to the socio-economic policies of states, for example in the field of competition or "anti-trust" law; exchange control designed to protect the national economy or its currency; laws designed to protect the environment. Or they may seek to regulate the contents of private contracts, requiring the inclusion of certain types of term, or prohibiting exclusion or exemption clauses or the imposition of unreasonable sanctions in penalty clauses. They may be designed to protect the interests of those seen as economically weak, such as workers (with rules as to health and safety at work and to safeguards from unfair dismissal) or consumers (with rules designed to help them in disputes with suppliers of goods and services). Or they may serve more general interests such as the proper administration of justice or the uniform regulation of an international industry such as aviation.[88]

Article 3(3) envisages a situation in which all elements of the factual situation are connected with Country A, the law of which contains a relevant rule which cannot be derogated from by agreement. The parties, for whatever reason, agree that the law of Country B is to govern their contract. They have that freedom of choice, and art.3(3) does not remove it; the law of Country B will indeed be the governing law. However, the non-derogable rules of Country A will also apply, and within its scope will override any different rule in the law of Country B.

The provision speaks of "all other elements relevant to the situation". What this may mean can be considered in the light of facts based on those of an Australian case[89]:

> X is an estate agency which specialises in selling retirement homes in the South of Queensland, advertising widely in newspapers circulating in the holiday areas of Queensland where potential purchasers may be staying. A contract is entered into which carries a commission much in excess of the maximum amount allowed under Queensland legislation; that legislation cannot under the law of Queensland be excluded by a contractual term. X's conditions of doing business specify that the law of Hong Kong should govern.

If all the elements are connected only with Queensland, there is no difficulty. If the estate agency is a company incorporated under the law of Hong Kong, or for

---

[86] See also Regulation, art.3(4), a similar rule as to non-derogable rules of Community law.
[87] The redraft was intended to make no substantial change: Regulation, Recital (15).
[88] See McClean, De Conflictu Legum (2000) 282 Hague Receuil des cours, Ch.V.
[89] *Golden Acres Ltd v Queensland Estates Pty Ltd* [1969] Qd.R. 378 (affd. on other grounds (1970) 123 C.L.R. 418). See *Caterpillar Financial Services Corp v SNC Passion* [2004] EWHC 569 (Comm); [2004] 2 Lloyd's Rep. 99; *Emeraldian Ltd Partnership v Wellmix Shipping Ltd, Guangzhou Iron & Steel Corp Ltd* [2010] EWHC 1411 (Comm); [2011] 1 Lloyd's Rep. 301.

that matter of New South Wales, or the purchase is made by a couple retiring from their present home in Tasmania, the factual elements are no longer all connected to Queensland. This raises the question, to which there is as yet no clear answer, as to whether the adjective "relevant" is to be interpreted so as to enable some minor non-Queensland elements to be ignored and the non-derogable rule applied.

Article 3(4) of the Regulation protects in the same manner the imperative norms of European law.[90]

Incorporation (by reference) of foreign law

15–023 A distinction must be drawn between the parties' express selection of the applicable law and their incorporation of some of the provisions of a foreign law (other than the applicable law) as a term or terms of the contract. It often happens that statutes governing the liability of a carrier, such as the Carriage of Goods by Sea Act 1971, are incorporated by what is known as a "paramount clause" in a contract governed by a law other than that of which the statute forms part. The statute then operates not as a statute but as a set of contractual terms agreed upon by the parties.[91]

The distinction between incorporation of foreign law by reference and an express choice of the applicable law is seen most clearly if there is a change in the law between the time of making the contract and its performance.[92] Where a foreign statute is incorporated in a contract as a contractual term, it remains part of the contract, although as a statute it may have been amended or repealed.

Article 4 of the Rome Convention: applicable law in the absence of choice

15–024 As the rules of the Convention and of the Regulation diverge at this point, they must be dealt with separately.

---

[90] See *Ingmar GB Ltd v Eaton Loenard Technologies Inc* [2000] E.C.R. I-09305. The inclusion of a provision on the applicability of European imperative norms in art.3 has been criticised. See Boele-Woelki and Lazić, 'Where Do We Stand on the Rome I Regulation?' in Boele-Woelki and Grosheide (eds) *The Future of European Contract Law, Liber Amicorum E H Hondius* (London & Boston: Kluwer, 2007) at 31. In their opinion it would have been better to deal with this issue in the general provision dealing with overriding mandatory rules (art.9).

[91] The practice is not free from difficulties as the statute incorporated may not be an ideal "fit" to the facts of the particular contract: see *Adamastos Shipping Co Ltd v Anglo-Saxon Petroleum Co* [1959] A.C. 133; *Seven Seas Transportation Ltd v Pacifico Union Marina Corp, The Oceanic Amity* [1984] 2 All E.R. 140. The distinction between incorporation by reference and choice of law is not always easy: *Shamil Bank of Bahrain EC v Beximco Pharmaceuticals Ltd* [2004] EWCA Civ 19; [2004] 1 W.L.R.1784. In *Kingspan Environmental Ltd v Borealis A/s* [2012] EWHC 1147 (Comm.) Danish law was applied to determine whether a seller's standard terms and conditions were incorporated into the contract of sale; the standard terms included a choice-of-law clause in favour of Danish law (at [559]–[568]). See also *Toyota Tsusho Sugar Trading Ltd v Prolat SRL* [2014] EWHC 3649 (Comm.); [2015] 1 Lloyd's Rep. 9.

[92] See above, para.15–021.

In the Convention, if there is no choice by the parties, the governing law is determined by the complex rules set out in art.4. The starting point is the clear principle set out in art.4(1):

> "To the extent that the law applicable to the contract has not been chosen in accordance with art.3, the contract shall be governed by the law of the country with which it is most closely connected."

In this context, as in art.3, there is room for *depéçage*: there is a, notably guarded, provision that "nevertheless" a severable part of the contract which has a closer connection with another country may "by way of exception" be governed by the law of that other country.[93] The Court of Appeal has held that this contemplates distinct provisions within a contract, which can be treated as separate from the rest of the contract.[94]

If art.4 had stopped at that point, it would have reflected the English common law position; but the authors of the Convention felt obliged to limit its flexibility. They felt it essential to give the courts more guidance as to the identification of the law of the country of closest connection. So art.4(2) provides:

> "Subject to the provisions of paragraph 5 of this article, it shall be presumed that the contract is most closely connected with the country where the party who is to effect the performance which is characteristic of the contract has, at the time of conclusion of the contract, his habitual residence, or, in the case of a body corporate or unincorporate, its central administration. However, if the contract is entered into in the course of that party's trade or profession, that country shall be the country in which the principal place of business is situated or, where under the terms of the contract the performance is to be effected through a place of business other than the principal place of business, the country in which that other place of business is situated."

This paragraph is best approached in a number of stages:

(1)   The first stage is the identification of the "party who is to effect the performance which is characteristic of the contract". This idea, made fashionable by its use in Swiss legal texts,[95] is explained in the Giuliano-Lagarde Report as one which "links the contract to the social and economic environment of which it will form a part".[96] It identifies a particular category of contract, an exercise more appealing to the civil law mind than that formed by the common law.

    In the normal case, one party to a contract provides consideration in the form of money. The performance which is characteristic of the contract is:

---

[93] Convention, art.4(1).
[94] *Bank of Scotland v Butcher* [1998] N.P.C. 144.
[95] See the Law on Private International Law of 1987, art.117; Vischer, "The Concept of Characteristic Performance reviewed" in Borras (ed.), *E Pluribus Unum: Liber Amicorum Georges A L Droz* (1996), 499; and Mankowski, "The Principle of Characteristic Performance Revisited Yet Again" in Boele-Woelki et al (eds), *Convergence and Divergence in Private International Law—Liber Amicorum Kurt Siehr* (Schulthess Juristische, 2010), 433.
[96] Giuliano-Lagarde Report, p.20.

"the performance for which the payment is due, i.e. depending on the type of contract, the delivery of goods,[97] the granting of the right to make use of an item of property, the provision of a service, transport, insurance,[98] banking operations,[99] security, etc. which usually constitutes the centre of gravity and the socio-economic function of the contractual transaction".[100]

If A pays B to act as the distributor of A's goods in a particular country, the characteristic performance of this distribution contract would seem to be that of B. The facts are seldom as simple as that, and the Court of Appeal has held on one set of facts that it was the supplier of the goods rather than their distributor who effected the characteristic performance.[101] There may, of course, be cases, such as complex financial services transactions, where this sort of analysis is unhelpful. A later provision in art.4 takes care of that problem.[102]

(2)   Having identified the relevant party, it must be determined whether in entering into the contract he was acting in the course of his trade or profession,[103] which is a matter of fact that will usually, but perhaps not always, present little difficulty.

If he was so acting, then it is to be presumed that the country with which the contract is most closely connected is that in which the party's principal place of business is situated.[104]

If, however, under the terms of the contract the performance is to be effected through some other place of business, the country is that in which that other place of business is situated. Plainly, a contractual term that performance by a London-based company was to be effected through its Rome office would come within this type of case. It is not wholly clear whether the Convention phrase "under the terms of the contract" would be satisfied by a term expressly requiring performance in Italy (in circumstances normally requiring action by a local representative) but making no

---

[97] e.g., the supply of whisky in *William Grant & Sons International Ltd v Marie Brizard Espana SA* 1998 S.C. 537; *Lupofresh Ltd v Sapporo Breweries* [2013] EWCA Civ 948; [2013] 2 Lloyd's Rep. 444.

[98] e.g., work as an insurance broker as in *Hogg Insurance Brokers Ltd v Guardian Insurance Co Inc* [1997] 1 Lloyd's Rep. 412.

[99] In the case of a contract between a bank and one of its customers, the bank will provide the characteristic performance, but (see point (iii), below) the location of the branch holding the account may be relevant: *Sierra Leone Telecommunications Co Ltd v Barclays Bank Plc* [1998] 2 All E.R. 821 at 826–827. More complex banking cases can require very careful analysis, often involving the use of agency concepts with the agent as the party regarded as providing the characteristic performance. See, e.g., *Bank of Baroda v Vysya Bank* [1994] 2 Lloyd's Rep. 87 (confirmation of letters of credit).

[100] Giuliano-Lagarde Report, p.20.

[101] *Print Concept GmbH v GEW (EC) Ltd* [2001] EWCA Civ 352, criticised (it is submitted correctly) by Hill (2004) 53 I.C.L.Q. 325 at 335–336.

[102] Convention, art.4(5), considered below, para.15–025.

[103] Note that this is the question; not whether *in effecting the characteristic performance* he would be so acting.

[104] Note that the test is as stated; the presumption in art.4(2) always identifies a place *of business*; the place *of performance* as such is not relevant for this purpose (though it may of course be crucial for the purposes of jurisdiction under art.5(1) of the Brussels I Regulation: see paras 6–016 and following).

reference to a place of business there. A stricter test was applied in
Ennstone Building Products Ltd v Stanger Ltd (No.2)[105]:

> E, an English company, supplied stone for use in building work. S, also an English company, provided testing and consultancy services through offices in England (its head office), Wales and Scotland. E supplied stone for a building in Edinburgh, but technical problems arose. A member of E's staff visited S's Scottish office, and it was agreed that S would conduct tests and report. A dispute arose and E brought a claim against S in England. The key issue was whether Scottish or English law applied; under Scottish law the claim might be time-barred.

(3)   The Court of Appeal held that unless a term of the contract would be broken by performance through a particular place of business, the last part of art.4(2) would not apply. The parties had anticipated performance of the contract through the defendant's Scottish office, but there was no contractual requirement to that effect. Article 4(2) therefore pointed to the country of the defendant's principal place of business, namely England.[106]
(4)   If the relevant party was not acting in the course of his trade or profession, the presumption is that the country with which the contract is most closely connected is that in which, at the time of the conclusion of the contract, he had his habitual residence, or in the case of a "body" its central administration.

Disregarding the presumption: Article 4(5)

The presumption created by art.4(2)[107] has a limited effect. It does not apply if   **15–025**
the characteristic performance cannot be determined; more significantly, it is to
be disregarded if it appears from the circumstances as a whole that the contract is
more closely connected with another country.[108]

The English courts, unlike some in other Member States, were used to a
flexible test of this sort, and might be expected to resort to the presumptions only
in "tie-break" situations. The English cases seem in general to confirm that
assessment[109]. In the earliest case, the presumptions pointing to the application of
the law of State A were disregarded because the relevant transaction was part of
linked series of transactions which as a whole were governed by the law of State
B.[110]

Morrison J in *Definitely Maybe (Touring) Ltd v Marek Lieberberg Konzertagentur GmbH*[111] referred to the fact that, under the common law approach, little

---

[105] [2002] EWCA Civ 916; [2002] 1 W.L.R. 1141.
[106] cf. the different view tentatively advanced in *Iran Continental Shelf Oil Co v IRI International Corp* [2002] EWCA Civ 1024 per Clarke LJ at para.[65].
[107] And the special presumptions in Convention, art.4(3)(4), to be considered below.
[108] Convention, art.4(5).
[109] e.g. *Bank of Baroda v Vysya Bank* [1994] 2 Lloyd's Rep. 87; *Definitely Maybe (Touring) Ltd v Marek Lieberberg Konzertagentur GmbH* [2001] 1 W.L.R. 1745; *Land Rover Exports Ltd v Samcrete Egypt Engineers and Contractors SAE* [2001] EWCA Civ 2019; [2002] C.L.C. 533; *British Arab Commercial Bank plc v Bank of Communications* [2011] EWHC 281 (Comm); [2011] 1 Lloyd's Rep. 664.
[110] Which just happened to be England: *Baroda v Vysya Bank* [1994] 2 Lloyd's Rep. 87.
[111] [2001] 1 W.L.R. 1745.

weight would be given to the place of business or residence of a party and much more weight to the place of performance; he spoke of "a natural tendency to wish to maintain the old, well-developed common law position where factors were weighed and attempts were made to ascertain the true intention of the parties". Article 4(2) reverses the order of priority. In *Definitely Maybe*:

> DM, agents with a principal place of business in England, arranged with MLK, a German company, for the rock band Oasis to appear at two concerts in Germany. The group appeared, but without its lead guitarist, Noel Gallagher. MLK refused to pay the agreed fee. The issue of jurisdiction depended on what law governed. DM was the party effecting characteristic performance of the contract.

Morrison J felt that prima facie the contract was nonetheless most closely connected with Germany. What weight, then, had to be given to the presumption? His answer was "due" weight. The burden of proof was on the party seeking to have the presumption disregarded to establish factors which pointed to another country. This would be more readily achievable where the place of performance was different from the place of the performer's business. "But in carrying out what must be regarded as a comparative exercise, due weight must be given to the factor identified in Art.4(2)." In the instant case, and despite his observation that giving wide effect to art.4(5) would render the presumption in art.4(2) of no value, Morrison J held that this burden had been discharged, and German law applied.

A similar approach can be seen in the later case of *Land Rover Exports Ltd v Samcrete Egypt Engineers and Contractors SAE*[112]:

> LR appointed T its distributor in Egypt. S, with a principal place of business in Egypt, entered into a contract of guarantee with LR guaranteeing, inter alia, T's debts. S was sued on the guarantee. As S was the party whose performance was characteristic of that contract, the presumption in art.4(2) clearly pointed to the law of Egypt. The Court of Appeal disregarded the presumption, applying English law as the place of payment under the guarantee was in England.[113]

It is difficult not to see these decisions as interpreting the Convention text to make it accord with the pre-Convention common law. There is in some other Contracting States a very different view of the relationship between arts 4(2) and 4(5). The best known example is the Dutch case of *Société Nouvelle des Papeteries de l'Aa v BV Maschinefabrieke BOA*.[114] The case involved the supply of machinery by a Dutch company, which clearly provided the characteristic performance. Delivery was to a French company in France; payment was in francs; the contract was negotiated in France. The Dutch court held that the presumption in art.4(2) should be disapplied only if, in the light of special factors,

---

[112] [2001] EWCA Civ 2019; [2002] C.L.C. 533, followed in *Commercial Marine & Piling Ltd v Pierse Contracting Ltd* [2009] EWHC 2241 (TCC); [2010] 1 All E.R. (Comm) 1087. See also *British Arab Commercial Bank plc v Bank of Communications* [2011] EWHC 281 (Comm); [2011] 1 Lloyd's Rep. 664.

[113] A second reason was that the place of performance by LR of its contract with T was also in England, but it is difficult to see the relevance of that.

[114] Hoge Raad, 25 September 1992; see Struycken, [1996] L.M.C.L.Q. 18. cf. the facts of the common law case of *The Assunzione* (above, para.15–004).

the country of habitual residence (or principal place of business) of the party carrying out the characteristic performance had "no real value as a connecting factor".

In the process that led to the adoption of the Rome I Regulation, the European Commission's Green Paper commented on the differing views as to the strength of the presumption in art.4(2). It expressly favoured the Dutch view:

> "Given the letter and spirit of the Convention, the courts might reasonably be expected to begin with the presumption of Art.4(2). Only if it emerged that the law designated is not appropriate because other circumstances clearly militate in favour of another law would the court then use the 'exception clause'."[115]

Special presumptions apply in certain cases. To the extent that the subject matter of a contract is a right in immovable property, or a right to use immovable property, it is presumed that the contract is most closely connected with the country where the immovable property is situated[116]; this reflected the usual position at common law.

In *Haeger & Schmidt GmbH v Mutuelles du Mans assurances IARD*[117] the European Court established that "an overall assessment of all the objective factors characterising the contractual relationship" was necessary in order to determine which of those factors are, in the view of the adjudicating court, most significant. In this case, involving the interpretation of art.4(5) of the Convention, the European Court referred to Recital (20) of the Rome I Regulation[118] to emphasise the significance of a close connection to another contract forming part of the same chain of contracts.[119]

Article 4 of the Rome I Regulation: applicable law in the absence of choice

Article 4 of the Regulation contains much more precise and detailed rules in the case in which the parties have not chosen the applicable law. The notion of "characteristic performance" is much less important. So is the notion of "the closest connection". There are no presumptions as such, but a series of rules each applying to a different type of contract with a limited power to depart from the relevant rule. The policy, hard fought over in the negotiations, is that the choice of law rules should be highly predictable, but that the courts should retain a degree of discretion to determine the law that is most closely connected to the situation.[120] The rules[121] are as follows:

15–026

Article 4 (1) provides that:

---

[115] Green Paper, para.3.2.5.3, which canvassed various means of ensuring that its preferred approach is generally adopted.
[116] Convention, art.4(3).
[117] Case 305/13; [2015] Q.B. 319
[118] See below, para.15–030.
[119] [2015] Q.B. 319, at [49].
[120] Regulation, Recital (16).
[121] Regulation, art.4(1).

"To the extent that the law applicable to the contract has not been chosen in accordance with Article 3 and without prejudice to Articles 5 to 8, the law governing the contract shall be determined as follows:

(a)   a contract for the sale of goods shall be governed by the law of the country where the seller has his habitual residence[122].

(b)   a contract for the provision of services shall be governed by the law of the country where the service provider has his habitual residence"

No further definition is given of "sale of goods" or "provision of services" but they are to be interpreted in the same way as in art.5 of the Brussels I Regulation.[123]

"(c)   a contract relating to a right in rem in immovable property or to a tenancy of immovable property shall be governed by the law of the country where the property is situated;

(d)   notwithstanding point (c), a tenancy of immovable property concluded for temporary private use for a period of no more than six consecutive months shall be governed by the law of the country where the landlord has his habitual residence, provided that the tenant is a natural person and has his habitual residence in the same country;

(e)   a franchise contract shall be governed by the law of the country where the franchisee has his habitual residence;

(f)   a distribution contract shall be governed by the law of the country where the distributor has his habitual residence;

(g)   a contract for the sale of goods by auction shall be governed by the law of the country where the auction takes place, if such a place can be determined;

(h)   a contract concluded within a multilateral system which brings together or facilitates the bringing together of multiple third-party buying and selling interests in financial instruments, as defined by art.4(1), point (17) of Directive 2004/39/EC, in accordance with non-discretionary rules and governed by a single law, shall be governed by that law."[124]

Habitual residence

15–027   To apply these rules, and some others, it is necessary to have a clear provision as to the meaning of habitual residence.[125] Article 19 accordingly provides that, for the purposes of the Regulation, the habitual residence of companies and other bodies, corporate or unincorporated, is the place of central administration; and the habitual residence of a natural person acting in the course of his business activity is his principal place of business.[126] In each case, the facts are taken as at the time of the conclusion of the contract.[127] However, where the contract is concluded in the course of the operations of a branch, agency or any other establishment, or if, under the contract, performance is the responsibility of such a branch, agency or

---

[122] e.g. *SSL International Plc v TTK LIG Ltd* [2011] EWCA Civ 1170; [2012] 1 W.L.R. 1842; *BNP Paribas SA v Anchorage Capital Europe LLP* [2013] EWHC 3073 (Comm.), at [64]; *Air Transworld Ltd v Bombardier Inc* [2012] EWHC 243; [2012] 1 Lloyd's Rep. 349; *Lupofresh Ltd v Sapporo Breweries Ltd* [2013] EWCA Civ 948; [2013] 2 Lloyd's Rep. 444.

[123] Regulation, Recital (17). See para.6–019.

[124] See Recital (18).

[125] Recital (39) refers to inappropriateness of having three criteria, as in art.60 of the Brussels I Regulation on the domicile of companies and other bodies.

[126] Regulation, art.19(1).

[127] Regulation, art.19(3).

establishment, the place where the branch, agency or any other establishment is located is to be treated as the place of habitual residence.[128]

The Regulation does not provide guidance as to the determination of the habitual residence of an individual not acting in the course of his business activity. In *Wrigley v Wood*[129] the habitual residence of a captain of a luxury yacht needed to be determined to apply the provisions of the Rome I Regulation for the sake of determining whether the contract was governed by English law (in order to decide on authorisation to serve out of the jurisdiction under the CPR gateways available when the English traditional rules of jurisdiction apply[130]). Captain Wrigley was from the UK but resided there only during his holiday period, five weeks a year. For the rest of the time, he was based at various locations around the world, with the yacht. This case is illustrative as to the difficulties that can appear when trying to apply this connecting factor,[131] which is essentially a factual determination.

The remaining relevance of the characteristic performance

Article 4(2) provides further guidance as follows: **15–028**

> "Where the contract is not covered by paragraph 1 or where the elements of the contract would be covered by more than one of points (a) to (h) of paragraph 1, the contract shall be governed by the law of the country where the party required to effect the characteristic performance of the contract has his habitual residence."

The problem with the aforementioned list is that some contracts may not be covered at all, and other contracts may combine elements of two or more entries. In both these cases, the Regulation provides that the contract is to be governed by the law of the country where the party required to effect the characteristic performance of the contract has his habitual residence.[132] Hence, the characteristic performance criterion discussed above in relation to the Rome Convention is also of application in relation to this provision of the Rome I Regulation. However, the characteristic performance criterion is overall less influential a criterion in the determination of the applicable law to contractual obligation in the Regulation than in the Convention.

A very common illustration would be a contract for the sale of machinery which also provided for the seller to carry out regular servicing of the machinery for a number of years. This combines the sale of goods (point (a)) and the supply of services (point (b)). Both those rules identify the habitual residence of the seller/provider of services, and it will be obvious that he is to affect the characteristic performance of the contract. The emphasis placed on the habitual residence of one party, even with the special understanding of habitual residence in branch and agency cases, may identify a state with a very slight connection with the substantial purpose of the contract.

---

[128] Regulation, art.19(2).
[129] [2014] EWHC 3684 (Comm.).
[130] See para.7–018.
[131] See para.3–004.
[132] Regulation, art.4(2).

The 'escape clause': the manifest closest connection

15–029   Article 4(3) provides:

> "3.   Where it is clear from all the circumstances of the case that the contract is manifestly
> more closely connected with a country other than that indicated in paragraphs 1 or 2,
> the law of that other country shall apply."

The Recitals indicate that account should be taken, inter alia, of whether the contract in question has a very close relationship with another contract or contracts.[133] The word "manifestly" is a signal to the courts to use this power only in very clear cases.[134] In *BNP Paribas SA v Anchorage Capital Europe LLP*[135] it was held that art.4(3) "deliberately places a high hurdle in the way of a party seeking to displace the primary rule"[136].

The 'default' provision: the closest connection

15–030   Finally, art.4(4) provides:

> "4.   Where the law applicable cannot be determined pursuant to paragraphs 1 or 2, the
> contract shall be governed by the law of the country with which it is most closely
> connected."

Recitals 20 ("manifestly more closely connected" test) and 21 ("most closely connected" test) of the Regulation provide further guidance on this point. Interestingly enough, both recitals finish with the same sentence, i.e. "In order to determine that country, account should be taken, inter alia, of whether the contract in question has a very close relationship with another contract or contracts."[137]

Contracts of carriage[138]

15–031   The Rome I Regulation, like the Rome Convention, contains special rules applying to contracts for the carriage of goods. This applies to contracts the main purpose of which is the carriage of goods,[139] even if they are classified as charterparties under national law.[140]

---

[133] Regulation, Recital (20).

[134] On the standard required by the Regulation as compared to the Convention, see Dickinson, [2010] L.M.C.L.Q. 27.

[135] [2013] EWHC 3073 (Comm.).

[136] Ibid at [64]. Article 4(3) was applied in *Wrigley v Wood* [2014] EWHC 3684 (Comm.).

[137] In Case 305/13 *Haeger & Schmidt GmbH v Mutuelles du Mans assurances IARD* [2015] Q.B. 319 the European Court took into consideration Recital (20) in a case involving Article 4(5) of the Rome Convention.

[138] See Morse, "Contracts of Carriage and the Conflict of Laws" in Boele-Woelki et al (eds), *Convergence and Divergence in Private International Law—Liber Amicorum Kurt Siehr* (2010), 463. See also Kenfack, 2009 Clunet 3.

[139] This is the European autonomous interpretation of the concept as confirmed in Case C–305/13 *Haeger & Schmidt GmbH v Mutuelles du Mans assurances Iard SA* [2015] Q.B. 319, at [25] and following. The Court held that the parties' categorisation of the contract is not determinative and an

In the Convention a special presumption favoured the country in which, at the time the contract was concluded, the carrier had its principal place of business if it was also the country in which the place of loading or the place of discharge or the principal place of business of the consignor was situated.[141]

This rule is replaced in the Regulation by a similar rule, making use of the concept of habitual residence, to which provisions dealing with the carriage of passengers are added.

In the case of the carriage of goods (including single-voyage charter parties and other contracts the main purpose of which is the carriage of goods)[142] where the parties have not chosen the applicable law, the law applicable to a contract for the carriage of goods is the law of the country of habitual residence of the carrier[143], provided that the place of receipt[144] or the place of delivery or the habitual residence of the consignor is also situated in that country.

If those requirements are not met, the law of the country where the place of delivery as agreed by the parties is situated applies.[145] "Consignor" means any person who enters into a contract of carriage with the carrier and the term "the carrier" should refers to the party to the contract who undertakes to carry the goods, whether or not he performs the carriage himself.[146] The passenger provisions are more complicated. The freedom of the parties to select the applicable law is limited. They (and in reality that means the carrier) may select only the law of the country where (a) the passenger has his habitual residence; or (b) the carrier has his habitual residence; or (c) the carrier has his place of central administration; or (d) the place of departure is situated; (e) the place of destination is situated. Where the parties have not chosen the applicable law, the law applicable is the law of the country where the passenger has his habitual residence, provided that either the place of departure or the place of destination is situated in that country. If these requirements are not met, the law of the country where the carrier has his habitual residence applies.[147]

---

examination of "the purpose of the contractual relationship, the actual performance effected and all of the obligations of the party who must effect the characteristic performance" is what should be considered in deciding whether the principal purpose of the contract is indeed the carriage of goods (ibid. at [28]).

[140] Case C-133/08 *Intercontainer Interfrigo SC v Balkenende Oosthuizen BV* [2009] ECR I-9687 at paras 33–35 of the judgment.

[141] Convention, art.4(4).

[142] Regulation, Recital (22).

[143] In Case C–305/13 *Haeger & Schmidt GmbH v Mutuelles du Mans assurances Iard SA* [2015] Q.B. 319 the European Court noted that "as the principal purpose of the contract is the transport of goods and the carrier's habitual residence [alone] has no objective connection with the contract" at [22].

[144] This may not be the same as the place of loading referred to in the Convention: a carrier may collect the goods at a place distant from that at which the goods are loaded on to the vehicle that is to carry them.

[145] Regulation, art.5(1). In the words of Advocate General Bot in Case C-133/08 *Intercontainer Interfrigo SC v Balkenende Oosthuizen BV* [2009] ECR I-9687, "legal certainty and foreseeability of the applicable law have taken preference over the flexibility of application of the conflict rule" (para.65 of the judgment).

[146] Regulation, Recital (22).

[147] Regulation, art.5(2).

In each case, where it is clear from all the circumstances of the case that the contract, in the absence of a choice of law, is manifestly more closely connected with a country other than that indicated in these rules, the law of that other country applies.

Particularly in relation to contracts for the international carriage of goods, there is usually a complex web of contractual relationships connected to any transaction. In *Haeger & Schmidt GmbH v Mutuelles du Mans assurances Iard SA*[148] the CJEU stated that the courts have to take into account "the purpose of the contractual relationship, the actual performance effected and all of the obligations of the party who must effect the characteristic performance" to decide whether a particular contract within that web is or is not a contract of carriage of goods for the purposes of art.5(1). This implies that "contracts for the carriage of goods" has a European autonomous interpretation for the purposes of the Regulation. In many cases, the matter may well fall within one or other of the well-established international transport conventions, which are not affected by the Regulation.[149]

THE PROTECTION OF WEAKER PARTIES

15–032   Changes in the vision of the role that private international law should have in Europe—and in the world at large—have had an impact on the provisions on choice of law, as is also the context of jurisdiction, as explained in a previous chapter.[150]

Consumer contracts

15–033   It is part of the policy of the Rome I Regulation,[151] as it was of the Convention,[152] that the weaker parties in consumer contracts should be protected by conflict of law rules that are more favourable to their interests than the general rules. So far as consumers are concerned, the Regulation contains a fairly extensive revision of the Convention text. The Convention's more beneficial treatment was limited to guaranteeing the consumer the protection afforded by the substantive law of his habitual residence and, in the absence of a choice of law by the parties, a rule that the law of the consumer's habitual residence is the applicable law. Article 6 of the Rome I Regulation provides[153] that a contract concluded by a natural person for a purpose which can be regarded as being outside his trade or profession (the consumer) with another person acting in the exercise of his trade or profession (the professional) is to be governed by the law of the country where the consumer has his habitual residence, provided that the professional:

---

[148] Case C-305/13; [2015] Q.B. 319.
[149] Regulation, art.25.
[150] See para.6–038.
[151] Regulation, Recital (23).
[152] See Giuliano-Lagarde report, p.23.
[153] Without prejudice to the rules in art.5 (carriage) and art.7 (insurance).

(a)   pursues his commercial or professional activities in the country where the consumer has his habitual residence; or

(b)   by any means, directs such activities to that country or to several countries including that country;

and the contract falls within the scope of such activities.[154] If the requirements in points (a) or (b) are not fulfilled, applicable law is determined under the general rules in arts 3 and 4.[155]

'Consumer'—European autonomous definition

A person is a "consumer" only if he or she concluded the contract for a purpose which can be regarded as being outside his or her trade or profession.[156] The CJEU has held that this brings within the consumer contract category only contracts concluded[157] for the purpose of satisfying an individual's own needs in terms of private consumption.[158] The definition used in the Rome I Regulation is in line with the definition used in the Brussels I *bis* Regulation, supporting the idea that European instruments of private international law need to be interpreted and applied consistently in civil and commercial matters.[159]

15–034

As explained in a previous chapter in relation to jurisdiction, if the trade or professional purpose of a particular contract was so limited as to be negligible in the overall context of the contract, the contract may still be considered as a consumer contract.[160]

'Protected Consumer contracts'

Article 6 applies to any contract that is a contract between a professional and a consumer, provided that the professional (i) pursues his commercial or professional activities in the country where the consumer has his habitual residence,[161] or (ii) by any means, directs such activities to that country or to several countries including that country, and the contract falls within the scope of such activities.[162] The idea is that not every consumer contract is protected by the special applicable law rules under the Regulation, but only those within the scope of application indicated by art.6(1); this is underlined by the provision in art.6(3)

15–035

---

[154] Regulation, art.6(1); and Recital (25).

[155] Regulation, art.6(3).

[156] reg.1215/2012 art.17(1); reg.44/2001 art.15(1). Assignees of the original consumer are not included: Case C-89/91 *Shearson Lehman Hutton Inc v TVB Treuhandgesellschaft fur Vermogensver-waltung* [1993] E.C.R. I-139; nor are consumer associations: Case C-167/00 *Verien fur Konsumenteninformation v Henkel* [2002] E.C.R. I-8111.

[157] Case C-96/00 *Gabriel v Schlank & Schick GmbH* [2000] E.C.R. I-6367; Case C-27/02 *Engler v Janus Versand GmbH* [2005] E.C.R. I-481; Case C-180/06 *Ilsinger v Dreschers* [2009] E.C.R. I-3961.

[158] Case C-269/95 *Benincasa v Dentalkit SRL* [1997] E.C.R. I-3767.

[159] Regulation, Recital (24).

[160] Case C-464/01 *Gruber v BayWa AG* [2006] Q.B. 204 (E.C.J.) (tiles for a farmhouse which was used both as a private house and for farm purposes).

[161] Regulation, art.6(1)(a).

[162] Regulation, art.6(1)(b).

that the law applicable to a contract between a consumer and a professional, outside the scope of art.6(1) must be determined under the general rules in arts 3 and 4 of the Regulation.

Furthermore, there are express exclusions from the scope of application of the protective choice of law rules, provided for in art.6(4) discussed below ('non-protected consumer contracts').

'Directing activities'

15–036 So far as the concept of "directed activity"[163] in point (b) is concerned, Recital (24) asserts that it must be interpreted harmoniously in the Brussels I Regulation and the Rome I Regulation, and cites the joint declaration by the Council and the Commission (on art.15 of the Brussels I Regulation) that:

> "the mere fact that an Internet site is accessible is not sufficient for Article 15 to be applicable, although a factor will be that this Internet site solicits the conclusion of distance contracts and that a contract has actually been concluded at a distance, by whatever means. In this respect, the language or currency which a website uses does not constitute a relevant factor".

In *Pammer v Reederei Karl Schlüter GmbH* and *Hotel Alpenhof GmbH v Heller*[164] the CJEU was asked for a preliminary ruling on, inter alia, the interpretation of "directing activities" in the context of what was then art.15 of the Brussels I Regulation. The European Court enumerated a non-exhaustive list of matters capable of constituting evidence from which it might be concluded that the trader's activity was directed to the Member State of the consumer's domicile.[165] In interpreting the corresponding provision of the Brussels I Regulation in *Emrek v Sabranovic*[166] the CJEU made clear that there was no need for a causal link between the directing of the activities and the conclusion of the contract; it was sufficient for the application of the protective rule in this context that the professional had directed his activities to the Member State of the consumer's habitual residence, even if such activities did not impact on the conclusion of the contract that was the basis of the claim. This sits uneasily with Recital 25 of the Regulation that states that the protection should be provided if "the contract is concluded as a result of such [directing] activities".[167]

---

[163] See Gillies, *Electronic Commerce and International Private Law* (Aldershot: Ashgate, 2008); Tang, *Electronic Consumer Contracts in the Conflict of Laws* (Oxford: Hart Publishing, 2009); Tang, (2010) 6 J.Priv.Int.L. 225; and Fawcett, Harris and Bridge, International Sales of Goods in the Conflict of Laws (Oxford: Oxford University Press, 2005), pp.1217–1321. See also *Pammer v Reederei Karl Schluter GmbH & Co KG* Case (C-585/08) (joined with case C-144/09); [2012] All E.R. (EC) 34.

[164] Joined Cases C-585/08 and C-144/09; [2012] All E.R. (EC) 34. See also Case C–419/11 *Česká spořitelna, as v Feichter* [2013] I.L.Pr. 375; Case C–375/13 *Kolassa v Barclays Bank Plc* [2015] I.L.Pr. 245.

[165] See para.6–042.

[166] Case 218/12 *Emrek v Sabranovic* [2014] I.L.Pr.39.

[167] Regulation, Recital (25), final words.

Consumer contracts and party autonomy

Article 6(2) or the Regulation provides that the parties may choose the law applicable to a "protected consumer contract" but such a choice cannot deprive the consumer of the protection afforded to him by provisions that cannot be derogated from by agreement by virtue of the law of the consumer's habitual residence.[168]   **15–037**

'Non-protected consumer contracts'

Certain types of contract that would otherwise fall within the consumer contract category are excluded from the effect of these rules. Article 6(4) provides that the protection does not apply to: (i) contracts for the supply of services where the services are to be supplied to the consumer exclusively in a country other than that in which he has his habitual residence[169]; (ii) contracts of carriage other than a contract relating to package travel[170]; (iii) contracts relating to a right in rem in immovable property or a tenancy of immovable property other certain timeshare contracts[171]; and (iv) certain contracts relating to financial instruments.[172]   **15–038**

Insurance contracts

One of the aims of the Rome I Regulation was to draw together relevant rules in a single instrument, and this was partially successful in the case of insurance contracts. Reference will not be made here to the complex position before the regulation.   **15–039**

Article 7 of the Regulation applies to insurance contracts covering a "large risk", whether or not risk covered is situated[173] in a Member State, and to all other insurance contracts covering risks situated inside the territory of the Member States.[174] It does not apply to reinsurance contracts.[175] A "large risk" is defined by reference to an earlier Directive[176] and includes such things as risks relating to damage to or loss of railway stock, aircraft, ships, vehicles, goods in transit, and export and instalment credit. An insurance contract covering a large risk is governed by the law chosen by the parties, and to the extent that the applicable law has not been so chosen, by the law of the country where the

---

[168] Regulation, art.6(2).

[169] Regulation, art.6(4)(a).

[170] Regulation, art.6(4)(b). See Council Directive 90/314/EEC of 13 June 1990 on package travel, package holidays and package tours, OJ L 158/59, 23 June 1990.

[171] Regulation, art.6(4)(c). See European Parliament and Council Directive 2008/122/EC of 14 January 2009 on the protection of consumers in respect of certain aspects of timeshare, long-term holiday product, resale and exchange contracts, OJ L 33/10, 3 February 2009.

[172] Regulation, art.6(4)(d) and (e). See Recitals (26)–(31).

[173] For the location of risks, see regulation, art.7(6) and the Directives there cited.

[174] Where such insurance contracts cover risks situated outside the Member States, the general rules in arts 3 and 4 will apply subject to any special rules in the specialised Directives.

[175] Regulation, art.7(1).

[176] The First Council Directive 73/239/EEC of 24 July 1973 on the co-ordination of laws, regulations and administrative provisions relating to the taking-up and pursuit of the business of direct insurance other than life assurance, art.5(d).

insurer has his habitual residence. Where, however, it is clear from all the circumstances of the case that the contract is manifestly more closely connected with another country, the law of that other country applies.[177]

In the case of all other insurance contracts, the ability of the parties (in practice the insurer) to select the governing law is limited. The parties may select only:

(a) the law of any Member State where the risk is situated at the time of conclusion of the contract;
(b) the law of the country where the policy holder has his habitual residence;
(c) in the case of life assurance, the law of the Member State of which the policy holder is a national;
(d) for insurance contracts covering risks limited to events occurring in one Member State other than the Member State where the risk is situated, the law of that Member State; or
(e) where the policy holder of a contract falling under this paragraph pursues a commercial or industrial activity or a liberal profession and the insurance contract covers two or more risks which relate to those activities and are situated in different Member States, the law of any of the Member States concerned or the law of the country of habitual residence of the policy holder.

Where, in the cases set out in points (a), (b) or (e), the Member States referred to grant greater freedom of choice of the law applicable to the insurance contract, the parties may take advantage of that freedom. To the extent that the law applicable has not been chosen by the parties, the contract is governed by the law of the Member State in which the risk is situated[178] at the time of conclusion of the contract.[179]

Where under the law of a Member State, insurance of a risk is compulsory, (a) the insurance contract shall not satisfy the obligation to take out insurance unless it complies with the specific provisions relating to that insurance laid down by the Member State that imposes the obligation. Where the law of the Member State in which the risk is situated and the law of the Member State imposing the obligation to take out insurance contradict each other, the latter prevails; and (b) by way of derogation from the usual rules (those in art.7(2) and (3)), a Member State may lay down that the insurance contract is to be governed by the law of the Member State that imposes the obligation to take out insurance.[180]

---

[177] Regulation, art.7(2).
[178] For this purpose, where the contract covers risks situated in more than one Member State, the contract is to be considered as constituting several contracts each relating to only one Member State: art.7(5).
[179] Regulation, art.7(3).
[180] Regulation, art.7(4).

Individual contracts of employment

Article 8 of the Rome I Regulation and art.6 of its predecessor the Rome Convention contain broadly similar provisions dealing with individual employment contracts.   **15–040**
Article 8 provides:

> "1.   An individual employment contract shall be governed by the law chosen by the parties in accordance with Article 3. Such a choice of law may not, however, have the result of depriving the employee of the protection afforded to him by provisions that cannot be derogated from by agreement under the law that, in the absence of choice, would have been applicable pursuant to paragraphs 2, 3 and 4 of this Article.
>
> 2.   To the extent that the law applicable to the individual employment contract has not been chosen by the parties, the contract shall be governed by the law of the country in which or, failing that, from which the employee habitually carries out his work in performance of the contract. The country where the work is habitually carried out shall not be deemed to have changed if he is temporarily employed in another country.
>
> 3.   Where the law applicable cannot be determined pursuant to paragraph 2, the contract shall be governed by the law of the country where the place of business through which the employee was engaged is situated.
>
> 4.   Where it appears from the circumstances as a whole that the contract is more closely connected with a country other than that indicated in paragraphs 2 or 3, the law of that other country shall apply."

Individual employment contract—European autonomous interpretation

There is no attempt to define "individual employment contract", though the Giuliano-Lagarde Report[181] observed that de facto employment situations (where, for example, the employer fails to issue any formal contract of employment) are included. This concept should be given an autonomous meaning consistent with the protective rules on jurisdiction provided for employment contracts in the European regime of jurisdiction.[182] Several broad characteristics have been identified as contributing to define the scope of this legal category: (a) one party—the employee—provides services to the other party—the employer— over a period of time for which remuneration is paid; (b) the provision of services is directed and controlled by the employer; and (c) the employee is in some way or another integrated in the organisational framework of the employer.[183] These characteristics will vary from contract to contract, and in many cases the terms of the contract will go a long way to showing how far these three criteria are met. The most difficult distinction will be usually between an individual employment contract and a contract for the provision of services provided by a self-employed individual. In *WPP Holdings Italy Srl v Benatti*,[184] it was considered that "it would be an unusual contract of employment which left the employee free to   **15–041**

---

[181] At p.26.
[182] See para.6–044. See further Merret, *Employment Contracts in Private International Law* (Oxford: Oxford University Press, 2011); Grušić, *The European Private International Law of Employment* (Cambridge: Cambridge University Press, 2015).
[183] See also case C-47/14 *Holterman Ferho Exploitatie v F.L.F. Spies von Büllesheim* [2015] I.L.Pr. 789, at [41] referring to concepts used in EU law more generally.
[184] [2007] EWCA Civ 263; [2007] 1 W.L.R. 2316.

decide how many hours and days he worked, when, and what holidays he took; or to spend as much time as he liked on other business activities".[185]

As a matter of general principle, the law most relevant to employment is that of the country in which the employee works. That statement fails, however, to reflect the fact that individual employees may work in several countries; they may have one fixed base but visit other countries for shorter or longer periods, but may also have a pattern of work which makes it difficult to identify any place as the base from which they work; and the employer may be located in a quite different country, having recruited the employee in yet another. The Regulation deals rather better with this range of fact-situations than does the Convention.

Under the Convention, an individual employment contract is, in the absence of choice in accordance with art.3, governed (a) by the law of the country in which the employee habitually carries out his work in performance of the contract, even if temporarily employed in another country[186]; or (b) if the employee does not habitually carry out his work in any one country, by the law of the country in which the place of business through which he was engaged is situated[187]; unless it appears from the circumstances as a whole that the contract is more closely connected with another country, in which case the contract is to be governed by the law of that country.[188] These provisions were examined in the first case to reach the ECJ on employment contracts under the Rome Convention, *Koelzch v Luxembourg*.[189]

> K was a German lorry driver employed by the Luxembourg subsidiary of a Danish company. The employer's business was the transport of flowers and other plants from Denmark to destinations situated mostly in Germany, but also in other European countries, by means of lorries stationed in Germany but registered in Luxembourg. The employer had no seat or offices in Germany. K's contract contained a clause selecting Luxembourg law as the applicable law and another giving exclusive jurisdiction to the courts of Luxembourg. After K was dismissed, he sued first in Germany (the German courts holding that they had no jurisdiction) and then in Luxembourg. K argued that under art.6 of the Convention [substantially reproduced in art.8 of the Rome I Regulation] the mandatory rules of German law applied, notwithstanding the choice of Luxembourg law, as he habitually carried out his work in performance of the contract in Germany.

In determining where an employee habitually carries out the work, a court:

> "must, in particular, find in which state is situated the place from which the employee carries out his transport tasks, receives instructions concerning his tasks and organises his work, and the place where his work tools are situated. It must also determine the places where the transport is principally carried out, where the goods are unloaded and the place to which the employee returns after completion of his tasks".[190]

Under the Regulation, to the extent that the law applicable to the contract has not been chosen by the parties, the contract is governed by the law of the country "in which or, failing that, from which" the employee habitually carries out his

---

[185] ibid., at [50].
[186] Convention, art.6(2)(a).
[187] Convention, art.6(2)(b).
[188] Convention, art.6(2) *in fine*.
[189] Case C-29/10; [2012] Q.B. 210; [2011] I.L.Pr. 25.
[190] See paras 40, and 43–50 of the judgment.

work in performance of the contract. The country where the work is habitually carried out will not be deemed to have changed if he is temporarily employed in another country.[191] It is only where the law applicable cannot be determined under these rules that contract is governed by the law of the country where the place of business through which the employee was engaged is situated.[192] Where it appears from the circumstances as a whole that the contract is more closely connected with a country other than that identified by these rules, the law of that other country applies.[193] Where there is a choice of law by the parties, it does not deprive the employee of the protection afforded to him by provisions that cannot be derogated from by agreement under the law that, in the absence of choice, would have been applicable under the rules just stated.[194] It is for the national law of which a particular rule forms part to determine whether a rule is non-derogable in the sense of art.8(1) of the Regulation.

SCOPE OF THE APPLICABLE LAW

The use of the term "applicable law" must not mislead the reader into supposing that the law so described necessarily governs all issues concerning a particular contract. That this is not the case is evident from the partial exclusion from its scope of questions of capacity, already noted.[195] The applicable law does, however, govern many questions, including the interpretation, performance, consequences of breach (including the assessment of damages), prescription and limitation of actions, and the consequences of the nullity of the contract. The list of matter included within the scope of the applicable law is not intended to be exhaustive.[196] Some of these matters require comment.

15–042

Interpretation

A contract must always be interpreted according to its applicable law; that is possibly the most obvious role of the *lex causae*. Where expressions are ambiguous or contradictory within a contract, the true intention of the parties is to be determined taking into account the canons of construction of the governing law. In English proceedings, when foreign law is the applicable law, expert evidence is most often used to prove the foreign rules of construction, but it is the court that applies these canons of construction to the contract in question and ultimately determines the meaning of the contractual bargain.[197]

15–043

---

[191] Regulation, art.8(2).
[192] Regulation, art.8(3).
[193] Regulation, art.8(4).
[194] Regulation, art.8(1).
[195] See para.15–011.
[196] Regulation, art.12(1): "in particular".
[197] e.g. *Svenska Petroleum Exploration AB v Republic of Lithuania (No.2)* [2005] EWHC (Comm.) (construction under Lithuanian law, expert evidence to that effect).

Performance

15–044 Article 12 of the Regulation, as well as its predecessor in the Rome Convention, makes two references to "performance". This is listed as one of the matters governed by the applicable law[198] but it is also provided that:

> "in relation to the manner of performance and the steps to be taken in the event of defective performance regard shall be had to the law of the country in which performance takes place."[199]

This latter provision does not displace the applicable law; the court is merely to "have regard to" the law of the place of performance. This is explained in the Giuliano-Lagarde Report[200] as empowering the court to consider the relevance of that law and, in its discretion, to apply it in whole or in part so as to do justice between the parties. The report provides also some illustrations, providing that issues such as the rules governing public holidays and the manner in which goods are to be examined would fall within this concept of "manner of performance".

At common law there was a familiar, if not clear-cut, distinction between the "substance of the obligation" and the "method and manner of performance". It was well established that the proper law of the contract governed the substance of the obligation; so, for example, in *Mount Albert Borough Council v Australasian Temperance and General Assurance Society*[201]:

> A New Zealand borough corporation borrowed £130,000 in 1926 from an insurance company incorporated in Victoria and carrying on business in Australia and New Zealand. To secure the loan the borough corporation issued debentures charged on the borough rates, and therefore on New Zealand land. The proper law of the contract was New Zealand law. Interest on the debentures at the rate of five and two-third per cent was payable in Victoria. In 1931, during the Great Depression, a Victorian statute reduced the rate of interest on all mortgages to 5 per cent. It was held that this statute did not apply to the debentures, although Victoria was the place of performance, because New Zealand law was the proper law of the contract.

It was also clear that excuses for non-performance such as the doctrine of force majeure were matters for the proper law. However, in establishing that proposition, the Court of Appeal, in *Jacobs v Credit Lyonnais*[202] said that the law of the place of performance might well regulate the "method and manner" of performance; but this was confined to matters of detail, matters which do not affect the substance of the obligation. If, for instance, under an English contract a seller undertook to deliver goods in Paris "during usual business hours", it would presumably be for French law to say what business hours were usual; but English law would determine whether performance was excused by frustration or to what extent the seller was liable for defects in the goods delivered. If, by an English contract, an English seller agreed to sell goods in Lisbon to an American buyer for export to East Germany, Portuguese law would say whether an export licence was required and whether the goods had to be cleared through the customs, but

---

[198] Convention, art.10(1)(b); Regulation, art.12(1)(b).
[199] Convention, art.10(2); Regulation, art.12(2).
[200] p.33.
[201] [1938] A.C. 224.
[202] (1884) 12 Q.B.D. 589.

English law would determine whether the seller or the buyer was under a duty to obtain the licence, and if no licence was obtained, which party had broken the contract or whether the contract had been frustrated.[203] If a New York contract made between an Australian and a Canadian provided for the payment of dollars in London, New York law would determine whether this means American or Australian or Canadian dollars (money of account), i.e. the extent of the debtor's indebtedness, but English law would determine whether payment might or had to be made in dollar bills or could be made in pound notes (money of payment), i.e. how the debtor's obligation was to be performed.

On the basis of the Giuliano-Lagarde Report[204] these English cases prior to the Convention and the Regulation would still be relevant: the report says that the distinction between "performance" and "manner of performance" is to be drawn by the *lex fori*. This is yet to be clarified by the courts. In any case it is clear that the impact of the law of the place of performance is limited to matters related to the mode, place and time of performance and does not extends to the substance of the obligation.

Consequences of breach

The applicable law governs, *within the limits of the powers conferred on the court*   **15–045**
by its procedural law, the consequences of breach, including the assessment of damages *in so far as it is governed by rules of law*.[205] This tortuous language reflects a hard-fought compromise, and its effects are not easily stated. The difficulty lies in the qualifications italicised above.

In general, the type of remedies which are to be made available, be they damages, injunctions, or orders for specific performance, will be determined by reference to the applicable law. However, and this is the point of the first qualification, a court will not be required to make an order unknown to its legal system or (less clearly) to make an order that its procedures regard as inappropriate, e.g., an order of specific performance in the context of an employment contract.

So far as the assessment of damages is concerned, one aspect of that exercise, the actual "quantification" was traditionally regarded as a matter for the court of trial, as one for the *lex fori* or simply a question of factual estimation. This however, under the Rome I Regulation, is within the scope of the applicable law. In *Excalibur Ventures LLC v Texas Keystone Inc*[206] it was held that the principles by reference to which damages are to be assessed are a matter for the law applicable to the contract.

---

[203] *Pound & Co Ltd v Hardy & Co Inc* [1956] A.C. 588.
[204] p.33.
[205] Convention, art.10(1)(c); Regulation, art.12(1)(c) (emphasis added).
[206] [2013] EWHC 2767 (Comm.), at [1422]–[1423].

Extinguishing obligations, prescription and limitation of actions

15–046 These matters are governed by the applicable law.[207] So far as limitation of actions is concerned, this reflects the position reached in English law in the Foreign Limitation Periods Act 1984; that the limitation rules of the *lex* causae govern.[208]

Material validity

15–047 Article 8 of the Regulation, and its predecessor art.10 in the Convention, address the question of "material validity" a term which includes a number of matters which English writers would more readily see as concerned with the "formation" of the contract, e.g., offer and acceptance.

So, the existence and validity of a contract, or of any term of a contract, is to be determined by the law which would govern it under the Convention or Regulation if the contract or term were valid.[209] This is to apply what is sometimes called "the putative applicable law", ascertained by applying the usual rules as set out in arts 3 and 4. It involves giving weight to any choice of law made by the parties, even though the legal existence or validity of the instrument in which that choice is expressed is ex hypothesi doubtful.

Illegality

15–048 One aspect of material validity is the question of illegality. At common law, the English courts had held that performance of a contract was excused (i) if it had become illegal by the proper law of the contract or (ii) necessarily involved doing an act which was unlawful by the law of the place where the act had to be done.[210] If the contract were governed by English law, the latter aspect of this rule could be seen as an application of the rule of English domestic law as to the effect of supervening illegality. It was never finally established whether there was an independent rule of the conflict of laws under which illegality could be a matter for the law of the place of performance.[211] This issue would only arise were the English court faced with a contract governed by the law of State A (not England), performance of which was illegal by the law of the place of performance, State B.

The position now is that illegality is a matter for the applicable law. This still means that where the applicable law is English, the English rule as to supervening illegality will apply. This can be illustrated by the facts of the pre-Convention case of *Ralli Brothers v Compania Naviera Sota y Aznar*[212]:

---

[207] Convention, art.10(1)(d); Regulation, art.12(1)(d).
[208] See below, para.9–002.
[209] Convention, art.8(1); Regulation, art.10(1).
[210] *Libyan Arab Foreign Bank v Bankers Trust Co* [1989] Q.B. 728.
[211] See *Zivnostenska Banka v Frankman* [1950] A.C. 57 at 59 per Lord Reid, but cf. the different view expressed by Lord Reid in a companion case, *Kahler v Midland Bank* [1950] A.C. 24 at 28.
[212] [1920] 2 K.B. 287.

A contract, governed by English law, for the carriage of jute by sea from Calcutta to Barcelona provided for the payment of freight on delivery of the cargo at Barcelona at the rate of £50 per ton. After the date of the contract, but before the arrival of the ship, a Spanish decree fixed the maximum freight on jute at £10 per ton and made it illegal to pay more. The shipowners' action to recover the difference between £10 and £50 per ton was dismissed.

The decision would be the same today, on the basis that illegality, performance and discharge of contractual obligations are all matters for the applicable law—English law—and by applying the rule of English domestic law as to the effect of supervening illegality. However, as will be seen, rules of the country in which a contract is to be performed may in some circumstances be given direct effect.[213]

Consent

Another aspect of material validity is that of consent; a contract cannot exist unless the parties consent to be bound by it, either by a positive giving of consent or, in some situations, by tacit acceptance. The latter possibility, in effect that in some legal situations silence may be held to indicate consent, has given rise to a great deal of debate. In practice the issue is likely to arise in less extreme circumstances, where the law as to the giving of consent varies as between the countries concerned.[214]   **15–049**

The general view is that it would be unfair to deem someone to have consented when his or her actions (or silence) would not have this effect under that person's "own" law. The European instruments express this thought, and identifies the country of a party's habitual residence[215] as the relevant one: a party may rely upon the law of the country in which he has his habitual residence to establish that he did not consent[216] if it appears from the circumstances that it would not be reasonable to determine the effect of his conduct in accordance with the putative applicable law.[217] "Reasonable" defies further definition, though it has been said that in applying it in this context the courts should take a "dispassionate, internationally minded approach".[218]

Formal validity

"Form" is defined in the Giuliano-Lagarde Report[219] as including "every external manifestation required on the part of a person expressing a will to be legally bound, and in the absence of which such expression of will would not be   **15–050**

---

[213] See below for "overriding mandatory provisions": paras 15–052 and following.
[214] In *Lupofresh Ltd v Sapporo Breweries Ltd* [2013] EWCA Civ 948; [2013] 2 Lloyd's Rep. 444, art.8(2) of the Rome Convention (Rome I Regulation, art.10(2)) was held to apply only to questions concerning the *existence* of consent, and not to questions concerning the *quality* or *validity* of that consent.
[215] Even in the case of corporations or other business associations.
[216] He is provided with a shield, not a sword; he can avoid being bound but not create a binding obligation.
[217] Convention, art.8(2); Regulation, art.10(2).
[218] *Egon Oldendorff v Libera Corp* [1995] 2 Lloyd's Rep. 64 at 70.
[219] p.29.

regarded as fully effective". This clearly includes a requirement that a contract is valid only if it is in writing, or witnessed in a particular way, or drawn up before a notary, or registered; though on the last point, the notion of form does not include questions as to what may be required to make a term binding on third parties. The test proposed in the report is not always easy to apply. As Floyd LJ observed in *Integral Petroleum SA v SCU-Finanz AG*,[220]

> "This definition is relatively easy to apply in the case of a natural person: there are numerous ways in which an individual can express the will legally to bind himself, and questions of his authority to do so will not arise. In the case of a corporation it is not easy to imagine what such an expression of will might consist of. A company can only act through natural persons, duly authorised to act on its behalf, and its ability to express its will is limited by the authority of those representing it".

The question of an agent's authority was not within the scope of "formal validity", and is in any event excluded from the scope of the Regulation.[221]

The Convention and Regulation favour the formal validity of agreements by listing a number of laws, compliance with the requirements of any of which will establish formal validity. The rules are somewhat confusingly set out, but their effect can be stated as follows:

(1)   It always suffices to comply with the formal requirements of the applicable law.[222]

(2)   A contract concluded between persons who are in the same country is formally valid if it satisfies the formal requirements of the law of that country.[223] The development of electronic means of communication means that it is not always possible for one party to know the whereabouts of the other, but this lack of knowledge is immaterial.

(3)   A contract concluded between persons who are in different countries is formally valid if it satisfies the formal requirements of the law of either of those countries,[224] or (under the regulation only) the law of the country where either of the parties had his habitual residence at that time.[225]

(4)   For the purposes of these rules, where a contract is concluded by an agent, the country in which the agent acts is the relevant country.[226]

(5)   However, none of the above rules can be relied on the case of consumer contracts within the relevant provisions of the Convention or Regulation.[227] The formal validity of such contracts is governed by the law of the country in which the consumer has his or her habitual residence.[228]

(6)   A contract, the subject matter of which is a right in immovable property or a right to use immovable property, remains subject to the mandatory (or non-derogable) requirements of form of the law of the country where the

---

[220] [2015] EWCA Civ 144; [2016] 1 All E.R. (Comm) 217, at [40].

[221] Regulation, art.1(2)(g).

[222] Convention, art.9(1)(2); Regulation, art.11(1)(2).

[223] Convention, art.9(1); Regulation, art.11(1).

[224] Convention, art.9(2); Regulation, art.11(2).

[225] Regulation, art.11(2).

[226] Convention, art.9(3); Regulation, art.11(1)(2).

[227] i.e. those to which Convention, art.5 or Regulation, art.6 applies.

[228] Convention, art.9(5); Regulation, art.11(4).

property is situated, if by that law those requirements are imposed irrespective of the country where the contract is concluded and irrespective of the law governing the contract.[229]

(7) Finally, and most obscure to the English reader, "a unilateral act [in the Convention, an act] intended to have legal effect relating to an existing or contemplated contract" is formally valid if it satisfies the formal requirements of the law which governs or would govern the contract, or of the law of the country where the act was done,[230] or, under the Regulation, of the law of the country where the person by whom it was done had his habitual residence at that time.[231] The Giuliano-Lagarde Report gives as examples notices of termination or of repudiation.[232]

Incapacity

In general, questions of capacity are excluded from the scope of the Convention and of the Regulation, and are therefore still governed by the common law rules. The Community texts do contain one limited provision. In a contract concluded between persons who are in the same country (not necessarily in one another's presence), a natural person (as opposed to a company or other entity) who would have capacity under the law of that country may invoke his incapacity resulting from another law only if the other party to the contract was aware of this incapacity at the time of the conclusion of the contract or was not aware thereof as a result of negligence.[233] The stringent requirements of this article will be noted, and also the fact that it is concerned only with the right of a person to invoke his own incapacity; were the other party to raise capacity issues, the common law rules would apply.

15–051

There is, however, an extraordinary dearth of English authority on the question of what law governs capacity to make a contract. There is only one decision (dating from 1800) and a few stray and contradictory dicta.

One approach, which has long seemed old-fashioned, is to regard a person's capacity to contract as an emanation of status and therefore as governed by the law of the person's domicile. Another is to consider it as a factor determining the validity of the contract and therefore as governed by its proper law. There is general agreement among writers that in this context the proper law must be ascertained objectively, i.e. by applying the test of closest connection. Any other view would lead to the unacceptable result that a child could confer capacity on himself or herself by agreeing that some more favourable system than the objectively ascertained proper law should govern the contract.[234]

A hypothetical case illustrates the difficulty of deciding between the law of the domicile and the proper law of the contract:

---

[229] Convention, art.9(6); Regulation, art.11(5).
[230] Convention, art.9(4); Regulation, art.9(3).
[231] Regulation, art.9(3).
[232] p.29.
[233] Convention, art.11; Regulation, art.13.
[234] cf. *Cooper v Cooper* (1888) 13 App. Cas. 88 at 108, where Lord Macnaghten said: "It is difficult to suppose that Mrs. Cooper could confer capacity on herself by contemplating a different country as the place where the contract was to be fulfilled".

A domiciled Ruritanian aged 20 buys goods on credit from a London shop. Could he refuse to pay for them on the ground that by Ruritanian law minority ends at 21 and contracts made by minors cannot be enforced against them?

Here we have a conflict of policy between Ruritanian law, anxious to protect its domiciliary (or national) from making an improvident bargain, and English law, which we may assume to be the putative proper law. Most students coming fresh to this topic say that the Ruritanian should be held liable because commercial convenience requires this result. In the great majority of cases this answer is surely correct. If we assume that the Ruritanian minor is in England, art.11 of the Rome Convention or art.13 of the Rome I Regulation will usually secure that result.

But if we change the facts and suppose (a) that the Ruritanian minor never left Ruritania, the contract being concluded by correspondence, or by email; (b) that the shopkeeper opened negotiations by sending him a catalogue depicting, e.g., attractive-looking motor-bikes or electric guitars; (c) that the letter of acceptance was posted in Ruritania; and (d) that the shop was owned and managed by Ruritanians, then the case for applying English law becomes progressively weaker. But in the normal case, where the contract is made *inter praesentes* in the London shop and the shop is English-owned and managed, then the case for applying English law is strong. It would lead to inconvenience and injustice if the validity of an ordinary contract made in England, of which English law was the putative proper law, were allowed to depend on the law of one party's foreign domicile with which the other party could not be expected to be familiar.

There may of course be no real conflict between the law of the domicile and the proper law of the contract. If we reverse the facts and suppose that a domiciled Englishman aged 20 buys goods on credit from a shop in Ruritania, and that law is the putative proper law, it could be plausibly argued that the customer is not entitled to the protection of English law, because by that law he is of full age, nor of Ruritanian law, because he is not a Ruritanian. If so, the contact should be valid and the Englishman liable. We have here what the Americans call a false conflict[235]; if this is recognised, there is no problem.

So far as the practice of the courts is concerned, dicta favouring the law of the domicile can be quoted,[236] but they were all delivered in cases concerning capacity to marry or to make a marriage settlement, and they have been much criticised. Although the place of contracting is commonly regarded as of little importance, as in modern commercial practice it may be fortuitous, dicta may also be cited in favour of the law of the place of contracting,[237] and so can one Scottish case[238] where a contract made in Scotland by a minor domiciled in

---

[235] For false conflicts, see above, para.2–012.

[236] *Sottomayor v De Barros (No.1)* (1877) 3 P.D. 1 at 5 (criticised in *Sottomayor v De Barros (No.2)* (1879) 5 P.D. 94 at 100, and in *Ogden v Ogden* [1908] P. 46 at 73); *Re Cookes Trusts* (1887) 56 L.J. Ch. 637 at 639; *Cooper v Cooper* (1888) 13 App.Cas. 88 at 99, 100 and 108.

[237] *Male v Roberts* (1800) 3 Esp. 163 (the nearest English case to a decision on the matter); *Simonin v Mallac* (1860) 2 Sw. & Tr. 67; *Baindail v Baindail* [1946] P. 122 at 128 (both cases of marriage). In *Republica de Guatemala v Nunez* [1927] 1 K.B. 669 at 689–690 and 700–701, Scrutton and Lawrence LJJ refused to decide between the *lex domicilii* and the *lex loci contractus*, because they coincided.

[238] *McFeetridge v Stewarts and Lloyds Ltd*, 1913 S.C. 773. See especially at p.789, per Lord Salvesen.

Ireland was held valid. In a Canadian case,[239] a husband and wife, domiciled in Quebec but resident for many years in Ontario, made a separation agreement in Ontario. When sued in Ontario for arrears of maintenance due under the agreement, the husband's executor pleaded that by the law of their domicile the spouses had no capacity to make such a contract. The court rejected this defence on the ground that capacity to contract is governed by the proper law of the contract. The court said that had the parties been resident as well as domiciled in Quebec, and had made the contract during a short visit to Ontario, "it would be against common sense to decide the parties' capacity by Ontario law". This dictum is perhaps more significant than the decision itself.

In one English case,[240] there is an indication that the judge would have held that incapacity was governed by the proper law, but the matter did not directly arise.

In view of what has been said, the law which an English court would apply to the question is obviously anybody's guess. The best solution, it is suggested, is to say that if a person has capacity either by the proper law of the contract or by the law of his domicile and residence, then the contract is valid, so far as capacity is concerned.

RESTRICTIONS ON THE REACH OF THE APPLICABLE LAW

Overriding mandatory provisions of the forum

One of the more troublesome aspects of the Rome Convention was its treatment of "mandatory rules". The phrase was used in two senses, and we have already encountered one, that of rules which cannot be derogated from by agreement between the parties. The second sense is clarified in the Regulation which speaks of "overriding mandatory provisions" and provides a definition:

15–052

> "Overriding mandatory provisions are provisions the respect for which is regarded as crucial by a country for safeguarding its public interests, such as its political, social or economic organisation, to such an extent that they are applicable to any situation falling within their scope, irrespective of the law otherwise applicable to the contract under this Regulation."[241]

This definition is based on the decision of the CJEU in *Arblade*.[242] English writers have used the expression "overriding statutes", legislative rules which override or preclude the normal rules of choice of law.[243] The European Commission had earlier explained in its Green Paper that:

---

[239] *Charron v Montreal Trust Co* (1958) 15 D.L.R. (2d) 240.
[240] *Bodley Head v Flegon* [1972] 1 W.L.R. 680.
[241] Regulation, art.9(1).
[242] Cases C-369/96 and C-374/96 [1999] E.C.R. I-8453 at para.31. See for criticism by (one of the negotiators of Rome I, Hellner, (2009) 5 J.Priv.Int.L. 447 at 460.
[243] An example is the Carriage of Goods by Sea Act 1971: *The Hollandia* [1983] 1 A.C. 565.

> "What is special about [this type of rule] or *lois de police*,[244] is that the court does not even apply its conflict rules to see what law would be applicable and assess whether its content might be repugnant to the public policy of the forum but automatically applies its own law."[245]

Both the Convention[246] and the Regulation provide, albeit in different language, that nothing they contain restricts the application of the overriding mandatory provisions of the law of the forum.[247] These provisions allow English courts to continue to apply the overriding provisions of English statutes. So, the Trade Union and Labour Relations (Consolidation) Act 1992[248] and the Employment Rights Act 1996[249] both provide that "for the purposes of this Act it is immaterial whether the law which (apart from this Act) governs any person's employment is the law of the United Kingdom, or of a part of the United Kingdom, or not". This does not mean that the Acts apply to all contracts of employment in the world, regardless of their connection with the UK, because another section of each Act lays down that certain of its provisions do not apply where under his contract of employment the employee ordinarily works outside Great Britain.[250] What it does mean is that the draftsman, instead of enacting (or leaving it to be assumed) that the Act only applies when the law governing the contract of employment is that of some part of the UK, has cut across the normal rules of the conflict of laws and laid down his own rules for the application of the Act. His method has two advantages. First, it prevents the parties evading the Act by choosing a foreign law as the law of the contract of employment. Second, it secures the benefits of the Act to employees who work in the UK for foreign employers and whose contracts of employment might well be governed by foreign law.

Another example is provided by the Unfair Contract Terms Act 1977.[251] That Act imposes severe restrictions on the validity of exemption clauses in many kinds of contract. The provisions of the Act are mandatory: the parties cannot contract out of them.[252] To prevent them from doing so indirectly by selecting a foreign law as the applicable law, s.27(2) provides that the Act has effect notwithstanding any contract term purporting to apply the law of some country

---

[244] The term used in the heading to art.7 in the French text of the Convention.

[245] Green Paper, para.3.2.8.1.

[246] Convention, art.7(2): "Nothing in this Convention shall restrict the application of the rules of the law of the forum in a situation where they are mandatory irrespective of the law otherwise applicable to the contract". The European Court gave a narrow interpretation to this provision in Case C–184/12 *United Antwerp Maritime Agencies NV (Unamar) v Navigation Maritime Bulgare* [2014] 1 Lloyd's Rep. 161. See also *Fern Computer Consultancy v Intergraph Cadworx & Analysis Solutions Inc* [2014] EWHC 2908 (Ch.), at [33]–[34].

[247] Regulation, art.11(2).

[248] s.289, re-enacting earlier legislation, on which see Mann, (1966) 82 L.Q.R. 316; Hughes, (1967) 83 L.Q.R. 180; Unger, (1967) 83 L.Q.R. 427 at 428–433; Mann, (1972–73) 46 B.Y.I.L. 177 at 136–137.

[249] s.204(1).

[250] 1992 Act s.285; 1996 Act s.215, re-enacting earlier legislation, which is also discussed in the articles cited above. For other cases, see *Ravat v Halliburton Manufacturing & Services Ltd* [2012] UKSC 1; [2012] 2 All E.R. 905.

[251] See, e.g., *Trident Turboprop (Dublin) Ltd v First Flight Couriers Ltd* [2009] EWCA Civ 290; [2010] Q.B. 86.

[252] Unless a contract is an "international supply contract" as defined in s.26. That definition follows closely the definition in the Uniform Laws on International Sales Act 1967.

outside the UK, if the term appears to have been imposed wholly or mainly for the purpose of enabling the party imposing it to evade the application of the Act. Similarly s.74 of the Consumer Rights Act 2015 provides that Pt 2 of the Act dealing with unfair terms applies whenever a consumer contract has a close connection with the UK notwithstanding a choice of the law of a non-EEA state.

The concept of 'overriding mandatory provisions' is to be interpreted narrowly[253]; and should only include provisions enacted to safeguard fundamental public interests in English law. In any case the adjudicating court has to consider the wording of the relevant provision and the overall purpose for which it was enacted in order to determine whether it is 'overriding' in the sense of art.(1) and therefore justifies the deviation from the otherwise applicable law.[254]

Overriding mandatory provisions of other states

What has been more controversial is the effect of overriding mandatory provisions of third states,[255] i.e., states which are neither the forum nor the state whose law is the applicable law.   **15–053**

Article 9(3) of the Rome I Regulation provides:

> "Effect may be given to the overriding mandatory provisions of the law of the country where the obligations arising out of the contract have to be or have been performed, in so far as those overriding mandatory provisions render the performance of the contract unlawful. In considering whether to give effect to those provisions, regard shall be had to their nature and purpose and to the consequences of their application or non-application."

The effect is much more limited if compared to the overriding mandatory provisions of the forum. (i) The countries whose mandatory rules may have an impact are those "where the obligations arising out of the contract have to be or have been performed" rather than those with which "the situation has a close connection" as it was in the Convention[256]; (ii) The types of mandatory provisions that may have an impact are only those of the foreign law that render the performance of the contract unlawful. The extent of 'unlawful' in this context is not yet clear; if it is to be limited to 'illegal' the use of this provision is likely to be rather limited.

---

[253] Case C–184/12 *United Antwerp Maritime Agencies NV (Unamar) v Navigation Maritime Bulgare* [2014] 1 Lloyd's Rep. 161.
[254] See also *Fern Computer Consultancy v Intergraph Cadworx & Analysis Solutions Inc* [2014] EWHC 2908 (Ch.), at [33]–[34].
[255] See Dickinson, (2007) 3 J.Priv.Int.L. 53; Kunda, *Internationally Mandatory Rules of a Third Country in European Contract Conflict of Laws* (Rijeka Law Faculty, 2007); Hellner, (2009) 5 J.Priv.Int.L. 447.
[256] Article 7 (2) of the Rome Convention.

The public policy of the forum

15–054   Article 16 of the Convention and art.21 of the Regulation contain a text, familiar in international instruments of this kind, allowing the disapplication of the applicable law if such application is "manifestly incompatible with the public policy (*ordre public*) of the forum".[257]

Public policy has been characterised as a "last-ditch weapon"[258] wielded at the *end* of the forum's choice of law process to resist the application of the rule which that process has identified (unlike the overriding mandatory provisions which operate to prevent that process operating). The disapplication of the provisions of the applicable law that are considered to be manifestly incompatible with the law of the forum is therefore to be cautiously assessed, and reserved for the rare cases where, if applied, those provisions would violate fundamental principles of the forum.[259] Putting it in a different way, it is the application of the foreign law to the particular case and not the provisions of the foreign law in the abstract which needs to be considered as incompatible with English public policy.[260]

VOLUNTARY ASSIGNMENT AND CONTRACTUAL SUBROGATION

15–055   Article 12 of the Rome Convention and art.14 of the Rome I Regulation deal with voluntary assignment.[261] The issue has become vital to the financial services sector in transactions such as securitisation and factoring.[262] However, the effectiveness of cross-border assignments raises long-vexed questions. The leading English case is *Raiffeisen Zentral Bank Osterreich AG v An Feng Steel Co Ltd*,[263] where the Court of Appeal decided that art.12(2) of the Convention covers "issues both as to whether the debtor owes monies to and must pay the assignee (their 'relationship') and under what 'conditions', e.g. as regards the giving of notice".

Article 12 of the Rome Convention reads as follows:

> "1.   The mutual obligations of assignor and assignee under a voluntary assignment of a right against another person ('the debtor') shall be governed by the law which under this Convention applies to the contract between the assignor and assignee.
> 2.   The law governing the right to which the assignment relates shall determine its assignability, the relationship between the assignee and the debtor, the conditions under which the assignment can be invoked against the debtor and any question whether the debtor's obligations have been discharged."

Article 14 of the Regulation provides:

---

[257] Article 21 of the Rome I Regulation.
[258] Jackson, "Mandatory Rules and Rules of *Ordre Public* in North", op. cit., (1892) p.62.
[259] See paras 4–002ff; see further Fresnedo de Aguirre, (2016) 379 *Recueil des Cours* 181.
[260] Giuliano-Lagarde report, p.38.
[261] See Le Verhagen and Van Dongen, (2010) 6 J.Priv.Int.L. 1.
[262] See Hartley, (2011) 60 I.C.L.Q. 29 and Møllmann [2011] L.M.C.L.Q. 262.
[263] [2001] EWCA Civ 68; [2001] Q.B. 825.

"1.   The relationship between assignor and assignee under a voluntary assignment or contractual subrogation of a claim against another person (the debtor) shall be governed by the law that applies to the contract between the assignor and assignee under this Regulation.

2   The law governing the assigned or subrogated claim shall determine its assignability,[264] the relationship between the assignee and the debtor, the conditions under which the assignment or subrogation can be invoked against the debtor and whether the debtor's obligations have been discharged.

3.   The concept of assignment in this article includes outright transfers of claims, transfers of claims by way of security and pledges or other security rights over claims."

The scope of the rule has been extended in the Regulation, as a result of which the provision also governs contractual subrogation. In comparison to its predecessor, the Regulation has made it clear that the law applicable to the contract between assignor and assignee also governs the property aspects of an assignment; however, it does not cover questions of effectiveness and priorities in relation to third parties.

---

[264] See Case C–396/13 *Sähköalojen ammattiliitto ry v Elektrobudowa Spólka Akcyjna*, 18 September 2014.

CHAPTER 16

TORTS AND OTHER NON-CONTRACTUAL OBLIGATIONS

As every law student knows, the law of torts is a core component not only of a law degree course but of the common law; yet for centuries the law of torts was almost ignored in the conflict of laws. Story, in his major nineteenth century treatise on the conflict of laws, did not refer to torts at all. Even the sixth edition of Dicey, published in 1949, contained only nine pages on torts compared with 175 pages on contracts. There is more to be said now, and developments in EU law place torts within a larger category; hence the compendious title to this chapter. Those same developments have, alas, made the topic more difficult.

16–001

All that calls for some explanation. As a matter of history, the law of torts is largely a creation of the twentieth century, a response to enormous changes in the manufacture and distribution of products and in transport and communication. Before that century, there was little to say about the law of torts even in domestic English law, and it is unsurprising that the same should be true of the conflict rules. In more recent times globalisation has meant that the area we know as "torts" has become much more important. Dangerous electrical machinery may cause fatal accidents in countries far removed from its place of manufacture; pharmaceutical products have caused babies to be born without arms or legs thousands of miles from the laboratory where the drugs were made. Foreign business travel and tourism has increased enormously: accidents occur and people are injured or killed far from home. Satellite television programmes and websites can be seen all over the world: private reputations sometimes suffer. Especially in the US, torts has become a favourite topic in the field of choice of law: in American writing, torts cases have come to be the focus of the discussion of methodological issues in the conflict of laws, or (in simpler language) the discussion of why courts apply foreign law, and on what basis they choose it.[1]

Unlike the law of contract, the law of torts lacks a single focus. Its content is very disparate, and different legal systems use the concept in different ways and to protect a range of interests which may vary from country to country. So in some countries, the protection of privacy is a function of this branch of the law whereas in England a law of privacy is still work in progress. The common law uses tort remedies, in the guise of detinue, conversion or wrongful interference

---

[1] See Currie, *Selected Essays on the Conflict of Laws* (Durham NH: Duke University Press, 1963), Chs 3, 7, 14; Cavers, *The Choice of Law Process* (Ana Arbor: University of Michigan Press, 1965), Chs 1, 2, 6; Hancock, *Torts in the Conflict of Laws* (Ana Arbor: University of Michigan Press, 1942); Stromholm, *Torts in the Conflict of Laws* (Stockholm: Norstedt, 1961); Kahn-Freund (1968) 124 Hague *Recueil des Cours*, 5 (a profound and penetrating study from the point of view of comparative law); Morse, *Torts in Private International Law* (Amsterdam: North Holland, 1978); McClean, *De Conflictu Legum* (2000) 282 Hague *Recueil des Cours*, Ch.VI.

with goods, as a means of trying title to movable property; such an idea is quite alien to civil law systems which use a different legal category, often derived from the Roman law *vindicatio*, for that purpose.

For EU legislation, the category of "torts" seemed problematic and that of "non-contractual obligation" was preferred. The demarcation of the boundaries of that new category will take some time but it clearly includes most of what English law regards as "torts".

The development of the English rules of the conflict of laws as to torts was not only slow but also unsatisfactory. There were few cases of any significance, and a leading decision of the House of Lords[2] created more uncertainty than clarity. In 1995, Parliament intervened and enacted new rules in Pt III of the Private International Law (Miscellaneous Provisions) Act of that year. Statutory reform was, however, incomplete: actions for defamation were excluded altogether, and it was 2013 before any relevant provisions as to defamation were enacted. The 1995 Act is in turn being replaced by European legislation in the form of the Rome II Regulation, formally European Parliament and Council Regulation 864/2007 of 11 July 2007 on the law applicable to non-contractual obligations[3] which has "(Rome II)" in its full title. These developments draw on a set of ideas debated over the years and outlined in the paragraphs that follow.

THE LAW OF THE PLACE OF THE TORT

16–002 In the course of the twentieth century, most legal systems developed conflicts rules which applied, or at least gave pride of place to, the law of the place of the tort, the *lex loci delicti*. In 1994, a survey by the Law Commission showed that the law of the place of the tort was the primary choice of law rule in almost all European countries, though the notion of the "place of the tort" was differently expressed and some countries[4] allowed the application of another law if that were more favourable to the injured party.[5] In the nineteenth century, some writers, notably Savigny,[6] had argued for the application of the *lex fori*, the law of the court seised of the case. English common law gave some weight to the *lex fori*, but except in countries which still follow the unreformed English doctrine, the use of the *lex fori* has been abandoned as impractical and unjust.[7]

The adoption of the law of the place of the tort as the prevailing doctrine reflected in part ideas as to the "territoriality" of law. It seemed natural to many lawyers to argue that the law of the place where events occur is the only law that can attribute legal consequences to them, an argument seen by some to follow

---

[2] *Boys v Chaplin* [1971] A.C. 356.
[3] O.J. L 199/40, 31 July 2007.
[4] Germany and Hungary.
[5] See HL Paper (Session 1194–95) 36, at pp.19–22; Morse, (1984) 32 Am.Jo.Comp.L. 51.
[6] *System des heutigen roemische Rechts* (1849), Vol. 8, pp.275 and following.
[7] See the decision of the Canadian Supreme Court in *Tolofson v Jensen* (1995) 120 D.L.R. (4th) 289 applying the law of the place of the tort as an invariable rule, and those of the High Court of Australia in *Pfeiffer Pty Ltd v Rogerson* (2000) 172 A.L.R. 625, noted Olbourne, [2002] C.L.J. 537 (adopting the same approach in an intra-Australian context) and *Regie National des Usines Renault SA v Zhang* [2002] 187 A.L.R. 1, noted Smart, (2002) 118 L.Q.R. 512 (reserving the issue in international cases).

from the, now long-abandoned, "vested rights" theory.[8] In what was for a century the leading English case, Willes J paid lip-service to this argument when he said that "the civil liability arising out of a wrong derives its birth from the law of the place, and its character is determined by that law".[9]

A more pragmatic argument in favour of applying the law of the place of the tort is that it usually accords with the legitimate expectations of the parties.[10] The law of torts attaches certain liabilities to certain kinds of conduct and to the creation of certain social risks. Those engaging in activities that may involve liability should be able to calculate the risks they are incurring, and to insure against them. Everyone should be entitled to adjust his or her conduct to the law of the country in which the conduct is to take place. The ancient adage "when in Rome, do as the Romans do" becomes, in modern life, "when in Rome see that your insurance policy covers the risks against which Romans insure".[11]

Certainty or Flexibility

However, there are strong arguments against a mechanical application of the law of the place of the tort to each and every issue arising out of each and every kind of tort. The very notion of "the place of the tort" raises questions. It may be difficult to determine, as in cases where the defendant's acts take place in one country, and the ensuing harm to the claimant is sustained in another. Even if the location is clear-cut, the place of the tort may be fortuitous. This is particularly true in transport accidents. An aircraft may disintegrate in flight, or may be forced off its course by bad weather and crash in a country in which neither the passengers nor the airline contemplated that the journey would end. A road accident may occur in Switzerland involving English and Italian lorry drivers: it might just as well have occurred in Italy or France.   **16–003**

The most important point, however, is that the application of the law of the place of the tort regardless of the habitual residence of the tortfeasor and the victim, and regardless of the type of issue and the type of tort involved, may lead to results which seem wholly inappropriate. If, for instance, a Scotsman employed by a Scottish firm, negligently driving his employer's lorry, causes the death of another Scotsman employed by the same firm who is a passenger in the lorry, so committing a tort under both English and Scots law, there is hardly a strong case for applying English law to the Scottish widow's claim for compensation, just because the accident happened at Shap in England, a mere 40 miles south of the border.[12]

Considerations of this kind led Dr Morris to suggest, in 1949, that tort liability should be governed by "the proper law of the tort", the law of the country with

---

[8] See Holmes J in *Slater v Mexican National Ry* (1904) 194 U.S. 120, 126, and *Western Union Telegraph Co v Brown* (1914) 234 U.S. 542, 547. cf. Cardozo J in *Loucks v Standard Oil Co of New York*, 224 N.Y. 99; 120 N.E. 198, 200 (1918): "A tort committed in one state creates a right of action that may be sued upon in another unless public policy forbids". For the theory, see para.2–006.
[9] *Phillips v Eyre* (1870) L.R. 6 Q.B. 1, 28.
[10] An argument accepted in the High Court of Australia in *Pfeiffer Pty Ltd v Rogerson* (2000) 172 A.L.R. 625, 645.
[11] Kahn-Freund (1968) 124 Hague *Recueil des Cours*, 44.
[12] These are the facts of *M'Elroy v M'Allister*, 1949 S.C. 110.

which the tort had its closest and most real connection.[13] The gist of this theory is that, while in many, perhaps most, situations there would be no need to look beyond the place of the tort, we ought to have a conflict rule broad enough and flexible enough to take care of the exceptional situations as well as the more normal ones; otherwise the results will begin to offend our common sense. It was suggested that a proper law approach, which the common law had used with great success in the field of contract, would, if intelligently applied, furnish a much-needed flexibility and enable different issues to be segregated, thus allowing a more adequate analysis of the social factors involved. It was also suggested that a proper law approach would facilitate a more rational solution of the problems that arise when acts are done in one country and harm ensues in another.

The proper law thesis can take a stronger or a weaker form. The stronger version places great emphasis on the virtue of flexibility, and argues that the primary choice of law rule should be that of the proper law. A court following that approach would start with a blank sheet of paper and examine the factors connecting the tort to particular countries without reference to any presumption giving priority to any one factor.[14] This stronger form of the proper law thesis was adopted by the American Law Institute's *Restatement Second of the Conflict of Laws*. The leading section on torts provides that "the rights and liabilities of the parties with respect to an issue in tort are determined by the local law of the state which, as to that issue, has the most significant relationship to the occurrence and the parties".[15]

On the other hand, the stronger form of the proper law doctrine has been criticised by some because it sacrifices the advantages of certainty, predictability and uniformity of result which are claimed to follow from the application of the law of the place of the tort. It is also said that the analogy from contract is not useful because the parties to a contract can avoid uncertainty by choosing the proper law,[16] whereas liability in tort is usually unexpected: road accidents are by definition never planned. Predictability of result may not be such an important factor in the law of torts as it is in the law of contract or the law of property but it is important in practice because it facilitates the lawyer's task of advising the client and negotiating a settlement.

The balance of argument may favour the weaker form of the proper law thesis. This accepts the value of having a clear rule, such as the application of the law of the place of the tort, to be applied in the majority, and perhaps the great majority, of cases. But it also stresses the value of flexibility: where a proper law analysis identifies another law with which the tort (or some issue in a tort case) is much more closely connected, it should be possible for a court to apply that other law.

---

[13] (1949) 12 M.L.R. 248, commenting on *McElroy v McAllister*, above; and (in more detail) (1951) 64 Harv.L.Rev. 881. See also Nygh, (1977) 26 I.C.L.Q. 932.

[14] An analogy would be the application in a contract case of art.4(1) of the Rome Convention without reference to the presumption in art.4(2); see para.15–024.

[15] *Restatement*, s.145.

[16] *Boys v Chaplin* [1971] A.C. 356, per Lord Hodson at pp.377–378; per Lord Wilberforce at p.391.

BEFORE THE ROME II REGULATION

The Rule in *Philips v Eyre*

It is necessary to give a brief account of the common law developments in
England: they profoundly influenced later legislation, and the rule they produced
still applies in defamation cases.

In 1870, the common law rule was formulated in a celebrated dictum by
Willes J in *Phillips v Eyre*[17]:

> "As a general rule, in order to found a suit in England for a wrong alleged to have been
> committed abroad, two conditions must be fulfilled. First, the wrong must be of such a
> character that it would have been actionable if committed in England. Secondly, the act must
> not have been justifiable by the law of the place where it was done."

This dictum was treated by later courts almost as if it were a statutory
provision, but their struggles with its interpretation are now happily of little
consequence.[18] The rule in *Phillips v Eyre* came eventually to be understood as a
rule of "double actionability". Its first limb was that a claim brought in England
on a tort committed abroad would fail unless the conduct complained of was
actionable as a tort by English domestic law.

It is this first limb, the application of the *lex fori*, which is the distinctive
feature of the Rule. Its survival for over a century is one of the oddities of English
legal history. Nowhere else in the English conflict of laws did a claimant have to
surmount a double hurdle and show that the claim was valid not only by the
appropriate foreign law, but also by English domestic law. Its second limb was
that the claim would also fail if there were no civil liability under the law of the
place of the tort as between the actual parties to the litigation. This was relatively
uncontroversial. Its effect can be seen from the facts of *Phillips v Eyre*[19] itself.

> An action for assault and false imprisonment was brought in England on the basis of events in
> Jamaica said to be the responsibility of the defendant, who was Governor of Jamaica. The
> defendant pleaded that the acts complained of were done by him in the course of suppressing
> a rebellion which had broken out, and that his acts were subsequently declared lawful by an
> Act of Indemnity passed by the island legislature.

The Court of Exchequer Chamber held that as the actions of the defendant
were not legally wrongful in the law of Jamaica, there was no liability in the law
of the place of the tort and so the action failed. After the speeches of the Law
Lords in *Boys v Chaplin*,[20] it was clear that the second limb would be satisfied if
there were civil liability between the parties in the law of the place of the tort.
There was no requirement that the defendant's conduct be classified as tortious

16–004

---

[17] (1870) L.R. 6 Q.B. 1, 28–29.
[18] See, e.g., *Machado v Fontes* [1897] 2 Q.B. 231; *McLean v Pettigrew* [1945] 2 D.L.R. 65.
[19] (1870) L.R. 6 Q.B.1.
[20] [1971] A.C. 356.

by the foreign law; it was sufficient if by that law the defendant's liability to pay damages was contractual, quasi-contractual, quasi-delictual, proprietary or sui generis.[21]

A more flexible approach

16–005   In *Boys v Chaplin*[22]:

> the plaintiff and defendant were both normally resident in England but temporarily stationed in Malta in the British armed services. While both were off duty, the plaintiff, riding as a pillion passenger on a motor scooter, was seriously injured in a collision with a car negligently driven by the defendant. By the law of Malta, he could only recover special damages for his expenses and proved loss of earnings, which in the circumstances amounted to no more than £53. By English law, he could recover general damages for pain and suffering, i.e., a further £2,250.

The plaintiff recovered the full sum, totalling £2,303. It is not at all easy to identify the ratio decidendi. In part the difficulty arises from the fact that the appeal raised two quite distinct issues. The first is essentially one of the classification of questions as to the heads of damage. The House of Lords held, surely correctly but by the slimmest of majorities, that the question as to available heads of damage—the extent of liability in terms of economic loss, pain and suffering, loss of amenities of life, etc.—was a substantive issue governed by the applicable choice of law rule rather than a procedural issue governed by the *lex fori*.[23]

That left the second issue before the House of Lords, the correct choice of law rule. It is difficult to find any proposition that commanded the support of a majority. Academic and professional opinion identified the speeches of Lord Hodson and, especially, Lord Wilberforce as authoritative, and later courts have associated *Boys v Chaplin* with their approach. It can be seen as embracing the weaker form of the proper law thesis. In essence, the "general rule" expounded by Willes J in *Phillips v Eyre* was made subject to exceptions: it might be departed from where the facts of the case so required. A particular issue might be governed by the law of the country that, with respect to that issue, had the most significant relationship with the occurrence and the parties.[24] The outcome in *Boys v Chaplin* was the application of the law of the forum, but the exception to the general rule was not in terms limited to cases where it would result in the application of that law. Might it be used to secure the application of the law of the place of the tort, or of a third country? In *Red Sea Insurance Co Ltd v Bouygues SA*,[25] a Privy Council case on appeal from Hong Kong, it was held that it could: on the facts and using the new flexibility, the whole case, and not just one limited issue, was held to be properly governed by the law of the place of the tort.

---

[21]   Lord Hodson at p.377 and Lord Wilberforce at p.389 both required "civil liability" (not tortious liability).

[22]   [1971] A.C. 356.

[23]   See the analysis of the speeches in *Boys v Chaplin* in *Harding v Wealands* [2004] EWCA Civ 1735; [2005] 1 All E.R. 415.

[24]   per Lord Hodson at p.380; per Lord Wilberforce at pp.390–392.

[25]   [1995] 1 A.C. 190, applied in *Pearce v Ove Arup Partnership Ltd* [2000] Ch. 403.

The 1995 Act

Before the uncertainties this decision produced could be worked out in further, and no doubt expensive, litigation, there was introduced into Parliament what became the Private International Law (Miscellaneous Provisions) Act 1995, Pt III of which reformed the law in this field.

16–006

The general effect was to abolish the double actionability rule and substitute a statutory general rule applying the law of the place of the tort with an exception derived from the common law developments in *Boys v Chaplin*[26] and *Red Sea Insurance Co Ltd v Bouygues SA*.[27]

Section 11(1) established a new "general rule": "The general rule is that the applicable law is the law[28] of the country in which the events constituting the tort in question occur". However, the new general rule could be "displaced" under s.12 when the special circumstances of the case so required.

THE ROME II REGULATION

Discussion of a European instrument on the law applicable to non-contractual obligations as a counterpart to the Rome Convention began in 1998. A preliminary draft was prepared in 2002, building on work by the European Private International Law Group, and a formal Proposal was submitted by the Commission in July 2003.[29] Despite some sharp criticisms, notably by the European Union Committee of the House of Lords,[30] the proposal made good progress and eventually emerged as the Rome II Regulation in July 2007. It applies to "events giving rise to damage which occur after its entry into force"[31] and the crucial question is whether the event causing damage (as opposed to the resulting damage) occurred on or after 11 January 2009.[32] But, as the entry into force and the application of a Regulation are not necessarily the same, it is possible that the Regulation applies where the events giving rise to the damage occurred on or after 20 August 2008. The Regulation does not apply to Denmark and "Member State" must be understood as excluding Denmark.

16–007

Interpretation

The European Court will have competence to interpret the Regulation in accordance with the usual rules applying to EU legislation. This jurisdiction is likely to have a particular importance in the case of this Regulation: as the

16–008

---

[26] [1971] A.C. 356.

[27] [1995] 1 A.C. 190.

[28] i.e., the internal law, not including choice of law rules, so excluding *renvoi*: 1995 Act s.9(5).

[29] COM(2003) 427 final. See Dickinson, *The Rome II Regulation: A Commentary* (Oxford: Oxford University Press, 2009).

[30] *The Rome II Regulation*, Eighth Report, Session 2003–2004 (HL Paper 66).

[31] Article 32.

[32] Article 31. See Case C-412/10 *Homawoo v GMF Assurances SA* [2011] E.C.R.I-11603 (date of claim irrelevant); *Allen v Depuy International Ltd* [2014] EWHC 753; [2015] 2 W.L.R. 442 (implant manufactured before 11 January 2009; injury after that date; Regulation held inapplicable).

Recitals recognise, the concept of a non-contractual obligation itself varies from one Member State to another and so must be understood as a European autonomous concept.[33] The substantive scope and provisions of the Regulation are intended to be consistent with the Brussels I *bis* Regulation and "the instruments dealing with the law applicable to contractual obligations", meaning the Rome Convention and the Rome I Regulation.[34]

The countries whose law may be made applicable are not limited to Member States; it is expressly provided that a law specified by the Regulation must be applied whether or not it is the law of such a State.[35] The law of a country means the rules of law in force in that country other than its rules of private international law; i.e., *renvoi* is excluded.[36]

In the case of federal or composite states in which each territorial unit has its own rules of law in respect of non-contractual obligations, each territorial unit is treated as a "country" for the purposes of the Convention and the Regulation.[37] A federal or composite State is not bound to apply the Convention or Regulation to conflicts solely between the laws of different units within that State.[38]

Scope

16–009 The Regulation applies, in situations involving a conflict of laws, to non-contractual obligations in civil and commercial matters. "Civil and commercial matters" will no doubt be given the same meaning as in the Brussels I *bis* Regulation;[39] expressly excluded are revenue,[40] customs and administrative matters and the liability of the State for acts and omissions in the exercise of State authority (*acta iure imperii*).[41]

Although there is no definition of "non-contractual obligations", there is, under that heading, a definition of "damage". It covers any consequence arising out of tort/delict,[42] unjust enrichment, *negotiorum gestio* or *culpa in contra-hendo*.[43] Some of these terms will be unfamiliar not only to many readers of this book but to English lawyers generally. *Negotiorum gestio*[44] concerns unauthorised interference in the affairs of another, a sort of unauthorised agency, in which the intervenor is entitled to recover the expenses incurred and to a degree of

---

[33] Recital (11), which adds the specific observation that the conflict of law rules set out in the Regulation should also cover non-contractual obligations arising out of strict liability.

[34] Recital (7).

[35] Article 3.

[36] Article 24. For *renvoi*, see further, Ch.20.

[37] Article 25(1).

[38] Article 25(2).

[39] See para.6–006.

[40] So, for example, claims for unjust enrichment based on the payment of tax where the demand for payment was ultra vires (as in *Woolwich Equitable Building Society v IRC* [1993] 1 A.C. 70) do not fall within the Regulation.

[41] Article 1(1). Claims arising out of *acta iure imperii* include claims against officials who act on behalf of the State and liability for acts of public authorities, including liability of publicly appointed office-holders: Recital (9).

[42] The "tort/delict" usage continues throughout; for convenience we shall refer simply to "tort".

[43] Article 2(1).

[44] Sheehan, (2006) 55 I.C.L.Q. 253.

immunity. *Culpa in contrahendo* relates to pre-contractual matters, but is dealt with under Rome II and not Rome I. Recital (30) explains that for the purposes of the Regulation it is an autonomous concept and should not necessarily be interpreted within the meaning of national law. It should include the violation of the duty of disclosure and the breakdown of contractual negotiations.[45] The Regulation deals with anticipated events in that it applies to non-contractual obligations that have not yet arisen but are likely to arise[46]; and similarly references to an event giving rise to damage includes events giving rise to damage that are likely to occur; and references to damage include damage that is likely to occur.[47]

Exclusions

Article 1(2) lists a number of matters which are excluded from the scope of the Regulation. Many are identical to those listed in the corresponding provision in the Rome I Regulation, and similar reasons apply[48]; but it must be admitted that it is difficult to identify what "non-contractual obligations" could arise in some of the listed cases. The matters excluded are: **16–010**

(a) non-contractual obligations arising out of family relationships[49] and relationships deemed by the law applicable to such relationships to have comparable effects[50] including maintenance obligations;

(b) non-contractual obligations arising out of matrimonial property régimes, property régimes of relationships deemed by the law applicable to such relationships to have comparable effects to marriage, and wills and succession;

(c) non-contractual obligations arising under bills of exchange, cheques and promissory notes and other negotiable instruments to the extent that the obligations under such other negotiable instruments arise out of their negotiable character;

(d) non-contractual obligations arising out of the law of companies and other bodies corporate or unincorporated regarding matters such as the creation, by registration or otherwise, legal capacity, internal organisation or winding-up of companies and other bodies corporate or unincorporated, the personal liability of officers and members as such for the obligations of the company or body and the personal liability of auditors to a company or to its members in the statutory audits of accounting documents;[51]

---

[45] See further para.16–022 below.

[46] Article 2(2).

[47] Article 2(3).

[48] See para.15–011.

[49] "Family relationships" covers parentage, marriage, affinity and collateral relatives: Recital (10). Rodriguez Pineau assumes ((2012) 8 J.Priv.Int.L. 113 at 124) that this excludes intra-family torts as where a father by negligence injures his son; but is the duty of care one "arising out of [the] family relationship"?

[50] The "comparable effects" provisions are to be interpreted in accordance with the law of the Member State seised of the case: Recital (10).

[51] The reference to the liability of auditors has no equivalent in the Rome I Regulation.

(e)   non-contractual obligations arising out of the relations between the settlors, trustees and beneficiaries of a trust created voluntarily[52];

(f)   non-contractual obligations arising out of nuclear damage;

(g)   non-contractual obligations arising out of violations of privacy and rights relating to personality, including defamation.

The last exclusion was particularly controversial and the debates reflected those in Britain which led to the exclusion of defamation from the 1995 Act. Article 30(2) of the Regulation requires the Commission, not later than 31 December 2008, to submit a study on the situation in the field of the law applicable to non-contractual obligations arising out of violations of privacy and rights relating to personality, taking into account rules relating to freedom of the press and freedom of expression in the media, and conflict-of-law issues related to Directive 95/46/EC.[53] The deadline was not met.

There is one further limited exclusion.[54] The Regulation does not apply to evidence and procedure, without prejudice to arts 21 and 22.[55]

Party autonomy

16–011   The Regulation adopts the notion of party autonomy, applying in the field of non-contractual obligations ideas more familiar in relation to contract disputes. At first sight the notion of a choice of law agreement in relation to a tort might seem improbable: the parties will not have foreseen the events giving rise to the claim. A choice of law agreement *after* the event may, however, be entirely sensible; and, as we have seen, the term "non-contractual obligations" is wider than "torts".

So in most cases,[56] the parties may agree to submit non-contractual obligations to the law of their choice by an agreement entered into *after* the event giving rise to the damage occurred.[57] Where all the parties are pursuing a commercial activity, effect will be given to an agreement freely negotiated *before* the event giving rise to the damage occurred.[58] The choice must be expressed or demonstrated with reasonable certainty by the circumstances of the case and must not prejudice the rights of third parties.

As in the case of contractual obligations, i.e. under the Rome I Regulation,[59] there are limitations on the parties' freedom of choice. Where all the elements

---

[52] The Rome I Regulation does not specify that the trust be created voluntarily; it was more important here to exclude constructive trusts.

[53] European Parliament and Council Directive 95/46/EC of 24 October 1995 on the protection of individuals with regard to the processing of personal data and on the free movement of such data.

[54] Article 1(3). See *Wall v Mutelle de Poitiers Assurances* [2014] 1 W.L.R. 4263 (expert evidence); *Actavis UK Ltd v Eli Lilly & Co* [2015] EWCA Civ 555 (conditions for obtaining declaration of non-infringement of patent).

[55] See para.16–028 and 16–029.

[56] Not in the context of unfair competition: art.6(4); nor that of the infringement of intellectual property rights: art.8(3).

[57] Article 14(1)(a).

[58] Article 14(1)(b).

[59] See para.15–016 ff.

relevant to the situation at the time when the event giving rise to the damage occurs are located in a country other than the country whose law has been chosen, the choice of the parties does prejudice the application of provisions of the law of that other country which cannot be derogated from by agreement.[60]

Torts

The primary rule

Article 4 of the Rome II Regulation contains general rules applicable to torts, saving certain other types of non-contractual obligation for later treatment. The primary rule is that in art.4(1):   **16–012**

> "the law applicable to a non-contractual obligation arising out of a tort shall be the law of the country in which the damage occurs irrespective of the country in which the event giving rise to the damage occurred and irrespective of the country or countries in which the indirect consequences of that event occur."

The policy behind this provision is set out in the Recitals. They note that the principle of the *lex loci delicti commissi* (the law of the place of the tort) is the basic solution for non-contractual obligations in virtually all the Member States, though the practical application of the principle where the component factors of the case are spread over several countries varies.[61] A connection with the country where the direct damage occurred (*lex loci damni*) strikes a fair balance between the interests of the person claimed to be liable and the person sustaining the damage, and also reflects the modern approach to civil liability and the development of systems of strict liability.[62] The law applicable should be determined on the basis of where the damage occurs, regardless of the country or countries in which the indirect consequences could occur, and so, in cases of personal injury or damage to property, the country in which the damage occurs should be the country where the injury was sustained or the property was damaged respectively.[63] As Andrew Smith J observed in *Hillside (New Media) Ltd v Baasland*,[64] this provides no guidance in cases in which financial loss is suffered in more than one country.

The question of where a tort should be located has been much debated. This question has been encountered in the context of the Brussels regime on jurisdiction, where it was possible for the European Court to give the claimant the option of locating the tort at the place where there occurred the damage *or* the event giving rise to that damage.[65] Such an option is not available when a single applicable law is to be identified. There is no difficulty where all the events, except the bringing of the action, occur within one country. It is not so simple

---

[60] Article 14(2); art.14(3) deals with the application of such rules in Community law.
[61] Recital (15).
[62] Recital (16).
[63] Recital (17). See *Fortress Value Recovery Fund I LLP v Blue Skye Special Opportunities Fund LP* [2013] EWHC 14 at [45].
[64] [2010] EWHC 3336 (Comm.).
[65] Case 21/76 *Bier v Mines de Potasse d'Alsace* [1976] E.C.R. 1735, [1978] Q.B. 708.

when the defendant's act takes place in one country, and the ensuing harm is inflicted on the claimant in another: for example, the defendant negligently manufactures poisoned chocolates in country A which are bought, perhaps at an airport,[66] in country B and consumed in country C, with the result that the consumer dies in country D. The first *Restatement* contained a rule of thumb that "the place of wrong is in the state where the last act necessary to make an actor liable for an alleged tort takes place".[67] This "last event" rule focuses on the question when the tort is constituted, and that is not necessarily the same question as where it should be located. Moreover, the "last event" rule is not easy to apply, as the facts just given illustrate. For this and other reasons, the "last event" approach has been cogently criticised by writers.[68]

Section 11(2) of the Private International Law (Miscellaneous Provisions) Act 1995 sought at least to minimise the difficulties. It provided that where elements of the events giving rise to the claim occurred in different countries, the applicable law for a cause of action in respect of personal injury was that of the country where the individual was when he or she sustained the injury; and for a cause of action in respect of damage to property, the law of the country where the property was when it was damaged. This is the same approach as is adopted in the Rome II Regulation, though the specific rules are in the Recitals and not the text of the Regulation.

Article 4(1) excludes a reference to the law of the country or countries in which only the indirect consequences of an event. This is similar to the *Dumez* principle developed in the context of the Brussels I Regulation.[69] Its application in the present context can be seen in *Lazar v Allianz SpA*[70]:

> L, a Romanian national, claimed in the Italian courts compensation for material and non-material damage sustained as a result of the death of his daughter, a Romanian national resident in Italy, in a road traffic accident in Italy. Where, as in this case, the damage was caused by an unidentified vehicle a claim could be brought against a guarantee fund operated by the defendant insurance company. The mother and grandmother of the victim, both Romanian nationals residing in Italy, intervened and sought similar compensation.

Under art.4(1), the applicable law would be the law of the State in which the "damage" occurred, and the place in which "indirect consequences" occurred would be irrelevant. The court recalled the provisions in the Recitals (16) and (17) that the damage which must be taken into account in order to determine the place where the damage occurred is the direct damage; and that in the event of physical injuries caused to a person, that the county of the place where the direct damage occurs is the country of the place where the injuries were suffered. It followed that, where it was possible to identify the occurrence of direct damage, as usually is the case with a road traffic accident, the place where the direct

---

[66] It will be immaterial whether the sale is before or after passing through immigration controls; the notice 'UK Border' is important for immigration purposes but not for choice of law. Torts taking place on ships or aircraft are generally treated as located in the State of registration of the ship or aircraft.

[67] Section 377.

[68] Rheinstein, (1944) 19 Tulane L.Rev. 4, 165; Cook, *Logical and Legal Bases of the Conflict of Laws* (Cambridge MA: Harvard University Press, 1942), Ch.13; Morris, (1951) 64 Harv.L.Rev. 881, 887–892; Webb and North, (1965) 14 I.C.L.Q. 1314.

[69] See Case 220/80 *Dumez France v Hessische Landesbank* [1990] E.C.R. I-49 and para.6–023.

[70] Case C-350/14 (CJEU, December 2015).

damage occurred is the relevant connecting factor for the determination of the applicable law, regardless of the indirect consequences of that accident. In the present case, the damage is constituted by the injuries which led to the death of Mr Lazar's daughter, which occurred in Italy; the damage sustained by the close relatives of the deceased was to be regarded as "indirect consequences".

The common habitual residence exception

The law of the place of the tort does not have unqualified sway under the Regulation. Where the person claimed to be liable and the person sustaining damage both have their habitual residence in the same country at the time the damage occurs, the law of that country applies.[71] Whether this would apply on facts similar to those in *Boys v Chaplin*[72] depends on the meaning to be given to "habitual residence", and the Regulation gives only a limited answer. Article 23 provides that, for the purposes of the Regulation, the habitual residence of companies and other bodies, corporate or unincorporated, is the place of central administration.[73] However, where the contract is concluded in the course of the operations of a branch, agency or any other establishment, or if, under the contract, performance is the responsibility of such a branch, agency or establishment, the place where the branch, agency or any other establishment is located is to be treated as the place of habitual residence.[74] The habitual residence of a natural person acting in the course of his or her business activity is the principal place of business.[75] The parties in *Boys v Chaplin* were both off-duty, so the Regulation offers the courts no guidance, and the European Court is likely to develop an autonomous meaning of habitual residence to cover such non-business cases.

16–013

The 'more closely connected' exception

Article 4(3) contains a more general exception to the primary rule:

16–014

> "Where it is clear from all the circumstances of the case that the tort is manifestly more closely connected with a country other than that indicated in paragraphs 1 or 2, the law of that other country shall apply. A manifestly closer connection with another country might be based in particular on a pre-existing relationship between the parties, such as a contract, that is closely connected with the tort in question".

Again the policy is explained in the Recitals, as combining legal certainty and the need to do justice in individual cases.[76] The latter is the basis for the 'escape clause' in art.4(3).[77]

---

[71] Article 4(2).
[72] [1971] A.C. 356; see para.16–005.
[73] Article 23(1).
[74] Article 23(1).
[75] Article 23(2).
[76] Recital (14).
[77] Recital (18).

There is as yet only limited authority on the operation of art.4(3). In *Winrow v Hemphill*[78] a motor accident occurred in Germany; on the facts both parties involved in the accident, English wives of men serving in the British Army, were habitually resident in Germany.[79] Slade J, held that the matters to be taken into account under art.4(3) included the matters mentioned in art.4(1) and 4(2), the country in which the accident and damage occurred, and the common habitual residence at the time of the accident of the claimant and the person claimed to be liable. Although under art.4(2), habitual residence was to be considered at the time when the damage occurred, under art.4(3), the habitual residence of the claimant at the time when consequential loss is suffered might also be relevant. Slade J also held that the consequences of the tortious events were a relevant factor, so that it was relevant where the greater part of loss and damage was suffered. She rejected an argument that the circumstances relevant under art.4(3) varied depending upon the issues to be determined or the stage reached in the proceedings. However, a court would make an assessment on the relevant facts as they stand at the date of their decision, including, for example, that current and future loss would be suffered in a particular country, or that, as in the instant case, the claimant and the defendant had both become habitually resident in another country.

In *Erste Group Bank AG v JSC "VMZ Red October*[80]:

> the claim alleged a conspiracy hatched in Russia to strip a borrower from the bank, and its guarantor of assets in Russia so preventing them repaying their debt to the bank. The Court of Appeal used an 'impartial observer' test: 'Any impartial observer of the alleged facts, posed with the question: "by reference to which system of law should it be adjudged whether the conduct complained of was unlawful?would answer "Russian law of course"'. The trial judge's view that English law might be applicable because the repayment would have been made there was dismissed as fanciful."

Product liability

16–015 The Regulation contains specific rules for certain types of tortuous liability, in the belief that in those cases "the general rule does not allow a reasonable balance to be struck between the interests at stake".[81] The first of these special cases is that of product liability. In that context the Recitals contain the unexceptionable but fairly unhelpful declaration that the choice of law rules in matters of product

---

[78] [2014] EWHC 3164. See also *Stylianou v Toyoshima* [2013] EWHC 2188 (a motor accident in Western Australia); claimant habitually resident in England, was a passenger in a car driven by the defendant, normally resident in Japan. The motorist was insured by a Queensland insurance company under a policy governed by the law of Western Australia; the case was not manifestly more closely connected with England so as to displace the law of Western Australia. cf. *Harding v Wealands* [2004] EWCA Civ 1735; [2005] 1 W.L.R. 1539, decided under the 1995 Act. This aspect of the case was not examined in the speeches in the later appeal to the House of Lords: [2006] UKHL 32; [2007] 2 A.C. 1.

[79] Their common UK nationality was also taken into account under art.4(3), even though that nationality does not refer exclusively to England. The insurance company, the second defendant, was habitually resident in England. Following *Jacobs v Motor Insurers Bureau* [2010] EWHC 231, it was held that that "the person claimed to be liable" for the purposes of art.4(2) was the driver not the insurance company.

[80] [2015] EWCA Civ 379.

[81] Recital (19).

liability should meet the objectives of fairly spreading the risks inherent in a modern high-technology society, protecting consumers' health, stimulating innovation, securing undistorted competition and facilitating trade.[82] It is not at all clear, to give one of a number of possible examples, how the choice of law rules adopted, or indeed any conceivable choice of law rules, can stimulate innovation.

The rules in art.5 are in the form of a "cascade", a device quite familiar in civil law systems. Unless the parties share a common habitual residence, in which case the law of that country applies by virtue of art.4(2), the applicable law is (a) the law of the country in which the person sustaining the damage had his or her habitual residence when the damage occurred, if the product was marketed in that country; or, if the product was not so marketed, (b) the law of the country in which the product was acquired, if the product was marketed in that country; or, if the product was not so marketed, (c) the law of the country in which the damage occurred, if the product was marketed in that country. In many cases, these three countries will in fact be the same, but it is quite possible for a person habitually resident in State A to buy a product at an airport in State B and consume it, with harmful effects, in State C. The Regulation assumes that a product will have been marketed in some country, but if the defendant could not reasonably foresee the marketing of the product, or a product of the same type, in the country the law of which is applicable under the cascade, the law of the country in which the defendant is habitually resident applies.[83] It is not clear what meaning is to be given to the notion of "marketing": it might refer to a process of stimulating interest amongst potential users of the product, e.g., by advertising, but is perhaps more likely to refer simply to the entry of the product into the "stream of commerce" in the particular country.

There is a 'more closely connected' exception, worded as in art.4(3).[84]

Unfair competition and acts restricting free competition

Unfair competition may have general effects on the market or affect a specific competitor. The general approach in the Regulation is to identify as the law applicable to non-contractual obligations the law of the country in which the damage occurs.[85] That principle is no less appropriate in the special context of unfair competition, and can readily be applied where only one specific competitor is affected, as for example passing-off and some cases of inducing breach of contract.[86] Where the effects are more general, as with misleading advertisements, some clarification is needed,[87] and art.6(1) applies the law of the country where competitive relations or the collective interests of consumers are, or are likely to be, affected.[88]

16–016

---

[82] Recital (20).
[83] Article 5(1).
[84] Article 5(2).
[85] Article 4(1).
[86] This is the effect of art.6(2).
[87] See Recital (21).
[88] Article 6(1).

Similarly, the law applicable to a non-contractual obligation arising out of a restriction of competition is the law of the country where the market is, or is likely to be, affected.[89] "Restriction of competition" is interpreted in Recital (23) as covering prohibitions on agreements between undertakings, decisions by associations of undertakings and concerted practices which have as their object or effect the prevention, restriction or distortion of competition within a Member State or within the internal market, as well as prohibitions on the abuse of a dominant position within a Member State or within the internal market, where such agreements, decisions, concerted practices or abuses are prohibited by European law or that of a Member State.

The law applicable under art.6 may not be derogated from by an exercise of party autonomy, i.e., an agreement within art.14.[90]

Environmental damage

16–017 Another case in which special provision is made is that of environmental damage, meaning adverse change in a natural resource, such as water, land or air, impairment of a function performed by that resource for the benefit of another natural resource or the public, or impairment of the variability among living organisms.[91] The primary rule in art.4(1) applies with one qualification: the person seeking compensation for environmental damage may choose to base his or her claim on the law of the country in which the event giving rise to the damage occurred.[92]

Infringement of intellectual property rights

16–018 It was formerly thought that the English court had no jurisdiction to entertain claims for infringement of foreign intellectual property rights, irrespective of whether issues of title or validity were involved. This was based on the *Moçambique* rule (which principally concerns jurisdiction over issues relating to foreign land)[93] and the act of state doctrine.[94] In *Lucasfilm Ltd v Ainsworth*[95] this understanding was not challenged so far as it was limited to patents and other intellectual property rights dependent on the grant or authority of a foreign state, and to cases where what is in issue is the validity of the patent, as opposed to its infringement. The Supreme Court held, however, that, in the case of a claim for infringement of copyright, the claim is one over which the English court has jurisdiction, provided that there is a basis for in personam jurisdiction over the defendant.

---

[89] Article 6(3)(a). See art.6(3)(b) for the cases in which the market is, or is likely to be, affected in more than one country.
[90] Article 6(4).
[91] Recital (24). An illustration would be the facts of Case 21/76 *Bier v Mines de Potasse d'Alsace* [1976] E.C.R. 1735; [1978] Q.B. 708.
[92] Article 7.
[93] See para.17–010.
[94] Both as applied notably by the High Court of Australia in *Potter v Broken Hill Pty Co Ltd* (1906) 3 C.L.R. 479.
[95] [2011] UKSC 39; [2011] 3 W.L.R. 487.

Where the claim can be heard in England, the choice of law rules will be those in the Rome II Regulation, which apply the *lex loci protectionis*, the law of the country for which protection is claimed.[96] For the purposes of the Regulation, the term "intellectual property rights" includes copyright, related rights, the sui generis right for the protection of databases and industrial property rights.[97] In the case of an infringement of a unitary EU intellectual property right, the law applicable, for any question that is not governed by the relevant EU instrument, is the law of the country in which the act of infringement was committed.[98] The law applicable under art.8 may not be derogated from by an exercise of party autonomy, i.e., an agreement within art.14.[99]

Industrial action

There is wide diversity in the law of the different Member States on such matters as the legal status of trades unions and the liabilities which may flow from certain types of "industrial action" such as a strike or a lock-out. The Regulation is drafted so as to respect national law[100] but does contain a choice of law rule. If the parties have a common habitual residence (as will very often be the case) the law of that country will apply.[101] Otherwise, the law applicable to a non-contractual obligation in respect of the liability of a person in the capacity of a worker or an employer or the organisations representing their professional interests for damages caused by an industrial action, pending or carried out, is the law of the country where the action is to be, or has been, taken.[102]   **16–019**

Unjust enrichment

Article 10 deals with cases of unjust enrichment.[103] Such cases are by their nature quite varied, and that fact is reflected in the text of the Regulation which attempts a categorisation with three different rules.   **16–020**

If a non-contractual obligation arising out of unjust enrichment, including payment of amounts wrongly received, concerns a relationship existing between the parties, such as one arising out of a contract or a tort, that is closely connected with that unjust enrichment, it is governed by the law that governs that relationship.[104] In English law, claims for unjust enrichment very commonly involve sums of money paid on the basis of a mistaken belief in liability, either contractual or tortuous, or in respect of consideration that has totally failed, and they will clearly fall within this provision. A not dissimilar case is that set out in s.7(4) of the Torts (Interference with Goods) Act 1977: "if a converter of goods pays damages first to a finder of the goods, and then to the true owner, the finder

---

[96] Article 8(1).
[97] Recital (26).
[98] Article 8(2).
[99] Article 8(3).
[100] See Recitals (27) and (28).
[101] Article 9 applies art.4(2) in this case.
[102] Article 9.
[103] See Chang, (2008) 57 I.C.L.Q. 863.
[104] Article 10(1).

is unjustly enriched unless he accounts over to the true owner ... and then the true owner is unjustly enriched and becomes liable to reimburse the converter of the goods." It remains to be seen how the terms "relationship ... arising" and "closely connected with" are interpreted. In the case of a man left injured by the roadside after an assault upon him, a passer-by who tends his wounds and takes him to a nearby inn, paying the inn-keeper to look after him, is entitled under some systems of law to recover his expenses from the injured man. There has clearly been a tort, but not one directly involving the passer-by. There is no (pre-) existing relationship between the passer-by and the injured man, so that it is not possible to identify a law governing such a relationship. It was held in *Banque Cantonale de Geneve v Polevent Ltd*[105] that the natural meaning of a relationship "existing" between the parties was that it was in existence before the facts which gave rise to the claim had occurred.

Where the applicable law cannot be determined on the basis of that rule and the parties had their habitual residence in the same country when the event giving rise to unjust enrichment occurred, the law of that country applies.[106] Taking the last example, were the kind passer-by to come from Samaria, not "the same country", this rule, too, would be inapplicable. Cases of proprietary restitutionary claims, for example where A's property or its proceeds comes into B's hands and A is able to assert a constructive trust or "trace" the goods, will often fall under this rule. The test of a common habitual residence may not seem entirely appropriate in such cases; its use avoids what can be a difficult issue under the next following rule, of deciding *where* the unjust enrichment occurred, but it will be necessary to decide what is often almost the same question: *when* it occurred.

Where the applicable law cannot be determined on the basis of either or those rules, the law of the country in which the unjust enrichment took place applies.[107]

There is an escape clause in the case of the obligation being manifestly more closely connected with a country other than that identified in these rules: in that case the law of that other country applies.[108]

Negotiorum gestio

16–021 A similar "cascade" applies in the case of *negotiorum gestio*, a non-contractual obligation arising out of an act performed without due authority in connection with the affairs of another person. So, the law governing the relevant relationship existing between the parties; or, failing that, the law of the country in which the parties both had their habitual residence when the event giving rise to the damage occurred; or, failing that, the law of the country in which the act was performed.[109] There is an escape clause in the case of the obligation being manifestly more closely connected with a country other than that identified in these rules: in that case the law of that other country applies.[110]

---

[105] [2015] EWHC 1968 (Comm.).
[106] Article 10(2).
[107] Article 10(3).
[108] Article 10(4).
[109] Article 11(1)–(3).
[110] Article 11(4).

Culpa in contrahendo

In this context, that of a non-contractual obligation arising out of dealings prior to   **16–022**
the conclusion of a contract, regardless of whether the contract was actually
concluded or not, the primary rule is that the obligation is governed by the law
that applies to the contract or that would have been applicable to it had it been
entered into.[111] Where the applicable law cannot be determined on the basis of
that rule, it is (a) the law of the country in which the damage occurs, irrespective
of the country in which the event giving rise to the damage occurred and
irrespective of the country or countries in which the indirect consequences of that
event occurred; or (b) where the parties had their habitual residence in the same
country at the time when the event giving rise to the damage occurred, the law of
that country; or (c) where it is clear from all the circumstances of the case that the
non-contractual obligation arising out of dealings prior to the conclusion of a
contract is manifestly more closely connected with a country other than that
identified in (a) and (b), the law of that other country.[112]

Reach of the applicable law

The applicable law identified under the Regulation governs a wide range of   **16–023**
issues. Article 15 sets out a long, but non-exclusive,[113] list:

(a)   the basis and extent of liability, including the determination of persons who
       may be held liable for acts performed by them;
(b)   the grounds for exemption from liability, any limitation of liability and any
       division of liability;
(c)   the existence, the nature and the assessment of damage or the remedy
       claimed;
(d)   within the limits of powers conferred on the court by its procedural law, the
       measures which a court may take to prevent or terminate injury or damage
       or to ensure the provision of compensation;
(e)   the question whether a right to claim damages or a remedy may be
       transferred, including by inheritance;
(f)   persons entitled to compensation for damage sustained personally[114];
(g)   liability for the acts of another person;
(h)   the manner in which an obligation may be extinguished and rules of
       prescription and limitation, including rules relating to the commencement,
       interruption and suspension of a period of prescription or limitation.

Point (c) calls for some comment. In the context of contractual obligations,
both the Rome Convention and the Rome I Regulation provide that the applicable
law governs, *within the limits of the powers conferred on the court by its
procedural law*, the consequences of breach, including the assessment of

---

[111] Article 12(1).
[112] Article 12(2).
[113] "Shall govern, *in particular* ...".
[114] See Case C-350/14 *Lazar v Allianz SpA* (CJEU, December 2015).

damages *in so far as it is governed by rules of law*.[115] The language of point (c) contains no such qualifications, and it seems that all aspects of the assessment of damages, including quantification, are referred to the applicable law. At common law, questions of liability and of heads of damage were matters for the governing law, but the matter of "quantification", arriving at a sum of money which compensates for the loss of a limb, for pain and suffering, the reduction in earning power, or whatever, was always been regarded as procedural, and so a matter for the *lex fori*. That was affirmed in *Boys v Chaplin*[116] and accepted as applying under the 1995 Act in *Roerig v Valiant Trawlers Ltd*,[117] but the position is changed by the Regulation. So, in *Wall v Mutuelle de Poitiers Assurance*[118] which concerned a traffic accident in France, the Court of Appeal held that it should seek to quantify damages as a French court would do, using whatever guidelines, conventions or practices were used by a French court.

This does not conflict with Recital (33), which refers to road traffic cases. It declares that "according to the current national rules on compensation awarded to victims of road traffic accidents, when quantifying damages for personal injury in cases in which the accident takes place in a State other than that of the habitual residence of the victim, the court seised should take into account all the relevant actual circumstances of the specific victim, including in particular the actual losses and costs of after-care and medical attention." The effect of this Recital has been much discussed. As was emphasised by the court in *Stylianou v Toyoshima*[119] it cannot override the rule as to applicable law in art.4(1); rather it encourages a court to look at the actual costs, for example, of aftercare in the victim's place of residence, and taking those into account when assessing damages, but only insofar as the applicable law permits it to do so.

Rules of safety and conduct

16–024 Despite the extensive reach of the applicable law, the Regulation recognises that in assessing the conduct of the person *claimed* to be liable, account must be taken, as a matter of fact and in so far as is appropriate, of the rules of safety and conduct which were in force at the place and time of the event giving rise to the liability,[120] even where the non-contractual obligation is governed by the law of another country.[121] "Rules of safety and conduct" means all regulations having any relation to safety and conduct, including, for example, road safety rules in the case of an accident.[122]

---

[115] Rome Convention, art.10(1)(c); Rome I Regulation, art.12(1)(c) (emphasis added). See para.15–045.
[116] [1971] A.C. 356.
[117] [2002] EWCA Civ 21; [2002] 1 W.L.R. 2304.
[118] [2014] EWCA Civ 138; [2014] 1 W.L.R. 4263; followed on this point in *Stylianou v Toyoshima* [2013] EWHC 2188.
[119] [2013] EWHC 2188.
[120] Article 17.
[121] See Recital (34).
[122] ibid.

Direct action against the insurer of the person liable

The person having suffered damage may bring his or her claim directly against **16–025**
the insurer of the person liable to provide compensation if the law applicable to
the non-contractual obligation or the law applicable to the insurance contract so
provides.[123] The effect of this is not entirely clear. Advocate-General Sharpston in
her Opinion in *ERGO Insurance SE v If P&C Insurance AS*[124] argued, without
giving full reasons, that:

> "Article 18 does no more than give the victim the option of proceeding directly against the
> insurer (rather than the perpetrator) whilst leaving untouched the basic parameters of the
> situation. Whether the victim can claim against the perpetrator will be governed by the law
> applicable to non-contractual obligations. Whether the insurer is legally required to pay
> compensation in place of the perpetrator will depend on the terms of the insurance contract as
> construed under the law applicable to the contract."[125]

Subrogation

Where a person (the creditor) has a non-contractual claim upon another (the **16–026**
debtor), and a third person *has* a duty to satisfy the creditor, or has in fact
satisfied the creditor in discharge of that duty, the law which governs the third
person's duty to satisfy the creditor determines whether, and the extent to which,
the third person is entitled to exercise against the debtor the rights which the
creditor had against the debtor under the law governing their relationship.[126]

Multiple liability (i.e. contribution)

If a creditor has a claim against several debtors who are liable for the same claim, **16–027**
and one of the debtors has already satisfied the claim in whole or in part, the
question of that debtor's right to demand compensation from the other debtors is
governed by the law applicable to that debtor's non-contractual obligation
towards the creditor.[127] The effect of this can be seen from this example:

> A, who is habitually resident in England, sustains damage in France. He has a claim in tort
> against B, also habitually resident in England, and C, who is habitually resident in Germany.
> The claim against B will be governed by English law, under the common habitual residence
> rule in art.4(2). If B pays damages, B's claim for contribution from C will also be governed by
> English law.

---

[123] Article 18. For the position in the UK, see the European Communities (Rights against Insurers)
Regulations 2002, SI 2002/3061.
[124] Joined Cases C-359/14 and C-475/14; Opinion given September 2015. See Case C-240/14
Prüller-Frey v Brodnig [2015] 1 W.L.R. 5031 (direct action permitted under law applicable to the
non-contractual obligation; that being so, fact that not permitted under law chosen to govern the
insurance contract immaterial).
[125] cf *Jacobs v Motor Insurers' Bureau* [2010] EWCA Civ 1208; [2011] 1 W.L.R. 2609 (claims
brought in England in Wales against the MIB under the Motor Vehicles (Compulsory Insurance)
(Information Centre and Compensation Body) Regulations 2003, SI 2003/37, reg.13 in respect of
injuries in other EU Member States to be assessed under English law).
[126] Article 19.
[127] Article 20.

Formal validity of "unilateral acts"

16–028   Article 21 provides that a unilateral act intended to have legal effect and relating to a non-contractual obligation shall be formally valid if it satisfies the formal requirements of the law governing the non-contractual obligation in question or the law of the country in which the act is performed. The meaning of this provision is obscure, at least to an English reader. In the contractual sphere, the term "unilateral act" can apply to formal notice of denunciation or rescission and there are analogous circumstances in some legal systems in relation to non-contractual obligations.[128]

Burden of proof

16–029   The law governing a non-contractual obligation under the Regulation applies to the extent that, in matters of non-contractual obligations, it contains rules which raise presumptions of law or determine the burden of proof.[129]

Limits on the reach of the applicable law

16–030   As in the case of the Rome I Regulation, there are certain limits on the reach of the applicable law. They are briefly noted here, as the principles have been discussed in the Rome I context. Article 16 provides that nothing in the Regulation restricts the application of the provisions of the law of the forum in a situation where they are mandatory irrespective of the law otherwise applicable to the non-contractual obligation.[130] Article 26 contains the usual *ordre public* provision, that the application of a provision of the law of any country specified by the Regulation may be refused only if such application is manifestly incompatible with the public policy (*ordre public*) of the forum.[131]

Actions in defamation

16–031   Neither the Regulation nor the 1995 Act applies to claims in defamation.[132] They remain governed by the common law rule, that of double actionability subject to the flexibility derived from *Boys v Chaplin*.[133] This meets the concerns of the press and other media: the continued relevance of the law of the forum via the first limb of the common law rule means that the defences of fair comment and qualified privilege remain available even where publication takes place abroad, and this goes some way to mitigate the advantages of England as a forum for defamation plaintiffs.[134]

---

[128] For the proof of such acts, see art.22(2).
[129] Article 22(1).
[130] cf. para 15–052.
[131] See para 15–054.
[132] Regulation, art.1(2)(g); 1995 Act s.13(1). Defamation is defined for this purpose in s.13(2): it includes claims for libel, slander, slander of title, slander of goods or other malicious falsehood.
[133] See above, para.16–005.
[134] See Hartley, (2010) 59 I.C.L.Q. 25.

CHAPTER 17

PROPERTY

This chapter examines the conflict of laws rules relating to property, rules which are generally much easier to grasp than those found in English domestic law. We need first to examine the way in which property is classified for the purposes of the conflict of laws. This involves distinctions between movables and immovables, and between tangible and intangible movables; the meaning of these terms will be explored shortly. The choice of law rules for each category (and in the case of immovables, some special rules as to jurisdiction) are then examined. Finally, we will examine the effect of governmental acts such as nationalisation.

17–001

The death of an individual will, and his or her marriage may, have a general effect on that individual's property rights. These are considered elsewhere[1]; the focus of this chapter is on specific as opposed to general transfers of property.

The Distinction Between Movables and Immovables

In English domestic law, the leading distinction between proprietary interests in things is the historical and technical distinction between realty and personalty. In the English rules of the conflict of laws, however, the leading distinction between things is the more universal and natural distinction between movables and immovables.[2] This approach produces rules which "work" even when the other system of law involved is one in which the English distinction between realty and personalty is unknown. "In order to arrive at a common basis on which to determine questions between the inhabitants of two countries living under different systems of jurisprudence, our courts recognise and act on a division otherwise unknown to our law into movable and immovable".[3]

17–002

The importance of the distinction between movables and immovables is most apparent in the context of succession, because succession to movables is

---

[1] See, for matrimonial property regimes, Ch.13; for succession, Ch.18.
[2] *Freke v Carbery* (1873) LR 16 Eq. 461; *Duncan v Lawson* (1889) 41 Ch.D. 394; *Re Hoyles* [1911] 1 Ch. 179; *Macdonald v Macdonald*, 1932 SC (HL) 79. See, generally, Falconbridge, *Selected Essays on the Conflict of Laws,* 2nd edn (Toronto: Canada Law Book, 1954), Ch.21; Cook, *Logical and Legal Bases of the Conflict of Laws* (Cambridge, MA: Harvard University Press, 1942), Ch.2; Robertson, *Characterization in the Conflict of Laws* (Cambridge, MA: Harvard University Press, 1940), pp.190–212; Smith, (1963) 26 M.L.R. 16.
[3] *Re Hoyles* [1911] 1 Ch. 179, 185, per Farwell LJ.

governed (in general) by the law of the deceased's domicile, whereas succession to immovables is in general governed by the *lex situs* (the law of the country of the location) of the property.[4]

Immovable property is essentially land, but different systems of law may characterise things as movable or immovable in different ways. In all systems, some physically movable things are so closely connected with the land that for legal purposes they are characterised as immovables. Thus, in English domestic law the title deeds to land and the keys of a house are characterised as real estate and therefore as immovable. In Scots law, the old form of security known as the heritable bond[5] was characterised, at least for some purposes, as immovable; and this was recognised by the English courts.[6] There may, therefore, be a conflict between the law of the forum and the law of the country in which the property is located (the *lex situs*) as to whether a particular thing is movable or immovable. In such a situation, it is well settled that it is the *lex situs* that determines the characterisation.[7]

Examples

17–003 For the purposes of the conflict of laws, leasehold interests in land in England are classed as interests in immovables,[8] and it is quite immaterial that English domestic law regards them as personal estate. The same is true of a mortgagee's interest in land in England, including the right to repayment of the debt.[9] But in Australia and New Zealand it is equally well settled that a mortgagee's interest in land is an interest in a movable, on the theory that the debt is the principal thing and the security only an accessory.[10]

Until the Trusts of Land and Appointment of Trustees Act 1996[11] a trust for sale of land notionally converted the interests of the beneficiaries from real estate to personal estate. On the conflicts plane, however, this application of the doctrine of conversion was treated by the English courts as irrelevant: the beneficiaries' interests were treated as immovables.[12]

---

[4] Below, Ch.18. The attempts made in this book to avoid the more arcane Latinisms must exclude the very convenient expressions *situs* and *lex situs* in relation to property.

[5] A bond for a sum of money to which is joined, for the creditor's further security, a conveyance of land or of heritage, to be held by the creditor in security of the debt.

[6] *Jerningham v Herbert* (1829) 4 Russ 388, 395; *Re Fitzgerald* [1904] 1 Ch. 573, 588.

[7] *Re Hoyles* [1911] 1 Ch. 179; *Re Berchtold* [1923] 1 Ch. 192, 199; *Macdonald v Macdonald*, 1932 SC (HL) 79, 84; *Re Cutcliffe* [1940] Ch. 565, 571. The *situs* of property is not always self-evident: see Dicey, Morris and Collins 15th edn (London: Sweet & Maxwell, 2012), Rule 129.

[8] *Freke v Carbery* (1873) LR 16 Eq. 461; *Duncan v Lawson* (1889) 41 Ch.D. 394; *Pepin v Bruyere* [1900] 2 Ch. 504.

[9] *Re Hoyles* [1911] 1 Ch. 179.

[10] *Re ONeill* 1922] N.Z.L.R. 468; *Re Young* [1942] V.L.R. 4; *Re Williams* [1945] V.L.R. 213; *Haque v Haque (No.2)* (1965) 114 C.L.R. 98, 133, 146; *Re Greeneld* [1985] 2 N.Z.L.R. 662.

[11] Section 3(1).

[12] *Re Berchtold* [1923] 1 Ch. 192. Compare the position of capital money arising under a sale of settled land, deemed by the Settled Land Act 1925, s.75(5) to be "land" and so necessarily treated on the conflicts plane as an immovable: *Re Cutcliffe* [1940] Ch. 565. The Trusts of Land and Appointment of Trustees Act 1996 prevented the creation of any further settlements under the Settled Land Act 1925.

Change in situs

Difficult problems arise if things that are physically movable are moved from a jurisdiction which regards them as legally immovable to a jurisdiction which regards them as legally movable. Logically, the new *lex situs* should determine their character. In *Re Midleton's Settlement*,[13] the proceeds of sale of Irish settled land were reinvested in English securities. It was held that for purposes of taxation the securities were situated in England. It seems to follow from that decision that, had it been necessary to determine for purposes of the conflict of laws whether the English stocks and shares were, as a matter of legal classification, movable or immovable, they would have been held to be movable. Under Irish law, a statutory doctrine of conversion[14] would treat them as land, but the property was no longer in Ireland.[15]

17–004

IMMOVABLES

Jurisdiction over immovables

Most legal systems accept that jurisdiction over immovable property is properly exercised exclusively by the courts of the country in which the land is situated. This principle is accepted in the Brussels I *bis* Regulation,[16] which gives exclusive jurisdiction, regardless of the domicile of the parties, "in proceedings which have as their object rights in rem in immovable property, or tenancies of immovable property" to the courts of the Member State in which the property is situated.[17]

17–005

This provision has proved surprisingly troublesome. One of the easier questions is its effect where a single land-holding straddles an international boundary. The European Court has held that in such a case separate actions will have to be brought in each Member State in respect of the parcel of land in that State, unless perhaps the land in one State is a very small fraction of the whole.[18]

Actions based on rights in rem

More fundamental difficulties concern the concepts of "rights in rem" and "tenancy". The former concept has very clear and precise meanings in many civil law systems, where the types of interest in land which may exist are strictly limited. In English law, the use of the trust device means that almost any interest

17–006

---

[13] [1947] Ch. 583; affirmed *sub nom Midleton v Cottesloe* [1949] A.C. 418.

[14] Settled Land Act 1882 s.22(5) (then unrepealed in its application to Ireland).

[15] What does make the result seem distinctly odd is that a similar rule was part of English law; but s.75(5) of the Settled Land Act 1925 did not apply to that case because the capital money did not arise "under this Act".

[16] European Parliament and Council Regulation No.1215/2012. For the other jurisdictional rules of the Regulation, see Ch.6.

[17] Article 24(1).

[18] Case 158/87 *Scherrens v Maenhout* [1988] E.C.R. 3791. See Hartley, (1989) 17 E.L.Rev. 57.

may be created as a term of the trust. The respective positions of trustee and beneficiary as legal and beneficial owner of land are not easily accommodated in the language of the Regulation.

The European Court explored this issue in *Webb v Webb*[19]:

> George Webb provided money with which his son Lawrence bought a flat in Antibes, France. The flat was used as a holiday home by both father and son. A dispute arose between father and son. The son claimed that the flat had been given to him by his father. The father claimed that the son held the flat on trust for him and sought an order that the son should transfer the legal ownership to him.

In one sense, the object of the proceedings was that George Webb should acquire full ownership, a right in rem, of the property; hence, it was argued that only the French courts had jurisdiction. The European Court held, however, that for the provision as to exclusive jurisdiction[20] to apply it was not sufficient that the action involved a right in rem; it had to be *based on* a right in rem. The father was not asserting that he already had such a right, enforceable against the whole world, but only a right as against his son.

A similar result was reached in the context of a matrimonial dispute in *Praciz v Praciz*[21]:

> H began divorce proceedings in France. W, anxious for the case to be heard in England, tried to begin divorce proceedings there but failed under the Brussels IIa Regulation as the French court was the court first seised. W next tried to bring a claim relating to certain property the couple had bought in London, relying on the Trusts of Land and Appointment of Trustees Act 1996 and Art.22 of the Brussels I Regulation.

The Court of Appeal refused to accept the art.22 argument: W was asserting an equitable right in personam and not a right in rem.[22] The boundaries of the concept of actions based on rights in rem were explored in two contrasting cases. In *Re Hayward*,[23] a trustee in bankruptcy claimed to be entitled, as legal owner, to a half-share of a villa in Spain: the Spanish courts had exclusive jurisdiction. A different result was reached in *Reichert v Dresdner Bank*[24]:

> Mr and Mrs R, German nationals residing in Germany, owned a property in Antibes, France. By a deed executed in a notary's office in France, they made a gift of the property to their son who also resided in Germany. A German bank, a creditor of Mr and Mrs R, brought in the French courts an *action paulienne*, seeking a declaration that the gift was void as a fraud on the creditors.

---

[19] Case C–292/92; [1994] E.C.R. I–1717, [1994] Q.B. 696. See Briggs, (1994) 110 L.Q.R. 526.

[20] Then art.16(1) of the Brussels Convention; now art.24(1) of the Brussels I *bis* Regulation.

[21] [2006] EWCA Civ 497; [2006] 2 F.L.R. 1128.

[22] The Court of Appeal also thoroughly disapproved of the attempt to rely on the 1996 Act when divorce proceedings were under way.

[23] [1997] Ch. 45.

[24] Case C–115/88; [1990] E.C.R. I–27. See also Case C-343/04 *Land Oberösterreich v EZ as* [2006] E.C.R. I-4557 (action for injunction against nuisance not a dispute having as its object rights in rem in immovable property; although the basis of such an action is the interference with a right in rem in immovable property, the real and immovable nature of that right was, in such a context, of only marginal significance).

The bank asserted that the French courts had jurisdiction under the predecessor of what is now art.24(1); the bank's argument failed, for the dispute was really concerned with the respective rights of creditors, not title to property.[25]

Tenancies

The concept of "a tenancy" is not defined but in some civil law systems leases fall outside the category of rights in rem and require separate mention in the text. It is not possible to read into the Regulation some of the distinctions, used for various purposes in English law, between a short-term letting and a longer lease, or between a contract to grant an interest and its actual grant.[26] In some cases the European Court has adopted a restrictive approach to the scope of art.22(1). So, in *Sanders v Van der Putte*[27] where the dispute concerned a florist's shop, it was held that there was no exclusive jurisdiction because the lease was essentially of the business carried out in the shop rather than of the shop as a building. Similarly, package holiday contracts fall outside art.22(1) even if they include accommodation not owned by the travel company.[28] But short-term holiday lets and time-share arrangements have been held to be within art.22(1).[29]

17–007

In *Rosler v Rottwinkel*,[30] a German landlord made a holiday cottage in Italy available on a short-term let. He brought an action in the German courts against the tenant claiming compensation under the terms of the lease for damage done to the property and sums due for gas and electricity, and also damages in respect of his own holiday in a neighbouring property, ruined by the behaviour of the defendants. The European Court held that the Italian courts had exclusive jurisdiction, applying to all the obligations of the parties under the lease, including any action for the recovery of possession, to collect rent or other charges due, and the cost of necessary repairs. The jurisdiction did not extend to issues only indirectly related to the lease, such as the claim for the ruined holiday.

The application of the exclusive jurisdiction rule to short-term holiday lettings was seen as undesirable, and some are now excluded. The Regulation provides that in the case of proceedings which have as their object tenancies of immovable property concluded for temporary private use for a maximum period of six consecutive months, the courts of the Member State in which the defendant is domiciled also have jurisdiction, provided that the tenant is a natural person (i.e. not a corporation) and that the landlord and tenant are domiciled in the same Member State.

---

[25] See also Case C-438/12 *Weber v Weber* (right of pre-emption having effects on non-parties).

[26] See *Jarrett v Barclays Bank Plc* [1999] Q.B. 1.

[27] Case 73/77; [1977] E.C.R. 2383.

[28] Case C–280/90 *Hacker v Euro-Relais GmbH* [1992] E.C.R. 1111.

[29] Case 241/83 *Rosler v Rottwinkel* [1985] E.C.R. 99; [1986] Q.B. 33; *Jarrett v Barclays Bank Plc* [1999] Q.B. 1.

[30] Case 241/83; [1985] E.C.R. 99; [1986] Q.B. 33. See also Case C–8/98 *Dansommer v Gotz* [2000] E.C.R. I–93; [2001] 1 W.L.R. 1069 (exclusive jurisdiction covered an action brought by a tour operator, not the owner of the relevant property, against a tenant for damages for taking poor care of premises and causing damage to holiday accommodation).

Claims in contract and concerning rights in rem

17–008   A different provision of the recast Brussels I Regulation enables the court of the *situs* of immovable property, where it is possible under the *lex situs* to combine an action relating to a contract with an action (against the same defendant, one domiciled in a Member State) relating to rights in rem in the property (for example an action both to enforce a mortgage debt and to obtain an order for the sale of the property), the courts of the *situs* may hear the former together with the latter, even if they would not otherwise have jurisdiction over the contractual action.[31]

Limits on jurisdiction

17–009   It follows from the above that where the land in question is situated in England and the issues fall within the scope of the recast Brussels I Regulation or the Lugano Convention, the English courts will have jurisdiction. If the land is in England and the Regulation and Convention do not apply, the English court may take jurisdiction by allowing service out of the jurisdiction under the Civil Procedure Rules on the basis that the whole subject matter of a claim relates to property within the jurisdiction.[32] Where the land is in another part of the UK or another Member State or State party to the Lugano Convention, the jurisdiction of the English court will be excluded. If the land is in some other State, or the issue is not within the scope of the Regulation or the relevant Convention, it is still necessary to explore what is known as the *Moçambique* rule.

The *Moçambique* rule: title to foreign land

17–010   As a general rule, English courts have no jurisdiction to entertain a claim for the determination of the title to, or the right to possession of, any immovable situated outside England.[33] The origins of this rule have been traced to the ancient common law practice whereby juries were chosen from persons acquainted with the facts of a case, who therefore decided questions of fact from their own knowledge and not from the evidence of witnesses. In order that the right jury might be empanelled it was necessary to lay the venue exactly. The consequence was that English courts had no jurisdiction to entertain actions where the facts occurred abroad. This led to such inconvenience that the rule was evaded by the fiction of *videlicet*, i.e. by the untraversable allegation[34] that a foreign place was situated in, e.g., the parish of St Marylebone.[35]

Unfortunately this relaxation applied only to "transitory" actions, that is, actions where the facts might have occurred anywhere (e.g., for breach of

---

[31] Article 8(4).

[32] CPR, r.6.36 and PD 3.1(11).

[33] *British South Africa Co v Companhia de Moçambique* [1893] A.C. 602.

[34] i.e., one that could not be denied.

[35] Holdsworth, *History of English Law*, Vol.5, pp.140–142.

contract). It did not apply to local actions, where the facts could only have occurred in a particular place (e.g., actions relating to foreign land).[36]

The rules as to venue were abolished by the Judicature Act 1873, and accordingly it was then arguable that there was no longer any reason for English courts not to decide questions of title to foreign land, or at least grant damages for trespass to such land. But in the leading case of *British South Africa Co v Companhia de Moçambique*[37] the House of Lords decided that:

> "the grounds upon which the courts have hitherto refused to exercise jurisdiction in actions of trespass to lands situated abroad were substantial and not technical, and that the rules of procedure under the Judicature Acts have not conferred a jurisdiction which did not exist before".

Unfortunately neither Lord Herschell nor Lord Halsbury, who delivered speeches in that case, vouchsafed a hint as to what these "substantial" grounds were.

The facts of the case were as follows:

> The plaintiff, a Portuguese chartered company, alleged that it was in possession of large tracts of lands in southern Africa, and that the defendant, an English chartered company, by its agents wrongfully broke and entered and took possession of the lands and ejected the plaintiff company therefrom. The plaintiff claimed (1) a declaration that it was lawfully in possession of the lands; (2) an injunction restraining the defendant from asserting any title to the lands; (3) £250,000 damages for trespass. The defendant pleaded that because the lands were outside the jurisdiction the statement of claim disclosed no cause of action.

In the Court of Appeal the plaintiff formally abandoned claims (1) and (2), and that court by a majority declared that the High Court had jurisdiction over claim (3). The House of Lords unanimously reversed that judgment and dismissed the action.

Section 30 of the Civil Jurisdiction and Judgments Act 1982 provides that English courts have jurisdiction to entertain proceedings for trespass to or other torts affecting foreign land, unless the proceedings are principally concerned[38] with a question of title to, or the right to possession of, the land. This section reverses the much-criticised decision of the House of Lords in *Hesperides Hotels Ltd v Aegean Turkish Holidays Ltd*[39] where the House refused to limit the *Moçambique* rule to cases where title or the right to possession was in issue, conceding only that it did not prevent an action for damages for trespass to the contents of a building situated abroad.

---

[36] For an attempt by Lord Mansfield to circumvent this distinction, see cases on land in "uncivilised" parts of Canada cited in *Mostyn v Fabrigas* (1774) 1 Cowp 161. The rule was re-asserted in *Doulson v Matthews* (1792) 4 T.R. 503, 504.

[37] [1892] 2 Q.B. 358; [1893] A.C. 602.

[38] This imprecise expression has been held to be "a matter of judgment, one of fact and degree": *Re Polly Peck International Plc (No.2)* [1998] 3 All E.R. 812, at 828. For the consequence that some thousands of actions arising from oil spillage would have to be analysed individually, see *Bodo Community v Shell Petroleum Development Co of Nigeria Ltd* [2014] EWHC 1973 (TCC) at [166].

[39] [1979] A.C. 508.

Effect of the recast Brussels I Regulation

17–011   It is arguable that the Brussels I Regulation affected the position and the same issue is relevant under the recast Regulation. If the defendant is domiciled in England, so that an English court has jurisdiction in a civil and commercial matter under what is now art.4 of the recast Regulation, can it refuse to exercise jurisdiction on the ground that the land is situated abroad, in a non-Member State? Strict logic would suggest a negative answer, but policy arguments, including the clear policy of the Regulation in respect of disputes as to title to land, strongly support the continued right of the English court to decline jurisdiction in these circumstances. This latter view has been supported, albeit obiter, by the Court of Appeal.[40] In the decision of the European Court of Justice in *Owusu v Jackson*[41] that the plea of forum non conveniens was generally unavailable where the English court had jurisdiction under art.2 of the Brussels I Regulation, the precise issue as to foreign land was expressly reserved, as it was not raised by the facts before the court. In *Lucasfilm v Ainsworth*[42] (which was primarily concerned with intellectual property rights) the Court of Appeal held in effect that the *Moçambique* rule was not affected by the Regulation and *Owusu v Jackson*. On appeal, the view of the Supreme Court on other issues meant that it did not address that specific matter.[43] In *Ferrexpo AG v Gilson Investments Ltd*[44] it was held that the exclusive jurisdiction provisions of the Brussels I Regulation could be given a certain "reflexive" effect in case where a non-Member State was involved.[45] There a court in Ukraine was dealing with company law issues within the scope of art.22 of the Regulation (now art.24 of the recast Regulation); the court held that despite the English domicile of the defendants, which gave the English court jurisdiction, it could as a matter of discretion stay the English proceedings, and was not prevented from doing so by the decision in *Owusu v Jackson*.

Scope of the Moçambique rule

17–012   If the *Moçambique* rule is one of policy, as the House of Lords insisted, the better opinion would seem to be that it cannot be waived by any agreement between the parties.[46]

The common law rule is subject to two not very well defined exceptions, both of which are derived from the practice of Courts of Equity. These will now be considered.

---

[40] *Re Polly Peck International Plc (No.2)*[1998] 3 All E.R. 812, at 829–830.
[41] Case C–281/02; [2005] E.C.R. I-1383; [2005] Q.B. 801.
[42] [2009] EWCA Civ 1328; [2010] Ch. 503.
[43] [2011] UKSC 39; [2011] 4 All E.R. 817.
[44] [2012] EWHC 721; [2012] 1 Lloyd's Rep 588.
[45] For the various types of argument as to "reflexive" effect, see Smith, Lasserson and Rymkiewicz, [2012] 8 J.Priv.Int.L.389.
[46] *The Tolten* [1946] P. 135, 166. Contrast *The Mary Moxham* (1876) 1 P.D. 107, 109 and *Re Duke of Wellington* [1948] Ch. 118, where waiver seems to have been allowed: but the latter case would now fall under the second exception to the rule, and the former would raise no jurisdictional problem in view of s.30 of the Civil Jurisdiction and Judgments Act 1982.

First exception: contracts and equities

If the court has jurisdiction in personam over a defendant, either because of **17–013** presence in England when a claim form is served, or because of submission to the jurisdiction, or because the court grants permission to serve the claim form out of the jurisdiction under the Civil Procedure Rules, the court has jurisdiction to entertain an action against the defendant in respect of a contract or an equity affecting foreign land.[47] In considering the scope of this exception, s.30 of the Civil Jurisdiction and Judgments Act 1982 must be borne in mind: there is no need to rely on this exception if proceedings are not principally concerned with a question of title to, or the right to possession of, the land.

Courts of Equity have, from the time of Lord Hardwicke's decision in *Penn v Baltimore*,[48] exercised jurisdiction in personam in relation to foreign land against persons locally within the jurisdiction of the English court in cases of contract, fraud and trust.[49] The facts of that case (slightly simplified) were as follows:

Penn was the owner of the then province of Pennsylvania. Lord Baltimore was the owner of the then province of Maryland. They made a contract to settle the boundaries between the two provinces. Lord Hardwicke decreed specific performance of the contract.

The obligations which the courts will thus enforce are not easily brought under one head. "They all depend", said Parker J, "upon the existence between the parties to the suit of some personal obligation arising out of contract or implied contract, fiduciary relationship or fraud, or other conduct which, in the view of the Court of Equity in this country, would be unconscionable, and do not depend for their existence on the law of the locus of the immovable property".[50]

The jurisdiction is substantially confined to cases in which there is either a contract or an equity between the parties. Examples of contracts are claims by a lessor to recover rent due under a lease of foreign land,[51] or claims by a vendor or purchaser of foreign land for specific performance of a contract of sale.[52] Examples of equities are claims to redeem[53] or foreclose[54] a mortgage on foreign land, or to prevent a creditor from purchasing foreign land at an undervalue by making unfair use of local procedure,[55] or to reclaim gifts made under undue influence,[56] or for a declaration that the defendant holds foreign land as trustee.[57]

The decided cases have emphasised the following general points:

---

[47] See Wass, (2014) 63 I.C.L.Q103.
[48] (1750) 1 Ves. Sen. 444.
[49] *Pattni v Ali* [2006] UKPC 51; [2007] 2 A.C. 85.
[50] *Deschamps v Miller* [1908] 1 Ch. 856, 863.
[51] *St. Pierre v South American Stores Ltd* [1936] 1 K.B. 382.
[52] *Richard West and Partners Ltd v Dick* [1969] 2 Ch. 424.
[53] *Beckford v Kemble* (1822) 1 S. & St. 7.
[54] *Toller v Carteret* (1705) 2 Vern. 494; *Paget v Ede* (1874) LR 18 Eq. 118.
[55] *Cranstown v Johnston* (1800) 5 Ves. 277.
[56] *Razelos v Razelos (No.2)* [1970] 1 W.L.R. 392.
[57] *Cook Industries Inc v Galliher* [1979] Ch. 439. The exception was applied in *Stevens v Hamed* [2014] EWCA Civ 911 to a claim in restitution for the repayment of a contractual payment where the consideration is said to have failed (but on the facts the claim was held not to be within the *Moçambique* rule itself).

(a)   The jurisdiction cannot be exercised if the *lex situs* would prohibit the enforcement of the decree. "If, indeed", said Lord Cottenham, "the law of the country where the land is situate should not permit, or not enable, the defendant to do what the court might otherwise think it right to decree, it would be useless and unjust to direct him to do the act".[58] What this means is far from clear. In the very case in which Lord Cottenham was speaking, a mortgagee by deposit of title deeds was held entitled to priority over the mortgagor's unsecured creditors, although by the *lex situs* of the land the deposit gave him no lien or equitable mortgage over the land at all.

(b)   The jurisdiction cannot be exercised against strangers to the equity unless they have become personally affected thereby. But it is difficult to determine what degree of privity prevents a defendant being a stranger to the equity. If A agrees to sell foreign land to B, but instead conveys it to C who has notice of the contract, C is a stranger to the equity against whom the jurisdiction cannot be invoked.[59] But if a company creates an equitable charge on foreign land in favour of debenture-holders, and sells the land to a purchaser "subject to the mortgage lien or charge now subsisting", and the purchaser expressly undertakes to pay the debentures and interest thereon, the court has jurisdiction to entertain an action by the debenture-holders against the purchaser to enforce their security.[60] The distinction between buying land with notice of a contract and buying land subject to a charge seems to be a tenuous one, not easily reconcilable with equitable doctrines of constructive notice.

(c)   The jurisdiction cannot be exercised if the court cannot effectively supervise the execution of its order. For this reason the court will not order a sale of foreign land at the instance of a mortgagee.[61] But it will order the foreclosure of a mortgage,[62] decree specific performance of a contract to sell foreign land,[63] and make an order for the inspection of foreign land.[64]

(d)   The jurisdiction cannot be exercised unless there is some personal equity running from the plaintiff to the defendant. Thus in *Re Hawthorne*,[65] by reason of an intestacy the title to a house in Dresden was in dispute between A and B. B sold the house and received part of the purchase-money. A brought an action against B to make him account for the purchase-money, but it was held that the court had no jurisdiction. And in *Deschamps v Miller*[66]:

> a man and woman, domiciled in France, married there. Their marriage contract adopted a matrimonial property régime including community of after-acquired property under French law. The husband acquired land in India, where he went through a bigamous ceremony of marriage with Q, and settled the land on trusts for the benefit of Q and her

---

[58] *Re Courtney, Ex p. Pollard* (1840) Mont & Ch. 239, 250.
[59] *Norris v Chambres* (1861) 29 Beav. 246; 3 D.F. & J. 583.
[60] *Mercantile Investment Co v River Plate Co* [1892] 2 Ch. 303.
[61] *Grey v Manitoba Rly Co* [1897] A.C. 254.
[62] *Paget v Ede* (1874) LR 18 Eq. 118, criticised by Falconbridge, op. cit., pp.618–620.
[63] *Richard West and Partners Ltd v Dick* [1969] 2 Ch. 424.
[64] *Cook Industries Inc v Galliher* [1979] Ch. 439.
[65] (1883) 23 Ch.D. 743.
[66] [1908] 1 Ch. 856.

children. After the deaths of the husband and wife the plaintiff, their only son, brought an action against the trustees of the settlement claiming his share of the land in India under French law. It was held that the court had no jurisdiction.

The equitable jurisdiction is anomalous and, as Lord Esher said,[67] "seems to be open to the strong objection that the court is doing indirectly what it dare not do directly". In the early cases in which the jurisdiction was invoked, the land was situated within British colonies with ill-developed court systems. In modern times, it is difficult to rely on any such rationale. A modern judge could hardly say, as Shadwell VC once said, "I consider that in the contemplation of the Court of Chancery every foreign court is an inferior court".[68]

Second exception: estates and trusts

If the court has jurisdiction to administer a trust[69] or the estate of a deceased person, and the property includes movables or immovables situated in England and immovables situated abroad, the court has jurisdiction to determine questions of title to the foreign immovables for the purposes of the administration. This formulation of the exception is based upon that of *Dicey, Morris and Collins*[70] because it has never been precisely formulated by English judges, though it has been approved by the Court of Session and referred to without dissent by the Court of Appeal.[71] But the existence of the exception can scarcely be doubted. The principal authority on which it rests is the case of *Nelson v Bridport*[72]:

17–014

> "The King of the Two Sicilies granted land in Sicily to Admiral Nelson for himself and the heirs of his body, with power to appoint a successor. By his will, which dealt also with property in England, the Admiral devised the land to trustees in trust for his brother William for life with remainders over. After the Admiral's death, and in the lifetime of William, a law was passed in Sicily abolishing entails and making the persons lawfully in possession of such estates the absolute owners thereof. Taking advantage of this law, brother William devised the land to his daughter Lady Bridport. The remainderman under the Admiral's will claimed to be entitled to the land. The court assumed jurisdiction."

Here, it will be noticed, there was no contract, no fiduciary relationship and no equity between the parties: nothing in the report suggests that they were other than complete strangers to each other. There was nothing but a mere naked question of title to foreign land, and therefore the case could not possibly have fallen under the first exception discussed above.

---

[67] *Companhia de Moçambique v British South Africa Co* [1892] 2 Q.B. 358, 404–405.

[68] *Bent v Young* (1838) 9 Sim. 180, 191.

[69] It may be that this should now be confined to trusts arising under wills or intestacies, since these are excluded from the Brussels I *bis* Regulation, whereas inter vivos trusts might fall within art.24(1), above, para.17–005.

[70] 15th edn (2012), Rule 131(3)(b).

[71] *Jubert v Church Commissioners for England*, 1952 SC 160, 162; *Polly Peck International Plc (No.2)* [1998] 3 All E.R. 812, at 828.

[72] (1846) 8 Beav. 547.

This second exception is also supported by a number of other cases.[73] These cases cannot be explained on the ground that the jurisdictional objection was waived because, as we have seen, the better opinion is that the *Moçambique* rule cannot be waived; and in any case it is difficult to see how waiver could be allowed in cases where the interests of minors or of unborn persons are involved. The cases may perhaps be justified on the ground that the court can make its adjudication effective indirectly through its control of the trustees or of the other assets situated in England.

Immovables: choice of law

17–015 One of the most deeply-rooted principles of the English conflict of laws, and of the corresponding rules in other legal systems, is that all questions relating to immovables are governed by the *lex situs*. The proposition may seem an almost self-evident one, for land can never be moved, and can be dealt with only in a manner permitted by the *lex situs*. Coupled with the *Moçambique* rule, the application of the *lex situs* ensures that virtually all disputes in the English courts about title to land are governed by English law.

However, the *situs* rule has been subjected to devastating academic criticism[74] on the ground that it is much too broad, hopelessly undiscriminating, and careless of the important policies of domestic law. Admittedly it achieves certainty, uniformity and symmetry in the law, and is easy to apply; but as we shall see it can lead to extremely harsh and inconvenient results. The first of the critics was Cook, who pointed out that when a court sitting at the *situs* of the land is confronted by a document (e.g., a deed or will) executed abroad by a person domiciled abroad, the real question is: should the court apply to such a document the same rule of decision that it would apply to a purely domestic document. He argued cogently that in matters of form, capacity, and matrimonial property it should not, but that in matters of essential validity it should.

Cook's analysis was carried several stages further by Hancock who, in an important series of articles, argued that, apart from questions of the marketability or use of land, the *situs*-forum should not necessarily apply the domestic law of the *situs* but should consider whether that law, properly interpreted and understood, was intended to apply to foreign-executed documents or to persons domiciled abroad.

The arguments of Cook and Hancock have not persuaded English judges to reconsider their traditional reliance on the *situs* rule as an all-embracing formula by which, in the absence of statute or judicial precedent to the contrary, all questions relating to land must be governed. But it may be pointed out that, long before Cook and Hancock, it was held that a foreign marriage contract or

---

[73] *Hope v Carnegie* (1866) LR 1 Ch. App. 320; *Ewing v Orr-Ewing* (1883) 9 App Cas. 34; *Re Piercy* [1895] 1 Ch. 83; *Re Moses* [1908] 2 Ch. 235; *Re Stirling* [1908] 2 Ch. 344; *Re Pearses Settlement* [1909] 1 Ch. 304; *Re Hoyles* [1911] 1 Ch. 179; *Re Ross* [1930] 1 Ch. 377; *Re Duke of Wellington* [1948] Ch. 118.

[74] Cook, op. cit., Ch. 10; Hancock, (1964) 16 Stanford L. Rev. 561; (1965) 17 Stanford L. Rev. 1095; (1966) 18 Stanford L. Rev. 1299; (1967) 20 Stanford L. Rev. 1; Weintraub, (1966) 52 Cornell L.Q. 1; Morris, (1969) 85 L.Q.R. 339.

settlement (even if it was not express but was imposed or implied by foreign law) could affect the devolution of land in England[75]; that wills of immovables are, as a general rule, interpreted by reference to the law of the testator's domicile[76]; that now by statute a will of immovables must be treated as properly executed if its execution conformed to the law of the country where it was executed, or where the testator was domiciled or habitually resident, or of which he or she was a national.[77]

Renvoi

Nearly all writers on the conflict of laws agree that, in the rare cases where an English court is dealing with a question of title to land situated abroad, it should apply whatever system of domestic law the *lex situs* would apply,[78] and there are cases in which this has been done.[79] In other words, this situation is one in which it is justifiable to apply the doctrine of *renvoi* in order to achieve uniformity with the *lex situs*.[80] Uniformity with the *lex situs* is important because in the last resort the land can only be dealt with in a manner permitted by that law. Consequently, any decision by a non-*situs* court which ignored what the courts of the *situs* had decided or would decide might well be of no value.

17–016

In what follows, it should be noted that the effect of grants of administration on immovables, succession to immovables, and marriage are reserved for separate discussion in later chapters.

Formal validity

There appears to be only one reported English case in which the formal validity of a deed affecting land has been considered. In *Adams v Clutterbuck*,[81] a domiciled Englishman conveyed to a purchaser domiciled in England a right of shooting over land in Scotland. The conveyance was made in England by an instrument in writing but not under seal. The law of England required such conveyances to be under seal, but the law of Scotland did not. It was held that the conveyance was valid.

17–017

Insofar as the instrument is to have effect as a contract, its formal validity is governed in the case of contracts concluded on or before concluded after 17 December 2009 by European Parliament and Council Regulation 593/2008 on the law applicable to contractual obligations ("Rome I").[82] The only special rule is that in art.9(6) of the Convention and (in a slightly different draft) in art.11(5) of the Regulation. The rule in its Regulation wording is that a contract the subject

---

[75] *Re De Nicols (No.2)* [1900] 2 Ch. 410; below, para.16–008.
[76] See below, para.18–022.
[77] Wills Act 1963 s.1; below, para.18–015.
[78] Falconbridge, op. cit., pp.141, 217–220; Cook, op. cit., pp.264, 279–280; Lorenzen, op. cit., p.78; Hancock, (1965) 17 Stanford L. Rev. 1095, 1096, n.4.
[79] *Re Ross* [1930] 1 Ch. 377; *Re Duke of Wellington* [1947] Ch. 506.
[80] See below, para.20–019.
[81] (1883) 10 Q.B.D. 403.
[82] Contracts concluded earlier are governed by the Rome Convention as given effect by the Contracts (Applicable Law) Act 1990.

matter of which is a right in rem in immovable property or a tenancy of immovable property is subject to the requirements of form of the law of the country where the property is situated if by that law (a) those requirements are imposed irrespective of the country where the contract is concluded and irrespective of the law governing the contract; and (b) those requirements cannot be derogated from by agreement.

Essential validity

17–018   Although all the cases concern wills, there can be no doubt that the essential validity of a deed affecting land in England is also governed by English law. That law will determine what estates can legally be created,[83] what are the incidents of those estates,[84] whether gifts to charities are valid,[85] and whether the interests given infringe the rule against perpetuities or accumulations.[86]

On the other hand, the material or essential validity of a contract affecting land is governed by the Rome I Regulation.[87] Under the earlier Rome Convention, if the parties have not chosen the governing law, that law would be determined by Article 4.[88] Article 4(3) provides that, to the extent that the subject matter of the contract is a right in immovable property or a right to use immovable property, it is presumed that the contract is most closely connected with the country in which the immovable is situated. Although this presumption will not apply if it appears from the circumstances as a whole that the contract is more closely connected with another country,[89] the likely result is that the *lex situs* will apply in almost every case. The Rome I provisions are likely to have the same effect. Article 4(1)(c) of the Regulation provides that a contract relating to a right in rem in immovable property or to a tenancy of immovable property is governed by the law of the country where the property is situated; but art.4(3) adds that where it is clear from all the circumstances of the case that the contract is manifestly more closely connected with another country, the law of that other country applies.

Capacity: land in England

17–019   There appears to be no reported case in which the English court has had to consider the question of capacity to transfer land in England when the transferor was domiciled abroad.[90] The relevant considerations are well illustrated by the American case of *Proctor v Frost*[91]:

> A married woman domiciled in Massachusetts became surety in that state for her husband and gave as security a mortgage on land she owned in New Hampshire. The mortgagee brought

[83] *Nelson v Bridport* (1846) 8 Beav. 547.
[84] *Re Miller* [1914] 1 Ch. 511.
[85] *Duncan v Lawson* (1889) 41 Ch.D. 394; *Re Hoyles* [1911] 1 Ch. 179.
[86] *Freke v Carbery* (1873) LR 16 Eq. 461.
[87] See para.15–047.
[88] See para.15–024.
[89] As a result of applying art.4(5) of the Convention.
[90] Issues as to capacity are generally excluded from both the Rome Convention and the Rome I Regulation.
[91] 89 N.H. 304, 197 A. 813 (1938).

proceedings in New Hampshire to foreclose the mortgage. The mortgagor's defence was that by a New Hampshire statute a married woman could not become surety for her husband.

The New Hampshire court rejected this defence on the ground that "the primary purpose of the statute was not to regulate the transfer of New Hampshire real estate, but to protect married women in New Hampshire from the consequences of their efforts, presumably ill-advised, to reinforce the credit of embarrassed husbands". This decision seems sound and sensible; but the reasoning is not entirely satisfactory because it emphasises the place where the mortgage was executed and not where the mortgagor was domiciled. The mortgagor was surely outside the scope of the New Hampshire statute, not because she executed the mortgage in Massachusetts but because she was domiciled there.[92]

If the laws of the two states had been reversed and the mortgagor was incapable of making the mortgage by the law of her domicile (Massachusetts), but capable by the *lex situs* (New Hampshire), there would have been something to be said for applying the *lex situs* and holding the mortgage valid, at any rate if the mortgagee was domiciled and resident in New Hampshire. New Hampshire mortgagees ought not to be deprived of their security because of some lurking incapacity in the law of the mortgagor's domicile.

Capacity to take (as opposed to transfer) land in England is governed by English domestic law. Perhaps the most striking illustration of this principle is the former rule, abolished in 1870,[93] that an alien could not own land in England. A more modern, but still obsolete, illustration is afforded by *Attorney General v Parsons*,[94] where the House of Lords held that a company incorporated in the Republic of Ireland could not hold land in England without a licence in mortmain from the Crown.

Capacity: land abroad

The question what law governs capacity to transfer land situated abroad came before the Court of Appeal in *Bank of Africa v Cohen*,[95] where the *lex situs* was applied. The reasoning is, however, most unsatisfactory.

17–020

> A married woman, domiciled and resident with her husband in England, executed a deed in England whereby she agreed to mortgage land in Johannesburg to an English bank as security for past and future advances by the bank to her husband. The bank sought specific performance of the deed. The mortgagor's defence was that by South African law a married woman was incapable, with limited exceptions inapplicable in the instant case, of becoming surety for her husband. The trial judge found as a fact that she knew quite well what she was doing.

It was held that her capacity to make the contract was governed by South African law and the contract was therefore void. This decision seems unjust. The bank was left without security for advances made on the strength of the

---

[92] The reasoning is criticised on this ground by Cook, p.275, n.48, and Hancock, (1967) 20 Stanford L.Rev. 1, 31, though both writers approve the result.
[93] Naturalisation Act 1870 s.2.
[94] [1956] A.C. 421.
[95] [1909] 2 Ch. 129; criticised by Falconbridge, op. cit., p.629.

mortgagor's promise; and she was allowed to break her promise with impunity although she knew quite well what she was doing. The court made no attempt to ascertain either the policy of the South African law, or whether a South African court would have applied South African domestic law to this very case. Had it done so, it might well have discovered that the South African law laid down a policy not for South African land but for South African married women, and that the defendant was outside the scope of that law because she was domiciled in England. Moreover, the court was dealing not with a mortgage but with a contract to make a mortgage. If, as seems likely, the law governing the contract (at that date, the proper law of the contract) was English law, what was there to prevent the court from making a decree of specific performance? The court made no attempt to determine the proper law of the contract, but baldly asserted that the defendant's capacity was governed by the *lex situs*, and mechanically applied the domestic provisions of that law.

TANGIBLE MOVABLES

17–021 We now turn to examine the question of what law governs the validity of particular transfers of movables and the effect on the proprietary interests of the parties and those claiming under them.[96] By a "particular" transfer is meant, for example, a transfer by way of sale, gift, pledge, hire-purchase, or conditional sale. We are not concerned with general transfers made on occasions such as marriage or death: these are considered elsewhere.[97]

It is convenient to consider first the transfer of what are called "tangible movables", i.e. chattels, ordinary objects such as furniture, cars, or jewellery. But much property is intangible: simple contract debts, shares in companies, intellectual property rights, and so on. Diverse in nature, they are referred to collectively as "intangible movables" and are considered in a later part of this chapter.

Where the situs remains constant

17–022 In simple cases where the *situs* of the chattel remains constant at all material times, the *lex situs* governs the validity and effect of the transfer.[98] There is a consistent line of authority to that effect. "I do not think", said Maugham J, "that anyone can doubt that, with regard to the transfer of goods, the law applicable must be the *lex situs*. Business could not be carried on if that were not so".[99] "There is little doubt", said Devlin J, "that it is the *lex situs* which, as a general

---

[96] See Lalive, *The Transfer of Chattels in the Conflict of Laws* (1955); Zaphiriou, *The Transfer of Chattels in Private International Law* (1955); Chesterman, (1973) 22 I.C.L.Q. 213.

[97] See Chs 13 (matrimonial property) and 18 (succession).

[98] *Inglis v Usherwood* (1801) 1 East 515; *City Bank v Barrow* (1880) 5 App.Cas. 664; *Inglis v Robertson* [1898] A.C. 616; *Government of the Islamic Republic of Iran v Barakat Galleries Ltd* [2007] EWCA Civ 1374; [2008] 1 All E.R. 1177. The same principle applies to the acquisition of title in newly-created goods: *Glencore International AG v Metro Trading International* [2001] 1 Lloyd's Rep. 284 at 296.

[99] *Re Anziani* [1930] 1 Ch. 407, 420.

rule, governs the transfer of movables when effected contractually".[100] "The proper law governing the transfer of corporeal movable property", said Diplock LJ, "is the *lex situs*".[101] More recently, the authorities were reviewed and the principle reasserted by Moore-Bick J in *Glencore International AG v Metro Trading International*.[102] Applying the *lex situs* has the great advantage of certainty because, except where goods are in transit from one country to another,[103] it is likely to be easily ascertainable.

The *lex situs* rule governs not only questions of ownership but also the location of a possessory title. The Court of Appeal has accepted that the *lex situs* governs the question whether a party has an immediate right to the possession of goods for the purpose of establishing a claim in tort for conversion.[104]

It is of course possible to argue for the application of some other law than that of the *situs*. It would plainly be inappropriate to apply a law identified by reference to characteristics of the parties, such as their domicile or place of business.[105] Nor in modern conditions would it be sensible to apply the law of the place in which the relevant transaction occurs, for this can be purely fortuitous. The claims of the law governing the transaction by which the transfer is effected may seem stronger. A transfer may be invalid as a transfer yet valid as an executory agreement to transfer; there are advantages in recognising the links between the contractual and proprietary issues.

The issue was very fully examined in *Glencore International AG v Metro Trading International*.[106] Counsel for the claimants argued that when issues relating to the passing of property arose as between the immediate parties to a contract, English law ought to resolve any conflict between the terms of the contract and the *lex situs* by recognising and giving effect to the contract in accordance with its governing law in preference to the *lex situs*. In rejecting this argument, Moore-Bick J referred to the two main justifications for the *lex situs* rule: that it accords with the natural expectations of reasonable men and facilitates business, and indeed was required by considerations of commercial convenience; and that it reflects the practical realities of control over movables. He did not favour an exception in those cases involving only the two parties to the contract: consistency of principle requires that the same rule should apply whether or not third party interests were affected. The very nature of title to movables is that it gives the person in whom it is vested rights which can be

---

[100] *Bank voor Handel en Scheepvaart NV v Slatford* [1953] 1 Q.B. 248, 257.

[101] *Hardwick Game Farm v Suffolk Agricultural Poultry Producers Association* [1966] 1 W.L.R. 287, 330; affirmed by the House of Lords [1969] 2 A.C. 31.

[102] [2001] 1 Lloyd's Rep. 284. See also *Macmillan Inc v Bishopsgate Investment Trust Plc (No.3)* [1996] 1 W.L.R. 387 (title to shares in a company).

[103] Slade J in *Winkworth v Christie Manson & Woods Ltd* [1980] 1 Ch. 496 quoted with evident approval a rule that where goods are in transit, and their *situs* is casual or not known, a transfer which is valid and effective by its proper law will be valid and effective in England: see now Dicey, Morris and Collins, op. cit., at the Exception to Rule 133.

[104] *Government of the Islamic Republic of Iran v Barakat Galleries Ltd* [2007] EWCA Civ 1374; [2008] 1 All E.R. 1177 (where the point was agreed by counsel for both parties).

[105] Early continental writers held that *mobilia sequuntur personam* (movables follow the person) but this is nowhere followed today.

[106] [2001] 1 Lloyd's Rep. 284. The complex facts involved dealings in the United Arab Emirates (the *situs*) with oil the subject of contracts governed by English law. *Glencore* was approved on this point in *Dornoch Ltd v Westminster International BV* [2009] EWHC 1782 (Admlty).

maintained against all other parties. Questions of title are most likely to be of importance when one party to the transaction became insolvent, where the interests of third parties in the form of a general body of creditors may clearly be affected. Practical control over movables can ultimately be regulated and protected only by the state in which they are situated and the adoption of the *lex situs* rule in relation to the passing of property recognised that fact. That is just as true in relation to the passing of property between the parties to the transaction as it is in relation to the passing of property between one or other of them and a third party.

It is also the case that a transfer may be by way of a gift, so that the transferor is under no contractual obligation at all.[107] There may be two independent transfers, each governed by the law of a different country, e.g., where the title to goods is in dispute between an unpaid seller and a pledgee from the purchaser.[108] Moreover, a problem may arise although there has been no transfer at all. For instance, A finds B's ring in Scotland, takes it to England, and possesses it there for a period sufficient to extinguish B's title under the English, but not the Scottish, Statute of Limitations.

Renvoi

17–023   An issue addressed in a number of cases but which still awaits a definitive ruling from an appellate court, is the availability of *renvoi* in applying the *lex situs*. It was rightly said in *Glencore International AG v Metro Trading International*[109] that:

> "if the *lex situs* rule rests, at least in part, on a recognition of the practical control exercised by the State in which they are situated, there is something to be said for applying whatever rules of law the Courts of that state would actually apply in determining such questions".

It was not necessary to resolve the issue on the facts, and the point had also been left unresolved in the earlier case of *Winkworth v Christie Manson & Woods Ltd*.[110] More recent cases, examined in a later chapter,[111] show a strong judicial disinclination to accept the application of *renvoi* in this context.

Public policy

17–024   There is at least one exception to the *lex situs* rule: the English court may decline to give effect to the relevant rules of the *lex situs* on the ground of public policy.[112] A second exception has been suggested, that of want of good faith on

---

[107] See *Cochrane v Moore* (1890) 25 Q.B.D. 57 (where, however, the *lex situs* was not pleaded).
[108] See, e.g., *Inglis v Robertson* [1898] A.C. 616.
[109] [2001] 1 Lloyd's Rep 284.
[110] [1980] 1 Ch. 496. cf. *McMillan Inc v Bishopsgate Investment Trust Plc (No.3)* [1996] 1 W.LR 387 (at first instance: *renvoi* held inapplicable, but a case on priority in respect of intangibles; the *renvoi* issue was not taken on appeal).
[111] See para.20–002.
[112] *Winkworth v Christie Manson & Woods Ltd* [1980] 1 Ch. 496; *Glencore International AG v Metro Trading International* [2001] 1 Lloyd's Rep. 284.

the part of the person acquiring title.[113] The existence of any such exception, at least as distinct from public policy considerations, was doubted by Moore-Bick J in the *Glencore* case.[114]

Where the situs changes

Much more complicated problems arise if the *situs* of the goods does not remain constant at all material times, so that a choice has to be made between two or more *leges situs*. For example, a car is delivered to a hirer in England under a hire-purchase contract, taken by the hirer to France, and sold there to a purchaser in circumstances which give the purchaser a good title under the general doctrine of French law *en fait de meubles, la possession vaut titre*.[115]

17–025

The leading English case is *Cammell v Sewell*[116]:

> A, a domiciled Englishman, bought some timber in Russia and shipped it to England in a Prussian ship. The ship was wrecked off the coast of Norway. B, the master of the ship, sold the timber in Norway to C in circumstances which gave C a good title by the law of Norway, but not by English law. C brought the timber to England. It was held that C's title conferred by the *lex situs* prevailed over that of A.

Cammell v Sewell was followed in *Winkworth v Christie*[117] where works of art were stolen from the plaintiff's house in England, taken to Italy without his knowledge or consent, and there sold to the second defendant, an Italian, who sent them to the first defendant in England to be auctioned. By Italian law the second defendant had a good title. It was held that Italian law governed.

Cammell v Sewell is usually cited for the proposition that the English owner's title, validly acquired in Russia where he bought the timber, was lost by what happened in Norway. But it also decides that the Norwegian buyer's title, validly acquired in Norway, was not lost when he brought the timber to England. This second aspect of the case is just as important as the first; and it leads to the following distinction[118]:

> "A title to a tangible movable acquired or reserved [under the *lex situs*] will be recognised as valid in England if the movable is removed from the country where it was situated at the time when such title was acquired, unless and until such title is displaced by a new title acquired in accordance with the law of the country to which it is removed."

For the sake of clarity, let us call the country of the first *situs* X, and the country of the second *situs* Y. The law can be stated in four propositions.

(a) A title to goods acquired in X will be recognised in England if the goods are subsequently removed to Y, until some new title validly acquired in Y overrides the title acquired in X. If no such new title is acquired in Y after

---

[113] *Winkworth v Christie Manson & Woods Ltd* [1980] 1 Ch. 496.
[114] *Glencore International AG v Metro Trading International* [2001] 1 Lloyd's Rep. 284 at 295.
[115] French Civil Code, art.2279.
[116] (1860) 5 H. & N. 728.
[117] [1980] Ch. 496.
[118] See Dicey, Morris and Collins, op. cit., r.134.

the removal of the goods to Y, the fact that the title acquired by the law of X would not have been acquired by the law of Y is immaterial, for the goods were in X at the material time. This is the result of the decision in *Cammell v Sewell*[119]:

> "If, according to Norwegian law, the property passed by the sale in Norway to Clausen as an innocent purchaser, we do not think that the subsequent bringing of the property to England can alter the position of the parties".

(b)   If a new title is acquired under the law of Y after the removal of the goods to Y, which has the effect of overriding prior titles, the title previously acquired under the law of X is displaced. It was for this reason that A's Russian title was displaced by C's Norwegian title in *Cammell v Sewell*, since the sale by the master of the ship had by Norwegian law the effect of overriding prior titles. It was for this reason that A's English title was displaced by C's Italian title in *Winkworth v Christie*, since the sale by the thief had by Italian law the effect of overriding prior titles. Other instances of transactions which override prior titles in English domestic law are sales by a mercantile agent under statutes such as s.2 of the Factors Act 1889, and sales by a buyer in possession with the consent of the seller under statutes such as s.25 of the Sale of Goods Act 1979.[120] That the goods were removed to Y without the owner's consent makes no difference: "We do not think that goods which were wrecked here would on that account be less liable to our laws as to market overt[121] or as to the landlord's right of distress, merely because the owner did not foresee that they would come to England".[122]

(c)   The difficult intermediate case is where A has acquired or reserved a title to goods in X, and B, the person in possession of the goods, takes them to Y, where they are sold by B to a purchaser, the sale not being one which overrides prior titles, or attached by B's creditors, not being creditors claiming a paramount lien. By the law of X, the owner's title prevails over that of the purchaser or creditors; by the law of Y, it does not. But the reason it does not is quite different from that in paragraph (b) above. Here the purchaser or creditors are not saying to A: "Our title prevails over yours because the sale to or attachment by us overrides all prior titles by the law of Y". They are saying: "Our title prevails over yours because your title, validly acquired or reserved by the law of X, was not validly acquired or reserved by the law of Y".

In this situation, most of the English, American and Canadian cases uphold the title of the owner A against that of purchasers from or creditors

---

[119] (1860) 5 H. & N. 728, 742–743; *cf. Todd v Armour* (1882) 9 R. 901.

[120] *Cammell v Sewell*, cited above, at p.744; *Alcock v Smith* [1892] 1 Ch. 238, 267; *Embiricos v Anglo-Austrian Bank* [1905] 1 K.B. 677; *Century Credit Corporation v Richard* (1962) 34 D.L.R. (2d) 291; *Price Mobile Home Centres Inc v National Trailer Convoy of Canada* (1974) 44 D.L.R. (3d) 443; *Re Fuhrmann and Miller* (1977) 78 D.L.R. (3d) 284; *Maden v Long* [1983] 1 W.W.R. 649.

[121] The special rules under which overriding title was acquired on a sale in market overt were abolished in England in 1995.

[122] *Cammell v Sewell*, above, at p.745.

of B.[123] The reason is simple: since the goods were in X when A's title was reserved, the law of X should govern that reservation of title. As the matter was put in the *Glencore* case,[124] English law recognises the effect which the *lex situs* gives to a transaction, but does not recognise any attempt by the *lex situs* to re-characterise a transaction which occurred when the goods were situated within another country.

Very often the law of Y differs from the law of X in that it requires hire-purchase or conditional sales contracts to be registered in Y. There is an observable tendency for courts, even courts in Y, to hold that the statutory registration requirements of the law of Y are confined to domestic transactions,[125] or can be satisfied if A registers soon after he becomes aware that the chattel has been removed to Y, even though this may not be until after it has been sold there to a purchaser.[126] Thus in a leading American case[127]:

> A & Co, a Californian corporation, sold a motor car in California to B, a Californian resident, on hire-purchase terms. It was agreed that title should remain with A until the price was fully paid and that until then B would not remove the car out of California. Before the price was fully paid, B took the car to New York without A's knowledge or consent and sold it there to C, a bona fide purchaser. By the law of California, A's title was superior to any title derived from B on resale, even to an innocent purchaser for value. By the law of New York, all such reservations of title were void against subsequent purchasers in good faith unless the contract was registered in New York. The contract never was so registered. The New York Court of Appeals held that A & Co's title was good against C.

It follows from what has been said that whether A loses his title when his goods are removed to Y and dealt with there depends entirely on why the law of Y would say that his title is lost.[128] It may do so, generally speaking, for one of two reasons: either because it says that an event which has occurred in Y has the effect of overriding prior titles, or because it does not recognise that the transaction whereby A acquired or reserved his title in X had this effect by the law of Y. In the former case, the law of Y governs, and A's title is lost, because the law of Y (*lex situs*) determines the effect of the transaction in Y when the goods were in Y, and the law of X is irrelevant to that transaction. In the latter case, the law of X governs, and A retains his title, because the law of X (*lex situs*) determines the effect of the transaction in X when the goods were in X, and the law of Y is irrelevant to that transaction. This conclusion is the necessary consequence of the proposition advanced in paragraph (a) above. If A acquires a valid title to goods in X, we have seen that A's title is upheld if the goods are removed to Y, even though A would not have acquired a good title by law of Y. Thus, if B

---

[123] *Simpson v Fogo* (1863) 1 H. & M. 195; *Goetschius v Brightman* (1927) 245 N.Y. 186; 156 N.E. 660; *Industrial Acceptance Corporation v La Flamme* [1950] 2 D.L.R. 822; *Rennie Car Sales v Union Acceptance Corporation* [1955] 4 D.L.R. 822.

[124] *Glencore International AG v Metro Trading International* [2001] 1 Lloyd's Rep. 284 at 295–296.

[125] See, e.g., *Goetschius v Brightman* (1927) 245 N.Y. 186; 156 N.E. 660.

[126] *Rennie Car Sales v Union Acceptance Corporation*, above; *McAloney v McInnes and General Motors Acceptance Corporation* (1956) 2 D.L.R. (2d) 666. See Davis, (1964) 13 I.C.L.Q. 53.

[127] *Goetschius v Brightman* (1927) 245 N.Y. 186; 156 N.E. 660.

[128] See Morris, (1945) 22 B.Y.I.L. 232, 238–246.

removes A's goods to Y, A's title is still good. If B now sells the goods in Y to C, there is no reason why B should be capable of passing a better title than he has himself, unless the law of Y attributes this special effect to the sale there.

This distinction was drawn very clearly in a Canadian case[129]:

> A & Co sold a motor car in Quebec to B, a resident of Quebec, under a conditional sales contract which provided that the car should remain the property of A & Co. until the price was fully paid. Before the price was fully paid, B took the car to Ontario without the knowledge or consent of A & Co and sold it there to C, a resident of Ontario, who had no knowledge of A & Co's rights in the car. The law of Ontario required conditional sales contracts to be registered; the law of Quebec did not. The Ontario Court of Appeal held that A & Co's title would have prevailed against C, but for the fact that B was a person who had agreed to buy goods and was in possession of them with the consent of the seller and could therefore pass a good title to C under s.25(2) of the Ontario Sale of Goods Act.

In the course of his judgment, Kelly JA said:

> "If the laws of Ontario were to seek to invalidate [A & Co's] title by refusing to recognise that the transaction which took place in Quebec had the effect of continuing the title in [A & Co], this attempt of Ontario law to invalidate a transaction taking place in Quebec would be bad because the validity of a Quebec transaction must be determined by the laws of Quebec, the *lex situs* . . . However, if the laws of Ontario provide that a later transaction which takes place wholly within Ontario has the effect of overriding prior titles, then since Ontario does not seek to give its laws any extra-territorial effect the laws of Ontario prevail and the title created under the laws of Ontario displaces the title reserved in the Quebec transaction".

(d)   In the situations so far discussed, it has been assumed that the law of Y affords greater protection to purchasers and creditors than the law of X. The reverse side of the usual picture is presented when chattels are taken into Y and dealt with there in circumstances which deprive the owner of title by the law of X, but not by the law of Y. Suppose that A delivers a chattel in State X to B, a broker, for the purposes of sale, but reserving title: no title is to pass to B. B takes the chattel to State Y and there sells it to C. By the law of State Y, A's reservation of title is good as against third parties. In the law of State X, the circumstances of the transaction are such that A's title was extinguished. A has good title, for the law of State X was not the *lex situs* at the time of the relevant transaction.[130]

---

[129] *Century Credit Corporation v Richard* (1962) 34 D.L.R. (2d) 291, 293–294; cf. *Traders Finance Corporation v Dawson Implements Ltd* (1959) 15 D.L.R. (2d) 515. Contrast *Industrial Acceptance Corporation v La Flamme* [1950] 2 D.L.R. 822, approved in *Century Credit Corporation v Richard*, but distinguished on the ground that the court overlooked s.25(2) of the Ontario Sale of Goods Act.

[130] See *Cline v Russell* (1908) 2 Alta. L.R. 79; *Rennie Car Sales v Union Acceptance Corporation* [1955] 4 D.L.R. 822; Morris, (1945) 22 B.Y.I.L. 232, 246–247.

INTANGIBLE MOVABLES

A valiant effort was made by counsel in *Raiffeisen Zentralbank Österreich AG v Five Star General Trading LLC*[131] to argue that the *lex situs* rule applied equally to intangible movables. The argument was rejected, not least because the allocation of a *situs* to an intangible is necessarily quite artificial.[132] (There are rules which do that, for example the rule that a debt is regarded by English law as located where it is enforceable).[133] Equally unsuccessful was the argument that in the case of intangibles there could be the same distinction as can be drawn in the context of tangibles: that between the contractual and proprietary aspects of transactions.[134] The various issues are clearly governed by the Rome I Regulation.

17–026

The *Raiffeisen* case also confirmed the significance of another distinction, that between voluntary and involuntary assignments. There are processes (such as garnishment, considered more fully below)[135] under which the debtor is obliged to pay not the original creditor, A, but some other person, and that transfer is involuntary on the part of A. An example is an attachment of earnings order, under which an employer must pay part of an employee's salary to satisfy a court order. Voluntary assignments, but not involuntary assignments, are now governed, in respect of contracts concluded after 17 December 2009, by art.14 of the Rome I Regulation. As the Court of Appeal observed in the *Raiffeisen* case, the difference between the consensual and non-consensual cases is such that it is neither surprising nor inconvenient that they have different choice of law rules.

Identifying the issues

The voluntary assignment of an intangible movable can raise a number of different issues, some of which can be illustrated by using the example of a simple contract debt, one created by a transaction between A (the creditor) and B (the debtor). By a further transaction, A assigns the benefit of the debt to C.[136]

17–027

One set of questions concerns the validity of that second transaction, as between A and C. Logically, that will be governed by the law applicable to that transaction. But there are other questions which cannot be referred to that law.

One is the prior question whether the debt is assignable at all, a question that can only be answered by reference to the law which governs the creation of the debt, the law applicable to the original transaction between A and B. Another issue is that of priorities, were A to assign the same debt, in separate transactions, to C and to D: has C or D the better claim? The issue (which may be simply a question of which transaction came first, but may involve a consideration of

---

[131] [2001] EWCA Civ 68; [2001] Q.B. 825; Briggs, (2001) 72 B.Y.I.L. 461.

[132] In the *Raiffeisen* case, the *situs* was said to be France the claim being on insurers resident in France. The deed of assignment was expressly governed by English law.

[133] See *Hillside (New Media) Ltd v Baasland* [2010] EWHC 3336 (Comm.).

[134] For discussion of this and related issues, see Moshinsky, (1992) 108 L.Q.R. 591; Struycken, [1998] L.M.C.L.Q. 345.

[135] See para.17–032.

[136] There are of course many more complex cases, and there may be special considerations in, for example, the field of intellectual property and in relation to various forms of financial instruments.

further steps such as giving notice to B or making an entry on a register of some sort) cannot be resolved by reference to the law governing either of the competing assignments. It is best also referred to the law applicable to the original transaction between A and B.

Intrinsic validity

17–028 The intrinsic validity of a voluntary assignment is governed by art.14(1) of the Rome I Regulation[137]: the relationship between assignor and assignee under a voluntary assignment or contractual subrogation of a claim against another person (the debtor) is to be governed by the law that applies under the Regulation to the contract between the assignor and assignee.[138] "Contractual subrogation" involves the creation of subrogation rights by contract, notably in an insurance context. It is clear that art.14(1) govern the proprietary as well as the contractual issues as between assignor and assignee.[139]

This law will govern issues as to the formal and essential validity of the assignment. The question of the capacity of the parties to make or to take under the assignment is more difficult; the Rome I Regulation does not address this issue.[140] It was considered in the leading case of *Republica de Guatemala v Nunez*.[141]

> In 1906, the President of Guatemala deposited £20,000 in a London bank. In 1919 in Guatemala, he assigned this sum to his illegitimate son, Nunez, a minor domiciled and resident in Guatemala. By English law the assignment was valid in all respects. By the law of Guatemala it was formally invalid and a minor could not accept a voluntary assignment unless a tutor had been appointed by a judge on his behalf; this was not done.

Unfortunately, the judges gave different reasons for their decision that the assignment was governed by Guatemalan law, and only Scrutton and Lawrence LJJ distinguished between the various grounds of invalidity. On the capacity point, both these judges held that the issue was governed either by the law of the domicile or by the law of the country in which the assignment took place. So do the judgments of Day and Wills JJ in *Lee v Abdy*[142]:

> H, domiciled in Cape Province, insured his life with an English insurance company and assigned the policy to his wife in Cape Province. The assignment was valid by English law but void by the law of the Cape as a gift between husband and wife. It was held that Cape law governed and that the assignment was void.

---

[137] cf. the rather different language of the Rome Convention, art.12, providing that the mutual obligations of the assignor and assignee are governed by the law which under the Convention applies to the contract between the assignor and assignee.
[138] Article 14(3) offers a partial definition of the concept of assignment, as including outright transfers of claims, transfers of claims by way of security and pledges or other security rights over claims.
[139] See Recital (38) to the Regulation and T.C. Hartley, (2011) 60 I.C.L.Q. 29.
[140] Save for the special rule in art.13 of the Regulation; see para.13–035 and following.
[141] [1927] 1 K.B. 669.
[142] (1886) 17 Q.B.D 309.

However, there can be no doubt that in the *Guatemala* case Guatemalan law was the law applicable to the assignment and that in *Lee v Abdy* it was the law of the Cape. It is submitted that the governing law of the assignment is a far better test of capacity than either the law of the domicile or the law of the place of the assignment. It also produces a result harmonising with the principle in art.12(1) and applying to other aspects of the mutual obligations of the assignor and assignee.

Assignability

In some systems of law some kinds of debts cannot be assigned at all, for obvious reasons of social policy: e.g. policies of life insurance, future wages, pensions, maintenance payable to a wife or child. By art.14(2) of the Rome I Regulation, the assignability of a right is determined by "the law governing the right", in the case of a contractual right that applying under the other provisions of the Regulation.

17–029

Other issues

The same rule determines the relationship between the assignee and the debtor, the conditions under which the assignment or subrogation can be invoked against the debtor and whether the debtor's obligations have been discharged.[143] This category of issues would seem to include such questions as the need for notice of the assignment to be given to the debtor, whether the assignee takes subject to equities, the effect of the debtor paying the assignee instead of the assignor, and that, once much debated, as to the priority between competing assignments of the same right.

17–030

That priority issues are included seems to have been the opinion of the Court of Appeal in *Raiffeisen Zentralbank Österreich AG v Five Star General Trading LLC*[144] but the debates surrounding the drafting of the Rome I Regulation suggest otherwise. The Commission's original proposal included a rule under which the issue of priority would be governed by the law of the country where the assignor was habitually resident. This rule could have been difficult for financial institutions to operate and was dropped; though the Commission is to return to the issue.[145] In its consultation document on whether the UK should opt in to the Regulation, the Ministry of Justice assumed that the Rome Convention did not address the issue and that national law governed. English law would seem to subject the priority issue to the law of the original claim, which happens to be the law identified by art.14(2) of the Regulation.[146]

---

[143] *Raiffeisen Zentralbank Österreich AG v Five Star General Trading LLC* [2001] EWCA Civ 68; [2001] Q.B. 825, declining to follow a Dutch decision, *Brandsma v Hansa Chemie AG* (Hoge Raad, May 16, 1997, N.J. 1998 No. 585) which gave a wider effect to art.12(1) (see Struycken, [1998] L.M.C.L.Q. 345 and more generally A. Flessner and H. Verhagen, *Assignment in European Private International Law* (2006)).

[144] [2001] EWCA Civ 68; [2001] Q.B. 825.

[145] See Regulation, art.27(2) on the duty to report on the matter.

[146] See *Kelly v Selwyn* [1905] 2 Ch. 117.

Legal subrogation

17–031   Although not really a case of assignment, similar issues may arise where a person (the creditor) has a contractual claim against another (the debtor) and a third person has a duty to satisfy the creditor, or has in fact satisfied the creditor in discharge of that duty. Article 15 of the Rome I Regulation provides that in such cases, the law which governs the third person's duty to satisfy the creditor determines whether and to what extent the third person is entitled to exercise against the debtor the rights which the creditor had against the debtor under the law governing their relationship.

GARNISHMENT: THIRD-PARTY DEBT ORDERS

17–032   The determined expulsion of traditional language from the Civil Procedure Rules means that "garnish" will soon be a forgotten term, depriving authors of the chance to deploy jokes of a culinary variety. The Rules now speak of "third-party debt orders": orders by which a judgment creditor secures the payment to him of money which a third party (referred to in the older cases as the garnishee) who is within the jurisdiction owes to the judgment debtor.[147] A similar process (called arrestment in Scotland) is allowed by the laws of other countries. In a purely domestic case, the third party is of course effectively discharged from further liability once he has paid the judgment creditor.[148] To that extent it amounts to an assignment of the debt, but it is not a voluntary assignment and is not affected by the Rome I Regulation.

The English court will have jurisdiction to make an order only if the third party is within the jurisdiction of the court.[149] Mere temporary presence at the time the initial "interim third-party debt order" is made may suffice, as will submission to the jurisdiction by a person physically absent.[150] The English court will not make an order in respect of a foreign debt, one governed by foreign law. There was some difference of emphasis in speeches in the House of Lords in *Société Eram Shipping Co Ltd v Compagnie Internationale de Navigation*[151] as to whether this was a rule of jurisdiction or a principle followed by the English courts; and indeed as to whether that difference of emphasis had any practical effect.

In some cases the third party is in double jeopardy. This can be illustrated by the facts of the *Eram* case:

> Eram, a Romanian company, obtained judgment against A Co and B (the judgment debtors, both resident in Hong Kong) in the French courts. The judgment was registered for

---

[147] CPR r.72.1(1).

[148] For this reason the process is only available where the debt is owed solely to one judgment debtor: CPR r.72(2)(1) as interpreted in *Taurus Petroleum Ltd v State Oil Marketing Co* [2013] EWHC 3494 (Comm.), [2014] 1 Lloyd's Rep. 432.

[149] CPR r.72.1(1).

[150] *SCF Finance Co Ltd v Masri (No.3)*[1987] Q.B. 1028.

[151] [2003] UKHL 30, [2004] A.C. 260, noted Rogerson, [2003] C.L.J. 576, Briggs, (2003) 74 B.Y.I.L. 511. See also the speeches in *Deutsche Schachtbau-und Tiefbohrgesellschaft mbH v Shell International Petroleum Co Ltd* [1990] 1 A.C. 295, where the debt was situated in England.

enforcement in England. The judgment debtors had an account with the third party, a Hong Kong bank,[152] to which Hong Kong law applied. Eram obtained an interim third party debt order in England requiring, in effect, the bank to apply the money in the account to pay the sums due under the French judgment.

The difficulty for the bank was that the courts in Hong Kong would not recognise a third party debt order made in England in relation to a debt situated in Hong Kong; as the House of Lords admitted, that was not "an unusual or idiosyncratic rule but one which reflects general international practice". The bank might therefore find that it had paid money in accordance with the third party debt order, but that under the law of Hong Kong this payment would not discharge its obligations to the judgment-debtor.

The House of Lords held that it was not open to the English court to make an order in circumstances, such as those of the *Eram* case, where it is clear or appears that the making of the order will not discharge the debt of the third party to the judgment debtor according to the law governing that debt.

The *Eram* decision was followed in a companion case decided on the same day, *Kuwait Oil Tanker SAK v Qabazard*[153] which also concerned the effect of provisions in the Lugano Convention, found also in the Brussels I Regulation. Article 22 of the latter provides:

"The following courts shall have exclusive jurisdiction, regardless of domicile:

. . .

5.   in proceedings concerned with the enforcement of judgments, the courts of the Member State in which the judgment has been or is to be enforced"

The judgment creditors sought a third-party debt order in respect of bank accounts in Switzerland.[154] The House of Lords held that Switzerland was the state in which the judgment was being enforced, and therefore the Swiss courts had exclusive jurisdiction. It follows from this decision and the *Eram* case that the English courts (a) have no jurisdiction to make a third party debt order where the debt is located in a Member State or a state party to the Brussels or Lugano Convention, and (b) will not make an order when the law of the State in which the debt is located will not recognise payment under the order as discharging the third party's obligations to the judgment debtor.

This is an area in which the European Community may take action. A Green Paper published in 2006 raised the possibility of creating a European order for the attachment of bank accounts.[155] An attachment order issued in one Member State would be recognised and enforceable throughout the EU without the need for a declaration of enforceability.

There is surprisingly little English authority on the converse question, namely, when will effect be given by English courts to a foreign garnishment order. Clearly, if no effect is given, there may be a risk that the third party will be

---

[152] The Hong Kong bank had branches in England and so was within the jurisdiction for the purpose of the Rules.

[153] [2003] UKHL 31; [2004] 1 A.C. 300.

[154] As in the *Eram* case, the Swiss bank had a branch in England and so was present within the jurisdiction.

[155] COM(2006) 618 final.

compelled to pay the debt twice. Here again it seems that the test is whether the debt is situated, in other words properly recoverable, in the foreign country where the order was made.[156]

GOVERNMENTAL SEIZURE OF PROPERTY

17–033   It is the practice of some governments to seize private property on various pretexts and in the supposed interests of the state, often with inadequate compensation payable to the owners, and sometimes with no compensation payable at all. The issue can be one of considerable political and economic importance, especially in the context of foreign investment.[157] The state may nationalise foreign companies, or requisition or expropriate property: nothing seems to turn on the precise terminology used.

Difficult questions in the conflict of laws are presented if such decrees purport to have extra-territorial effect, or if the property affected by the decree is later brought to England. The questions tend also to be associated with two important principles which are discussed elsewhere in this book. These are: first, the principle that English courts will not enforce directly or indirectly a foreign penal law[158]; and, secondly, the principle that English courts have in general no jurisdiction to entertain an action which affects a foreign sovereign's interest in property.[159]

The principle on which English courts proceed when deciding whether to recognise foreign governmental decrees purporting to seize private property is comparatively simple to state but often difficult to apply. The principle is that the decree will be recognised as having deprived the owner of property if the property was within the territory of the foreign state at the time of the decree,[160] but not otherwise.[161] The application of the principle in any particular case involves answering three questions. First, what was the legal situation of the property at the time of the decree? Secondly, did the decree purport to affect property situate at that place? Thirdly, is the decree a part of the law of a place which the English courts can recognise? These three questions will now be discussed in turn.

---

[156] See *Rossano v Manufacturers Life Insurance Co Ltd* [1963] 2 Q.B. 352, 374–383; *Deutsche Schachtbau v Shell International Petroleum Co Ltd* [1990] 1 A.C. 295, 354.

[157] See Asante, (1988) 37 I.C.L.Q. 588.

[158] Above, para.4–006.

[159] Above, para.8–002.

[160] *Luther v Sagor* [1921] 3 K.B. 532; *Princess Paley Olga v Weisz* [1929] 1 K.B. 718; *Re Banque des Marchands de Moscou* [1952] 1 All E.R. 1269; *Jabbour v Custodian of Israeli Absentee Property* [1954] 1 W.L.R 139; *Re Helbert Wagg & Co Ltd's Claim* [1956] Ch. 323, 344–349; *Williams & Humbert Ltd v W & H Trade Marks (Jersey) Ltd* [1986] A.C. 368.

[161] *Lecouturier v Rey* [1910] A.C. 262; *The Jupiter (No.3)* [1927] P. 122, 250; *Re Russian Bank for Foreign Trade* [1933] Ch. 745, 766–767; *Government of the Republic of Spain v National Bank of Scotland*, 1939 S.C. 413; *Frankfurther v W L Exner Ltd* [1947] Ch. 629; *Novello & Co Ltd v Hinrichsen Edition Ltd* [1951] Ch. 595; *Bank voor Handel en Scheepvart NV v Slatford* [1953] 1 Q.B. 248; *Attorney General of New Zealand v Ortiz* [1984] A.C. 1; affd. on other grounds ibid., p.41.

The situation of property

The property may be movable or immovable, tangible or intangible. Artificial **17–034** rules have to be adopted in order to ascribe a location, a *situs*, to intangible things or choses in action. The general principle is that choses in action are situated where they are properly recoverable. Thus a simple contract debt is situated where the debtor resides and can be sued and presumably keeps his or her assets.[162] This is so even if the contract provides for payment at another place.[163] There may of course be a number of countries in which the debtor can be sued, and it may well be that the residence of a company for this purpose can be equated with its domicile for the purposes of the Civil Jurisdiction and Judgments Act 1982. If the debtor resides in more countries than one, and the creditor either expressly or impliedly stipulates for payment at one of them, then the debt will be situated there.[164] If there is no such stipulation, the debt is situated at that place of residence where it would be paid in the ordinary course of business. Shares in a company are situated where, as between the shareholder and the company, they can be effectively dealt with according to the law under which the company was incorporated. Thus if shares are transferable only upon a register they will be situated at the place where the appropriate register is kept.[165] Where they are transferable upon more than one register they will be situated at the register where they would be dealt with in the ordinary course by the registered owner.[166] Intellectual property rights owe their origin to the law of a particular country, and are said to be situated in that country.[167]

Tangible objects are, as a general rule, legally situated where they physically are. But ships and aircraft may be an exception. There are dicta indicating (though somewhat faintly) that a ship on the high seas is deemed to be situate at her port of registry.[168] But this applies only to ships on the high seas. When a ship is in territorial or national waters, the artificial *situs* is displaced by the actual *situs*, and the ship is treated like any other chattel.[169] Hence, a foreign governmental decree requisitioning a ship registered in that foreign State will not be recognised if, at the time of the decree, the ship is in an English port.[170] What has been said about ships may also be true of aircraft. An aircraft in flight over the high seas or over a no man's land such as the North Pole or the Antarctic might well be held to be situate in its country of registration.[171]

---

[162] *New York Life Insurance Co v Public Trustee* [1924] 2 Ch. 101; *Deutsche Schachtbau v Shell International Petroleum Co Ltd* [1990] A.C. 295.

[163] *Re Helbert Wagg & Co Ltd's Claim* [1956] Ch. 323.

[164] *Jabbour v Custodian of Israeli Absentee Property* [1954] 1 W.LR 139 (insurance by English company of property in Israel; company resident in both England and Israel; debt held situated in Israel).

[165] *Brassard v Smith* [1925] A.C. 371; *R. v Williams* [1942] A.C. 541.

[166] *R. v Williams*, above; *Treasurer of Ontario v Aberdein* [1947] A.C. 24; *Standard Chartered Bank Ltd v I.R.C.* [1978] 1 W.L.R. 1160.

[167] *Lecouturier v Rey* [1910] A.C. 262; *Novello & Co Ltd v Hinrichsen Edition Ltd* [1951] Ch. 595.

[168] *The Jupiter* [1924] P. 236, 239; *The Cristina* [1938] A.C. 485, 509.

[169] *Trustees Executors and Agency Co Ltd v IRC* [1973] Ch. 254.

[170] *Government of the Republic of Spain v National Bank of Scotland*, 1939 SC 413; *Laane v Estonian State Cargo and Passenger Line* [1949] 2 D.L.R. 641.

[171] *Blue Sky One Ltd v Mahan Air* [2010] EWHC 631 (Comm.).

The interpretation of the decree

17–035 Whether the decree purports to affect the property in question can only be answered by interpreting the decree. There is an observable tendency for English courts to hold whenever possible that the decree does not purport to have extra-territorial effect,[172] since this will often provide an easy answer to the dispute between the parties.

Recognition of the foreign act

17–036 If the seizure is to be recognised in England it must have some standing in the law of the place where it occurs; forcible seizure by a revolutionary mob will not be recognised. But what is one day a revolutionary mob may the next day be the effective government of an existing or a newly independent State. It was formerly the convenient practice of the UK Government to accord recognition to foreign governments, either de jure or de facto. The courts would recognise an act of a foreign government accorded at least de facto recognition, even if the recognition came after the act in question.[173] The acts of an unrecognised government might be given effect if it could be treated as a subordinate body set up by another (recognised) government; this approach was applied to acts of the former East German Government as a subordinate body of the Soviet Union.[174] However, in 1980 the UK Government announced that it would no longer accord recognition to governments, although it would continue to accord recognition to states in accordance with international practice.[175] For the purposes of legal proceedings, the attitude of the Government as to whether a new régime qualified to be treated as a government would have to be inferred from the nature of the dealings, if any, that the Government might have with it, and in particular whether it dealt with the régime on a normal government-to-government basis.[176] In *Republic of Somalia v Woodhouse Drake and Carey (Suisse) SA*,[177] the absence of such dealings was taken into account, along with other factors such as the extent of the control exercised by the "interim government" whose acts were in issue.

---

[172] e.g., *Lecouturier v Rey* [1910] A.C. 262; *The Jupiter (No.3)* [1927] P. 122, 145; *Re Russian Bank for Foreign Trade* [1933] Ch. 745. 767.

[173] *Luther v Sagor* [1921] 1 K.B. 456.

[174] *Carl Zeiss Stiftung v Rayner & Keeler Ltd (No.2)* [1967] 1 A.C. 853. See also *Gur Corp v Trust Bank of Africa Ltd* [1987] Q.B. 559.

[175] For the complications ensuing, see *R. (Kibris Turk Hava Yollari) v Secretary of State for Transport* [2009] EWHC 1918 (Admin.); [2010] 1 All E.R. (Comm) 253 (re the so-called Turkish Republic of N Cyprus).

[176] See (1980) 51 B.Y.I.L. 367–368; Warbrick, (1981) 30 I.C.L.Q. 568, 576–592.

[177] [1993] Q.B. 54.

Property within the confiscating state

If a foreign decree is entitled to recognition under these principles, the effect to be given to it depends upon the location of the property it purports to seize. It will operate to affect rights to property if the property is within the territory of the foreign state and the foreign state has reduced the property to possession.[178] The leading case is *Luther v Sagor*[179]:

> A & Co, a Russian company, had a factory or mill in Russia where in 1919 they had a large stock of manufactured boards. The Soviet Government promulgated a decree vesting the property of all sawmills and woodworking establishments in the state. In reliance on this decree State officials seized A & Co's timber and sold it to B, an American firm carrying on business in London. B imported the timber into England. A & Co claimed a declaration that the timber was their property. Roche J granted the declaration, on the ground that His Majesty's Government had not recognised the Soviet Government as the government of a sovereign State. B appealed. Before the hearing of the appeal the Foreign Office informed B's solicitors that His Majesty's Government recognised the Soviet Government as the *de facto* government of Russia. The Court of Appeal gave judgment for B.

17–037

The principle in *Luther v Sagor* was accepted and applied by the House of Lords in *Williams & Humbert Ltd v W&H Trade Marks (Jersey) Ltd*.[180] The underlying dispute in that case concerned the "Dry Sack" sherry trademark which had belonged to the plaintiff English company, a wholly-owned subsidiary of R, a Spanish company. The Spanish Government compulsorily acquired all the shares in R and this act was recognised as effective. It did not seek to change the ownership of the shares in the English company; they remained the property of R (though of course the English company was now subject to the control of R's new owner, the Spanish authorities).

Property outside the confiscating state

The approach of the English courts to foreign decrees is quite different where the property is outside the territorial limits of the foreign state. As Lord Templeman put it in *Williams & Humbert Ltd v W&H Trade Marks (Jersey) Ltd*[181]:

> "There is undoubtedly a domestic and international rule which prevents one sovereign state from changing title to property so long as that property is situate in another state. If the British government purported to acquire compulsorily the railway lines from London to Newhaven and the railway lines from Dieppe to Paris, the ownership of the railway lines situate in England would vest in the British government but the ownership of the railway lines in France would remain undisturbed."

17–038

Accordingly, the English courts will not give effect to a foreign decree so far as it purports to deal with rights in property in England.

---

[178] *Brokaw v Seatrain UK Ltd* [1971] 2 Q.B. 476; *Government of the Islamic Republic of Iran v Barakat Galleries Ltd* [2007] EWCA Civ 1374; [2009] Q.B. 22.

[179] [1921] 3 K.B. 532. See also *Princess Paley Olga v Weisz* [1929] 1 K.B. 718.

[180] [1986] A.C. 368.

[181] [1986] A.C. 368. See also *Kuwait Airways Corp v Iraqi Airways Co (Nos 4 and 5)* [2002] UKHL 10; [2002] 2 A.C. 883.

Public policy

17–039   In *Bank voor Handel en Scheepvaart NV v Slatford*,[182] Devlin J, after an
exhaustive review of the authorities, refused to give effect to a decree of the
Netherlands Government-in-exile in England which purported to transfer to the
state the property in England and elsewhere of persons resident in enemy-
occupied Holland. He refused to follow the anomalous decision in *Lorentzen v
Lydden & Co Ltd*[183] where effect had been given to a not dissimilar decree of the
Norwegian Government-in-exile; that case, which is no longer good law, was
based on the desirability of enforcing an act of an allied Government acting at a
critical time in its, and England's, history. Devlin J rejected the idea that the
English court should consider what he described as "the political merits" of such
a decree. The same view was taken by the Court of Appeal in *Peer International
Corp v Termidor Music Publishers Ltd*[184]: the court refused to give any weight to
an argument that, because a Cuban decree was made for "benevolent" reasons, it
should be treated as having effect on property in England. A public policy
exception to the principle that a foreign decree cannot affect property in England
was rejected for a set of reasons advanced by counsel and accepted by the Court
of Appeal:

(1)   it would subordinate English property law to that of a foreign state;
(2)   the rule would be founded and would operate by reference to public policy
       which could change from time to time and could be uncertain;
(3)   it would require the English courts to assess the merits of the foreign
       legislation;
(4)   it would lead to intractable problems when the property was situated in a
       third state;
(5)   it would require the court to balance one public policy against the public
       policy that states do not interfere with property situated abroad, and
(6)   it would lead to great uncertainty.

There are, however, grounds upon which the English courts may refuse to
recognise or to give effect to a foreign decree, even in cases where the property
was in the foreign state at the time of the decree. They were analysed by Nourse
J at first instance in *Williams & Humbert Ltd v W&H Trade Marks (Jersey)
Ltd*,[185] an analysis subsequently adopted by the Court of Appeal.[186] English law
will not recognise certain foreign confiscatory laws: those which are discriminatory on grounds of race, religion or the like and constitute a grave infringement of
human rights.[187] Similarly the English courts will not recognise decrees which
discriminate against British nationals in time of war by purporting to confiscate

---

[182] [1953] 1 Q.B. 248.
[183] [1942] 2 K.B. 202.
[184] [2003] EWCA Civ 1156; [2004] Ch. 212.
[185] [1986] A.C. 368.
[186] See *Settebello Ltd v Banco Totta & Acores* [1985] 1 W.L.R. 1050.
[187] See *Oppenheimer v Cattermole* [1976] A.C. 249.

their movable property situated in the foreign State.[188] Nor will the English court enforce a foreign law confiscating property in a foreign State if the law is categorised as penal.[189]

However, Nourse J held that there was no additional category of decrees which would be denied recognition merely because they purport to confiscate the property of particular individuals[190] or categories of individuals.[191] There also seems to be no place in modern English law for an argument that a decree should be denied recognition or enforcement because no compensation, or inadequate compensation, is payable to the owner under the decree. In one case,[192] Scott LJ considered that a decree providing for only 25 per cent compensation was obviously penal. In two later cases,[193] Nazi decrees directed against Jewish businesses were treated as penal not so much because the owners of the businesses were Jews as because the decrees were confiscatory and no compensation was payable. On the other hand, in *Luther v Sagor*[194] and *Princess Paley Olga v Weisz*[195] the decrees were not treated as penal although no compensation at all was payable. The better view would seem to be that whether or not compensation is payable is irrelevant.[196] This is certainly the more convenient view: it would be a thankless task for a court to have to decide what amount of compensation is adequate, and whether a promise to pay compensation at some time in the future is worth more than the paper it is written on.

---

[188] *Wolff v Oxholm* (1817) 6 M. & S. 92; *Re Fred Krupp AG* [1917] 2 Ch. 188; *Re Helbert Wagg & Co Ltd's Claim* [1956] Ch. 323 at 345.

[189] *Banco de Vizcaya v Don Alfonso de Borbon y Austria* [1935] 1 K.B. 140.

[190] cf. *Banco de Vizcaya v Don Alfonso de Borbon y Austria* [1935] 1 K.B. 140, which Nourse J would rest on the fact that the decree was penal in the criminal law sense; *The Rose Mary* [1953] 1 W.L.R. 246, as explained in *Re Helbert Wagg & Co Ltd's Claim* [1956] Ch. 323, 346, an explanation rejected by Nourse J.

[191] See the decree confiscating the property of the House of Romanov mentioned in *Princess Paley Olga v Weisz* [1929] 1 K.B. 718, 722. The plaintiff's property was not caught by the decree because her marriage to the Grand Duke Paul was morganatic.

[192] *A/S Tallina Laevauhisus v Estonian State SS Line* (1947) 80 Ll.L.R. 99, 111. cf. *Laane v Estonian State Cargo and Passenger Line* [1949] 2 D.L.R. 641.

[193] *Frankfurther v W L Exner Ltd* [1947] Ch. 629; *Novello & Co Ltd v Hinrichsen Edition Ltd* [1951] Ch. 595.

[194] [1921] 3 K.B. 532.

[195] [1929] 1 K.B. 718.

[196] See especially the judgments of Devlin J in *Bank voor Handel en Scheepvaart NV v Slatford* [1953] 1 Q.B. 248, 258, 260–263, and of Upjohn J in *Re Helbert Wagg & Co Ltd's Claim* [1956] Ch. 323, 349 (declining to follow *The Rose Mary* [1953] 1 W.L.R. 246, a decision of the Supreme Court of Aden which concerned facts of some political sensitivity and so enjoyed more attention than it deserved).

CHAPTER 18

SUCCESSION AND THE ADMINISTRATION OF ESTATES

In their treatment of the estates of deceased persons, English law and the systems **18–001** based on it differ widely from modern civil law systems. In English law the general principle is that no one is entitled to deal with the property of a deceased person without first obtaining the authority of the court.[1] If the deceased made a will appointing an executor who is willing to act, the necessary authority is acquired by the executor obtaining a grant of probate of the will. If the deceased died intestate, the necessary authority is acquired by some person (for example one of the next of kin, or a creditor) obtaining a grant of letters of administration. Where there is a will but no executor, the letters of administration are "with will". The executors or administrators (generically called the personal representatives) succeed to the property of the deceased, and are bound to clear the estate of debts, duties and expenses; this is the process of administration of the estate. The personal representatives then distribute the surplus among the persons entitled under the deceased's will or intestacy. Issues of "succession" concern this beneficial distribution of the net surplus of the estate.

In civil law countries, the general rule is that the property of a deceased person passes directly to the deceased's heirs or universal legatee; personal representatives in the English sense need not be appointed and when personal representatives are appointed, their duties are usually of a supervisory nature, quite different from those of English personal representatives.[2] But, whatever the foreign law may say, no property in England may pass directly to a foreign heir or universal legatee: an English grant must be obtained.

Within the EU the inconsistencies and incompatibilities between national systems were addressed in a Regulation of 2012, the Succession Regulation.[3] However, the UK is not bound by this Regulation; Ireland took a similar decision not to "opt-in".

---

[1] *New York Breweries Co Ltd v Attorney General* [1899] A.C. 62. There are statutory exceptions, e.g. Administration of Estates (Small Payments) Act 1965.
[2] See *Re Achillopoulos* [1928] Ch. 433.
[3] European Parliament and Council Regulation No.650/2012 of 4 July 2012 on jurisdiction, applicable law, recognition and enforcement of decisions and acceptance and enforcement of authentic instruments in matters of succession and on the creation of a European Certificate of Succession, [2012] O.J. L 201, p. 107.

ADMINISTRATION OF ESTATES

English grants of administration

18–002　The practice concerning grants of administration is governed by the Non-Contentious Probate Rules 1987 as amended. These give wide discretion to the court, in practice the officials of the probate registries. Disputes concerning the administration of estates, however, are the subject of proceedings in the Chancery Division.

Until 1932, the English court could make a grant only if there were property of the deceased situated in England. This restriction could be very inconvenient. When a person died domiciled in England but leaving property in a civil law country, the foreign court would sometimes refuse to make a grant of representation until a grant had been obtained in England. If the deceased left no property in England, the result was an impasse.[4] The Administration of Justice Act 1932[5] therefore provided that the court should have jurisdiction to make a grant in respect of any deceased person, even if the deceased left no property in England. But if there is no property of the deceased in England and the deceased died domiciled abroad, the court is very reluctant to make a grant.[6]

Separate wills

18–003　Testators sometimes make separate wills disposing of their property in England and abroad. If one instrument confirms the other, they both together constitute the last will of the testator, and an executor seeking a grant of representation must take probate of both. But if the wills are independent of each other, the practice is to admit only the English will to probate unless there is some reason for also making a grant of probate in respect of the foreign will.[7]

Person to whom the grant will be made

18–004　When a person dies domiciled in a foreign country, the court will make a grant in the first instance to the person entrusted with the administration of the estate by the court of the deceased's domicile.[8] If there is no such person, for example because no application for a grant has yet been made in the country of the domicile or because its courts do not appoint personal representatives in the English sense, the grant will be made to the person entitled to administer the estate by the law of the domicile.[9] But the making of such a grant is discretionary,

---

[4] *In the Goods of Tucker* (1864) 3 Sw. & Tr. 585.

[5] Section 2(1). This Act was repealed by the Supreme Court [now the Senior Courts] Act 1981 Sch.7, but in substance kept alive by s.25(1).

[6] *Aldrich v Attorney General* [1968] P. 281, 295.

[7] *Re Wayland* [1951] 2 All E.R. 1041.

[8] Non-Contentious Probate Rules 1987 r.30(1)(a) (r.30 is amended, as to the titles of the officers acting, by SI 1991/1876). The English administration is said to be "ancillary" to the "principal" administration in the domicile.

[9] Non-Contentious Probate Rules 1987 r.30(1)(b). Where the English estate consists wholly of immovables, a grant limited thereto may be made to the person who would have been entitled if the

and the court may make a grant to such other person as it thinks fit, either because there is no one who qualifies under these rules or because there are special circumstances which appear to require it.[10]

If the deceased left a formally valid will in English or Welsh which names an executor as such, or which describes (in any language) the duties of a named person in terms which according to English law are sufficient to constitute an executor "according to the tenor", probate may be granted to that person.[11] If the law of the domicile restricts the powers of the representative to a fixed period from the death of the deceased, such restriction will be disregarded in England.[12]

The foreign personal representative must be a person to whom a grant can properly be made in English law. Thus the court will not make a grant to a foreign personal representative who is a minor.[13] And if there is a minority or a life interest arising under a will or intestacy, the court must normally[14] make a grant to not less than two individuals or a trust corporation; it will therefore not make a grant to a single individual even if that individual is entitled to administer the estate by the law of the domicile.[15]

Under the Consular Conventions Act 1949, the court may make a grant to a consular officer of a foreign State to which the Act has been extended by Order in Council, if a national of that state is entitled to a grant of probate or administration in respect of property in England, is not resident in England, and has not by an attorney applied to the court for a grant.

Effect in England of Scottish, Northern Irish and Commonwealth grants

Scottish and Northern Irish grants

Section 1 of the Administration of Estates Act 1971 provides that where a person dies domiciled in Scotland or Northern Ireland, a Scottish "confirmation" or Northern Ireland grant will be treated without further formality as if it had originally been made by the English High Court. There are of course reciprocal provisions for the direct recognition of English grants in Scotland and Northern Ireland,[16] and as between Northern Ireland and Scotland.[17]

18–005

---

deceased had died domiciled in England: Non-Contentious Probate Rules 1987 r.30(3)(b). Under the EU Succession Regulation, where an administrator is appointed it will normally be the person identified in the law governing the succession.
[10] Non-Contentious Probate Rules 1987 r.30(1)(c); *In the Goods of Kaufman* [1952] P. 325; see also *Practice Direction* [1953] 1 W.L.R. 1237.
[11] Non-Contentious Probate Rules 1987 r.30(3)(a).
[12] *In the Estate of Goenaga* [1949] P. 367, a case difficult to reconcile with *Laneuville v Anderson* (1860) 2 Sw. & Tr. 24; see Morris, (1950) 3 Int.L.Q. 243; Lipstein, (1949) 26 B.Y.B.I.L. 498.
[13] *In the Goods of HRH the Duchesse d'Orleans* (1859) 1 Sw. & Tr. 253.
[14] See Supreme Court [now Senior Courts] Act 1981 s.114(2), under which the court has a discretionary power to make a grant to one individual if it thinks fit.
[15] See Non-Contentious Probate Rules 1987 r.30(2).
[16] Administration of Estates Act 1971 ss.2(1), 3(1).
[17] Administration of Estates Act 1971 ss.2(2), 3(1).

Commonwealth grants

18–006 Under the Colonial Probates Act 1892, a grant of representation made in a country to which the Act has been applied by Order in Council may be sealed with the seal of the probate registry and will thereafter have the same effect as an English grant. The Act has been applied to almost the whole Commonwealth.[18] The Act does not require that the deceased should have been domiciled in the country where the grant was made, but the probate registry has a discretion whether or not to reseal. Unless there are special reasons, a grant not made by the court of the domicile will not be resealed unless it was made to a person who would have been entitled to an original grant in England, e.g. as an executor named in a will written in English or Welsh, or as the person entitled to administer the estate by the law of the domicile.[19]

Effect of an English grant

18–007 An English grant vests in the personal representatives all property of the deceased, movable or immovable, which at the time of the death is situated in England[20]; and also, probably, any movables of the deceased which are brought to England after that time.[21] But, although there is no authority on the point, it would be consistent with principle to recognise the title of a third party who under the *lex situs* had obtained a good title to such movables before they were brought to England.[22] Even if the deceased died domiciled in England, an English grant does not of its own force vest in the personal representatives any property which is and remains outside England: at most it gives the personal representative a "generally recognised claim" to be appointed as such by the courts of the country where the movables are situated.[23]

An English personal representative may legitimately take such steps as are open to him or her to recover property of the deceased wherever situated. Whether there is a positive duty to recover assets situated outside England is less clear. Usually the English personal representative will be unable to recover such assets without first obtaining a grant of representation from the foreign court. Anyone attempting to deal with foreign assets without a grant may be liable as an executor *de son tort* under the foreign law. In practice, therefore, an English personal representative will be concerned with foreign assets only if the deceased died domiciled in England, since only in such a case has the English personal representative a "generally recognised claim" to a grant from the foreign court. If there are sufficient assets in England to pay the debts and duties, an English personal representative is not obliged to collect a specifically bequeathed chattel

---

[18] See the Colonial Probates Act Application Order 1965, SI 1965/1530, SI 1976/579 (Vanuatu), and SI 1997/1572 (continued application to Hong Kong Special Administrative Region). The Act continued to apply to South Africa during the period when that country was outside the Commonwealth.

[19] Non-Contentious Probate Rules 1987 r.39(3).

[20] Administration of Estates Act 1925 s.1.

[21] *Whyte v Rose* (1842) 3 Q.B. 493, 506, per Parke B.

[22] See above, para.17–025.

[23] *Blackwood v R* (1882) 8 App.Cas. 82, 92.

situated abroad, and may simply assent to its vesting in the legatee and leave the latter to bear the expense of bringing it home[24] or paying any foreign duty which it may have attracted.[25]

A personal representative will be liable to account for assets under an English grant only if he or she received them in the character of English personal representative. An English personal representative who also has a grant from a foreign court is not accountable in England qua personal representative for assets recovered in that capacity.

Choice of law

The administration of a deceased person's estate is governed wholly by the law of the country in which the personal representative obtained the grant.[26] Every question as to the admissibility of debts and as to the priority in which debts are to be paid is governed by the *lex fori*. Foreign creditors rank equally with English creditors, whether the English administration is principal or ancillary.[27] The only difference is that the English ancillary administrator need not advertise for foreign claims.[28] **18–008**

Administration does not include the distribution of surplus assets to beneficiaries under the deceased's will or intestacy. That is a matter of succession. If the deceased died domiciled abroad, the English administration is ancillary to that which takes place in the country of the domicile, and the English ancillary personal representative will normally hand over the surplus to the principal representative appointed by the courts of the domicile.[29] However, the court has a discretionary power to restrain the English personal representative from so doing. This power has been exercised where the domiciliary representative would have applied the surplus to pay debts which by English domestic law were statute-barred[30]; or would have distributed the surplus in accordance with a will which by the English rules of the conflict of laws had been revoked.[31] In both these cases the court ordered the English representative not to hand over the assets but to distribute them to the persons entitled under English law.

---

[24] *Re Fitzpatrick* [1952] Ch. 86.
[25] *Re Scott* [1915] 1 Ch. 592.
[26] *Preston v Melville* (1841) 8 Cl. & F. 1. Under the EU Succession Regulation, an administrator's powers are those identified in the law governing the succession.
[27] *Re Kloebe* (1884) 28 Ch.D. 175.
[28] *Re Achillopoulos* [1928] Ch. 433, 445.
[29] *Re Achillopoulos* [1928] Ch. 433; *In the Estate of Weiss* [1962] P. 136.
[30] *Re Lorillard* [1922] 2 Ch. 638; approved by Lord Simonds in *Government of India v Taylor* [1955] A.C. 491, 509.
[31] *Re Manifold* [1962] Ch. 1.

Foreign personal representatives

18–009 A foreign personal representative who wishes to represent the deceased in England must obtain an English grant.[32] Anyone else intermeddling with the assets of the deceased incurs all the liabilities but none of the privileges of such a representative.[33] However, a foreign personal representative who has obtained a judgment against a debtor of the estate in the foreign country can enforce the judgment in England in a personal capacity without taking out an English grant.[34]

A foreign personal representative without an English grant cannot be made liable in England for property held or acts done in the capacity of foreign representative.[35] The foreign personal representative may be liable in England through acts attracting liabilities as a debtor or trustee, for example by entering into a contract in England in respect of the estate, or by making an improper investment;[36] and, by intermeddling with English assets, will become liable as an executor *de son tort*.[37]

SUCCESSION

18–010 When the estate of a deceased person has been fully administered, that is to say when all debts, duties and expenses have been paid, the question arises by what law the beneficial distribution of his or her net estate is to be governed. As a general rule, succession to immovables is governed by the *lex situs*, and succession to movables by the law of the deceased's last domicile.[38] Few qualifications need to be made to these propositions so far as intestate succession is concerned. But in succession under wills it may sometimes be necessary to look at the law of the testator's domicile at the date on which the will was executed; other laws are made relevant by statute if the question is one of formal validity.

---

[32] *Carter and Crosts Case* (1585) Godb. 33; *Tourton v Flower* (1735) 3 P. Wms. 369; *New York Breweries Co Ltd v Attorney General* [1899] A.C. 62; *Finnegan v Cementation Co Ltd* [1953] 1 Q.B. 688.

[33] *New York Breweries Co Ltd v Attorney General* [1899] A.C. 62. cf. the recognition of a foreign trustee in bankruptcy as a matter of course.

[34] *Vanquelin v Bouard* (1863) 15 C.B. (N.S.) 341; *Re Macnichol* (1874) L.R. 19 Eq. 81.

[35] *Jauncy v Sealey* (1686) 1 Vern. 397; *Beavan v Hastings* (1856) 2 K. & J. 724; *Flood v Patterson* (1861) 29 Beav. 295; *Degazon v Barclays Bank International* [1988] F.T.L.R. 17.

[36] *Harvey v Dougherty* (1887) 56 L.T. 322.

[37] *New York Breweries Co Ltd v Attorney General* [1899] A.C. 62.

[38] Under the European Union Succession Regulation, the general rule is that the law applicable to the succession as a whole is the law of the State in which the deceased had his habitual residence at the time of death. Where, by way of exception, it is clear from all the circumstances of the case that, at the time of death, the deceased was manifestly more closely connected with another State the law applicable to the succession is the law of that other State (art.21). A person may choose as the law to govern his succession as a whole the law of the State whose nationality he possesses at the time of making the choice or at the time of death (art.22).

Intestate succession

Movables

It has been settled law for over 200 years that intestate succession to movables is governed by the law of the deceased's last domicile.[39] This subject to the application of *renvoi*, which has been developed very largely in this context.[40]

18–011

But this rule applies only to succession in the strict sense of that term. It does not apply to the right of the Crown or of a foreign government to take ownerless property as bona vacantia or under a *jus regale*.[41] The title to movables so claimed is governed by the *lex situs* and not by the law of the deceased's last domicile. Thus if a person dies intestate domiciled in a foreign country and without next of kin, and the foreign state claims his or her movables in England as ownerless property, the Crown's claim to the movables as bona vacantia will be preferred.[42] In such a case the foreign state claims not by way of succession but because there is no succession. It is otherwise, however, if the foreign state claims as *ultimus heres* (last heir)[43] under the foreign law and not under a *jus regale*. In such a case there is a true claim of succession which is governed by the law of the domicile, and the claim of the foreign State will be preferred to that of the Crown.[44]

Immovables

According to the traditional rule of the English conflict of laws, intestate succession to immovables is governed by the *lex situs*. This was confirmed, albeit with reluctance, in *Re Collens*.[45]

18–012

The scission principle

The "scission" principle under which intestate succession to immovables is governed by the *lex situs* has been abandoned by almost all countries outside the common law world. The principle made some sense before 1926 when there were two systems of intestate succession in English domestic law, one for realty and the other for personalty. It makes no sense today when England and all other

18–013

---

[39] *Pipon v Pipon* (1744) Amb. 799; *Somerville v Somerville* (1801) 5 Ves.750.
[40] See para.20–015.
[41] Both these concepts allow the Crown or the State to take ownerless property as, in effect, a prerogative right.
[42] *Re Barnett's Trusts* [1902] 1 Ch. 847; *Re Musurus* [1936] 1 All E.R. 1666.
[43] A typical civil law code will list heirs in an order of priority, with the state as the final heir in default of all others.
[44] *Re Maldonado's Estate* [1954] P. 223. This is an extreme example of characterisation in accordance with the *lex causae* (below, para.20–007) and as such it has been much criticised: see Gower, (1954) 17 M.L.R. 167; Cohn, (1954) 17 M.L.R. 381; Lipstein, [1954] Camb. L.J. 22. The decision does seem to treat the form of the foreign law as more important than its substance.
[45] [1986] Ch. 505. The existence of the rule was assumed in *Balfour v Scott* (1793) 6 Bro. P.C. 550; *Brodie v Barry* (1813) 2 v & B. 127, 131; *Dundas v Dundas* (1830) 2 Dow & Cl. 349; *Freke v Carbery* (1873) L.R. 16 Eq. 461; *Duncan v Lawson* (1889) 41 Ch.D. 394; *Re Berchtold* [1923] 1 Ch. 192; and *Re Cutcliffe* [1940] Ch. 565.

countries in the world have adopted one system of intestate succession for all kinds of property. It has been more fully argued elsewhere[46] that the "scission" principle has outlived its usefulness in England and should be abandoned in favour of the law of the intestate's domicile.

The Hague Conference on Private International Law at its Sixteenth Session in 1988 drew up a Convention on the Law Applicable to Succession to the Estates of Deceased Persons, which adopts the unitary approach; having received only one ratification, it is a dead letter. However the European Union Succession Regulation also adopted a unitary approach, succession to the entire estate being governed by the law of the habitual residence of the deceased.[47]

The retention of the *situs* rule frequently frustrates the intention of Parliament. For when Parliament passes a modern statute on intestate succession, it seeks to give effect to what the average intestate would have wished to do with his or her property, if he or she had made a will. What average intestate? Surely the obvious answer is, an English intestate if the statute applies to England, and a Scottish intestate if the statute applies to Scotland; and indeed legislative action follows sample surveys of wills conducted on this basis.

Even within the UK there are striking differences between the English, Scottish, and Northern Ireland laws of intestate succession, particularly with regard to the rights of the surviving spouse. In England, a surviving spouse is now entitled to a statutory legacy of £250,000 if the intestate left issue and £450,000 otherwise.[48] A similar rule is found in Northern Ireland. Suppose that a man dies intestate domiciled in Northern Ireland leaving a widow and no issue, and leaving movables in Northern Ireland worth £200,000 and land in England worth the same amount. Would the widow be entitled to two statutory legacies, one under the English and a second under the Northern Ireland legislation, thereby leaving nothing for the next of kin (perhaps the mother of the intestate)?

It should not be supposed that this is a mere hypothetical case, far removed from reality. In *Re Collens*[49]:

> C died intestate domiciled in Trinidad and Tobago leaving a substantial estate there, another in Barbados, and a comparatively small estate, including some land, in England. After litigation in Trinidad between his widow and G, his ex-wife, G accepted $1 million in full settlement of her claims against the Trinidad estate. G then successfully asserted a claim to the statutory legacy (then only £5,000) under English law.

The Vice-Chancellor reached this conclusion with regret, and expressed the hope that the Law Commission would review the "scission" principle in the light of the criticisms made of it by Dr Morris.

---

[46] Morris, (1969) 85 L.Q.R. 339.
[47] Article 21.
[48] Administration of Estates Act 1925 s.46 as amended. The figure is increased from time to time by the Lord Chancellor under powers created by the Inheritance and Trustees' Powers Act 2014.
[49] [1986] Ch. 505. See also *Re Rea* [1902] Ir. R. 451 and *Re Ralston* [1906] V.L.R. 689.

Wills

Capacity

The law of the testator's domicile determines whether the testator has personal capacity to make a will of movables.[50] "Personal capacity" is here used to denote such questions as whether a minor or a married woman or a person suffering from bodily or mental illness[51] can make a valid will. It does not include what are sometimes called questions of proprietary capacity, for example, whether a testator can leave property away from his or her spouse and children. Such questions are best regarded as questions of material or essential validity and will be dealt with later under that heading.[52]

18–014

There is no difficulty in applying the principle stated above if the testator's domicile is the same at the date of death as at the date of the will. But if the domicile changes between these two dates, and the two laws differ, it is necessary to choose between them. It is submitted that, on principle, the law of the domicile at the date of the will should govern.[53] Hence, if the testator makes a will at the age of 18 while domiciled in a country where minority ends at 21 and minors cannot make wills, and dies domiciled in England, the will would be void. Conversely, if the testator makes a will at the age of 18 while domiciled in England, and dies domiciled in a country where minority ends at 21 and minors cannot make wills, the will should be valid. It may be noted that by English domestic law (and presumably by the domestic laws of other countries) a testator must have personal capacity to make a will at the date when the will is made, and capacity at the date of death is neither necessary nor sufficient.

So far as capacity to *take* movables under a will is concerned, it has been held that a legacy can be paid to a legatee who is of age to receive it by the law of his or her domicile or by the law of the testator's domicile, whichever happens first.[54]

There is no English authority on what law governs capacity to make a will of immovables. Probably the *lex situs* would be held to govern.[55] This seems to have been the assumption in *Re P (Statutory Will)*[56] where the deceased was domiciled in California and the court ordered the making of a statutory will dealing with immovable property in England as the deceased lacked capacity under the Mental Capacity Act 2005.

---

[50] *In bonis Maraver* (1828) 1 Hagg. Ecc. 498; *In bonis Gutteriez* (1869) 38 L.J.P. & M. 48; *In the Estate of Fuld (No.3)*[1968] P. 675, 696.

[51] *In the Estate of Fuld (No.3)*, above.

[52] Below, para.18–021.

[53] Most writers adopt this view: Story, s.465; Savigny, s.377; Wolff, s.557; F. A. Mann (1954) 31 B.Y.I.L. 217, 230–231. *Re Lewal's Settlement* [1918] 2 Ch. 391 supports the statement in the text; but that was a case on the exercise of a power of appointment by will.

[54] *Re Hellman's Will* (1866) L.R. 2 Eq. 363.

[55] See *Bank of Africa v Cohen* [1909] 2 Ch. 129, above, a case on capacity to transfer land *inter vivos*.

[56] [2009] EWHC 163 (Ch.); [2010] Ch. 33.

Formal validity

18–015 At common law, a will of immovables had to comply with the formalities prescribed by the *lex situs*,[57] and a will of movables had to comply with the formalities prescribed by the law of the testator's last domicile.[58] This latter rule led to much inconvenience and hardship when, for example, the domicile of the testator changed after the execution of the will, or the testator became mortally ill while travelling in a country other than that of his or her domicile. After various attempts by the courts[59] and Parliament[60] to remedy the situation, the modern law was enacted in the Wills Act 1963, which gives effect to the Hague Convention of 1961 on the Formal Validity of Wills.[61]

Section 1 of the Act provides that a will shall be treated as properly executed if its execution conformed to the internal law in force in the territory where it was executed, or in the territory where, at the time of its execution or of the testator's death, he was domiciled or had his habitual residence, or in a State of which, at either of those times, he was a national. This section applies to wills of movables and to wills of land; and s.2(1)(b) additionally provides that a will of immovables shall be treated as properly executed if its execution conformed to the internal law in force in the territory where the property was situated.

Under s.1, if a testator is domiciled in one country, habitually resident in a second, and a national of a third, and changes all three between the time of execution of the will and the time of death, there are no fewer than six systems of law by which the formal validity of the will may be tested, or seven if the testator makes the will in a yet different country. This should be enough to save most wills from formal invalidity so far as the conflict of laws is concerned. There is no requirement in the Act that all the testamentary instruments executed by a testator must conform to the same system of law. Hence, a will and six codicils could each derive its formal validity from a different system.

The law of the testator's nationality

18–016 The reference to the law of the testator's nationality is an even greater innovation than the reference to the law of habitual residence. If the testator is a national of a federal or composite state comprising many countries, like the USA or the UK, there is an obvious difficulty in ascertaining his nationality for the purposes of the Act. Section 6(2) attempts to solve this problem. It provides as follows: (a) if there is in force throughout the state in question a rule indicating which of its systems of internal law can properly be applied in the case in question, that rule

---

[57] *Coppin v Coppin* (1725) 2 P. Wms.291; *Pepin v Bruyere* [1900] 2 Ch. 504.

[58] The leading case is *Bremer v Freeman* (1857) 10 Moo. P.C. 306.

[59] *Collier v Rivaz* (1841) 2 Curt. 855; *In bonis Lacroix* (1877) 2 P.D. 94. This, as a matter of history, is how the doctrine of *renvoi* obtained a foothold in English law, obviously as an escape device: see para.20–015.

[60] The notoriously ill-drafted Wills Act 1861 (Lord Kingsdown's Act).

[61] The Act was based on the recommendations in the Fourth Report of the Private International Law Committee, Cmnd. 491 (1958). For comments on the Act, see Kahn-Freund, (1964) 27 M.L.R. 55; Morris, (1964) 13 I.C.L.Q. 684. On the Convention, see Neels, (2007) 56 I.C.L.Q. 613.

shall be followed; but (b) if there is no such rule, the system shall be that with which the testator was most closely connected at the relevant time.[62]

It is not easy to imagine circumstances in which the provisions of s.6(2)(a) will be applicable, or to assign a precise meaning to the provisions of s.6(2)(b). One has to think of a testator who is, for example, a British citizen or a citizen of the US, who is domiciled and habitually resident elsewhere and who makes a will elsewhere, the will being formally invalid by the law of the place where it was made and of the testator's domicile and habitual residence, so that it is necessary to invoke the law of the testator's nationality in order to admit the will to probate. Section 6(2)(a) can rarely help in circumstances like these, because it is doubtful if there is a composite State in the world which has a uniform conflicts rule but different rules of domestic law for the formal validity of wills. Certainly the UK has not, nor has the US. And as for s.6(2)(b), how can we determine whether our hypothetical testator is "most closely connected" with, England or Scotland or New York or California, when ex hypothesi he or she is domiciled and habitually resident outside the UK or the US?

The only possible answer seems to be, look and see where the testator keeps the bulk of the property. This answer will not help if, as is likely in the circumstances here envisaged, the property is kept in the country where the testator is domiciled or habitually resident, and not in the State of nationality. It might have been more sensible to make the formalities of the *lex situs* available for wills of movables, as they are for wills of immovables.[63] The reference to the law of the nationality will not work for British or American citizens: but it does them no obvious harm and will be beneficial in relation to citizens of many other countries.

Wills made on ships and aircraft

The law of the country where the will was executed is given an extended meaning in the case of wills made on board a vessel or aircraft "of any description". In addition to the law of the place where the vessel or aircraft happens to be (including, no doubt, the country in whose territorial waters the vessel is sailing or the country over which the aircraft is flying), s.2(1)(a) of the Act allows as an alternative the internal law in force in the territory with which, having regard to its registration (if any) and other relevant circumstances, the vessel or aircraft may be taken to have been most closely connected. This will normally be the law of the flag or, in the case of ships wearing flags like the Red Ensign, the law in force at the port of registration. The cautious drafting is presumably designed to allow for exceptions in the case of flags of convenience. There is no requirement that the vessel or aircraft should be in motion when the will is made. Hence a will formally valid by French law would be admissible to probate in England if executed on board a French ship alongside in an English port, or on board a French aircraft on the runway at Heathrow Airport.

18–017

---

[62] "The relevant time" is defined (very obscurely) as the time of the testator's death where the matter is to be determined by reference to circumstances prevailing at his death, and the time of execution of the will in any other case.
[63] Section 2(1)(b).

Changes in the relevant law

18–018   Section 6(3) of the Wills Act 1963 provides that regard is to be had to the formal requirements of a particular law at the time of execution, but that this is not to prevent account being taken of an alteration of the law affecting wills executed at that time if the alteration enables the will to be treated as properly executed. Thus, retrospective alterations in the law are relevant if they *validate* a will, but irrelevant if they *invalidate* it. This subsection is not in terms confined to alterations in the law made before the death of the testator; and there is no reason to read into it words that are not there.[64]

Special requirements as to form

18–019   Under some foreign systems of law, certain classes of testators can make wills only in a special form. For example, testators over 16 and under 18 years of age may be able to make wills only in notarial form. It has long been controversial among continental jurists whether such provisions relate to form or to capacity. Section 3 of the Wills Act 1963 settles this question by providing that where a law in force outside the UK falls to be applied (whether in pursuance of the Act or not), any requirement of that law whereby special formalities are to be observed by testators answering a particular description, or witnesses to the execution of the will are to possess certain qualifications, shall be treated as a formal requirement, notwithstanding any rule of that law to the contrary. So, if a German national, domiciled and habitually resident in Germany and aged 17, makes a will in Germany in holograph form, the will would not be admitted to probate in England because it was not made in notarial form as required by German law. If, however, the will had been made in France and was formally valid by French law, it would be admitted to probate: the testator had capacity by the law of his domicile, and the will was formally valid by the law of the country where it was executed.

Renvoi

18–020   It will be seen that the Act refers throughout to the "internal law" of the various systems which it allows. Thus, any reference to another system from the conflicts rules of the systems of law authorised by the Act is excluded. But the Act does not abolish, either expressly or by implication, the doctrine of *renvoi* in relation to the formal validity of wills, nor the rule of common law that the formal validity of a will of movables is governed by the law of the testator's last domicile.[65] Hence, if a British citizen with an English domicile of origin and an Italian domicile of choice makes a will of movables which is formally valid by English domestic law but formally invalid by Italian domestic law, and it is proved that

---

[64] If this is right, the subsection renders *Lynch v Provisional Government of Paraguay* (1871) L.R. 2 P. & M. 268 obsolete. See below, para.20–033.

[65] For *renvoi*, see below, para.20–011 ff.

the Italian courts would regard the will as formally valid, it could be admitted to probate in England by way of *renvoi* from Italian law instead of under ss.1 and 6(2) of the Act.

Material or essential validity

The material, or essential, validity of a will of movables, or of any particular gift of movables contained therein, is governed by the law of the testator's domicile at the time of death.[66] The term material or essential validity includes such questions as whether the testator must leave a certain proportion of his estate to his children or widow,[67] and whether gifts to attesting witnesses are valid.[68] But if the will bequeaths property on trusts, any question as to whether the trust offends against a rule against perpetuities or accumulations is determined by the law governing the trust under the Recognition of Trusts Act 1987 and not by the law governing the validity of the will.[69]

18–021

The material or essential validity of a gift by will of immovables is governed by the *lex situs*. That law will determine what estates can legally be created,[70] what are the incidents of those estates,[71] whether gifts to charities are valid,[72] and whether the testator is bound to leave a certain proportion of his estate to his children or widow.[73]

Closely analogous to the question whether a testator is bound to leave a certain proportion of the estate to his or her spouse or children (as is the case under the laws of Scotland, France and many continental European countries) is the question whether the court can make an order for the payment of part of the income of the estate to any dependants (as it can in England under the Inheritance (Provision for Family and Dependants) Act 1975). In England the statute itself limits the court's power to cases where the testator died domiciled in England, whether the property is movable or immovable.[74]

Construction (or interpretation)

The construction of a will of movables is governed by the law intended by the testator. In the absence of indications to the contrary, this is presumed to be the

18–022

---

[66] *Whicker v Hume* (1858) 7 H.L.C. 124; *Dellar v Zivy* [2007] EWHC 2266 (Ch), [2007] I.L.Pr. 868.
[67] *Thornton v Curling* (1824) 8 Sim. 310; *Campbell v Beaufoy* (1859) Johns. 320; *Re Groos* [1915] 1 Ch. 572; *Re Annesley* [1926] Ch. 692; *Re Ross* [1930] 1 Ch. 377; *Re Adams* [1967] I.R. 424.
[68] *Re Priest* [1944] Ch. 58; see now Wills Act 1968.
[69] See para.19–003.
[70] *Nelson v Bridport* (1846) 8 Beav. 547.
[71] *Re Miller* [1914] 1 Ch. 511.
[72] *Duncan v Lawson* (1889) 41 Ch.D. 394; *Re Hoyles* [1911] 1 Ch. 179.
[73] *Re Hernando* (1884) 27 Ch.D. 284; *Re Ross* [1930] 1 Ch. 377.
[74] Inheritance (Provision for Family and Dependants) Act 1975 s.1(1). See, e.g., *Cyganik v Agulian* [2006] EWCA Civ 129; [2006] 1 F.C.R. 129. The Law Commission recommended (*Inheritance and Family Provision Claims on Death*, 2011) a widening of the jurisdictional grounds but this recommendation was rejected.

law of the testator's domicile at the time the will was made;[75] but this is only a rebuttable presumption.[76] An illustration is provided by *Dellar v Zivy*[77]:

> Z, French by nationality, lived in England for many years managing the UK subsidiary of the family company. His will disposed of French shares, and in it he declared himself to be domiciled in England. In fact he may well have retained his French domicile of origin, but the making of the declaration, the use in the will of the trust for sale, unknown in French law, and the direction that English solicitors be consulted over the administration of the estate all made it clear that he intended the will to be interpreted in accordance with English law.

A change of domicile between the time the will was made and the time of the testator's death does not affect the construction of the will:

> "If a question arises as to the interpretation of the will, and it should appear that the testator has changed his domicile between making his will and his death, his will may fall to be construed according to the law of his domicile at the time he made it".[78]

This is reinforced by s.4 of the Wills Act 1963, which provides that the construction of a will shall not be altered by reason of any change in the testator's domicile after the execution of the will.

The term "construction" includes not only the meaning of words and phrases used by the testator, but also the way in which the law fills up gaps in the dispositions when the testator has failed to foresee and provide against certain events (for example, that one of several named residuary legatees might predecease the testator). This of course is not construction in the sense that it has reference to the intentions of the actual testator, for ex hypothesi the testator never had in mind the events which have happened. But it is construction in the sense that the law supposes that the average testator would wish the gap to be filled in a particular way.

A good instance of construction in accordance with the law of the testator's domicile is afforded by *Re Cunnington*,[79] where a British subject domiciled in France made a will in the English language and form in which he gave his residue on trust for division between ten named legatees, most of whom resided in England. Two of these legatees predeceased him. It was held that their shares were divisible among the survivors in accordance with French law, and did not lapse to the next of kin as they would have done by English domestic law. Again, if a testator domiciled in one of the US were to give legacies expressed in dollars to legatees resident in Canada and Australia, there can be little doubt that the amount of the legacies would be calculated in American dollars.[80]

If a testator domiciled in England gives movables to the "heirs" or "next of kin" of a person who died domiciled in a foreign country, should the heirs or next of kin be ascertained in accordance with English law or the law of the foreign

---

[75] *Anstruther v Chalmer* (1826) 2 Sim. 1; *Re Fergusson* [1902] 1 Ch. 483; *Re Cunnington* [1924] 1 Ch. 68.
[76] *Bradford v Young* (1885) 29 Ch.D. 617; *Re Price* [1900] 1 Ch. 442, 452, 453; *Re Adams* [1967] I.R. 424; *Curati v Perdoni* [2012] EWCA Civ 1381.
[77] [2007] EWHC 2266 (Ch); [2007] I.L.Pr. 868.
[78] *Philipson-Stow v IRC* [1961] A.C. 727, 761 per Lord Denning.
[79] [1924] 1 Ch. 68.
[80] *Saunders v Drake* (1742) 2 Atk. 465.

country? The English courts have adopted the former solution,[81] and the Scottish courts the latter.[82] The view of the Scottish courts seems preferable. For surely the question is not "Who would have been A's next of kin if he had died domiciled in England?" but rather "Who are A's next of kin having regard to the fact that he died domiciled abroad?'[83]

There is no reason to suppose that a different general rule applies to the construction of wills of immovables. However, the use of technical language of the *lex situs* may indicate an intention that its law should govern the construction of the will.[84] Difficult problems arise when the testator devises land in two different countries and aims at producing identical results by the use of the technical language of one system of law only. The court, when interpreting the will in accordance with the law of the testator's domicile, will endeavour to see that the dispositions will operate in the country in which the land is situated to the fullest extent possible under the *lex situs*.[85] But if the *lex situs* makes it illegal or impossible to give effect to the terms of the will as construed by the law of the testator's domicile, then the *lex situs* will prevail.[86]

Revocation

The question as to what law determines whether a will has been revoked is one of considerable nicety.[87] A will may be revoked either (a) by a later will or codicil, or (b) by some other testamentary mode of revocation, for example in English domestic law by burning, tearing or destroying, or (c) by a change of circumstances, for example in English domestic law by the subsequent marriage of the testator, or in some other systems by the testator's subsequent divorce or by the birth of children. Each of these modes requires separate discussion.

18–023

Revocation by later will or codicil

A later will or codicil may revoke an earlier will either expressly or by implication. It may do so expressly, as when the testator says "I hereby revoke all testamentary dispositions heretofore made by me". In such a case the question whether the second instrument revokes the first depends on the intrinsic validity of the second will, especially with regard to the capacity of the testator and the formal validity of the will.[88] Both these matters have already been discussed.[89] It may be added that under s.2(1)(c) of the Wills Act 1963 a later will, in so far as it revokes an earlier will or any provision therein, will be treated as properly executed if its execution conformed to any law by reference to which the revoked will would be so treated. So, if the testator is domiciled in one country, habitually

18–024

---

[81] *Re Fergusson's Will* [1902] 1 Ch. 483.
[82] *Mitchells Trustee v Rule* (1908) 16 S.L.T. 189; *Smiths Trustee v Macpherson*, 1926 S.C. 983.
[83] *Smith's Trustee v Macpherson*, 1926 S.C. 983, 991–992, per Lord Sands.
[84] *Bradford v Young* (1885) 29 Ch.D. 617, 623.
[85] *Studd v Cook* (1883) 8 App.Cas. 577, 591, per Lord Selborne.
[86] *Re Miller* [1914] 1 Ch. 511; *Philipson-Stow v IRC* [1961] A.C. 727, 761.
[87] For comparative material, see Neels (2007) 56 I.C.L.Q. 613.
[88] *Cottrell v Cottrell* (1872) L.R. 2 P. & M. 397; *Re Manifold* [1962] Ch. 1.
[89] Above, paras 18–014 and 18–015.

resident in a second, and a national of a third, and changes all three between the execution of the earlier and the later will, and again between the execution of the later will and the time of death, there may be a choice of nine systems of law for the formal validity of the revoking (as opposed to the disposing) provisions of the later will, or eleven if the wills are made in different countries.

However, if one will deals only with property in a foreign country and is made in foreign form, and the other deals only with property in England, the later will does not necessarily revoke the earlier one even if it contains a revocation clause.[90]

If the later will does not contain an express revocation clause, it may nevertheless revoke the first will by implication, for example if it is described as a "last" will (though this is not sufficient by English domestic law), or if its provisions cannot stand with those of the earlier will, as when the earlier will gives property to A and the later will gives the same property to B. In such cases, the question is one of construction and is governed prima facie by the law of the testator's domicile at the time of making the later will, though this presumption may be rebutted if there sufficient indication that the testator intended to refer to some other law.[91]

Other testamentary modes of revocation

18–025   The question as to whether a will is revoked by burning, tearing or destroying or the like is no doubt governed by the *lex situs* in the case of immovables or by the law of the testator's domicile in the case of movables. If the testator's domicile is the same at all material times there is no difficulty. But if the domicile changes between the date of the alleged act of revocation and the date of death, and the two laws differ, it is necessary to determine which law governs. They may differ, for example because in English law the will must be destroyed in the presence of the testator,[92] but in other systems (such as Italian law[93]) this is not necessary. If a testator domiciled in Italy writes to the solicitor who holds the will instructing the solicitor to destroy it, and by Italian law this amounts to an effective revocation, it is thought that the will would be revoked even if the testator died domiciled in England. For the will is effectively revoked by the law of the testator's domicile: it ceases to exist as a will just as though it had never been made, so that there is no will upon which English domestic law can operate. The converse case is perhaps more difficult: a testator domiciled in England writes to the solicitor instructing him to destroy his will, and dies domiciled in Italy. Here again it is thought that the law of the testator's domicile at the date of the alleged act of revocation would govern, with the result that the will would not be revoked. For at the time when the act was done there was no revocation in law,

---

[90] *Re Wayland* [1951] 2 All E.R. 1041; *Re Yahudas Estate* [1956] P. 388.
[91] *Curati v Perdoni* [2012] EWCA Civ 1381.
[92] Wills Act 1837 s.20.
[93] See *Velasco v Coney* [1934] P. 143.

and at the time when the act might have amounted to revocation in law the act did not in fact occur. There is however no English authority on either of these questions.[94]

Revocation by subsequent marriage

In English domestic law a marriage revokes any previous will made by either party to the marriage.[95] In the laws of most other countries (including Scotland) it does not. It is well settled that the question as to whether a will is revoked by subsequent marriage is governed by the law of the testator's domicile at the time of the marriage. Thus in the leading case of *Re Martin*,[96] a lady domiciled in France made a will, married a domiciled Englishman (thereby, as the law then stood, acquiring an English domicile by operation of law), and died domiciled in France: it was held that her will was revoked. Conversely, in *In the Estate of Groos*[97] a lady domiciled in Holland made a will, married a domiciled Dutchman, and died domiciled in England: it was held that her will was not revoked.

Of course, a subsequent marriage will not revoke a will if the marriage is void under English rules of the conflict of laws, for example because the parties are within the prohibited degrees of consanguinity or affinity.[98] But it will revoke a will if the marriage is voidable.[99]

18–026

---

[94] See Mann (1954) 31 B.Y.B.I.L. 216, 231.

[95] Wills Act 1837 s.18, as substituted by Administration of Justice Act 1982 s.18, where some exceptions are stated.

[96] [1900] P. 211.

[97] [1904] P. 269. cf. *In bonis Reid* (1866) L.R. 1 P. & M. 74; *Westerman v Schwab*, 1905 S.C. 132.

[98] *Mette v Mette* (1859) 1 Sw. & Tr. 416.

[99] *Re Roberts* [1978] 1 W.L.R. 653.

CHAPTER 19

TRUSTS

The trust is perhaps the most distinctive contribution made by English law to the **19–001** science of general jurisprudence. It is therefore surprising that there was at common law a dearth of authority on what law governs the validity and administration of trusts in the conflict of laws. Those issues are made all the more important by the fact that although many countries in the civil law tradition have legal devices that serve some of the purposes for which trusts are used, none have a fully-developed trust on the English model. The position was transformed by the enactment of the Recognition of Trusts Act 1987 which gave effect in the law of the UK to the Hague Convention on the law applicable to trusts and on their recognition of 10 January 1986,[1] and was later complicated by the appearance of the Rome II Regulation.[2] In what follows, the Convention and its implementation in England are considered first, and then the rather difficult question of the, limited, impact of the Rome II Regulation.

The Hague Convention's authors had an ambitious aim, to "establish common provisions on the law applicable to trusts and to deal with the most important issues concerning the recognition of trusts",[3] for a variety of legal systems, some of which had a highly developed law of trusts, some of which were wholly without the trust, and others again had devices analogous to the trust in function or structure. This diversity required the inclusion of a description of the trust in the Convention as a means of indicating the range of legal institutions within its scope, and also to exclude from the scope of the Convention some uses of the trust familiar to English lawyers but not clearly linked to property interests, for example constructive trusts used as a form of remedy.[4]

The Convention describes the trust as the legal relationship created, inter vivos or on death, by a person, the settlor, when assets have been placed under the control of a trustee[5] for the benefit of a beneficiary or for a specified purpose.[6] It

---

[1] The text, with certain omissions, is scheduled to the 1987 Act. For commentaries, see the official Explanatory Report by von Overbeck, *Actes et Documents de la 15e Session*. p.370; Hayton, (1987) 36 I.C.L.Q. 260; Harris, *The Hague Trust Convention* (Oxford: Hart Publishing, 2002); Gaillard and Trautman, (1987) 35 Am.J.Comp.L. 307; Hayton (2014) 366 Recueil des cours 9.

[2] European Parliament and Council Regulation No.864/2007, [2007] O.J. L 199, p.40.

[3] Preamble (not art.7(1). As Harris observes, the choice of law rules have more in common with those for contracts than property: see Fawcett (ed.), *Reform and Development of Private International Law* (Oxford: Oxford University Press, 2002) p.187.

[4] See Hayton, (1987) 36 I.C.L.Q. 260, 264.

[5] This includes the case of a settlor declaring himself a trustee: *Akers v Samba Financial Group* [2014] EWCA Civ 1516; [2015] Ch. 451.

[6] Article 2(1). The last phrase will include charitable trusts and Scottish public purpose trusts.

applies only to trusts created voluntarily and evidenced in writing.[7] Some resulting trusts will be included, such as those arising where a trustee continues to hold property after the exhaustion of express trusts[8] but it is far from clear whether other types of resulting trusts, even if later evidenced in writing, will be caught.[9] Trusts created by judicial decisions are not included, but Contracting States are free to extend the provisions of the Convention to such trusts.[10]

The Recognition of Trusts Act 1987 adopts the principles of the Convention. Although the Convention itself came into effect in 1992, and then only as between three States,[11] the Act applies to trusts regardless of the date on which they were created[12] but this does not affect the law to be applied to anything done or omitted before 1 August 1987.[13] Section 1(2) of the Act applies the Convention's provisions not only in relation to the trusts described in arts 2 and 3 but also in relation to any other trusts of property arising under the law of any part of the UK or by virtue of a judicial decision, whether in the UK or elsewhere.[14] The first of these extensions is in very general terms, and will include trusts created orally and never evidenced in writing, and trusts created by statute or under statutory powers[15]; the only requirement is that the trust must "arise under the law of" some part of the UK, a requirement which may prove unclear in some types of case. The second extension, to trusts created by judicial decisions, indicates no pre-requisites for the recognition of the decision in question. It was designed to enable the UK to meet its obligations under the Brussels Convention 1968, now replaced by the Brussels I *bis* Regulation. In its operation in respect of decisions reached outside the Member States, the English courts will, it seems, require the decision to be capable of recognition in England under the applicable rules as to foreign judgments.

Some trusts, for example a trust created orally in the Irish Republic, fall outside the scope of the Recognition of Trusts Act 1987. This does not mean that such trusts will be invalid or incapable of recognition. The principles applicable to trusts generally before the coming into force of the 1987 Act will continue to apply in such cases; the Act is consistent with what limited authority exists as to the position at common law,[16] and it is likely that the courts will seek to ensure that no inconsistencies develop in future.

There is an important distinction between questions relating to the settlement, will, or other instrument which operates inter alia to vest property in trustees and

---

[7] Article 3.

[8] See von Overbeck, Explanatory Report, para.51.

[9] cf. Hayton, (1987) 36 I.C.L.Q. 260, 263–264.

[10] Article 20, not reproduced in the 1987 Act.

[11] Australia, Italy and the UK. There are now 12 Contracting States.

[12] Article 22.

[13] Recognition of Trusts Act 1987 s.1(5). The position resulting from a combination of this provision and art.22 was described with some restraint as "obscure" in *Armenian Patriarch of Jerusalem v Sonsino* [2002] EWHC 1304.

[14] See Barnard, [1992] C.L.J. 474.

[15] See e.g. Law of Property Act 1925, ss.34–36 (co-ownership); Administration of Estates Act 1925 s.33 (trust for sale on intestacy), in each case as amended by Trusts of Land and Appointment of Trustees Act 1996.

[16] *Attorney General v Campbell* (1872) L.R. 5 H.L. 524; *Duke of Marlborough v Attorney General (No.1)* [1945] Ch. 78; *Iveagh v IRC* [1954] Ch. 364; *Chellaram v Chellaram* [1985] Ch. 409. See Evans, (1986) 102 L.Q.R. 28; Wallace, (1987) 36 I.C.L.Q. 454.

questions relating to the validity and operation of the trust provisions contained in it. The line is drawn once the assets are transferred to the trustee.[17] In the negotiations at The Hague, delegates used the expression "rocket-launcher" for the former type of question, as opposed to the "rocket" of the trust itself.[18] The Hague Convention, and so the 1987 Act, does not apply to what it styles "preliminary issues", those falling into the former category[19]; an English court will continue to deal with those issues under the existing rules of the conflict of laws. If in the case of a testamentary trust the testator had no capacity to make the will or the will is formally invalid or has been revoked, it will not be admitted to probate and any trust contained therein will fail. Similarly, a marriage contract or settlement may fail because of incapacity or invalidity in point of form. The essential validity of a gift of movables contained in a will is governed by the law of the testator's domicile at the time of his or her death[20]; that law will determine, e.g. whether the testator is free to deal in the will with the whole of his or her estate or whether a testator's powers are limited by a rule that a fixed proportion of the property must go to the spouse and children.[21] A will of movables or immovables will be interpreted in accordance with the law intended by the testator, which in the absence of any indication to the contrary, is presumed to be the law of the testator's domicile at the time the will is made.

THE GOVERNING LAW

Articles 6 and 7 of the Hague Convention, as given effect by the Recognition of Trusts Act 1987, contain two rules as to the law governing the validity, construction, effects and administration of a trust. The primary rule[22] is that a trust is governed by the law chosen by the settlor. The choice must either be express or be implied in the terms of the instrument creating or the writing evidencing the trust interpreted, if necessary, in the light of the circumstances of the case.[23] There is no doubt that at common law a settlor was able to select the governing law of a trust.[24] A testator or settlor domiciled in England is free to set up a trust governed by some foreign law, and conversely such a person domiciled in a foreign country may establish an English trust.[25]

19–002

---

[17] *Akers v Samba Financial Group* [2014] EWCA Civ 1516; [2015] Ch. 451 at [50].

[18] The Court of Appeal found this "academic" terminology unhelpful, "but at least it emphasises that article 4 is about matters that are preliminary to the final establishment of the trust (presumably when the rocket is in orbit)": *Akers v Samba Financial Group* [2014] EWCA Civ 1516; [2015] Ch. 451 at [38].

[19] Article 4.

[20] See para.18–024.

[21] *Thornton v Curling* (1824) 8 Sim. 310; *Re Annesley* [1926] Ch. 692; *Re Ross* [1930] 1 Ch. 377; *Re Adams* [1967] I.R. 424.

[22] Article 6. For change of the governing law, see art.10 and para.19–005, below.

[23] It is only when determining whether there is an *implied* choice that resort may be had to the circumstances of the case: *Tod v Barton* [2002] EWHC Ch 264 at para.[33].

[24] See *Este v Smyth* (1854) 18 Beav. 112, 122; *Re Hernando* (1884) 27 Ch.D. 284, 292–293; *Re Fitzgerald* [1904] 1 Ch. 573, 587.

[25] See e.g. *Attorney General v Campbell* (1872) L.R. 5 H.L. 524. cf. *Mayor of Canterbury v Wyburn* [1895] A.C. 89. See *Re Pollaks Estate* [1937] T.P.D. 91, as explained in *Chellaram v Chellaram* [1985] Ch. 409, 431–432.

If the settlor makes no choice of the governing law, or selects some law which does not provide for trusts or the category of trust involved,[26] the secondary rule applies. This is that the trust is governed by the law with which it is most closely connected.[27] The same rule appears to apply at common law.[28] In cases within the 1987 Act, the ascertainment of the law with which a trust is most closely connected involves making reference in particular to four factors:

(a)   the place of administration of the trust designated by the settlor;
(b)   the *situs* of the assets of the trust;
(c)   the place of residence or business of the trustee; and
(d)   the objects of the trust and the places where they are to be fulfilled.[29]

There is among these factors "a certain implicit hierarchy",[30] but also a considerable overlap as (a) and (c) will usually coincide. Although not expressly stated in the Hague Convention, it is clear from other provisions of the Convention[31] that these factors are to be considered as at the moment of creation of the trust.[32]

Despite the identification of the four factors, the court must carry out a careful examination of all the circumstances. For example, in *Chellaram v Chellaram*,[33] a case decided before the Act, the settlor and beneficiaries were all domiciled in India. However, the parties were found to have contemplated that the trust would be administered in England; the assets of the trust were shares in a holding company in Bermuda, the underlying assets being in 12 countries (none of which was India); the trustees were either ordinarily resident in, or closely connected with, England; and the purpose of the whole arrangement was to avoid Indian taxation and exchange control regulations. The court was not required to resolve the question as to whether the proper law was Indian or English, a question which would be made no easier by the guidance in the 1987 Act: the factors there set out will be taken into account in cases not falling within the Act.[34] Other factors, also relied on in the cases at common law[35] can also be weighed in applying art.7. These will include the domicile of the settlor, especially if the trust is created by

---

[26] See art.6(2).
[27] Article 7(1). As Harris observes, the choice of law rules have more in common with those for contracts than property: see Fawcett (ed.), op. cit. 187.
[28] *Duke of Marlborough v Attorney General (No.1)* [1945] Ch. 78, 83; *Iveagh v IRC* [1954] Ch. 364; *Chellaram v Chellaram* [1985] Ch. 409.
[29] Article 7(2). See *Gorgeous Beauty Ltd v Liu* [2014] EWHC 2952.
[30] von Overbeck, Explanatory Report, p.386.
[31] See art.10 dealing inter alia with changes in the governing law.
[32] cf. von Overbeck, Explanatory Report, p.387. cf. *Chellaram v Chellaram (No.2)* [2002] EWHC Ch 632; [2002] 3 All E.R. 17: for jurisdictional purposes, the applicable law falls to be determined at the date of the proceedings.
[33] [1985] Ch. 409. See also *Armenian Patriarch of Jerusalem v Sonsino* [2002] EWHC 1304.
[34] In *Chellaram v Chellaram (No.2)* [2002] EWHC Ch 632; [2002] 3 All E.R. 17 at paras [164]–[167], Lawrence Collins J considered it "likely" that Indian law governed. See also *Martin v Secretary of State or Work and Pensions* [2009] EWCA Civ 1289.
[35] See the analysis by Wallace, (1987) 36 I.C.L.Q. 454, 468–469.

a will or a marriage settlement,[36] the legal style of the trust instrument, the domicile of the beneficiaries, and the place of execution of the trust deed.

The weight to be given to all these factors, whether or not listed in art.7, must vary with the circumstances. The *situs* of the assets of the trust may deserve little weight: the movables included in a trust are usually intangible, e.g., stocks, shares and bonds; and the *situs* of an intangible movable is a fiction. The place where a trust deed is executed may not be sufficiently related to the substance of the transaction; it may be fortuitous, or worse still, carefully contrived so as to take advantage of a favourable law.

Article 5 of the Convention provides that the Convention does not apply to the extent that the law specified by Ch.II as the applicable law does not provide for trusts or the category of trusts involved. This provision, as given effect in the 1987 Act seems not to have been considered by an English court. If the Convention does not apply for the reason stated, recourse would be had to the common law. Whether a court applying the common law to identify the governing law would have regard to the fact that one possibly applicable law did not provide for trusts is an unresolved question.[37]

The freedom of choice given to the settlor is qualified by art.18 which allows the provisions of the Convention to be disregarded when their application would be manifestly incompatible with public policy. At common law, it seems that the settlor's freedom of choice might similarly be subject to the requirements of English public policy; for example, an English court would presumably not allow a settlor creating an essentially English trust to evade the English rule against perpetuities by selecting, as the proper law of the trust, the law of some foreign country where the rule does not apply.[38]

SCOPE OF THE GOVERNING LAW

The law identified by art.6 or 7 of the Convention governs the validity of the trust, its construction, its effects, and the administration of the trust.[39] In particular it governs:

19–003

"the appointment, resignation and removal of trustees, the capacity to act as a trustee, and the devolution of the office of trustee;

the rights and duties of trustees among themselves;

the right of trustees to delegate in whole or in part the discharge of their duties or the exercise of their powers;

the power of trustees to administer or to dispose of trust assets, to create security interests in the trust assets, or to acquire new assets;

the powers of investment of trustees;

restrictions upon the duration of the trust, and upon the power to accumulate the income of

---

[36] See especially *Iveagh v IRC* [1954] Ch. 364 (domicile of settlor and beneficiaries decisive, despite execution of settlement and location of assets in England).

[37] See *Berezovsky v Abramovich* [2011] EWCA Civ 153 at [108]ff.

[38] See also art.13, which is not included in the text as given effect by the 1987 Act. It provides that no state is bound to recognise a trust the significant elements of which (except for the choice of the applicable law) i.e., the place of administration and the habitual residence of the trustee, are more closely connected with states which do not have the institution of the trust or the category of trust involved.

[39] Article 8(1).

the trust;
    the relationships between the trustees and the beneficiaries including the personal liability
of the trustees to the beneficiaries;
    the variation or termination of the trust;
    the distribution of the trust assets; and
    the duty of trustees to account for their administration.[40]"

So far as the appointment of trustees is concerned, there is no legal bar to the appointment of trustees resident abroad as trustees of an English trust: but such an appointment is improper except in exceptional circumstances, e.g., where all the beneficiaries have become resident in the foreign country concerned.[41] On the other hand there is no power to appoint the English Public Trustee as trustee of a foreign trust, even though all the beneficiaries are domiciled and resident in England, the trust property is situated in England, and the trustees who wish to retire from the trust are all resident in England.[42]

It is desirable that a trust should be treated as a unit and that the trusts of all the property comprised therein should be governed by a single law. The fact that some of the property is movable and some immovable does not necessarily defeat this policy.

In *Re Fitzgerald*[43] the Court of Appeal held that a marriage settlement in Scottish form made by a lady domiciled in Scotland before her marriage to a domiciled Englishman was governed by Scots law. Most of the settled property (to the amount of £13,200) was invested in Scottish heritable bonds, i.e. in immovables; the only movable was a sum of £500 in cash. One reason given by Cozens-Hardy LJ for holding that Scots law was the proper law was the following:

"It can scarcely be denied that the *lex loci*—i.e., the law of Scotland—must apply to the extent of the £13,000. There was £500 cash belonging to the lady which was paid over to the trustees for investment. It seems to me that this sum cannot fairly be treated as intended to be subject to a different law from that which is applicable to the bulk of the property."

But if the trust property had consisted of £13,000 worth of movables and a cottage in England worth £500, the same reasoning inverted would have led to the conclusion that the land in England was subject to the same law as the movables, i.e. Scots law.

Similarly, it seems advisable to avoid a rigid distinction between the validity, interpretation and effect of a trust on the one hand and questions of "administration" on the other. It has sometimes been suggested that the latter should be governed by the law of the place of administration of the trust. Such a rigid distinction was rejected in *Chellaram v Chellaram*.[44] But as in the case of the manner of performance of a contract,[45] regard must be had to the law of the place of administration so far as the detailed procedures for the administration of

---

[40] Article 8(2).
[41] *Meinertzhagen v Davis* (1844) 1 Coll.N.C. 335; *Re Smith's Trusts* (1872) 20 W.R. 695; *Re Liddiard* (1880) 14 Ch.D. 310; *Re Whitehead's Trusts* [1971] 1 W.L.R. 833.
[42] *Re Hewitt's Settlement* [1915] 1 Ch. 228.
[43] [1904] 1 Ch. 573.
[44] [1985] Ch. 409.
[45] See para.15–044.

the trust are concerned. In a similar context, it has been held that the English courts will not administer a foreign charity under the supervision of the court, nor will they settle a scheme for such a charity.[46] They may, however, authorise an application to the appropriate foreign court to frame such a scheme.[47] But if the foreign objects of an English charitable trust fail, the court will direct an application of the trust funds cy-près.[48]

The Hague Convention gives effect to these policies, but also admits the possibility of *depeçage*. Article 9 provides that a severable aspect of the trust, particularly matters of administration, may be governed by a different law. A deliberate choice by the settlor of two different laws to govern different issues or different types of property will therefore be respected.

Cases at common law before the 1987 Act established that the proper law of the trust governed the material or essential validity of the trust,[49] its interpretation,[50] and its effect, e.g. the question whether a beneficiary can alienate his or her interest in the trust and whether that interest can be reached by the beneficiary's creditors.[51]

RECOGNITION OF TRUSTS

The Recognition of Trusts Act 1987, despite its Short Title, is, like the Hague Convention to which it gives effect, primarily about the law applicable to trusts. Where a trust is valid under the governing law (and where no "preliminary issue" can be raised as to the validity of the will or trust instrument) its recognition necessarily follows. Article 11(1) of the Convention, which provides that a trust created in accordance with the law specified in the Convention must be recognised as a trust, is almost tautologous. However,   **19–004**

> "judges of civil law countries ... might stand perplexed before the pure and simple affirmation that a trust ... should deploy effects in their countries ... It is necessary that [the Convention should] indicate at least on the principal points, what recognition will consist of and what the effects will be that the trust will deploy".[52]

Accordingly, art.11 provides that recognition implies,

> "as a minimum, that the trust property constitutes a separate fund, that the trustee may sue and be sued in his capacity as trustee, and that he may appear or act in this capacity before a notary or any person acting in an official capacity."

---

[46] *Provost of Edinburgh v Aubrey* (1754) Ambler 256; *Attorney General v Lepine* (1818) 2 Swanst. 181; *Emery v Hill* (1826) 1 Russ. 112; *New v Bonaker* (1867) L.R. 4 Eq. 655.
[47] *Re Fraser* (1883) 22 Ch.D. 827; *Re Marr's Will Trusts* [1936] Ch. 671.
[48] *Re Colonial Bishoprics Fund* [1935] Ch. 148.
[49] *Lindsay v Miller* [1949] V.L.R. 13; *Augustus v Permanent Trustee Co (Canberra) Ltd* (1971) 124 C.L.R. 245. cf. art.8(2)(f) for the similar position under the 1987 Act.
[50] *Perpetual Executors and Trustees Association of Australia Ltd v Roberts* [1970] V.R. 732; cf. art.8(1).
[51] *Re Fitzgerald* [1904] 1 Ch. 573; cf. art.8(1).
[52] von Overbeck, Explanatory Report, p.377.

Further, in so far as the law applicable to the trust requires or provides, recognition implies in particular:

(a)   that personal creditors of the trustee can have no recourse against the trust assets;

(b)   that the trust assets do not form part of the trustee's estate upon his insolvency or bankruptcy;

(c)   that the trust assets do not form part of the matrimonial property of the trustee or his spouse nor part of the trustee's estate upon his death; and

(d)   that the trust assets may be recovered when the trustee, in breach of trust, has mingled trust assets with his own property or has alienated trust assets.

However, the rights and obligations of any third party holder of the assets remain subject to the law determined by the choice of law rules of the forum.[53] These provisions, like the description of the trust in art.2, concentrate on the position of the trustee, and deal less than satisfactorily with that of beneficiaries. In particular a beneficiary's right to trace trust assets is restricted, especially where the relevant assets are situated in a country the law of which does not have the concept of the trust.[54]

An important practical aspect of the recognition of trusts is the inclusion of trusts in registers of title, a matter of some difficulty in civil law countries. Article 12 seeks to facilitate such registration, but only in so far as this is not prohibited by, or inconsistent with, the law of the state where registration is sought.

The effect of art.11, and indeed of the Hague Convention as a whole, is qualified by the savings for mandatory rules in arts 15 and 16, of which the former is remarkable for the looseness of its drafting. It provides that the Convention "does not prevent" the application of the law designated by the conflicts rules of the forum, in so far as it cannot be derogated from by voluntary act, "relating in particular"[55] to various matters: the protection of minors and incapable parties; the personal and proprietary effects of marriage; succession rights, testate and intestate, especially the indefeasible shares of spouses and relatives; the transfer of title to property and security interests in property; the protection of creditors in matters of insolvency; and the protection, in other respects, of third parties acting in good faith.[56]

If recognition of a trust is prevented by the application of art.15, the court is directed to try to give effect to the objects of the trust by other means.[57] Article 16 similarly protects the mandatory rules of the forum.

---

[53] Article 11(2)(3). See Harris in Fawcett (ed.), op. cit. at 196–197.

[54] See Hayton, (1987) 36 I.C.L.Q. 260, 275–276; Harris, (2002) 73 B.Y.B.I.L. 65.

[55] The Court of Appeal emphasised in *Charalambous v Charalambous* [2004] EWCA Civ 1030, [2004] 2 F.C.R. 721 that "the liberation from arts 6 and 8 which art.15 provides" was not limited to the six specified cases.

[56] Article 15(1).

[57] Article 15(2).

VARIATION OF TRUSTS

Under s.1(1) of the Variation of Trusts Act 1958, the High Court or a county **19–005** court[58] has power to approve any arrangement varying or revoking all or any of the trusts on which the property is held under any will, settlement or other disposition. In cases decided before the Recognition of Trusts Act 1987 it was held that this jurisdiction was unlimited, applying even to trusts governed by a foreign law[59] but that an English court would hesitate before exercising its jurisdiction in such cases.[60] In cases within the Recognition of Trusts Act 1987, the variation of trusts is one of the matters governed by the law identified by arts 6 or 7 as the law governing the trust.[61] This is a choice of law rule and does not directly affect the jurisdiction of the English courts, but it may make it more likely that an English court would disclaim the exercise of jurisdiction, treating the courts of the relevant foreign country as a more appropriate forum. Such an approach was expressly contemplated in *Re Pagets Settlement*.[62] There, Cross J, while accepting that he had jurisdiction to vary a settlement assumed to be governed by the law of New York, said:

> "Where there are substantial foreign elements in the case, the court must consider carefully whether it is proper for it to exercise the jurisdiction. If, for example, the court were asked to vary a settlement which was plainly a Scottish settlement, it might well hesitate to exercise its jurisdiction to vary the trusts, simply because some of, or even all, the trustees and beneficiaries were in this country. It may well be that the judge would say that the Court of Session was the appropriate tribunal to deal with the case."

It is important that the power of a divorce court to vary a settlement made by the parties to a marriage, under s.24 of the Matrimonial Causes Act 1973 after granting a decree, and under s.17 of the Matrimonial and Family Proceedings Act 1984 after a foreign decree, should be exercised in accordance with the English *lex fori* as part of the whole range of powers exercisable in those contexts. The Recognition of Trusts Act 1987 does not affect that position.[63]

The law applicable to the validity of the trust determines whether that law, or the law governing a severable aspect of the trust, may be replaced by another law.[64] The governing law may be changed by the court on an application under the Variation of Trusts Act 1958. In *Re Seale's Marriage Settlement*[65] it was held that the court has power under the Variation of Trusts Act 1958 to approve an arrangement revoking the trusts of an English settlement, substituting the trusts of a foreign settlement and appointing a foreign trustee. In that case the husband and wife and their children had all immigrated to Canada many years before the

---

[58] County Courts Act 1984 s.23(b).
[59] *Re Ker's Settlement* [1963] Ch. 553.
[60] *Re Paget's Settlement* [1965] 1 W.L.R. 1046; *Mubarak v Mubarak* [2007] EWHC 220 (Fam.), [2007] 2 F.L.R. 364.
[61] Hague Convention, art.8(2)(h).
[62] [1965] 1 W.L.R. 1046 at p.1050.
[63] *Charalambous v Charalambous* [2004] EWCA Civ 1030; [2004] 2 F.C.R. 721 (noted Harris, (2005) 121 L.Q.R. 16), applying the principle in art.15.
[64] Hague Convention, art.10.
[65] [1961] Ch. 574.

application was made to the court. But in *Re Weston's Settlements*[66] the Court of Appeal refused to approve a similar arrangement where the settlor and his two sons (on whom the settlements in question had been made) emigrated from England to Jersey a bare three months before the application was made. Although the parties' evidence that they intended to remain permanently in Jersey was uncontradicted, the court obviously disbelieved it: the application was "an essay in tax avoidance naked and unashamed".

In that case it appeared that there was no Trustee Act in force in Jersey and that the courts there had never made an order executing the trusts of a settlement, though there was also evidence that they would probably do so if required. But the inexperience of the Jersey courts in matters of trusts does not prevent the English court from approving a revocation of an English settlement and the substitution of a Jersey settlement in a proper case. Thus in *Re Windeatt* the court made such an order. It distinguished *Re Weston's Settlements* on the ground that the life tenant had been living in Jersey for 19 years before the application was made, that she was probably domiciled there, and that her children were born there.

The powers of the court to vary trusts under the Matrimonial Causes Act 1973 and the Variation of Trusts Act 1958 extend to trusts of immovables as well as to trusts of movables.

THE EUROPEAN REGULATIONS

19–006   The Rome I Regulation on the law applicable to contractual obligations[67] does not apply to the constitution of trusts or the relationship between settlors, trustees and beneficiaries.[68] The Rome II Regulation on the law applicable to non-contractual obligations[69] is prima facie of greater relevance. In that Regulation there is also an exclusion dealing with trusts, but it is in qualified terms: "non-contractual obligations arising out of the relations between the settlers, trustees and beneficiaries of a trust created voluntarily".[70] It will be recalled that the scope of the Hague Convention is limited to trusts created voluntarily and evidenced in writing,[71] and the earlier discussion of the effect of that provision is equally applicable to the Rome II Regulation exclusion. The intention is clearly that where the Convention applies, it prevails over the Regulation, and art.28(1) of the Regulation gives effect to that intention. However, the Recognition of Trusts Act 1987, as we have seen, has a scope wider than that of the Convention and goes beyond even the extension to trusts created by judicial decision, an extension expressly allowed by the Convention.[72] There are therefore some trusts within the 1987 Act but beyond the scope of the

---

[66] [1969] 1 Ch. 223.
[67] European Parliament and Council Regulation 593/2008, [2008] O.J. L177, p.6.
[68] Rome I Regulation, art.1(2)(h).
[69] European Parliament and Council Regulation No.864/2007, [2007] O.J. L 199, p.40.
[70] Rome II Regulation, art.1(2)(e).
[71] Article 3.
[72] Convention, art.20.

Convention to which the Rome II Regulation will apply. The courts have yet to grapple with the implications of this awkward conclusion.

CHAPTER 20

SOME CONFLICTS TECHNICALITIES

As promised, some matters of fundamental importance identified in the first chapter have been reserved for discussion at the end of the book. These are characterisation (on which there is a measure of agreement on the solution, but no clarity as to the identity of the problem), the incidental question (which is incapable of any overall solution), *renvoi* (on which the English courts have thus far adopted a common approach, and where European regulations have clarified the issue in relation to the applicable law to several legal categories), and the whole issue of the time factor in the conflict of laws. These matters will be examined in turn.

20–001

CHARACTERISATION

The issue of characterisation[1] has been regarded by many continental and some English and American writers as the fundamental methodology in the conflict of laws. It was 'discovered' independently and almost simultaneously by the German jurist Kahn[2] and the French jurist Bartin[3] at the end of the nineteenth century, and was introduced to American lawyers by Lorenzen in 1920[4] and to English lawyers by Beckett in 1934.[5]

20–002

The methodology and its problems

The conflict of laws exists because there are different systems of domestic law. But systems of the conflict of laws also differ. Yet all systems have at least one thing in common. They are expressed in terms of juridical concepts or categories, and localising elements or connecting factors. This may be seen by considering

20–003

---

[1] There is a vast literature on this subject and the following is only a selection: Lorenzen, *Selected Articles on the Conflict of Laws* (New Haven: Yale University Press, 1947), Chs 4 and 5; Beckett, (1934) 15 B.Y.B.I.L. 46; Robertson, *Characterisation in the Conflict of Laws* (Cambridge MA: Harvard University Press, 1940); Falconbridge, *Selected Essays on the Conflict of Laws*, 2nd edn, (Toronto: Canada Law Book, 1954), Chs 3–5; Wolff, *Private International Law* (Cambridge MA: Harvard University Press, 1942), ss.138–157; Cook, *Logical and Legal Bases of the Conflict of Laws*, Ch.8; Rabel, *Conflict of Laws: A Comparative Study* (Ann Arbor: University of Michigan Press, 1947), Vol. I, pp.47–72; Inglis, (1958) 74 L.Q.R. 493 at 503–516; Kahn-Freund, (1974) 143 Hague *Recueil des cours*, 369–382; Forsyth (2006) 2 J.Priv.I.L. 425.
[2] (1891) 30 Jhering's Jahrbücher 1.
[3] (1897) Clunet 225, 466 and 720.
[4] (1920) 20 Col.L.Rev. 247; reprinted in Lorenzen, Ch.4.
[5] (1934) 15 B.Y.B.I.L. 46.

some typical rules of the English conflict of laws familiar from earlier chapters of this book: "succession to immovables is governed by the *lex situs*"; "the formal validity of a marriage is governed by the law of the place of celebration". In these examples, succession to immovables and formal validity of marriage are the categories, while *situs* and place of celebration are the connecting factors.

In the majority of cases it is obvious that the facts must be subsumed under a particular legal category, that a particular conflict rule is available, and the connecting factor indicated by that conflict rule is unambiguous. But sometimes it is not obvious. Even if the forum and the foreign country have the same conflict rule and interpret the connecting factor in the same way, they may still reach different conclusions because they characterise the question in different ways. For instance, the forum may regard the question as one of succession, while the foreign law may regard the same question as one of matrimonial property. That is the problem of characterisation.

Two illustrations will show the precise nature of the problem.

(1)   A woman buys a ticket in London for a train journey from London to Glasgow. She is injured in an accident in Scotland. Is her cause of action for breach of contract, in which case English law may govern as the law applicable to the contract, or for tort, in which case Scots law may apply? By which law, English or Scots, is this question to be answered?[6] Or, as the issues are now governed by EU Regulations, is there an autonomous European rule that might apply?

(2)   A Frenchman under the age of 21 marries an Englishwoman in England without obtaining the consent of his parents as required by French law. The French and English conflict rules agree that the formalities of marriage are governed by the law of the place of celebration (English law), and also that the husband must have capacity to marry by his personal law (French law).[7] But is the issue in the case one of formalities (in which case the French rule will be irrelevant) or of capacity (in which case the French rule will be apply and the marriage will be void for want of capacity)?[8] Or, analysing the question in different terms, is the French rule to be characterised as one dealing with formalities (and so inapplicable) or with capacity?

The subject matter of characterisation

20–004   Before we go further, we need to ask what exactly is it that we characterise? In earlier editions of this book, Dr Morris argued that in illustration (1) above, the answer was the nature of the cause of action; in illustration (2) the relevant rule of French law. In practice, attempts to characterise particular rules of law can produce serious difficulties.

---

[6] See *Horn v North British Rly* (1878) 5 R. 1055; *Naftalin v L.M.S. Rly*, 1933 S.C. 259.

[7] The fact that the personal law means the law of the nationality in France and the law of the domicile in England is immaterial if we assume that the husband was French by nationality and French by domicile.

[8] *Ogden v Ogden* [1908] P. 46.

An example is provided by *Re Cohn*[9]:

> A mother and daughter, both domiciled in Germany but resident in England, were killed in an air raid on London by the same high explosive bomb. The daughter was entitled to movables under her mother's will if, and only if, she survived her mother. By the English conflict rules, succession to movables is governed by the law of the domicile, but questions of procedure are governed by the *lex fori*. By s.184 of the Law of Property Act 1925, the presumption was that the elder died first; but by art.20 of the German Civil Code the presumption was that the deaths were simultaneous.

Uthwatt J first decided that the English presumption was substantive, not procedural, and therefore did not apply. He next decided that the German presumption was also substantive and not procedural, and therefore did apply. He reached this conclusion for himself by examining the terms of art.20 in its context in the German Civil Code, uninfluenced by the characterisation placed upon it by the German courts or by the characterisation which he had already placed upon s.184. Had he reached different conclusions, the difficulties latent in his approach would have become obvious. If s.184 had been characterised as substantive and art.20 as procedural, then neither rule would have applied.[10] If, on the other hand, s.184 had been characterised as procedural and art.20 as substantive, both rules would apply: the court would have been faced with conflicting presumptions and would have had to choose between them.

It seems better to say that what has to be characterised is the issue in the case, the "question in issue".[11] As Auld LJ put it in *Macmillan Inc v Bishopsgate Investment Trust Plc (No.3)*[12] (where the issue concerned a claim viewed as either restitutionary or proprietary):

> "The proper approach is to look beyond the formulation of the claim and to identify ... the true issue or issues thrown up by the claim and defence. This requires a parallel exercise in classification of the relevant rule of law."

"Parallel" cannot mean "simultaneous". Although Forsyth has argued,[13] in effect, that the issues can be identified only via the relevant rules of law, it seems more accurate to say that the relevant rule can only be discovered by the process of characterisation of the issue. As we have seen, the typical conflicts statement is that issue A is governed by rule B, and the logical approach is one that starts with the issue.

---

[9] [1945] Ch. 5; discussed by Morris, (1945) 61 L.Q.R. 340.

[10] The practical result would be that those interested in the daughter's estate would not have been entitled to the mother's movables, because they would have been unable to prove that the daughter survived her mother.

[11] See *Macmillan Inc v Bishopsgate Investment Trust Plc (No.3)* [1996] 1 W.L.R. 387, where the different members of the court use various terms to express the point.

[12] *Macmillan Inc. v Bishopsgate Investment Trust Plc (No.3)* [1996] 1 W.L.R. 387 at 407.

[13] (1998) 114 L.Q.R. 141.

The methodology and its various solutions

20–005 Although various compromise solutions have been advocated, the principal contenders are characterisation by the *lex fori* and by the *lex causae*. These, together with one other approach, will be examined in turn.

Characterisation by the *lex fori*

20–006 The great majority of continental writers follow Kahn and Bartin in thinking that, with certain exceptions,[14] characterisation should be governed by the law of the forum, the *lex fori*.

The strongest reason for relying on characterisation by the *lex fori* is that the exercise is essentially concerned with identifying the relevant legal category and so the applicable English conflicts rule, leading in turn to the identification of the governing law. Any reference to potentially applicable foreign law (except perhaps to inform an understanding of legal concepts) is premature until that has been done.

The continental writers tend to argue their case in terms of the characterisation of rules of law rather than issues. They assert that the forum should characterise rules of its own domestic law in accordance with that law, and should characterise rules of foreign law in accordance with their nearest equivalents in its own domestic law. This is in substance what was done in *Ogden v Ogden*, illustration (2), above.

The main argument in favour of this view is that if the foreign law were allowed to determine in what situations it is to be applied, the law of the forum would lose all control over the application of its own conflict rules, and would no longer be master of its own house. The main objections to this view are as follows. In the first place, to argue by analogy from a rule of domestic law to a rule of foreign law is to indulge in mechanical jurisprudence of a particularly objectionable kind, and may result in the forum seriously distorting the foreign law, applying it in cases where it would not be applicable and vice versa, so that the law applied to the case is neither the law of the forum nor the foreign law nor the law of any country whatever. In the second place, this view breaks down altogether if there is no close analogy to the foreign rule of law or institution in the domestic law of the forum.

Characterisation by the *lex causae*

20–007 A few continental writers[15] believe that characterisation should be governed by the *lex causae*, i.e. the appropriate foreign law. According to Wolff,[16] "every legal rule takes its characterisation from the legal system *to which it belongs*".

---

[14] One of Bartin's exceptions was the characterisation of interests in property as interests in movables or immovables, which he said must be determined by the *lex situs*.

[15] e.g., Despagnet, (1898) Clunet 253; Wolff, op. cit., ss.138–157.

[16] At p.154 (Wolff's italics).

This view was in substance adopted in *Re Maldonado*,[17] where the Court of Appeal had to decide whether the Spanish Government's claim to the movables in England of a Spanish intestate who died without next of kin was a right of succession (in which case the Spanish Government was entitled to the movables) or a *jus regale* (in which case the English Crown was entitled to them). The court held that this question must be decided in accordance with Spanish law, with the result that the Spanish Government was entitled. The argument in favour of this view is that to say that the foreign law governs, and then not apply its characterisation, is tantamount to not applying it at all.

But this view is open to even more serious objections than the first one. In the first place, it is a circular argument to say that the foreign law governs the process of characterisation before the process of characterisation has led to the selection of the foreign law. Secondly, if there are two potentially applicable foreign laws, why should the forum adopt the characterisation of one rather than the other?

Analytical jurisprudence and comparative law

Other writers[18] argue that the process of characterisation should be performed in accordance with the principles of analytical jurisprudence and comparative law. This view has its attractions, because judicial technique in conflicts cases should be more internationalist and less insular than in domestic cases.   **20–008**

But the objections to this view are that there are very few principles of analytical jurisprudence and comparative law of universal application: "international agreement on analytical concepts is a utopia".[19] While the study of comparative law is capable of revealing differences between domestic laws, it is hardly capable of resolving them. For instance, comparative law may reveal that parental consents to marriage are sometimes regarded as affecting formalities and sometimes as affecting capacity to marry, or that statutes of limitation are sometimes treated as procedural and sometimes as substantive: but how can comparative law determine the way in which these matters should be characterised in a particular case? Moreover, the method proposed seems quite inconsistent with the pragmatic spirit and traditions of the common law. There is no reported case in which this method has been adopted by an English court.

An internationalist approach?

In *Macmillan Inc v Bishopsgate Investment Trust Plc (No.3)*[20] the Court of Appeal characterised property by the *lex* fori, though the parties were agreed on that point. Auld LJ did, however, place an important gloss on the *lex fori* approach: **20–009**

> "However, classification of an issue and rule of law for this purpose, the underlying principle of which is to strive for comity between different legal systems, should not be constrained by

---

[17] [1954] P. 223; above, para.18–011.
[18] e.g. Rabel, op. cit., Vol. I, pp.54–56; Beckett, (1934) 15 B.Y.B.I.L. 46 at 58–60.
[19] Kahn-Freund, op. cit., p.227.
[20] [1996] 1 W.L.R. 387.

particular notions or distinctions of the domestic law of the *lex fori*, or that of the competing system of law, which may have no counterpart in the other's system. Nor should the issue be defined too narrowly, so that it attracts a particular domestic rule under the *lex fori* which may not be applicable under the other system".

This seems to be a call for an "internationalist" application of the *lex fori*.[21] It is certainly the case that for some purposes of the conflict of laws, the English courts use categories unknown in domestic law (preferring, for example, the distinction between movables and immovables to the domestic division of property into realty and personality).

It is far from clear how far this notion can be generalised in the characterisation process, and its limitations were exposed in its examination by a sharply divided Court of Appeal in *Haugesund Kommune v Depfa ACS Bank*.[22] The case concerned the capacity or power of Norwegian municipalities to enter into certain types of financial transaction. Aikens LJ (with whom Pill LJ agreed) characterised the issue as one of the "capacity" of a corporation. He continued, referring to the relevant rule in *Dicey, Morris and Collins*[23]:

"The rule as framed assumes that the legal concept of 'capacity' has a commonly understood content and significance so far as concerns non-English corporations. But because this is a conflict of laws rule, the corporations to be considered may, by definition, be non-English, and matters concerning their constitution may be governed by laws other than English law. That is the case here. As Mance L.J. points out in his judgment in *Raiffeisen Zentralbank Österreich AG v Five Star Trading LLC*,[24] classes or categories of issues which are recognised by English conflicts rules are man-made, not natural; they have no inherent value beyond their purpose of assisting in the selection of the most appropriate law to deal with them. They may need redefinition or modification. That must be so whether the conflicts rule is one agreed internationally, as with the Rome Convention, or is the product of the English common law."

In Aikens LJ's view, what was said by Auld LJ about legal issues was equally applicable to the legal concepts that go to make up issues, and so to the concept of "capacity". It would be legal parochialism to insist that the legal concepts used to make up the rule had to conform to English common law concepts. "Capacity" had to be given a broader, "internationalist", meaning and not be confined to the narrow definition accorded by domestic English law.

Etherton LJ was scathing. To say, with Auld LJ, that the underlying purpose of classification for settling a conflict of laws rule is "to strive for comity between competing legal systems" said nothing as to what the limits of such comity should be as a matter of policy. Aiken LJ's analysis led to a result which was counter-intuitive to an English lawyer and judge, was in marked contrast to the English law concept of corporate capacity, was not consistent with a sound policy objective, and was capable of producing bizarre consequences. Given the context, of contracts governed by English law, there was no authority which required giving the word "capacity" any meaning other than its meaning in domestic English jurisprudence.

---

[21] For some similar notions in the theoretical literature, see Forsyth (1998) 114 L.Q.R. 140 at 153–156.
[22] [2010] EWCA Civ 579; [2012] 2 W.L.R. 199.
[23] Rule 162(1) in the 14th edn, 2006.
[24] [2001] Q.B. 825.

English law is rich in cases raising questions of characterisation,[25] but poor in judicial discussion of the problem. It is well settled that the *lex situs* determines the characterisation of property.[26] But apart from that, it cannot be said that English courts have adopted any consistent theory of characterisation in accordance with the *lex fori*, of which *Ogden v Ogden*[27] is perhaps the most celebrated example, or in accordance with the *lex causae*, exemplified by *Re Maldonado*.[28]

It remains to add that, the problems of characterisation do not detract from the importance of characterisation as an essential methodology in the conflict of laws. The methodology can be said to be common to all legal disciplines; however, in the conflict of laws it has a particular role to play in the management of legal diversity. Through characterisation, different national legal systems can relate to each other. This "accommodation" is indeed vocational to the conflict of laws and characterisation is therefore a necessary stepping-stone in the conflicts process. It is true that conflicts of characterisation have arisen in relatively few cases, and that the process of characterisation is frequently simple and even obvious. But in some cases it is difficult, and these are the cases which have been most discussed and the results of which have been received with least enthusiasm. Hence the problem of characterisation does seem to have practical importance as well as academic interest; and some knowledge of its nature is essential for any serious student of the conflict of laws.

THE INCIDENTAL QUESTION

A problem similar to that of characterisation was discovered or invented by the German jurist Wengler in 1934.[29] It is called the incidental question,[30] and it arises in this way.   **20–010**

Suppose that an English court is considering a main question that has foreign elements, in the course of which other subsidiary questions, also having foreign elements, arise incidentally. Suppose that by the appropriate rule of the English conflict of laws, the main question is governed by the law of a foreign country. Should the subsidiary questions be governed by the English conflict rule

---

[25] In addition to the cases discussed in the text, see *Leroux v Brown* (1852) 12 C.B. 801 (Statute of Frauds 1677 s.4: substance or procedure); *Re Martin* [1900] P. 211 at 240 (Wills Act 1837 s.18: testamentary or matrimonial law); *Re Wilks* [1935] Ch. 645 (Administration of Estates Act 1925 s.33(1): administration or succession); *Re Priest* [1944] Ch. 58 (Wills Act 1837 s.15: formal or essential validity of wills); *Apt v Apt* [1948] P. 83 (proxy marriages: formal validity or capacity to marry); *Re Kehr* [1952] Ch. 26 (Trustee Act 1925 ss.31 and 32: administration or succession); *In the Estate of Fuld (No.3)* [1968] P. 675 at 696–697 (onus of proof of testamentary capacity: substance or procedure). For other examples, see Robertson, op. cit., pp.164–188 and 245–279; Falconbridge, op. cit., pp.73–123; Beckett (1934) 15 B.Y.B.I.L. 46 at 66–81.

[26] Above, para.17–002.

[27] [1908] P. 46.

[28] [1954] P. 223.

[29] Wengler, (1934) 8 Rabel's Zeitschrift, 148–251; Robertson, op. cit., Ch.6; Wolff, op. cit., ss.196–200; Gotlieb, (1955) 33 Can. Bar Rev. 523–555; Wengler, (1966) 55 Rev. Crit. 165–215; Hartley, (1967) 16 I.C.L.Q. 680–691; Gotlieb, (1977) 26 I.C.L.Q. 734.

[30] This term was used by Wolff and is considered the most suitable English expression. The French and German terms are, respectively, "*question préalable*" and "*Vorfrage*".

appropriate to such questions, or should they be governed by the appropriate conflict rules of the foreign law that governs the main question? An illustration will make this clearer.

Suppose that a testator domiciled in France gives movables in England to his "wife". The main question here is the succession to the movables, governed by French law, the law of the testator's domicile. The incidental question is the validity of the marriage, which may in turn depend on the validity of some previous divorce. Should these questions be referred to the English or the French rules of the conflict of laws relating to the validity of marriages and the recognition of divorces?

In order that a true incidental question may squarely be presented, three conditions must be fulfilled. First, the main question must by the English conflict rule be governed by the law of some foreign country. Second, a subsidiary question involving foreign elements must present itself and be capable of arising in its own right or in other contexts, and for which there is a separate conflict rule. Third, the English conflict rule for the determination of the subsidiary question must lead to a different result from the corresponding conflict rule of the country whose law governs the main question. Such cases are rare. Thus, in a case of succession to movables, the first condition would not be satisfied if the deceased died domiciled in England. The third condition would not be satisfied if a testator domiciled abroad gave a legacy to his or her legitimate children, but the English and the foreign conflict rule agreed that the children were or were not legitimate.[31]

Decisions, or even dicta, involving the incidental question in English, Commonwealth or American case law, are extremely rare.

In *Schwebel v Ungar*[32]:

> A husband and wife, both Jews, were domiciled in Hungary. They decided to immigrate to Israel. While en route to Israel they were divorced by a Jewish *ghet* (or extra-judicial divorce) in Italy. This divorce was not recognised by the law of Hungary (where they were still domiciled) but was recognised by the law of Israel. The parties then acquired a domicile in Israel, and the wife while so domiciled went through a ceremony of marriage in Toronto with a second husband, who subsequently petitioned the Ontario court for a decree of nullity on the ground that the ceremony was bigamous.

The main question here was the wife's capacity to remarry, which by the conflict rule of Ontario was governed by the law of Israel. The incidental question was the validity of the divorce. This was not recognised as valid by the conflict rule of Ontario but was recognised as valid by the conflict rule of Israel. The Supreme Court of Canada, affirming the decision of the Ontario Court of Appeal, held that the remarriage was valid, because by the law of her antenuptial domicile the wife had the status of a single woman. Thus, the incidental question was determined by the conflict rule of Israeli law, the law governing the main question, and not by the conflict rule of the forum.

---

[31] cf. *Doglioni v Crispin* (1866) L.R. 1 H.L. 301.

[32] (1963) 42 D.L.R. (2d) 622; (1964) 48 D.L.R. (2d) 644; discussed by Lysyk (1965) 43 Can. Bar Rev. 363; approved by Simon P in *Padolecchia v Padolecchia* [1968] P. 314 at 339. The facts of *Schwebel v Ungar* are misstated by Gotlieb in (1977) 26 I.C.L.Q. 734 at 775 and 793.

In *R. v Brentwood Marriage Registrar*[33]:

> An Italian husband married a Swiss wife and later obtained a divorce from her in Switzerland, where they were both domiciled. After the divorce the wife remarried. The husband wanted to marry, in England, a Spanish national domiciled in Switzerland. But the Registrar refused to marry them because in his view there was an impediment. By Swiss law, capacity to marry is governed by the law of the nationality; and Italian law did not recognise the divorces of Italian nationals.

The main question here was the husband's capacity to remarry, which by the English conflict rule was governed by Swiss law, the law of his domicile. The incidental question was the validity of the divorce. This was recognised as valid by the English conflict rule; but was not recognised by the Swiss conflict rule as entitling the husband to remarry. The Divisional Court upheld the Registrar's objections to the remarriage. Thus the incidental question was determined by the conflict rule of Swiss law, the law governing the main question, and not by the conflict rule of the forum.

The actual decision in *R. v Brentwood Marriage Registrar* would now be different because s.50 of the Family Law Act 1986 provides that where a foreign divorce (or nullity decree) is recognised in England, the fact that the divorce is not recognised elsewhere shall not preclude either party from remarrying in England or cause the remarriage of either party to be regarded as invalid in England.[34]

In *Baindail v Baindail*,[35] Lord Greene MR, in the course of a discussion of the extent to which polygamous marriages might be recognised in England, said:

> "If a Hindu domiciled in India died intestate in England leaving personal property in this country, the succession to the personal property would be governed by the law of his domicile; and in applying the law of his domicile effect would have to be given to the rights of any children of the Hindu marriage and of his Hindu widow."

Thus, this dictum recognises that the incidental questions of the validity of the marriage and the legitimacy of the children would be governed by Indian law (the law governing the main question, of succession) and not necessarily by the English conflict rule.

In *Haque v Haque*,[36] a succession case on appeal from Western Australia, the High Court of Australia applied the conflicts rule of the *lex successionis* (Indian law) and not that of the *lex fori* to determine the formal validity of a marriage celebrated in Western Australia.

Thus the weight of English, Canadian, and Australian authority (so far as it goes) seems to indicate that the incidental question is usually determined by the conflict rule of the foreign law governing the main question and not by the conflict rule of the forum.

The writers who have discussed the incidental question are equally divided in opinion between those who think it should be determined by the conflict rule of the foreign law and those who think it should be determined by the conflict rule

---

[33] [1968] 2 Q.B. 956.
[34] See above, para.11–020.
[35] [1946] P. 122 at 127.
[36] (1962) 108 C.L.R. 230.

of the forum.[37] They usually discuss the classic case of the testator domiciled in France who gives movables in England to his "wife". The writers who take the first view mentioned above emphasise that the question is not the abstract question, "was the claimant the wife of the deceased?" but rather, "was she his wife according to the law of his domicile at the time of his death and as such entitled to succeed to his movables under his will?" Those who take the second view emphasise that since ex hypothesi the incidental question is capable of arising in its own right or in other contexts than the one before the court, and has conflict rules of its own available for its determination, the court (if it applied the foreign-conflict rule) might have to give a decision contrary to its own conceptions of justice, and different from what it would have decided if the question had been presented to it in some other form. Thus, if the husband had petitioned for nullity on the ground of consanguinity, the court would have applied its own conflict rules, and might have dismissed the petition and held the marriage valid. But if the wife claimed to succeed to the husband's movables on his death, the court, if it applied the conflict rule of the law governing succession, might have to hold that she was not entitled to succeed because the marriage was invalid.

The first view harmonises well with the tendency of English courts to decide questions of succession to movables in the same way as the courts of the deceased's domicile would decide them, so as to promote uniformity of distribution. But this international harmony has to be purchased at the price of internal dissonance: sometimes the price may seem too high.

Suppose, for instance, that a Mexican national domiciled in England obtains a divorce from his wife in the English court. The divorce is, of course, valid in England, but it is not valid in Mexico. After the divorce the husband, while still domiciled in England, marries a second wife. He dies intestate domiciled in Mexico leaving movables in England. By the English conflict rule the succession to these movables is governed by Mexican law as the law of the intestate's domicile (main question); and by Mexican law the intestate's wife is entitled to a share: but which wife is entitled, the first or the second or neither (incidental question)? By Mexican law, the first wife is entitled, because she was never validly divorced and therefore the husband's remarriage was invalid. But the English court might well be reluctant to deny the validity of its own divorce decree, and if it were, the second wife should be entitled.

Such cases show that the problem of the incidental question is not capable of a mechanical solution and that each case may depend on the particular factors involved. As one writer puts it, "there is really no problem of the incidental question, but as many problems as there are cases in which incidental questions may arise".[38] The incidental question is seldom discussed by courts, but it does seem to involve a problem which is necessarily present in certain types of case.

---

[37] See the analysis in Gotlieb, (1977) 26 I.C.L.Q. 734, 751–760.
[38] Gotlieb, above, at p.798.

RENVOI

Renvoi[39] comes into play whenever a rule of the conflict of laws refers to the "law" of another country, but the conflict rule of the foreign country would have referred the question to the "law" of the first country or to the "law" of some third country. Suppose, for instance, that a British citizen dies intestate domiciled in Italy, leaving movables in England; and that by the English conflict rule, succession to movables is governed by the law of the domicile (Italian law), but by the Italian conflict rule succession to movables is governed by the law of the nationality (English law). Which law, English or Italian, will regulate the distribution of the English movables? This is a relatively simple case of remission from Italian law (the law identified by the English choice of law rule, the *lex causae*) to English law (the law of the forum or *lex fori*). Had the intestate been a German instead of a British citizen we should have had a more complicated case of transmission from Italian to German law. It will be as well to focus attention on cases of remission at the outset.[40]

20–011

It is possible to identify three approaches to the use (or exclusion) of *renvoi* in the choice of law process.

The internal law solution (exclusion of *renvoi*)

The English court might apply the purely domestic rule of Italian law applicable to Italians, disregarding the fact that the intestate was a British citizen, which is in any case irrelevant in the English conflict of laws. This method requires proof of Italian domestic law, but not of its choice of law rules. It has been recommended (obiter) by two English judges on the ground that it is "simple and rational",[41] but rejected in another case after a comprehensive review of the authorities.[42]

20–012

Partial or single *renvoi* theory (accepting the *renvoi*)

The English court might accept the reference back from Italian law and apply English domestic law, disregarding the fact that the intestate was domiciled in Italy. This process is technically known as "accepting the *renvoi*".[43] This method requires proof of the Italian conflict rules relating to succession, but not of the

20–013

---

[39] There is an immense literature on this subject, and the following is only a selection: Wolff, op. cit., ss.178–195; Falconbridge, op. cit., Chs 6–10; Cook, op. cit., Ch.9; Lorenzen, op. cit., Chs 2, 3, 5; Morris, (1937) 18 B.Y.B.I.L. 32; Griswold, (1938) 51 Harv.L.Rev. 1165; Inglis, (1958) 74 L.Q.R. 493; Kahn-Freund, op. cit., 431–437; Briggs, (1998) 47 I.C.L.Q. 877; op. cit., Kassir, *Réflexions sur le renvoi en droit international privé comparé* (Bruylant, Brussels, 2002).

[40] Transmission is briefly considered below, para.20–022.

[41] *Re Annesley* [1926] Ch. 692 at 708–709, per Russell J; *Re Askew* [1930] 2 Ch. 259 at 278, per Maugham J.

[42] *Re Ross* [1930] 1 Ch. 377 at 402.

[43] This expression must be distinguished from accepting the doctrine of the *renvoi*, which the forum may do without necessarily accepting the first reference back. The former expression means stopping the game of tennis with the return of serve. The latter means continuing the game until the other player gets tired of it.

Italian rules about *renvoi*. It is the practice in many of the countries of continental Europe,[44] but it is not the current doctrine of the English courts.

Total or double *renvoi*

20–014 The English court might decide the case in the same way as it would be decided by the Italian court. If the Italian court would refer to English "law" and would interpret that reference to mean English domestic law, then the English court would apply English domestic law. If on the other hand the Italian court would refer to English "law" and interpret that reference to mean English conflict of laws and would "accept the *renvoi*" from English law and apply Italian domestic law, then the English court would apply Italian domestic law. This method requires proof not only of the Italian conflict rules relating to succession but also of the Italian rules about *renvoi*, requiring a high degree of expertise from witnesses (and creating a risk that the experts will disagree).

How this theory works in practice can best be seen by comparing two leading cases. In *Re Annesley*[45]:

> T, a British subject of English domicile of origin, died domiciled in France in the English sense, but not in the French sense.[46] She left a will that purported to dispose of all her property. By French law, T could dispose of only one-third of her property because she left two surviving children. Evidence was given that a French court would refer to English law as T's national law and would accept the *renvoi* back to French law. French domestic law was applied and T's will was only effective to dispose of one-third of her property.

In *Re Ross*,[47] on the other hand:

> T, a British subject domiciled in Italy, died leaving movables in England and Italy and immovables in Italy. She left two wills, one in English and the other in Italian. By her English will she gave her property in England to her niece X. By her Italian will she gave her property in Italy to her grand-nephew Y, subject to a life interest to his mother X. She left nothing to her only son Z. Z claimed that by Italian law he was entitled to one-half of T's property as his *legitima portio*. By the English conflict rules, the validity of T's will was governed by Italian law as the law of her domicile in respect of movables and by Italian law as the *lex situs* in respect of immovables. Evidence was given that an Italian court would refer to English law as T's national law in respect of both movables and immovables, and would not accept the *renvoi* back to Italian law. English domestic law was applied and Z's claim was rejected.

Origin and development

20–015 The doctrine of *renvoi* obtained a foothold in English law in 1841 via cases on the formal validity of wills. In that context, three factors favoured its recognition. First, the English conflict rule was at that time unduly rigid. It insisted on compliance with one form and one form only for wills, that of the testator's last

---

[44] Including Austria, France, Germany, Monaco, Spain and Switzerland; by contrast, Denmark, Greece, Italy, the Netherlands, and Norway reject *renvoi*.
[45] [1926] Ch. 692.
[46] Because she had not obtained authority to establish her domicile in France as required by art.13 of the Civil Code (since repealed).
[47] [1930] 1 Ch. 377.

domicile.[48] Second, in neighbouring European countries (where people of English origin were likely to settle) there was a more flexible conflict rule, which allowed compliance with the forms prescribed by either the testator's personal law or the law of the place where the will was made. Third, there was a judicial bias in favour of upholding wills which admittedly expressed the last wishes of the testator and were defective only in point of form.

The fountain-head of authority is *Collier v Rivaz*,[49] where the court had to consider the formal validity of a will and six codicils made by a British subject who died domiciled in Belgium in the English sense, but not in the Belgian sense.[50] The will and two of the codicils were made in Belgian form and were admitted to probate in England without argument. Four of the codicils were opposed because they were not made in local Belgian form, though they were made in English form. Upon proof that by Belgian law the validity of wills made by foreigners not legally domiciled in Belgium was governed by "the laws of their own country", Sir H. Jenner admitted these codicils to probate, remarking that "the court sitting here to determine it, must consider itself sitting in Belgium under the peculiar circumstances of this case". He did not consider the possibility that a Belgian court might have accepted the *renvoi* from English law and applied Belgian domestic law.

So the doctrine of *renvoi* was invoked, obviously as an escape device, in order to get round the rigidity of the English conflict rule. The fact that the will and the two codicils made in Belgian form were admitted to probate as well as the four codicils made in English form means that the English conflict rule was interpreted as a rule of alternative reference either to the domestic rules or to the conflict rules of Belgian law. A rule of alternative reference, while practicable for the formal validity of wills, is impracticable for the essential (or intrinsic) validity of wills or for intestacy. In such cases the court must choose between the domestic rules and the conflict rules of the foreign law. It cannot apply both, for it must decide whether or not the testator had disposing power, whether or not the deceased died intestate, and if so who were the next of kin. It is one thing to uphold a will if it complies with the formalities prescribed by either the domestic rules or the conflict rules of the foreign law. It is quite another thing to allow the next of kin entitled under the domestic rules of the foreign law to share the property with the next of kin entitled under its conflict rules.

Collier v Rivaz was disapproved in *Bremer v Freeman*,[51] where on almost identical facts the Privy Council refused to admit to probate the will of a British subject who died domiciled in France in the English sense, but not in the French sense, on the ground that it was made in a form acceptable in English but not in French law.

Until 1926, the few decisions and dicta which recognised the *renvoi* doctrine were all consistent with a theory of partial or single *renvoi*. That is to say, the

---

[48] The law has since been amended, first by the Wills Act 1861, and then by the Wills Act 1963. See above, para.18–015.

[49] (1841) 2 Curt. 855.

[50] Because he had not obtained the authority of the Belgian Government to establish his domicile in Belgium as required by art.13 of the Code Napoléon.

[51] (1857) 10 Moo. P.C. 306 at 374; followed in *Hamilton v Dallas* (1875) 1 Ch.D. 257 (partial intestacy).

English court first referred to the conflict rules of the foreign law and then applied the domestic rules either of English law or of the law of a third country,[52] without considering the possibility that the foreign court might accept the *renvoi* from English law and apply its own domestic law. In *Re Annesley*,[53] Russell J introduced the doctrine of double or total *renvoi* (but without citing any authority or giving any reasons for doing so) and applied French domestic law as the law of the domicile on the ground that a French court would have done so by way of *renvoi* from English law. He expressed his personal preference for reaching this result by a more direct route, that is, by the application of French domestic law in the first instance without any *renvoi* at all[54]; but this part of his judgment has not been followed.[55] This theory of double *renvoi* is of course quite different from the theory of single or partial *renvoi* because, by inquiring how the foreign court would decide the case, it envisages the possibility that the foreign court might "accept the *renvoi*" and apply its own domestic law, as happened in *Re Annesley*.

Confusion between the two theories was, however, introduced by an obiter dictum of the Privy Council in *Kotia v Nahas*,[56] which appeared to speak in terms of single or partial *renvoi*. It was the principal authority relied upon for the application of the *renvoi* doctrine in *Re Duke of Wellington*[57]:

> The testator, who was a British subject domiciled in England, made a Spanish will giving land and movables in Spain to the person who should fulfil two stated qualifications, and made an English will giving all the rest of his property on trust for the person who should fulfil one of the qualifications. At his death there was no person who fulfilled both qualifications, and questions arose as to the devolution of the property in Spain. It appeared that Spanish law, as the *lex situs* of the land, referred questions of succession to the national law of the testator and would not accept the *renvoi* back to Spanish law. Wynn Parry J therefore applied English domestic law and held that the gift in the Spanish will failed for uncertainty and that the Spanish property fell into the residue disposed of by the English will.

However, it was nowhere stated that the construction of the Spanish will would have been different in Spanish domestic law; and, indeed, if the construction of the Spanish will was the only point at issue, it would seem that English domestic law should have been applied without any reference to Spanish law because the testator was domiciled in England.[58] One of the counsel engaged in the case later furnished the information that by Spanish domestic law the testator could in the circumstances only dispose of half of his property and that the other half passed to his mother as heiress. It may be that this is the explanation of the decision; but it must be admitted that there is no trace of this to be found in the report. Whatever may have been the reason for referring to Spanish law, it is clear that the judge, although he relied mainly on a dictum

---

[52] As in *Re Trufort* (1877) 36 Ch.D. 600, and *Re Johnson* [1903] 1 Ch. 821, a much criticised decision.

[53] [1926] Ch. 692.

[54] At pp.708–709.

[55] *Re Ross* [1930] 1 Ch. 377 at 402. See, however, *Re Askew* [1930] 2 Ch. 259 at 278.

[56] [1941] A.C. 403 at 413.

[57] [1947] Ch. 506; affirmed on other grounds, [1948] Ch. 118; discussed by Morris, (1948) 64 L.Q.R. 264; Jennings, (1948) 64 L.Q.R. 321; Mann, (1948) 11 M.L.R. 232; Falconbridge, op. cit., pp.229–232.

[58] See above, para.18–022.

enunciating a theory of single *renvoi*, was in fact adopting a theory of double *renvoi*. Otherwise, there would have been no occasion to inquire whether Spanish law would "accept the *renvoi*" from English law, an inquiry which occupied much space in the judgment.

General conclusion from the English cases

The history of the *renvoi* doctrine in English law is the history of a chapter of accidents. The doctrine originated as a device for mitigating the rigidity of the English conflict rule for the formal validity of wills. The passing of Lord Kingsdown's Act in 1861 rendered this mitigation no longer necessary, at any rate in cases where the testator was a British subject. But the doctrine was applied in cases falling within that Act, and was extended far beyond its original context to cases of intrinsic validity of wills and to cases of intestacy. In 1926, the theory underlying the doctrine underwent a significant change, but no authorities were cited nor reasons given for making the change.[59] Two of the cases that have been relied upon as establishing the doctrine have been subsequently overruled or dissented from.[60] In three other cases, the decision would have been the same if the court had referred to the domestic rules of the foreign law in the first instance.[61] And in three further cases,[62] none of the parties was concerned to argue that the foreign law meant foreign domestic law. It follows that the whole question of *renvoi* can be reviewed by any appellate court. In *Macmillan Inc v Bishopsgate Investment Trust Plc* at first instance,[63] Millet J noted that the *renvoi* doctrine had often been criticised, and said:

20–016

> "It is probably right to describe it as largely discredited. It owes its origin to a laudable endeavour to ensure that like cases should be decided alike wherever they are decided, but it should now be recognised that this cannot be achieved by judicial mental gymnastics but only by international conventions".

The issue was not pressed on appeal,[64] and a later court noted Millet J's observations but nonetheless applied the doctrine.[65]

It is certainly the case that the English doctrine was formulated before many important developments in the methodology of the conflict of laws, notable the recognition of the significance of "mandatory rules". Those developments point to a need for the reconsideration of the nature and purpose of the doctrine.

---

[59] *Re Annesley* [1926] Ch. 692.
[60] *Collier v Rivaz* (1841) 2 Curt. 855, see above, para.20–015; *Re Johnson* [1903] 1 Ch. 821, see *Re Annesley* [1926] Ch. 692 at 705; *Re Askew* [1930] 2 Ch. 259 at 272.
[61] *Re Annesley* [1926] Ch. 692; *Re Askew* [1930] 2 Ch. 259; *In the Estate of Fuld (No.3)* [1968] P. 675.
[62] *Re Johnson* [1903] 1 Ch. 821; *Re O'Keefe* [1940] Ch. 124; *Re Duke of Wellington* [1947] Ch. 506. In *Re O'Keefe*, the originating summons did not even suggest the possibility that Italian domestic law was applicable.
[63] [1995] 1 W.L.R. 978.
[64] [1996] 1 W.L.R. 387.
[65] *Glencore International AG v Metro Trading International Inc* [2001] 1 Lloyd's Rep. 284.

An Australian approach

20–017   That reconsideration must take into account the judgments of the High Court of Australia in *Neilson v Overseas Projects Corporation of Victoria Ltd*[66]:

> N's husband was employed by an Australian company to work on a project in China. N went with him, and was injured when she fell down the stairs of the flat provided by the company. The company, as occupier, was in breach of the duty of care it owed N, but a limitation of actions issue arose. The law of Western Australia referred liability to the law of the place of the tort, China, but Chinese law provided that where the parties are nationals of the same country, the law of their own country 'maybe applied.'

The High Court of Australia was divided and the case is made more difficult by the inadequacy of some of the evidence as to Chinese law. All the judgments repay study; what follows is an exposition of the leading judgment by Gummow and Hayne JJ.

Their Honours examined the development of the *renvoi* doctrine and described how, in their words, "metaphorical references to renvoi ('return' or 'reference back') entered the English legal lexicon",[67] the problem being presented, artificially, as if some dialogue occurred between jurisdictions. Would a foreign jurisdiction to whose law the forum had referred, "refer" the issue back to the forum and say that forum law should be applied? Would the forum "accept" the reference back? In their Honours' view, scholarly debate had "focused more upon theoretical explanations for the method of solution than upon the principal and essentially practical concern of the courts, which is to decide the controversies that are tendered by the parties for decision."[68]

They argued that the most important premise was that the rules adopted should, as far as possible, avoid parties being able to obtain advantages by litigating in a particular (in the instant case, an Australian) forum which could not be obtained if the issue were to be litigated in the courts of the jurisdiction whose law is chosen as the governing law. A party could gain an advantage by litigating in the courts of the forum rather than the courts of the foreign jurisdiction only if the forum were to choose to apply only *some* of the law of that foreign jurisdiction. (In the terms of the traditional debate, this is to reject the internal law solution, which was favoured by the dissenting judge, McHugh J).

Their second premise was that certainty and simplicity are desirable characteristics; they cite Kahn-Freund[69] as saying that the intellectual challenge presented by questions of conflict of laws is its main curse, and that in this field dogmatism must yield to pragmatism.[70] To take no account of what a foreign court would do when faced with the facts of the case would not assist the pursuit of certainty and simplicity, because it would require the law of the forum to divide the rules of the foreign legal system, which must be assumed to be

---

[66] [2005] HCA 54; (2005) 233 C.L.R. 331. See Briggs, [2006] L.M.C.L.Q. 1; Dickinson (2006) 122 L.Q.R. 183.

[67] At para.86.

[68] At para.87.

[69] Kahn-Freund, *General Problems of Private International Law*, 1976, p.320.

[70] Kahn-Freund, *General Problems of Private International Law*, 1976, p.290.

intended to constitute an integrated system of interdependent rules, between those rules that are to be applied by the forum and those that are not. They illustrate this with a worked example[71]:

> "A foreign legal system may make separate provision for the kinds of loss sustained by a person as a result of a traffic accident, recoverable from the party whose negligence caused that loss, according to whether the negligent party was a national of, or domiciled in, that foreign country. The differences may reflect not only different insurance arrangements for 'local' drivers from those applying to others but also different social security and health arrangements. That is, the foreign legal system may also make provision in its social security and health legislation for giving larger benefits to those who are nationals of, or domiciled in, the country than the benefits allowed to others. If the Australian choice-of-law rules look only to the 'domestic' law of that country, what account is to be taken of these different social security and health provisions in deciding the extent of the liability to an Australian citizen of the Australian employer of a negligent 'local' driver sued in an Australian court? Is reference to be made only to the foreign law that deals with recovery of damages? Is reference to be made to the social security and health provisions? Any division that is made is necessarily an incomplete and incoherent reflection of the law of that place."

The argument seems to be leading to the double *renvoi* solution, but their Honours reject the traditional scholarly analyses as not providing a sure footing upon which to construct applicable rules. They reject the traditional distinction between a foreign legal system's rules of "domestic law" and its choice of law rules[72]:

> "Choosing a single overarching theory of *renvoi* as informing every question about choice of law would wrongly assume that identical considerations apply in every kind of case in which a choice of law must be made. But questions of personal status like marriage or divorce, questions of succession to immovable property, questions of delictual responsibility and questions of contractual obligation differ in important respects. Party autonomy may be given much more emphasis in questions of contract than in questions of title to land. Choice of governing law may be important in creating private obligations by contract but less important when the question is one of legal status. Choosing one theory of *renvoi* as applicable to all cases where a choice of law must be made would submerge these differences."

In the field of tort, the Australian choice-of-law rule applies the law of the place of the tort, the *lex loci delicti*. In that context, their Honours held that the *lex loci delicti* is the whole of the law of that place. If the foreign jurisdiction would choose to apply the law of the forum, and not the law of the place where the wrong was committed, the forum should apply its own law. If the law of the place where the wrong was committed would look to a third jurisdiction to provide the relevant law governing the resolution of substantive questions, the forum should look to and apply the law of that third jurisdiction. Scholars (and they include Dr Morris) whose writings showed great antipathy to *renvoi* did accept that the doctrine should be invoked if it is plain that the object of the relevant choice of law rule, in referring to a foreign law, will on balance be better served by construing the reference to foreign law as including the conflict rules of that law. A choice of law rule for foreign torts which requires reference to and application of the *lex loci delicti*, without exception, was such a case.[73]

---

[71] At para.95.
[72] At para.99.
[73] At paras 109–111.

It is perhaps a fair summary to say that the case endorses the application of a double *renvoi* approach if, but only if, the nature of the dispute and the underlying purpose of the forum's choice-of-law rule justify its application.

Scope of the doctrine in England

20–018   The English *renvoi* doctrine has been applied to the formal[74] and intrinsic[75] validity of wills and to cases of intestate succession.[76] It has been applied when the reference has been to the law of the domicile,[77] the law of the place where a will was made,[78] and the law of the place where an immovable was situated (*lex situs*).[79] Outside the field of succession, it seems to have been applied only to legitimation by subsequent marriage[80] and, with unfortunate results, in the context of child abduction.[81] There are indications that it might be applied to the formal validity of marriage[82] and to capacity to marry.[83] It no longer applies to the formal validity of wills in cases falling within the Wills Act 1963. *Renvoi* is excluded by the Rome Convention, its successor (the Rome I Regulation), reflecting the common law rule that "the principle of *renvoi* finds no place in the field of contract",[84] and, in the field of tort, by the Rome II Regulation. Renvoi is however permitted in the Brussels I *bis* Regulation, in relation to the law applicable to the substantial validity of a choice of court agreement.[85]

Even in the sphere in which the doctrine has been most frequently applied, namely succession to movables and immovables, it must be stressed that for every case which supports the doctrine there are hundreds of cases in which the domestic rules of the foreign law have been applied as a matter of course without any reference to its conflict rules, though it must be admitted that most of these can be explained on the ground that no one was concerned to argue that the reference to foreign law included its rules of the conflict of laws. There is, therefore, no justification for generalising the few English cases on *renvoi* into a general rule that a reference to foreign "law" always means the conflict rules of

---

[74] *Collier v Rivaz* (1841) 2 Curt. 855; *In the Goods of Lacroix* (1877) 2 P.D. 94; *In the Estate of Fuld (No. 3)* [1968] P. 675.

[75] *Re Trufort* (1887) 36 Ch. D. 600; *Re Annesley* [1926] Ch. 692; *Re Ross* [1930] 1 Ch. 377; and (perhaps) *Re Duke of Wellington* [1947] Ch. 506.

[76] *Re Johnson* [1903] 1 Ch. 821; *Re O'Keefe* [1940] Ch. 124; *Haji-Ioannou v Frangos* [2009] EWHC 2310 (QB); [2010] 1 All E.R. (Comm) 303 (were the doctrine was applied, without any discussion, to intestate succession to rights under a judgment).

[77] *Collier v Rivaz*; *Re Trufort*; *Re Johnson*; *Re Annesley*; *Re Ross*; *Re Askew*; *Re O'Keefe*; *In the Estate of Fuld (No.3)*, all cited above.

[78] *In the Goods of Lacroix*, above.

[79] *Re Ross*, above; *Re Duke of Wellington*, above.

[80] *Re Askew*, above.

[81] e.g., *Re JB (Abduction) (Rights of Custody: Spain)* [2003] EWHC 2130; [2004] 1 F.L.R. 976.

[82] *Taczanowska v Taczanowski* [1957] P. 301 at 305 and 318; above, para.11–008.

[83] *R. v Brentwood Marriage Registrar* [1968] 2 Q.B. 956; above, para.11–020.

[84] The leading common law authority was *Re United Railways of the Havana and Regla Warehouses Ltd* [1960] Ch. 52 at 96–97 and 115.

[85] Reg. 1215/2016, art.25 and Recital (20).

the foreign law, and no justification for the statement that "the English courts have generally, *if not invariably*, meant by 'the law of the country of domicile' the whole law of that country".[86]

Much of the discussion of the *renvoi* doctrine has proceeded on the basis that the choice lies in all cases between its absolute acceptance and its absolute rejection. Even before *Neilson v Overseas Projects Corporation of Victoria Ltd*,[87] it was clear that in some situations the doctrine is convenient and promotes justice, and that in other situations the doctrine is inconvenient and ought to be rejected. In some situations the doctrine may be a useful means of arriving at a result which is desired for its own sake; but often this is because the English conflict rule is defective. For instance, if the court wishes to sustain a marriage which is alleged to be formally invalid, or to promote uniformity of distribution in a case of succession to movables where the deceased left movables in more countries than one, or to avoid conflicts with the *lex situs* in a case of title to land or conflicts with the law of the domicile in a case involving personal status, then the doctrine of *renvoi* may sometimes be a useful (though troublesome) device for achieving the desired result. On the other hand, in all but exceptional cases the theoretical and practical difficulties involved in applying the doctrine outweigh any supposed advantages it may possess. The doctrine should not, therefore, be invoked unless it is plain that the object of the English conflict rule in referring to a foreign law will on balance be better served by construing the reference to mean the conflict rules of that law.[88]

When will this be so? A number of types of case can be considered in which the arguments for *renvoi* have been advanced:

Title to land situated abroad[89]

If the question before the English court is whether a person has acquired a title to land situated abroad, the court (in so far as it has jurisdiction to deal with the matter at all) will apply the *lex situs*, the law of the place where the land is situated. One of the reasons for applying the *lex situs* is that any adjudication which was contrary to it would in most cases be a *brutum fulmen*, a waste of judicial breath, since in the last resort the land can only be dealt with in a manner permitted by the *lex situs.*

20–019

This reason requires that the *lex situs* should be interpreted to mean the law that the *lex situs* would apply. Suppose, for instance, that a British citizen domiciled in England dies intestate leaving land in Spain; and that by Spanish domestic law X is entitled to the land, but that Spanish courts would apply English domestic law according to which Y is entitled. It would be manifestly useless for an English court to decide that X was entitled to the land, because X

---

[86] *Re Ross* [1930] 1 Ch. 377 at 390, per Luxmoore J (italics added).

[87] [2005] HCA 54; (2005) 233 C.L.R. 331. See Briggs, [2006] L.M.C.L.Q. 1; Dickinson (2006) 122 L.Q.R. 183.

[88] See Lawrence Collins J in *Barros Mattos v MacDaniels Ltd* [2005] EWHC 1323 (Ch) at [108] citing language to this effect in *Dicey, Morris and Collins*. See also *Blue Sky One Limited v Mahan Air* [2010] EWHC 631 (Comm).

[89] See Falconbridge, op. cit., pp.141 and 217–220; Cook, op. cit., pp.264 and 279–280; Lorenzen, op. cit., p.78.

could never recover it from Y in Spain.[90] However, the Wills Act 1963 excludes *renvoi* even in the case of immovables so far as the formal validity of wills is concerned.

Movables

20–020   A similar argument suggests that when the English court applies the *lex situs* to determine the title to movables situated abroad, it should interpret the *lex situs* broadly so as to include whatever the courts of the *situs* have decided or would decide. However, the argument is not so strong as in the case of land, because the movables may be taken out of the jurisdiction of the foreign court; the application of the *renvoi* doctrine in this type of case was rejected in *Islamic Republic of Iran v Berend*,[91] in which Eady J referred with some approval to the non-dogmatic approach taken in *Neilson v Overseas Projects Corporation of Victoria Ltd*.[92] In *Dornoch v Westminster International NV*,[93] Tomlinson J, having reviewed the earlier dicta, thought that were he to apply *renvoi* in a case involving movables he would be "rowing against a strong tide". He would be reluctant to apply in a commercial context, concerning marine insurance and title to a ship, a doctrine "hitherto applicable only in fields such as the formal and intrinsic validity of wills, intestate succession and legitimation by subsequent marriage when in the fields of contract, tort, restitution and trusts a deliberate decision has apparently been taken to eschew the doctrine of *renvoi*." Having referred to the Australian approach, the judge refused to reach a definitive answer to the *renvoi* issue, given the incomplete evidence of the foreign law then available to him. Finally, in *Blue Sky One Ltd v Mahan Air*[94] Beatson J rejected the use of *renvoi* in a commercial context (the mortgage of an aircraft located abroad). He criticised elements in Tomlinson J's reasoning, and by implication that of the High Court of Australia in *Neilson*:

> "to leave the applicability of the *renvoi* doctrine to a case by case analysis depending on the identification of the policy behind the private international law of the particular country under consideration is likely to lead to a very uncertain legal regime. Indeed it could lead to a Tennysonian wilderness of single instances. Moreover, as Fentiman states,[95] it would mean 'that the identity of the applicable law cannot be known without a judicial determination, even in a case where the location of the property is known to the parties'."

So title to movables is one area in which the use of *renvoi* is excluded.

---

[90] For this reason it is thought that the decision in *Re Ross* [1930] 1 Ch. 377 was correct so far as the immovables were concerned, subject to what is said later about the difficulty arising from the reference by the foreign law to the national law of a British citizen.

[91] [2007] EWHC 132; [2007] 2 All E.R. (Comm) 132.

[92] [2005] HCA 54; (2005) 233 C.L.R. 331. See Briggs, [2006] L.M.C.L.Q. 1; Dickinson (2006) 122 L.Q.R. 183.

[93] [2009] EWHC 1782 (Admlty); [2009] 2 Lloyd's Rep. 420.

[94] [2010] EWHC 631 (Comm).

[95] *International Commercial Litigation* (Oxford: Oxford University Press, 2010), para.5.57.

Formal validity of marriage

Factors similar to those which originally favoured the application of the *renvoi*   **20–021**
doctrine as a device for sustaining the formal validity of wills also favour its
application as a device for sustaining the formal validity of a marriage celebrated
abroad. These factors are, first, a rigid rule of the English conflict of laws which
normally requires compliance with the law of the place of celebration (the *lex loci
celebrationis*); secondly, a more flexible rule in neighbouring European countries
(where English people frequently get married) which allows compliance with
either the *lex loci* or the personal law of the parties; and thirdly, a strong judicial
bias in favour of the validity of marriage. There is, however, no English case
which actually sustains the validity of a marriage on the ground that it was
formally valid by the law which the *lex loci celebrationis* would apply. But it is a
legitimate inference from *Taczanowska v Taczanowski*[96] that such a marriage
would be upheld. This does not mean that a marriage would be held formally
invalid for failure to comply with the formalities prescribed by whatever system
of domestic law would have been referred to by the conflict rules of the *lex loci
celebrationis*. It merely means that a marriage may be formally valid if the parties
comply with the formalities prescribed by either the domestic rules of the *lex loci
celebrationis*, or by whatever system of domestic law the *lex loci celebrationis*
would apply. Thus, the reference to the *lex loci celebrationis* in the case of
formalities of marriage is an alternative reference to either its conflict rules or its
domestic rules, just as it was in the case of formalities of wills.

Certain cases of transmission[97]

Where the foreign law referred to by the English court would refer to a second   **20–022**
foreign law, and the second foreign law would agree that it was applicable, the
case for applying the second foreign law is strong.

Thus, if a German national domiciled in Italy died leaving movables in
England, and Italian and German law both agreed that German domestic law was
applicable because the *propositus* was a German national, the English court
should accept that situation and apply German domestic law. For the practical
advantages of deciding the case the way the Italian and German courts would
decide it (especially if the *propositus* left movables in Italy and Germany as well
as in England) seem to outweigh the theoretical disadvantages of this mild form
of transmission.

If, on the other hand, the second foreign law would not agree that it was
applicable, then there seems no reason for it to be applied. Thus, if a Danish
national domiciled in Italy died leaving movables in England, and Italian law
would apply the law of the nationality, while Danish law would apply the law of
the domicile, neither law recognising any *renvoi* from the other, then the English
court should apply Italian domestic law, thus ignoring *renvoi* altogether.[98]

---

[96] [1957] P. 301 at 305 and 318.
[97] Griswold, (1938) 51 Harv.L.Rev. 1165 at 1190; Lorenzen, op. cit., pp.76–77; cf. *Re Trufort* (1887)
36 Ch.D. 600; *R. v Brentwood Marriage Registrar* [1968] 2 Q.B. 956.
[98] Wolff, op. cit., p.203.

Difficulties in the application of the doctrine

20–023 It remains to discuss certain difficulties in the application of the English *renvoi* doctrine, emphasised by Beatson J in *Blue Sky One Ltd v Mahan Air*.[99] These are as follows.

Unpredictability of result

20–024 The doctrine makes everything depend on "the doubtful and conflicting evidence of foreign experts".[100] Moreover, it is peculiar to this theory of *renvoi* that it requires proof, not only of the foreign choice of law rules, but of the foreign rules about *renvoi* and there are few matters of foreign law about which it is more difficult to obtain reliable information. In continental countries, decided cases, at least of courts of first instance, are not binding as authorities to be followed, and doctrine changes from decade to decade. Consequently, we find Wynn Parry J saying in *Re Duke of Wellington*[101]:

> "It would be difficult to imagine a harder task than that which faces me, namely, of expounding for the first time either in this country or in Spain the relevant law of Spain as it would be expounded by the Supreme Court of Spain, which up to the present time has made no pronouncement on the subject, and having to base that exposition on evidence which satisfies me that on this subject there exists a profound cleavage of legal opinion in Spain and two conflicting decisions of courts of inferior jurisdiction."

The English cases show that the effect of acquiring a domicile in a foreign country may sometimes be to make the foreign domestic law applicable,[102] sometimes English domestic law,[103] sometimes the law of the domicile of origin,[104] and sometimes the law of yet a fourth country.[105] There is no certainty that different results will not be reached in any future case in which the same foreign laws are involved, because foreign law is a question of fact and has to be proved by evidence in each case. Moreover, if the evidence of foreign law is misleading or inadequate, the English court may reach a result which is unreal or unjust to the point of absurdity.

Thus, in *Re O'Keefe*[106] the intestate had lived in Italy for the last 47 years of her life and was clearly domiciled there. Yet the effect of the English *renvoi* doctrine was that her movables were distributed not in accordance with the Italian domestic law with which she might be expected to be most familiar, and in reliance on which she may have refrained from making a will, but in accordance with the domestic law of the Irish Free State, of which she was not a citizen,

---

[99] [2010] EWHC 631 (Comm).

[100] *Re Askew* [1930] 2 Ch. 259 at 278, per Maugham J, cited with approval in *Blue Sky One Ltd v Mahan Air* [2010] EWHC 631 (Comm) at [178].

[101] [1947] Ch. 506 at 515.

[102] *Re Annesley* [1926] Ch. 692; *Re Askew* [1930] 2 Ch. 259.

[103] *Re Ross* [1930] 1 Ch. 377.

[104] *Re Johnson* [1903] 1 Ch. 821; *Re O'Keefe* [1940] Ch. 124.

[105] *Re Trufort* (1887) 36 Ch.D. 600; *R. v Brentwood Marriage Registrar* [1968] 2 Q.B. 956.

[106] [1940] Ch. 124; a much criticised decision. The short unreserved judgment has given rise to "a flood of writings in all corners of the world, but particularly in Italy": Nadelmann, (1969) 17 Am. J. Comp. L. 418 at 444.

which only came into existence as a political unit during her long sojourn in Italy, and which she had never visited in her life except for a "short tour" with her father 60 years before her death. The only possible justification for such a result is that it may have enabled the movables in England to devolve in the same way as the movables in Italy. But of course in many cases uniformity of distribution is unattainable so long as some systems of law refer to the national law and others to the law of the domicile. For instance, uniformity of distribution would be impossible on any theory if an Italian national died intestate domiciled in England, for the English and Italian courts would each distribute the movables subject to its control in accordance with its own domestic law.

The national law of a British citizen

The most frequent occasion for applying the *renvoi* doctrine has been the conflict between English law, which refers succession to movables to the law of the domicile, and the laws of some continental countries, which refer to the law of the nationality. If the *propositus* is a British or an American citizen, the foreign court's reference to his or her national law is meaningless, for there is no such thing as a "British" or "American" or even a "Canadian" or "Australian" law of succession, nor, conversely, is there any such thing as "English" nationality. If the English court decides for itself how the foreign court might be expected to interpret its reference to the national law of a British citizen, as has been done in some cases, it is not necessarily deciding the case as the foreign court would decide it. Thus in *Re Johnson*[107] and *Re O'Keefe*[108] it was assumed, without any evidence of foreign law, that the national law of a British subject meant the law of his domicile of origin. If, on the other hand, the English court allows a foreign expert witness to assume that the national law of a British citizen is English law, as has been done in other cases,[109] it is basing its decision on a manifestly false premise. Thus in *Re Ross*[110] the evidence was that "the Italian courts would determine the case on the footing that the English law applicable is that part of the law which would be applicable to an English national [sic] domiciled in England". In *Re Askew*,[111] the expert witness stated: "I am informed and believe that John Bertram Askew was an Englishman [sic]. Therefore English law would be applied by the German court". Of course it can be argued that if the English court seeks to discover what decision the foreign court would reach, the grounds on which the foreign court would arrive at its decision are irrelevant.

20–025

---

[107] [1903] 1 Ch. 821.
[108] [1940] Ch. 124 at 129: "Italian lawyers cannot say what is the meaning of the law of the nationality when there is more than one system of law of the nationality".
[109] e.g., *Re JB (Child Abduction) (Rights of Custody: Spain)* [2003] EWHC 2130; [2004] 1 F.L.R. 976.
[110] [1930] 1 Ch. 377 at 404.
[111] [1930] 2 Ch. 259 at 276.

Circulus inextricabilis

20–026   As we have seen,[112] the effect of applying the doctrine of double *renvoi* is to make the decision turn on whether the foreign court rejects the *renvoi* doctrine altogether or adopts a doctrine of single or partial *renvoi*. But if the foreign court also adopts the doctrine of double *renvoi*, then logically no solution is possible at all unless either the English or the foreign court abandons its theory, for otherwise a perpetual *circulus inextricabilis* would be created. So far, this difficulty has not yet arisen, because English courts have not yet had occasion to apply their *renvoi* doctrine to the law of a country that adopts the same doctrine. (That, in turn, is due to the fact that most Commonwealth countries, which are likely to adopt the double *renvoi* doctrine, also follow the English choice of law rules, so that a reference back to English law from the law of such a country is unlikely.) Yet the possibility remains, and the *circulus inextricabilis* cannot surely be dismissed as "a (perhaps) amusing quibble".[113] "With all respect to what Maugham J. said in *Re Askew*," said the Private International Law Committee, "the English judges and the foreign judges would then continue to bow to each other like the officers at Fontenoy".[114] It is hardly an argument for the doctrine of double *renvoi* that it will only work if the other country rejects it.

In *Neilson v Overseas Projects Corporation of Victoria Ltd*,[115] Gummow and Hayne JJ considered the possibility of what they called "an infinite regression of reference." Their Honours held that there was no evidence suggesting that China would apply a "double *renvoi*" approach, but recognised that the problem could arise. They seem to favour the application of the law of the forum in such a case.[116]

Conclusion

20–027   As a purely practical matter it would seem that a court should not undertake the onerous task of trying to ascertain how a foreign court would decide the question, unless the situation is an exceptional one and the advantages of doing so clearly outweigh the disadvantages. In most situations, the balance of convenience surely lies in interpreting the reference to foreign law to mean its domestic rules. Although the doctrine of *renvoi* was favoured by Westlake[117] and Dicey,[118] the great majority of writers, both English and foreign, are opposed to it. Lorenzen said: "Notwithstanding the great authority of Westlake and Dicey, it may reasonably be hoped that, when the doctrine with all its consequences is squarely

---

[112]   Above, para.20–014.
[113]   *Re Askew* [1930] 2 Ch. 259 at 267, per Maugham J.
[114]   First Report (1954) Cmd. 9068, para.23(3).
[115]   [2005] HCA 54; (2005) 233 C.L.R. 331. See Briggs, [2006] L.M.C.L.Q. 1; Dickinson (2006) 122 L.Q.R. 183.
[116]   At paras 130–134.
[117]   Chapter 2.
[118]   3rd edn, Appendix I.

presented to the higher English courts, they will not hesitate to reject the decisions of the courts that have lent colour to *renvoi* in the English law".[119]

THE TIME FACTOR

The conflict of laws deals primarily with the application of laws in terms of geography, of place. Yet as in other branches of the law, so in the conflict of laws, problems of time cannot altogether be ignored. There is a considerable continental literature on the time factor in the conflict of laws, and a growing awareness of the problem by English-speaking writers[120] though, as might be expected, the English courts have dealt with it in a somewhat empirical fashion.

20–028

Three different types of problem have been identified by writers. The time factor may become significant if there is a change in the content of the conflict rule of the forum (called *le conflit transitoire* by French writers), or in the content of the connecting factor (which the French call *le conflit mobile*), or, most important of all, in the content of the foreign law to which the connecting factor refers. These will now be discussed in turn.

Changes in the conflict rule of the forum

A change in the conflict rule of the forum does not differ from a change in any other rule of law and its effect must therefore be ascertained in accordance with the familiar English rules of statutory interpretation and of judicial precedent.

20–029

Judge-made law is retrospective in operation, whereas statute law is usually prospective. Very strange consequences sometimes follow from a retrospective alteration in a conflict rule of the forum by judicial or legislative action, especially in the field of family relations. Thus, the English conflict rule for the recognition of foreign divorces was radically altered by judicial action in 1953[121] and again in 1967,[122] and by legislative action in 1971[123] and 1986.[124] In *Hornett v Hornett*[125]:

> A man domiciled in England married in 1919 a woman domiciled before her marriage in France. They lived together in France and England until 1924, when the wife obtained a divorce in France. The husband heard about this divorce in 1925. He then resumed cohabitation with his wife in England until 1936, when they parted. No children were born of this cohabitation. In 1969 the husband petitioned for a declaration that the divorce would be recognised in England.

---

[119] Lorenzen, op. cit., p.53. The sentence was first published in 1910, but the learned author left it unchanged in 1947.

[120] See F. A. Mann (1954) 31 B.Y.I.L. 217; Grodecki, (1959) 35 B.Y.B.I.L. 58; Spiro, (1960) 9 I.C.L.Q. 357; Rabel, op. cit., Vol. 4, pp.503–519; Grodecki, *International Encyclopaedia of Comparative Law* (Nijhoff, Tübingen, 1976), Vol. III, 8; Pryles, (1980) Monash U.L. Rev. 225; Fassberg, (1990) 39 I.C.L.Q. 856.

[121] *Travers v Holley* [1953] P. 246.

[122] *Indyka v Indyka* [1969] 1 A.C. 33.

[123] Recognition of Divorces and Legal Separations Act 1971.

[124] Family Law Act 1986 ss.44–49; for the retrospective effect of the relevant provisions see Recognition of Divorces and Legal Separations Act 1971 s.52.

[125] [1971] P. 255; discussed by Karsten, (1971) 34 M.L.R. 450.

Although it could not have been recognised before 1967, the divorce was recognised under the new judge-made rule declared by the House of Lords in that year.[126]

If we alter the facts a little, the consequences of this retrospective alteration of the conflict rule are startling:

(1) If children had been born of the resumed cohabitation between the parties after the divorce, they would have been legitimate when born, but rendered illegitimate by the subsequent recognition of the decree.

(2) If the husband had gone through a ceremony of marriage with another woman in 1945, his second marriage had been annulled for bigamy in 1950, and his second wife had then remarried, would the result of recognising the divorce in 1971 be to invalidate the nullity decree and also the second wife's second marriage?

(3) If the husband had died intestate in 1940, and a share in his property had been distributed to his French wife as the surviving spouse, would she have had to return it when the new conflict rule declared by the House of Lords in 1967 validated her French divorce?

Changes in the connecting factor

20–030   From the temporal point of view, the connecting factor in a rule of the conflict of laws may be either constant or variable. It may be of such a character that it necessarily refers to a particular moment of time and no other, or it may be liable to change so that further definition is required. For instance, a conflict rule which referred the question of capacity to make a will to the law of the testator's domicile would be meaningless unless it defined the moment of time at which the domicile was relevant.

Examples of constant connecting factors in the English conflict of laws include the *situs* of an immovable, the place where a marriage is celebrated, a will executed, or a tort committed, and the domicile of a corporation.[127] Examples of varying connecting factors include the *situs* of a movable, the flag of a ship, and the nationality, domicile or residence of an individual.

In these cases, it is simply a question of formulating the most convenient and just conflict rule, and the time factor, though it cannot be disregarded, is not the dominant consideration. For this reason, it has been doubted whether it is appropriate to treat a change in the connecting factor as a problem of time in the conflict of laws.[128]

---

[126] See the powerful arguments adduced by Latey J in the court of first instance and by Russell LJ (dissenting) in the Court of Appeal in *Indyka v Indyka* [1967] P. 233 at 244–245 and 262–263.
[127] A corporation, unlike an individual, cannot at common law change its domicile.
[128] See Grodecki, (1959) 35 B.Y.B.I.L. 58.

Changes in the *lex causae*

Changes in the *lex causae* present the most important and difficult problems of 20–031
time in the conflict of laws, especially when the change purports to have
retrospective effect. The overwhelming weight of opinion among writers is that
the forum should apply the *lex causae* in its entirety, including its transitional
rules. This is certainly the prevailing practice of courts on the mainland of
Europe. It is arguably the prevailing practice of the English courts, although there
is one case, *Lynch v Provisional Government of Paraguay*,[129] which is often cited
for the contrary proposition.

   Much confusion has resulted from ambiguous formulations of the conflict
rule, and these in turn have suffered from a failure to distinguish between
constant and variable connecting factors. If, for example, the forum's conflict rule
says that succession to immovables is governed by the *lex situs*, the connecting
factor is constant, no further definition is required, and it is natural and proper for
courts to apply the *lex situs* as it exists from time to time. But if the forum's
conflict rule says that succession to movables is governed by the law of the
deceased's domicile, the connecting factor is variable, and further definition is
required to make the rule more precise. So the words "at the time of his death"
are added in order to define the time at which his domicile is relevant. The effect
of this is to exclude reference to any earlier domicile, but courts have sometimes
assumed that the effect is also to exclude retrospective changes in the law of the
domicile made after the death of the deceased. This assumption seems
unnecessary and improper, for the two questions are really quite distinct.

   Although it must be emphasised that the problem is always basically the same,
namely, should the forum apply or disregard subsequent changes in the *lex
causae*, it will be convenient to deal with it under the following heads arranged
according to subject matter: succession to immovables; succession to movables;
torts; discharge of contracts; and validity of marriage. In conclusion, something
will be said on the extent to which public policy may occasionally induce the
forum to refuse recognition to foreign retrospective laws.

Succession to immovables

In *Nelson v Bridport*[130]: 20–032

> The King of the Two Sicilies granted land in Sicily to Admiral Nelson for himself and the heirs
> of his body, with power to appoint a successor. By his will the Admiral devised the land to
> trustees in trust for his brother William for life with remainders over. After the Admiral's
> death, and in the lifetime of William, a law was passed in Sicily abolishing entails and making
> the persons lawfully in possession of such estates the absolute owners thereof. Taking
> advantage of this law, brother William devised the land to his daughter, from whom it was
> claimed by the remainderman under the Admiral's will.

---

[129] (1871) L.R. 2 P. & D. 268.
[130] (1846) 8 Beav. 547.

In giving judgment for the defendant, Lord Langdale MR took it for granted that he had to apply the law of Sicily as it existed from time to time and not as it was at the time of the original grant or at the time of the Admiral's death.

Succession to movables

20–033   However, an opposite result was reached in *Lynch v Provisional Government of Paraguay*[131]:

> A testator who had been dictator of Paraguay died domiciled there having by his will left movable property in England to his mistress, the plaintiff. Two months after his death, but before probate of the will had been granted in England, there was a revolution in Paraguay, and the new Government passed a decree declaring all the testator's property wherever situate to be the property of the state and depriving his will of any validity in England or elsewhere. This decree purported to relate back to the time of the testator's death. The plaintiff applied for a grant of probate as universal legatee under the will.

Her application was opposed by the new government. The Government's opposition was bound to fail, because the decree was penal[132] and because property in England could not be confiscated by a foreign government.[133] But Lord Penzance, in granting probate to the plaintiff, preferred to rest his judgment on the ground that English law adopts the law of the domicile "as it stands at the time of the death" and does not undertake to give effect to subsequent retrospective changes in that law. In support of this proposition he quoted Story's formulation that succession to movables is governed by the law of the domicile "at the time of the death", without appearing to realise that the last six words were intended to qualify "domicile" and not "law", and that Story never considered the effect of subsequent retrospective changes in the law.

Lord Penzance's manifest inclination to uphold the will on the peculiar facts of the case is understandable, but his wide formulation has been much criticised by writers[134] on the ground that it failed to give effect to the transitional law of the *lex causae*, and appeared to do so irrespective of the content of that law. If, for example, the will had been defective in point of form, say, because the law of Paraguay required all wills to be witnessed by a notary public, and after the testator's death it was discovered that a witness, though practising as a notary, was not qualified to do so, and the will had been validated by retrospective legislation in Paraguay, it is hard to suppose that Lord Penzance would have thought it "inconvenient and unjust" to give effect to that legislation.

The decision was followed without much discussion in the curious case of *Re Aganoor's Trusts*[135]:

---

[131] (1871) L.R. 2 P. & D. 268.

[132] See *Banco de Viscaya v Don Alfonso de Borbon y Austria* [1935] 1 K.B. 140.

[133] See above, para.17–038.

[134] See Mann (1954) 31 B.Y.B.I.L. 217 at 234; Grodecki (1959) 35 B.Y.B.I.L. 58 at 67–69, where various interpretations of the decision are discussed.

[135] (1895) 64 L.J.Ch. 521; criticised by Mann, (1954) 31 B.Y.BI.L. 217 at 234; Grodecki (1959) 35 B.Y.B.I.L. 58 at 69–70.

> A testatrix died in 1868 domiciled in Padua having by her will given a settled legacy to A for life and if he died without children to B for life and then to B's children living at B's death. This was valid by the Austrian law in force in Padua in 1868; but on 1 September 1871, the Italian Civil Code came into force and forbade trust substitutions, dividing the ownership between the persons in possession on that date and the first persons entitled in remainder who were born or conceived before then. B died in 1891 leaving children. A died in 1894 without children.

It was held that the settled legacy was valid and that the change in the law in force in Padua made after the death of the testatrix would be ignored. This result is diametrically opposite to that which was reached in *Nelson v Bridport*.[136]

If it is true that in succession to movables no account is to be taken of subsequent changes in the *lex causae* made after the death of the testator, that proposition is subject to an important qualification so far as the formal validity of wills is concerned. For s.6(3) of the Wills Act 1963 provides that retrospective alterations in the *lex causae* made after the execution of the will are relevant in so far as they validate but irrelevant in so far as they invalidate the will. This enactment is not in terms confined to alterations in the law made before the death of the testator, and there seems no reason to read into it words that are not there.

Torts

In *Phillips v Eyre*, already discussed in the context of torts[137]:

20–034

> An action for assault and false imprisonment was brought in England against the ex-Governor of Jamaica. The acts complained of took place in Jamaica while the defendant was engaged in suppressing a rebellion which had broken out in the island. The acts were illegal by the law of Jamaica as it stood at the time of the tort; but the defendant pleaded that they had been subsequently legalised by an Act of Indemnity passed in Jamaica with retrospective effect.

The Court of Exchequer Chamber gave effect to this defence. It follows from this decision that even in 1870 English law had no objection to foreign retrospective legislation as such; and what was true in 1870 must be even more true today when retrospective legislation has become a more familiar phenomenon in English domestic law. It will be noted that the Court of Exchequer Chamber adopted a wholly different approach from that of Lord Penzance in *Lynch*'s case. It is thought that a similar result would follow from the application of the rules in the Rome II Regulation, given the approach, already noted,[138] prevalent in European legal systems generally.

Discharge of contracts

The discharge of a contractual obligation is a matter for the applicable law, determined under the Rome I Regulation. There seems little doubt that this means the applicable law as it exists from time to time, so that legislation enacted in the country of the applicable law after the date of the contract may have the effect of

20–035

---

[136] (1846) 8 Beav. 547.
[137] (1870) L.R. 6 Q.B. 1.
[138] At para.16–004.

discharging or modifying the obligations of the parties. This was certainly the case under the common law rules in respect of changes in the content of the proper law of the contract.[139]

In *Adams v National Bank of Greece*[140] the House of Lords refused to apply a Greek law which purported retrospectively to exonerate a Greek bank from liability under an English contract of guarantee. The House was not unanimous in its reasons for reaching this conclusion[141]; but the main reason seems to have been that since the proper law of the contract was English, no Greek law could discharge one party's obligation thereunder.[142] In other words, Greek law was not the *lex causae*. The case is noteworthy in the present context because all five Law Lords went out of their way to approve the principle of *Lynch*'s case.[143] But only Lord Tucker based his judgment squarely on that decision, and Lord Reid was not satisfied that it should be applied to a case like the one before him. This is surely the better view.

Validity of marriage

20–036   In *Starkowski v Attorney General*[144]:

> H1 and W, both Roman Catholics domiciled in Poland, went through a ceremony of marriage in Austria in May 1945 in a Roman Catholic church. They lived together until 1947, when they separated, having acquired a domicile of choice in England. In 1950 W went through a ceremony of marriage in England with H2, a Pole domiciled in England. In May 1945 a purely religious marriage without civil ceremony was void by Austrian law. But in June 1945 a law was passed in Austria retrospectively validating such marriages if they were duly registered. By some oversight, the marriage between H1 and W was not registered until 1949, by which time they had acquired a domicile in England and separated.[145]

The House of Lords held that the Austrian ceremony was valid and the English ceremony was bigamous and void. Lord Reid stated the question to be decided as follows: "Are we to take the law of that place [of celebration] as it was when the marriage was celebrated, or are we to inquire what the law of that place now is with regard to the formal validity of that marriage?" He answered the question by saying "There is no compelling reason why the reference should not be to that law as it is when the problem arises for decision".[146] Lord Cohen[147] distinguished the *Lynch* case somewhat faintly on the ground that it involved a remotely

---

[139] See, e.g., *Re Chesterman's Trusts* [1923] 2 Ch. 466 at 478; *Perry v Equitable Life Assurance Society* (1929) 45 T.L.R. 468; *De Beeche v South American Stores Ltd* [1935] A.C. 148; *R. v International Trustee for the Protection of Bondholders AG* [1937] A.C. 500; *Kahler v Midland Bank Ltd* [1950] A.C. 24; *Re Helbert Wagg & Co. Ltd's Claim* [1956] Ch. 323 at 341–342.

[140] [1961] A.C. 255.

[141] See, for a detailed analysis of the judgments, Grodecki, (1961) 24 M.L.R. 701 at 706–714.

[142] See, in particular, the judgment of Lord Reid and that of Diplock J in the court of first instance: [1958] 2 Q.B. 59.

[143] [1961] A.C. 255.

[144] [1954] A.C. 155.

[145] Mann thought that the breakdown of the marriage before the registration of the Austrian ceremony should have led the House of Lords to an opposite conclusion: (1954) 31 B.Y.B.I.L. 217 at 243–245. But this seems unacceptable for the reasons given by Grodecki, (1959) 35 B.Y.B.I.L. 58 at 75–76.

[146] [1954] A.C. 155 at 170 and 172.

[147] At p.180.

different subject matter. Lord Tucker[148] agreed with Barnard J in the court of first instance[149] that *Lynch*'s case would have been of more assistance if the second ceremony had preceded the registration of the first. But these distinctions are illusory because, as is shown by Lord Reid's formulation quoted above, the problem was basically the same. The House of Lords adopted a different approach and surely a preferable one from that of Lord Penzance in *Lynch*'s case.

Public policy

The prevailing practice of the English courts thus seems to be to apply the *lex causae* as it exists from time to time and to give effect if need be to retrospective changes therein. But the consequences of giving effect to retrospective changes in the law are sometimes so extraordinary that public policy must occasionally impose qualifications and exceptions. There is an almost complete lack of English authority on this question. The discussion that follows is therefore highly speculative. It will throw the problem into the clearest possible relief if we consider some variations on the facts of the *Starkowski* case and consider what decision an English court might be expected to reach.   **20–037**

(1)   If the Austrian marriage had been valid originally but had later been retrospectively invalidated by Austrian legislation, it would seem that, on grounds of policy, the marriage should be held valid in England.

(2)   If either party had obtained an English nullity decree annulling the Austrian marriage for informality before it was registered, it would seem that the foreign retrospective legislation should not be allowed to invalidate the English nullity decree.[150]

(3)   What would the position have been if the English ceremony had preceded and not followed the registration of the Austrian ceremony? The majority of the House of Lords expressly left this question open in the *Starkowski* case.[151] It is thought that the English ceremony should have been held valid. A similar point was decided by the British Columbia Court of Appeal in *Ambrose v Ambrose*[152]:

> A wife obtained an interlocutory judgment for divorce from her first husband in California, where they were domiciled, on 25 November 1930. This judgment could become final, and so entitled either party to remarry, at the expiration of one year, either on the application of either party or on the court's own motion. It was not in fact made final until 1939. Meanwhile, in 1935, the wife went through a ceremony of marriage in the State of Washington with her second husband, who was domiciled in British Columbia. They lived together in British Columbia until 1956, when they separated. The wife then took advantage of a Californian statute passed in 1955 and obtained an order from the Californian court in 1958 which retrospectively back-dated the divorce to 25 November

---

[148]   At p.175.
[149]   [1952] P. 135 at 144.
[150]   See *Von Lorang v Administrator of Austrian Property* [1927] A.C. 641 at 651, per Lord Haldane.
[151]   [1954] A.C. 155 at 168, 176 and 182.
[152]   (1961) 25 D.L.R. (2d) 1; criticised by Castel, (1961) 39 Can. Bar Rev. 604, by Hartley, (1967) 16 I.C.L.Q. 680 at 699–703; and by Grodecki, op. cit., Vol. III, Ch.8, para.34(1).

1931, the earliest date on which final judgment could have been obtained. The second husband then petitioned for nullity in British Columbia on the ground that the second ceremony was bigamous.

The court granted a decree. It distinguished *Starkowski v Attorney General* on two grounds. First, the defect in that case was formal and could be corrected by the law of the place of celebration, which remained constant throughout; whereas the defect in the *Ambrose* case related to capacity to marry, a matter which was governed by the law of the wife's antenuptial domicile: but she ceased to be domiciled in California in 1939, and was therefore domiciled in British Columbia, and not in California, when she obtained her order from the Californian court in 1958.[153] Second, in *Starkowski v Attorney General* the retrospective validation of the Austrian ceremony preceded the English ceremony, whereas in the *Ambrose* case the Washington ceremony preceded the retrospective validation of the Californian divorce.

---

[153] In Canadian law, the domicile of a married woman was the same as that of her husband, but a woman whose marriage was void acquired the domicile of the man if she lived with him in the country of his domicile. Therefore W remained domiciled in California until her divorce from H1 was made final in 1939, whereupon she became domiciled in British Columbia because she had been living there with H2 since 1935 on the ground that she was married to him.

INDEX

This index has been prepared using Sweet and Maxwell's Legal Taxonomy. Main index entries conform to keywords provided by the Legal Taxonomy except where references to specific documents or non-standard terms (denoted by quotation marks) have been included. These keywords provide a means of identifying similar concepts in other Sweet and Maxwell publications and online services to which keywords from the Legal Taxonomy have been applied. Readers may find some minor differences between terms used in the text and those which appear in the index. Suggestions to *sweetandmaxwell.taxonomy@thomson.com*.

All references are to paragraph number